AUSTRALIAN
FISHING
ENCYCLOPEDIA

AUSTRALIAN
FISHING
ENCYCLOPEDIA

Bill Classon • Frank Prokop • Peter Horrobin • Geoff Wilson

AFN
AUSTRALIAN FISHING NETWORK

Cover Photograph: Doug Blair with a 10 kg plus clear water cod taken on a Bassman DT spinnerbait.

This Edition published in 2010
Australian Fishing Network
PO Box 544
Croydon Victoria 3136
Tel: (03) 9729 8788
Fax: (03) 9729 7833
Email: sales@afn.com.au

Hard Cover: 9781 8651 3172 6
Flexibound: 9781 8651 3177 1

CONTENTS

ACKNOWLEDGEMENTS

Producing a publication such as this is a significant undertaking and the authors would like to thank all the anglers throughout Australia who, over the years, have contributed to this book, even if unknowingly!

Combined, the authors have over 60 years experience as editors of Australia's premier fishing magazines and have met anglers around the country, picking up hints and ideas. To all of those anglers go our thanks.

This publication also required a huge number of diagrams to get our message across. Our thanks goes to Geoff Wilson for allowing us to use the diagrams produced for the Australian Fishing Network journal library over the years. Geoff is the doyen of technical angling illustrations and we thank him for his generosity and participation.

We would also like to thank our fish artists Trevor Hawkins and Bernard Yau: their contributions of fish paintings have really enhanced fish identification.

The other illustrators include Dennis Keys, Ian Warnecke and Petra Hanzak who have worked for the Australian Fishing Network in the past and our thanks go to all of them.

Thanks for the production of the lure section of this encyclopedia must go to Steve Kovacs and Russell Breed, Rod Cockburn, John Wakeford and Alan Faulkner, Les Rochester, Adam Neilson, Matthew Hodge, Dean Skelly and Clinton Engel, Bill Classon, Helen Classon, Dr Norm Hall of Murdoch University, Dr Frank Prokop—dad, John Wakeford of Australian Maritime College, Peter Coulson, David Roche and finally to Frank's wife Sonja and kids Frank and Natasha.

INTRODUCTION

The changes in the management of our fisheries, especially in the restriction and removal of commercial fishers from the areas that recreational anglers enjoy, has produced a great improvement in the results obtained by recreational anglers. Bays and estuaries, as well as rivers like the Murray have improved out of sight since being the sole domain of recreational anglers. Also, the development of new fisheries such as the barra lakes of Queensland, the bass fisheries of New South Wales and Queensland, and the expansion of stocking in both location and numbers in so many of our waters are presenting many more angling opportunities than ever existed before.

Fishing tackle has improved out of sight over the last two decades. In those early times if you bought at the low end of the tackle market you took your chances. These days even the modestly priced tackle has the legacy of high-end technological and material development, while the high-end tackle is to marvel at. Lures that once were merely a piece of shiny metal with hooks attached are now computer designed, tested and built with components and dimensions that are accurate to fractions of a millimetre. These lures perform consistently and reliably and are strong enough to handle the big fish found in Australia's waters.

Tactics too have improved with fishing with artificials—lures and flies—experiencing a massive surge in popularity along with catch and release as anglers only keep what they need rather than fill freezers.

Fishing overall is experiencing a general increase in popularity and with the fish seeing more anglers they are becoming more difficult to catch. The information within this book will enable you to become a better and more proficient angler, enable you to make better informed decisions about the choice of tackle, including lures, and introduce you to tactics that leading anglers are developing to ensure their ongoing success.

The information in this book is presented with the hope that you will take part in this great sport, enjoy your interaction with nature and the environment and pass those feelings and skills on to the next generation.
Get out and give fishing a go.

CHAPTER ONE

UNDERSTANDING
FISH

FISH BIOLOGY

ABILITIES AND WEAKNESSES

Fish have amazing abilities! They can, according to body shape and musculature, swim either very slowly or with astonishing speed. Some fish are incredibly adept leapers. Others have astonishing eyesight. Many fish can change colour or even body shape, almost at will, while some can cease feeding for long periods, with little or no long-term ill effect. Whatever the fish's physical characteristics and habits, they are important for fishermen to identify so correct fishing tackle and techniques can be selected to counter their abilities and make the most of their weaknesses. If, for instance, you are targeting free-swimming pelagics, use finer lines and fluorocarbon leaders to counter their great eyesight.

Be aware too that what sometimes appears to be the strength of the fish in natural surroundings may also be the factor that enables it to be more easily caught. Fish that are omnivorous and aggressive may well ensure their own survival in the natural environment with these characteristics but they will also make them far more vulnerable to anglers' baits, lures and flies. The key to success is to present the fish with an instant choice of whether to eat or not, or whether to fend off intruders or not. To achieve this, present your offering as close to the fish's nose as you can.

BASIC NEEDS

All fish need to feed, to find shelter from the elements and predators, to conserve energy, to spawn, to find habitat and environments that suit their particular metabolisms. Ideal habitats will always carry all or most of these features and successful angling depends largely on being able to identify these places, as directing your fishing effort elsewhere is a waste of time.

When everything comes together in the one place, fish are usually so abundant there, and so readily caught, that such places become recognised as 'hot spots'.

BODY SHAPE AND LIFESTYLE

The body shapes of fish provide clues to where the fish might be found and how they live and feed. Some fish with large eyes capable of gathering even faint light, are more likely to be caught at night, at dawn or dusk, or when conditions are overcast. Streamlined and smooth-skinned fish are built for speed and running down active prey or escaping from fast predators. These fish are generally found in open water where such hunting and danger avoidance tactics are possible. Fish with shorter, more robust, or flattened bodies are more likely to move relatively short distances to feed or escape from predators.

Some of these fish have rotund, muscular bodies, heavily scaled and well able to withstand the rigours of living in turbulent wave-washed coastal water. Others have bodies that are laterally compressed, i.e. they are higher than they are wide across the back. These typically (though not always) frequent some form of vertical structure, against which their body shape can take maximum advantage of cover and respite from strong water movement. Others have vertically compressed or flattened bodies, indicating their

The body shape, colouration and musculature of flathead make them ideally suited to bottom feeding

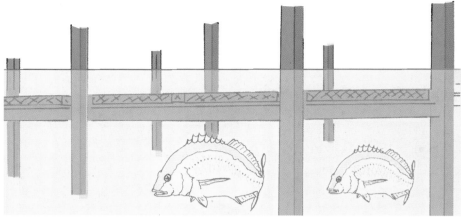
Bream will often hide under oyster racks or rafts of floating weed.

Barramundi have a reflective element in their eyes that enables feeding in low light conditions.

preference for feeding and conducting their lifestyle near the bottom.

BODY SHAPE AND FISHING TECHNIQUES

Fish accustomed to running their food down, respond well to wide-scope, rapid presentations of baits and lures, which is why high-speed spinning, and trolling are such productive techniques for fish such as billfish, tuna, mackerel, kingfish, barracuda, queenfish, trevally and other pelagic species. Some of these fish are more or less cylindrical in body shape and can follow lures, or sweep in from considerable distances to strike them. Other fish, with varying degrees of flattening of their flanks have correspondingly shorter attack ranges.

Fish with flattened sides and shorter bodies, like trout, bream, bass, Murray cod and both golden and silver perch, respond better to techniques that present baits and lures close to their holding position. Generally too, the ideal retrieve speed

will be slow or intermittent, allowing the fish to strike from cover and 'catch' the lure. While these fish can sprint for short distances, they generally don't respond to presentations that demand they chase a lure at high speed or for any distance.

The same applies to bait presentations, whether cast and brought past such fish, or drifted to their positions with the aid of wind or tide or a moving boat. Examples abound, with sea fish like morwong, snapper, jewfish and others that are effectively targeted by baits presented right in their faces or at least within a fairly specified area.

Bottom-dwelling fish like flathead and flounder are not fussy about where the lure or bait lands, as long as it comes past them at close range. That means you have to make the bait or lure travel close to the bottom, and not too quickly. Species like tailor, Australian salmon and pike will chase lures and baits but bite better when they have the angler's offering delivered right to their doorstep.

Similar tactics work for barramundi, threadfin salmon, mangrove jack and so on.

COLOUR AND CAMOUFLAGE

Counter-shading on fish, dark above and light beneath, indicates they live and feed in the open ocean or other large bodies of water. This shading affords them camouflage from above against the dark background of the depths, or allows them to blend in against the silvery glare of the surface when viewed from underneath. Still others, habituated to stony bottomed streams, or areas of mottled light and shade in rivers, are camouflaged by skin markings and spots and variegated skin tones.

COMFORT ZONES

Conditions in which fish can survive, and those in which they can breed, feed and become catchable, can be significantly different. Australian bass, for example, are able to survive in water temperatures ranging from three degrees Celsius to 27 degrees, but are most readily caught when the water temperature is between 18 and 21 degrees.

Similarly, light levels need to be strong enough for fish to see their prey and avoid predators, but not so strong that the fish become blinded by it. In the same way, levels of pH (how acidic or alkaline the water is) are very important in fresh water (less so in salt water, where pH is buffered somewhat by the salinity). Fish obtain all their oxygen in a dissolved form directly from the water, so the levels of dissolved oxygen can be critical in determining how actively and aggressively fish feed. That in turn determines how readily your baits, lures or flies will be attacked or accepted.

FISH SENSES

Fish 'hear' sounds as variations in pressure, registered both through the inner ear (not very efficiently) and the lateral line, an enormously sensitive array of sensory organs arranged down the fish's flanks and usually visible as a distinct

Schooling behaviour of some species like Queenfish often enables anglers to secure multiple hook ups as several fish strike at once.

line or colour change, running from gill plate to tail.

The fish's olfactory sense is much more sensitive than that of humans, as they can literally taste what they smell, which is why berley works so well. Sharks have an additional sensory system that can detect minute electrical fields that are emitted by every living creature.

Fish eyesight is similar to that of humans, although there is debate about whether or how fish see colours. They are certainly able to detect changes in hue or shading however and some fish can see quite well in darkness so profound that we would not be able to see at all.

Fish are so generally light sensitive in fact that they seldom spend much time close to the surface unless the light intensity is diminished by surface ripples or wave chop, or there are cloudy skies or some solid form of shade is available. This is why in part that many fish hunt along the edge where darkness meets the light and why many fish only become active and feed at the surface at dusk or at night.

GROWTH RATES

How much and how rapidly fish grow is determined to some extent by their genetic characteristics. Bream, for example, rarely grow larger than snapper, and tailor are mostly smaller than Australian salmon, but within each species,

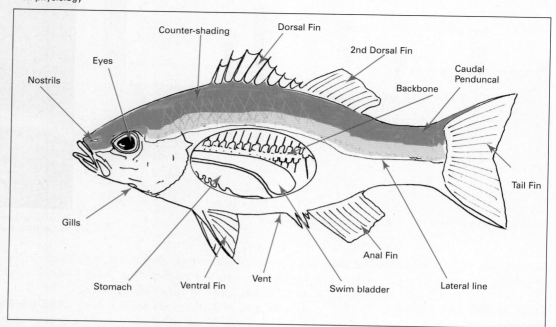

Fish physiology

there can be variations in maximum size and growth rates.

These are affected by environmental factors like the abundance and types of food, the presence or absence of competitors, the likely suppression of growth by predatory species and year-round temperature regimes. For example, tailor from some parts of Western Australia, such as Cloughs Bar in the Shark Bay region, will often exceed 4 kilograms and may infrequently attain 8 kilograms.

However, these fish pale into insignificance against the 14.4 kilogram fish taken in 1972 from Hatteras in North Carolina USA. It matters little that these in America are known as 'bluefish'.

They are one and the same general species, simply a localised version.

Of interest, similar disparities in growth rate and potential are being realised now within the Australian bass fishing scene, with fish of 2 kg being a rarity in most river systems, but increasingly common within certain freshwater dams in south-east Queensland and mid-New South Wales.

SPAWNING CYCLES

Most fish spawn once on a more or less annual basis, although there are some that spawn more than once annually, and others that spawn several times within a given season. Usually, spawning times come about when conditions occur that will give progeny the best chance of survival. These conditions may include water temperatures within a given range, water chemistry regimes, or the relative absence of predators. Those fish that form part of the food chain for a large number of other species, are usually the most fecund or prodigious spawners, producing such vast numbers of offspring that some just have to survive.

Different species of freshwater fish spawn at different times, for example, most trout spawn from late autumn through winter, while bass and estuary perch do so from winter through spring. Murray cod on the other hand, spawn from spring through early summer, depending on the availability of suitably warm water and snaggy shallows.

In salt water too, spawning times vary between types of fish, and even within the same species, according to location. Generally, spawning periods in tropical latitudes start earlier and finish later than those in more southern climes, which have relatively short spawning seasons.

The mottled gold colouration of this brown trout from a shallow Tasmanian lake enables it to blend in with the general water colour and bottom hues. Camouflage is important to both predator and prey species, enabling them to escape detection in a deadly game of hide and seek.

Black bream like this one migrate upstream in summer to spawn in river reaches where salinity is diluted by freshwater inflows.

Yellowfin bream for example generally spawn from winter to spring, as do black bream, but the latter's spawning period gets progressively later the further west you go. Yellowtail kingfish on the other hand spawn off Coffs Harbour in winter, around Jervis Bay in spring and further south around Narooma in summer. Spanish mackerel spawn off north Queensland reefs during the making tides of late October through early December, and black marlin spawn northeast of Cairns during spring and early summer. In most of these cases, the critical factor in timing has to do with suitable water temperatures, which occur earlier in the north than in the south.

SPECIALISED ATTRIBUTES

Fish will evolve special attributes to better adapt them for particular environments. One example is the threadfin salmon, of which there are 4 recognised types: the King threadfin salmon, the blue threadfin, the seven-fingered threadfin and the striped threadfin.

These fish all vary in size and colouration, but they all share one thing in common: the attenuation of their pectoral fins into free filaments, or 'fingers'. Fisheries scientists have thought this specialised fin development helps the fish to locate prey in the muddy and silt-laden bottoms of tropical waters. This may well be so, but recent observations by anglers and fishing guides have revealed what seems to be a more immediate and direct use. As threadfin swim toward groups of prey such as baitfish and jelly prawns, they use these long 'finger-fins' like outstretched arms, to corral their food into more densely packed feeding targets.

Many fish gather in schools to feed because it enables greater efficiency in herding prey.

Schooling Behaviour

Once they have them moving, they pivot the fins forward, literally shovelling the herded prey in front of their hungry mouths and feeding with much greater efficiency than they could if they simply had to run down smaller and more scattered prey.

FISH HABITAT

COVER AND STRUCTURE

'Structure', used in a fishing context, refers to the physical features of a waterway. It includes both natural features such as rocks, reeds, reefs, trees, snags, weed beds, mangroves, dips and rises in the floor of the waterway, as well as man-made features such as pylons, groynes, wharves, artificial reefs and so on. Fish will use structure as cover, either permanently or temporarily, for habitat for concealment from predators and prey, for protection from strong currents or other external forces, as an aid in food collection and for camouflage. Structures are prime spots for anglers to target for fish.

FLOW RATES AND TURBULENCE

Most fish feed more actively when there is some form of water movement, such as down-stream flows, tidal flows or coastal longshore currents,

These are the jaws of a sizeable mulloway, revealing a surprisingly fearsome array of teeth that help these fish seize live prey.

as well as large swells and heavy wind chop caused by water rebounding from shoreline structures such as rocky cliffs, breakwalls or beaches.

When water flow strikes hard, submerged features like boulders, estuary corners and man-made structures like wharf or bridge pylons and so forth, it is deflected into whirling areas of turbulence. The main advantage of this for fish is that this turbulence can disorient weak-swimming prey and make them easier for predatory fish to catch.

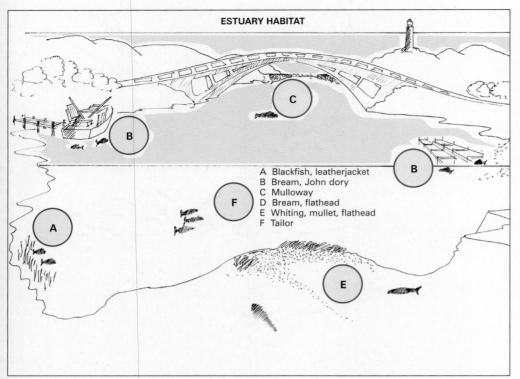

ESTUARY HABITAT

A Blackfish, leatherjacket
B Bream, John dory
C Mulloway
D Bream, flathead
E Whiting, mullet, flathead
F Tailor

Estuary fish habitat

hold position there comfortably, with the worst of the current rushingpast them.

SAND AND MUD FLATS

Sand and mud flats carry an astounding array and quantity of food. Enormous numbers of worms, insect larvae, shellfish and crustacea live in the substrate of freshwater sand and mud flats and a similar supply lives beneath the apparently empty surface of those in salt water.

These areas also have underwater of weed beds and algae, and many have bottom shapes scoured out by water movement that provide feeding points for a variety of fish. For example, sand flats in estuaries will generally feature a series of hollows and hummocks, and moving water frets away at these, exposing food items to such species as bream, whiting, flathead and blackfish. In fresh water, mud flats can be veritable hothouses of larval life, with bass, golden perch, trout and cod all prowling over them looking for signs of movement that indicate food.

The sandy margins of freshwater lakes too can provide excellent gathering grounds for smooth-shelled yabbies, Cherax destructor, that prowl over them at night and can be gathered with the aid of a torch and strong nerves.

Some species have adapted to life in rough water conditions. For example, black drummer, a fish of the rugged coastal rock fringes, will feed most energetically when big sea conditions would spell almost certain injury or death to other fish. By comparison, it is rare to find trout vigorously feeding in heavy weather. Most of their feeding takes place either as they cruise through relatively calm lake waters or when they are holding in sheltered spots within rivers, but close enough to the flow to swing out and grab passing food. Many fish species also take advantage of wave action, which pummels food loose from weed beds, rock faces and snags, providing any fish that can handle the conditions with a supermarket of forage they may not otherwise be able to get.

REEFS AND ROCKY SHORES

Submerged rocks offer many benefits to fish. Underwater weeds and plants grow on them for one thing, their required nutrients brought to them by passing currents or surges, These in turn provide homes, food and shelter for a host of small prey, ranging from crustacea, through worms and other invertebrates to small fish.

There are always eddies and conflicting currents surrounding reefs and rocks too — spaces of low water pressure, created by a phenomenon known as laminar flow. This deflects current, skidding it away from the hard object and creating a 'cushion' of slow moving water between the full force of the flow and the hard surface of the underwater object. If there is enough space in this 'laminar cushion', fish can

Below: Freshwater fish habitat

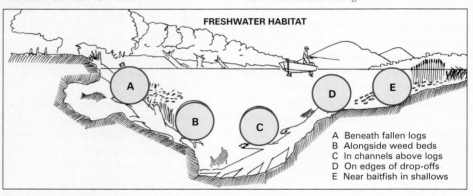

FRESHWATER HABITAT

A Beneath fallen logs
B Alongside weed beds
C In channels above logs
D On edges of drop-offs
E Near baitfish in shallows

Below: These drowned trees in Lake Windamere, NSW, provide plenty of cover and feeding opportunities for golden perch.

Eddies and wave action as well as long-shore currents wash ocean rock platforms like this, accumulating fish foods and creating feeding eddies.

WATER DEPTH

Deep water is not necessarily required for catching good fish but many beginners still throw their baits and lures well past many fish that are waiting right in shallow waters close to the shore. Generally, what determines how much water a fish will want over its head is how safe it feels (the less safe it feels, the more water it will want overhead), and where the available food is located.

Marlin for example, hunt and feed in water from the abyssal depths of the Continental Shelf, to waters as shallow as 10 or 20 metres, either close in to some coastal rock platforms or even just behind the surf break of some ocean beaches. Recent discoveries about Australian bass in deep freshwater impoundments too have indicated that while these fish might school up in water 50 metres deep or more, they may actually be encountered at depths of three to five metres below the surface.

Often the bass are there to feed on suspended forage, such as small fish or shrimps, which in turn are feeding on clouds of daphnia, or water fleas. Primary food chain items like daphnia and plankton are usually found suspending over the thermocline but not in or below it. Use a quality sounder to pinpoint the thermocline and the location of fish and their food.

What is certain is that you must present your lures, flies or baits close enough to the depth at which the fish are holding for them to feed comfortably.

WATER QUALITY

There are a number of factors that determine water quality, but for fish, the most critical factors are the water's dissolved oxygen levels, temperature, chemical composition, and pollution levels. Fish obtain life-sustaining oxygen from dissolved oxygen in the water but the amount in the water will vary. Water temperature is a key factor indetermining how quickly dissolved oxygen is lost back to the atmosphere—warm water releases dissolved oxygen to the atmosphere faster

than cold water. The levels of dissolved oxygen will improve when the water cools or more of it is aerated by greater exposure to air, such as when it moves and splashes over rocks or is choppy.

The distribution of most fish species on our planet is determined by water temperature with most able to sustain life within a given water temperature range; however most feed and breed within a narrower temperature range still. These two factors by themselves can create difficult environments for fish. Sometimes the colder water that fish find more comfortable can be very low in dissolved oxygen too. In extreme summer conditions for example, fish like trout in lakes may have the choice of either suffocating down deep where it is acceptably cold, or being practically cooked in the upper layers where there is still enough dissolved oxygen but temperatures are high enough to be lethal.

Chemicals in the water, which will determine its acidity or alkalinity, will also determine whether or not it can sustain fish. Ordinarily, fresh water is neutral or slightly acidic or alkaline. Whichever it is will depend on the chemical composition of the surrounding soil and underlying bedrock. Fresh water that is slightly alkaline is nutrient-rich, food-rich and weed-rich and will produce bigger fish. However too much alkalinity is a negative as algae take over, reducing oxygen levels and suffocating the fish. In coastal salt water, some chemical releases occur naturally when soils with high acid sulphate content are disturbed when floods or tidal waters wash over them.

Waters can also be artificially loaded toward acidity or alkalinity by the introduction of chemicals in the form of agricultural, household or industrial effluents, creating polluted environments in which fish may not be able to survive. Good water conditions for fish then are a complex web of interlocking and interacting factors.

These tropical flats clearly show the channel formation of a wilderness estuary. At high tide, both the sandy mid sections and the muddy fringes will be inundated, with hungry fish foraging along their edges.

Above: In the shallows, these anglers can look forward to catching fish such as bream, whiting, flathead and mullet. The darker line of water in the background indicates a deeper channel, which could yield tailor, more bream and perhaps blackfsh as well.

Below: Even shallow riffle water like this can hold fish if the oxygen content and light diffusion is great enough, but it would fish better in low light.

WEED BEDS

The importance of weed beds to fish is often underrated. Weed beds can provide structure and cover for fish, and are important as feeding stations, since many forms of fish food live or grow within and around them. Weed beds thrive in slightly alkaline water, and act to filter suspended matter from the water, creating clearer and cleaner water. They also have a vital role in converting the sun's energy into plant growth through photosynthesis. One of the outcomes of this process is that they contribute to dissolved oxygen levels in the water which fish need to live.

FISH AND WEATHER

BAROMETRIC EFFECTS

There are many indications that shifts in barometric pressure affect the way fish behave. It is widely held that rising barometric pressure (high pressure system) results in good fishing, and dropping barometric pressure (low pressure system) results in relatively poor fishing. While reasonable fishing can be maintained with a rising barometer and dropping water levels, the worst fishing conditions are usually those that feature dropping barometric pressure and dropping water levels. There are however exceptions to every rule and some fish, like Australian bass, which are very sensitive to barometric pressure, typically exhibit feeding frenzies before summer storms when the barometric pressure is dropping. Generally, barometric pressure appears to affect freshwater fish more than marine fish which would experience variations in pressure as they move through the different depths of water of the oceans.

Barometric pressure may also affect fishing indirectly by its influence on other aspects of weather like temperature and humidity levels. An example of this would be the propensity of insects to end up as food on the water's surface during periods of high humidity caused by barometric pressure. The humidity can affect their ability to fly.

LIGHT EFFECTS

Since fish have no eyelids and cannot shut light out, they react instead to intense or uncomfortable light levels by moving away from the light source and into a less well lit area. Many species of predatory fish use the interchange area between light and dark areas (such as the illuminated areas beneath a road bridge at night) to hunt for baitfish, drawn there by the strong lights. The periods just before and after both sunrise and sunset also are prime feeding times for fish, which suggests there is some correlation between light intensity, or at least the angle at which light strikes the water, and fish feeding patterns.

Big fish often feed at night. Big trout and mulloway are examples of prime sport fish that feed under the cover of darkness.

RAINFALL EFFECTS

Rain has an obvious effect on freshwater rivers, causing them to rise and increase in flow rates. Heavy rain may also wash in surface material from the ground surrounding waterways and discolour a stream or dam. In summer and autumn, rainwater also tends to be somewhat colder than standing water and these sudden drops in temperature can slow fish feeding activity down. Conversely, in

While redfin tend to feed voraciously most times, they will definitely be easier to catch when the barometer and insect activity are both high.

winter and in many large dams that hold native fish, the first rainfalls of spring can actually infuse slightly warmer water into a dam from its feeder streams, attracting fish into the area.

In salt water, rain also has an effect, lowering the salinity of estuaries. Since this fresher water is less dense than full strength seawater, it will tend to stratify on top and this can send fish deeper, into the more dense lower layers of salty water. In flood time, whole river populations of fish can be swept out to sea by the torrent, where large predators, such as sharks and mulloway feast on the hapless mullet, whiting, bream, flathead and blackfish that have been flushed from their estuary homes. Offshore anglers will also note that a sudden heavy

downpour, such as is common in tropical regions, can flatten an otherwise boisterous and choppy sea. These passing tropical squalls can be followed in the brief calm afterward by a sudden surge of fish activity.

TEMPERATURE EFFECTS

All fish have reasonably broad tolerance ranges of temperature, but much narrower ones of 'preferred' thermal limits. Changes in weather can bring changes in water temperature and these can have a marked effect on where fish will be found and how willing or able they are to feed when you do find them. Shallow standing water or rivers with low flow rates can become quite warm during

Light effects

SHADE

Fish tend to seek shade when light levels are strong and for this reason can often be found within the shaded areas of riverbanks and other habitats.

Rain changes salinity in estuaries, flattens wind chop and in sufficient quantities, can cause flooding that drives baitfish out into coastal seawaters, where big predators like mulloway hunt them down. This angler, knowing heavy rain was likely to trigger such activity, braved the conditions and has just hooked up on a big mulloway on a feather lure.

Barramundi are one species of fish noticeably affected by water temperatures. Usually they will not feed aggressively until the water temperature approaches and surpasses 23 degrees Celsius. This fish hit in water that was tested with a thermometer and predictably revealed a temperature of 25 degrees.

protracted periods of hot weather. This is less likely to have negative effects on warmth-loving species like barramundi, but may completely shut down a local trout fishery until things cool off again.

WIND EFFECTS

Wind can have many positive results for the angler. When wind blows across a freshwater lake for example, it creates wind chop, which lowers light penetration levels and brings fish closer to the surface (where anglers can get at them). And, because the surface of the lake is ruptured by wave action, more atmospheric oxygen is infused into the water, further heightening the ability of fish to expend energy by feeding vigorously.

On the shore toward which the wind is blowing, wave action can knock food loose from bankside crannies and weed beds, and create a curtain of suspended silt under which predatory fish can hunt.

Wind also creates feeding lanes for fish as diverse as trout in alpine lakes and striped tuna in 100 metre depths of sea water. Weak-swimming or planktonic food items are shovelled into concentrated streams by the wind and the fish simply swim along those lines of floating forage, taking advantage of the bounty. Anglers in the know can of course, do the same thing.

FISH CHARACTERISTICS

AMBUSHING

Fish have many ways of gathering food. Some species are entirely herbivorous fish and rely on their environment to provide food, but by far, the majority of fish live by finding and eating

Above: Wind can encourage fish to feed under the cover of ripples and also tends to shovel food into defined 'wind lane' feeding areas.

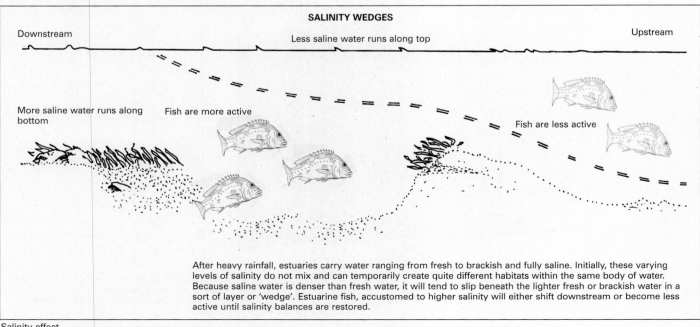

SALINITY WEDGES

Downstream

Less saline water runs along top

Upstream

More saline water runs along bottom

Fish are more active

Fish are less active

After heavy rainfall, estuaries carry water ranging from fresh to brackish and fully saline. Initially, these varying levels of salinity do not mix and can temporarily create quite different habitats within the same body of water. Because saline water is denser than fresh water, it will tend to slip beneath the lighter fresh or brackish water in a sort of layer or 'wedge'. Estuarine fish, accustomed to higher salinity will either shift downstream or become less active until salinity balances are restored.

Salinity effect

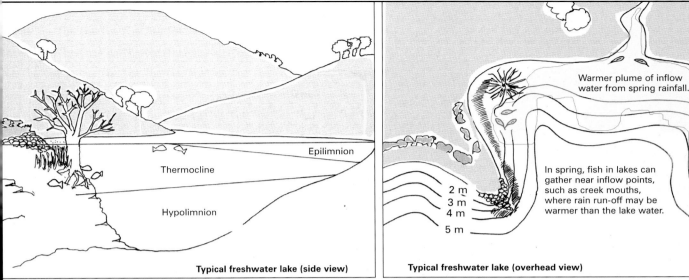

Epilimnion

Thermocline

Hypolimnion

Typical freshwater lake (side view)

Warmer plume of inflow water from spring rainfall.

2 m
3 m
4 m
5 m

In spring, fish in lakes can gather near inflow points, such as creek mouths, where rain run-off may be warmer than the lake water.

Typical freshwater lake (overhead view)

Water temperature strongly determines the location of fish within freshwater dams and lakes. Depending on the season, there can be one or several distinct thermal layers from the surface of the water to the bottom. When these thermal layers form, usually in summer and winter, the upper or surface layer is called 'the epilimnion', the lower or bottom layer is called 'the hypolimnion' and the intervening layer is known as 'the metalimnion' or more commonly, as 'the thermocline'. Usually fish will be found within, just above, or just below the thermocline.

NB: Fish will usually be found either where there is structure of some sort or where temperatures best suit their needs.

Temperature effects

other aquatic creatures. This may not be easy, as speed and agility are often the characteristics of the forage species. Predators that are not built for sustained high speed, those species usually flatter or chunkier in build, rely instead on ploys like ambushing to get a regular meal.

Reefs, rock walls, wharves and jetties, bridge pylons and midstream boulders are structures that provide suitable cover for predators to ambush prey. Weed beds qualify here too, as do areas of scattered light and shade, such as the foamy white water around islands and headlands, or the roiled water of a surf beach. Fish like flathead and flounder actually bury themselves partially in loose bottom strata, such as sand and mud and leap up at passing prey with lightning speed. Strangely enough, even bluewater speedsters like marlin, which are perfectly capable of running down the fastest fish, will also ambush prey from the dark blue depths of the ocean, perhaps 50 or 60 metres below their target.

CAMOUFLAGE

When threatened, fish may hide by burying in soft bottom strata (a ploy used by whiting) or by slipping quietly into standing weed beds (used by a whole host of fish species). Some fish dash for crevices in local rock formations, others, equipped with brilliantly reflective scales and colouration, hide by swimming toward the silvery underside of the water's surface, while still others with darker backs, dive for the depths to blend in there.

Others, like flathead and flounder have mottled markings that help camouflage them making them almost indistinguishable from the sort of sand, mud and weed bottom that they favour. For sheer chromatic versatility though no

Midstream rocks and holes provide predatory fish with ambush points where they can wait in concealment for passing victims.

fish are as adept as squid and octopus. These creatures are able, by rapid opening and closing of pigment cells in their skin, to disappear against virtually any colour or pattern of backdrop in the blink of an eye.

SYMBIOSIS

Some fish species make use of companion creatures in their environment to scare away potential predators, unearth or reveal food for them, or simply provide free transport. Small clown fish on the Great Barrier Reef have developed immunity to the sting of certain sea anemones and can actually nestle down within

the tentacles that would spell instant death to many other fish. Whiting in estuaries commonly follow large stingrays around, picking up stray bits of food uncovered by the ray's vigorous movement of its broad swimming flaps. A similar relationship can be seen where cobia follow giant manta rays around, using them almost like a mobile reef. Lastly, the curious and somewhat comical suckerfish often swims with large sharks and manta rays, picking off the small fish that often surround such big creatures. When it gets tired, it applies the powerful sucking plate on top of its head to the underside of its mobile host and is carried along without any effort.

Trout's natural camouflage helps conceal them from both predators and prey, requiring anglers to look carefully into the water Polarising sunglasses help.

These 'snowy' bream, so-called because of their light clean colouration, were part of a seasonal spawning migration working its way up the NSW coast during winter. Their open ocean surroundings and essentially baitfish and crustacean diet at this time changed their general colouration and improved their table value as well.

Quite commonplace fish work in concert with one another when feeding. These tailor and the bonito shown here were working baitfish at the surface, while the bream was scavenging scraps that fell down from the carnage above.

TRAVELLING

Many fish species will travel or shift from one location or another to ensure a constant food supply or to spawn. There are many such instances of marine fish moving up and down the coast into warmer or more food-rich places and most of these events happen on a semi-regular and seasonal basis. Other major movements that fish undertake have to do with spawning runs. Tailor for example are known to travel right from the southern states of Australia up to the waters off Fraser Island in Queensland, where they form massive spawning aggregations. Freshwater fish also have spawning runs, some of which are anadromous, like those of trout, which take them up into the shallow gravelly headwaters of alpine streams. Species like Australian bass and barramundi on the other hand are both catadromous, which means they run down from fresh water to salt water to spawn.

FINDING FISH

ATTRACTING FISH

Berley is used to attract and bring fish within the fishing distance of the angler. For example anglers can bring fish from one part of a river or estuary to another by spreading berley down a tidal or river current, or dispensing berley into an oceanic current at sea to bring fish from sometimes considerable distances down current, right to the back of the boat. Rock fishers and even beach anglers can do this as well, utilising longshore currents to carry the smells of berley to where fish are cruising by and help steer them into where the anglers are fishing.

LOOKING FOR FISH

Signs of fish activity at sea include splashes from surface breaking fish as they feed, or perhaps, concentrations of seabirds, whirling above a particular spot. You can also narrow the search for fish out at sea by identifying current lines, along which both baitfish and major predators swim. A smaller scale version of this activity can be applied on freshwater lakes containing bass, by using an echo sounder and searching for signs of fish schools suspended in mid-water. Even anglers chasing bream and trout use this method to some extent when they go looking for places to cast lures or flies, in the expectation that fish will be in residence because various factors like food supply, cover and water movement past structure are in evidence.

LOCATIONS

This is a common practice of anglers who target structures that hold fish, such as snags in rivers and estuaries, rocky points and drop-offs in large freshwater dams or reefs out at sea. Rock fishermen nearly always apply this form of fishing strategy, often without realising it, by picking rock platforms to fish from that are adjacent to areas of deep water or wave washed rubble and foam.

Sometimes, because of combinations of water movement, wind direction and seasonal factors, fish will be there and on the bite when you arrive. At other times, you will need to wait for them to work their way along to where you are fishing. This is particularly the case when working sections of coastal rocks or wash areas where mulloway are known to have travelling paths that they follow with some regularity. You go there to the place where fish have been encountered before, hopefully at a time when similar conditions of tide and weather and moon phase are operative. You set your baits out and you wait. The rest is up to the fish.

Below: You can attract fish into the area you are fishing by using wind and current to disperse berley, which is simply foodstuffs that fish find appealing. They can be either cereal-based or fish products, such as these pellets and this concentrated fish oil.

Above: Angler observation is often critical in finding fish. An unwatchful eye could miss this school of foraging golden trevally, were it not for their tails breaking the surface.

Below: Any constriction, whether natural or man made in a waterway, is a prime place to start looking for fish.

CHAPTER TWO

TACKLE

FISHING TACKLE

Welcome to the wonderful world of fishing tackle – the gadgets, gizmos, fundamentals and flummery that fits under the general heading of 'stuff you need to go fishing'. A good way to start on this voyage of discovery is to think about the different kinds of fishing there are and some typical tackle set-ups you will need to enjoy it.

Fishing tackle covers an enormous range of gear and equipment. To begin with, there are four major types of reels – overheads, threadlines, centrepins and closed face types. The many versions of these will increase that number significantly. When you add in the range of sizes and variations in levels of performance, the list can become enormous. Fishing rods differ too. They can be short, long, or somewhere in between. They can also be large or small diameter, solid or tubular and, if the latter, have walls that are thick and heavy or quite thin and light. Rods can also be supple or stiff, as well as light or powerful, and can come in a variety of materials, each of which has particular performance characteristics.

SPECIALISE OR GENERALISE?

The tackle you choose will depend on what you want to catch – whether that's as many different kinds of fish as you can, or perhaps just one special target species.

Take fishing rods for example. If you want to do a bit of beach and rock fishing, you could use a rod about 3.0 to 3.6 m long, capable of fishing 6 to 10 kg line and casting weights from 10 to 85 grams. If you were planning to shore-fish in estuaries, then a rod of 2.0 to 2.7 m, capable of fishing 3 to 6 kg line and casting weights from 5 to 40 g would be better. To fish those same estuaries from a boat, the same line rating and weight casting capabilities would apply, but it's doubtful you'd need anything longer than a rod of 1.8 to 2.0 metres. Depending on how much casting you need to do, and how far and how accurately you need to cast, these rods could be very light-tipped, or perhaps could be a little stiffer and more able to lift heavy rigs. Gamefishermen and offshore anglers seldom use a rod more than 1.5 to 1.8 m long because they need to consider forces such as leverage when fighting large, powerful fish. Freshwater fishermen targeting trout on the other hand, hardly ever need to think about such matters – their main concerns are about rod sensitivity, light weight and responsiveness. The rod lengths

Soft plastics are used more widely than ever as anglers discover their potential.

usually required for general freshwater fishing range from around 1.8 to 2.0 m, which would also suit light estuary boat fishing.

A single-handed rod for instance, which would be ideal for golden and silver perch would probably suit big bass as well. At a pinch, it could even be used for light tropical fishing for barramundi, threadfin salmon, tarpon, sooty grunter and saratoga. Rods needed to cope with tropical species in larger sizes, could well also suit large Murray cod, or offer the option of light offshore fishing.

Factors such as rod length, rod power, and weight casting capabilities are key elements in rod selection. Fish size and fighting ability also come into the equation, as do the difficulties presented by the terrain where the fish lives. You also need to consider whether the rod is needed to cast with, or simply to drop baits and jigs down or to troll.

If taken to the extreme, a rod's casting abilities and fish fighting power can call up quite opposite characteristics. In practice, every rod is a compromise between two conflicting requirements – being light enough to cast with and powerful enough to land the target fish. Whatever the sort of fishing you want to do, some rod and reel combination will do that job brilliantly. If it is good quality, the outfit will also probably suit a range of other fishing tasks as well. The more specialised your preferred fishing style however, the more specialised the tackle you will need to do it.

Regardless of the type of tackle you choose, the important factor is how well it works. If you need to cast a lot, then the outfit should do that job as effectively as possible. If the main game is stopping hefty fish, then the rod should be capable of sapping the fish's energy without wearing you out in the process.

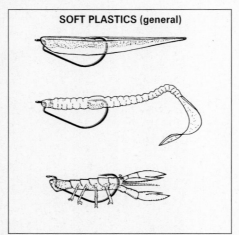

SOFT PLASTICS (general)

Slug-go rigged on Mustad Big Mouth hook, worm and crayfish.

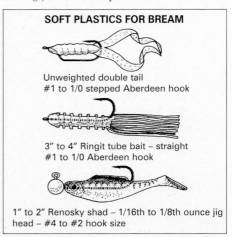

SOFT PLASTICS FOR BREAM

Unweighted double tail
#1 to 1/0 stepped Aberdeen hook

3" to 4" Ringit tube bait – straight
#1 to 1/0 Aberdeen hook

1" to 2" Renosky shad – 1/16th to 1/8th ounce jig head – #4 to #2 hook size

Soft Plastics for bream.

Don't confuse cheap tackle with good tackle – and that applies right the way through from 'big-ticket' goods like boats and echo sounders, rods and reels and so on, to less expensive items such as hooks, line, snaps and lures.

Electric trolling motors offer the same ability as anchors to fish a specific place without moving off it, but can also be used to slowly explore along a riverbank or lake shore, or sneak up on nervous fish.

ANCHORS, CHAINS AND ROPES

Anchoring tackle is used in fishing to keep the boat in position so you can reach fish with baits or lures. Over sand and mud, use a flat-bladed anchor such as a Danforth or 'sand-anchor'. Over rocky bottom, use a grapnel type anchor or 'reef pick'. In calm water, with no wave action and little current or wind, you may not need to use anchor chain, but wherever water or boat movement is likely to lift the anchor from the bottom, a length of chain is a good idea. This is attached between the anchor and anchor rope and will help keep the anchor in secure contact with the bottom.

ANTI-TWIST RIGS

In deep water, it is very likely that turbulence, wave action or currents will swing the boat around at anchor or on the drift and in some cases, the boat will describe a series of circles as the eddying water pulls it about. The same thing can happen to deep water fishing rigs and if this happens enough, rigs can tend to rotate and twist the fishing line into tangles. Various methods can be used to minimise or block this line twist, including the use of keels, swivels or the incorporation of small aluminium triangles fitted between sinkers and hook traces and the main line.

BAGS

While you can use almost any form of bag for carrying fishing tackle (or fish for that matter) there are several specific types that suit fishing particularly well. Beginning at the simple end, there is nothing wrong with a plain hessian sack for carrying and holding fish. The open weave and natural fibres of the sack allow you to keep the fish moist and cool by periodically dunking the bag into the water and allowing the cooling effect of natural evaporation to prevent spoilage. Dedicated beach anglers sometimes make use of canvas or plastic sheet shoulder bags into which they can dump fish as they are caught. This enables them to remain in the one spot, taking advantage of a bite that may only run for a few minutes, or could go on for hours on end. Fishing tackle requires similar thought when deciding on carry bags. You can use shoulder bags but these do not make it easy to carry tackle for any distance over rough terrain as you may need to do when hiking into remote freshwater streams or negotiating beaches and coastal rock platforms. The best kinds of tackle bags for leaving your hands free are the haversack type. These allow you to carry a significant amount of gear and fishing rods, while not interfering too much with your ability to climb in and out of some fishing locations.

BAIT DRIFTING TACKLE

The art of bait drifting is a skill that is particularly rewarding. Bait drifting tackle can be as simple as a 9 ft fly rod and an ordinary fly reel loaded with 2 to 3 kg monofilament.

White this form of angling has suffered a decline in popularity, it is one of the most effective ways to catch trout in streams. The idea is to cast and present unweighted natural baits such as worms, grasshoppers and mudeyes.

The technique involves stripping line off the reel, carefully holding it in your stripping hand in loops and casting the unweighted bait upstream to drift down naturally. The weight to cast is achieved by using a heavy suicide hook.

Above: Baitcasters are used extensively for barramundi fishing because they suit trolling and repetitive, accurate, short-range casting.

Below: Worms, grasshoppers and mudeyes are a great trout bait

A size 4–6 long shanked keeper hook attached to a 2 kg line. A mudeye is impaled through the front of the thorax and/the hook is drawn along abdomen to exit throughthe rear orifice. Swimming action is simulated by cast and retrieve with jerky movement.

The Dual Leader Rig

Brass ring

Short leader

Size 4–1 hook is used to hold a heavy bait.

Long leader—

Ensure that there are plenty of wriggling ends to draw a trout's attention and interest.

Size 12–8 hook used to present a lighter bait.

Three grasshoppers provide extra weight for easier casting. The first two are threaded 'head to toe' to attract trout through their sense of smell. The last one is barely nipped, so the movement visually attracts the fish.

BAITDRIFTING TECHNIQUES

The Conventional Rig

The Conventional Rig with Bait Shandy

Flat Wine Wrap Rig

A size 4–2 hook with a 1.5 cm square of lead-like wine bottle wrap which provides the weight necessary to cast a single March fly or other light bait.

Size 4 hook attached to a 2 kg monofilament line.

Size 2–4 hook with a worm threaded onto the shank provides sufficient weight to cast even the lightest baits.

A fine nip in a lower segment of the abdomen or through the wing buds of a mudeye by a size 12 hook barely inhibits natural movements.

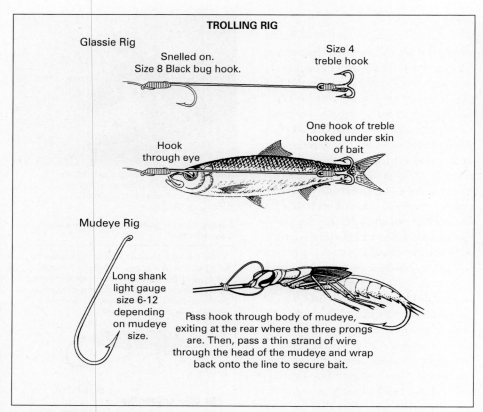

TROLLING RIG

Glassie Rig

Snelled on.
Size 8 Black bug hook.

Size 4
treble hook

Hook
through eye

One hook of treble
hooked under skin
of bait

Mudeye Rig

Long shank
light gauge
size 6-12
depending
on mudeye
size.

Pass hook through body of mudeye,
exiting at the rear where the three prongs
are. Then, pass a thin strand of wire
through the head of the mudeye and wrap
back onto the line to secure bait.

Bait trolling rigs.

Bass and perch are best chased with light single handed rod and reel outfits but will take baits, lures or flies.

BAIT TROLLING TACKLE

The tackle used to troll baits for trout needs to be slightly heavier than normal trout tackle. A long bait casting rod with a good tip action is ideal when matched with 4 kg line and a baitcaster reel that incorporates a ratchet.

There's little action on trolled baits, so there's no need to monitor the rod tip. The heavier tackle ensures a solid hook set when a trout takes the bait. The two best rigs for bait trolling are shown here. The stinger treble hook on the glassie bait should increase hook ups.

A fine piece of copper fuse wire is used to hold the mudeye on the hook.

BARRAMUNDI TACKLE

Typically, rods used for barramundi fishing are from 1.5 to 1.8 m long (when used with baitcasters) and from 1.8 to 2.1 m long (when used with threadlines). Lines are usually 4 to 8 kg breaking strain, with about a metre of heavier leader material, say, 15 to 25 kg fluorocarbon. Lures for barramundi are most often bibbed minnows from 75 to 120 mm long and should carry heavy-duty split rings and treble hooks to withstand the stresses of fighting these powerful fish. Other lures that will take barramundi include soft plastics, heavy-duty spinnerbaits, surface poppers, rattling spot type lures and large, bushy streamer flies. Top baits, depending on location, are live Machrobrachium shrimp and pop-eye mullet (in billabongs and estuaries), while around ocean fronting headlands

MANNS BOOF BAIT

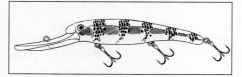

These and similar minnow lures are standard fare for barramundi fishing. The model shown is a deep diver, but other versions have smaller bibs and suit shallow water work as well.

and inshore reefs saltwater barramundi will take almost any small live fish, and just love large banana prawns.

BASS AND PERCH TACKLE

Australian bass and estuary perch are two very closely related freshwater fish, with distribution zones that can overlap according to season and regional weather conditions. The same tackle is ideal for either – usually baitcaster reels mounted on rods from 1.6 to 1.8 m long, or threadline reels matched with rods from 1.7 to 1.9 m long. In either case, suggested line classes range from 2 to 4 kg and lures can be surface poppers, bibbed plugs, surface paddling lures, soft plastics, spinnerbaits, small rattling spot style lures, and flies — from streamers to Dahlberg Divers and frog patterns. Baits for these fish include earthworms, cicadas and either live prawns or shrimp.

BERLEY

You can use various substances such as berley to attract fish into the area you are fishing and get them into a feeding mood. Berley can be such

things as prawn heads and shells, or fish flesh, or perhaps crushed crabs and shellfish.

For luderick, the best berley is a quantity of the green weed they naturally eat and that you will also use for bait. As a rule, the best berley is the same as, or similar to, some locally available fish food, but even substances quite foreign to fish's usual diets will work. Such things as bread or any number of other cereal-based products can work. When fishing for bream, crushed oyster shells will often bring them on the bite, just be sure you're not vandalising someone's oyster lease in the process.

BERLEY BAGS

Often, the method of dispensing berley can be just as important as its content. A sneaky

Perch tackle

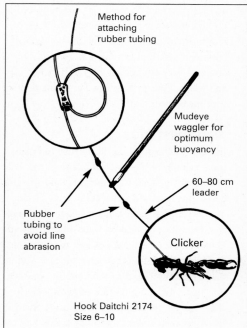

Method for
attaching
rubber tubing

Mudeye
waggler for
optimum
buoyancy

60–80 cm
leader

Rubber
tubing to
avoid line
abrasion

Clicker

Hook Daitchi 2174
Size 6–10

method of dispensing berley at a depth is to pack berley into a strong paper bag and tie this to your fishing line at a point some way above the hook. The rig is lowered down into the water and as the water seeps into the paper bag and weakens it, the berley is allowed to escape, right down where your baited hook is. When you catch a fish or bring your rig in to re-bait it, another sack of berley is wrapped onto the line and sent down with the fresh bait.

BERLEY BOMBS
Berley bombs are designed to release berley below the surface at specific depths. This localises fish feeding activity beneath the boat and is a particularly good method when surface currents are strong and might otherwise spread the berley and take fish away from your baits. Berley bombs can be anything you can cobble together, or can be purpose-built commercially available versions. Most are cylindrical containers with holes drilled in the sides to allow the slow escape of berley particles, or are designed with hinged panels that flip open when a release cord is pulled to spill a quantity of berley in a specific place.

BERLEY BUCKETS
Berley buckets are open-top pots attached to the backs of boats. Berley is dropped into these and dispensed through a series of holes drilled in the pot walls and bottom. They are particularly useful for using a whole tuna frame or similar, as with a berley masher you can agitate or break up large lumps of berley matter, allowing smaller pieces to gradually escape through the holes in the pot. For a berley masher, you can use any sufficiently sharp and heavy-bladed arrangement that has a handle attached. The method suits many shallow reef-fishing situations, but because the berley is all released at the surface, it may not be as effective in deep water as the berley bomb. It is particularly good for bringing baitfish to the surface where they can be line caught and is also a good method for attracting species such as mackerel, kingfish, tuna and snapper to the boat.

BERLEY CUBING
When offshore fishing for species such as yellowfin tuna or albacore, 'cubes' or biscuit-sized pieces of fish can be cut up onboard and flipped over the stern into the current to bring fish into the area. Make the size of the pieces small enough for a fish to sip them in easily as it swims by, but large enough to completely bury a strong short-shank hook. Typical hook examples include 5/0 to 7/0 Mustad 9174 KEBR, Black Magic KS, or Eagle Claw L317MG. Some anglers now use circle hooks for this work, such as the Mustad 3997 or Eagle Claw 190.

Ordinary laundry buckets like this one make excellent accessories for beach fishing and anywhere that tackle has to be carried a short way.

BINOCULARS
The notion of using binoculars as a fishing tool might seem odd at first, until you consider that many fast-moving fish, such as tuna do not always reveal themselves to unaided vision. In fact, these fish can be so mobile you could spend a lot of time and fuel chasing them all over a large waterway, never see a fish, yet be sharing the water with thousands of them. A good pair of sufficiently large and powerful binoculars, about 7 x 50 (seven times magnification and 50 mm lens diameter), will gather enough light and allow sufficient long sight to be able to spot tuna working the surface from several kilometres away. Binoculars can also be useful when confirming distant landmarks, identifying vessels and reconnoitering unfamiliar territory.

BUCKETS AND BINS
The fishing uses of buckets are manifold. Carrying bait, washing down the boat, providing somewhere to drop hooks and lures in a hurry, using them to bail out a swamped boat and even serving as a handy helmet during sudden hail storms (use a plastic one, the metal ones can deafen you). Bins are just buckets without handles and can be fixed to the sides of boats or incorporated into seats and console areas. They can take hand tools like knives and pliers, hold bait and ice, serve as temporary storage for rig components while you are rigging up in a pitching boat, or simply be

somewhere to drop rubbish until you are ready to dump it properly back at port.

CHEMICALLY SHARPENED HOOKS
These are extremely sharp hooks right out of the box and don't require any further sharpening after purchase. That might seem an odd thing to say, but for years, serious anglers knew that to be sure of having a hook point go in, they would first have to take to the hook with a sharpening stone or file. This was because for many years, hook metallurgy was not sufficiently advanced to produce a needle sharp point that would not fold over or break. The vast majority of fish hooks were deliberately made blunt enough for the hook point to survive. This required light tackle anglers especially to be aware of this fact and to 'touch up' the hook before use. The chemicals in the process are used more to remove minute surface irregularities and grinding marks prior to final hook plating. If these imperfections were not removed this way, they would hinder the smooth penetration of the hook point. Such highly processed hooks are not cheap, but they do work better, right from new, without any modification by the angler. This is not to say that such hooks will not become blunt or damaged over time and with use. When and if they do however, they can easily be honed again and continue to give good service.

CIRCLE HOOKS
At one time, the only consumers of these funny-looking hooks were deep sea and longline commercial fishermen. As these commercial fishing lines are left essentially unattended for long periods, during which time the fish are obliged to hook themselves, these fishers needed a hook that would penetrate a fish's jaw easily without the need to strike or 'set' the hook in any way. The peculiar design and shape of the circle hook does this perfectly, the re-curved point tending to roll around in the fish's mouth until the point slides over a bone or sinew and pops through an area of thin membrane. As the fish tries to swim away, pressure comes onto the hook and it rolls even further until it is centralised on the bend, with the re-curved point now imprisoning the jaw or other solid mouth part, ensuring the fish cannot dislodge the hook or tear it free from soft tissue. Offshore recreational fishermen have only recently become aware of the many good properties of these hooks and they are now being pressed into service for everything from serious bottom fishing to game fishing. They are particularly well-suited to catch and release fishing, as they are seldom swallowed like conventional hooks, more usually taking hold right in the corner of a fish's jaw where release is both less injurious to the fish and easier and safer for the angler.

SALTWATER CHEMICALLY SHARPENED HOOK GUIDE

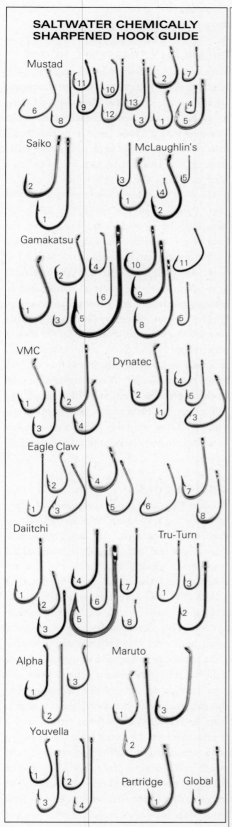

Mustad
Saiko
McLaughlin's
Gamakatsu
VMC
Dynatec
Eagle Claw
Daiitchi
Tru-Turn
Alpha
Maruto
Youvella
Partridge
Global

Above: Saltwater chemically sharpened hooks.

Right: List of saltwater chemically sharpened hooks.

SALTWATER CHEMICALLY SHARPENED HOOKS

Manufacturer	Model	Style	Size Range	Point Style
Mustad	1.Big Red (92554NPNR)	Heavy Beak	8/0 – 6	Needle Suicide Point
Good Tackle Shops	2.Hoodlum (10827NPBLN)	Heavy Live Bait	11/0 – 1/0	Needle Straight Point
	3.Bloodworm (90234NPNR)	Extra Long Shank Beak	3/0 – 6	Needle Point
	4.Needle Sneck (3331NPG)	Square Bend	2/0 – 12	Needle Point
	5.Big Gun (10829NPBLN)	Heavy Saltwater	12/0 – 6	Kirbed Needle Point
	6.Big Mouth (37753NPNP)	Wide Gap	7/0 – 6	Needle Point
	7.Red Baitholder (92668NPNPN)	Baitholder	4/0 – 1/0	Needle Point
	8.Aberdeen (3261NPBLN)	Light Gauge	1/0 – 8	Needle Bend Point
	9.Needle Tarpon (7766NPNR)	Heavy Straight	7/0 – 6	Turned-in Needle Point
	10.Needle Tarpon (77662NPBL)	Open Eye Gang	1 – 6	Needle Point
	11.Demon Fine Wire (39952NPBL)	Circle Style	11/0 – 2/0	Kirbed Point
	12.Saltwater Fly (34039NPSS)	Extra Long Stainless	4/0 – 1/0	Needle Point
	13.Saltwater Fly (34005KESS)	Stainless	2/0 – 1	Knife Edge
Saiko	1.Special Sea Hook	Long Shank	6/0 – 4	Needle Point
K & M Tackle	2.Extra Strength	Micro Barb, Heavy Wire	8/0 – 3/0	Needle Point
015 852 505				
McLaughlin's	1.Snapper	Heavy Duty Beak	4/0	Turned-in Needle Point
03 9555 5433	2.Mulloway	Heavy Duty Beak	6/0	Turned-in Needle Point
	3.Whiting	4x Long Shank	6	Needle Point
	4.Blackfish	Extra Short 200 Shank Bend	8	Needle Point
	5.Gar/Yakka	4x Long Shank	12	Needle Point
Gamakatsu	1.Octopus	Octopus	10/0 – 12	Needle Point
Offshore Sports	2.Octopus Circle	Circle	8/0 – 2/0	Turned-in Needle Point
02 9319 2986	3.Baitkeeper	Double sliced long shank	4/0 – 8	Needle Point
	4.Baitholder	Double sliced long shank	4/0 – 14	Needle Point
	5.Oceania Long Shank	2x Long Shank	2/0 – 12	Needle Point
	6.Worm Hook	Fine Gauge Long Shank	1 – 6	Needle Point
	7.O'Shaughnessy	Heavy Duty Straight	10/0 – 8	Needle Point
	8.SL12S Big Game	Fine Gauge Tinned	10/0 – 4/0	Needle Point
	9.Big Bait	Extra Strong Offset	10/0 – 1/0	Needle Point
	10.Big Bait Circle	Circle	8/0 – 2/0	Turned-in Needle Point
	11.Shiner	Super Bend Circle	1 – 6	Turned-in Needle Point
VMC	1.Octopus (7299SS)	Stainless Octopus		Cone Cut Point
Freetime Group	2.O'Shaughnessy (7255SS)	Stainless O'Shaughnessy		Needle Point
02 9793 2999	3. Baitholder (7292RO)	Baitholder		Cone Cut Point
	4.Octopus (7299RD)	Octopus		Cone Cut Point
Dynatec	1.Long Shank	2x Long Shank	4/0 – 12	Needle Point
VFSD	2.Suicide	Offset Point	8/0 – 8	Turned-in Needle Point
03 9764 9799	3.Wide Gap	Super Bend Circle	4/0 – 6	Turned-in Needle Point
	4.Baitkeep	Double Slice Offset	6/0 – 10	Turned-in Needle Point
	5.O'Shaughnessy	Straight	5/0 – 6	Needle Point
Eagle Claw	1.LT6088R	Long Shank Double Barb	2 – 8	Needle Point
Tacspo	2.LT226RD	Suicide Double Barb	9/0 – 6	Needle Point
07 3390 4399	3.LT141	Kahle Wide Gap	7/0 – 8	Needle Point
	4.L318N	Live Bait Straight	9/0 – 6/0	Needle Point
	5.L7042	Wide Bend	2/0 – 8	Turned-in Needle Point
	6.L741	Kahle Wide Gap	5/0 – 10	Needle Point
	7.L054SS	O'Shaughnessy Stainless	4/0 – 1/0	Needle Point
	8.L067	Straight	5/0 – 6	Needle Point
Daiitchi	1.2546 Stainless	Straight Eye O'Shaughnessy	6/0 – 6	Needle Point
Juro	2.3000 Red	2x Short Shank Beak	10/0 – 4	Turned-in Needle Point
03 9555 5433	3.3111 Black	2x Short Shank Beak	10/0 – 4	Turned-in Needle Point
	4.2451 Black	Straight Eye O'Shaughnessy	4/0 – 8	Needle Point
	5.7000 Stainless Steel	Extra Heavy Duty Game	10/0 – 6/0	Knife Edge
	6.1720 Red	4x Long Shank	2 – 12	Needle Point
	7.1750 Bronze	4x Long Shank	2 – 12	Needle Point
	8.2174 Green	Short Shank Weed/Shrimp	2 – 12	Needle Point
Tru-Turn	1.Bait Holder	2x Long Shank	1/0 – 6	Spear Point
M & N Umbers	2.XX Strong	2x Strong	4/0 – 2/0	Spear Point
02 9871 3459	3.Long Shank	Forged	4 – 10	Spear Point
Maruto	1.MS-4310	Beak	10/0 – 12	Needle Point
Top End Tackle	2.3300	Long Shank Carlisle	6/0 – 6	Needle Point
08 8948 0378	3.DS-4310	Baitholder	10/0 – 10	Needle Point
Alpha	1.Bait Holder	Forged Shank	2/0 – 10	Turned-in Needle Point
M.B. Wraggs	2.Long Shank	4x Long Shank	2/0 – 12	Needle Point
03 9376 2411	3.Suicide	Forged Shank	6/0 – 8	Needle Point
Youvella	1.Octopus (121462XB)	2x Beak	10/0 – 1/0	Turned-in Needle Point
Gus Veness	2.Baitholder (11716B)	Baitholder	4/0 – 4	Turned-in Needle Point
02 9540 2955	3.Kirby (424142XB)	2x Strong Kendall Kirby	10/0 – 1/0	NeedlePoint
	4.Carlisle (11605B)	4x Long Shank	2/0 – 12	Needle Point
Partridge	1.Sea Prince (C552)	Stainless O'Shaughnessy	6/0 – 10	Turned-out Needle Point
Clarkson Imports				
03 9755 5377				
Global	1.44007S	O'Shaughnessy	6/0 – 8	Needle Point
Clarkson Imports				
03 9755 5377				

Note there is no industry standard for hook sizing. Similar patterns from different manufacturers will be the close to the same size, however different patterns will be different in physical size.

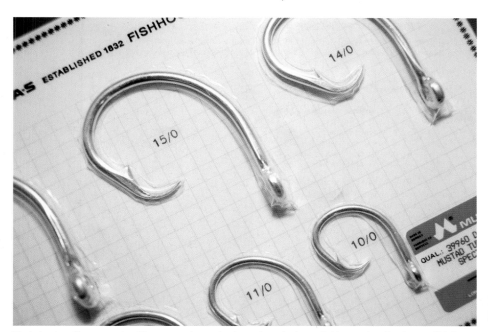

Circle hooks offer secure hooking properties and suit catch and release fishing as they hook most fish in the corner of the mouth, allowing clean release.

fishing as they resist scuffing by the bodies of big fish, but are very well behaved in the water, allowing excellent presentation of lures and baits, which enhances the chances of a hook up in the first place. Sometimes this tough outer skin is achieved by passing the line through a chemical bath, a process claimed by some manufacturers to inhibit the absorption of water by the line. This is important because, it is maintained, line can lose a percentage of its breaking strength to the degree by which water is absorbed.

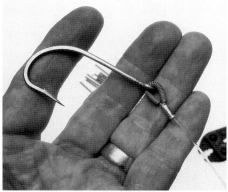

Co-polymer lines such as this hard-skinned game fishing trace make excellent leaders for fishing situations that call upon durability in the terminal rig.

CLOTHING

You might think this is a bit silly – considering what forms of specialised clothing to wear fishing. If you think about it, most people do that to some extent already, even if it is only to be careful not to wear their best shirt and pants fishing. In fact, fishing clothing does need to be a bit special if you are to remain comfortable, effective and in some cases unseen. This can be very important in fishing situations that require stealth, such as trout fishing on streams, or flats fishing for sharp-eyed species like bream, flathead and bonefish. You need to be sensible about sleeve and trouser leg lengths, striking a balance between comfort and coolness (or warmth) and to consider such things as the dangerous effects of prolonged exposure to sunlight and the future risk of skin cancer.

CO-FILAMENT FISHING LINES

Co-filament lines are made by bonding two separate extrusions – one within the other. This provides product technicians with the ability to combine several different line characteristics within the one product. For instance, it is possible to make a tough-skinned line with a low-density core, so that the line tends to float. This is a very useful attribute when float fishing for luderick from the ocean rocks, where wave action tends to pull slack line under the surface, slowing down angler response times to sudden and subtle submersions of the float as a fish takes the bait. Conventional fishing line in this situation is traditionally greased with Vaseline or something similar to keep it up on top of the water, but here, the product's inherent buoyancy does the job without the need for messy lubricants. Other combinations of suppleness and

sinking behaviour can be achieved, such as low stretch and hard wearing characteristics.

COOL CHESTS, FISH BOXES AND ICE SLURRIES

If every time you caught a fish you had to rush home and put it in the fridge, you wouldn't be able to stay out very long or catch more than a single fish in a session. To get around this problem, fishermen use insulated plastic cool chests or fish boxes that can be refrigerated by dropping in ice or a frozen freezer block. A very effective way of keeping fish in good order until you go home and clean them is to create a water and ice slurry by dumping crushed ice into about 20-25 cm of water. Fish caught and intended for table use can be dropped live into this slurry, where they quickly and painlessly fall asleep. In effect, they die without stress, as the cold simply shuts their metabolisms down to zero. Fish killed this way will actually taste better than those knocked on the head or allowed to flip and flop all over the place until they asphyxiate. This is because stress releases certain enzymes that can materially affect the taste and texture of fish flesh and usually for the worse. This is how premium fish is cared for by professional fishermen looking for top dollar for their catch and recreational anglers can learn a valuable lesson here about preserving the very best eating quality in the fish they catch.

CO-POLYMER FISHING LINES

Co-polymer fishing lines are created by combining two formulations or specifications of nylon within the one extrusion, usually seen as a soft supple core with a hard wearing outer skin. Such lines are very useful for leader materials for game

CUTTING BOARDS

Whenever you need to use a knife, you also need to use a cutting board to protect the edge of the knife and whatever surface you are working on from damage. Cutting boards can be made from 9 mm-thick scrap plywood (20 x 30 cm is a realistic minimum size) or if using solid timber, then 12 mm is probably a minimum thickness. Nylon cutting boards are readily available from supermarkets and vary in thickness from 9 to 11 mm. If you want to create a fixed cutting board for use in a boat however, you can buy nylon sheeting from industrial plastics providers and in this case, since the sheet is supported by another structure, you can get away with using only 2 mm or 3 mm thick material. It is important for reasons of hygiene to be able to wash and scrub cutting boards. Loose boards are easy to scrub on both sides and around the edges, but in-built sheet ones should be fixed at multiple points to ensure the edges don't curl with sunlight. The edges should also be sealed with a bead of Sikaflex to fill any gaps that might be created underneath which can harbour bacteria. There is also an excellent range of moulded plastic cutting boards made for fishing boats by the Bermuda Fishing Accessories company.

DECK WINCHES

Deck winches are simply large diameter centrepin reels, mounted vertically on 'U' brackets and bolted onto a railing or gunwale cover. Most

TWISTED DROPPER LOOP

Dropper loops facilitate the easy attachment of hooks. Twisting the line before tying a dropper loop stiffens the dropper so that it is less likely to tangle around the main line. This strategy, which has applications in deep sea and surf fishing, eliminates the need for rings and swivels.

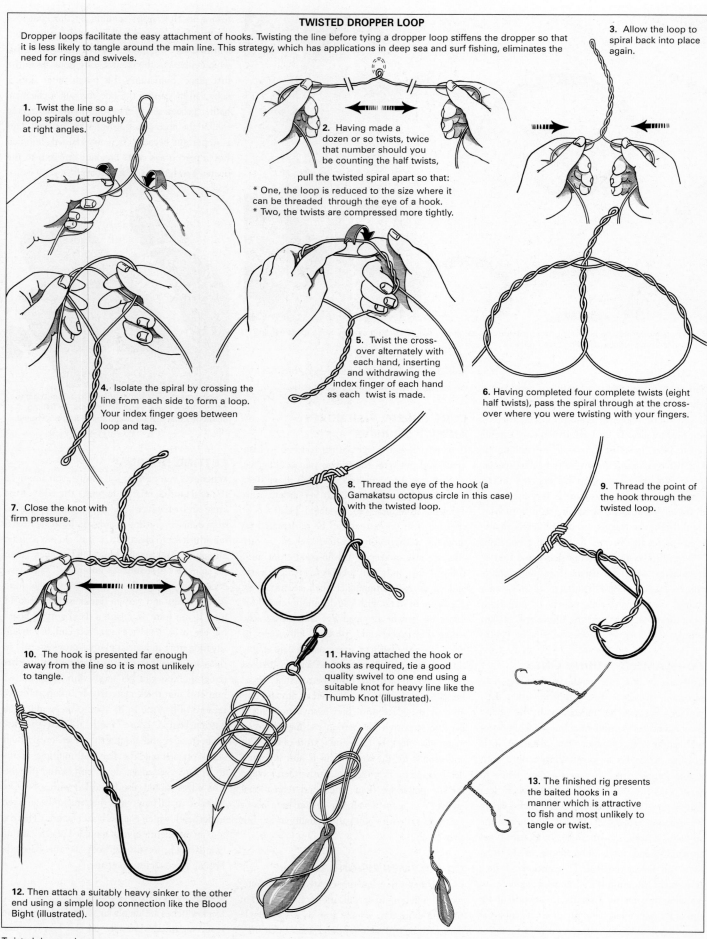

1. Twist the line so a loop spirals out roughly at right angles.

2. Having made a dozen or so twists, twice that number should you be counting the half twists,

pull the twisted spiral apart so that:
* One, the loop is reduced to the size where it can be threaded through the eye of a hook.
* Two, the twists are compressed more tightly.

3. Allow the loop to spiral back into place again.

4. Isolate the spiral by crossing the line from each side to form a loop. Your index finger goes between loop and tag.

5. Twist the cross-over alternately with each hand, inserting and withdrawing the index finger of each hand as each twist is made.

6. Having completed four complete twists (eight half twists), pass the spiral through at the cross-over where you were twisting with your fingers.

7. Close the knot with firm pressure.

8. Thread the eye of the hook (a Gamakatsu octopus circle in this case) with the twisted loop.

9. Thread the point of the hook through the twisted loop.

10. The hook is presented far enough away from the line so it is most unlikely to tangle.

11. Having attached the hook or hooks as required, tie a good quality swivel to one end using a suitable knot for heavy line like the Thumb Knot (illustrated).

12. Then attach a suitably heavy sinker to the other end using a simple loop connection like the Blood Bight (illustrated).

13. The finished rig presents the baited hooks in a manner which is attractive to fish and most unlikely to tangle or twist.

Twisted dropper loop.

Dropping heavy weights and multiple baits down to deep water fish means large diameter centrepin reels like these are a good choice.

have some form of a line guard incorporated into their framing and this makes it easier to keep line under control when paying it out or winding it in. They are very popular on multi-client charter boats where dozens of fishers at a time might be fishing baits on the bottom. Usually, they are spooled with heavy line (20 to 30 kg) and use heavy sinkers to take baited multiple dropper rigs to the bottom.

DEEPWATER OFFSHORE TACKLE

Some tackle requirements of deep sea bottom fishing have a lot in common with bait fishing, but others are more specialised. Noted angler Geoff Wilson has developed a twisted dropper loop rig that he calls the 'Deep Sea Tangle-Free Rig'. This arrangement allows the increased stiffness of the twisted line to make the dropper stand out proud from the main line. This, in turn, reduces the tendency of droppers to wrap around the main line and so helps prevent tangles. Sinkers for this work are usually snapper leads or bomb sinkers and range in weight from 500 g to 1.5 kilograms. In extremely deep water however, where fish like hapuku, oilfish or gemfish are pursued and currents can be strong, deep-sea anglers have been known to use window sash weights or even short lengths of railway line for sinkers!

Reels should be large capacity and capable of retrieving considerable weight, which is why centrepin boat reels and deck winches are so popular, but within reason, using weights up to 0.5 kg or so, large overhead reels can be pressed into service. When rods are used, they must, of necessity, be short and stout. Hook sizes generally range from 6/0 upward to 10/0 with occasional very large baits calling up larger hooks again. Line is usually heavy, from 15 to 50 kg breaking strain and this is one area where gelspun lines have made a big difference. You can fish 50-pound braid and land most deep sea angling species.

Aside from the disadvantage of purchase cost, there are two distinct advantages of braid over conventional mono line. There is virtually no stretch, so hook sets are better and bites are more readily felt, and since the diameter of the line is much less than equivalent-strength mono, water resistance is reduced, meaning smaller sinker weights can be used.

DEPTH SOUNDERS

Depth sounders, sometimes called 'fish finders', are an extremely useful tool for many forms of fishing. They have obvious applications in terms of telling you how deep the water is beneath your boat. They can do more though. For instance, they can also show the type of bottom, whether it is hard or soft, the general bottom shape, and also reveal salient fish-holding features, such as drop-offs, pinnacles, rubble bottom, sloping terrain and thermoclines. They will also show suspended fish, and good ones can let you tell the difference between large and small fish, isolated fish and groups, and whether or not the fish are actively feeding or

acting defensively. Also, with practice, you can learn to recognise the typical signals returned by particular species, enabling you to target the fish beneath you with greater efficiency and expectation of results. Good sounders offer high definition images, drawn clearly because of high pixel counts in their screen displays. They filter out irrelevant signals and 'clutter' with suitable suppression circuitry and enable you to distinguish between bottom formations and bottom-hugging fish though a system variously described by different brands as 'grey line', 'white line' and so on.

DOWNRIGGERS

Downriggers are essentially a form of deck winch, spooled with thin but strong, multi-strand wire cable. They use a heavy lead weight called a 'bomb' to set a fishing rig at a specific depth. Good ones have counters that indicate the depth at which the bomb is set and when used in conjunction with a depth sounder, will let you match the depth of your bait or lure presentations exactly to the depth at which fish are showing. A release clip system allows the fishing line to be held close to the

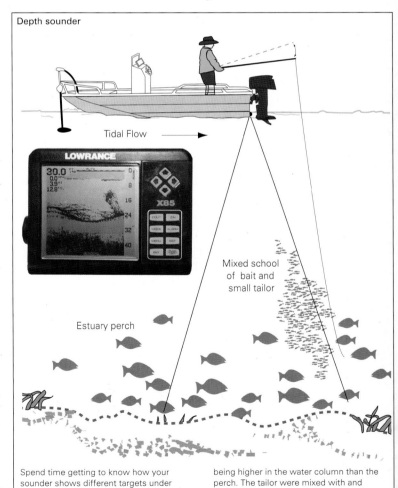

Spend time getting to know how your sounder shows different targets under varying conditions. The signals on this screen shot proved to be small tailor and reasonable estuary perch. Both species took vertically jigged soft plastics, with the tailor being higher in the water column than the perch. The tailor were mixed with and feeding on a cloud of whitebait and prawns. The estuary perch were preying on these same food items and possibly also on the smaller tailor.

back of the bomb with the length between the bomb and the hook being set by you, topside, before the rig is deployed. When a fish hits the rig, the clip releases, allowing you to fight the fish unimpeded by the weight of the bomb. In this respect alone, downriggers are far superior to planer boards, paravanes, lead-core line or heavy trolling sinkers, all of which have to be wound in along with the hooked fish.

Downrigging tackle must be just right. Larger, high quality threadlines with front drags are very good. Baitrunner style reels are also ideal as the baitrunner setting can be used when the bomb is lowered.

Rods should be around 1.8 m and be progressively tapered so they can be bent over and well tensioned in the downrigger troll position so bites can be easily monitored.

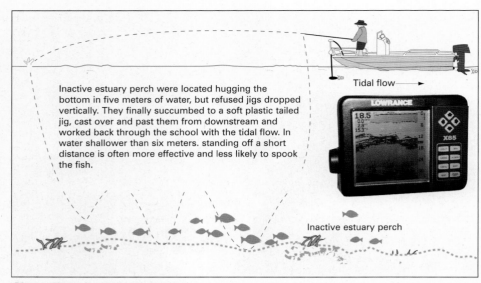

Inactive estuary perch were located hugging the bottom in five meters of water, but refused jigs dropped vertically. They finally succumbed to a soft plastic tailed jig, cast over and past them from downstream and worked back through the school with the tidal flow. In water shallower than six meters. standing off a short distance is often more effective and less likely to spook the fish.

Tidal flow ⟶

Inactive estuary perch

Above: Alternative presentation strategies.

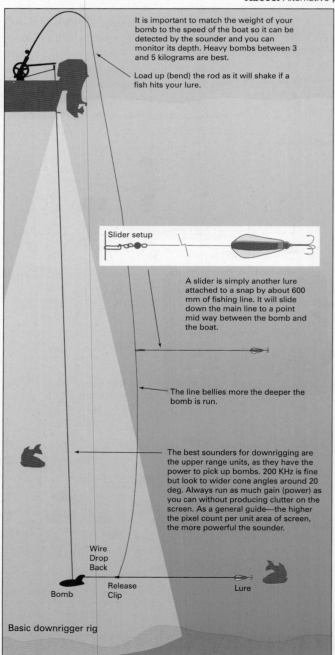

It is important to match the weight of your bomb to the speed of the boat so it can be detected by the sounder and you can monitor its depth. Heavy bombs between 3 and 5 kilograms are best.

Load up (bend) the rod as it will shake if a fish hits your lure.

Slider setup

A slider is simply another lure attached to a snap by about 600 mm of fishing line. It will slide down the main line to a point mid way between the bomb and the boat.

The line bellies more the deeper the bomb is run.

The best sounders for downrigging are the upper range units, as they have the power to pick up bombs. 200 KHz is fine but look to wider cone angles around 20 deg. Always run as much gain (power) as you can without producing clutter on the screen. As a general guide—the higher the pixel count per unit area of screen, the more powerful the sounder.

Wire Drop Back

Bomb

Release Clip

Lure

Basic downrigger rig

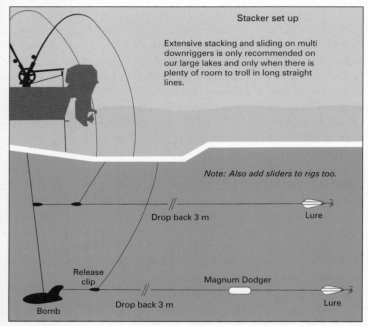

Stacker set up

Extensive stacking and sliding on multi downriggers is only recommended on our large lakes and only when there is plenty of room to troll in long straight lines.

Note: Also add sliders to rigs too.

Drop back 3 m

Lure

Release clip

Magnum Dodger

Drop back 3 m

Lure

Bomb

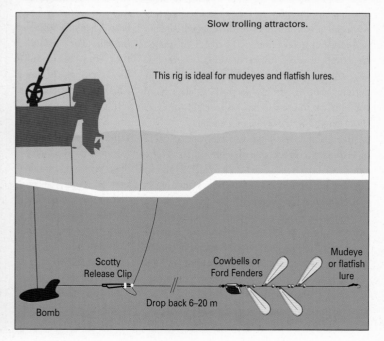

Slow trolling attractors.

This rig is ideal for mudeyes and flatfish lures.

Scotty Release Clip

Cowbells or Ford Fenders

Mudeye or flatfish lure

Drop back 6–20 m

Bomb

Magnum controlled slider

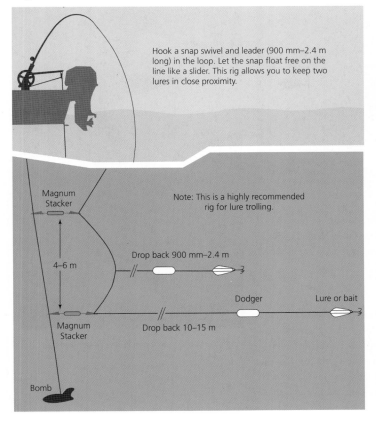

Hook a snap swivel and leader (900 mm–2.4 m long) in the loop. Let the snap float free on the line like a slider. This rig allows you to keep two lures in close proximity.

Magnum Stacker

Note: This is a highly recommended rig for lure trolling.

4–6 m

Drop back 900 mm–2.4 m

Magnum Stacker

Drop back 10–15 m

Dodger

Lure or bait

Bomb

Magnum dodger rig

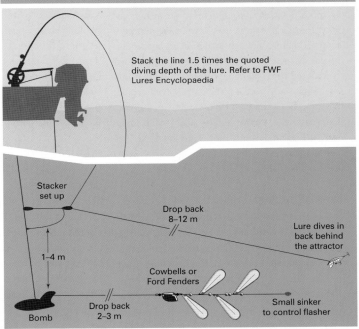

Note: With this rig as with others, the deeper you go to the shorter the drop back is required.

Magnum Stacker

Drop back 4–21 m

Small Dodger

Magnum J Plug or Tassie lure

1–2 m

Drop back 3–20 m

Dodger Chain or Dodger

Small sinker to control dodger action

Rigging a down-rigger bomb in this manner gives it a stumpjumper effect and is very helpful in snaggy impoundments. To rig simply drill a hole in the nose of the bomb and use loop of wire or heavy plastic passed through the hole to connect to cable. This way it becomes much more difficult for the bomb to snag.

Stack the line 1.5 times the quoted diving depth of the lure. Refer to FWF Lures Encyclopaedia

Stacker set up

Drop back 8–12 m

Lure dives in back behind the attractor

1–4 m

Cowbells or Ford Fenders

Drop back 2–3 m

Bomb

Small sinker to control flasher

DRY FLIES

Dry flies are those built so the fly floats at, or on the surface, or in some cases, within the surface film or meniscus. Sometimes this flotation comes from using inherently buoyant materials in the fly's construction. In other cases, it is the stiffness of radiating hackle points that together allow the light weight of the fly to be supported by surface tension. Dry fly fishing is essentially a visual form of angling, relying on the angler's observation skills to indicate when a fish has taken the fly. In the case of bulky bass flies, such a take is not hard to see at all, or to hear, but when a trout takes a tiny dry fly, the surface disturbance can be minimal. This demands the angler remains watchful at all times and react appropriately by lifting the rod tip to set the hook.

Right:
Fast trolling attractors

Below:
Flies of all descriptions can be used to take a variety of fish species. These shown range from tiny dry flies (on the right) to large saltwater streamer flies.

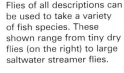

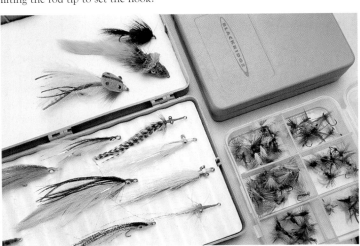

Below: This downrigger would suit either heavy freshwater or light saltwater use.

FISH MEASURERS

With the advancing coverage of all species by fisheries management regulations, more and more anglers are required to measure how long their fish are to stay within the law and avoid costly and embarrassing fines. Most state fisheries organisations print and distribute free self-adhesive stickers that can be applied to boat gunwales or side decks, while other commercially available fish tapes and measuring boards also allow you to stay on the right side of the law. Of interest, scientific research and some fishing tournaments require fish with forked tails be measured from the nose to the inside of the tail fork, as this style of measuring results in less variation of method and results. All fisheries regulations though at present allow you to measure from the nose of the fish to the tips of the tail, something more than one angler has breathed a sigh of relief about when his catch is examined by fisheries inspectors.

FISH PREDICTORS

These vary from complex and sophisticated electronic computers to simple tables and disc-dials with readouts indicating suggested best times for fishing effort to be applied. Based mostly on lunar and solar cycles and tides and seasonal factors, these are regarded by some anglers as gospel, while to others, they seem to be mumbo-jumbo. There is enough evidence on both sides of this discussion for these devices to be at least considered when planning fishing trips. Even the staunchest advocate of them, however, would have to admit they are by no means fool-proof. Fish have the innate ability to do what they want to do and when they want to do it, for reasons which sometimes simply elude the most meticulous anglers.

FISH SCALERS

It is a truism with few exceptions that any fish you intend to eat has to be prepared for the table. By far the most common method to do this is to remove the scales from the body first, then to take fillets or to gut and cook the fish whole. Removing fish scales is relatively easy if it is done immediately after the fish expires and becomes progressively more difficult the longer this chore is left. Tools for this job vary, from serrated back edges of knives (perhaps the worst and most damaging of all scaler types) through serrated metal rings on handles (the next most injurious to the flesh). Plastic forms of these scalers do the job of removing the scales just as well but with less skin tearing, while some anglers use electric powered rotary scalers that literally flog the scales from the fish. Some species of fish, such as whiting, have scales that are easily removed. Indeed, there is a form of knotted nylon mesh keeper bag used in some states that is known as

This form of net is a wire cage of expandable mesh and is used to keep the catch fresh without refrigeration by immersing it in the water until it can be cleaned and iced down.

a 'scaler bag' for its ability to remove most if not all of the scales from a bag full of whiting. This is done by simply towing the bag of fish at low speed behind the boat for a short distance.

FISH SMOKERS

There are two ways of smoking fish. 'Hot' smoking involves the fish being enclosed in a sealed metal box on a rack suspended above a scattering of sawdust that is charred by the application of a spirit-fueled flame source beneath the box. 'Cold' smoking can utilise much more substantial fuel and smoking agents by having a firebox located some distance away from the smoking chamber, which is connected to it by a length of horizontal flue or chimney pipe. By the time the smoke reaches the smoking chamber in which the fish have been suspended, most of heat has escaped, leaving only the curing effect of the smoke to do its work without the heat of the fire drying the flesh of the fish out so much.

FISHING HATS

Hats for fishing should offer protection from the harmful effects of UV sunlight, keep the rain off your head and offer some warmth when conditions are cold. For night fishing or keeping warm on cold winter days, a beanie or balaclava is a good idea. For mild weather, peaked baseball caps are easy to stow and convenient to wear. In strong sunlight however, a broad-brimmed hat is much more practical in terms of face, ears and neck protection.

FISHING KNIVES

Knives are needed for several tasks when fishing. While a single knife can serve many purposes, it's a good idea for the well-equipped fisher to have three main types. A strong-bladed bait knife is helpful for chopping through fish bones and general knockabout cutting work. For filleting, a knife with a slender and flexible blade will do a much better job. Lastly, a good quality, folding pocketknife is always an asset, particularly when fishing on foot around freshwater streams. All knives should be kept clean and sharp and

Whether you use a heavy knife for general bait work, or a fine-bladed filleting knife for dressing fish, keep it clean, sharp and in a protective scabbard between uses.

handled with the respect they warrant if you are to avoid mishaps.

FISHING LIGHTS

Fishing at night is often productive as fish become emboldened by the darkness and generally tend to feed more aggressively. For you to see what you are doing however, some form of light is necessary and there are several different types of torches and lanterns that you will find helpful. The standard flashlight-style of torch, with its narrow cylindrical body and globe and lens on the front end, will suffice for a great amount of this work. Occasionally, however, you will need a torch that throws a broader or more powerful beam. This is particularly so when walking over rough terrain or lighting a general work area. You can also buy small battery-pack fluorescent lanterns that can be stood on any level surface and provide steady wide area illumination. There are times too when you need to have a light that lets you work hands-free. In this situation, such as beach fishing, a headlamp style light is excellent. You can get models that clip onto a hat or others that have a strap and clip to hold them on your forehead like a miner's light. Yet another useful style is the penlight kind, which clips onto a shirt pocket or fishing vest. The flexible illumination head on these is quite tiny, yet perfectly adequate for illuminating small areas such as your hands when tying a fly or lure on or sorting out a tangle. As much as possible, you should try to ensure that all fishing lights are waterproof.

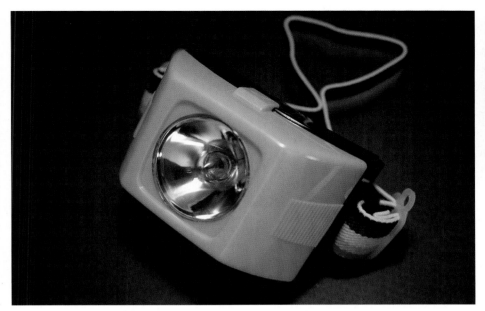

Headlamps like this one are very practical as they allow hands-free illumination of whatever you are looking at.

By gluing sections of bathroom mirror to this snapper lead, it now doubles as a fishing weight and a fish attractor, an excellent option when fishing for sand flathead offshore.

FISHING MAPS AND CHARTS

Once you get to know a fishing area intimately, it is unlikely you will need a map or chart to find your way around. For most of us though, available fishing time is limited and the desire to fish in new and interesting places is strong. This makes such aids essential. Some show terrain and localities in perfect scale and great detail, while others may give only an approximate idea of the lay of the land. When hiking through bush to get to freshwater streams, topographical maps are helpful as they show contours and slopes in detail, as well as land information features such as cliffs, forests and watercourses. Admiralty charts provide coastal shapes and features and detailed depth information. Tourism maps show main and connecting roads, and may show important information like accommodation, food and fuel outlets as well as local emergency services. Some specialised fishing maps show just enough of all of these kinds of information with the occasional addition of other interesting details such as which fish are available there and when, and on what tackle and methods.

FISHING SCISSORS

Sometimes, the best cutting tool for fishing line or even baits is a sharp pair of scissors. Gelspun line for example, is great to fish with but very difficult to cut neatly with a knife or standard line clippers. A good pair of sharp, serrated-blade scissors will cut through this tough stuff like a hot knife through butter. Likewise, when preparing fillet baits, the shape and neatness of the cut can play a big part in how attractive the bait is to a fish. A good pair of general utility scissors (kitchen scissors are great) will let you cut baits quickly, neatly and safely while other fishermen are struggling with knives.

FISHING SINKERS

Sinkers are usually moulded from lead or an alloy of lead and some other metal. Sinkers provide casting weight for bait rigs, and help position a bait where the fish are most likely to be. Factors such as local terrain, depth and water movement will dictate the size, shape and weight of the sinker required. Some sinkers, like balls, beans, bugs and barrels, have holes though them and are threaded onto the line and usually allowed to run freely to either the hook or a swivel or ring above a trace.

Others, including spoons, snapper leads, bomb sinkers, grapnels, star sinkers and ring sinkers have holes through which the line is passed and knotted, which means they are designed to be rigged at the end of a length of line. These types are often rigged in what is called a 'Paternoster' style rig, with the sinker below the hooks, which stand out from the main line on short dropper lines. Another kind of sinker is the split-shot, a ball-shaped sinker that is cut across the middle, providing a groove into which the line can be slipped. These sinkers are then held in place by squeezing the soft lead shut against the line. More sophisticated forms of sinkers such as bullet weights are used to weight soft plastic lures, while a specially shaped sinker with little wings on it called a trolling sinker, is used to add depth to trolled lure presentations in freshwater.

FISHING TACKLE LUBRICANTS

Like any form of machinery or equipment with moving parts, many items of fishing tackle require some form of lubrication or protection against corrosion. Reels, for example, need waterproof greases and oils inside their bodies to keep gears and axles working smoothly. Roller runners on game fishing rods should be sprayed regularly

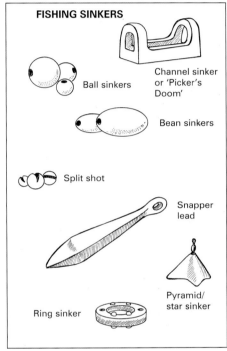

FISHING SINKERS

Ball sinkers

Channel sinker or 'Picker's Doom'

Bean sinkers

Split shot

Snapper lead

Ring sinker

Pyramid/star sinker

Fishing sinkers.

after outings with WD40 or a similar product, while reel seats will also benefit from a spray and wipe down with the same substance to keep them from developing salt or dirt build up and jamming.

FISHING TACKLE MAINTENANCE

From time to time, all fishing tackle needs to be maintained, as there are a lot of damaging forces at work to reduce their serviceability. Fishing line becomes frayed and damaged with use, especially on big fish or around rough terrain like bushes, sand or rocks. Reels should be washed and wiped down each time you bring them home and before you put them away. Line loads should be checked and any damaged line removed and the spool topped up with fresh line. Rusty hooks should be discarded, as if left in with the other good hooks they will send them rusty too. Sand needs to be washed or brushed out of sinker holes and swivels, float eyes can become squashed and

Water displacing sprays and Teflon-based lubricants like these can improve the performance of your fishing tackle and greatly prolong its useful life.

These split ring pliers and line cutters make an ideal minimal tool kit for the freshwater angler.

will need to be opened out or replaced, while rod runners, if allowed to develop cracks, can shred fishing line and cost you fish. Check the hooks and rings on lures and replace as necessary, or at least check them for sharpness and hone them to a razor point again if required.

FISHING TACKLE TUNING

Most quality tackle performs well, however there are always ways in which you can improve its performance or correct minor problems that occur through use and natural wear and tear. Fishing reels, for example, can develop a rough drag system, so that instead of line peeling smoothly from the spool under pressure, it comes off in fits and starts. You can pull the drag system apart, which usually consists of a series of metal and compression material discs and wash them in white spirits, removing any build up of grease or dirt that is causing the drag to jump. In extreme cases you may need to lap any roughness off the metal discs with 600 to 1000 grit wet and dry emery paper. Clean and then reassemble them again, being careful to do so in the correct order.

Lures can be bent out of shape as a result of knocks and torsional stresses when fighting fish, but can be carefully adjusted to swim correctly again. If a swimming lure is veering off to one side or the other, use a pair of long nosed pliers and carefully bend the towing eyelet – in the direction the lure is swimming towards – and this should correct any misalignment and allow it to track straight and true again.

FISHING TOOL KIT

Here's a handy short list of useful fishing tools. First, a sharp knife in a scabbard, or being a good quality folding type, so both you and the blade are protected. Next, a good pair of long-nosed pliers, for removing hooks from fish, making minor adjustments to wire traces or doing running repairs on tackle. At least two screwdrivers, one flat bladed and the other a Phillips head (good mini kits can be purchased at a reasonable cost

that have interchangeable screw driver heads and small sockets with a ratchet driver). An electrical test light to track down circuit problems in boats. If you run an outboard motor, a spark plug spanner will be needed sooner or later for changing outboard spark plugs. It's also a good idea also to throw in a clean cloth and some sort of lubricant or grease for freeing up stuck or corroded boat or tackle bits.

FISHING TOWELS

It is impossible to keep bait off your hands when bait fishing, but having a small towel with you can let you rinse your hands and then dry them again, so the bait doesn't get all over you and your tackle. In winter particularly, you will appreciate being able to fish with dry hands as cold winds can cause the skin of your fingers and palms to crack quite painfully, especially if handling astringent baits, such as squirt worms which exude a substance that strips natural oils from your skin. You can also use a towel to grip a fish when removing hooks, saving your hands from damage by the fish's spines. The same towel can be used wet for releasing fish, as handling fish with dry hands or cloths can remove the protective slime from the fish and cause fungal infections, whereas a wet towel is much less likely to do so.

FISHING WITH THERMOMETERS

Many species of fish become more or less active and therefore harder or easier to catch when the temperature of the water changes. Each species has an optimum range of water temperatures in which it is most likely to take a bait or lure. Knowing what these are and being able to measure the temperature of the water gives you a significant fishing advantage. Trout, for example, prefer water temperatures to be low, something below 16ºC as a rule, while bass and golden perch are most active when the water temperature reaches 19ºC and above. Thermometers come in various forms, mercury tubes (the most usual

kind) and digital readout thermometers with metal probes on the end of a length of cable, and analogue or dial readout temperature gauges.

FLOAT FISHING

The whole purpose of float fishing is to present baits to fish that characteristically suspend and feed at specific depths. Often, the same species of fish will feed at differing depths at different times, so being able to adjust the depth at which the bait is suspended beneath the float can be important. Floats can be rigged as fixed, but adjustable, or as running rigs, where the float is able to slide down the line quite close to the hook and allow easy casting with a relatively short trace. Its upward movement is limited by the inclusion of some form of stopper in the rig. This needs to be something small enough to pass through the rod runners when casting, yet large and firm enough to hold the float and not be pushed up the line when a fish strikes.

FLOAT STOPPERS

You can tie an effective stopper knot onto your line with wool, simply by making an overhand knot, pulling that snug, then tying another. A more effective way is to create a loop of wool around the line, then wrap the ends of the wool several times round one another before pulling the knot down firmly. You can also buy soft rubber float stopper beads that come pre-threaded onto a series of short wire loops. To fit them, pass one end of the fishing line through the wire loop, then pinch a bead stopper and slide it down off the wire loop and over both legs of the fishing line until the tag end of the line pops free. This will leave the stopper firmly in place on just the one strand of line where it can now be slid up and down as required.

FLOAT TUBES

This rather comical-looking form of boating is actually a very effective way of fishing in calm, yet deep water, where wading is impossible. Originally, these were developed by sewing cloth or canvas into 'saddle seats', then attaching them to truck tyre inner tubes. The angler then sits in the 'saddle' with his legs hanging down below the tube and paddles his way about by using his hands or legs. At some point, swim fins were incorporated into this product assembly and now specially designed float tube fins, shaped so you can get maximum thrust and manoeuvrability from a sitting position, have become available. These days, float tubes come in full ring and horseshoe shapes and are usually encased in a high denier nylon or Cordura material. They have such refinements as inflatable back rests, zip-up tackle pockets, mesh lap panels and even Velcro rod holder loops. They are quite safe to fish from in still water but are inadvisable to use in fast flowing streams.

FLUOROCARBON FISHING LINES

These are specially formulated and processed nylon fishing lines using a fluorocarbon bath to produce a combination of stiffness and hard skin. The line type is most suitable for leader material, but there are some examples of it being used as general fishing line. Its main features are its low refractive index, which can make it less visible to fish underwater, and its hard wearing characteristics.

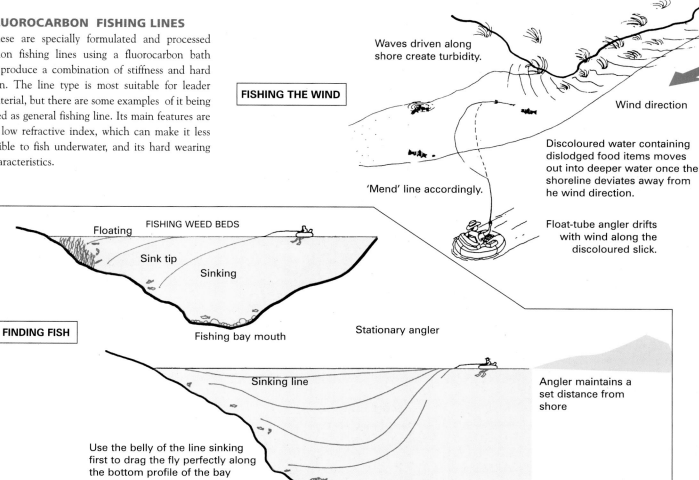

FISHING THE WIND

Waves driven along shore create turbidity.

Wind direction

'Mend' line accordingly.

Discoloured water containing dislodged food items moves out into deeper water once the shoreline deviates away from he wind direction.

Float-tube angler drifts with wind along the discoloured slick.

FISHING WEED BEDS

Floating

Sink tip

Sinking

Fishing bay mouth

Stationary angler

FINDING FISH

Sinking line

Angler maintains a set distance from shore

Use the belly of the line sinking first to drag the fly perfectly along the bottom profile of the bay

WATER TEMPERATURE EFFECTS ON AUSTRALIAN FRESHWATER FISH

	RANGE		MOST ACTIVE		SPAWNING	
NATIVES	**C**	**F**	**C**	**F**	**C**	**F**
Australian Bass	2 to 36	34 to 97	15 to 25	60 to 78	14 to 20	58 to 69
Barramundi	20 to 40	69 to 105	24 to 29	77 to 85	25 to 30	78 to 86
Estuary Perch	10 to 25	50 to 78	15 to 22	60 to 72	1.45 to 16	58 to 61
Clarence River Cod	Assumed to be the same as Murray Cod					
Golden Perch	4 to 37	40 to 100	14 to 27	58 to 82	23 to 26	74 to 79
Gulf Saratoga	7 to 40	45 to 105	24 to 29	77 to 85	30	86
Macquarie Perch	4 to 28	40 to 83	10 to 17	50 to 63	14 to 20	58 to 69
Murray Cod	2 to 34	34 to 94	16 to 25	61 to 78	17 to 22	63 to 72
River Blackfish	0 to 28	32 to 83	15 to 23	60 to 74	16	61
Saratoga	7 to 40	45 to 105	25 to 31	20 to 88	20 to 23	63 to 74
Silver Perch	4 to 38	40 to 101	14 to 26	58 to 79	24 to 27	77 to 82
2-Spined Blackfish	0 to 25	32 to 78	15 to 23	60 to 74	16	61
Trout Cod	4 to 28	40 to 83	13 to 19	56 to 67	15 to 21	60 to 70
INTRODUCED						
Atlantic Salmon	3 to 25	37 to 78	10 to 18	50 to 65	7 to 10	45 to 50
Brook Trout	0 to 25	32 to 78	10 to 15	50 to 60	7 to 12	45 to 55
Brown Trout	3 to 25	37 to 78	13 to 20	56 to 69	7 to 10	45 to 50
Chinook Salmon	3 to 25	37 to 78	10 to 18	50 to 65	7 to 10	45 to 50
European Carp	0 to 41	32 to 106	15 to 32	60 to 90		
Redfin	0 to 36	32 to 98	8 to 27	47 to 82	10 to 20	50 to 69
Rainbow Trout	3 to 25	37 to 78	10 to 18	50 to 65	7 to 10	45 to 50
Roach	0 to 38	32 to 101	8 to 25	47 to 78	15	60
Tench	0 to 39	32 to 102	20 to 26	69 to 79	16	61

How temperatures affect freshwater fish in Australia

FLY FISHING TACKLE

This comprises a long, slender, supple rod matched to a specially manufactured flyline with a braided core and an extruded plastic sheathing. The rod imparts the necessary line speed that catapults the line and fly to its target and the flyline provides the casting weight for the tiny fly. Lines are designed to have a specific weight, expressed as a 7-weight or 8-weight and so on, which must correspond to the rod. Flyline weights range from 1-weights for delicate freshwater fishing, right up to 15-weights for heavy-duty saltwater work and even some heavier sinking lines are rated in terms of so many 'grains'.

The buoyancy, shape and weight distribution of flylines can also vary. Some will float, others will sink, some float for most of their length and only the tip will sink. They can also have their weight and thickness evenly distributed along the whole line length (level lines), concentrated in the mid-section (double tapers), concentrated in the front half (weight-forwards) or in the very tip end section (shooting heads). They also come in a variety of colours, including lines that are perfectly clear.

Thin leaders (either tapered or level) are attached to the forward end of the flyline so flies can be tied on and the line and cast. Fly reels are of simple centrepin design, and often have their side plates drilled to reduce weight and allow the flylines to dry after use.

FLY FLOATANTS AND SINK AGENTS

Finely-built dry flies, which only use hackles to support the fly's weight, can become waterlogged over time or in rough conditions and will require some form of water repellant treatment to retain their buoyancy. You can apply this in the form of a lotion or gel squeezed from specially manufactured dispensing bottles. Use just enough to achieve flotation and wipe any excess away with a clean cloth, as if you don't, it will simply seep into the water around the fly and may discourage a fish from taking it. Other flies intended for use under the water surface, can tend to float because of air trapped between the fibres of the fly. These will require a wetting agent to be applied so they are able to break through the surface tension and sink. This preparation is also available in a handy squeeze bottle and can be applied in an instant.

FOOTWEAR

There are some situations in which bare feet are the best option, for a host of reasons, however there are practical considerations here too. For example, if you are fishing from a small open aluminium boat and you are not wearing shoes, the soles of your feet can instantly detect even minute changes in surface water temperature as the boat moves through a warm current or cold patch of

Fly reels, as shown, are light centrepin types, loaded with thick fly line that is cast on long fly rods.

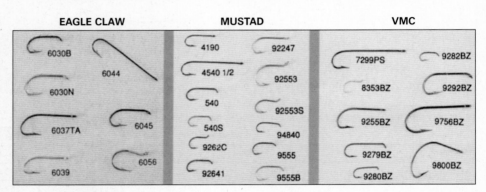

Freshwater bait hooks.

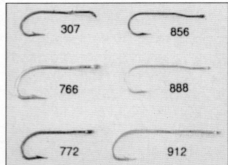

Tru Turn Freshwater bait hooks.

water. This can be vital information when fishing for temperature sensitive species such as trout (which seek out cold water) or tuna (which tend to gravitate toward warmer water).

You need to temper your desire to do a Huckleberry Finn and go barefoot though. Consider the wisdom of having good, solid footwear when fishing from ocean rocks, hiking through dense scrub where snakes, sharp sticks and spiders might be a problem, or when walking around estuary shorelines that may be studded with oysters. Some fly fishers who want the dryness and comfort of waders without the weight of moulded-in gum boots on the end of them, can opt for what is called a 'stocking-foot' style of wader. These are worn with either (oversized) sneakers for good hiking and wading protection or specialised wading boots. These wading shoes are designed with high traction soles, good ankle protection from midstream boulders and the ability to drain water quickly so you don't have to carry half the river with you when you leave it.

FRESHWATER HOOKS FOR LURES AND BAITS

The hook is our basic piece of tackle and for freshwater bait fishing the correct choice of hook is critical.

It is important to match hook size to bait size and type being used, keeping in mind the type of tackle being used. The chart on the following page will give a guide on how to get started and sort out what hook to use.

FRESHWATER BAIT HOOKS

COMMON BAITS & TECHNIQUES	BEST HOOK STYLES	TYPICAL SIZE RANGE	RECOMMENDED PATTERNS
Live maggots (gentles), small grubs, under a float or unweighted.	Offset, short shank, straight or turned down eyes. Strong.	No. 22 – 12	MUSTAD: 9555, 9555B, 92641 & 540 etc, EAGLE CLAW: 6030B, 6045B & 6039B.
Dragonfly nymphs (mudeyes), small shrimps, 'hoppers' etc, under floater drifted. Hook through wings.	Offset, short to medium shank, straight or down-turned eye.	No. 16 – 10	MUSTAD: 9555, 9555B, 92641, 92553S, 94840 & 540. EAGLE CLAW: 6030B, 6045B & 6039B VMC: 9282.
Slow trolled dragonfly nymph Hook up through body – Fred Jobson style.	Straight (non-offset), straight or upturned eye, round bend, slightly extra length shank. Fine to medium wire.	No. 10 – 6	MUSTAD: 2212, 9672 & 94840(mudeye). EAGLE CLAW: 6044B. VMC: 9280 & 9289.
Earthworms, scrub worms, tiger worms, etc. Float fished, bottom fished or drifted	Offset, round bend, long shank, fine to medium wire. Bait holder slices an advantage.	No. 10 – 4/0	MUSTAD: 9555, 9555B, 92641, 92553S, 540 & 5450. EAGLE CLAW: 6030B, 6044B & 6030N. VMC: 8353, 9292 & 9255.
Slow trolled earth or scrub worms.	Straight (non-offset), round bend, straight eye, light to medium wire.	No. 8 – 2/0	MUSTAD: 540, 542, 9555, 9262C, 92553, 92247 & 37140. EAGLE CLAW: 6030B, 6045B & 6030N. VMC: 9292, 7299, 9756 & 9800.
Large shrimps and small to medium crayfish (yabbies). Also frogs, where legal.	Offset, up or down eyes, round bend, straight or slightly re-curved point. Medium to heavy wire.	No. 4 – 3/0	MUSTAD: 540, 542, 9555, 9262C, 92553, 92247 & 37140. EAGLE CLAW: 6039B, 6030B, 6030N & 6037T.
Large crayfish (yabbies), alive or "bobbed".	Offset, up or down eyes, round bend, straight of slightly re-curved point. Medium to heavy wire.	No. 2 – 6/0	MUSTAD: 540, 542, 540S, 92555, 92555B, 92553, 9262C, 92600. EAGLE CLAW: 6030B, 6056N & 6037T.
Bardi, wood, wattle and witchetty grubs.	Offset, round bend, slightly long shank, straight or down eye, medium to heavy wire. Bait holder slices an advantage.	No. 1 – 5/0	MUSTAD: 540, 542, 540S, 92555, 92555B, & 9262C. EAGLE CLAW: 6039B, 6030B, 6030N & 6037T.
Live baitfish. *(Galaxias gudgeons, herring, smelt, goldfish, (etc.))	Offset, up or down eye, short to standard shank, slightly re-curved point, wide gape, medium to heavy wire.	No. 6 – 8/0	MUSTAD: 540, 542, 540S, 9262C, 92553, 4190, 92641 & 7140, 9263. EAGLE CLAW: 6056N, 6030B & 6030N
Heavy set lines (all baits).	Offset, up or down eye, round bend, re-curved point, heavy wire.	No 1/0 – 8/0	MUSTAD: 542, 92641, 92553, 4190 & 92600. EAGLE CLAW: 6037T.

FRESHWATER LURE HOOKS

LURE TYPE	IDEAL HOOK FEATURE	SIZE RANGE	RECOMMENDED PATTERNS
Small metal casting lures: spinners, spoons, lead fish, etc.	Light gauge trebles with straight or EAGLE CLAW: 374, 375, 974, 975, 954, plugs, etc.	No. 12 – 6	MUSTAD: 3562, 3565, 35647 & 36145. Also small minnows, poppers,
AS ABOVE (Alternative)	Light gauge, non-offset singles with large, ringed eyes.	No. 8 – 2	MUSTAD: 34007 & 3407. EAGLE CLAW: 210.
AS ABOVE (Alternative)	Light gauge double hooks.	No. 12 – 6	MUSTAD: 3674 & 3582F.
Medium to large plugs minnows, spoons, straight or re-curved points.	Light to medium gauge trebles with poppers, etc.	No. 6 – 3/0	MUSTAD: 3562, 3563, 3565, 33592H & 9430A. EAGLE CLAW: 374, 375, 974, 975, 954, 474 & 475.
AS ABOVE (Alternative)	Medium gauge, non-offset singles with large, ringed eyes.	No. 2 – 4/0	MUSTAD: 34007, 3407 & 9510. EAGLE CLAW: 210 & 208SS.
AS ABOVE (Alternative)	Medium gauge double hooks.	No. 4 – 4/0	MUSTAD: 7897DT & 7982HS.
Trolling spoons, flutter spoons, Tassie lures etc.	Light to medium gauge, trebles with straight or re-curved points.	TNo. 6 – 3/0	MUSTAD: 3562, 3563 & 3565. EAGLE CLAW: 374, 375, 974, 975, 954,
AS ABOVE (Alternative)	Medium gauge, non-offset singles with large, ringed eyes.	No. 2 – 4/0	MUSTAD: 9510. EAGLE CLAW: 210, L308 & 208SS.
Lead-head jigs	Special, single point jig hooks, suitable for moulding in lead heads.	No. 10 - 4/0	MUSTAD: 32755 & 32756 EAGLE CLAW: 410, 570, 575, 630, 640 & 730.
Soft plastic worms, grubs (Rigged straight or "Texan" bend, style.)	Straight (non-offset) shank, round straight point single hooks with bait holder barbs and/	No. 6 – 4/0	MUSTAD: 32813 lizards, etc. EAGLE CLAW: 41, 45, 95 & 357.
AS ABOVE (Alternative)	AS ABOVE with weed/snag guard	No. 4 – 4/0	EAGLE CLAW: 151, 249 & 449. TRU-TURN: 125.

FRESHWATER LURES

Lures used in freshwater are of six main types. Bibbed swimming lures, surface lures, spinnerbaits, axis spinners, swimming spoons and various kinds of jigs.

Bibbed swimming lures can be slender (minnows) or fat (plugs). Surface lures can be poppers or paddlers such as Crazy Crawlers and Jitterbugs; prop-baits, like Heddon Tiny Torpedos; or buzz-baits, hich are wire-frame lures with a single hook and trailing skirt and either single or double churning blades.Spinnerbaits are similar in design to buzz- baits except they incorporate a heavier leadhead and are intended for use beneath the surface. They too have a single hook and trailing skirt (sometimes with a secondary or 'stinger' hook attached) and can have one or more fluttering blades that spin on clevises or swivels. There are two blade shapes used, a slender 'willow-leaf' style and a fatter rounder 'Colorado' style.

Axis spinners (like Mepps, Celtas and Vibraxes) have a heavy body and a clevis and blade arrangement threaded onto a central wire shaft that has the hook attached at one end and a towing eyelet at the other.

Swimming spoons can be made from pressed metal (like Wonder Wobblers) or moulded from plastic with a lead core body and transparent 'wings' (Tassie Devils, Cobras and the like). Jigs can be leadheads with single hooks moulded into them or solid banana-shaped bodies with a line eyelet mounted in the centre of the back and hooks at either end and underneath (such as ice-jigs).

These metal lures are (left to right) a spoon type, and three different weights and sizes of bladed axis spinners.

REBEL POP-R

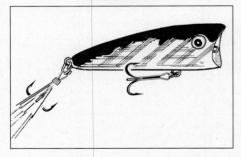

Surface poppers, like the Rebel Pop-R can be used for bass, cod, golden perch or even large trout. They are generally retrieved with a stop-start action, using sudden jerks of the rod tip to submerge the cupped face of the lure and create a 'blooping' sound.

GAFFS, NETS AND TRAPS

Fish are hard to grab with your bare hands and you can do a lot of unnecessary damage to fish and yourself by attempting to do this. Gaffs, nets and traps allow you to pin, scoop or otherwise imprison fish so they can either be extracted and kept or released after the hook is removed.

Gaffing fish intended for capture should be down somewhere near the head and shoulder region where the flesh is thickest and firm. Gaffs can also be handy for controlling fish you intend to release. You do, however, need to take more care as to where you put the gaff. Don't pierce the main body of the fish anywhere, but instead, carefully bring the gaff point up from beneath the bottom jaw, penetrating only the thin mouth membrane and carrying the fish's weight entirely on the much stronger and less vulnerable jawbone. Even so, fish gaffed this way should not be lifted from the water without supporting the rest of the body.

When netting fish, bring the fish to the net, don't chase the fish with the net. There is no way you can push a net faster through the water than a fish can swim. Tire the fish out and then swim it straight into the submerged net. Once it is more than halfway in, just lift the net. Regulations regarding fish and crab traps vary from state to state so you should check with local fisheries offices before using them.

GAME FISHING TACKLE

Game fishing tackle must take into account the size and power of the fish being targeted, some of which may reach 500 kg or more. Accordingly, lines used for this style of fishing can range from as light as 6 kg to as heavy as 60 kg. Again, because of the generally large and potent nature

Below: Squid jigs like these can help you gather effective bait for other fish or be the means of collecting a meal of delicious calamari.

of these fish, leader materials must be strong and tough enough to withstand incredible stresses and abrasions. In the case of large-toothed game fish, such as wahoo, sharks and mackerel, wire traces are advisable if not mandatory. But even fish like kingfish, cobia and dolphinfish (mahi-mahi) have villiform teeth and can damage line over a prolonged fight. Tunas have sharp but small conical teeth which do not slice but can nick or pinch line and marlin and other billfish have very hard bony mouth parts that are rough on lines too. Characteristics of good game fishing leaders are that they are supple enough not to tangle, but must be hard-skinned enough to withstand significant abrasion and compression, hence why fluorocarbon has proven so popular for game fishing in recent years.

Penn reel

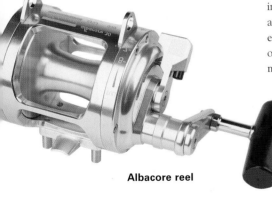

Tiagra reel

Albacore reel

Duel reel

Game fishing reels

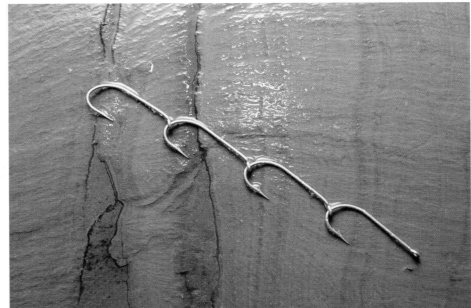

This flight of four ganged hooks would be an ideal rig for mounting a whole fish bait such as a pilchard or garfish for tailor, salmon, snapper, kingfish or mulloway.

Reels must hold up to 1000 m of the chosen line class to cope with the often huge runs of these fish. Rods should be short and powerful, able to provide the angler with enough leverage to control a fish and steer it where it can be landed. Of necessity, sundry terminal items like hooks and swivels suddenly assume very important status and must be of first class quality and strength. Ball-bearing swivels are used almost exclusively for game fishing and hooks are always of forged design and carry plenty of high tempered metal in their shanks and points.

GANGING HOOKS

For using long, whole fish baits such as pilchards and garfish, ganged hook rigs were developed after innovative work on tailor by the late Len Thompson. 'Thommo' was a champion Queensland angler who single-handedly popularised the system of passing the point and bend of one hook through the slightly opened eye of the hook in front, creating 'gangs' or flights of hooks that could carry the longest bait available. As each hook is passed through the eye of the one in front, pliers are used to gently squeeze the eye shut again. This was a problem with hooks that had been tempered to a brittleness that would not allow such bending, but Thommo got them to develop a slightly softer tempered hook, which became known as the #4200. This hook was silver in colour and available in the critical 3/0 to 4/0 sizes that suited garfish baits. It could withstand the eye being prised open and squeezed shut again and was also amenable to having its shank bent down at about 50 degrees to allow the shank of the hook in front to lie perfectly in line with that of the following hook. Eventually,

the hook style became available a in larger range of sizes, to suit both larger and smaller baitfish types.

Soon after, a pre-bent version of the 4200, called the 4202 was developed, and this came with the eye already partially opened, needing only to be squeezed shut once the hook gang had been assembled.

Other hook patterns can be ganged with care but breakage rates are much higher. As such, various other methods of ganging have come into vogue, including snooding several hooks in line with lengths of plastic spaghetti tubing in between the eyes.

GELSPUN LINE

Gelspun polyester fishing lines have been around for some time, but for a long period they suffered from various manufacturing faults and quality control problems. They did not really take off until the development of the Dyneema and Spectre thread types. Sometimes called 'braids' these multi-fibre lines also come in heat fused forms and have become known either as braids, gelspuns or simply 'super lines'. These lines generally have very low stretch factors and are extremely strong for their diameters when compared to similar thickness monofilaments.

GENERAL ESTUARY TACKLE

For estuary fishing, you can get away with nothing more complicated than a handline, a few sinker and hooks and some bait. That's okay for fishing from a boat on the drift or at anchor, but when casting or trolling is involved, a rod and reel will make things much easier. Hooks should suit the species being targeted and the size of the bait being presented. Sinkers should generally be

COLLAR AND CAPSTAN

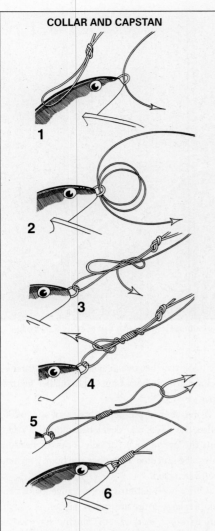

1

2

3

4

5

6

This knot was developed for anglers who insist on tying fine gelspun lines directly to the towing eye of the lure. It tests a good deal higher than any other knots tested.

1. First tie a loop in a piece of monofilament of similar breaking strain to the gelspun line. This will be used later as a pull-through to finish the knot.
Thread the gelspun line through the towing eye of the lure.
2. Do this 3 times to produce a capstan effect.
3. Introduce the monofilament loop as shown and begin wrapping it with the tag back toward the lure.
4. Continue to make about 10 wraps before feeding the tag through the monofilament loop, taking care to leave enough slack in the last wrap to prevent it jamming.
5. Withdraw the mono loop, drawing the tag of the gelspun line back through the knot producing the collar.
This step is easy enough provided there was some slack in the last wrap of the gelspun line. If there was not, the tag may jam.
6. Slide the collar (which you have just tied in the tag), down onto the capstan nd trim the tag.

Tested in 24 lb Spiderwire Fusion, (which actually tested over 25 lb), the Collar and Captstan broke at 22 lb against the Braid Ring Knot 19.6 lb, Triple Palomar 19.6 lb and the Palomar at 16.5 lb.

TWISTED LEADER KNOT FOR GELSPUN LINES

Twisted Leader Knot for Gelspun Lines

This is the strongest method I know of tying a single strand of gelspun line to a monofilament leader. It is also a useful knot for tying a double gelspun to a mono leader. I tested it six times with a sample of Berkley Fireline, which was labelled 14 pounds. When tied to a 12.5 kg Maxima monofilament leader, the highest test obtained was 9.4 kg (20.7 pounds). Only one knot tested below 8 kg (17.6 pounds). (Geoff Wilson)

1
Wind the gelspun line (black) around one end of the monofilament leader. I suggest doing this twenty times.

2
Tie a knot in the twisted lines and pull the entire monofilament leader through.

3
Do the same again so another wrap is added.

4
Do this two more times so four wraps are made.

5
Then, with firm but gentle pressure on all four legs, close the knot.
Should a loop of slack gelspun line appear within the knot as it closes, release the mono leader tag and apply tension to the gelspun line until the loop disappears.

6
Close the knot firmly and trim the tags.

Above: Twisted leader knot for gelspun lines.

Left: Collar and capstan knot,

SILLY SNELL

1

2

3

4

5

Silly snell.

small when fishing slow or still water, gradually increasing in size as the water being fished speeds up with tidal movements.

GENERAL FISHING HOOKS

Depending on the target species and the shape and size of the baits being used to catch them, hooks can vary between tiny size 12 long-shanks for mullet, yellowtail and leatherjackets to hefty 6/0 and 7/0 suicides or 'French' hooks used for big mulloway. Flathead bait fishing hooks are usually long-shanked, both to carry the whole

One of the easiest of all hook attachments, the Silly Snell is a very strong join and the simplest hook to join to return very high tests using the new super lines like æSpiderwire' by Spectra and 'Ultramax' and 'Gorilla Braid' by Berkley.

1. Pass the line through the eye of the hook and wrap it around the shank away from the end of the wire forming the eye.
2. Begin wrapping back up the shank of the hook with the tag.
3. Continue almost back to the eye of the hook then simply tuck the tag under the last wrap as shown.
4. Slide the wraps up to the eye of the hook, pulling the line to tighten it.

THE 2-HOOK WHITING RIG
The 2-hook whiting rig

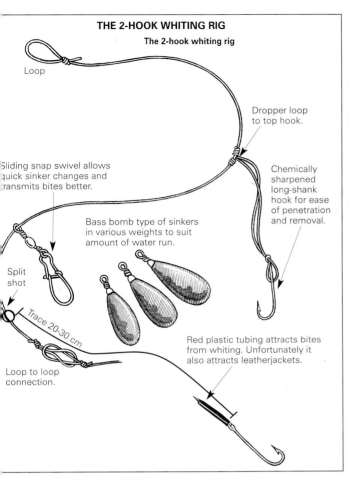

Loop

Dropper loop to top hook.

Sliding snap swivel allows quick sinker changes and transmits bites better.

Chemically sharpened long-shank hook for ease of penetration and removal.

Bass bomb type of sinkers in various weights to suit amount of water run.

Split shot

Trace 20-30 cm

Red plastic tubing attracts bites from whiting. Unfortunately it also attracts leatherjackets.

Loop to loop connection.

The 2-hook whiting rig.

This kirbed 7/0 hook is rigged on heavy trace and would be an ideal choice for bait fishing for mulloway.

prawn baits or long fish strips that work well for this species and also to offer some protection for the line against the flathead's array of small sharp teeth. Bream like a short hook, something like a 9263 suicide or a 4190 pattern, while tailor will take just about any bait on any hook and bite you off in a wink if you don't use some kind of trace, of either wire or heavy monofilament. Luderick have small mouths and therefore are best targeted with short shanked hooks in about size 6 to 10.

GLOVES

Anyone who has handled spiky fish like bream and flathead, soon drops any pretense of being macho and will gladly slip on a pair of lightweight fishing gloves. The best ones have partial fingers, leaving the tips of your fingers free to maintain maximum feel and dexterity when rigging up, are light and cool to wear and have leather palm pads to protect your hands from unnecessary injury. Fishermen working cold country in the depths of winter will also appreciate being able to wear warm gloves made of either neoprene or greasy wool that allow you to have wet hands without suffering from the cold. There are also gloves now available that offer UV protection for those vulnerable areas such as the backs of your hands, where skin cancers are most commonly found to develop.

HARNESSES

These are waistcoat-like devices with straps through which you put your arms or secure about your waist and others that come forward off the harness and clip onto your reel. They are only ever used for really big fish and as such are most often seen on game fishing boats or sportfishers where the anglers are expecting to tangle with a big yellowfin or marlin.

HAVERSACKS

Originally designed and developed for campers and hikers, these backpacks have been eagerly taken up as useful fishing accessories by anglers who need to travel some distance on foot to their fishing destinations. They suit beach and rock fishing and have also won a place in the kit of anglers who trudge many hours into the wilderness in search of pristine freshwater fishing.

HOOK REMOVERS

These extended plier-like tools are very handy for getting hooks out of fish's mouths, particularly when those fish have teeth that could shred a finger. They are especially useful when a fish has taken a hook deeply and it cannot be reached by any other means.

Neoprene fishing gloves are ideal for cold weather fishing. The fingers are cut short to enable better dexterity when rigging or handling fish.

General fishing hooks

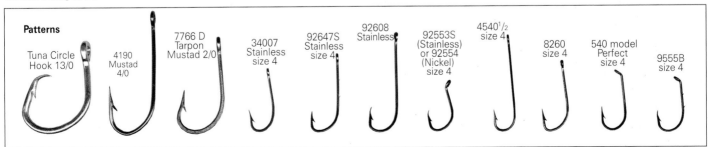

Patterns

Tuna Circle Hook 13/0 · 4190 Mustad 4/0 · 7766 D Tarpon Mustad 2/0 · 34007 Stainless size 4 · 92647S Stainless size 4 · 92608 Stainless · 92553S (Stainless) or 92554 (Nickel) size 4 · 4540½ size 4 · 8260 size 4 · 540 model Perfect size 4 · 9555B size 4

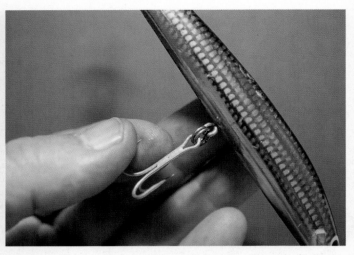

Above and right: With time, hooks on saltwater lures can become corroded and less serviceable. You can change these easily however with a pair of split ring pliers and some brand new sharp hooks from your local tackle store. The first pic shows the pliers holding the split ring apart to remove the old hook and the second shows the new hook in place.

HOOKS FOR LURES

Most lures have free swinging treble hooks attached directly to the lure body by a saddle, or by way of split rings connecting the hook eye to metal loop eyelets that emerge from the lure body. Exceptions include the single hook style of lead head jig, some of the newer soft plastic lure arrangements that utilise single hooks to better present the lure, and lure versions such as ice jigs that have single hooks protruding from either end and a treble hanging from the belly eyelet.

Some anglers argue that single hooks on other lure types offer better holding properties than trebles, which may allow fish to tear free, as the gap of each hook bend on the treble is much smaller.

Some magnum-sized saltwater bibbed swimming lures carry heavy-duty double hooks. These are made, by forging a single piece of heavy hook wire into a hook at each end, and bending it, so the two hooks lie side by side and slightly splayed.

INFLATABLE KIDDIES POOLS

Anglers fishing for large gamefish from the ocean rocks can keep live baits healthy and frisky for hours by taking along a plastic blow up paddle pool. Inflating it, filling it with sea water and tossing live slimy mackerel, garfish or yellowtail into it will keep them alive until they are required. The large surface area of the pool allows oxygen to be absorbed from the atmosphere, meaning weighty and problematic batteries and aerators are not necessary. From time to time, if the baits start to stress out or act sluggishly, you can spill a little of the stale water out and top it up again with a bucket.

JIG HEAD WITH LONG WORM TAIL

The combination of a long standard worm with a standard jig head is quick and easy. It works well

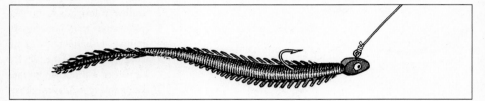

Jig head with standard worm tail

in open areas when the hook doesn't need to be buried in the worm tail.

KAYAK TACKLE

Many people fish from small boats like kayaks. Often they will drift in small lakes and estuaries. The gear preferred is a short, light baitcasting rod and reel. Such tackle prevents the angler having to lean too far over the edge of the kayak, which can cause it to tip.

The best rig to use from a kayak is shown here, along with some tips from Rob Paxevanos, an expert on fishing from a kayak.

LEAD CORE TROLLING TACKLE

Trolling with a lead core main line is a very effective method of taking trout when they are living and feeding over the vast underwater weed areas in many of our lakes and impoundments.

The depth of these beds or 'fields' can be quantified as aquatic weed requires light and, as we know, the deeper in the water we travel, the less the light is able to penetrate. This fact then restricts these vast aquatic weed beds to depths in the range of 3 to 6 m, depending upon the water clarity of each individual lake. Trolling lures at these depths and just over the top of the weed beds is what lead core trolling achieves.

The tackle required is, of course, a lead core lure or leadline. Leadline is a thin lead wire surrounded by a dacron line and comes in a breaking strain of between 18 to 36 pound. It is supple, but not supple enough to be used on a

threadline reel. The reel should be a centrepin, like an Alvey (which can take a full 100 m spool of leadline) or a big baitcaster like a Shimano TR 200 G or ABU 7000 that can handle perhaps 70 m of leadline.

The rod should be soft and parabolic and within the 3 to 6 kg class. A soft rod will balance forward and backward giving extra life and action to the lure.

LEADER SPOOLS

You can keep pre-rigged leaders ready for instant use and in un-kinked condition by winding them onto large diameter plastic leader spools. These have slots and holes moulded into them to take rings or swivels and the hook end of the trace can then be secured by pushing the hook point into the soft plastic of the spool ring.

LEADER STRAIGHTENERS

Fly fishers sometimes need to remove kinks and wriggles from their fly leaders which have formed through tangles, etc. This can be done with a leader straightener, which is simply a folded leather patch lined with either rubber sheet or felt. The wrinkled line is gripped between the folds of the straightener, then pulled through under moderate pressure. The combination of pressure and friction heat re-aligns the molecules within the nylon line and allows the kinks to be removed. They work fairly well for moderate to minor kinks but really severe ones should be cut out and replaced with a new section of leader

KAYAK DRIFTER RIG

It is important to note that lengths A, B and C can be adjusted quickly to suit the conditions. This is possible because the whole rig is made up from one piece of line. A plastic stopper is used to hold length A, B and C as required. The plastic stopper or ring replaces the standard three-way swivel. (Line twist is usually not a problem if the bait is secured correctly to prevent twist.) The loop length C is passed through the stopper, the stopper is secured and the main line snap swivel is clipped on to the loop. The line may have to be put through the stopper several times to prevent slippage. Alternatively a small ring or similar item may be tied onto the line at this point. The important thing is to form a secure joint that is easily undone to facilitate quick adjustment — there are many other ways to do this.

My rig is fished with a sinker heavy enough to maintain contact with the bottom. The sinker can be dragged through weed and whatever else is down there. The important fact is that the bait is always at the present height above the sinker (ignoring any height errors caused by line angle). The beauty of this rig is that with a little experimentation the rig can be quickly adjusted to hold the bait in the established strike zone regardless of the drift speed. It works a treat and it's heaps of fun to experience this method.

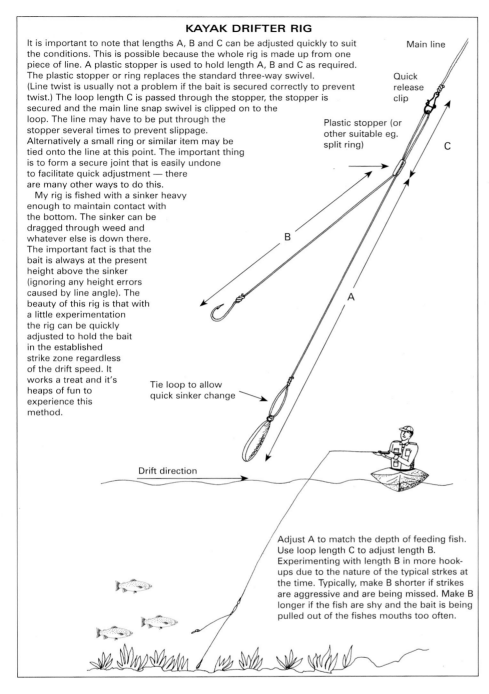

Main line

Quick release clip

Plastic stopper (or other suitable eg. split ring)

C

B

A

Tie loop to allow quick sinker change

Drift direction

Adjust A to match the depth of feeding fish. Use loop length C to adjust length B. Experimenting with length B in more hook-ups due to the nature of the typical strkes at the time. Typically, make B shorter if strikes are aggressive and are being missed. Make B longer if the fish are shy and the bait is being pulled out of the fishes mouths too often.

LEADLINE CHARACTERISTICS

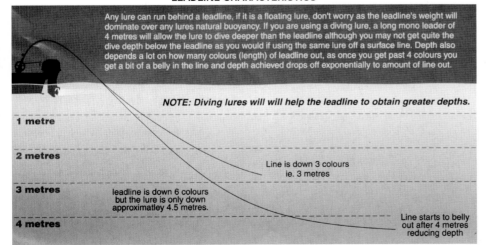

Any lure can run behind a leadline, if it is a floating lure, don't worry as the leadline's weight will dominate over any lures natural buoyancy. If you are using a diving lure, a long mono leader of 4 metres will allow the lure to dive deeper than the leadline although you may not get quite the dive depth below the leadline as you would if using the same lure off a surface line. Depth also depends a lot on how many colours (length) of leadline out, as once you get past 4 colours you get a bit of a belly in the line and depth achieved drops off exponentially to amount of line out.

NOTE: Diving lures will will help the leadline to obtain greater depths.

1 metre

2 metres

Line is down 3 colours ie. 3 metres

3 metres

leadline is down 6 colours but the lure is only down approximatley 4.5 metres.

4 metres

Line starts to belly out after 4 metres reducing depth

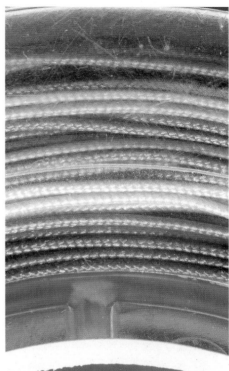

Lead core trolling line like this is colour coded every 10 m so you know how much line you have out and how deep you are fishing.

material. Bear in mind too, by heating the leader like this, you are gradually weakening it. If you find you need to straighten a leader more than two or three times in a fishing session, cut it off and start with some fresh line to be on the safe side.

LEVER DRAG GAME FISHING REELS

Game fishing reels are required to handle big, fast and heavy fish that can create a lot of heat build-up in a reel's drag system when they run and take line. Heat build-up is the enemy of a smooth drag and can even lead to glazing of the metal drag washers as the softer compression material reaches critical temperatures. It starts to burn or melt, leaving a deposit on the metal washer and creating an uneven drag.

Lever drag reels have superior performance to star drag reels for the simple engineering reasons of having a much greater drag surface area. This dissipates heat better than small washers can and so maintains a generally cooler drag and ultimately a smoother one.

Star drag reels can only have their fighting pressure set. The only other adjustment available is full free spool. Some additional drag can be applied mid-fight through thumb pressure on the spool or, you could take the gamble and rely on turning the star wheel until some appreciable difference in the fish's behaviour is felt. This, however, is a very inexact system of adjustment and can easily result in a fish breaking off because too much drag was applied to the line.

Lever drags on the other hand, provide a much more controllable amount of pressure manipulation through the use of a lever that moves through a quadrant, a very precise and controllable way of adjusting drag pressures within preset limits governed by the line class in use. Lever drags also have an intermediate and readily found reference point in the middle of that range, called the 'strike' or 'hookset' drag setting. This enables a lever drag reel to be in free spool and instantly adjusted to enough pressure to set the hook with a single movement of the lever up to the strike position. When the fight begins to get underway, the lever can then be deliberately pushed past this point by depressing a button. Again, at the end of the fight when a fish may make a last minute surge, the drag can be instantly backed off to the 'strike' setting again, preventing any mishaps and losing the fish.

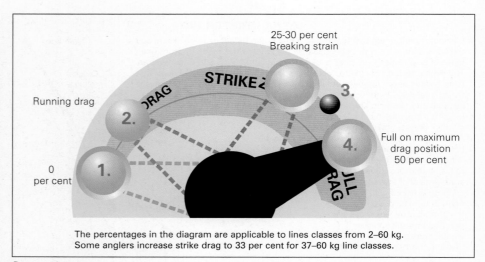

25-30 per cent
Breaking strain

STRIKE

DRAG

Running drag

0
per cent

3.

Full on maximum
drag position
50 per cent

4.

1.

2.

The percentages in the diagram are applicable to lines classes from 2–60 kg.
Some anglers increase strike drag to 33 per cent for 37–60 kg line classes.

Drag quadrant.

Lever drag reels have the ability to apply precise drag pressures throughout a wide range and can also be preset to suit particular line classes.

LIGHT ESTUARY TACKLE
Most of the fish species encountered in estuaries are relatively small, meaning they can often be landed on quite light tackle.

LINE CLIPPERS
The need for neatness in rigging is not just a matter of making your rigs look as presentable as possible, it's also avoids having fish taking fright at the rig behaving unnaturally. This means trimming your knots so the tag end is as short as you can make it without risking the knot slipping and the end pulling through. This kind of critical rig shaping is much easier with a tool to help trim these tag ends quickly, neatly and reliably. For this work, there is nothing as effective as a set of line clippers. Ordinary nail clippers will do the job, but tend to be bulky and rather too shiny for some fishing situations, such as trout fishing. Specialist line clippers are usually slender, sharp and easy to operate and best of all, inconspicuous, being either a matt silver or black colour. Don't

use your teeth unless you like pain and sending your dentist on expensive holidays every year. The dearest pair available is still more affordable than the cheapest dental consultation!

LINE FEEDING OPTIONS
In many fishing situations, you will need to feed line out off a reel, either to control the drift of a bait or to allow a tentative fish to pick up a bait and run with it unimpeded. Depending on the type of reel, the procedure for this will vary slightly. With centrepin reels, commonly used for float fishing for luderick, cradle the rod and reel in one hand, using the extended fingers of that hand to reach beneath the reel spool and flip it, so line is fed off to follow a drifting float. Overruns are prevented by instantly applying fingertip pressure to the spool and stopping the line flow. Alvey sidecasts can be handled in much the same way, except because of their diameter you will need to use two hands, one to hold the rod and the other to manage the spool. To control line feed, all you need do is feather the spool with the fingers of your rod hand and pull line off with the other.

Overhead reels can be taken out of gear and line pulled from the spool by hand, or allowed to be pulled off by the current. Be careful to have a thumb resting lightly on the spool to prevent overruns should a fish grab the bait while this is going on. Threadline reels are simplicity itself, you simply open the bail arm and allow line to peel off the spool at its own accord, being ready to close the bail and set the hook if a fish grabs the bait and runs. Some threadline reels have a free spool device that allows you to feed line off the spool with the bail arm still closed, yet simply stop the spool revolving instantly by flipping a switch or turning the reel handle.

LIVE BAIT CAGES
Rock fishermen can catch livebaits such as garfish, slimy mackerel and yellowtail and keep them alive

in natural rock pools, provided they have enough clean water being washed into them by wave action on a semi-regular basis. To prevent baits escaping back out of these pools when a wave sloshes over the edge, you can use a simple expanding link wire mesh bait cage. These have either a spring-loaded lid or a clip-shut wire top door and can be roped off within a rock pool and will hold up to a dozen good sized baits provided the pool is large and cool and deep enough.

LIVE WELL OPTIONS
When using live baits that normally live in the water, such as prawns, shrimp, squid, or small fish, it is more efficient to gather a number of these and keep them alive in a tank or well of water until required. Sometimes all you need do to keep the baits alive and healthy is to replenish the oxygen lost from the water by a simple aerator. You may find it will also be necessary to change the water regularly to cleanse the tank of bodily wastes eliminated by the captive baits. If you don't do this, the baits can stress and die. You can tip water out and bucket it back into the well, but this is laborious and messy and can result in some baits escaping in the process. The best way to keep the water clean and fresh is to use a battery-powered submersible pump. This exchanges the water in the well on a continuous or intermittent basis. Alternatives include using live bait cages or a live bait bucket, hung over the side of the boat and roped off.

LURES FOR DOWNRIGGING
Shown here in diagram form are ideal set-ups and lures match for down rigging. The basic premise is that you need to troll higher action lures on the deep sets. The reason for this is that as the depth increases, water pressure also increases and effectively kills lure action. In the case of trolling minnows, the action on a deep-set minnow can be increased by attaching it to your line with a clinch knot tied hard against the lure's eye.

Lures for downrigging.

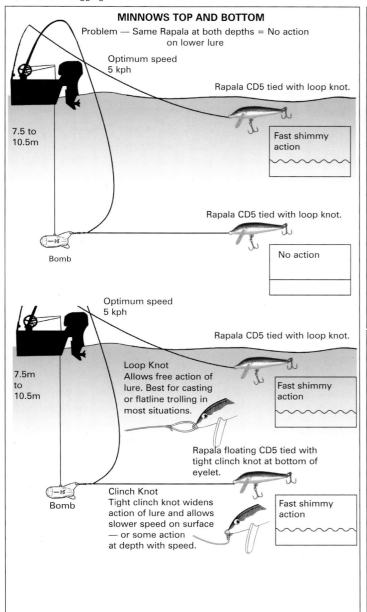

MINNOWS TOP AND BOTTOM

Problem — Same Rapala at both depths = No action on lower lure

Optimum speed 5 kph

Rapala CD5 tied with loop knot.

Fast shimmy action

7.5 to 10.5m

Rapala CD5 tied with loop knot.

No action

Bomb

Optimum speed 5 kph

Rapala CD5 tied with loop knot.

7.5m to 10.5m

Loop Knot
Allows free action of lure. Best for casting or flatline trolling in most situations.

Fast shimmy action

Rapala floating CD5 tied with tight clinch knot at bottom of eyelet.

Clinch Knot
Tight clinch knot widens action of lure and allows slower speed on surface — or some action at depth with speed.

Fast shimmy action

Bomb

MINNOW AND TASSIE DEVIL

Different lures and different depths, same speed and right for both.

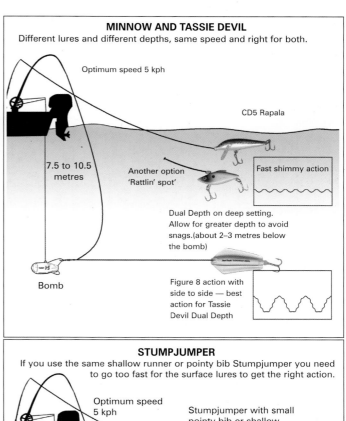

Optimum speed 5 kph

CD5 Rapala

Fast shimmy action

7.5 to 10.5 metres

Another option 'Rattlin' spot'

Dual Depth on deep setting. Allow for greater depth to avoid snags.(about 2–3 metres below the bomb)

Bomb

Figure 8 action with side to side — best action for Tassie Devil Dual Depth

STUMPJUMPER

If you use the same shallow runner or pointy bib Stumpjumper you need to go too fast for the surface lures to get the right action.

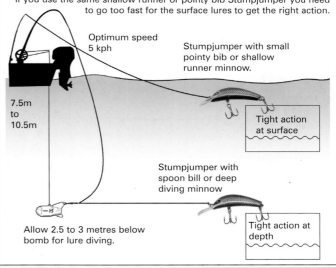

Optimum speed 5 kph

Stumpjumper with small pointy bib or shallow runner minnow.

7.5m to 10.5m

Tight action at surface

Stumpjumper with spoon bill or deep diving minnow

Allow 2.5 to 3 metres below bomb for lure diving.

Tight action at depth

FORD FENDER ATTRACTORS WITH MUDEYES

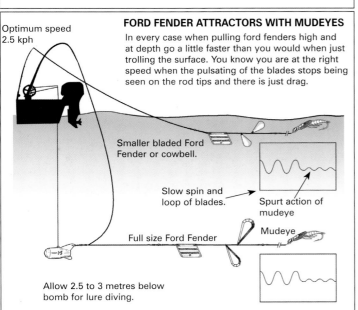

Optimum speed 2.5 kph

In every case when pulling ford fenders high and at depth go a little faster than you would when just trolling the surface. You know you are at the right speed when the pulsating of the blades stops being seen on the rod tips and there is just drag.

Smaller bladed Ford Fender or cowbell.

Slow spin and loop of blades.

Spurt action of mudeye

Full size Ford Fender

Mudeye

Allow 2.5 to 3 metres below bomb for lure diving.

FLATFISH STYLE LURES

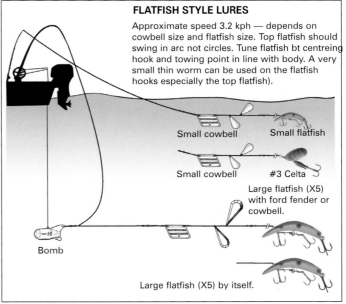

Approximate speed 3.2 kph — depends on cowbell size and flatfish size. Top flatfish should swing in arc not circles. Tune flatfish bt centreing hook and towing point in line with body. A very small thin worm can be used on the flatfish hooks especially the top flatfish).

Small cowbell   Small flatfish

Small cowbell   #3 Celta

Large flatfish (X5) with ford fender or cowbell.

Bomb

Large flatfish (X5) by itself.

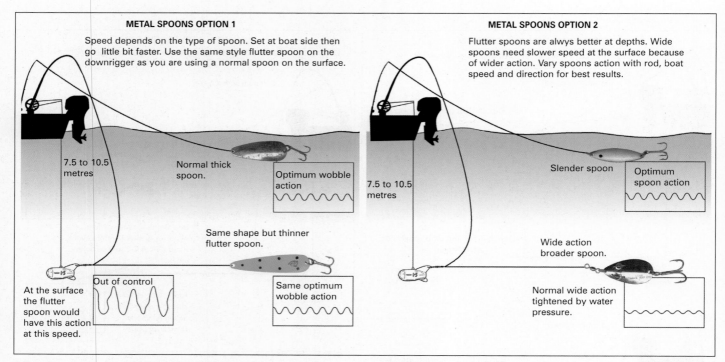

METAL SPOONS OPTION 1

Speed depends on the type of spoon. Set at boat side then go little bit faster. Use the same style flutter spoon on the downrigger as you are using a normal spoon on the surface.

7.5 to 10.5 metres

Normal thick spoon.

Optimum wobble action

Same shape but thinner flutter spoon.

At the surface the flutter spoon would have this action at this speed.

Out of control

Same optimum wobble action

METAL SPOONS OPTION 2

Flutter spoons are alwys better at depths. Wide spoons need slower speed at the surface because of wider action. Vary spoons action with rod, boat speed and direction for best results.

Slender spoon

Optimum spoon action

7.5 to 10.5 metres

Wide action broader spoon.

Normal wide action tightened by water pressure.

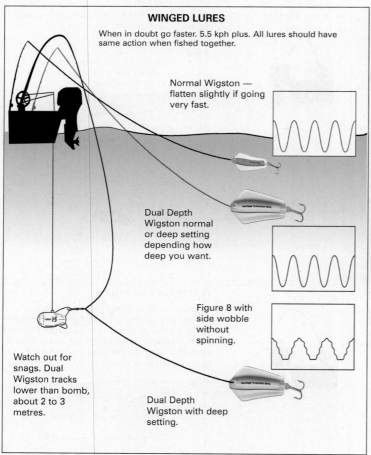

WINGED LURES

When in doubt go faster. 5.5 kph plus. All lures should have same action when fished together.

Normal Wigston — flatten slightly if going very fast.

Dual Depth Wigston normal or deep setting depending how deep you want.

Figure 8 with side wobble without spinning.

Watch out for snags. Dual Wigston tracks lower than bomb, about 2 to 3 metres.

Dual Depth Wigston with deep setting.

Above: This lure retriever uses entangling chains to snare a snagged lure and the heavy line allows it to be pulled free and brought back up to the surface.

LURE RETRIEVERS

When fishing with lures around the sort of places that hold fish, it is inevitable that sooner or later, you will get a lure stuck on something submerged and solid, like the branch of a sunken tree, a rocky outcrop or oyster clump – a snag. There are several versions of lure retrievers available but basically only two types.

The first has a loop or spiral or notch of heavy wire or metal attached to the end of a long stout pole, and these are used to push the lure off the offending structure. The other is of more use when the lure is stuck down really deep, perhaps beyond the reach of a push pole. It comprises a weight of some sort attached to a heavy cord and having wire line loops sticking out of it that

enable the unit to be clipped onto the angler's line and slid down to where the lure is stuck. Some form of entangling device is then used (lengths of chain links or a shaped strong wire loop is the usual) to snag onto the lure body or hooks. Then, the heavy cord is used to drag the lure off, often breaking the branch (or piece of shell or rock) or simply straightening the hook out enough for it to lose its grip on the problem.

MARKER FLOATS

Floats with string and a lead weight attached can be tossed overboard by anglers to mark a spot where some sub-surface feature worth fishing attention has been noticed, or to show where crab pots and lobster pots have been set. Usually, they are deployed after an interesting piece of underwater structure or active fish have been registered on the screen of an echo sounder. In

Pic. 2.30: With a marker float, you can mark a spot where you have struck a fish before or where your echo sounder indicates fish or interesting structure is below the boat. The lead weight makes the float flip, releasing line until it hits bottom or reaches the end of the string.

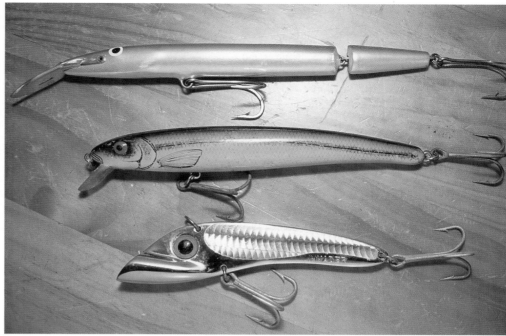

These saltwater minnow lures do different jobs. The top one is for medium pace deep trolling work, while the second is for slow trolling, spinning or jerk baiting and the heavy metal bibless version is a high speed trolling lure that can also be deep jigged.

some cases, the angler will turn the boat around and go back and fish the area immediately. In others, such as when tournament fishing, where time is precious, the angler may continue his search pattern, marking a range of spots with floats that are identifiably his and then come back and begin to work each spot systematically.

MINNOW LURES

Any slender bibbed lure that has a 'swimming' or linear wagging action as it is moved through the water can be broadly classified as a minnow. There are many different kinds of minnows. Some are very slim, while others are more rounded. Others are almost perfect cylinders, or have compound body shapes, involving curves, bends and swoops and even shaped keel sections. The size, shape and angle of the bib can dramatically alter the action of the lure (how fast and how far it wags from side to side) and also, how deep it will dive before its path flattens out into a maximum swimming depth. Generally, large bibs set at a flat angle to the body will make the lure dive deep and will also generally operate at higher speeds than others. Short and steeply angled bibs will give less diving depth and tend not to work well at anything above a slow or intermittent and jerking style of movement.

Each has its place and its optimum field of application, with slender deep divers being used for fast swimming saltwater fish, such as kingfish, tuna and mackerel. Trolling those same lures a little slower and in different places can yield tailor, Australian salmon and flathead. Stouter or flat-bodied lures with pronounced body curves are best for slower-moving freshwater native fish such as Murray cod, golden and silver perch and bass. Slender lures with short bibs are often best used with a slow twitch and pause style of movement and, depending on their size, can

suit various fishing situations. Lures 70 to 120 mm long suit fish like barramundi, mulloway, threadfin salmon and mangrove jacks, while the mini-end of this lure style (35 to 60 mm) can suit fish such as trout, bass, redfin perch, bream, whiting and flathead.

MONOFILAMENT FISHING LINES

'Monofilament' lines are manufactured from liquified nylon by being extruded through a die as a single continuous filament. Over 90 per cent of all fishing line is manufactured this way, but there exists an enormous range of characteristics that can be built into the line, by varying the exact formulation of the plastics used to make the line. Other performance characteristics can be achieved by changing the speed, pressure and temperature at which the line is extruded also.

Many currently accepted fishing knots did not even exist before nylon fishing came along and demanded their invention, but they have now passed into such common usage that most fishermen assume they must have been there since the beginning of fishing itself. The fact is that monofilament lines require a particular style of knot to hold and not slip, yet at the same time, avoid creating weak spots through excessive heat buildup or compression as the knot is tied. Whatever knot you choose to tie, you should tie it slowly and carefully, and moisten the line in your mouth before pulling the knot down tight. This lubricates the line and it slips easily across itself as the knot is tied, avoiding the creation of localised hot spots of friction damage that can weaken the line.

MULLET TRAPS

Small juvenile mullet (often called 'poddy' mullet) can be trapped easily in various devices, for use as bait. Clear plastic cylindrical traps that have inward-facing funnels at either end are available, or you can construct a trap yourself with a wire or wooden frame and fly gauze walls. Bread is placed in these traps as bait and the fish swim in through small openings to eat it and can't find their way out again.

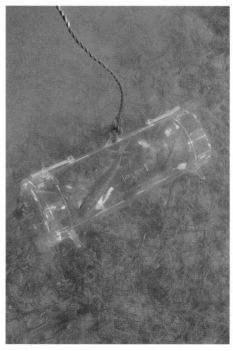

This mullet trap obviously works, with small mullet having been lured into it by the attraction of plain white bread bait.

MULTI-STRAND WIRE LINES

Wire traces come in many forms including single strand extrusions, cable-laid multi-strand versions and braided wire trace. Single strand wire is usually secured with a series of 45° twists (known as 'haywire' twists) and a series of locking wraps at 90 degrees around the main strand (barrel twists).

Multi-strand cable wire is secured by passing both the leading and return legs of the join through the hollow core of soft metal sleeves (called 'crimps') that are squeezed shut with special pliers to provide a non-slip join. To enhance the security of this join and also provide additional robustness in the loop of wire that will take all the wear and pressure when fishing, a twisted loop called a 'flemish eye' is usually formed. Braided wire trace may or may not have a central core of nylon or other soft material and this can usually be knotted, just as you would knot conventional nylon line. Some cable laid wire traces can be knotted too, but these joins are always suspect, since the individual small filaments of wire are easily crushed by the pressure of a standard fishing knot.

NATIVE TAIL KICKER

Use your favourite deep diving lure, the larger the better, and run a tail kicker worm off the first hook tow point.

NETS

Catching the fish means you have to get them into the boat and the traditional method has always been with a net. The basic fact that all anglers come across at some point in their fishing experience is that the net can be too small!
Our advice is always to err on the side of optimism and up-size your net rather than down-size it. Obviously, space storage, whether you're fishing from a boat or on foot, will always alter your choice.

Folding and collapsible nets are great if you're walking the bank or shore, but they can be a handful to open if you've got a big trout going berserk on the other end of your line! Many anglers prefer the wooden New Zealand 'snow shoe' style that clips to the back of your vest.

In saltwater, the nets are made from stainless steel or aluminium construction. It takes a strong net to get a 10–20 kg fish into the boat. An important hint when lifting big fish in a net is to always lift the fish with the net in the vertical plane once the fish is netted. To try to lift it horizontally takes much more strength on the part of the angler due to leverage and could even break the net.

NIPPER PUMPS

Pink nippers, known under a variety of names including ghost shrimp, yabbies or bass-yabbies, can be pumped from sand flats at low tide with a nipper pump. This is a cylindrical tube with a vacuum plunger arrangement inside and a stout handle fixed to the outside at 90 degrees. The plunger comprises rubber friction washers between two metal plates, threaded onto a long central shaft with a 'T' handle on the top end. With the handle fully down, the lower end of the pump is placed over a nipper hole and simultaneously, the pump barrel is pushed down into the sand as the plunger is withdrawn. If the sand is wet enough, this will drive the pump down below the sand surface to where the nipper's underground galleries are. Withdrawing the handle sucks liquified sand and any nippers present into the tube, the pump is then withdrawn from the sand and the plunger is pushed back down to eject the pump contents. Any nippers discharged with the sand are picked up, washed and dropped into a bucket of clean saltwater. If you are pumping a sand flat that is already covered with water, you can tow along a floating sieve arrangement and discharge the pump contents into that each time. The sand simply sinks through the sieve mesh, leaving the nippers behind.

NOISY CAROLINA RIG

Wake up shutdown fish by adding an extra worm weight.

NYMPHS

These are flies (usually) for use in freshwater fishing situations. They represent the aquatic, larval stage of many stream and lake insects. In fact, insects at this stage of their life cycle probably

This angler is using a nipper pump on a tidal flat at low water to gather live nippers for bait. In this shot he has just discharged the pump's contents onto the ground and will then look through the pumped slurry of sand for signs of movement.

represent the vast bulk of many freshwater fishes' diets. They are fished as 'wet' flies, i.e. they are presented below the surface, or in the case of mudeyes (the larval stage of the dragonfly), within the meniscus or surface film of the water.

PEGGED TEXAS RIG

If you're fishing in really heavy timber and snags, peg your worm weight so the weight stays near the worm.

POLARISING SUNGLASSES

Sunglasses with the ability to polarise light rays will enable you to see through the surface glare and into the water far better than is possible without them. This polarising effect is usually the product of using specially formulated laminates within

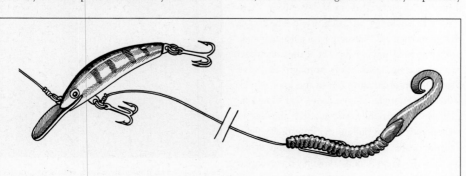

Native tail kicker.

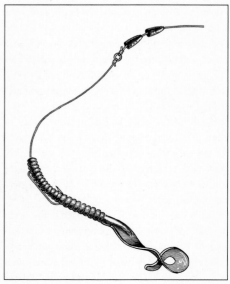

Noisy Carolina rig.

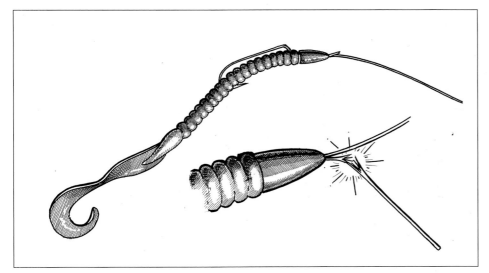

Pegged Texas rig

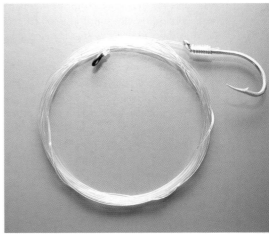

You can save valuable fishing time by pre-rigging traces before you leave home. This one is intended for use as a live bait trace for kingfish.

the lens construction of the glasses, which capture the light and split it into different parts of the light spectrum. The effect is to allow you to visually penetrate the water surface and to see more; such as weed beds, bottom detail, snags, holes and depth changes and also any fish that are moving about. Good quality polarising sunglasses can also reduce angler fatigue by minimising eye strain due to glare. If you need to wear prescription glasses for any reason, your optometrist can usually organise to incorporate a polarising ability into your next prescription adjustment.

PRAWNING LIGHTS

Sometimes, prawns can be gathered during the day by pushing a garden rake through shallow weed beds and scooping any fleeing prawns up with hand net. Most times, however, prawning is best done at night with lanterns of some sort to illuminate the prawn's highly reflective eyes and give you a target to scoop at. Prawning lights can be gas or kerosene lanterns mounted on the side of a boat or carried by prawners wading the shallows. It is very important to shield the light so it only shines downward, or you will be blinded by the light and see nothing at all. You can also use powerful torches, such as the Eveready Dolphin lantern, a fully waterproof and floating torch that runs on a 6 volt dry cell battery. Another option available to wading prawners is a waterproof battery-powered spotlight, which can be mounted on the end of a wand. This light can actually be submerged, allowing full illumination of the prawns and surrounding shallows without any surface glare. To run one of these, you will need a 12 volt battery, such as a small motorcycle battery. There are miniature versions of these weighing less than a kilogram and you can carry them in a small pouch on a belt. On a full charge, these should run a small spotlight for about two hours.

PRAWNING NETS

There are basically two types of prawning nets: drag nets, which are a panel style net with a pocket sewn into the middle: and scoop nets, which are either round or roughly triangular in shape and mounted on the end of a handle. Drag nets require two people to use them properly, one person standing at either end of the net and using a long pole or stake to push or drag the net along between them. Generally, this sort of prawning is done 'blind', simply by walking the nets along a shallow lake or estuary margin, wherever there are tidal currents and weed beds. Scoop nets are always hand-held and used in conjunction with a prawning. Once you spot one or more prawns, the scoop net is pushed forward and down beneath them, then lifted to get them out of the water.

PRE-RIGGING BAITS

Experienced game fishing crews often use the time spent running from homeport to the fishing grounds by rigging up several baits they expect to be using when they get there. These can then be kept chilled on ice and ready to use at a moment's notice. Examples include swimming mullet baits, slimy mackerel or garfish skipping baits, and hook-less teasers, made from the rolled belly flap or fillet of shiny-skinned fish like queenfish, tuna and mackerel.

PRE-RIGGING TRACES

You can save a lot of valuable fishing time before you even set out on a trip by pre-rigging several traces and such the night before. Rigs such as traces can be assembled, then coiled neatly and stored flat in zip-lock plastic bags. It helps to label these bags in some way, i.e. '40 kg live bait trace – 3 m – 6/0 suicide hook', or, perhaps, 'Saltwater fly leader – 1.5 m, 24 to 6 kg'. Baitfishing rigs can also be pre-rigged, complete with hooks, swivels and traces, and wrapped around blocks

of polystyrene foam. Cut a notch in the foam to take the swivel or ring at the top of the rig, then wrap the trace around the foam and secure the hook by pressing the point into the foam block. Several traces can be assembled this way on a single flat piece of foam about 30 cm x 10 cm in size.

REEL BAGS

Fishing reels can be kept in good order and protected from impact marks and damage by keeping them in a padded cloth bag. These rarely cost more than $10 or $20 and represent good value when you consider they can prolong the appearance and function of a reel worth more than 10 times that much.

REEL LINE CAPACITY

How much line a reel holds is rarely of real consequence during most forms of fishing, except on those occasions when a really big fish takes the lure or bait and runs for a

Closed face reels like this one are good for short range casting and fish that will not take a lot of line. They do not have the line capacity to handle long runs from powerful fish.

considerable distance before you can stop it. A more important consideration is how full the reel spool is as this can affect casting distance, drag performance and how long you can go before you need to fill the spool again to have enough line for practical fishing purposes. If you are chasing large gamefish then you may well need every metre of line you can pack onto a reel. For the rest of the time, think in terms of fishing with a full reel all the time and you will usually have enough line for any fishing purpose.

REEL RETRIEVE RATES

The rate at which a fishing reel can retrieve line is governed by four factors. Of these, two are things beyond your control and two are things you can consciously do something about. The two things you do have some control over are how fast you can wind the reel handle and how thick or thin the line is you are using. Line thickness affects line recovery rates in terms of how much line load diameter will be lost by removing a certain length of line from the spool. Thick line drops the line load diameter very quickly when stripped from a reel. Thin line reduces it much less for a given length of line.

The first fixed factor in this business of line recovery rate, is the spool's diameter. The other fixed factor is the gear ratio, i.e. how many times the line is wrapped around the spool for every turn of the reel handle. Large diameter reel spools (when full) will lose less line load diameter for a given length of line out and will recover line more quickly with each revolution of the spool. High gear ratios of around 6:1 mean the spool will revolve many more times per turn of the reel handle than is the case with a lower gear ratio of around 3:1. In fact, it will gather line in exactly twice as fast. How much actual line that is coming back onto the reel will be determined by the diameter of the line load at the commencement of the retrieve. A half full spool of line on a fast retrieve reel may not recover as much line as a slower retrieve reel with a much larger diameter line load on the spool.

ROD BUCKETS

Rod buckets are simply a leather or plastic or metal pouch or cup held around the angler's waist by a stout leather or webbing belt. The cup is where the rod butt is pushed when a fish is being fought. This saves some discomfort for the angler, as the rod bucket provides a padded fulcrum point for all the angler's fighting effort on the rod. This can greatly improve angler comfort and efficiency levels and considerably shorten fights with big fish.

ROD CARRIERS

When you want to carry long, one-piece rods any distance in a car, rod racks on the roof allow

There are many kinds of rod buckets. This one is made of leather and would suit light boat fishing work, or fishing from the rocks or beaches.

the rods to be kept entirely within the outline of the vehicle and safe from colliding with roadside trees, signs, or worse, pedestrians. Standard car roof racks are good enough for short journeys as the rods can be held on with bungee cords, light rope or special clamp-type rod holders and carriers can be employed.

ROD RESTS AND SPIKES

Shore fishermen often need to lay down their rods when some other task is at hand or when the fishing is very slow. Estuary and freshwater bank anglers can use a variety of rod rests and cradles that allow the rod to be positioned low and almost horizontal – a good angle when bait fishing for sensitive species like trout, carp and bream.

Beach fishermen also often need to stand their rod upright and give themselves a break from holding it. In this case, a sand spike is a great investment as it keeps the reel up out of the sand and can even allow a fish to take a set bait without the angler having to hold the rod all the time.

ROD STORAGE IN BOATS

Rods can be stored in boats either horizontally (good for when a lot of casting is going on) or vertically, which is a space-efficient way of storing rods so they don't take up floor space. For horizontal or flat storage of rods, you can use commercially made rod cradles (or make your own from jig-sawed plywood). Some small boat anglers are also storing rods in a rod box below a casting platform built into the boat. Game fishing boats and offshore sportfishers often run a vertical or slightly slanted rod rack called a 'rocket launcher'. These comprise a battery of rod tubes set side by side so the rods resemble a picket fence. The key to all rod storage in boats is to have them safe from harm, out of everyone's way, yet within easy reach when required.

ROD TUBES AND BAGS

Rods that perform well and deliver great fishing pleasure do not come cheaply. As such, you need to protect your investment by looking after them. Travelling anglers, in particular, know only too well that most rod damage occurs in and around vehicles, on aeroplanes, or when rods are being transported any distance. To preserve your fishing rods on a trip, wrap each rod in a soft, protective cloth bag and put those bagged rods into a tough PVC or metal tube to save them being damaged by severe knocks. This particularly applies to fly rods, most of which, if they are of any quality, come already in a rod bag and tube anyway. But you can extend this to ensure the long life and service of other kinds of rods by applying the same principles.

If you are travelling any distance over country roads and at high speed, it might be worth considering a large diameter PVC tube, in which the rods can be made perfectly safe and secure. The tube can be lashed or bolted to the roof rack or if short enough kept inside the car. It should also have a screw end cap that can be locked for security when the car is left unattended.

This sand spike rod holder enables you to rest your rod when you are rigging without having the reel fall into the sand. They are also good for setting baits and waiting for fish to come along when the fishing is slow.

ROD WRAPS

Anglers who have learned there is a need for several rods will appreciate the difficulty in moving bunches of rods around from place to place. There is an answer to this problem and it lies in the form of Velcro-fastened rod wraps. These can be either padded material or rubberised foam. The rods are simply stood up (butts down and tips up), with their runners all facing outward. The rod wraps are then wrapped around them, self-securing with the Velcro patches on the ends.

SALTWATER LURES

What a great range of options there are here, although, like freshwater lures, there are only a few basic types, with countless permutations of the main ideas into more specialised forms and myriad colours. The main types are: skirted trolling lures, meant for relatively high speed presentations for gamefish; metal jigs and spoons, which can be dropped down to fish beneath a boat or cast from boat or shore-based spots; bibbed (and bibless) swimming lures; leadhead jigs, soft plastics and surface poppers.

Aside from the maelstrom of colour choices that would take a whole book on their own to examine, the main features of lures to look for are size, overall body shape and profile, and degree of reflectivity or counter-shading.

Lure size relates sometimes to the size of your target fish, but not always. For example, big tuna will often take quite tiny metal lures, but much more consistently, marlin will take larger lures rather than smaller ones, and bream will take smaller lures rather than bigger ones. Overall body shape determines how fast or slow the lure is best presented and to some extent also dictates which fish it will suit. Reflectivity is a much-underestimated factor in lure performance. It partly relates to light conditions on the day (on dull days, very shiny lures seem to work better than they do on bright days). Lure reflectivity also relates to how shiny the natural prey is, such as baitfish or squid, where you are fishing. This is important as the local fish may have become conditioned to striking at either bright or dull-coloured prey on the day and you need to be aware of which is the operative choice. Counter-shading is also an important piece in the lure puzzle, as fish tend to key in on certain combinations of dark back/light belly or vice-versa, again in relation to locally available prey.

SINGLE STRAND WIRE LINES

Wire traces used for many species may need to be fairly flexible. Cable wire is usually best, but there are times when cable wire spooks fish too much and the much thinner and less conspicuous single strand wire is a better choice. Live baiting

This collection of lures would suit a variety of saltwater fishing situations. Despite their size differences, all these lures have one thing in common; they are meant to imitate small baitfish.

for Spanish mackerel is one instance that comes to mind.

SNAPPER TACKLE

Snapper tackle tends to vary a little depending on where in the country you are fishing for them, but there are enough basic similarities to be able to suggest a useful general approach. For boat fishing with a threadline reel, something capable of holding 200 m of 10 kg line. Line can be anywhere between 4 and 10 kg and a rod some 2.1 to 2.4 m long will allow you to throw unweighted baits and fish for snapper up to and including some very big fish. Overhead tackle can be an Abu 7000 sized reel or one a bit larger, with a rod from 1.8 to 2.1 m long and line in the 6 to 10 kg bracket.

Sidecast fishermen can catch snapper very well too. These large diameter reels allow unweighted or heavily rigged baits to be cast with equal ease. Rod length can be a 2.1 to 2.4 m fast taper casting rod or a moderately stiff 1.8 to 2.1 m model for use as a bottom bouncing outfit in deep water. Hooks should be sized to carry the baits being used and since this will vary from place to place it is probably best to suggest a range, which would be from 3/0 right up to 6/0 or 7/0. Sinkers can vary according to water conditions at the time and how far the baits need to be thrown. Generally, for running sinker work, ball sinkers from 5 to 35 g are usually employed, while snapper leads can be as light as 30 g or as heavy as 500 g, with a rough median weight of something like 100 to 200 g most of the time. Shore anglers need only alter the length of the

rods and the leaders being used as most of the baits, reels, hooks and rigs will remain the same as used for boat work. One exception is that Paternoster rigs used from the rocks are often rigged as sliders, so the drop from rod tip to sinker and bait can be kept suitably shorter.

SNAPS, SWIVELS AND RINGS

Snap clips, with or without swivels attached, are a very handy way of achieving a quick-connect system for rig changes. The swivel helps if the rig will be prone to line twist. Swivels themselves are theoretically used to prevent line twist, but in fact, very few, other than ball-bearing swivels, will work unfailingly to do this. There are significant engineering problems with the ability of most barrel swivels to rotate freely when under direct linear pressure, although good quality crane swivels and some better barrels do a fairly good job. Swivels do, however, provide a strong, secure and slim profile connection for bait rigs, and handle any incidental rig rotation problems arising from turbulent water.

For sheer strength, though, nothing beats brass rings as a metal connector between lines. But there is a down side. Brass rings are not always as inconspicuous as some fishing applications require a join to be. A case in point is when fishing for inveterate line choppers like tailor, mackerel or wahoo, which can zero in on any conspicuous element in a rig and strike at it, severing the line in the process. As such, many anglers prefer black swivels, believing them to be less easily seen and therefore less likely to attract unwanted toothy attention.

Various snaps.

SNAPS

Crosslock snap

Coastlock snap

Hook snap

Speed clip

Interlock snap

Hawaiian snap

Doulock snap

Snap system snap

WHAT SNAPPER RODS ARE AVAILABLE

Manufacturer	Model	Material	Butt Length	Guides	Guide Type	Rod Style	Overall Length	Line
MCLAUGHLINS 03 9555 5433	Bayfisher	E Glass	36.5	7 plus tip	Hardloy	Threadline	210	6 kg
	Strategy	Graph./E Glass	38	7 plus tip	Silicone	Threadline	205	8 kg
PENN 03 9764 8688	PSP7001SSH	Graph./E Glass	35	5 plus tip	Hardloy	Threadline	215	8 kg
	PSP6001OHM	Graph./E Glass	29.5	6 plus tip	Hardloy	Overhead	180	9 kg
	PSP6601SSM	Graph./E Glass	29	5 plus tip	Hardloy	Threadline	198	9 kg
	PSP7001OHM	Graph./E Glass	41	8 plus tip	Hardloy	Overhead	215	9 kg
JARVIS WALKER WHITETAIL 03 9764 8688	SB7001TLM	Graph./E Glass	35	6 plus tip	SiC	Threadline	215	8 kg
	GB6001TLM	Graph./E Glass	40	5 plus tip	SiC	Threadline	180	8 kg
	GB6601TLM	Graph./E Glass	40	5 plus tip	SiC	Threadline	200	8 kg
	SB7001TLH	Graph./E Glass	37.5	6 plus tip	SiC	Threadline	215	9 kg
	SB6301OHM	Graph./E Glass	31.5	7 plus tip	SiC	Overhead	193	10 kg
SHAKESPEARE 02 9820 9600	Ugly Stik 2000 plus	Graph./E Glass	34	5 plus tip	Hardloy	Threadline	210	5 kg
	Ugly Stik OHD66A	Graph./E Glass	36	7 plus tip	Hardloy	Threadline	198	10 kg
	Ugly Stik Custom	Graph./E Glass	33	9 plus tip	Hardloy	Overhead	210	10 kg
SHAKESPEARE TACKLE WORLD 02 9820 9600	Ugly Stik SP	Graph./E Glass	31	6 plus tip	Hardloy	Threadline	200	6 kg
	Ugly Stik SP	Graph./E Glass	35	6 plus tip	Hardloy	Threadline	210	8 kg
	Ugly Stik OH	Graph./E Glass	39	7 plus tip	Hardloy	Overhead	210	10 kg
	Ugly Stik SR	Graph./E Glass	37	7 plus tip	Hardloy	Overhead	210	10 kg
INNOVATOR 03 9620 3320	Shogun Barrier	Graphite	33	7 plus tip	Hardloy	Overhead	198	7 kg
RHINO SKIN 03 9620 3320	CA70	E Glass	31.5	7 plus tip	Hardloy	Threadline	210	8 kg
	CA70MB	E Glass	33	7 plus tip	Hardloy	Threadline	210	10 kg
SHIMANO DUNPHY SPORTS 02 9526 2144	Baitrunner Medium	Graphite	33	7 plus tip	SiC	Threadline	210	7 kg
	Snapper Special	E Glass	33	7 plus tip	SiC	Threadline	225	7 kg
	Taipan TP1702	Graphite	32	8 plus tip	SiC	Overhead	215	8 kg
	Calcutta Heavy	Graphite	29.5	8 plus tip	SiC	Overhead	198	8 kg
	TLD Special	Graphite	32	8 plus tip	SiC	Overhead	198	12 kg
G LOOMIS EJ TODD 02 9533 7700	L842-2-B	Graphite	30.5	7 plus tip	Hardloy	Threadline	215	7 kg
	SW84-16	Graphite	36.5	6 plus tip	Hardloy	Threadline	215	7 kg
	SW843	Graphite	32	6 plus tip	Hardloy	Threadline	215	7 kg
	SW844	Graphite	35	6 plus tip	Hardloy	Threadline	215	7 kg
	SW84-20	Graphite	35	6 plus tip	Hardloy	Threadline	215	10 kg
DAIWA 02 9938 2899	FW-B701MFS	Graphite	32.5	7 plus tip	Hardloy	Threadline	213	7 kg
	FW-B701MHFS	Graphite	36.5	7 plus tip	Hardloy	Threadline	213	8 kg
	SL-XB701MLF-1	Graphite	32	0	Internal	Threadline	213	10 kg
	SL-XB661MHR-1	Graphite	34	0	Internal	Overhead	213	15 kg
SILSTAR FREETIME GROUP 02 9792 4599	PX-561CAH	Graphite	19	8 plus tip	SiC	Overhead	165	6 kg
	PF-661SWM	Graph./E Glass	33	8 plus tip	SiC	Overhead	200	7 kg
	PC-701SSL	Graph./E Glass	35.5	6 plus tip	SiC	Threadline	210	7 kg
	PC-661SWM	Graph./E Glass	33	8 plus tip	SiC	Overhead	200	8 kg
	PC-701SWM	Graph./E Glass	34	8 plus tip	SiC	Overhead	210	9 kg
WILSON LIVE FIBRE L. WILSON & CO. 07 3890 2288	ZWS65LJ	Graphite	32.5	6 plus tip	Hardloy	Threadline	198	5 kg
	ZWS65LJ	Graphite	29	8 plus tip	Hardloy	Overhead	198	5 kg
	ZWS65MJ	Graphite	33	8 plus tip	Hardloy	Overhead	198	7 kg
	ZWS65MJ	Graphite	33	5 plus tip	Hardloy	Threadline	198	7 kg
	Jigger	Graphite	34	8 plus tip	Hardloy	Overhead	180	7 kg
	BWS70LJ	Graphite	26	6 plus tip	Hardloy	Threadline	210	7 kg
	BWS70LJ	Graphite	26	9 plus tip	Hardloy	Overhead	198	8 kg
	BWS70MJ	Graphite	32.5	9 plus tip	Hardloy	Overhead	210	10 kg
THUNDER RODS 03 9714 8482	Light Snapper	E Glass	29	6 plus tip	Hardloy	Threadline	210	4 kg
	Black Sooty	Graph./E Glass	29	7 plus tip	Hardloy	Threadline	180	4 kg
	Black Shag	Graph./E Glass	29	8 plus tip	Hardloy	Threadline	195	5 kg
	Snapper	Graph./E Glass	35	8 plus tip	Hardloy	Overhead	198	7 kg

Note that the given line rating is a recommendation by the manufacturer and most rods can comfortably use one line class heavier and two line classes lighter without risking the blanks safety.

SNAP SWIVELS

Supplier	Model	Locking Mechanism	Construction Material	B/S Range (kg)	Anodised	Size Range	Swivel Type	Colour
Wilson	SureCatch	Interlock	Brass	9 – 35	No	14 – 1/0	Barrel	Brass
	Interlock	Interlock	Brass	18 – 45	Yes	4 – 1/0	Crane	Black
	SureCatch	Coastlock	Brass	18 – 65	Yes	5 – 1	Crane	Black
	Coastlock	Coastlock	Brass	20 – 100	Yes	8 – 3	Ball Bearing	Black
	SureCatch	Hook	Brass	12 – 60	Yes	12 – 4	Rolling	Black
Goodsport	Coastlock	Coastlock	Brass	17 – 45	Yes	5 – 1/0	Crane	Black
	Hawaiian	Hawaiian	Brass	24 – 80	Yes	7 – 2	Ball Bearing	Black
	Coastlock	Coastlock	Brass	15 – 85	Yes	8 – 1	Ball Bearing	Black
Hawk	Italian	Italian	Brass	7 – 21	No	9 – 2	Rolling	Black
	Hawk	Interlock	Brass	9 – 36	No	14 – 6/0	Barrel	Polished
	Hawk	Interlock	Brass	9 – 36	Yes	14 – 6/0	Barrel	Black
Pisces	Crane	Coastlock	Brass/Stainless Steel	35 – 120	Yes	7 – 1	Crane	Black
	Black Snap	Interlock	Brass/Stainless Steel	6 – 45	Yes	14 – 6/0	Barrel	Black
	Brass Snap	Interlock	Brass/Stainless Steel	6 – 45	No	15 – 6/0	Barrel	Brass
	Rolling Snap	Hook	Brass/Stainless Steel	9 – 39	Yes	7 – 1	Rolling	Black
	Hawaiian	Hawaiian	Brass/Stainless Steel	22 – 80	Yes	7 – 1	Ball Bearing	Black
	Black Snap	Interlock	Brass/Stainless Steel	6 – 23	Yes	14 – 6	Barrel	Black
SeaHorse	SBKIS	Interlock	Brass	7 – 36	Yes	14 – 2/0	Barrel	Black
	SBIS	Interlock	Brass	7 – 36	No	14 – 2/0	Barrel	Brass
	SBCWS	Coastlock	Brass	16 – 180	Yes	5 – 5/0	Crane	Black
	SBBIRS	Coastlock	Brass	20 – 40	Yes	7 – 1	Ball Bearing	Black
	SRBHS	Hooked	Brass	20 – 40	Yes	12 – 8	Rolling	Black
	BBWS	Coastlock	Stainless Steel	24 – 240	Yes	24 – 240	Ball Bearing	Black
	CSWS	Coastlock	Stainless Steel	17 – 150	Yes	17 – 150	Crane	Black
Halco	Snap	Interlock	Stainless Steel		No		Barrel	Brass
Black Magic	Black Barrel	Interlock	Stainless Steel	4 – 20	Yes	4 – 20	Barrel	Black
Wasabi	Rolling	Hooked	Stainless Steel	2 – 20	Yes	2 – 20	Rolling	Black
Sampo	X3RTB	Tournament	Stainless Steel Snap	30 – 150	No	8 – 3	Ball Bearing	Silver
	BX4RCB	Coastlock	Stainless Steel	15 – 100	Yes	6 – 1	Ball Bearing	Black
EJ Todd	Dickson	Coastlock	Stainless Steel	5 – 35	Yes	6 – 5/0	Crane	Black
	Dickson	Coastlock	Brass/Stainless Steel	12 – 120	Yes	1 – 7	Ball Bearing	Black
	Dickson	Interlock	Brass/Stainless Steel	6 – 50	Yes	14 – 4/0	Barrel	Black/
Brass	Dickson	Coastlock	Brass/Stainless Steel	15 – 55	Yes	12 – 4	Rolling	Black
Pacific Lures	Shogun	Coastlock	Stainless Steel	15 – 55	Yes	7 – 1	Ball Bearing	Black
	Shogun	Coastlock	Brass/Stainless Steel	15 – 80	Yes	5 – 5/0	Crane	Black
	Shogun	Interlock	Brass/Stainless Steel	30	Yes	8 – 1/0	Rolling	Grey
	Shogun	Interlock	Brass/Stainless Steel	25 – 50	Yes	14 – 5/0	Barrel	Black

SNAP SWIVELS

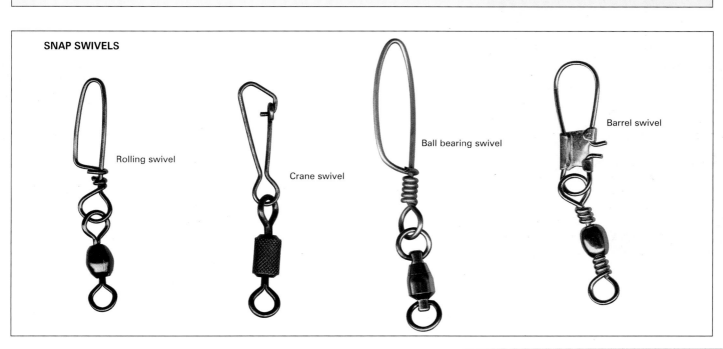

Rolling swivel

Crane swivel

Ball bearing swivel

Barrel swivel

<table>
<tr><td colspan="8">SNAPS</td></tr>
<tr><th>Supplier</th><th>Model</th><th>Locking Mechanism</th><th>Construction Material</th><th>B/S Range (kg)</th><th>Anodised</th><th>Size Range</th><th>Colour</th></tr>
<tr><td>Wilson</td><td>SureCatch</td><td>Coastlock</td><td>Brass</td><td>17 – 90</td><td>Yes</td><td>6 – 1</td><td>Black</td></tr>
<tr><td>Goodsport</td><td>Hawaiian</td><td>Hawaiian</td><td>Brass</td><td>18 – 85</td><td>Yes</td><td>6 – 2</td><td>Black</td></tr>
<tr><td></td><td>Coastlock</td><td>Coastlock</td><td>Brass</td><td>17 – 85</td><td>Yes</td><td>6 – 16</td><td>Black</td></tr>
<tr><td></td><td>Interlock</td><td>Interlock</td><td>Brass</td><td>5 – 30</td><td>Yes</td><td>6 – 1</td><td>Black</td></tr>
<tr><td></td><td>Crosslock</td><td>Crosslock</td><td>Brass</td><td>18 – 85</td><td>Yes</td><td>4 – 1</td><td>Black</td></tr>
<tr><td></td><td>Hooked</td><td>Hook and eye</td><td>Brass</td><td>25 – 55</td><td>Yes</td><td>6 – 3</td><td>Black</td></tr>
<tr><td>Hawk</td><td>Fastlock</td><td>Fastlock</td><td>Brass</td><td>9 – 18</td><td>Yes</td><td>3 – 1</td><td>Black</td></tr>
<tr><td></td><td>Hooked</td><td>Hooked</td><td>Brass</td><td>18 – 96</td><td>Yes</td><td>6 – 1</td><td>Black</td></tr>
<tr><td></td><td>Interlock</td><td>Interlock</td><td>Brass</td><td>10 – 36</td><td>No</td><td>6 – 1</td><td>Polished</td></tr>
<tr><td></td><td>Italian</td><td>Italian</td><td>Brass</td><td>7 – 40</td><td>No</td><td>5 – 1</td><td>Black</td></tr>
<tr><td>Pisces</td><td>Coastlock</td><td>Coastlock</td><td>Stainless Steel</td><td>41 – 118</td><td>Yes</td><td>6 – 1</td><td>Black</td></tr>
<tr><td></td><td>Hook</td><td>Hook</td><td>Stainless Steel</td><td>15 – 41</td><td>Yes</td><td>6 – 1</td><td>Black</td></tr>
<tr><td></td><td>Duolock</td><td>Duolock</td><td>Stainless Steel</td><td>8 – 58</td><td>Yes</td><td>6 – 1</td><td>Black</td></tr>
<tr><td>Mustad</td><td>Fly Snap</td><td>Snap System</td><td>Carbon Steel</td><td>3.3 – 4.8</td><td>No</td><td>3 – 1</td><td>Bronze</td></tr>
<tr><td>SeaHorse</td><td>ISB</td><td>Interlock</td><td>Stainless Steel</td><td>12 – 60</td><td>No</td><td>6 – 1</td><td>Bras</td></tr>
<tr><td></td><td>ISBK</td><td>Interlock</td><td>Stainless Steel</td><td>12 – 60</td><td>Yes</td><td>6 – 1</td><td>Black</td></tr>
<tr><td></td><td>DSBK</td><td>Duolock</td><td>Stainless Steel</td><td>15 – 37</td><td>Yes</td><td>6 – 1</td><td>Black</td></tr>
<tr><td></td><td>HSBK</td><td>Hooked</td><td>Stainless Steel</td><td>15 – 36</td><td>Yes</td><td>6 – 1</td><td>Black</td></tr>
<tr><td></td><td>CLSBK</td><td>Coastlock</td><td>Stainless Steel</td><td>25 – 80</td><td>Yes</td><td>5 – 1</td><td>Black</td></tr>
<tr><td></td><td>S</td><td>Coastlock</td><td>Stainless Steel</td><td>16 – 150</td><td>Yes</td><td>16 – 150</td><td>Black</td></tr>
<tr><td>Cotton</td><td>L9</td><td>Coastlock Cordell</td><td>Stainless Steel</td><td>Suitable for lures 7 – 28 grams in weight</td><td>No</td><td>9051 – 9053*</td><td>Silver</td></tr>
<tr><td>Pacific Lures</td><td>Shogun</td><td>Coastlock</td><td>Stainless Steel</td><td>15 – 80</td><td>Yes</td><td>1 – 6</td><td>Black</td></tr>
<tr><td>Tacspo</td><td>Speed clip</td><td>Hawaiian</td><td>Stainless Steel</td><td>10 – 20</td><td>No</td><td>Magnum & Standard*</td><td>Silver</td></tr>
</table>

*AMERICAN SIZING

SPINNERBAITS

Spinnerbaits have had a chequered history of acceptance by Australian anglers. They have only recently come into their own as a standard freshwater lure option. The best way to fish them is to bear in mind the depth and flow-rate of the water being fished and the likely attack speed of the species being targeted.

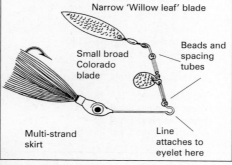

Narrow 'Willow leaf' blade

Small broad Colorado blade

Beads and spacing tubes

Multi-strand skirt

Line attaches to eyelet here

Spinnerbait.

For example, Murray cod will readily take spinnerbaits, but only if they enter and remain in the cod's strike zone (very close to the bottom or structure) and are moved quite slowly. For this work, heavy-headed spinnerbaits with large blades and lots of natural-coloured skirt material can be best.

Bass will strike at small to medium-sized spinnerbaits, with some flash in the tail and a combination of willow leaf and Colorado style blades. These fish often hit a spinnerbait on the drop, so they should be cast right into the back of sunken brush and log country and allowed to helicopter down with frequent upward snaps of the rod tip.

Golden perch in dams will pursue spinnerbaits. An effective retrieve is to let the lure sink and wind it in very slowly, feeling for the blade and head to make intermittent contact with the bottom. Another is to cast into heavy cover and jig it out in a series of snatches of the rod tip, allowing it to flutter and fall between rod movements.

Barramundi will also take spinnerbaits, but casting has to be accurate and the retrieve erratic and persistent enough to evoke a strike.

STAR DRAG REELS

Star drag reels are a very good option for smaller baitcasters and medium surf and jigging reels, as the drag is contained in a very compact housing. This minimises the overall weight of the reel and allows for repetitive casting without minimal fatigue on the angler. Generally, the drag performance is adequate for most species targeted on such gear.

As a rule of thumb, star drags should not be fished at full lock. Instead, it's a good idea to back the drag off just a notch and apply any additional pressure with your thumb. This allows you to back off instantly should a fish take the line close to failure.

Provided the drag is backed right off before the reel is stored away after each fishing session, you will avoid creating any flat spots on the pressure discs. Failing to back the drag off can mean disc deformation that will detract from the reel's performance.

SUBMERSIBLE PUMPS

Submersible electric pumps generally run off a 12-volt battery and can be used to replenish the water supply in live-wells and live bait tanks, as well as helping you make it home safely if the boat is swamped or taking water.

Spinnerbaits have plenty of casting weight in their lead head and great fish-holding ability with that big single hook. The whirling blades and skirt add to the lure's appeal to fish, which explains the popularity of this style of lure with many freshwater anglers.

Bait buckets like these can be clipped to a belt and save you walking back out of the surf each time you need a fresh bait.

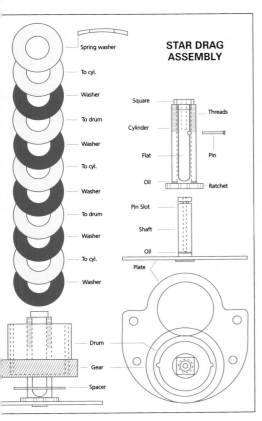

STAR DRAG ASSEMBLY

Spring washer
To cyl.
Washer
To drum
Washer
To cyl.
Washer
To drum
Washer
To cyl.
Washer

Square
Cylinder
Flat
Oil
Pin Slot
Shaft
Oil
Plate

Threads
Pin
Ratchet

Drum
Gear
Spacer

SURF FISHING ACCESSORIES

Accessories you will need when surf fishing include: a fish bag, a belt- mounted bait bucket, a sheath knife, a hand towel, one or more rod spikes and a headlamp for night fishing. You should also think about a gaff for big fish like sharks, rays and mulloway, a bucket for collecting beach worms or pipis and a cutting board for rigging baits. You may also need a good pair of pliers, a hook remover and a haversack for carrying all the incidental gear. For long range beach trips, the most important accessory may well be a suitable four wheel drive that will enable you to cover all the available fishing options.

Surf rods are generally long and powerful both to handle big fish and cast heavy weights a long way, but also to hold the line aloft above the surf.

SURF FISHING TACKLE

Rods for big surf should be 3 to 3.6 m long, fitted with either a large threadline, an Alvey sidecast reel or an overhead reel capable of holding 250 m of line in your chosen line class. A range of hooks in suicides for bream and mulloway, some French style hooks up to 7/0 for big mulloway and several 4200 and 4202 ganging pattern hooks in sizes 2/0 3/0 and 4/0. Some 2/0 long shank hooks for flathead would be useful as would some size 4 and 6 hooks for whiting and dart.

Swivels should be small to medium sized, with some three-ways swivels for Paternoster rigs. Sinkers for Paternoster rigs can be spoons, stars, grapnels, or ring styles, with a range of sizes in ball sinkers and bean sinkers for running sinker rigs. Baits can be nippers, beach worms, pipis, pilchards, garfish, tailor strips or peeled prawns or bloodworms.

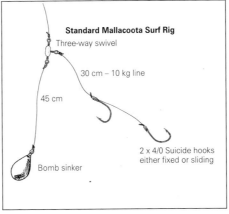

Standard Mallacoota Surf Rig

Three-way swivel

30 cm – 10 kg line

45 cm

Bomb sinker

2 x 4/0 Suicide hooks either fixed or sliding

Above: Standard Mallacoot surf rig.

Below: Surf popper rig.

Surf Popper Rig (for when crabs are about)

Surf poppers are basically a foam-bodied chugger, deployed on the bottom dropper of a tandem Paternoster rig. They are used because while salmon will feed near the bottom, they can't always beat the local sand crabs to a bait and this can prove frustrating. A natural bait is set on the top dropper, up away from the bottom. This makes it harder for the crabs to reach and the combined result is that you have two kinds of 'bait' that salmon will take but since the bottom one is an artificial, you are less likely to be pestered by crabs.

Just about any Victorian tackle shop will carry surf poppers, but anglers elsewhere can make their own from Styrofoam and a single 2/0 straight shank hook. Shape the foam into a wide-faced popper and cut a slot along the centre-line of the bottom (you can buy ready made versions from some fly-tying suppliers—just be sure you get one large enough to suspend the weight of the hook and feathers). Bind and epoxy the butts of four feathers to the shank of the hook and then epoxy the whole thing into place in the slot of the body. Good colours are red and white both for the feathers and the paintwork on the popper head.

The lure will not appeal to crabs, but will often take salmon in the surf, even when a natural bait is suspended above it.

Three-way swivel

Sliding snood

30 cm

30 cm

Three-way swivel

30 cm

30 cm

Surf popper

Bomb sinker

TACKLE BOXES

Various kinds of tackle boxes suit particular fishing situations. For the shore-based angler a standard cantilevered multi tray tackle box is fine. Larger tray boxes are good for home storage, or for use in a large boat that has plenty of floor space. A better system for on the water might be a series of separate flat tackle boxes that can be carried in a soft pack or mop bucket, or slotted into tackle drawers and cabinets. Small pocket-sized tackle boxes are good for carrying the small amount of tackle needed to walk and fish along streams and estuary shores.

There are many kinds of tackle boxes. These small modular types can be filled with specific kinds of tackle for different kinds of fishing and then taken out on fishing excursions as required in a general haversack or carry bag.

TASSIE TYPE LURES

An all-Australian success story, the Tassie Devil or Cobra style lure is unique to Australia. Invented by Brian Johnstone, in Tasmania, more trout have been caught on these than any other lure, and there are now over a dozen manufacturers of this type of lure.

These are essentially a form of spoon lure in that they have a curved heavy body that catches water on its two tapered wings and wags from side to side when trolled or retrieved. The body is plastic or resin based, with a heavy lead core in the centre, between the wings. There is a hole through the centre of this lead core body and line is threaded through here and tied directly to a single or treble hook, sometimes with a bead in between the knot and the hook eye to prevent it becoming jammed and sticking out to the side. They are most often trolled from boats or cast and retrieved from the shore.

The ideal tackle to use with Tassie Devil lures is a threadline reel loaded with 3 kg line and a trout rod around 2 m long that has a degree of tip action built into it. This tip action allows the angler to monitor whether the lure is working correctly. When a Tassie lure is working correctly the tip of a troll rod will pulse evenly. If it stops your lure will have picked up some weed or you could be moving too fast or too slow.

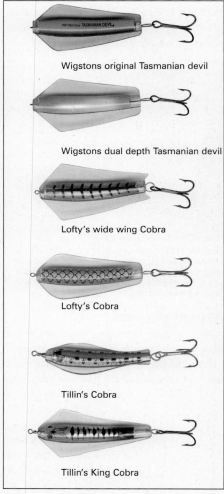

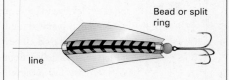

Tassie type lures

RIGGING A WIDE WING COBRA

Rigging a Wide Wing Cobra entails running the line through the centre of the body starting from the end that is widest. The line is then run through the supplied bead and tied off to a treble hook. Alternatively, you can also tie the line off to a treble hook rigged on a split ring. Riging in this manner allows the Wide Wing Cobra to reach depths of 3.2 metres, although this will vary with trolling speed and line diameter.

RIGGING A DUAL DEPTH TASMANIAN DEVIL

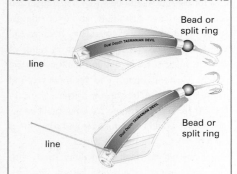

Rigging the Dual Depth Tasmanian Devil in the standard mode entails running the line through the cente of the body, then through a bead and finally tying it onto the hook. This can be varied by passing the line through the body, then tying it directly to a split ring which has a hook attached to it. This allows the lure's action to be far more pronounced. Rigged in this method the Dual Depth Tasmanian Devil runs at 2.5 metres in depth.

Rigging in the deep running mode, the line is passed through the moulded hole in the nose of the lure, through the body, through the bead and then it is tied to the hook, or you can use the split ring method. Rigged in the deep running mode, the Dual Depth Tasmanian Devil reaches a depth of 3.6 metres. It must be noted that these depths can vary with line diameter and boat speed.

SINGLE HOOKS VERSUS TREBLE HOOKS

Single hook rigs are becoming more popular with anglers who troll winged lures for salmonoids in Australia. They have several advantages over the traditional treble hook that most anglers use. The major advantage is their resistance to weed collection. In shallow lakes that are filled with ribbon or strap weed, there is often a lot of broken strands that constantly foul on the treble hook rig. With a single hook, the incidence of fouling is reduced markedly and means that you spend more time productively fishing. As a bonus a single hook provides a better hook up ratio because there is only one hook trying to penetrate the hard mouth. This means that all the pressure applied with the strike drag goes directly to the one hook point and is not spread over three hook points as is the case when using a treble hook. Also during the fight as the fish shakes its head, the pressure between the hook points on the treble may be great enough for one or two hook points to be removed. With a single there is no opposing force to remove the hook so they hold onto fish far better than a treble hook.

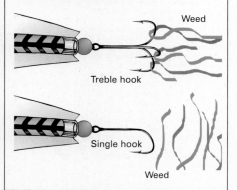

RIGGING FOR SHALLOW RUNNING

Trolling in waters that contain weed beds extending almost to the surface, can call for a different approach to lure presentation. If the forage fish you're attempting to imitate are very small the 7 gram size Cobra or Tasmanian Devil may be the answer. If your offering needs to be larger, but still run shallow, consider trying a technique shown to me by a good friend a few years ago. With a standard 13 gram lure take a sharp knife and pare the clear plastic wings of the lure. What you want to end up with is a wing that is 3–4 mm wide at the head of the lure tapering to about 1–2 mm at the tail. Altering the lure this way will allow it to swim much shallower (approx 0.4 m), but still retain the same action and great for targeting shallow weed beds.

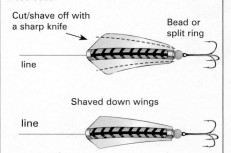

A last option if you do not want to alter your lures is to turn them around so that the tail end points towards the rod tip. Rigged in a similar fashion (line through centre of lure, through bead and tied off to the hook), a tighter action is achieved and the trolling speed can be increased without the lure blowing out. The reduced action and higher speed of trolling reduce the running depth of the lure and can be an easy way to troll above weed beds.

TIDE CHARTS

Tide charts give you a predictive model for tidal movements, showing each high and low tide with times and datum water heights. They also often show phases of the moon and should give locally adjusted delays or advance times for the tide calculation. It is very important to note that all times given as highs and lows are for a specific area and all other places listed will either be slightly earlier or later than the theoretical time stated.

TROLLING ATTRACTORS

Attractors are attached to your line ahead of a lure. Different attractors must be trolled at different speeds. For example, Ford Fenders must be trolled slowly; Cowbells can be trolled in the medium range, while Dodgers can be trolled faster.

Ford Fenders are a very popular choice with Flatfish lures or trolled mudeyes. Cowbells can be used with almost any lure but were designed originally to troll very small lures like spinners, that on their own wouldn't troll. If trout are taking tiny lures and you can't troll one down on their own, put one behind a Cowbell and use it that way. Dodgers are used for medium to fast lures, often behind down riggers.

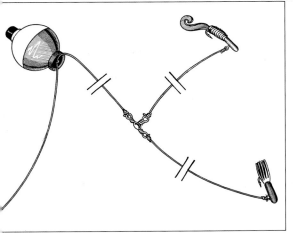

Trout jig rig.

TROUT JIG RIG

The best way to catch trout on soft plastics is to use small jigs with tiny tails. Rig them under a bobber float and use your long 3 m 'mudeye' rod or 'jig flicker' to work the float.

TROUT TROLLING TACKLE

Rods used for trout trolling should be long and limber enough to soak up the fight of a hooked trout, yet stiff enough and with sufficient backbone to troll sometimes high-resistance rigs. When downrigging, the rod is usually fairly long, up to 2.7 m, but most often 2.1 to 2.4 metres. Rods used for trolling strong-actioned lures such as bibbed plugs and Tassie Devils need to be a fairly fast taper, with light tips and strong butt sections. Reels can be threadlines or baitcasters, with some anglers also using small centrepin reels. Additional devices sometimes used for trolling for trout include sinkers, planer boards and paravanes, all of which are designed to take lures and bait rigs down deeper than they would usually travel.

WADERS

Waders are very popular for freshwater fishing. You may need waders if you have to walk into the water to make a cast past some stream obstruction, or perhaps to reach a spot further out in a lake. Waders are also useful when fishing streams in the Australian bush, as often the low shrubbery is quite hard on bare legs and they also offer protection against snakebite. Waders can also be used to help you stay dry in winter. This applies not only to freshwater fishing situations, but also to winter beach fishing in areas south of Brisbane.

WEIGHING SCALES

Scales are required to accurately weigh fish intended for recognition as record claims, or to tell your mates exactly what your fish weighed. Governing bodies, such as the Australian National Sportfishing Association (ANSA), Game Fishing Association of Australia (GFAA) and the International Game Fishing Association (IGFA) all scales are government certified, to attest to their accuracy.

Another use for scales is to accurately set drag levels on reels intended for use in line class fishing. The line is threaded from the reel, through the rod runners and then tied to a set of scales (usually spring balances), and the rod is bent into a working curve. The drag is then adjusted until line slips smoothly from the reel when the required amount of pulling pressure is applied to the line. Usually, this pressure is something between 25 and 33 per cent of the line's stated breaking strain, i.e. 10 kg should have the drag set to release line when the pulling force reaches between 2.5 and 3.3 kilograms.

WET FLIES

Flies fished beneath the surface are generally grouped together under the heading of 'wet flies'. Mostly, these are of the streamer type, but the classification also includes various crustacean imitations, such as shrimp, scuds, prawns, crayfish and crabs. Nymphs (the aquatic larval forms of insects) are also wet flies. As they are tied to represent a distinct phase of aquatic insect life, they have name and classification all their own.

WET WEATHER GEAR

Your comfort levels and therefore your fishing performance will be improved if you are able to fish through occasional rainfall, or to cope with windblown spray when travelling in a boat. Staying dry in cool climates can even be critical to survival as hypothermia can set in very quickly when the ambient air temperature drops and wind adds to the chill factor. As such, don't skimp on your rain gear. Ensure the material is able to breathe so you don't sweat inside the coat or trousers and that all seams are fully waterproof. Zips should be sturdy enough to take sometimes rough use and large enough for cold fingers to operate. A second stage of Velcro closures is also helpful to stop water incursions and the raincoat should have a hood.

If you often need to wear substantial rain gear in a boat, be sure there is sufficient flotation built into the clothing in case you find yourself washed overboard. This wet weather clothing costs more than plastic raincoats, but if you are fishing alpine lakes and encounter rough weather, you may be glad of the investment.

Trout trolling tackle.

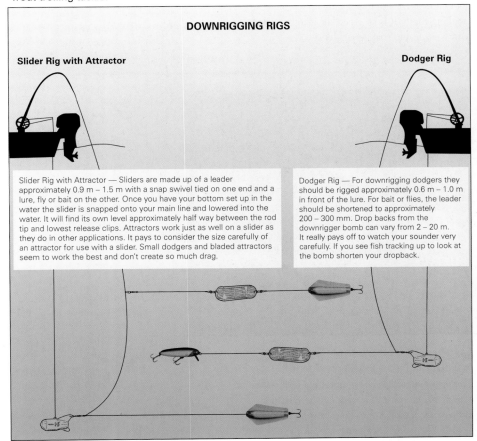

DOWNRIGGING RIGS

Slider Rig with Attractor

Dodger Rig

Slider Rig with Attractor — Sliders are made up of a leader approximately 0.9 m – 1.5 m with a snap swivel tied on one end and a lure, fly or bait on the other. Once you have your bottom set up in the water the slider is snapped onto your main line and lowered into the water. It will find its own level approximately half way between the rod tip and lowest release clips. Attractors work just as well on a slider as they do in other applications. It pays to consider the size carefully of an attractor for use with a slider. Small dodgers and bladed attractors seem to work the best and don't create so much drag.

Dodger Rig — For downrigging dodgers they should be rigged approximately 0.6 m – 1.0 m in front of the lure. For bait or flies, the leader should be shortened to approximately 200 – 300 mm. Drop backs from the downrigger bomb can vary from 2 – 20 m. It really pays off to watch your sounder very carefully. If you see fish tracking up to look at the bomb shorten your dropback.

CHAPTER THREE

KNOTS & RIGS

KNOTS
LINE TO TERMINAL TACKLE

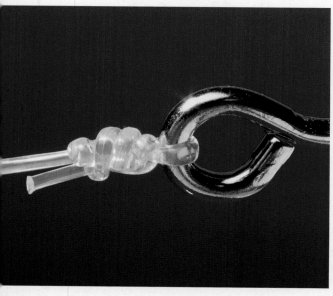

1. Thread the eye of your hook or swivel and twist the tag and main line together.

2. Complete three to six twists and thread the tag back through the first twist. The heavier your line, the less twists you will use.

3. Pull the line so that the knot begins to form. Do not pull it up tight yet or you will have an unlocked half blood which may slip should you be tying new line to a shiny metal surface.

4. To lock the knot, thread the tag through the open loop which has formed at the top of the knot.

5. Pull the knot up firmly and the result should be something like this. Should a loop form within the knot, simply pull on the tag until it disappears.

LOCKED HALF BLOOD KNOT

This simple and strong knot is adequate for tying hooks and swivels to line testing up to 25 kg breaking strain. It is an especially firm favourite with whiting and snapper anglers.

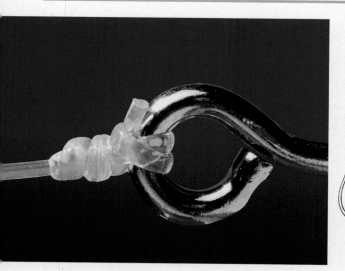

1. Thread the eye of the hook with the line.

2. And make an extra wrap.

3. Then wrap the tag around the main line from three to five times. The heavier the line you are using, the less the number of wraps. The lighter the line, the more wraps you use.

4. Complete the knot by passing the tag back through the first two wraps you made before pulling the knot tight.
   The best result is achieved when the loops through the eye of the hook retain their wrapping sequence and don't spring apart.

CLINCH OR BLOOD KNOT
A Geoff Wilson preferred knot

This is undoubtedly the strongest knot for tying a medium size hook to a medium size line such as hook size 4 to 4/0 onto line size 3 kg to 15 kg.

REVERSE TWIST OR BLOOD KNOT

The following knot illustrates how additional wraps can be made to blood knots by making at least half the wraps required in the usual direction, the rest in the opposite direction.

1. First, when tying on a hook, thread line through the eye of the hook.

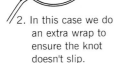

2. In this case we do an extra wrap to ensure the knot doesn't slip.

3. Twist the tag and standing part of the line together.

4. Do this three times, then wind the tag back in the other direction around the first wraps as shown.

5. Wind the tag back three times and thread it through the centre of the double loop on the eye of the hook so you have three turns up and three turns back. (This is for monofilament. Do six up and six back for gelspun lines but more on those later).

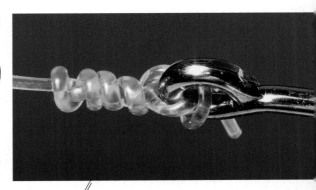

6. Finish the knot with pressure on the standing part against the hook. Some pressure on the tag may be required to take up the slack here as well.

PALOMAR KNOT

The Palomar knot is quick to tie and sufficiently strong for most fishing situations.

1. Make a loop in the leader and pass it through the eye of the hook.

2. Form an overhand knot on the eye of the hook.

3. Extend the loop and pass it over the hook.

4. Close the knot by pulling tag and leader. Trim the tag when complete.

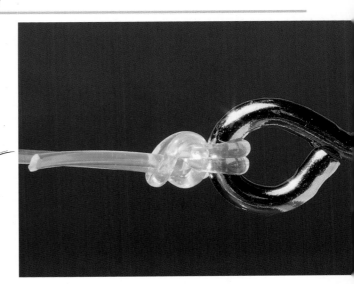

GARY MATIN'S WORLD'S FAIR KNOT

Gary Martin called this knot the 'World's Fair Knot' after being selected the winner from 498 entries in an international, original, fishing knot competition conducted by Du Pont at the Knoxville, USA, World's Fair in 1982. It is quick and easy to tie yet shows no tendency to slip.

1. Make a loop in your line and pass it through the hook eye or swivel.

2. Fold the protruding section of the loop back over the double strand.

3. Now bend the tag back and pass it over the folded loop and under the doubled strand as shown.

4. Now pass the tag through the loop formed by the previous step.

5. Shown is the finished knot formed with gentle but firm pressure on the main line.

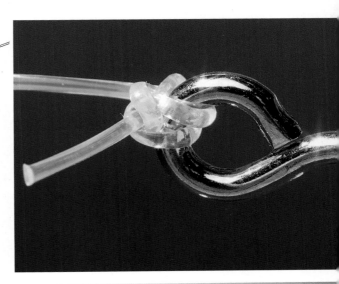

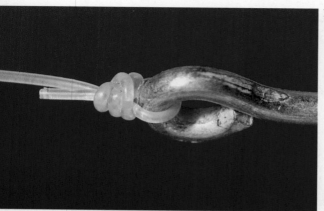

CENTAURI KNOT
A Geoff Wilson preferred knot

First published by fishing writer Dick Lewers, the Centauri knot is useful over a wide range of line diameters because it forms with a minimum of friction and therefore does not distort the line. Ideal for small hooks, rings and swivels.

1. Thread the eye of hook or swivel with the tag and make the configuration shown, first passing the tag behind the main line. The crossover is held between thumb and index finger of the left hand to facilitate tying.

2. The first step is repeated and the second crossover also held between thumb and index finger of the left hand.

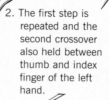

3. Again, the tag is passed behind the main line and the crossover held between thumb and finger. I will point out that some anglers make only two wraps, not three, but this produces a weaker knot.

4. Now tuck the tag through the centre of the three loops you have made and form the knot by pulling gently on the tag against the hook or swivel. Ideally the loops should close up evenly.

5. Having formed the knot, the loop will have enlarged. Simply slide the knot down the leader onto the eye of the hook or swivel.

6. The finished knot should lock down onto the hook eye with the tag pointing back up the leader.

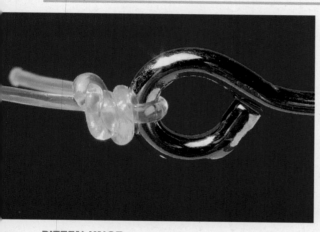

PITZEN KNOT

Credited to Edgar Pitzenbauer of Germany, the Pitzen knot is useful for tying monofilament to hooks, rings and swivels.

The chief advantage of the Pitzen Knot is that it is very small which makes it a favourite with fly fishermen. It is also very strong when tied correctly.

1. Thread the eye of the hook and loop the tag back under the standing part.

2. Wind the tag back around the loop so another smaller loop is formed at the beginning of the knot.

3. Make three wraps in all then pass the tag back through the small loop.

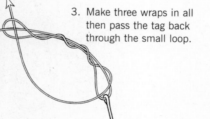

4. With gentle pressure on the tag, close the knot around the standing part of the line but not too tight; just like I've drawn it here. If you tighten it right up now, the strength of the final knot will be reduced quite a bit.

5. Slide the knot down the standing part, onto eye of the hook and tighten, this time with firm pressure until you feel the knot sort of click into place. Then trim the tag.

MARSHALL'S SNARE

This method of tying on a hook was introduced to anglers by Australian fishing writer Frank Marshall some decades ago. It is simple to tie in the dark and adequately strong for most situations.

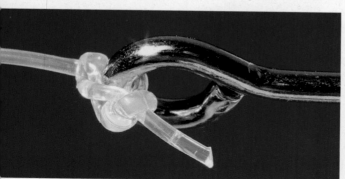

1. First make a loop in the end of your line and tie an overhand knot with the tag, encircling the main line.

2. Pass the loop through the eye of your hook.

3. Pass the loop entirely over the hook and pass the tag through the loop as well.

4. Close the overhand knot and pull the noose up tight around the hook.

REBECK KNOT

Introduced to anglers by Barry Rebeck of South Africa, the Rebeck knot provides a simple and secure hook connection.

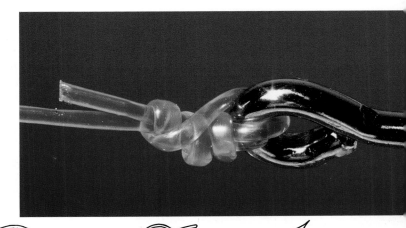

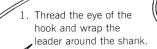

1. Thread the eye of the hook and wrap the leader around the shank.

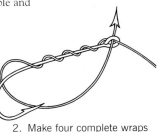

2. Make four complete wraps and thread the eye of the hook once more.

3. Take a firm hold of the hook in both hands as shown.

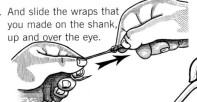

4. And slide the wraps that you made on the shank, up and over the eye.

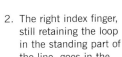

5. At this stage the knot looks like this.

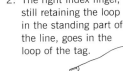

6. Close the knot by pulling gently on the main line, then on the tag to close the second loop.

PENNY KNOT

This excellent method of attaching a hook or fly is named after Ron Penny. This description of the knot, and technique of tying it, is by Peter Hayes of Premier Guides.

1. Thread the hook, which is held between thumb and third finger of the left hand. The tag, which is extended in a loop, is held between index finger and thumb. The standing part of the line is held in the palm of the right hand and looped over the right index finger as shown.

2. The right index finger, still retaining the loop in the standing part of the line, goes in the loop of the tag.

3. Pulls it back over the standing part, which was looped over the right index finger.

4. And rotates it anti-clockwise around the standing part.

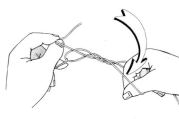

5. A complete rotation is made, then the right thumb is inserted into the loop beside the index finger to grip the tag on completion of another half rotation.

6. The tag is pulled free of the left thumb and finger grip and through the loop as shown.

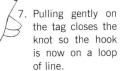

7. Pulling gently on the tag closes the knot so the hook is now on a loop of line.

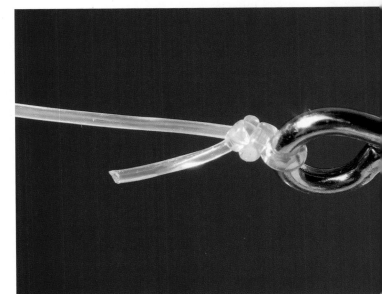

8. The knot is slid down onto the eye of the hook and locked in place with firm, but gentle pressure, on the standing part of the line. The tag is trimmed short.

UNI KNOT

The Uni Knot is widely used for attaching hooks, rings and swivels to the end of the line.

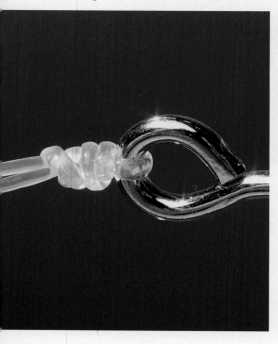

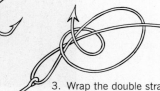

1. Thread the eye of the hook with the line so the hook is suspended on a loop.

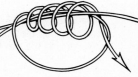

2. Encircle the main line with the tag so another loop is formed.

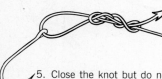

3. Wrap the double strand inside the loop with the tag.

4. Make four wraps in all, leaving the tag protruding from the loop.

5. Close the knot but do not pull it tight just yet.

6. Slide the knot down onto the eye of the hook, pull it tight and trim the tag.

THUMB KNOT

This knot is used for attaching hooks, rings or swivels to the very heaviest nylon monofilament.

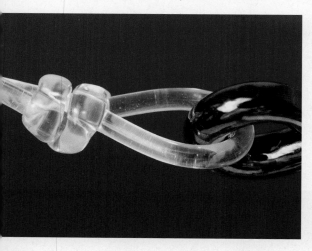

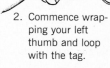

1. Thread your hook with the line and make a loop so that the hook is suspended from the loop. Pinch the cross-over between the thumb and finger of your left hand.

2. Commence wrapping your left thumb and loop with the tag.

3. Make three wraps in all, working from the base of your thumb toward the thumbnail.

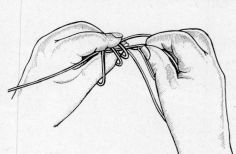

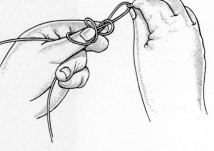

4. Push the tag back under those three wraps alongside your thumb. Push it all the way back toward the base of your thumb.

5. Secure the tag against your left thumb with your middle finger. Then take the hook loop in your right hand and ease the wraps off your thumb, one at a time, in sequence.

6. Close the knot by exerting pressure on the loop against the tag.

NAIL KNOT WITH LOOP

This knot is used for tying hooks to heavy monofilament leaders because it pulls up without damaging the line.

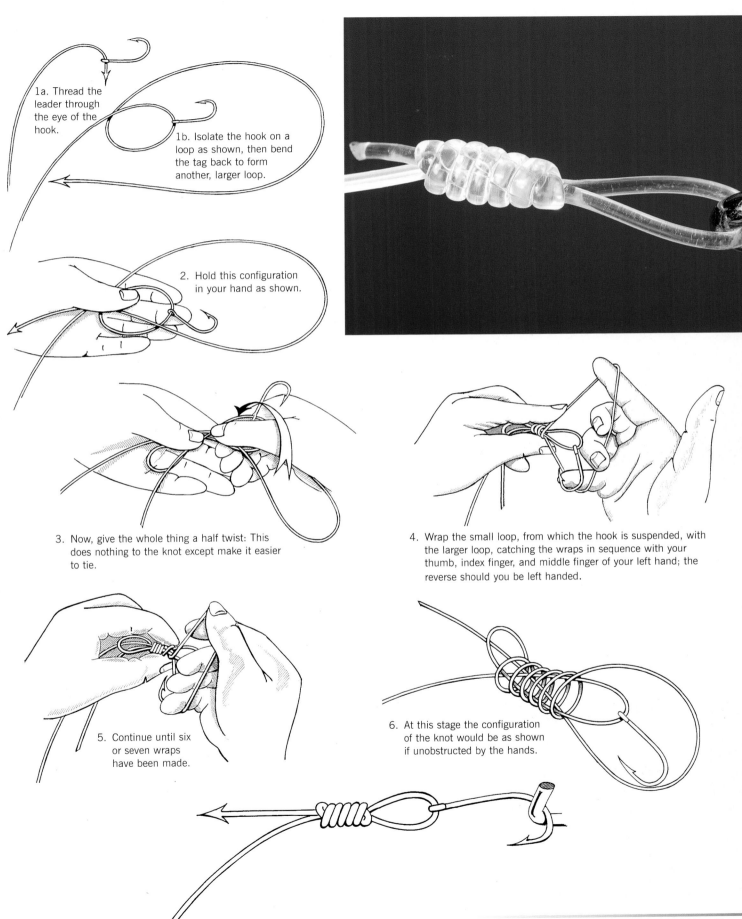

1a. Thread the leader through the eye of the hook.

1b. Isolate the hook on a loop as shown, then bend the tag back to form another, larger loop.

2. Hold this configuration in your hand as shown.

3. Now, give the whole thing a half twist: This does nothing to the knot except make it easier to tie.

4. Wrap the small loop, from which the hook is suspended, with the larger loop, catching the wraps in sequence with your thumb, index finger, and middle finger of your left hand; the reverse should you be left handed.

5. Continue until six or seven wraps have been made.

6. At this stage the configuration of the knot would be as shown if unobstructed by the hands.

SNELLS
LINE TO TERMINAL TACKLE

SIMPLE SNELL

This is the first fishing knot I ever learned. My father showed it to me at age five or six. It is a safe and sound way of attaching a hook to a snood but it requires a upturned eye hook like the Mustad 92554, or an downturned eye hook like the Mustad 540 (illustrated) to be effective. It also requires both ends of the snood line to be free because both have to be threaded through the eye of the hook.

After discarding this attachment for many years, I am using it again for tying the hooks onto bait jigs because it provides a particularly quick and satisfactory method of not only attaching the hook, but also facilitating the easy addition of a small piece of wool to the hook to act as a fish attractor.

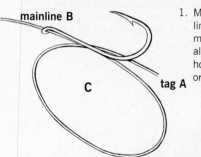

1. Thread the tag end of the snood line through the eye of the hook from underneath and bend it back against the shank of the hook.

2. Wrap both the tag and the shank of the hook with the main line of the snood.

3. Having completed nine or ten wraps, thread the other end of the snood line through the eye of the hook, once again from underneath, and pull the line up tight.

4. Trim the tag to finish the knot and the result should look like this. The main line runs over the wraps, not underneath as in the common snell, avoiding the risk of a separation through the line being cut by a partially open eye.

COMMON SNELL

Originally introduced for hooks with spatulate eyes, the Snell is appropriate for hooks with up or down turned eyes when the leader needs to be aligned along the shank of the hook. This knot is most important in many two-hook rigs. The eye of the hook need not be threaded.

mainline B

C   tag A

1. Make this configuration in the line against the hook. The eye may be threaded, but it is not always preferred. Indeed, using hooks with spatulate, knobbed or flattened eyes it is impossible.

2. Pull loop C over so that loop D is formed and commence wrapping the shank of the hook and the tag.

3. Your snell should begin to look something like this.

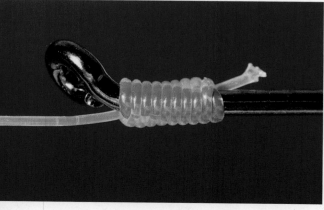

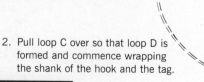

4. Continue until the required number of wraps is in place.

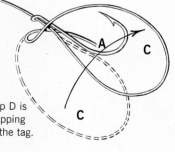

5. Pull on main line B against tag A until the knot is formed on the shank. When the eye of the hook is threaded, it is preferred that the snell is formed down a little from the eye so that the chances of a separation occurring from a roughly turned or sharp eye are reduced.

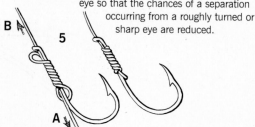

MULTIPLE HOOK RIGS: SLIDING SNELL

This is the adjustable two-hook rig I use for mulloway. The hooks can be drawnapart or closed up depending on the size of bait being used. It is a bit tricky to make but works well.

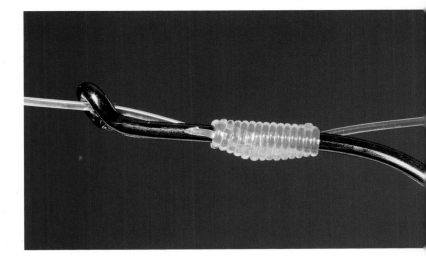

1. Take one hook and a length of line, (separate from, and lighter than, the leader) then make this configuration.

2. Roll the loop around the hook. You will need to do this a number of times.

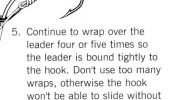

3. This I how I do it – it's really quite easy provided the tags are not too long.

4. Continue until you have made at least six wraps. I usually do a few more. Then introduce the leader through the eye of the hook.

5. Continue to wrap over the leader four or five times so the leader is bound tightly to the hook. Don't use too many wraps, otherwise the hook won't be able to slide without damaging the leader.

6. Tighten the snell on the hook and leader, then pull enough leader through so that you can snell on the other hook this time, directly onto the leader.

KNOTS
TYING LOOPS

Shown are the steps in attaching a lure to a heavy monofilament leader using the Perfection Loop.

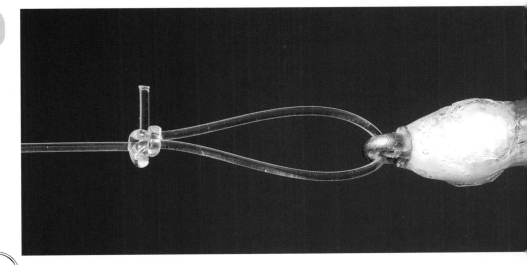

1. Tie an ordinary underhand knot in your leader but don't close it up. Then pass the tag of your leader through the eye of your lure.

3. Now comes the tricky part: the tag has to bend back, go over the main line, up through the crossover forming the underhand knot, then up through the gap between where the tag was passed through the knot in step 2.

4. Close the knot with pressure on the loop against the main line.

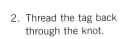

2. Thread the tag back through the knot.

HOMER RHODE LOOP

This is a useful loop for attaching rapid action lures to heavy monofilament leaders.

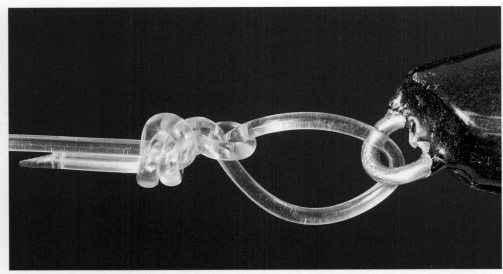

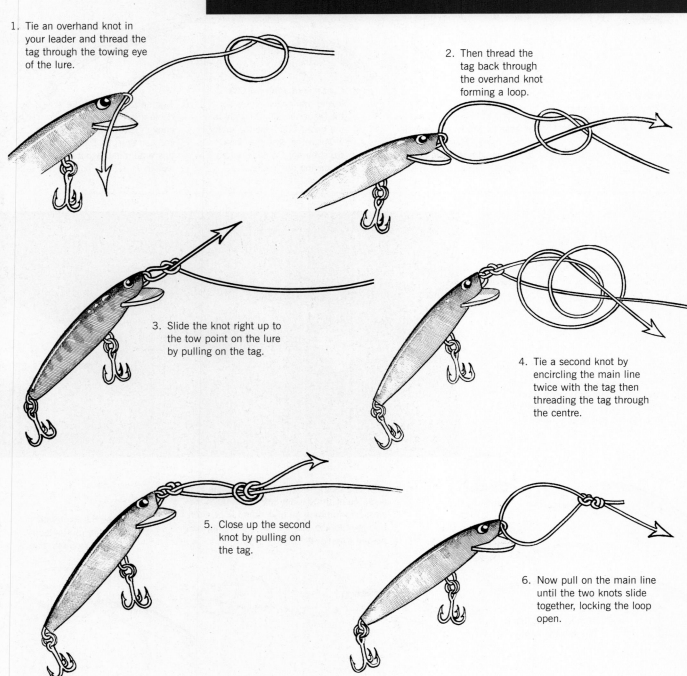

1. Tie an overhand knot in your leader and thread the tag through the towing eye of the lure.

2. Then thread the tag back through the overhand knot forming a loop.

3. Slide the knot right up to the tow point on the lure by pulling on the tag.

4. Tie a second knot by encircling the main line twice with the tag then threading the tag through the centre.

5. Close up the second knot by pulling on the tag.

6. Now pull on the main line until the two knots slide together, locking the loop open.

DROPPER LOOP

This loop can be tied anywhere along a length of line for the attachment of a hook or leader.

1. Make a generous loop in your line where the dropper is to be tied, then pull out a section of the loop so that it crosses over the main line at one side forming a second smaller loop.

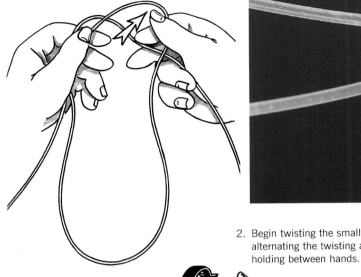

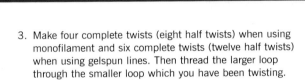

2. Begin twisting the smaller loop, alternating the twisting and holding between hands.

3. Make four complete twists (eight half twists) when using monofilament and six complete twists (twelve half twists) when using gelspun lines. Then thread the larger loop through the smaller loop which you have been twisting.

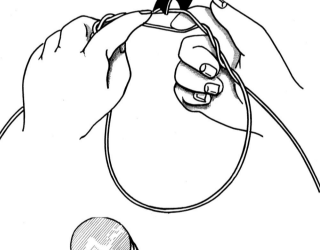

4. Put your larger loop around a peg or the like and gently tension the line both sides of the knot until it pulls up nicely. Particular care needs to be taken with this step when using gelspun or the line can be sheared off at either side of the knot.

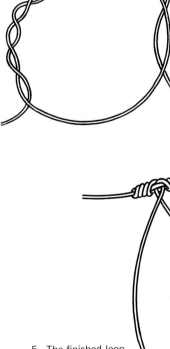

5. The finished loop is neat and of adequate strength for the majority of fishing situations.

TWISTED DROPPER LOOP

Dropper loops facilitate the easy attachment of hooks. Twisting the line before tying a dropper loop stiffens the dropper so that it cannot tangle around the main line.

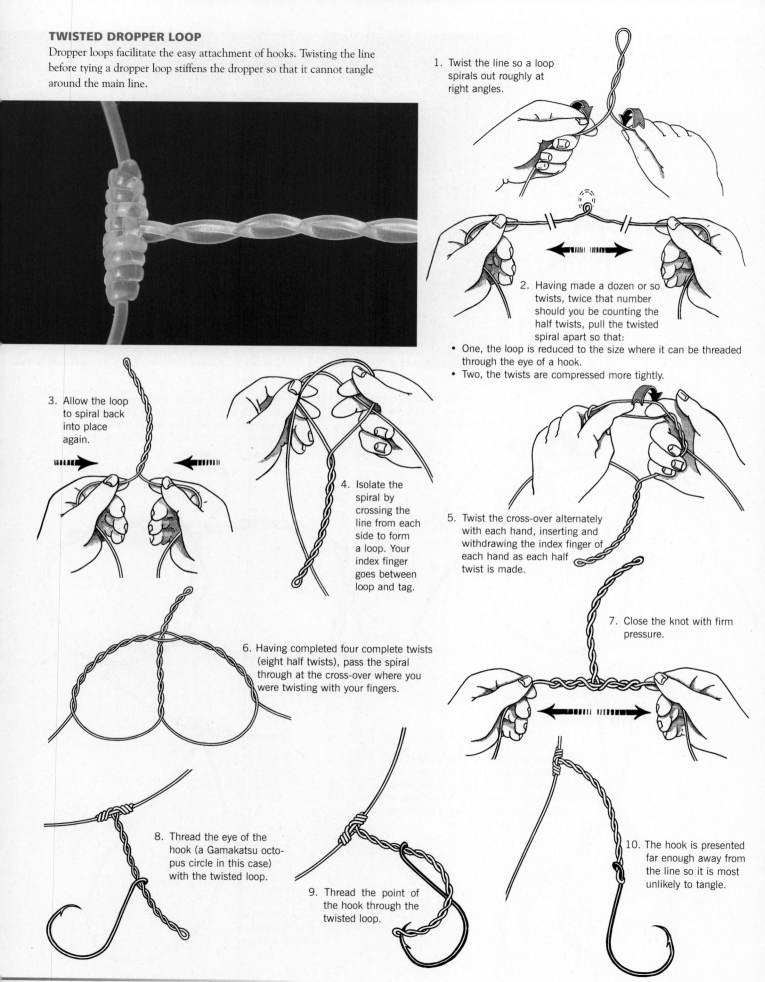

1. Twist the line so a loop spirals out roughly at right angles.

2. Having made a dozen or so twists, twice that number should you be counting the half twists, pull the twisted spiral apart so that:
- One, the loop is reduced to the size where it can be threaded through the eye of a hook.
- Two, the twists are compressed more tightly.

3. Allow the loop to spiral back into place again.

4. Isolate the spiral by crossing the line from each side to form a loop. Your index finger goes between loop and tag.

5. Twist the cross-over alternately with each hand, inserting and withdrawing the index finger of each hand as each half twist is made.

6. Having completed four complete twists (eight half twists), pass the spiral through at the cross-over where you were twisting with your fingers.

7. Close the knot with firm pressure.

8. Thread the eye of the hook (a Gamakatsu octopus circle in this case) with the twisted loop.

9. Thread the point of the hook through the twisted loop.

10. The hook is presented far enough away from the line so it is most unlikely to tangle.

END LOOP

This is one of the quickest and strongest ways of tying an End loop, or Short Double, in monofilament.

1. Make a loop in the end of your mono and wind it back around the doubled strand of tag and main line.

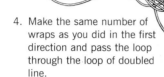

2. Wind it back two or three times. Two for heavy line, three for lighter line.

3. Then wind it back the other way.

4. Make the same number of wraps as you did in the first direction and pass the loop through the loop of doubled line.

5. Close up the knot with firm, but gentle pressure, aganst the loop and doubled strand of tag and main line.

DOUBLE OVERHAND LOOP

A quick and easy way to tie a loop on the end of your line.

1. Form a loop in the end of your line.

2. Tie the loop in an Overhand knot.

3. Add another wrap to the knot.

4. Close the knot up tight.

FIGURE OF EIGHT KNOT OR BLOOD BIGHT

Used for loop to loop connections, usually between a short dropper and a dropper loop in the main line.

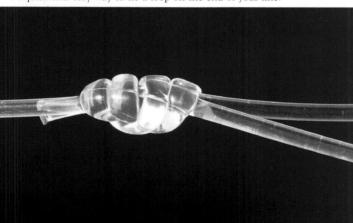

1. Bend the line back upon itself to form a loop.

2. Bend the loop back on itself to form a loop in the double strand.

3. Wind the loop over the double strand then through the loop in the double strand giving the knot its characteristic figure of eight appearance.

4. Close the knot up tight and trim the tag.

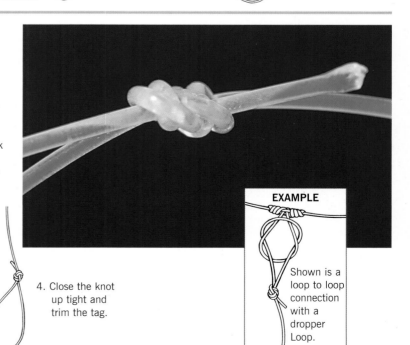

EXAMPLE

Shown is a loop to loop connection with a dropper Loop.

RIGGING WITH SUPER LINES

Polyethylene gelspun fishing lines are new, and with these products being improved constantly, there are no absolute rules. However these super lines generally share several properties which include, very high strength for a given diameter and very little stretch; they are also very sheer or slippery.

These properties make rigging difficult, but there are knots and rigging strategies for these lines that work very well.

Here we examine some knots and rigging strategies for super lines, but I do point out that my tests on a number of these lines indicated that the breaking strain stated by the manufacturer was usually lower than the actual breaking strain.

This could easily give the illusion of very high knot strengths, even with badly chosen or poorly tied knots.

To illustrate my point, I will quote the percentage of manufacturers breaking strain, and probable actual breaking strain, retained by the knots discussed in just two of the several super line products I tested.

One of those products was Berkley Fireline. My tests with 6 and 10 pound Berkley Fireline indicated actual breaking strains of 15 and 25 pounds (6.8 and 11.35 kg) respectively.

Another product was 30 pound Spiderwire (Spectra 2000). Its actual breaking strain was difficult to ascertain but was at least 33 pounds (15 kilograms).

TRIPLE PALOMAR KNOT

The Triple Palomar Knot is recommended for tying super lines to metal rings, towing eyes on lures, and hooks.

When tied in Berkley Fireline this knot retained 217% of the manufacturers breaking strain (86% of the actual breaking strain).

When tied in 30 lb Spiderwire, this knot broke at 25.3 pounds (11.49 kg), 85% of the manufacturers breaking strain (74.5% the probable actual breaking strain).

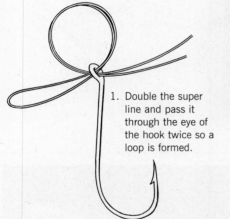

1. Double the super line and pass it through the eye of the hook twice so a loop is formed.

2. Repeat this step twice so three loops of doubled line have been formed on the eye of the hook.

3. Close the three loops around the eye of the hook, then wrap the protruding loop of doubled line back around the mainline and tag. Then pass it back through the loop so an overhand knot is formed.

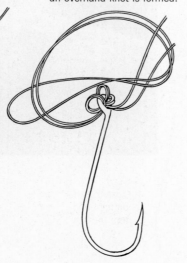

4. Now, loop the doubled line right over the hook.

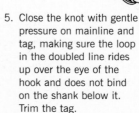

5. Close the knot with gentle pressure on mainline and tag, making sure the loop in the doubled line rides up over the eye of the hook and does not bind on the shank below it. Trim the tag.

SILLY SNELL

Although, like the Braid Snell, this very easy hook attachment was unsuitable for use with the finest super lines, it proved suitable for most super lines. It broke at 27 pounds (12.26 kg) when tied in 30 pound (13.62 kg) Spiderwire 90% of the manufacturer's breaking strain, (80% of the probable actual breaking strain).

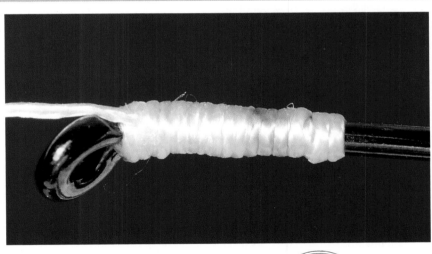

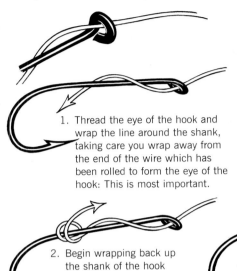

1. Thread the eye of the hook and wrap the line around the shank, taking care you wrap away from the end of the wire which has been rolled to form the eye of the hook: This is most important.

2. Begin wrapping back up the shank of the hook with the tag.

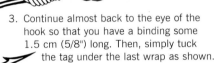

3. Continue almost back to the eye of the hook so that you have a binding some 1.5 cm (5/8") long. Then, simply tuck the tag under the last wrap as shown.

4. Slide the wraps up to the eye of the hook, pulling on the line to tighten the snell.

BRAID SNELL

This knot proved unsatisfactory with the very fine super lines like Berkley Fireline because the line slipped between the rolled down eye and the shank of the hooks I was using.

However, it worked well in most lines: In 30 pound Spiderwire this knot broke at 32 pounds (14.53 kg), 106% of manufacturers breaking strain (94% of the probable actual breaking strain).

1. Hold the hook with the eye to the left and the bend to the right. Extend a 30 cm (one foot) tag and wrap it around the shank of the hook in an anti-clockwise direction as shown.

2. Having completed a spiral of five or six turns, commence a tight binding back in the opposite direction.

3. Keep the wraps as close as you possibly can, and continue binding almost, but not quite, up to the eye of the hook.

4. Now turn the hook around. Fold back the tag so a loop is formed, and finish the binding clockwise.

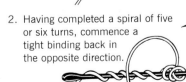

5. Rotating the loop as shown, over-bind the tag all the way up to the eye of the hook. Should you have difficulty doing this, chances are you commenced binding in the opposite direction than what was indicated.

6. Close the remaining loop by pulling out the tag.

7. Shown is the finished snell with the tag trimmed short. The main line emerges from the snell a short distance back from the eye of the hook, although not as far back as it appears to be in this diagram due to the exaggerated thickness of the line.

COLLAR & CAPSTAN

This knot was developed for anglers who prefer tying fine gelspun lines directly to the towing eye of a lure. It tests a good deal higher than most other knots tested.

Tested in 24 lb Spiderwire Fusion, (which actually tested over 25 lbs – 11.35 kg), the Collar and Capstan broke at 22 lbs (9.99 kg) against the Braid Ring Knot 19.6 lbs (8.9 kg), Triple Palomar 19.6 lbs (8.9 kg) and the Palomar at 16.5 lbs (7.49 kg).

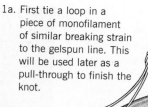

1a. First tie a loop in a piece of monofilament of similar breaking strain to the gelspun line. This will be used later as a pull-through to finish the knot.

1b. Thread the gelspun line through the towing eye of the lure.

2. Do this at least three times to produce a capstan effect.

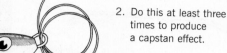

3. Introduce the monofilament loop as shown and begin wrapping it with the tag back toward the lure.

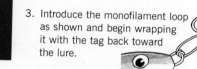

4. Continue to make about ten wraps before feeding the tag through the monofilament loop, taking care to leave enough slack in the last wrap to prevent it jamming.

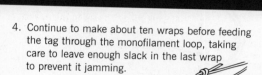

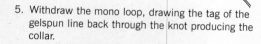

5. Withdraw the mono loop, drawing the tag of the gelspun line back through the knot producing the collar.
   This step is easy enough provided there was some slack in the last wrap of the gelspun line. If there was not, the tag may jam.

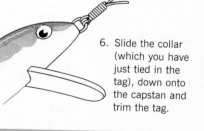

6. Slide the collar (which you have just tied in the tag), down onto the capstan and trim the tag.

BRAID RING KNOT

This is simply a basic blood knot (with two wraps around the eye of the hook in this case) but with quite a few more wraps (or twists) than usual, with the tag and standing part.

We use more wraps in super lines (than with monofilament) to ensure the knot will not slip undone. When tied in Berkley Fireline, this knot retained 191% of the manufacturer's breaking strain (76% of the actual breaking strain).

When tied in 30 lb Spiderwire, this knot broke at 25.3 pounds (11.49 kg), 85% of the manufacturer's breaking strain (74.5% of the probable, actual breaking strain).

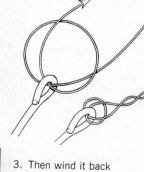

1. Pass the line through the hook eye, or ring, twice leaving plenty of tag.

2. Wind the tag around the main line five or six times.

3. Then wind it back again the same number of times.

4. Thread the tag through the centre of both ring wraps.

5. Slide the knot closed with gentle pressure on the main line, stroking the knot back periodically as you do so to keep the wraps in sequence. This prevents them bunching up as the knot closes.

BIMINI CAT'S PAW SPLICE

The Bimini Cat's Paw Splice is a most satisfactory way of joining two gelspun lines. In this case, the line from the spool (right) is being added to the line already on the reel.

When tied in 10 lb Berkley Fireline the Cat's Paw sheared at 8 kg (17.6 lbs) 176% of lines stated b/s. (70% of the probable, actual b/s).

When tied in 30 lb Spiderwire the Cat's Paw broke at 12.5 kg (27.5 lbs), 91.5% of line's stated b/s. (83% of the probable actual b/s.)

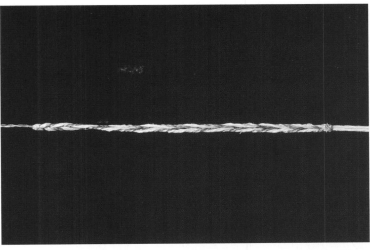

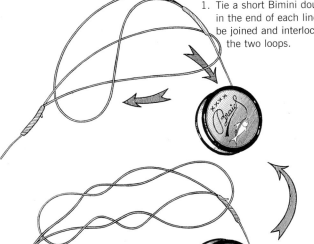

1. Tie a short Bimini double in the end of each line to be joined and interlock the two loops.

2. Rotate the spool of line through the loop of the line coming from the reel so a Cat's Paw effect is produced.

3. Make at least ten folds in your Cat's Paw Splice and spread the splice right out with your hands. This is to straighten out any twists or tangles.

4. Finally, with firm pressure from each side, close the splice up tight.

TWISTED LEADER KNOT FOR GELSPUN LINES

This is the strongest method I know of tying a single strand of gelspun line to a monofilament leader.

I tested it six times with a sample of Berkley Fireline, which was labelled 14 pounds. When tied to a 12.5 kg Maxima monofilament leader, the highest test obtained was 9.4 kg (20.7 pounds). Only one knot tested below 8 kg (17.6 pounds).

1. Wind the gelspun line (black) around one end of the monofilament leader. I suggest doing this twenty times.

2. Tie a knot in the twisted lines and pull the entire monofilament leader through.

3. Do the same again so another wrap is added.

4. Do this two more times so four wraps are made.

5. Then, with firm but gentle pressure on all four legs, close the knot. Should a loop of slack gelspun line appear within the knot as it closes, release the mono leader tag and apply tension to the gelspun line until the loop disappears.

6. Close the knot firmly and trim the tags.

RIGGING FOR SPORT, GAME, AND DEEP SEA FISHING

The physical properties of gelspun lines suit them admirably to sport, game and deep-sea fishing. However, should you be fishing line class with a view to recording captures under ANSA or IGFA, then it is your responsibility to ensure your line does in fact, test within that designated line class.

For sport, game and deep-sea fishing applications, all terminals are rigged on extended monofilament leaders, which are attached to Bimini doubles tied in the gelspun super line. This is how we add that extended monofilament leader.

Braid Leader Knot

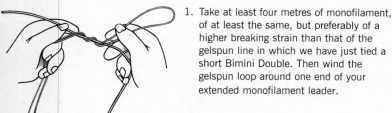

1. Take at least four metres of monofilament, of at least the same, but preferably of a higher breaking strain than that of the gelspun line in which we have just tied a short Bimini Double. Then wind the gelspun loop around one end of your extended monofilament leader.

2. Make at least ten wraps if the breaking strains of the gelspun and the monofilament are similar, but reduce the number of wraps if the monofilament is stronger.
   Then thread the tag of the monofilament through the loop in the gelspun line.

3. Hold the tag of the monofilament as shown and tension the join so: One, the monofilament tag begins to spiral around the wraps, and Two, the loop in the gelspun line closes.

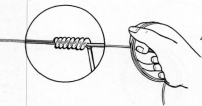

4. Take a firm grip both sides of the join and increase tension until the join closes up. Make sure the join is completely closed before trimming the tag.

Cautionary Note

While attaching extended monofilament leaders of sufficient length to be wound through the rod guides and onto the reel to gelspun lines, is recommended for the purposes described, it may not be suitable where long casts need to be made.

This is because leader knots, travelling through the rod guides at the extremely high speeds associated with long distance casting, may disintegrate after only a few casts.

Should an extended monofilament shock-leader be required in a long distance-casting situation, then the solution is to use the dacron leader-splice described in this publication.

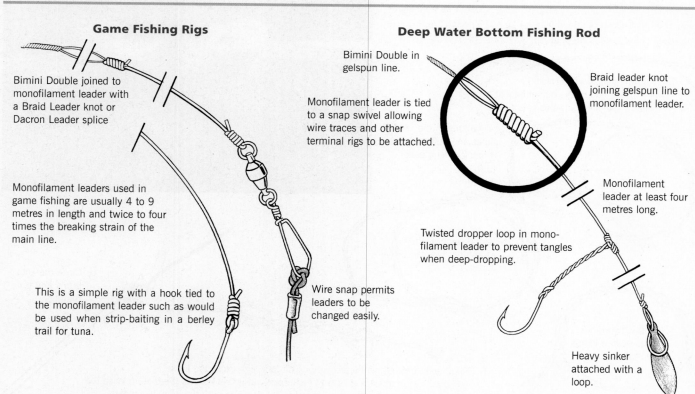

Game Fishing Rigs

Bimini Double joined to monofilament leader with a Braid Leader knot or Dacron Leader splice

Monofilament leaders used in game fishing are usually 4 to 9 metres in length and twice to four times the breaking strain of the main line.

This is a simple rig with a hook tied to the monofilament leader such as would be used when strip-baiting in a berley trail for tuna.

Wire snap permits leaders to be changed easily.

Deep Water Bottom Fishing Rod

Bimini Double in gelspun line.

Monofilament leader is tied to a snap swivel allowing wire traces and other terminal rigs to be attached.

Braid leader knot joining gelspun line to monofilament leader.

Monofilament leader at least four metres long.

Twisted dropper loop in mono-filament leader to prevent tangles when deep-dropping.

Heavy sinker attached with a loop.

DOUBLE UNI KNOT

Another join worth knowing is the double uni knot, sometimes called a grinner. The double uni-knot is used for joining lines of either similar or different diameters.

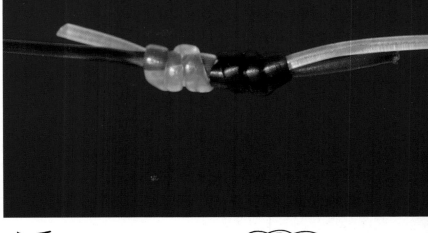

1. Overlap the lines to be joined and encircle one line with the tag of the other.

2. Wrap the double strand inside the loop formed.

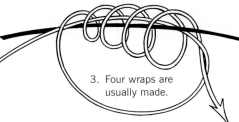

3. Four wraps are usually made.

4. Close the knot, but not too tightly, then do the same with the other length of line.

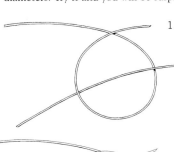

5. Two knots are formed, one in each line, around the other.

6. Slide the knots together, tighten each in turn, and trim the tags.

DOUBLE CENTAURI KNOT FOR JOINING LINES

The Centauri knot was introduced to Australian anglers by fishing writer Dick Lewers as a sound knot for tying on hooks, swivels and rings. However, when two Centauri knots are tied around separate lengths of line, one encircling the other, the join created is strong and durable.

While the best results were obtained when using lines of similar diameter, a satisfactory join could be created in lines of different diameters. Try it and you will be surprised at how strong it is.

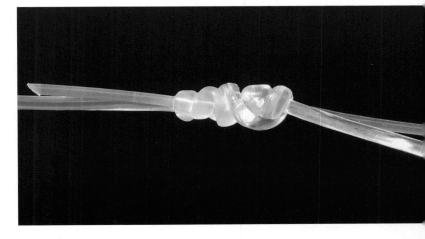

1. Place the two ends to be joined together and encircle one with the other.

2. Make three circles altogether and pass the tag through the middle as shown. Count one and two and three and through.

3. Do exactly the same with the opposite number so each length of line encircles the other.

4. Pull each knot up firmly, but not tight.

5. Gently slide both knots together and tighten each in turn. Slide them together once more to close them completely.

DOUBLE FOUR FOLD BLOOD KNOT

Sometimes, we have to join two similar size lines. The Double, Four-Fold Blood knot is widely used because it is neat, easy to tie, and retains adequate strength for most situations. This knot is useful for joining two lines of the same or similar diameters. It is not satisfactory when there is a significant difference in the diameters of the two lines.

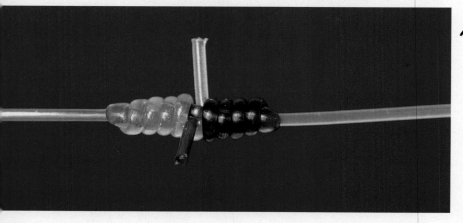

1. Overlap the two lines to be joined. (I have shaded one to make the operation easier to follow).

2. Twist both ends together.

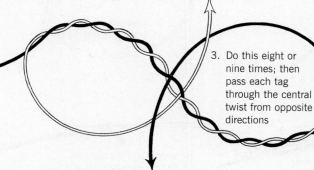

3. Do this eight or nine times; then pass each tag through the central twist from opposite directions

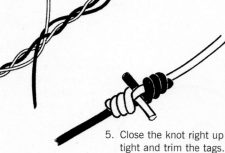

4. Close the knot gently with tension on the line each side.

5. Close the knot right up tight and trim the tags.

REVERSE TWIST BLOOD KNOT FOR JOINING LINES

The double blood knot requires four wraps each side so it won't slip undone. However, by doubling the wraps each side from four to eight the strength of the knot is substantially increased. We add the four extra wraps each side using the reverse twist principle.

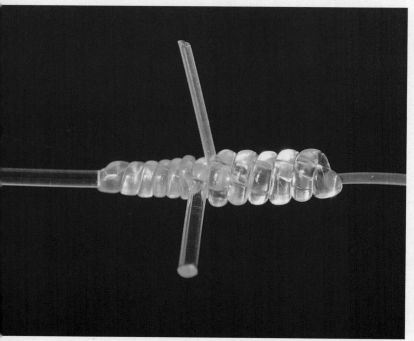

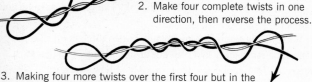

1. Overlap the lines to be joined by a generous margin and twist them together.

2. Make four complete twists in one direction, then reverse the process.

3. Making four more twists over the first four but in the other direction. Thread the tag between the lines before the first crossover.

4. Now, do the same with the tag of the other line from the opposite side.

5. Thread the tag through, what has now become the central wrap, alongside the tag of the other line but from the opposite direction.

6. Close the knot up with gentle, but firm, pressure on the line each side of the knot.

OPPOSED NAIL KNOT

Opposed Nail Knots provide a sound connection between monofilament lines of either the same or different diameters. To tie them you will need a metal tube. Those made by K&S and sold in model aircraft shops are ideal. The smallest tubes, those with an outside diameter of 1/16" will handle lines to 36 kg.

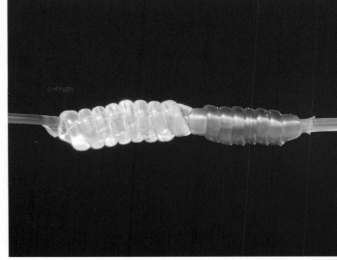

1. The lines to be joined are marked A and B. B is shown beside the tube while A encircles both tube and B.

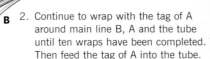

2. Continue to wrap with the tag of A around main line B, A and the tube until ten wraps have been completed. Then feed the tag of A into the tube.

3. Extract the tube and close the resulting knot with gentle pressure, do not pull it tight.

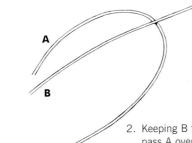

4. Now lay the tube parallel with line A, extend tag B through the knot and wrap the tube and main lines A and B.

5. Complete ten wraps and extract the tube. Close the resulting knot with gentle pressure, do not pull it tight.

6. Lubricate, pull the knots together, then tighten each in turn. Pull together once more and trim the tags with nail clippers.

PLAITED SPLICE

Method of joining two lines for maximum strength.

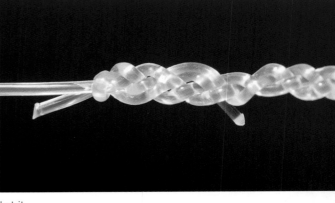

2. Keeping B tight, pass A over B so that A is now between B and C.

3. Pass C over A so that it is now between B and A. Keep the legs tight so that the plait is firm.

1. Ideally, line B should be the line coming from the new spool of line, C should be the line coming from your reel. While it is harder to plait like this because the line from the spool is difficult to keep tight, it is better because the leading end of the plait will go out through the runners first. This is desirable because the finish of the plait, where the ends are secured, is likely to bunch up if pulled out through the runners under tension. Lay the two ends to be joined as shown.

LOOP B

4. Continue to plait for the required length, as we do in the Plaited Double, then we make a loop out of one of the loose legs, in this case B. So instead of plaiting with leg B, we now plait with loop B. Remember to keep plenty of tension on the legs as you plait, or the plait will be too loose.

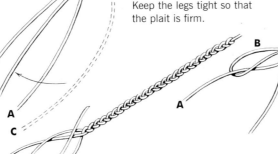

5. Having plaited with loop B for several steps, thread the other loose end, which is A, through loop B.

6. Pull end B against A and C to secure the plait and your two lines are joined.

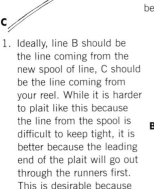

7. The join is complete and, although it takes longer to tie than ordinary joins, it is very strong and does not increase the diameter of the line very much.

ALBRIGHT KNOT

Shown is an improved method of tying the Albright Knot.

1. Double the last few centimetres of the heavier monofilament leader and thread the lighter line through, then around, the resulting loop.

2. Continue wrapping down the loop in the heavier monofilament leader with the lighter monofilament line.

3. Make five wraps down the loop then commence wrapping in the other direction, back over the first wraps you made.

4. Complete five wraps in each direction and thread the tag back through the loop alongside the main line.

5. Partially close the knot first with gentle pressure on the main line and tag of both leader and line.

6. When the knot begins to tighten, let both the tag of the line, and tag of the leader, go. Then tighten the knot with firm pressure on line against leader.

7. Close the knot and trim the tags.

IMPROVED BLOOD KNOT

The improved blood knot is used for joining two monofilament lines of different diameters. For example, when a heavier leader is attached to a lighter main line.

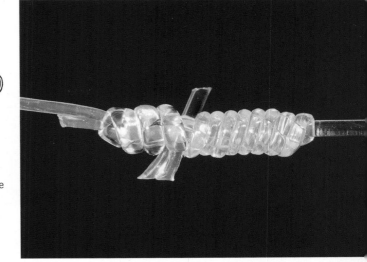

1. Double the lighter line and overlap with the heavier line or leader.

2. Wind the doubled lighter line along one end of the heavier line.

3. Push the tag of the heavier line through the third or fourth wrap and continue to wrap with the lighter line as before.

4. Make an additional five or six wraps then pass the looped tag end of the lighter line through the same wrap as you passed the tag of the heavier line through. As you can see, I have made five wraps; three up, and two back, before threading with the looped tag end of the lighter line.

5. Close the knot with firm but gentle pressure on the line each side of the knot, taking particular care that no loops of slack line appear in the doubled strand.

6. When the knot has been pulled up really tight, trim the tags.

SLIM BEAUTY

Slim Beauty is a knot used to connect a monofilament main line to a heavier monofilament leader. These are the steps as demonstrated by prominent Australia angler and fishing writer Dean Butler.

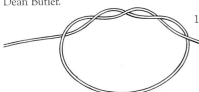

1. Tie a double overhand knot in the heavy monofilament leader.

2. Close the knot until it shows this figure of eight configuration.

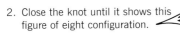

3. Make a loop in the end of the monofilament main line and thread it through the figure of eight configuration as shown.

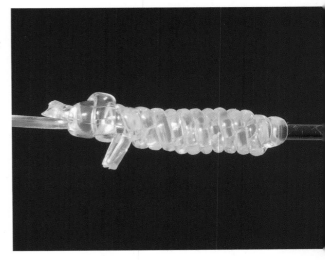

4. Wind the mono-filament loop down the heavier leader four times, then wind it back again.

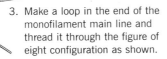

5. Having made four wraps down and four wraps back, thread the remaining monofilament loop between the leader and the descending double strand.

6. Tension the knot by pulling gently, but firmly, on both strands of the monofilament main line, against the heavier monofilament leader. Trim the tags and the join is complete.

SHOCK TIPPET AND LEADER KNOT

This is the strongest method for connecting a class tippet to a shock tippet, without first securing a double with either a Bimini or plait, that I have tested. It also provides a strong join between a monofilament main line and a heavier leader and is particularly useful for making wind-on leaders.

1. Tie a double overhand knot in one end of your mono leader or shock tippet.

2. Tension the knot to the point where a double loop is formed but no more.

3. Thread the class tippet or mono main line through the double loop configuration as shown.

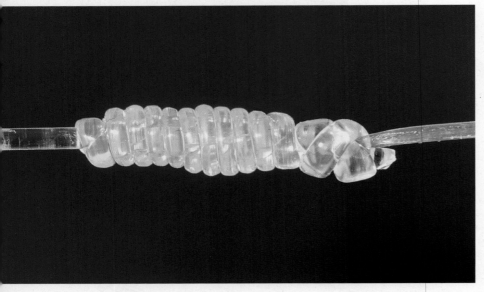

4. Pull the double overhand knot in the heavy line really tight so that some flattening or deformity is noticeable.

5. We need to tie a nail knot in the class tippet or mono main line using a fine metal tube. I use a Lumbar Puncture which is a coarse surgical needle. I have also used a 1/16" OD, K&S brass tube, like those used in model aircraft.

6. Wrap you tube or needle with the class tippet or mono main line eleven or twelve times.

7. Then thread the class tippet or mono main line into the tube.

8. Slide the tube out from under the wraps.

9. Slide the two knots together, Close up the nail knot but don't pull it too tight or you could break the class tippet and have to start again.

10. Trim the tags and the attachment is complete.

I tested this knot using a connection between a class tippet line marked Stren, High Impact, Hard Mono Leader, 20 lb Test, Dia. .022" (0.55 mm), and a heavier line marked Jinkai 150 lb, Dia. 1.04 mm (.04"). In the first test the class tippet broke within the knot at 9.1 kg (20 lbs). In the second test the class tippet broke within the knot at 9.25 kg (20.38 lbs).

WIND ON DACRON LEADER SPLICE

Described is the process of threading a heavy monofilament leader into the free end of a dacron fishing line so it may be wound through the rod guides and onto the reel. The leader is usually from five to ten metres in length and twice to three times the breaking strain of the dacron.

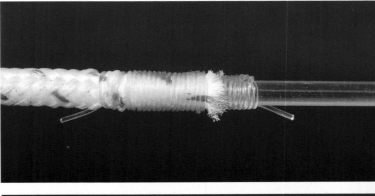

1. Sharpen the end of the monofilament leader to a point, but don't make it sharp enough to spear through the weave of the dacron.

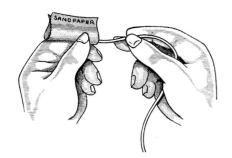

2. Remove any rough edges using fine sandpaper.

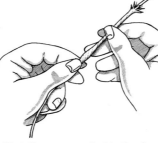

3. Push the tapered end of the monofilament leader inside the hollow dacron line.

4. Work the mono up inside the dacron by alternately bunching up the dacron over the mono, then stretching it out again.

5. Having pushed the mono some 30 cm or so inside the dacron line, trim the frayed dacron ends.

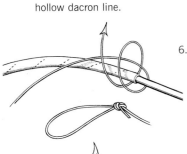

6. Take a length of fine thread, tie a loop in one end, then cut the loop off to use a pull-through to finish off the binding. Then commence a firm binding on the join.

Having threaded the monofilament leader into the dacron as described, it can't be pulled out. This is because pulling on the dacron contracts the weave, holding the monofilament firm. However, the mono may be released by pushing the dacron off so the weave expands. For this reason we must put a binding on the join. Fine waxed thread is most often recommended, but I now use a fine gelspun fishing line like Gorilla Braid or Spectra with a nominated breaking strain of 20 or 30 pounds.

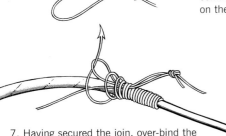

7. Having secured the join, over-bind the loop you made for at least the same distance as the existing binding, then thread the tag through the loop.

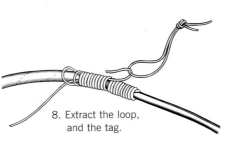

8. Extract the loop, and the tag.

9. Pull the binding tight, trim the tags, then saturate the entire binding with a pliable rubber sealant like Pliobond or Aquaseal.

Caution:

The join between leader and line is now secure: However, separtion may occur when rigging skirted trolling heads directly onto the leader. This is because a hooked fish taking line causes the lure to run back to the splice. While this is itself would not cause a separation, a situation which can occur — and one which I have experienced personally — is the lure riding backwards, hard up against the joining splice, may be struck by another game fish, and with sufficient force, to cause a separation.

WIND ON LEADERS FOR GAME FISHING

This version of Steve Morris' Top Shot, Wind-on Leader features "Shigeshi Tanaka's Loop Splice," an innovation which holds the dacron loop firmly in place, a most desirable feature when large fish need to be played out over a long period of time.

Although you can use a doubled length of single strand wire as a needle, this connection is best performed using the Top Shot dacron splicing needles produced by Top Shot Tackle in South Australia who export most of their products to the United States. Top Shot glues are recommended for sealing the splice, but suitable alternatives include Aquaseal and Pliobond.

Other materials include a five to ten metre length of monofilament three to five times the breaking strain of the line already on the reel, and some hollow dacron line about twice the breaking strain of the line on the reel. There is room for some variation with sleeve and leader size, but heavier, or lighter monofilament leaders, require a compatible dacron sleeve.

You will also need a sharp knife or scalpel for sharpening one end of the monofilament leader, and loop gauge or pencil to keep your loop open. A fine waxed thread, or other strong binding thread, is used for finishing off.

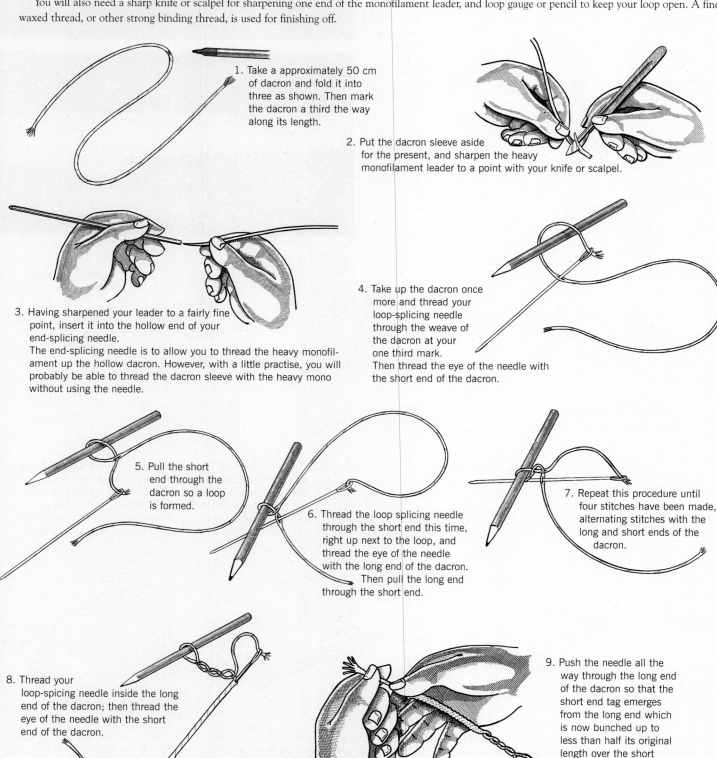

1. Take a approximately 50 cm of dacron and fold it into three as shown. Then mark the dacron a third the way along its length.

2. Put the dacron sleeve aside for the present, and sharpen the heavy monofilament leader to a point with your knife or scalpel.

3. Having sharpened your leader to a fairly fine point, insert it into the hollow end of your end-splicing needle.
The end-splicing needle is to allow you to thread the heavy monofilament up the hollow dacron. However, with a little practise, you will probably be able to thread the dacron sleeve with the heavy mono without using the needle.

4. Take up the dacron once more and thread your loop-splicing needle through the weave of the dacron at your one third mark.
Then thread the eye of the needle with the short end of the dacron.

5. Pull the short end through the dacron so a loop is formed.

6. Thread the loop splicing needle through the short end this time, right up next to the loop, and thread the eye of the needle with the long end of the dacron. Then pull the long end through the short end.

7. Repeat this procedure until four stitches have been made, alternating stitches with the long and short ends of the dacron.

8. Thread your loop-spicing needle inside the long end of the dacron; then thread the eye of the needle with the short end of the dacron.

9. Push the needle all the way through the long end of the dacron so that the short end tag emerges from the long end which is now bunched up to less than half its original length over the short end.

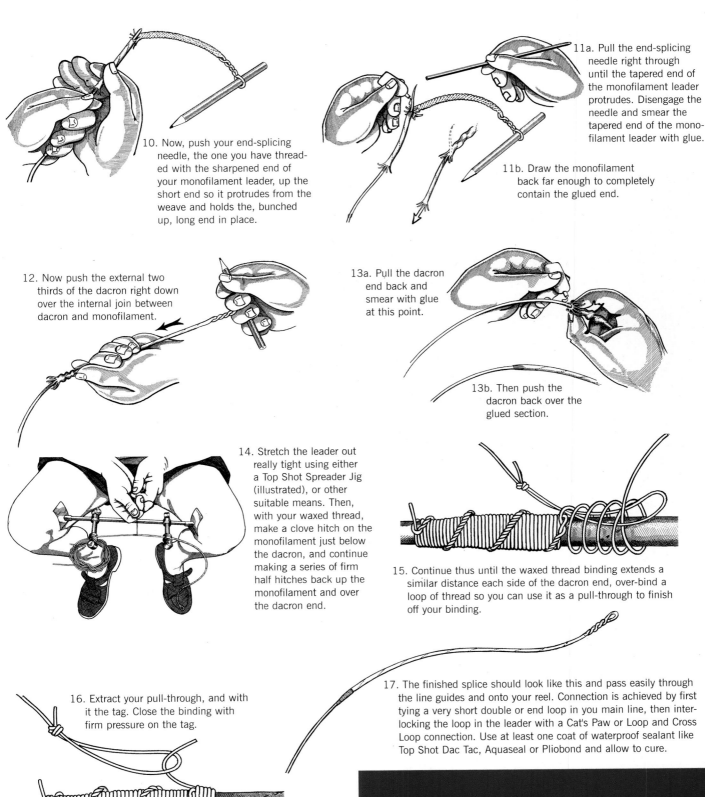

10. Now, push your end-splicing needle, the one you have threaded with the sharpened end of your monofilament leader, up the short end so it protrudes from the weave and holds the, bunched up, long end in place.

11a. Pull the end-splicing needle right through until the tapered end of the monofilament leader protrudes. Disengage the needle and smear the tapered end of the monofilament leader with glue.

11b. Draw the monofilament back far enough to completely contain the glued end.

12. Now push the external two thirds of the dacron right down over the internal join between dacron and monofilament.

13a. Pull the dacron end back and smear with glue at this point.

13b. Then push the dacron back over the glued section.

14. Stretch the leader out really tight using either a Top Shot Spreader Jig (illustrated), or other suitable means. Then, with your waxed thread, make a clove hitch on the monofilament just below the dacron, and continue making a series of firm half hitches back up the monofilament and over the dacron end.

15. Continue thus until the waxed thread binding extends a similar distance each side of the dacron end, over-bind a loop of thread so you can use it as a pull-through to finish off your binding.

16. Extract your pull-through, and with it the tag. Close the binding with firm pressure on the tag.

17. The finished splice should look like this and pass easily through the line guides and onto your reel. Connection is achieved by first tying a very short double or end loop in you main line, then interlocking the loop in the leader with a Cat's Paw or Loop and Cross Loop connection. Use at least one coat of waterproof sealant like Top Shot Dac Tac, Aquaseal or Pliobond and allow to cure.

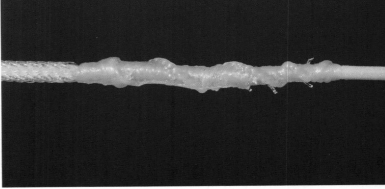

Caution:

The join between leader and line is now secure: However, separation may occur when rigging skirted trolling heads directly onto the leader. This is because a hooked fish taking line causes the lure to run back to the splice. While this is itself would not cause a separation, a situation which can occur — and one which I have experienced personally — is the lure riding backwards, hard up against the joining splice, may be struck by another game fish, and with sufficient force, to cause a separation.

WIND ON WIRE LEADERS

This method of rigging full-length IGFA wind-on wire leaders was devised by Steve Morris of Top Shot Tackle in Adelaide Australia.

Nylon or plastic coated, 49 strand cable is best.

The specimen used for these illustrations was rigged from 400 pound, nylon coated, 49 strand cable and 130 pound IGFA dacron. A Top Shot, loop splicing needle was used to make the loop in the dacron sleeve, but you can use a doubled length of single strand wire as a substitute.

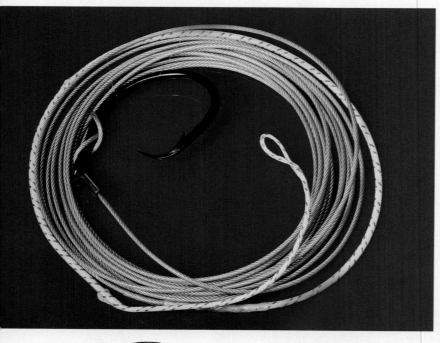

PREPARATION OF THE WIRE

1. Remove the last couple of centimetres of nylon or plastic coating from the wire.

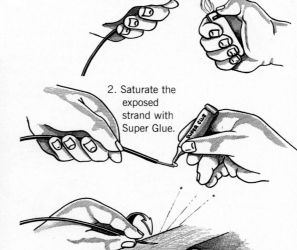

2. Saturate the exposed strand with Super Glue.

3. Allow the strands to fuse, then shave the fused strands to a taper using a belt sander like I did or similar device.

These steps prepare the wire so it will slide into the dacron sleeve without catching. However, because there may be some loose strands, it is advisable to give the wire another application of Super Glue and a sprinkling of talcum powder to make it smooth. An alternate treatment is to use Hot Melt Glue to cover the exposed wire taper and allow it to cool.

PREPARATION OF THE SLEEVE

4. Take about 50 cm (20 inches) of 130 pound IGFA dacron and fold it into three roughly equal lengths, then mark one of the folds.

5. Take an object to use as a loop gauge like a pencil or a pen, pass one third of the line around it and push your loop splicing needle or doubled wire through at the mark you made in the previous step.

6. Pull the dacron end through.

7. Now, thread the dacron splicing needle sideways through the weave of the short end, the opposite end to the one you threaded before.

8. Pull the long end through, then thread the needle sideways through the weave of the long end once more.

9. Finally, the loop splicing needle, or doubled wire, is threaded length wise through the long end of the dacron so the short end can be drawn right through.

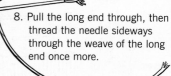

10. Draw out the short end so the long end is now bunched up over the short end.

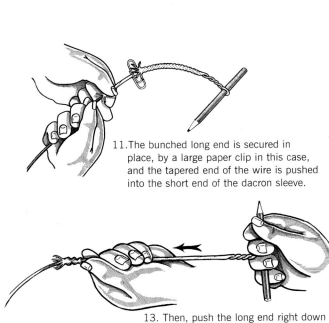

11. The bunched long end is secured in place, by a large paper clip in this case, and the tapered end of the wire is pushed into the short end of the dacron sleeve.

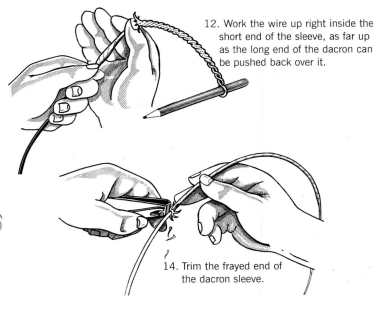

12. Work the wire up right inside the short end of the sleeve, as far up as the long end of the dacron can be pushed back over it.

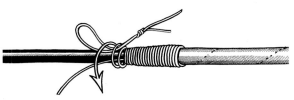

13. Then, push the long end right down over the short end sleeving the wire.

14. Trim the frayed end of the dacron sleeve.

FINISHING OFF

There needs to be a binding on the dacron sleeve overlapping the wire. This may be done with waxed thread, or — as I did when preparing this example — with fine gelspun line.

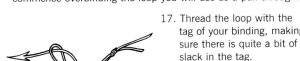

16. Continue your binding past the overlap and onto the wire and commence overbinding the loop you will use as a pull through.

17. Thread the loop with the tag of your binding, making sure there is quite a bit of slack in the tag.

15. Attach the loop splice in your dacron to a hook or the like so you can tension the wire where the dacron overlaps.

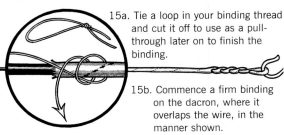

15a. Tie a loop in your binding thread and cut it off to use as a pull-through later on to finish the binding.

15b. Commence a firm binding on the dacron, where it overlaps the wire, in the manner shown.

18. Pull the loop out, and with it the tag. Then tension both tags so the binding is really firm.

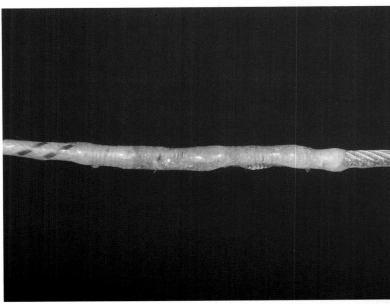

19. Apply a coating of a pliable adhesive like Aquaseal or Pliobond to the binding and work it right into the binding and adjacent dacron with your fingers, preferably with a surgical clove so it doesn't get on your fingers and under your fingernails.

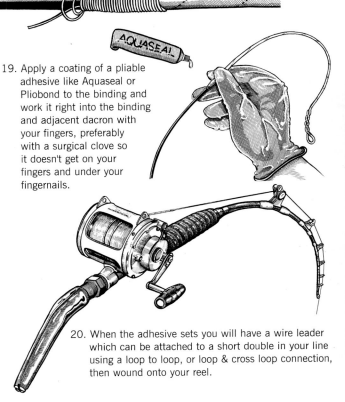

20. When the adhesive sets you will have a wire leader which can be attached to a short double in your line using a loop to loop, or loop & cross loop connection, then wound onto your reel.

DACRON JOINING SPLICE

This method of joining two lengths of IGFA, line class dacron, is used and recommended by Steve Morris of Top Shot Tackle in South Australia. A dacron splicing needle is required.

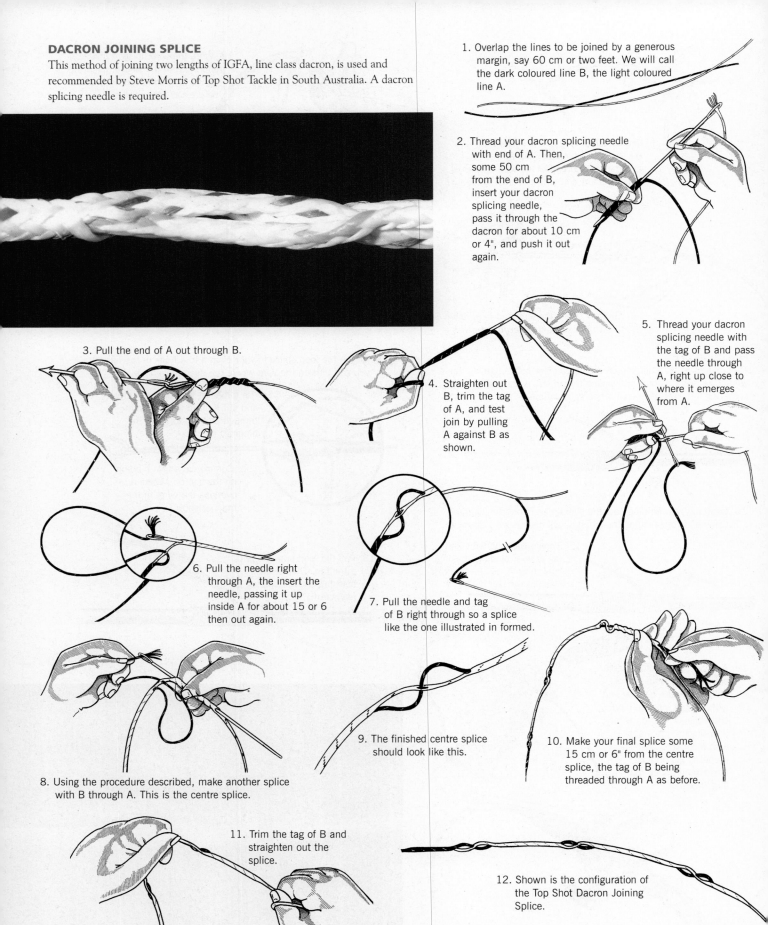

1. Overlap the lines to be joined by a generous margin, say 60 cm or two feet. We will call the dark coloured line B, the light coloured line A.

2. Thread your dacron splicing needle with end of A. Then, some 50 cm from the end of B, insert your dacron splicing needle, pass it through the dacron for about 10 cm or 4", and push it out again.

3. Pull the end of A out through B.

4. Straighten out B, trim the tag of A, and test join by pulling A against B as shown.

5. Thread your dacron splicing needle with the tag of B and pass the needle through A, right up close to where it emerges from A.

6. Pull the needle right through A, the insert the needle, passing it up inside A for about 15 or 6 then out again.

7. Pull the needle and tag of B right through so a splice like the one illustrated in formed.

8. Using the procedure described, make another splice with B through A. This is the centre splice.

9. The finished centre splice should look like this.

10. Make your final splice some 15 cm or 6" from the centre splice, the tag of B being threaded through A as before.

11. Trim the tag of B and straighten out the splice.

12. Shown is the configuration of the Top Shot Dacron Joining Splice.

TANAKA'S LOOP

This method of splicing a loop in dacron, heavy gelspun or other hollow braided leader material, was created by celebrated stand-up game fisherman, Shigeshi Tanaka, of Japan.

This loop is totally secure with no movement at all making it ideal for the Cat's Paw, and similar connections used with wind-on leaders. It is best performed using a Top Shot dacron loop-splicing needle made by Top Shot Tackle, Australia.

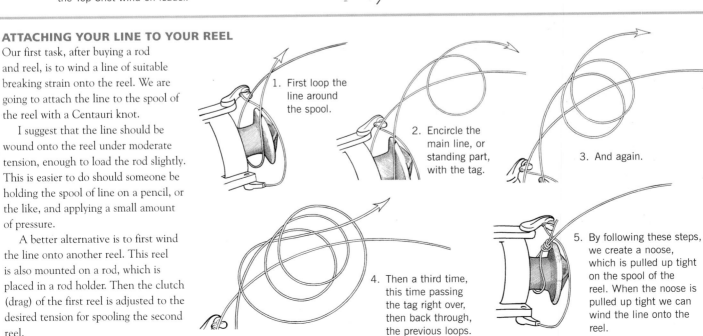

1. Select a length of dacron or other hollow braided line of suitable diameter for the wind-on leader you intend building. Pass the loop-splicing needle through the weave, more or less at right angles, about one third the way along, and thread the needle with the short end tag. The pencil represents the need to hold the loop open during the initial stages of forming the splice.

2. Pull the short end tag right through the weave.

3. Now thread the loop-splicing needle through the weave of the short end and thread the eye of the needle with the long end. This step will determine the size of your loop.

4. Continue in the same manner, alternately threading each end through the weave of the opposite length making each stitch as close to the last as you can manage.

5. The splice may be finished off by simply trimming the short tag after the third stitch, or . . .

6. You can thread the loop splicing needle with the tag or the short end and pull it down inside the long end.

7. Having pushed your needle down through the longer length of the dacron, which is now bunched over the shorter length, you may follow from step 9 on page 30 to complete the Top Shot wind-on leader.

ATTACHING YOUR LINE TO YOUR REEL

Our first task, after buying a rod and reel, is to wind a line of suitable breaking strain onto the reel. We are going to attach the line to the spool of the reel with a Centauri knot.

I suggest that the line should be wound onto the reel under moderate tension, enough to load the rod slightly. This is easier to do should someone be holding the spool of line on a pencil, or the like, and applying a small amount of pressure.

A better alternative is to first wind the line onto another reel. This reel is also mounted on a rod, which is placed in a rod holder. Then the clutch (drag) of the first reel is adjusted to the desired tension for spooling the second reel.

1. First loop the line around the spool.

2. Encircle the main line, or standing part, with the tag.

3. And again.

4. Then a third time, this time passing the tag right over, then back through, the previous loops.

5. By following these steps, we create a noose, which is pulled up tight on the spool of the reel. When the noose is pulled up tight we can wind the line onto the reel.

PLAITING A DOUBLE

Although plaiting is considered a little too slow and inconvenient for most sportfishing situations it is the most satisfactory way of tying a full length I.G.F.A. double, retaining the full breaking strain of the line being used. This is how it is done.

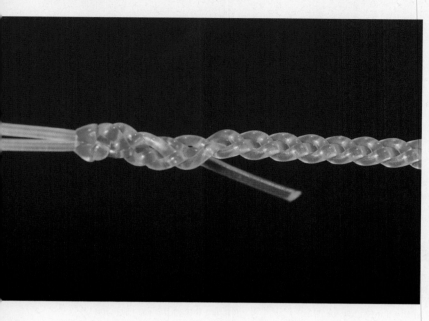

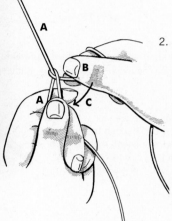

1. Measure off just over twice the length of line your finished double will be. Say our double will finish up at 4.5 metres, then you will need to double 9 metres of line plus half a metre or so for your tag. The main line or standing part is A. The returning length is B, and the tag is C. Let's call the loop formed, D.

2. As with the Bimini, your rod should be firmly in a rod holder and the clutch of the reel set on strike drag. Keeping the line tight by pulling away from your rod and reel, pass C over B (alongside A). Pull B tight. Because tension must be maintained throughout the plaiting process, it helps to wrap each successive leg in turn, around your finger as shown.

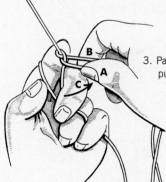

3. Pass A over C and pull C tight.

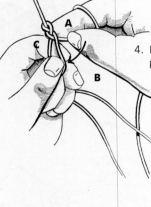

4. Pass B over A and pull A tight.

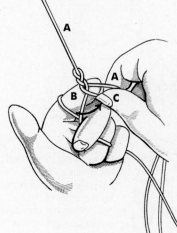

5. Pass C over B and pull C tight. Having completed the first cycle of the plait, increase tension on the line, even though some distortion may appear at the beginning of the plait. This is normal.

6. Now you are getting the idea, A goes over C then C is pulled tight. Always pull the leg you have just crossed, really tight against the line coming from your rod and reel. That way your plait will be nice and firm.

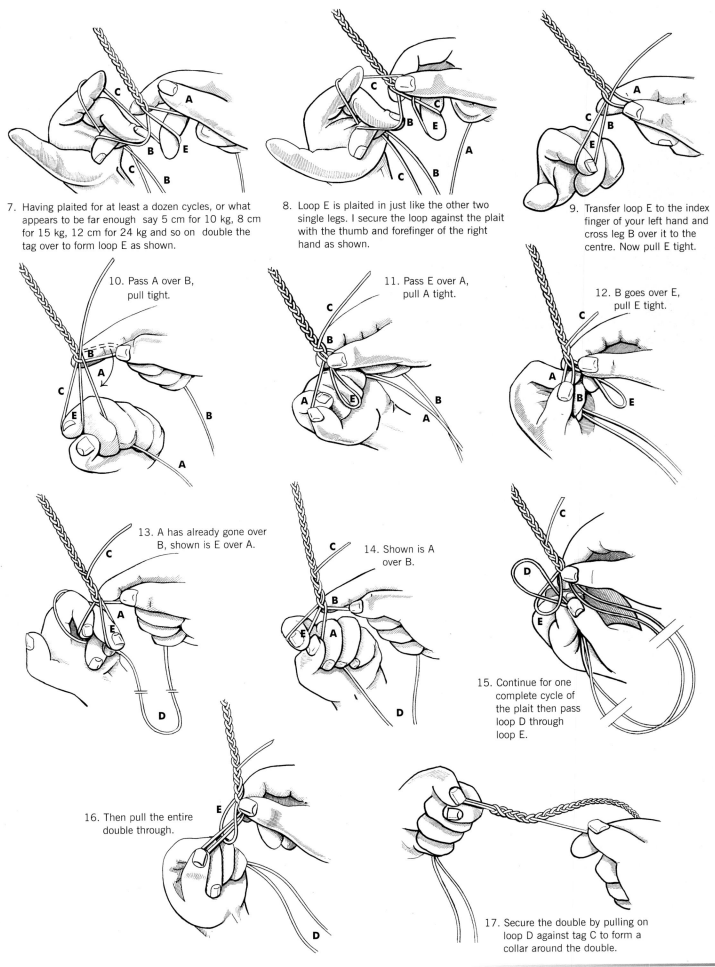

7. Having plaited for at least a dozen cycles, or what appears to be far enough say 5 cm for 10 kg, 8 cm for 15 kg, 12 cm for 24 kg and so on double the tag over to form loop E as shown.

8. Loop E is plaited in just like the other two single legs. I secure the loop against the plait with the thumb and forefinger of the right hand as shown.

9. Transfer loop E to the index finger of your left hand and cross leg B over it to the centre. Now pull E tight.

10. Pass A over B, pull tight.

11. Pass E over A, pull A tight.

12. B goes over E, pull E tight.

13. A has already gone over B, shown is E over A.

14. Shown is A over B.

15. Continue for one complete cycle of the plait then pass loop D through loop E.

16. Then pull the entire double through.

17. Secure the double by pulling on loop D against tag C to form a collar around the double.

BIMINI TWIST

Short doubles or end loops like those used in sport and fly fishing, are easily secured with a Bimini Twist which retains the full breaking strain of monofilament and most other lines.

Several ways of tying a Bimini Twist have evolved. The method shown here, with the rod placed firmly in a rod holder, is easiest to master and should enable the angler to graduate, more easily, to hand-tensioned Biminis later on.

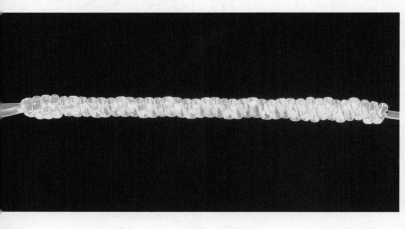

1a . Thread the line through your line guides of your rod and place your rod securely in a rod holder with your reel on strike drag.

1b. Tie a small loop in the end of your line, then cut it off and put it aside. This is to act as a pull-through to finish off the Bimini later on.

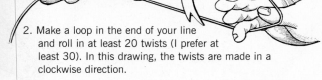

2. Make a loop in the end of your line and roll in at least 20 twists (I prefer at least 30). In this drawing, the twists are made in a clockwise direction.

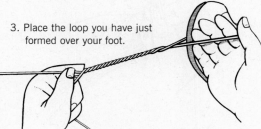

3. Place the loop you have just formed over your foot.

4a. Keeping the maximum tension on your line that your drag setting allows, compress the twists tightly together.

4b. Fold the tag back so it will spiral back over the twists as you increase tension with your right hand.

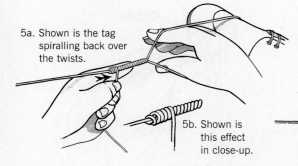

5a. Shown is the tag spiralling back over the twists.

5b. Shown is this effect in close-up.

6. Allow the tag to spiral right up to the crotch in the double and insert the short loop of line marked 1B as a pull-through.

7a. Over-bind the pull-through three or four times, taking care to continue (in this case) anti-clockwise, then thread the tag through the loop in the pull-through.

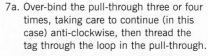

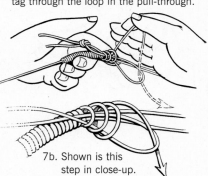

7b. Shown is this step in close-up.

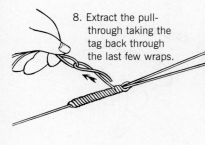

8. Extract the pull-through taking the tag back through the last few wraps.

9a. Pull gently, but firmly, on the tag and rotate the Bimini (anti-clockwise) until several twists form in the loop. Don't pull too hard on the tag because you may shear it off and have to retie the whole thing again.

9b. Trim the tag and the Bimini is finished.

HAND TENSIONED BIMINI DOUBLE

We have already discovered how to tie a Bimini double with the rod in a rod-holder to tension the line. Now we examine how to tie a hand-tensioned Bimini.

1a. Begin by tying a small loop in the end of your line then cutting it off. You will need this loop as a pull-through to finish off the Bimini later on, so don't lose it.

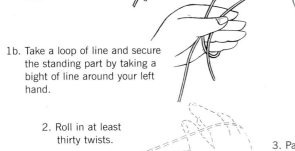

1b. Take a loop of line and secure the standing part by taking a bight of line around your left hand.

2. Roll in at least thirty twists.

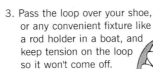

3. Pass the loop over your shoe, or any convenient fixture like a rod holder in a boat, and keep tension on the loop so it won't come off.

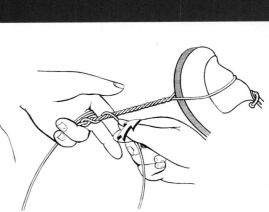

4. Keeping pressure on the standing part, rotate the tag between thumb and forefinger of the right hand to make the tag spiral back over the twists.

5. Hold the tag between thumb and middle finger of the left hand and put your right hand inside the loop over your shoe and open the loop by spreading your fingers and sliding your right hand toward the left hand.
This will cause the tag to spiral back over the twists while tension on the tag is controlled by the pressure of your thumb against the middle finger.

6. When the tag has spiralled back to the crotch in the loop, place your left index finger in the crotch to secure the tag. Then take the small loop you first made and commence wrapping it with the tag.

7. Wrap the loop, and both strands of the Bimini, three or four times then pass the tag through the loop.

8. Withdraw your loop, drawing the tag back out from under the last few wraps.

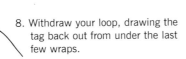

9. Pull gently on the tag, rotating the Bimini as you do so until a couple of twists appear in the loop, then stop. If you pull tag out too far you will shorten the splice.

SPIDER HITCH

Unlike the Bimini Twist and Plait, which are progressive splices, the Spider Hitch is a knot, which retains around 80% of line strength in monofilament. However, tied in gelspun lines it retains only 40 to 60% of the actual breaking strain.

Although lacking the strength of the Bimini and Plait the Spider Hitch does produce a double strand with which to attach terminals and leaders and it is quick and easy to tie.

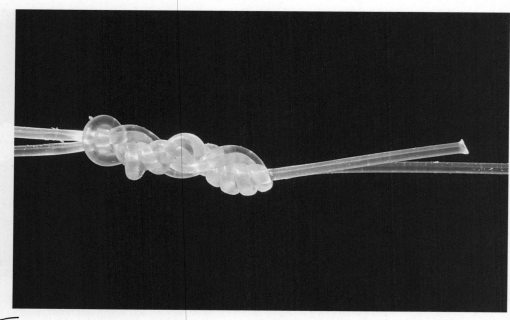

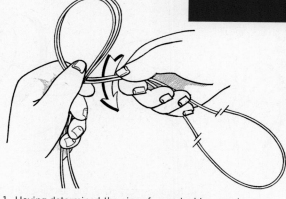

1. Having determined the size of your double or end loop, twist in a second loop just above the tag end and hold it between the thumb and finger of your left hand.

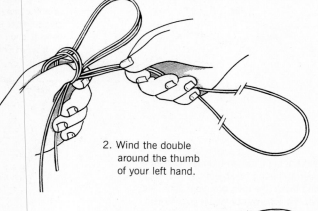

2. Wind the double around the thumb of your left hand.

3. Make four or five complete wraps.

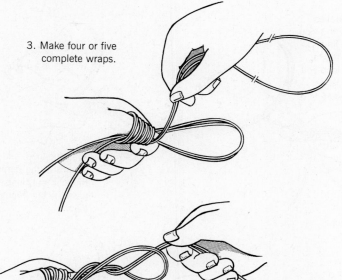

4. Then pass the loop in the double through the second loop.

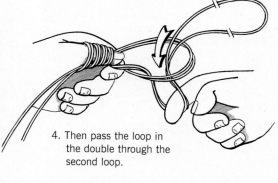

5. Pinching thumb and finger of the left hand firmly together so the loops disengage one at a time, pull gently but firmly on the double until all the loops have slid from your left thumb.

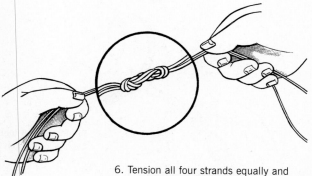

6. Tension all four strands equally and your Spider Hitch should look something like this.

TONY JONES' LEADER KNOT

I call this Tony Jones' Leader Knot because I learned it from Captain Tony Jones of Ra Charters.

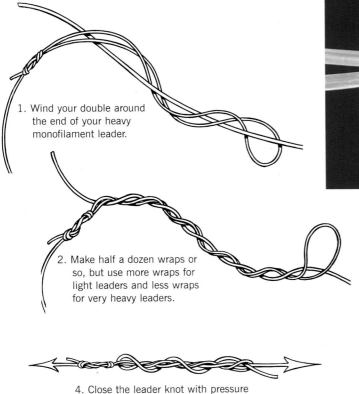

1. Wind your double around the end of your heavy monofilament leader.

2. Make half a dozen wraps or so, but use more wraps for light leaders and less wraps for very heavy leaders.

3. The wind the tag of the leader back around the knot and thread it through the loop in the double.

4. Close the leader knot with pressure on the leader against the main line.

5. The finished should join allow the heavy monofilament leader to be wound onto your reel.

CATS PAW TO RING OR SWIVEL

Bear in mind a double can be tied to a swivel or ring using the same knot as you would use to attach a single strand of line. However, to retain the intact double for the purpose of officially recording captures in sport or game fishing we use a Cat's Paw.

The Cat's Paw is usually tied to a high quality snap swivel so leaders can be changed as circumstances dictate. The swivel I've drawn here has a larger eye than usual so you can see more clearly what is happening.

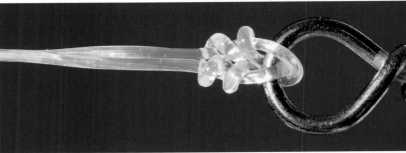

1. Thread the loop end of your double through the eye of the snap swivel and pass the swivel through the loop.

2. Fold the loop end of the double back against the standing part of the loop.

3. Rotate the swivel through the central loop formed.

4. Do this from three to six times depending on the thickness and pliability of the line.

5. Close up the Cat's Paw. Chances are you won't close your Cat's Paw as tight as this one unless you are using a supple braided line. Monofilament can be closed satisfactorily by lubricating with dry lubricant or powdered graphite. Lubrication with saliva is unsatisfactory for this purpose.

LOOP & CROSS-LOOP CONNECTIONS

Loop & Cross Loop Connections are used for joining two lines, each with a loop at the end to be joined. In this case, a Wind-on Leader, which has been loop-spliced at one end, is being attached to a short Bimini double in the end of the line coming from the reel: There are other applications as well.

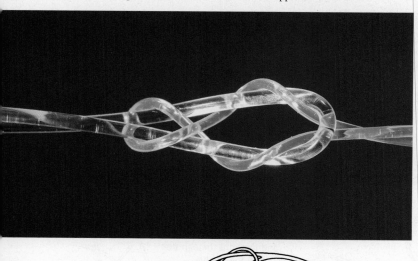

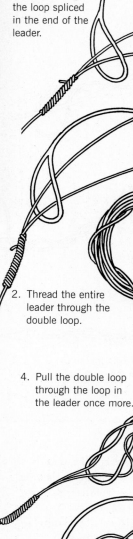

1. Roll up the leader then thread the loop of the short double through the loop spliced in the end of the leader.

2. Thread the entire leader through the double loop.

3. Close the two loops, but not too tightly. (Some anglers finish the connection at this point. However, this is an unstable connection and a "cutting girth hitch" may form, weakening the connection)

4. Pull the double loop through the loop in the leader once more.

5. Rotate the double loop through 360 degrees.

6. Thread the entire leader through the double loop once more.

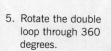

7. Close the loops together.

8. Loop & Cross Loop connections remain stable under extreme tension.

DUNCAN'S LOOP

Sometimes confused with the Uni Knot which looks similar but is not the same, Duncan's Loop provides a simple fixed loop attachment for fly to tippet or hook to leader. Peter Hayes of "Guided Fishing" provided the demonstration on which these drawings are based.

1. Thread the eye of the hook and roll a loop into the tippet.

2. Thread the tag back through the loop and commence wrapping both strands.

3. Continue till four wraps have been made.

4. Close the knot and adjust the loop size but do not pull it tight just yet.

5. When the loop is of the desired size, pull the knot tight.

LEFTY'S LOOP

When desirable for the fly to have free movement at the end of the tippet, it is rigged on a small loop. This knot is easy to tie and retains a substantial percentage of the line's breaking strain.

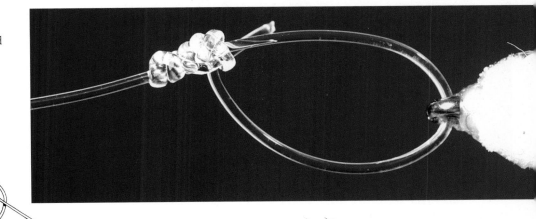

1. First make an overhand knot configuration in the leader, pass the tag through the eye of the hook, then back through the overhand knot.

2. Wrap the leader and tag together from three to five times.

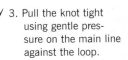

3. Pull the knot tight using gentle pressure on the main line against the loop.

IMPROVED TURLE KNOT

This knot provides a strong, neat connection to flies tied on hooks with turned-down eyes.

1. Thread the tippet trough the eye of the hook and over the body of the fly.

2. Then thread the tippet back through the eye of the hook.

3. Tie and overhand knot in the tag around the standing part of the tippet.

4. Add a second wrap to the overhand knot.

5. Close the overhand knot, but do not pull it really tight yet.

6. Pull the knot up with gentle pressure on the tippet so the knot slides right down into the eye of the hook. Pull the knot up tight and trim the tag.

BLOOD KNOT

Possibly the strongest method of attaching a fly to a monofilament leader is the Blood knot. It differs from the Half Blood in that the line is passed through the eye of the hook twice. This limits its use on very small hook eyes.

To retain the full potential strength of this knot, the loop sequence on the eye of the hook must be retained until the knot is pulled tight.

HALF BLOOD KNOT

The simplest, and most commonly used knot for attaching flies is the simple Half Blood. This knot should be used with caution, because under some circumstances it is inclined to slip. This knot is tied by passing the line through the eye of the hook, wrapping the tag around the main line three to six times, then passing the tag back through the first loop made around the eye of the hook. The finer the diameter of the line in relation to the diameter of the hook eye, the greater the number of turns (up to six), that should be made.

LOCKED HALF BLOOD KNOT

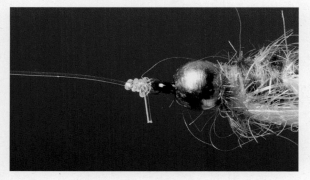

The Half Blood can be locked so that it won't slip. This is done by first forming the knot, then tucking the tag back through the transverse loop before pulling the knot up tight.

ATTACHING FLY LINE TO HOLLOW BRAIDED BACKING

This method of attaching a fly line to a hollow braided backing is used and recommended by Rob Meade of Clear Water Tours.

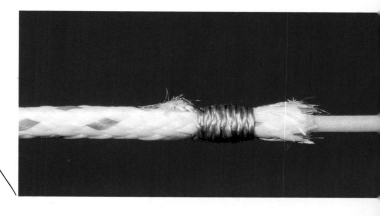

1. The fly line has to go inside the hollow backing so it is advisable to first insert a coarse needle inside the backing to open the weave.

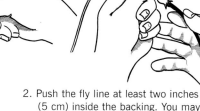

2. Push the fly line at least two inches (5 cm) inside the backing. You may have to jiggle it back and forth if it gets stuck, but it should go in.

3. You won't be able to pull the fly line out from the backing because the increased tension makes the backing contract. However, the fly line can easily removed by pushing the backing off the fly line. To prevent this from happening we make a lashing with very fine fishing line, preferably gelspun fishing line, to make the join secure. In this case we over-bind a loop of line to use as a pull-though to finish off.

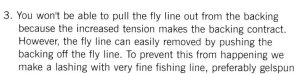

4. Make ten or a dozen wraps over the pull-though loop, then thread the tag through the loop.

5. Pull the loop out, and with it the tag.

6. Tighten the binding with pressure on both side, trim the tags and backing fringe with a set of nail clippers, the cover the lashing with a waterproof sealant like Aquaseal or Pliobond.

MONOFILAMENT LOOP TO FLY LINE

The following process was shown to me by Rob Meade of Clear Water Tours. It enables loop to loop connections with fly leaders in trout fishing.

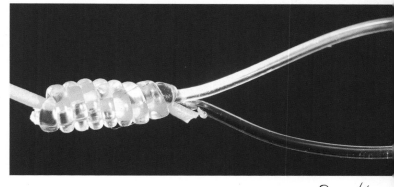

1. Take half a metre or so of monofil-ment with a diameter of about 0.5 mm and make the double loop configuration shown at the end of your fly line (black). Note that one loop is larger than the other.

2. Wrap the fly line and smaller monofilament loop with the larger monofilament loop.

3. Make at least six wraps.

4. Holding the loops together on the fly line so they don't spring apart, hook the smaller loop over a fixed hook or similar object and close the knot by pulling on both tags against the loop, but not too firmly at this stage. This will cause the loops at each end of the knot to close and the loop on the hook to open.

5. At this point you will be aware that one side of the loop is fixed, because it is tied to the fly line, and the other side of the loop will slide because the knot it is simply pinned against the fly line by the knot. Spread a small amount of suitable glue, like "Zap a Gap" on the side of the loop that slides.

6. Ascertain which of the two tags slides the loop closed. We will call that tag A and the other tag, the one forming the knot, tag B. Close the loop on the fixed hook by holding tag A firmly and sliding the loop up on the hook so the glued section is within the knot.

7. Adjust the loop to the size required by alternating tension between tag A and tag B. Then, and this is important, increase pressure on tag B until the knot closes down really firmly on the fly line, pinning the glued side of the loop firmly so it wont slip. Remember, only one side the loop is tied. The loop is secured by the tension of the knot and the glue which you have applied.

8. Trim the tags and protruding fly line and your monofilament loop is complete.

NAIL KNOT USING TUBE

This is an easier way to tie the nail knot for some. It requires a slender, stiff, tube onto which the leader is tied. The fly line is then inserted into the tube and the knot held by the thumb and forefinger while the tube is pulled away, this leaves the knot positioned perfectly over the fly line.

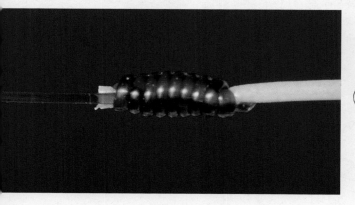

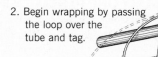

2. Begin wrapping by passing the loop over the tube and tag.

1. Shown is the tube with a monofilament leader coiled beside.

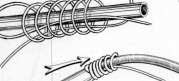

3. Continue to wrap in this way until a snell is formed on the tube.

4. Close the snell tightly on the tube by pulling the tag against the standing part. Then insert the fly line in the tube.

5. Transfer the snell from the tube onto the fly line.

6. Pull the snell up tightly on the fly line so that it bites down into the fly line making a smooth join.

INDICATOR KNOT

This knot produces a sliding loop in the leader for the purpose of securing a small piece of yarn to act as a visible strike indicator.

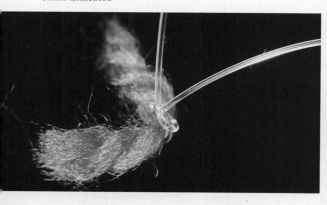

1. Make this configuration in the leader where the indicator is to be secured.

2. Pull one of the crossed legs out through the loop so that another loop is formed with a knot around it.

3. Close the knot and insert the piece of yarn in the loop.

4. Close the loop to secure the piece of yarn to the leader.

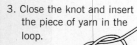

SURGEONS KNOT FOR ATTACHING DROPPER

The Surgeons Knot is used for building fly fishing leaders and multihook bait catching rigs. It can also be used for attaching a short dropper near the end of your main line. Its chief advantage over other knots used for the same purpose are its simplicity and speed.

Bear in mind that large loops are easier to work with when tying this knot so dropper or tippet sections should be cut somewhat longer than when using other joins.

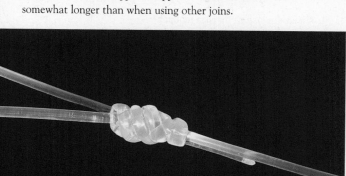

1. Shown is the main line, white, and the tippet or dropper, black. Lay them alongside each other as shown with an overlap of at least 15cm.

2. Tie an overhand knot in both main line and dropper.

3. Make a second wrap in your overhand knot so that four wraps and five crossovers are formed.

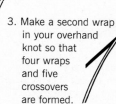

4. With equal pressure on each strand, pull the knot tight. Should the knot fail to close properly, pull gently on each end in turn until the knot is closed before trimming the tag end of the dropper.

HOW TO SPLIT LEADERS

'Splitting' leaders is the term used to describe the process by which one single strand of monofilament becomes two with minimal interruption to the 'lay' of the line, and without significant loss of strength.

This method was shown to me by fellow angling scribe Peter Horrobin who 'splits' flyfishing leaders to present multiple offerings. However, any monofilament line may be 'split' in this manner, either for multiple lure presentation or for rigging with hook and sinker for whiting etc.

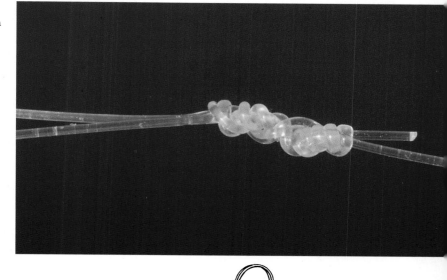

1. Anglers will recognise the configuration of the Spider Hitch, but instead of tying the hitch over our thumb, we use the stem of a float or a pencil (illustrated). The reason why we use a stem and not our thumb is because we are working with considerably shorter lengths of line when splitting leaders than we would be when tying a double for sportfishing, and wrapping the double strand around one's thumb uses up too much line.

2. Holding the loop of the double strand between the finger and stem commence wrapping the loop against the stem.

3. Continue until five wraps have been made.

4. Then pass the final wrap through the loop followed by the entire double strand.

5. Having threaded the entire double strand through the loop, pull the hitch off the stem turn by turn.

6. Close the hitch and cut the loop to produce a double strand, preferably so that one strand is approximately twice as long as the other.

7. Shown is a simple application of split leaders which is useful for multiple presentations when flyfishing.

MAKING SLATWATER FLY FISHING LEADERS

I.G.F.A. makes provision for some saltwater species to be claimed as line class records provided the line class leader and shock tippet (hook length) comply with the following specifications:

• The line class leader be at least 15 inches in length measured between any knot, splice or loop.

• The shock tippet or hook length be no longer than twelve inches including all knots, splices or loops. The following diagrams show rigging strategies which comply with these requirements.

Braided butt or heavy monofilament leader with a loop at each end.

Loop to loop connection between fly line and braided butt section or heavy mono leader.

Loop to loop connection between heavy mono leader or braided butt section and line class tippet or leader.

Bimini

Line class tippet or leader.

Shock Tippet

Huffnagle Knot

Bimini

Bimini to Heavy Monofilament Leader (Huffnagle Knot)

The Huffnagle principle allows a heavy monofilament leader to be tied flush with a double splice, in this case a Bimini, to control the overall length of a shock tippet with no loss of breaking strain to the leader.

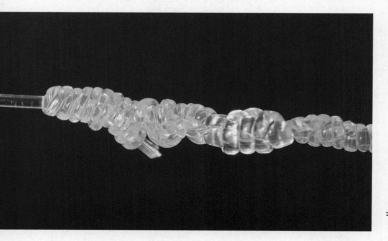

1. Take your heavy monofilament leader and tie it tightly around the Bimini Loop. In this case a nail knot is produced in the heavier line with the aid of a fine metal tube, but an overhand knot may be used provided it is pulled up really tight.

2. Wrap the Bimini Loop and tube with the heavy monofilament four of five times and thread the heavy mono through the tube.

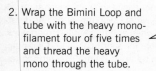

3. Remove the tube and pull the nail knot tight, right up against the Bimini.

4. Begin making a series of half hitches, with the Bimini loop, around the heavy monofilament leader and pulling them up tight against the nail knot.

5. Continue half hitching the leader up to half a dozen times with the loop, in the same direction, until a spiral rib effect is produced.

6. Extend the loop back down the leader and commence wrapping the end of the loop back up the leader under the extended loop, toward the series of half hitches you just made.

7. Do this several times.

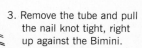

8. Then wind the extended loop back over those wraps in the same direction.

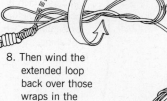

9. Continue thus until the twists are now transferred from the double strand on the inside to the double strand on the outside.

10. Pull out the loop leaving the outer double strand twisted tightly around the inner double strand, and the leader, which are now both straight.

11. Trim the tags and the join is complete.

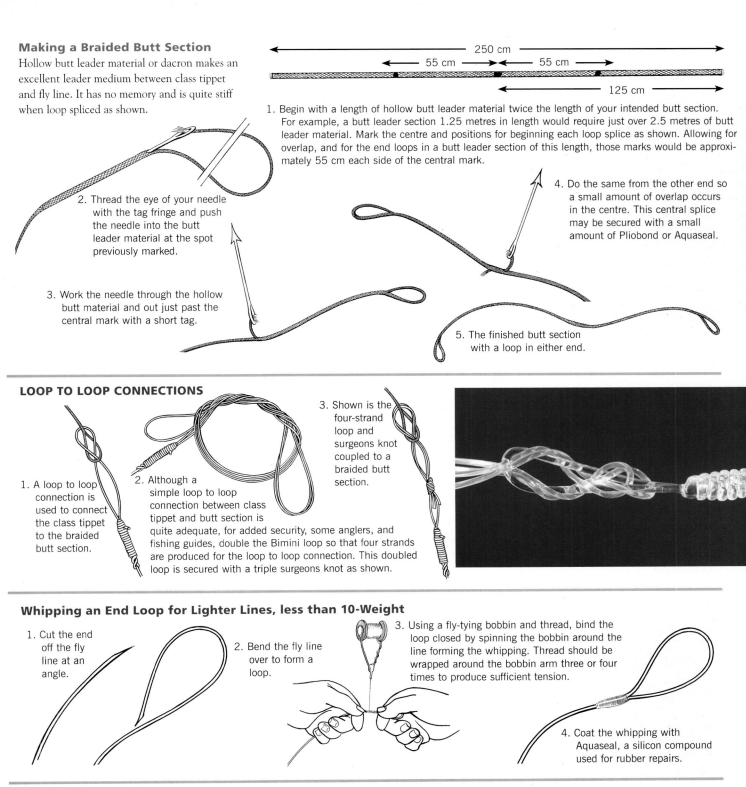

Making a Braided Butt Section

Hollow butt leader material or dacron makes an excellent leader medium between class tippet and fly line. It has no memory and is quite stiff when loop spliced as shown.

1. Begin with a length of hollow butt leader material twice the length of your intended butt section. For example, a butt leader section 1.25 metres in length would require just over 2.5 metres of butt leader material. Mark the centre and positions for beginning each loop splice as shown. Allowing for overlap, and for the end loops in a butt leader section of this length, those marks would be approximately 55 cm each side of the central mark.

2. Thread the eye of your needle with the tag fringe and push the needle into the butt leader material at the spot previously marked.

3. Work the needle through the hollow butt material and out just past the central mark with a short tag.

4. Do the same from the other end so a small amount of overlap occurs in the centre. This central splice may be secured with a small amount of Pliobond or Aquaseal.

5. The finished butt section with a loop in either end.

LOOP TO LOOP CONNECTIONS

1. A loop to loop connection is used to connect the class tippet to the braided butt section.

2. Although a simple loop to loop connection between class tippet and butt section is quite adequate, for added security, some anglers, and fishing guides, double the Bimini loop so that four strands are produced for the loop to loop connection. This doubled loop is secured with a triple surgeons knot as shown.

3. Shown is the four-strand loop and surgeons knot coupled to a braided butt section.

Whipping an End Loop for Lighter Lines, less than 10-Weight

1. Cut the end off the fly line at an angle.

2. Bend the fly line over to form a loop.

3. Using a fly-tying bobbin and thread, bind the loop closed by spinning the bobbin around the line forming the whipping. Thread should be wrapped around the bobbin arm three or four times to produce sufficient tension.

4. Coat the whipping with Aquaseal, a silicon compound used for rubber repairs.

Whipping an End Loop for Heavier Lines, less than 10-Weight & Upwards

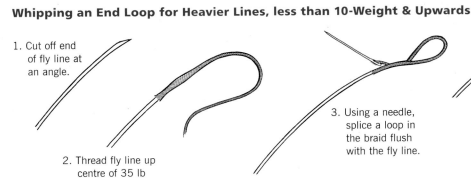

1. Cut off end of fly line at an angle.

2. Thread fly line up centre of 35 lb Gudebrod braid.

3. Using a needle, splice a loop in the braid flush with the fly line.

4. Using your fly-tying bobbin once more, whip the braid down onto the fly line and finish off like a rod binding, using a loop of binding thread as a pull-through. The finished loop is coated with Aquaseal.

   This method of whipping a loop may also be used for heavier fly lines provided the Gudebrod butt leader is substituted with 24 or 37 kg class dacron.

WESTY'S DROPPER

Shown to me by Peter West, this knot allows an additional dropper to be attached to a fly tippet.

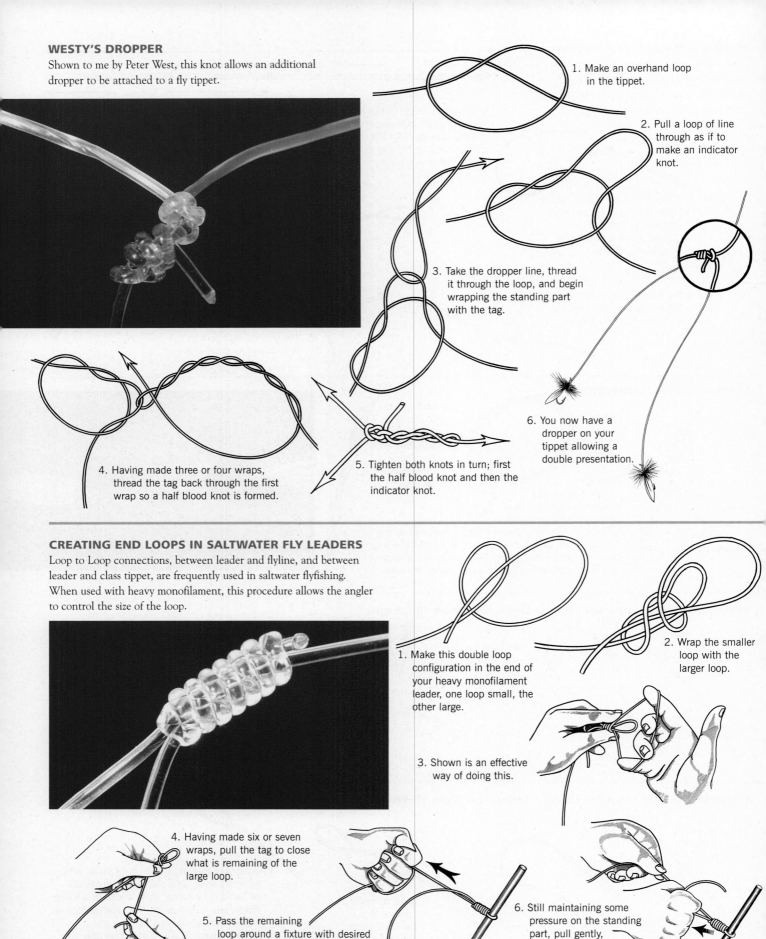

1. Make an overhand loop in the tippet.

2. Pull a loop of line through as if to make an indicator knot.

3. Take the dropper line, thread it through the loop, and begin wrapping the standing part with the tag.

4. Having made three or four wraps, thread the tag back through the first wrap so a half blood knot is formed.

5. Tighten both knots in turn; first the half blood knot and then the indicator knot.

6. You now have a dropper on your tippet allowing a double presentation.

CREATING END LOOPS IN SALTWATER FLY LEADERS

Loop to Loop connections, between leader and flyline, and between leader and class tippet, are frequently used in saltwater flyfishing. When used with heavy monofilament, this procedure allows the angler to control the size of the loop.

1. Make this double loop configuration in the end of your heavy monofilament leader, one loop small, the other large.

2. Wrap the smaller loop with the larger loop.

3. Shown is an effective way of doing this.

4. Having made six or seven wraps, pull the tag to close what is remaining of the large loop.

5. Pass the remaining loop around a fixture with desired diameter to act as a loop gauge, and close the knot, first by pulling firmly on the main or standing part of the leader.

6. Still maintaining some pressure on the standing part, pull gently, but very firmly on the tag until you feel the knot lock the loop in position. Trim the tag.

The most basic application of a float is to suspend your bait below the surface. Some floats are fixed on the line so the hook remains a constant distance below the float. Others are designed to slide along the line to make casting easier when the bait needs to be presented deeper than usual. There are enough floats, in all types, shapes and sizes, to fill a book. Fortunately, we can get by with just a few. Let's look at some basic floats and ways of fishing with them.

FIXED STEM FLOATS

Stem floats consist of a stem, usually with a pear or cigar-shaped body for added buoyancy. Those stem floats without the body are referred to as pencil floats or quills.

Stem floats used to be made from wooden stems with cork bodies. These days, many are made from plastic. Most have a plastic or rubber sleeve, which fits over the stem at the top to fix the float in position on the line.

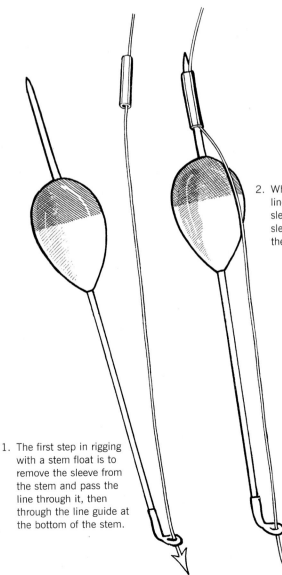

1. The first step in rigging with a stem float is to remove the sleeve from the stem and pass the line through it, then through the line guide at the bottom of the stem.

2. When the required amount of line has been passed through sleeve and line guide, slide the sleeve back over the stem to fix the float in position on the line.

3. Having fixed your float in position on the line, tie on your hook and weight the line with sufficient split shot to keep the float in an upright position. The split shot are clamped at intervals along the ine above the hook.

    We use a number of small weights (split shot) instead of one larger weight, firstly, to allow us to ballast the float more accurately, and secondly, to minimise the pendulum effect caused by a single large weight.

    While the pendulum effect does not seem to deter predatory fish like bonito, barracouta, tailor and salmon, it is to be avoided when seeking shy biters like luderick. It can also cause the leader to tangle around the main line when casting out.

    Some stem floats (like those used for luderick) carry sufficient ballast at the bottom of the stem to keep the float upright. This feature allows the angler to use, just enough weight (split shot) to present his bait in respect to depth and tide.

BOB FLOAT

Bob floats are popular among pier fishermen seeking mullet and garfish. The floats come in several sizes and consist of a plastic sphere, usually red and white, with a spring-loaded catch to fix them onto the line.

Although Bob floats are among the easiest floats to use, their application is limited. They tend to slide along the line and the spring mechanism corrodes fairly rapidly.

FIXED WAGGLER FLOAT

Wagglers are stem floats, and stem floats can be rigged as wagglers. However floats designed to be rigged as wagglers carry their body (if they have a body), lower on the stem, and the line guide at the bottom of the float is straight.

ALTERNATIVE RUNNING FLOAT

A running float may also be rigged by attaching a leader of heavy line to the lighter main line; say a 30 kg leader to a 10 kg mainline. We do this using the Improved Albright knot I have already described.

This rig is favoured by anglers live baiting from the rocks for pelagic fish such as tuna. You will appreciate that once the leader knot is on the reel, the angler has more control over the fish below. He may even be able to lift smaller fish like bonito straight out onto the rocks without gaffing them.

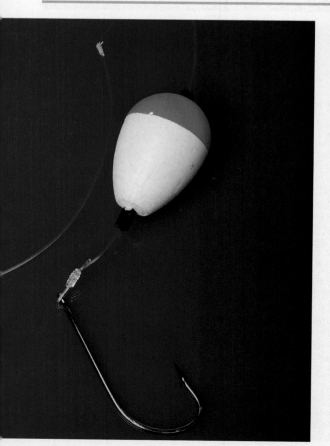

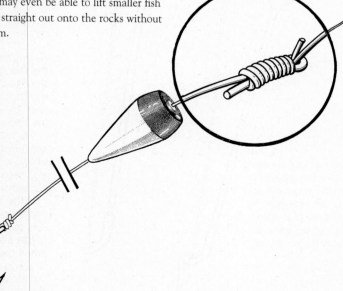

FIXED SINKER RIGS

Paternoster, or Fixed Sinker Rig, using Locked Half Blood Knot for all connections.
A preferred option when rigging for maximum strength such as in surf casting.

PATERNOSTER RIG

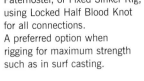

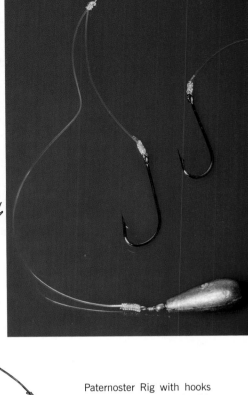

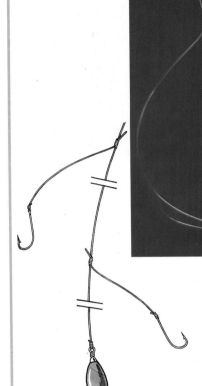

Paternoster Rig with hooks on droppers secured with triple surgeon's knot

RUNNING SINKER RIGS

1. Shown is the simplest of all running sinker rigs with the sinker running all of the way down to the hook. Although simple and effective, this rig has its limitations.

   Firstly, the sinker can't be too large because it may crush any of the bait threaded up the line above the hook. Secondly, no provision can be made for using a heavier leader to the hook, a desirable feature when seeking large fish like mulloway and big snapper.

2. Shown is a more complex running sinker rig featuring two hooks on a separate leader one sliding along the leader and one tied on the end. At the other end of the leader is a solid metal ring to which the hook leader is tied, the knot shown in both cases is a blood knot.

3. Shown is the Ezy Rig which slides along the line like a running sinker. It allows a bomb sinker, which would normally be tied on the end of the line, to be used as a running sinker.

   It consists of a plastic barrel, which slides along the line, to which is attached a metal snap for changing sinkers as required.

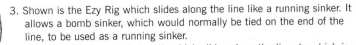

ROUGH BOTTOM RIG

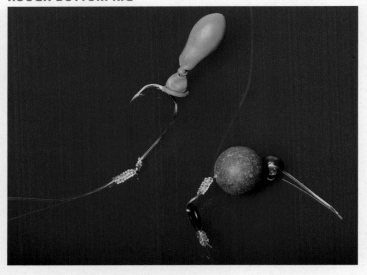

A. Big splash water bomb balloon inflated to thumbnail size to buoy bait up from bottom.

B. Bait rigged on two hooks and secured with hosiery elastic (Bait Mate).

C. Solid metal ring or swivel.

D. Ball sinker threaded on knot tag from main line.

F. Main line to rod and reel.

E. Removable split shot clamped onto knot tag to hold sinker in place.

BAITING UP AND FISHING WITH TUNA CIRCLES

Tuna circles are fish hooks which differ from conventional hooks in that the point of the hook faces back toward the shank at something approaching a right angle.

The tuna circle is designed to trap any ridge of cartilage, bone, gill-arch, lip, tongue, jaw hinge etc, in the gap between the point of the hook and the shank, a situation once initiated is almost impossible to reverse, hence their effectiveness.

Tuna circles have long been used by commercial long-liners, particularly for large pelagic fish like tuna, but they work equally well on all species from broadbill to bream.

They are especially effective in game and sportfishing situations where the fish may take a long time—sometimes hours—to bring in. This is because, once they are in place, tuna circles are very difficult to dislodge.

They are also particularly effective in bottom bouncing in the deep sea where any fish, once hooked, must be brought up a very long way, sometimes several hundred metres. Tuna circles save the disappointment many deep sea anglers experience on battling a really heavy blue eye trevalla, trumpeter or whatever, only to lose it when the hook tears out as it is nearing the boat.

Anglers rarely use tuna circles: Firstly, this is because they are usually forged in very heavy gauges to withstand the stresses of large fish hooked on heavy long-lines: Secondly they must be baited correctly or they will not work.

The first situation is being remedied by hook manufacturers: To date I have a sample of light gauge "Wasabi" tuna circles in sizes 1/0 to 5/0 from the New Zealand firm "Black Magic" and have been assured by other hook manufacturers their products will be soon be available as well.

The second situation is remedied by this article which details some deadly methods of baiting with tuna circles. Let's see how the job is done.

1. This simple method of rigging a strip of fish or squid is surprisingly effective when fish are "on the go". The main disadvantage of baiting like this, particularly with soft baits, is that the bait is likely to be pulled right off the hook by small, unwanted species before a big fish comes along.

2. This is the first step to making a strip bait more secure when the fishing is a bit slow, or, when the bait is deployed at some depth where it may be inconvenient to check it often. The diagram shows the leader being pulled right through the bait.

3. Next we fold the strip and impale the fold with the point of the hook. Not too deep mind you because we don't want to obstruct the gap between the point and the shank. If we do this, then the hook becomes ineffective.

4. This is a more secure bait presentation. Some anglers may be deterred by seeing how proud the hook sits out from the bait, but that is a situation which can be easily remedied.

5. The first step in making the hook appear less conspicuous is to cut the strip off below the hook.

6. Fold the cut section over tightly and impale the fold.

7. Push the folded strip down into the curve of the hook. This is a very effective bait presentation which substantially hides the hook without reducing its efficacy. Its disadvantage is that the bait is inclined to spin on the retrieve or when fished in a current.

The spinning bait problem is substantially solved in deep sea presentations when the hook is rigged on a twisted dropper loop which is far less inclined to spin and tangle around the main line.

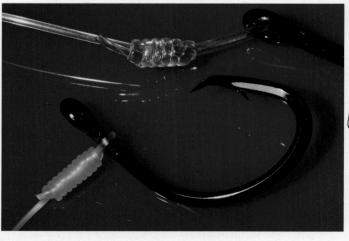

DOUBLE PINCH METHOD OF STRIP BAITING CIRCLES

When baiting strips of squid or fish on circle hooks, care needs to be taken not to obscure the gap between the point and the shank. The double pinch method of baiting strip baits on circles meets that requirement.

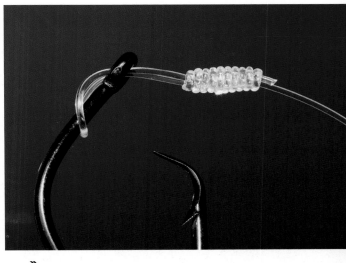

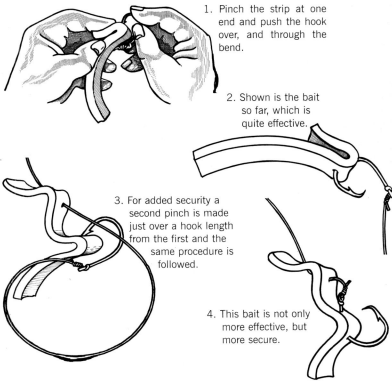

1. Pinch the strip at one end and push the hook over, and through the bend.

2. Shown is the bait so far, which is quite effective.

3. For added security a second pinch is made just over a hook length from the first and the same procedure is followed.

4. This bait is not only more effective, but more secure.

5. The bait may be made more attractive by first, trimming the ends off the strip.

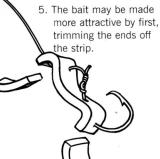

6. Then impaling those ends on the hook.

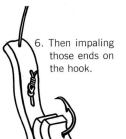

The knot used here is the Nail Knot with Loop refer to page 59.

RIGGING CIRCLES ON CABLE

Circle hooks, like the Mustad 39960, may be rigged on 7 strand or 49 strand cable to great effect on sharks and other game fish.

1. Thread the cable through a suitable size metal sleeve, then through the eye of the hook from the front.

2. Loop the cable around the front of the shank, back through the eye of the hook and then through the sleeve.

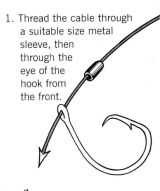

3. Extend the loop of cable, put in a half twist, and loop it over the point of the hook.

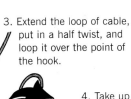

4. Take up the loop, slide the sleeve right up the hook, then — using a set of crimping pliers — crimp the sleeve firmly so the cable cannot slip.

5. Trim the tag from the cable and the hook is secure, but kicked out at a sharp angle to the cable.

6. The bait, in this case a fish fillet, is secured to the leader using electrical cable ties, taking care that the hook remains kicked out from the bait at an angle.

LIVE BAITING WITH TUNA CIRCLES

Tuna circles are probably the best live baiting hooks ever designed. This is how to bait them.

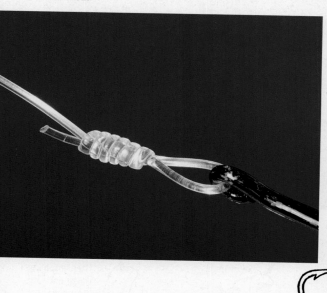

1. Impale the bait fish sideways through the nose.

2. This is the finished bait. Note particularly that the gap between the point and the shank is not obstructed.

BAITING TUNA CIRCLES WITH SOFT BAITS

Tuna flesh without any skin on it, a handful of pipis, mussels oysters, pieces of cray-tail and bait fish like slimy mackerel and pilchards which have been frozen then thawed out again are soft baits.

We attach these soft baits to tuna circle hooks using hosiery elastic which is sold in fishing tackle outlets as Bait Mate. Here is how we bait up with a pilchard. A slimy mackerel requires the same treatment.

1. Drive the point into the bait just behind the breast bone, but not too deep. Then push it forward and bring it back out again.

2. Lay the leader alongside the bait with a strand of Bait Mate, preparatory to commencing a binding down the bait from the tail wrist.

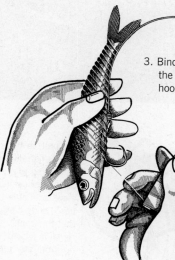

3. Bind the bait tightly all the way down to the hook.

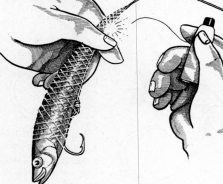

4. Then bind it all the way back again, continuing right past the tail, then back to the tail wrist before snapping the elastic so that it bites into the bait and will not come undone. These baiting methods ensure excellent results with conventional hooks as well, but they are particularly suited to tuna circles because they do not obstruct the gap between the point and the shank.

FISH HEAD ON TWO HOOKS

When pickers and lice are on the job, flesh baits do not last very long. That is why fish heads, like this small barracouta head, are preferred when seeking large fish like snapper which may take their time in coming along.

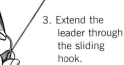

1. Tie one hook to the end of your trace of leader and bind the other in place using hosiery elastic (Bait Mate) so that it slides under pressure.

2. Pin the jaws with the sliding hook.

3. Extend the leader through the sliding hook.

4. Take a half wrap around the head with the leader and pin the head above the gill cover as shown.

5. Close up the two hooks once more by pulling the leader gently through the binding on the second hook.

RIGGING WITH WIRE: FLEMISH EYE

The Flemish Eye is used to attach hooks, rings and swivels to seven and forty-nine strand wire when sport and game fishing. The Flemish Eye is secured with a sleeve, which is firmly crimped with a special pair of pliers called a crimping tool.

1. First slide a sleeve of the correct size over the wire you are using. The size of sleeve required is specified on the packaging of the wire. Sleeves may also be supplied with the wire.

2. Thread on the hook and make an overhand knot in the wire on the eye of the hook.

3. Add one more wrap so that you have an overhand knot with two wraps, not one.

4. Thread the tag through the sleeve alongside the standing part.

5. Slide the Flemish Eye up tight on the eye of the hook, slide the sleeve right up against that, then crimp the sleeve with the crimping tool.

6. Trim off the tag and your hook is secure. Or, an alternative is to leave a short tag which is taped to the standing part to avoid injury from wire splinters.

MULTIPLE HOOK RIGS: DOUBLE RIGGING ON WIRE

Two-hook rigs are used in game fishing, particularly when trolling lures. This rig, which consists of two hooks, a swivel, a length of multi-strand wire and crimped sleeves, is assembled using a series of Flemish Eyes, a configuration described above.

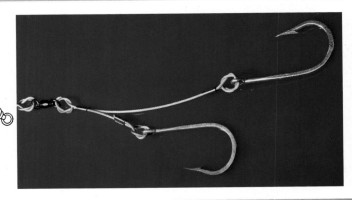

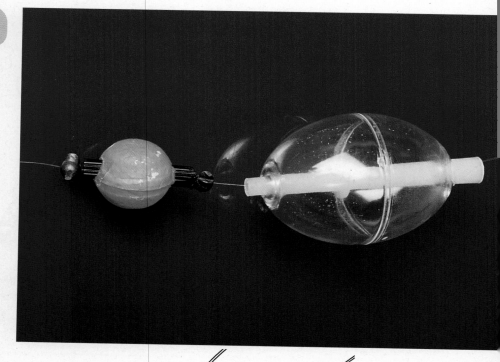

RIGGING WITH AN EGG-SHAPED BUBBLE FLOAT

Bubble floats are used in freshwater fishing. They are made from clear plastic and may be spherical or egg-shaped. Bubble floats are designed to be partially filled with water to give them added weight for casting. This is achieved by removing bungs in the spherical float and by displacing the central tube in the egg-shaped float.

The bubble float is rigged as a running float but differs from most running floats in that it does not suspend the baited hook. The baited hook is suspended from a tiny secondary float which is fixed on the line to regulate the depth at which the bait will be presented, and as a stopper on which the bubble rests when being cast out or retrieved.

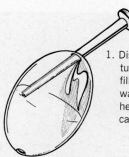

1. Displace the central tube and partially fill the float with water so it will be heavy enough to cast out.

2a. Replace the tube and thread your line through the float.

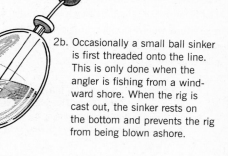

2b. Occasionally a small ball sinker is first threaded onto the line. This is only done when the angler is fishing from a windward shore. When the rig is cast out, the sinker rests on the bottom and prevents the rig from being blown ashore.

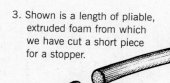

3. Shown is a length of pliable, extruded foam from which we have cut a short piece for a stopper.

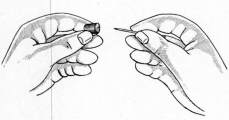

4. Make a hole right through the piece of foam with a needle. Should you use a piece of cork, you will need to heat the needle first so you can burn a hole through it.

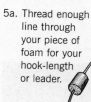

5a. Thread enough line through your piece of foam for your hook-length or leader.

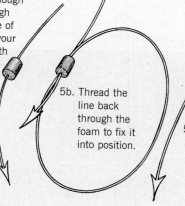

5b. Thread the line back through the foam to fix it into position.

5c. I suggest threading the line through the foam a second time, just to make sure it won't slip when you cast out.

6. Shown is the completed rig baited with a dragon fly larva. The baited hook is suspended from the tiny piece of foam so that the fish can take the bait without having to move the bubble float which would probably scare it off.

BUMPER KNOT OR SALMON EGG LOOP

This knot produces a loop along the shank of the hook enabling the use of soft, delicate baits like salmon roe. When tested this knot retained the full breaking strain of the line.

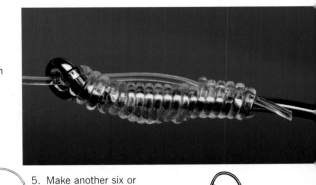

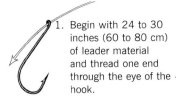

1. Begin with 24 to 30 inches (60 to 80 cm) of leader material and thread one end through the eye of the hook.

2. Adjust the length of the tag to the length of the hook and begin wrapping the shank of the hook, and tag, with the standing part of the leader. Wrapping in an anti-clockwise direction is suggested because this makes finishing the knot easier.

3. Make a series of tight wraps down the shank of the hook. Eight wraps are shown here but the number of wraps is determined by the size of loop required. Then thread the other end of the leader back through the eye of the hook leaving a loop large enough to make several more wraps around the hook.

4. Turn the hook around the other way and commence wrapping the entire hook and standing part of the leader – the part you just passed back through the eye of the hook – with the loop.

5. Make another six or seven wraps.

6. Close the loop by extracting the standing part of the leader with one hand while holding the wraps against the hook with the other.

7. Trim the tag up short and the knot is finished.

DOUBLE HOOK BUMPER KNOT

Used for slow-trolling, and drifting with small, live and dead fish baits for a variety of salt and freshwater predators, the double hook Bumper knot is well worth learning how to tie.

After adding a second hook to the leader, it was shown during testing that premature separations could occur if the eye of the hook was threaded before wrapping was commenced. This happened when weight was exerted on the bottom hook causing the line to pinch down into the gap between the end of the wire forming the eye and the shank of the hook. The problem was completely overcome by using the following strategy.

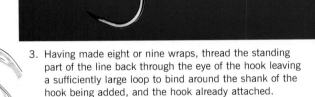

1. Lay the standing part of the line alongside the second hook to be added and twist a loop into the line near the eye of the hook as shown.

2. Commence a series of tight wraps down the shank of the hook, just as we did when attaching the first hook.

3. Having made eight or nine wraps, thread the standing part of the line back through the eye of the hook leaving a sufficiently large loop to bind around the shank of the hook being added, and the hook already attached.

4. The method of wrapping the added hook is shown and becomes relatively easy with practice.

5. Close the loop as we did with the single hook Bumper knot and trim the tag.

RIGGING SPINNERBAITS

Cameron Jones devised this inventive method to allow quick changing spinnerbaits.

3. This can be prevented by a short length of plastic tube, the type used for aquarium aerators.

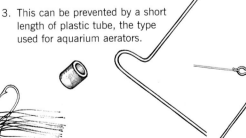

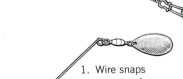

1. Wire snaps are great for attaching spinner baits, no doubt of that.

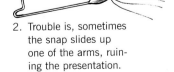

2. Trouble is, sometimes the snap slides up one of the arms, ruining the presentation.

4. Just slide the piece of hose over the bend in the wire before attaching the snap.

5. The problem is solved.

HOW TO HOOK FRESHWATER BAITS

SCRUBWORMS

Earthworms and scrubworms are excellent bait for most freshwater species. They may be used singly or in a bunch of two or more as shown in these diagrams.

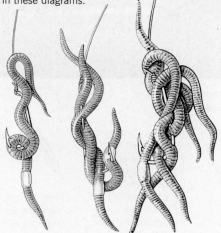

BARDI GRUBS

Bardi grubs are a great Murray cod bait. They are best fished alive but will soon die and discolour if pierced with the hook. This is why we bind bardi grubs to the hook with the elastic thread Bait Mate to which we referred earlier.

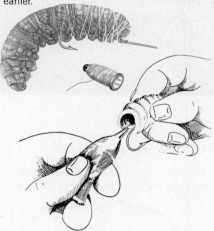

BARDI GRUB TIPS

To best prepare bardi grubs for storage, blanche grubs in boiling water for 28 seconds and freeze overnight. Then store in freezer bags—almost as good as fresh baits and will keep for ages.

Try Fred Jobson's method to make bardi grubs irresistible by cutting a large fresh grub in half and filling the body of the grub with a fish scent, such as Halco Scent.

CATERPILLAR

Best hooked through the body.

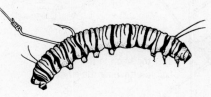

MUDEYES

Mudeyes, the aquatic larval form of various dragon flies, are prized for bait. Mostly they are used live, the hook penetrating their newly forming wings.

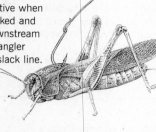

GRASSHOPPERS

Grasshoppers are most effective when lightly hooked and drifted downstream while the angler feeds out slack line.

MAGGOTS

Blowfly maggots are used in fresh water for a wide variety of fish, but will take saltwater species like garfish, bream and whiting to name just a few.

Maggots are hooked in the tail (large) end on a small hook say size 12 down to 16. They may be used singly or several at a time.

FRESHWATER CRAYFISH

Freshwater crayfish are usually fished live with the hook through the tail, with or without a running sinker. Remove or break the moveable joint on pincers to prevent it from crawling under snags.

When using dead crayfish crush the body to bet out all juices. Place a piece of bardi grub on hook end as shown.

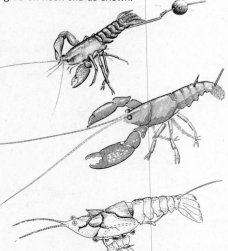

SHRIMPS

Hook in tail and always use live if possible. They can be single hooked backwards or double rigged with the hook through both tails.

MINNOWS & GALAXIDS

Minnow are used for trout in fresh water. Two minnow hooked on the same hook will often be taken eagerly when single presentations are ignored. Try any of the presentations shown, twin minnow hooked through tail, above the lateral line behind the shoulder, through the upper jaw or with two hooks and a half hitch on the tail.

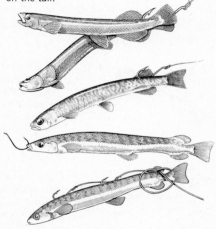

WHITEBAIT & GLASSIES

Hook through gill and eye with a half hitch on the tail. Also can employ a free running hook and attach just forward of tail. To rig whitebait for trolling behind a downrigger hook through the jaw and again under the belly.

SOFT PLASTIC RIGS

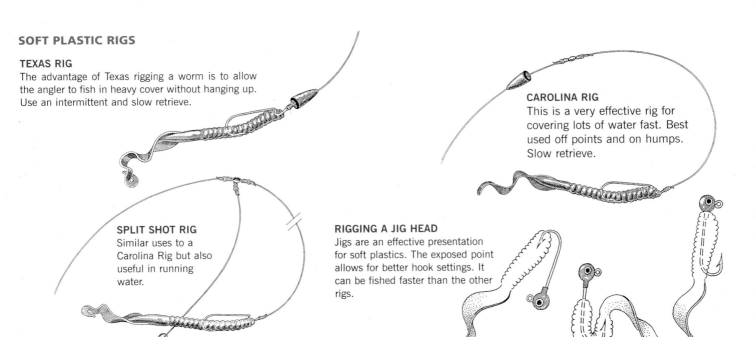

TEXAS RIG
The advantage of Texas rigging a worm is to allow the angler to fish in heavy cover without hanging up. Use an intermittent and slow retrieve.

CAROLINA RIG
This is a very effective rig for covering lots of water fast. Best used off points and on humps. Slow retrieve.

SPLIT SHOT RIG
Similar uses to a Carolina Rig but also useful in running water.

RIGGING A JIG HEAD
Jigs are an effective presentation for soft plastics. The exposed point allows for better hook settings. It can be fished faster than the other rigs.

RIGGING RUBBER WORMS ON WORM HOOKS

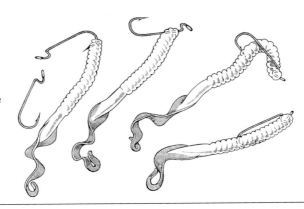

HOW TO RIG A RUBBER WORM HOOK: BERKLEY
To rig a worm, start the hook in the nose of the bait and bring it out 1/4 inch from the nose. Slide the worm up over the eye and rotate the hook 180° and re-enter and push the hook back until it's just under the surface of the worm.

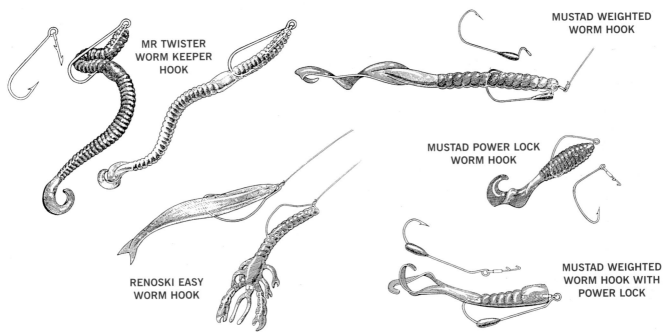

MR TWISTER
WORM KEEPER
HOOK

MUSTAD WEIGHTED
WORM HOOK

MUSTAD POWER LOCK
WORM HOOK

RENOSKI EASY
WORM HOOK

MUSTAD WEIGHTED
WORM HOOK WITH
POWER LOCK

RIGGING A STRIP BAIT

This is an excellent way of rigging an unweighted strip bait on heavy tackle. It is ideally suited for drifting down a berley trail because it can be deployed and retrieved continually without deforming or spinning. Your leader may be heavy nylon monofilament or multistrand wire and your hook should be straight, not kirbed or reversed, because this may cause the bait to spin.

In addition to your hook, leader and bait, you will need a length of .7 mm galvanised tie wire which is available from almost every hardware store. Should .7 mm not be available, you can use .8 mm.

1. First cut a suitable strip, either from a small tuna or other oily fish. The strip should be in the shape of an elongated, isosceles triangle.

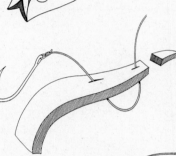

2. Cut off the pointed end so there is some width to the narrowest end. Then, using your hook as a needle, draw your leader through at the narrow end, then back again about a third of the way down.

3. Turn you hook around and, with the point of the hook facing away from the leader and down toward the end of the bait, push it into the skin side of the strip.

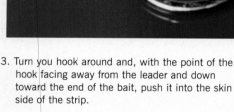

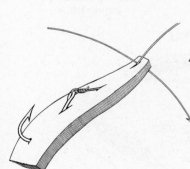

4. Then back out the same side so the point of the hook emerges from the bait near the end of the strip.

Having secured the hook in the bait, we now need to secure the leader to the bait with the galvanised tie wire. Push a 30 cm or so length through the bait where you first punctured it with the hook.

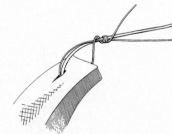

5. With the bait central on the wire, bend both wire tags back along the leader and, beginning as close as practical to the end of the strip, wind one tag tightly around the other, and the leader, in series of barrel rolls.

6a. Having completed about eight wraps, wrap the protruding tag tightly around the leader also, making sure that you leave about 10 cm of tag sticking out from each wrap.

6b. To break the tags off close to the wraps, we bend the tag over so that it forms a handle or crank. Do this with each tag in turn.

6c. Using the handle you have made, wind the tag around until it breaks off. Do each in turn so that there are no sharp tags to catch in your hand or clothing.

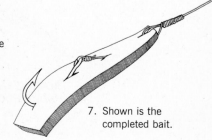

7. Shown is the completed bait.

MAKING A DOUBLE LOOP BRIDLE FOR LIVE BAIT TROLLING

Towing bridles for live bait trolling vary a good deal. We use the double-loop bridle pre-tied in monofilament because it allows the bait to be attached and placed back in the water in the shortest possible time: This is around 15 seconds for practised operators.

To make a double-loop bridle we need a rigged leader with a suitable hook attached, a length of 24 kg monofilament or thereabouts, an open-eye live-baiting needle and a loop gauge which can be a pencil or pen.

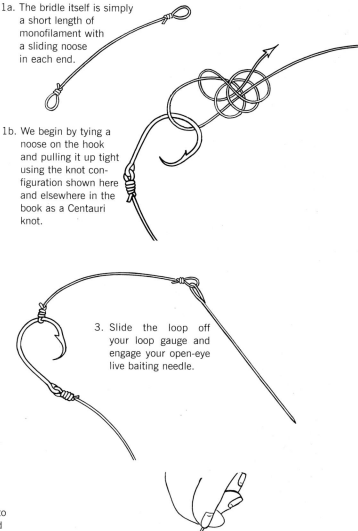

1a. The bridle itself is simply a short length of monofilament with a sliding noose in each end.

1b. We begin by tying a noose on the hook and pulling it up tight using the knot configuration shown here and elsewhere in the book as a Centauri knot.

2a Then we tie another sliding noose in the other end of the monofilament, keeping in mind the bridle needs to be quite short, say 100 mm for towing striped tuna and about 75 mm for slimy mackerel or frigates. Tying bridles of this short length does take a little practice.

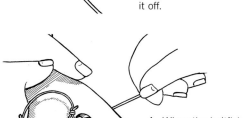

2b. Close the loop up on your loop gauge or pen, but not so tight that you can't get it off.

3. Slide the loop off your loop gauge and engage your open-eye live baiting needle.

4. When the baitfish comes aboard, the hook is usually cut straight off to save time, and the needle is passed straight through the eye tunnel of the baitfish taking care not to damage the eyes.

5. Pull the second loop right though and hook it over the point of the hook. Then disengage the loop from the open-eye needle.

6. The bait is placed back in the water and trolled slowly, usually as slow as the boat can go — and if possible — back toward the shoal of fish from which the bait was caught.

   Note there is a little slack in the bridle. This allows the hook to fold bait easily when it is taken by the game fish. Anglers who rig the hook too tightly on the head miss fish because of this.

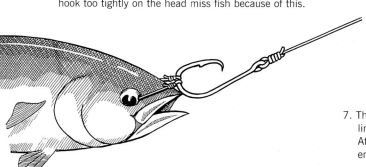

7. The angler holds the line by hand and pulls about twenty metres of line from the reel to act as a drop back when the fish takes the bait. At this point the drag adjustment on the reel should be just heavy enough to prevent an over-run when the drop-back is taken up.

   The fish is struck by the angler by placing the reel in strike drag, and signalling to the boat driver to accelerate the boat forward. This takes up any slack line in the water and, hopefully, hooks the fish.

RIGGING A GARFISH AS A SKIP BAIT

Garfish may be rigged as skip baits on either heavy monofilament or wire. This method deals with rigging a garfish on monofilament but 49 strand cable could be substituted where mackerel or other "toothy critters" are sought.

To rig this bait you will need a large garfish, a length of heavy monofilament or 49 strand cable with a suitable size hook for the garfish you are using, and a roll of 0.7 or 0.8 mm galvanised tie wire which is available in hardware stores. An awl or stout needle is also useful for making pilot holes for the wire.

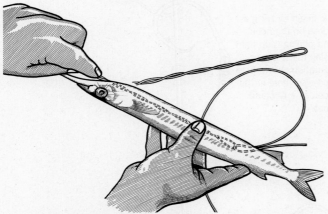

1. Begin by taking 60 cm or so of the galvanised wire, bending it over and twisting it together to form a baiting needle.
   Push the rounded end into the gills of the gar, down through body and out of its anus. Then , thread the bend in the wire with your leader and draw it inside the body of the gar.

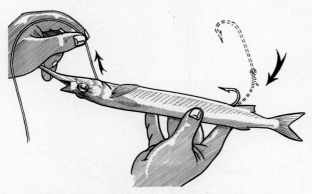

2. Pull the leader all of the way through until only the curve and spear of the hook protrude.

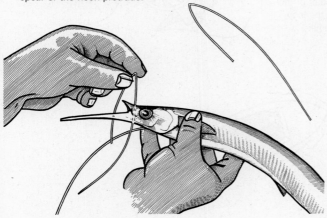

3. Take a 30 cm length of your galvanised wire and bend it into a V shape but with one side of the V about twice as long as the other.
   Push the long side of your wire V down through the centre of the gar's jaw hinge. Then, push the short side of the V through the gar's beak, right at the apex of the bottom jaw.
   You may need to use an awl or stout needle to make the pilot holes for the wire.

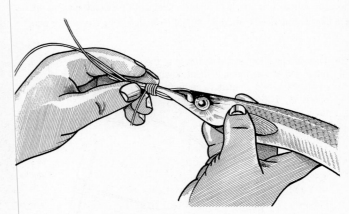

4. Push the wire V right down so it's flush with the jaw hinge and the longer side of the wire now faces forward alongside the bill.
   Next, wrap the short piece of wire around the bill of the gar, the leader, and the longer piece of wire.

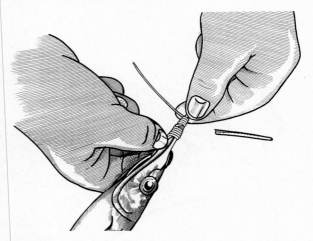

5. Having used up the short piece of wire wrapping the bill, leader and long end of the wire, snip the bill off just ahead of the wraps, then wrap the leader tightly with the longer wire until it too is used up.

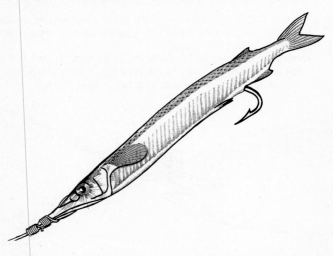

6. Rigged this way the gar can be trolled as a skip bait to entice a wide range of pelagic fish including tuna, sailfish and marlin.

CHAPTER FOUR

LURE FISHING &
LURE GUIDE

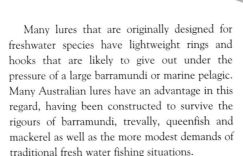

Using lures is fun. Casting and trolling them everywhere from bluewater for gamefish, through mangrove creeks, inshore reefs, rocks and estuaries to alpine rivers, lakes, slower rivers in the tropics and inland can be the most successful and satisfying way to fish in many situations. It is simply a matter of tying on a lure, chucking it out and either retrieving it or letting it swim behind the boat while you cruise around. Right?—Wrong! Very wrong.

There is a whole lot more to fishing with lures, although the chuck and chance brigade often has terrific fun catching the odd aggressive fish. But if you want to improve your catches and meet the challenge of successful lure fishing and enjoy it more, then here is a whole host of hints and information for you to digest and try.

Most anglers have definite ideas about what constitutes a good lure. Usually their favourite lure is determined by a history of success. This success generally develops on the basis of pub talk, what the fishing magazines say is hot, what your mates are using, local knowledge and what your recent results have been.

The adage that you can only use lures one at a time is certainly true and most anglers, resplendent with bulging tackle boxes containing hundreds of the latest lure offerings will continue to drag the same two or three around for hour after hour, even when getting no hits whatsoever. Consequently, favourite lures catch more fish than those that slowly rust in the bottom of the tackle box.

Let's assume that we were going to start selecting lures based upon their quality, special features and versatility. What factors are important in selecting the best lures? To be objective, we will ignore the rumour that your best mate caught heaps on his own special 'one-off' lure last week.

Some of the most important considerations for purchasing lures are the finish, price, action, size, and availability. The finish gives a good indication of how the lure will perform when you are using it. Splotchy paint work, crooked bibs and poor sanding on wooden lures or rough joins, bubbled finishes and glue globs on plastic lures gives an indication that something else is probably not right. If you have several examples of one lure type, all of which are difficult to tune, forget them. Often the hooks or hook attachments are of inferior quality and may give out on that trophy fish.

Many lures that are originally designed for freshwater species have lightweight rings and hooks that are likely to give out under the pressure of a large barramundi or marine pelagic. Many Australian lures have an advantage in this regard, having been constructed to survive the rigours of barramundi, trevally, queenfish and mackerel as well as the more modest demands of traditional fresh water fishing situations.

The price and availability of a lure are particularly important if it is successful. Very expensive and hard to get lures may not catch as many fish, as anglers are overly cautious with them. It is frustrating to lose the last one of a special lure or that productive colour and not be able to replace it.

It is true to say that highly priced lures represent good quality. However, cheaper lures do not automatically represent poor quality. Lures such as River2Sea, McLaughlin's, Juro and the Producers lures offer a lower price while still delivering products that catch fish and perform very well. Other value for money lures such as the spoons, Tasmanian Devils and spinnerbaits have the advantage of sinking and working the strike zone close to cover on the cast. These underutilised lures need to be cheap, because their life expectancy is less than for standard diving lures, many of which can float back out of snags.

It's an advantage if the lure is available in a variety of sizes. This will allow you to change size without altering other lure characteristics. This is important when targeting different species and sizes of fish and imitating different sizes of prey. Lures with wider ranges such as Halco, Bomber, Rebel, Bill Norman, Predatek, Rapala, Storm, Majik and Custom Crafted have an edge in this area.

In looking for the perfect lure, we give you the thoughts of long time lure making master Steve Kovacs of Custom Crafted lures. Nothing has changed since 1991, when Steve first gave me this insight, to make this comment any less relevant to lure manufacturers or users of today and tomorrow.

'There are a lot of novice fishermen around so one of the most important features is to design a lure which will track true and maintain a good depth at a variety of trolling speeds. Many anglers, both experienced and new, cannot, or do not know how to, tune a lure and aren't interested in learning! If the lure maker can design a lure which is very easy to tune and rarely plays up then he is well in front of his competitors. Rattles or not, sinking or floating, size of bib, location of pull point, angle and shape of bib, size of lure including size of hooks, action required etc, etc, etc. All are thoughts and considerations that race through a dedicated lure maker's mind each time a new lure is created and there is always another design on the backburner.'

Our tests provided us with the perfect forum to see if the perfect lure has been created. The verdict—there is always room for improvement, and we will still most likely tie on our favourite lure first.

THE BEST LURES

Action is by far one of the most important key attributes of a good lure. Key actions include a tight sway, wobble or vibrating action for trout and a medium or wide sway for native fish. Metal lures and poppers are particularly successful for the pelagic marine species.

There are basically three directions which a lure can move in while being trolled or retrieved. With the action description these are described as sway (side to side action), wobble (rolling action) and pitch (bucking up and down action).

There are very few lures that can move in all three directions without losing control and threatening to blow out. A lure travelling at the right speed will sway and wobble. It may occasionally dart out from side to side, which is particularly enticing to fish. As the speed increases, these darts to the side become wider and the recovery of the lure becomes more difficult. Finally the lure 'blows out' and rolls over onto its back and planes to the surface.

Few lures have the capacity to also move in the third direction—which is pitch. In most instances, once a lures starts 'bucking', it is likely to blow out at any increase in speed. With most lures, once they started to increase their pitch (bucking), they needed to be run more slowly and then they ran much more stably. It can be a very fine line between great, erratic action and a lure that is deemed unreliable because it is too fussy with its speed and keeps coming to the surface.

The assessment of action and quality is somewhat subjective. What looks attractive to us standing outside the flume tank might not look nearly as attractive to the fish.

However, after testing 1065 lures, I am willing to go out on a limb and nominate the 'Best' lure in the tests. It is the **DK Lures Scale Raza 20+.** The Yo-Zuri Hydro Squirt, Rapala Jointed Shad Rap 5, Reef Runner Deep Diver, Small Dinkum Yabby, MinMin Deep and Magnum Hellbender were also deemed to be exceptional lures.

THE ATTRACTIVE QUALITIES IN A LURE—THE 'SO DAM HOT' FORMULA

Since most lures are supposed to imitate food or stimulate an aggressive response in fish, it is necessary to look at the important factors that put a fish on your line. Each time I have published this formula it has evolved slightly and it has again. This is because of the importance of angler controlled factors such as experience and flexibility that make an enormous difference to results. It is up to you to practise and keep trying things on a day when it seems all the fish have lockjaw.

> THE CRUCIAL FACTORS IN ORDER ARE:
> 1. Skill (Knowledge)
> 2. Objectivity (Flexibility)
> 3. Depth
> 4. Action
> 5. Mass (Size)
> 6. Haste (Speed)
> 7. Outline (Shape)
> 8. Tone (Colour)
>
> This gives SO DAM HOT
> The formula for the successful use of lures.

SKILL

Knowledge, skill and experience are extremely important attributes for the successful use of lures. It is independent of the lures themselves and needs to be gathered yourself or learned from watching or fishing with someone who knows what works best.

While books like this and fishing magazines provide wonderful tips and hints to make you more successful, there is no substitute for getting out there and having a go yourself. It is only when you start getting hits on casts that land right next to the snag for bass or barramundi that you can see just how important it is. And with practice and good equipment, putting the lures into the right spot more often means that your catches will improve. Those without a lot of experience will catch fish, but those with it will catch them much more consistently.

OBJECTIVITY (FLEXIBILITY)

Some anglers have one or two tried and true lures or techniques and will stick with them through thick and thin. These old favourites have consistently performed and as a consequence get a swim most often. This is fine when things are going well, but I firmly believe that the truly great anglers are not the ones who catch 12 when everyone else is catching 6 or 7 fish, but the angler that catches one or two when everyone else is coming back empty handed.

It is really important to be open-minded and keep trying new things and not just as a last resort. Over the years I have immensely enjoyed fishing with Rod Harrison who is one of the most innovative anglers I know. Rod is always trying something new, a bit different and coming up with the goods on a regular basis.

Try a larger lure or a smaller one, use a suspending lure instead of a floater or give a spinnerbait or rattlin' spot lure a go. If you are getting follows but not hits, experiment until you get the right combination that turns a day of frustration into a day to remember.

DEPTH

Successful anglers are those who keep their lures in areas where they can be eaten by the most fish for the longest possible time. The strike zone is three dimensional and although fish will move upwards more readily than they will move downwards to take a lure, you need to get the lure close enough to the fish to evoke a response.

Most fish are lazy. They want to get the best possible return in food for expending the least possible energy. If your lure is right in front of their nose you will get many more hits than if they have to move up 5 metres in the water column (which is about equivalent to about one atmosphere of pressure).

Put in its simplest terms, it is no good trolling for trout at one metre deep when the surface temperature is 26 degrees Celsius, or trolling with lead core line if actively feeding fish are rising all around you.

In practice, the use of depth can dramatically improve your lure fishing results. Presenting your lure (or bait if you are using more active methods) where target fish can take it, must, logic dictates, improve your results.

Shallow divers, like this Shakespeare minnow can take bottom dwellers such as this flathead. Most fish will move much further up in the water column to take a lure and active fish will hungrily chase lures of the right size and action.

ACTION AND MASS

Action and mass (size) can be varied regularly with different lures trolled at the same time—such as a Rapala Fat Rap, a Spinnerbait and a Flatfish. It is possible to quickly confirm which size and action type is working best, and alter the other lures to further explore these areas.

Some action types work better for some species and it pays to match the hatch in terms of what the fish are eating to maximise strikes.

Better use of things such as trolling sinkers, different trolling lengths, lighter or heavier line or braid lines will enable you to present a much wider variety of lures at the same depth. If your sounder is telling you that fish are there, you should experiment to see if you can catch them.

HASTE (SPEED)

Speed (haste) is more difficult to experiment with and often needs a complete change of lure type. As a result, anglers do not change speeds too often whilst fishing.

For example, lures such as the Flatfish and Tasmanian Devil are incompatible when trolling. You either troll with medium paced lures such as the Rapala Countdown minnows, other spoons or a Tasmanian Devil, or with slow running lures to use with a Flatfish, Mann's, or Hot Shot.

This is an area worth investigating if other tactics are not working.

OUTLINE (SHAPE)

I have included outline (shape or profile) because there are times when it makes a dramatic difference. In fresh water, many baitfish such as smelt and gudgeons are long and skinny. Lures like the McGrath diver and Rapala minnows are excellent imitations and do very well. In salt water, whitebait, pilchards and prawns also have a narrow profile and many metal and diving lures imitate these common foods.

However, bony bream and goldfish are more bulky, so lures with a wider profile can work better. Yabbies provide yet another outline that can be imitated. In salt water, bony herring, small trevally, bream and snapper and cuttlefish have a broader profile.

In low light conditions or murky water, the general profile of your lure or their prey would be all that would register with a fish. A quick inspection of the stomach contents of your first fish should provide a short-cut to the size and profile departments.

TONE (COLOUR)

Lastly there is colour (tone). It is truly said that colour catches more fishermen than fish. I am not suggesting that colour is irrelevant, but to change colour ten times before experimenting with the other factors is not making best use of your fishing time.

In the flume tank, the contrast of light and dark colours showed up extremely well under water. The classical coachdog or striped patterns were far more visible than single colour lures. Even the stripes on a Fat Rap perch colour, which are difficult to see out of water, were very obvious in the tank. The new holographic colours and metallic finishes did add extra flash and have an important place.

With some of the Chinese lures, fantastic colours can mask ordinary action and performance, so don't just fall for a pretty face with a lure.

It is interesting to note that red lures are much more popular than black ones, yet at a trolling depth of 5 metres, the red washes out completely. Therefore, in a fishing sense, red is, and has been for a long time the 'new' black.

Research has shown that fluorescent colours are a definite turn on for some species at some times while they can be a turn off at other times. Colour is one area where fishes' underwater perception may be vastly different to ours, but in my experience, the times when only one colour works effectively are far fewer than the tales in pubs would have you believe.

At the end of the day, changing colours increases confidence and improves the way we fish. This, and a tendency to need to own every lure in every colour, not only helps the economy of Australia, it adds to the overall enjoyment of lure fishing.

LURE FISHING TACTICS

All this information is of only passing interest if it can't be put into practical use. The lure depths are much easier to use if you have a good quality depth sounder.

If the sounder is able to identify where the fish are, it is a matter of presenting a lure that will have the right action and run at the right depth. This is where these tables come into their own.

Many of us are guilty of trolling past a fish on the sounder and shaking our heads if we don't get a strike. Comments like 'Probably a carp or redfin' or 'school of baitfish', often follow. We ignore the fact that last week those same blips were good fish that were taking lures.

Although depth is perhaps the most critical element in successful trolling, it needs to be considered as only part of the overall SO DAM HOT picture.

With many cover-orientated species, locating a fish is only the beginning of the battle. With perseverance, and the patience to experiment until a successful formula is reached, many of these fish can be coaxed into striking.

ACTIVE NEUTRAL AND PASSIVE FISH

Fish can be loosely grouped into active, neutral and passive in their behaviour.

How they react to your lure will be determined by a variety of factors relating to the weather, season, availability of food and your presentation.

Contrary to local belief, it is very rare that fish aren't hungry. They are all designed to feed well while food is plentiful and this helps growth or the development of eggs or sperm. Some species such as golden perch will develop thick bands of fat if they remain where food is plentiful, while tailor simply regurgitate their food to keep feeding.

ACTIVE FISH

Active or aggressive fish are the stuff of fishing dreams. This is when trout and bass hit anything you put in front of them and fresh and saltwater fish will chase lures anywhere.

At times when fish are particularly active, the main objective is to put a lure close enough for the fish to see and eat it. Active fish will often move great distances to catch food, especially at their preferred depth.

It is possible to fish too deep at these times and this can be a big risk. Active fish will readily move up to take a lure, but will rarely move deeper. It is therefore possible to be dragging your lure through a fish desert even though you could be only slightly too deep.

Catching active fish is well illustrated when trolling lures like the Tasmanian Devil in fresh water. They run shallowly, but give off strong vibrations, are highly visible and attract active, feeding trout like magnets.

The factors which trigger large numbers of fish to become active include a rising water level or low level floods, rising barometer (although local storms often make bass very active). Pre-spawning or post- spawning behaviour, moon phases, tidal conditions and the availability of preferred food items. Spawning aggregations in particular can make fish very aggressive, either because the competition for available food is intense or as part of protecting their areas from other fish.

Kurt Blanksby, using baits and lures, hooked this big tailor at Kalbarri.

Even a small fingermark can test tackle with its explosive strike and speed to return to its home snag. Drag must be set correctly and knots tested.

NEUTRAL FISH

Neutral fish are still catchable but require a better presentation. Factors such as lure size and action may mean the difference between success and failure.

Most of the native fish and reef species spend a great deal of their time in a neutral mode. They will feed when the right food presents itself, but they will not expend a lot of energy in catching it. They may move a few metres to hit a lure, but they may just nudge it, or swipe and miss.

When there are large numbers of neutral fish, you have to work at it. But your efforts will be rewarded. Experiments pay off and what works for one area, specific spot or even fish, may not be the answer around the corner.

With trout, additional attractors such as cowbells are often the trigger that induces strikes. Sometimes fluorescent colours help, but your lure needs to be closer to the fish to get a strike. Conditions that result in neutral fish include constant or slowly falling water levels, long term stable barometer, continuing clear or foul weather spawning behaviour and an overabundance of food.

PASSIVE FISH

Passive or inactive fish present a real challenge. This is when the tough get going and only the best anglers can consistently take fish.

There is no doubt that there is an element of luck, as finding the one active fish on a day when everything else is holed up can be the only fish taken. However, to consistently take fish under these circumstances takes real skill and perseverance.

Presentations can be perfect and still not get a response. You can often drag a lure past the nose of a passive brown trout or Coral trout forever without ever getting a response. However,

cod, yellowbelly and barramundi often reward persistence and will often get sick of a lure if you don't get tired of putting it in front of them first.

Conditions that turn fish off include falling water levels, falling barometer, unsuitable water, pH or oxygen levels and cyclonic activity.

TACTICS FOR ADVERSE CONDITIONS

Even in the most adverse conditions there will still be the odd neutral or active fish, so a mobile approach often works.

Dams or estuaries, which have had strong winds for several days, are good examples. This frequently means that the usual tactics produce little more than a wet and uncomfortable day. Most anglers head for the lee shore and a bit of peace. Wrong!

A much better tactic is to cast or troll the windward shore. Often there is a well defined line of muddy water where the waves have disturbed the shore. That mud is full of food that is either eaten by predators or attracts forage fish. Fish the current line just like you would out at sea. Adverse conditions can often be used to advantage with a careful plan of attack.

ACHIEVING MAXIMUM DEPTH

There is a perception that you can let out unlimited amounts of line to get a lure to run deeper. This is not the case.

There is a point at which the drag on the line through the water is greater than the diving ability of the lure's bib and the lure will actually run shallower with more line out. There is an optimum drop back for all lures: for deep divers it is generally around twenty metres, and with marine trolling it is around thirty metres.

Speed, too, is important. If you get above or below the optimum speed, the lure action changes, often resulting in below par performance.

Another disadvantage of trolling with long lines is the enormous stretch in monofilament line that reduces your hook-setting ability. You are also very restricted in your ability to manoeuvre, especially if there are several lines out at once, or you are trolling in close around snags.

As a result I generally prefer to troll a deeper running lure on a shorter line to achieve the same depth, even in most saltwater trolling situations. This means that I have good contact with the lure; I can troll a lot tighter to the shore or have greater control in or near the wake and hopefully keep the lure in the strike zone for longer.

There is some variability in the diving ability of the tested lures. Some lures such as the Magnum Hellbender are renowned for their 'crash dive' capability, while many of the medium diving barramundi lures, for instance, do not dive much deeper on a longer cast or with more line out on the troll.

TARGETING ONE DEPTH

All right, let's get into an actual fishing scenario and see what we can do with our lures. Let's suppose we get a lot of fish showing at 4 metres on the sounder in a typical freshwater dam with good populations of trout and native fish. What should three anglers in a boat troll, and how?

Our list shows some terrific lures in the 4 metre range so we'll start with a Deep Shad Rap 7, a Pee Wee 15+ and a KK Medium by Custom Crafted. With these great lures out we should be on easy street, but no go! Perhaps they are only carp on the sounder?

After we have gone over quite a few fish with no success it is time to change lures, so we put on a Boomerang 65 Medium, a Deep Merlin and a Hot'N Tot 5. This time we should make it, but again no luck. Is this starting to sound familiar?

Quite often anglers will give up at this point. Note what has been happening. These anglers can't see past the dangerous tendency only to select larger lures that go deep and smaller lures that run shallow.

So what they should try now are two small lures down deep, let's say a Predatek Micro-Min on 30 metres of 6 pound line and a Halco Laser Pro 45 with a light trolling sinker. However, don't go overboard; retain the good old Hot n Tot 5 and use it as our control. Bang! We pick up a couple of small trout on the Laser Pro and a golden perch on the Micro-Min. A change to smaller lures brought some success.

But remember our third lure is the Hot'N Tot that hasn't been catching fish. The angler should work the rod to impart extra action. This action then inspires a neutral two kilo golden to strike.

Now that we know there are trout in the area we could give a Blue Fox Spinner a run with a medium trolling sinker. Hey presto the small trout like the different action of the spinner and fish are coming regularly.

During the course of the day you can try a Kadaitcha at about 10 metres, which will mean it will run at four metres down behind the boat, to see if any of the sounder readings are cod. If any lure proves to be a winner, you can troll a couple and experiment with different colours. Eventually, the other guys can change to different sizes and types of the successful lure (in this case a spinner). Don't change lures or tactics every few minutes, but don't think that picking up a fish or two for the day is the best that you can do. It may be that the fish are switched off and two fish is a great catch, but how often do you see a few guys with much better catches? If you think about your fishing and look to maximise the time that your lure spends in the strike zone, your catches must improve in the long term.

TRYING DIFFERENT DEPTHS

The above scenario is made more difficult if fish are showing at a variety of depths. It pays to keep in mind that the fish may be more active at one level than another.

Trout in Wyangala Dam, for example, often demonstrate this. Frequently, large numbers will show on the sounder near the thermocline (around 4–6 metres) with the odd fish near the surface. Concentrating on the deep fish can be a waste of time as the surface fish are often actively feeding and able to be caught more easily.

Because the effectiveness of specific lures can vary from day to day, try to cover your options quickly. I will always accept a partner's strike as incidental, but if they pick up two hits in a row, I want to know what I'm doing wrong.

CASTING WITH DIVING LURES

There is at least as much speculation about the performance of diving lures when cast and retrieved as there is about their trolling depth. The classical floating diving lure has a lot of faults when it comes to many casting situations.

Perhaps the best example is in bass fishing. It is well known that to catch bass, your cast has to land within 30 cm (a foot) or so of the snag. If you are further out you can usually forget about it. This leaves an effective strike zone of much less than a metre.

Because of the constraints of the flume tank, we were not able to run any further casting tests. However, we have run a variety of casting tests during the previous two lures' tests and the general principles still apply. As a rough guide, you can use the trolling depth to get an idea of the performance of the tested lures when cast and retrieved.

The average deep diving lure only reaches about 25 percent of its running depth (20 metres of line) after 1.5 metres of the retrieve. For a lure that trolls at 4 metres, it will be only one metre deep at this point.

For a fish near the bottom of a snag in four metres of water, the fish will have to move nearly the full 4 metres to eat your lure if you merely cast straight to the snag. This distance is much further with shallow diving lures like the floating Rapala series.

This information is very interesting, because although a lure which trolls at four metres gets down a metre deep after a metre and a half (5 foot) of the retrieve, it takes another 5 metres of winding to get down to two metres. The fish has to move a hell of a long way to eat it and it is only active fish that are really chasing these lures.

Generally, most lures reach about 33 percent (one third) of the listed trolling depth (on 20 metres of line) after 3 metres of the retrieve. This goes down to around 45 percent after 6 metres and approximately 50–60 percent after ten metres.

There is considerable variation in the maximum depth reached by lures on the retrieve. This is difficult to test due to the variability of casting performance of each lure. While fishing, wind, angler ability and different spool levels vary the cast distance, and hence the maximum depth that a lure could reach on any given cast.

But it is really the critical part of the cast, where it is closest to fish holding cover that is important. For many cover-associated fish, this is at the beginning of the cast. With species like flathead and flounder, this critical part of the cast could be at the end of the cast, where the lure comes up over a sand bank onto shallows.

The maximum cast depth varied from 50 percent to nearly 90 percent of the trolled depth. A very rough average was around 75 percent. This means that a lure which trolls at 4 metres deep should get down to around 3 metres or so on a long cast and this depth is achieved at around 75 percent of the distance retrieved.

CASTING TACTICS

It can be to very difficult to catch passive fish with a standard cast and retrieve. Most lures are going so far over their heads that they won't even bother the fish. There are two changes of tactic that work very well in these circumstances. The first is to change the angle of attack.

If possible, cast well beyond the place where you think the fish is. This will put the lure much deeper when it passes. If the fish doesn't have to move so far, more fish will be inclined to strike.

You should use far more parallel casts. Instead of just casting directly at the fish holding cover all the time, make your casts along it. This gets the lure closer to where the fish are most likely to be. This is also highly successful when fish are patrolling the outer edges of weedbeds or reefs. Placing a cast where the lure stays in 'fishy' looking water for the longest possible time will, in the long run, increase your fishing success.

There are also times when it pays to cast out from shore, even if you have a boat. Always try to work the shore, casting the lure so that it is at the right depth at the right place.

The other tactic, which has been largely ignored in Australia, is to use a sinking lure. In this way, your retrieve can begin right in the strike zone. Hits are often hard and after only one or two cranks of the handle.

This is one of the reasons why jigs are so successful for so many species and why spinnerbaits have exploded in popularity. These lures are presented where they can be eaten with the minimum amount of energy wasted.

Spoons, rattlin' spot lures and spinnerbaits are relatively cheap and do the job on a wide range of species very well. They sink right next to cover and can start the retrieve right on a fish's nose that is sitting at the bottom of a snag or ledge. Many other lures are slow sinkers and can drift slowly down a rocky ledge or next to drowned timber. I know that it is expensive to lose sinking lures like some of the Bagley's and Rapala Count-downs, but they work very well. You can even add a split shot to the line or Storm suspend dot to the lure to make a floating lure into a slow sinker. However, the action will be slightly different with this 'doctoring'.

In impoundments big bass are being increasingly taken with spinnerbaits or by vertical jigging to fish spotted with a depth sounder.

Another thing to bear in mind when casting is the way the lure finishes the retrieve. Most diving lures continue to dive, though at a slower rate, until they are nearly back to the rod. Some lures such as the Fat Raps and Hellbenders actually go under the boat before turning around as they rise to the surface.

With native fish, and many tropical creek species such as barramundi, you will get lots of hits at the point where the lure stops diving and starts to come back up to the surface. With a bit of practice you can feel that the lure changes its beat at this point. Use one of the best tricks going—pause.

A pause of as little as half a second when the lure starts to plane upwards will greatly increase the number of strikes you will get from native fish. I have watched golden perch for many hours in fish tanks. They will swim up to a baitfish to watch it and even nudge it with their nose. The instant the fish makes a move to escape it is gulped down.

By pausing, native fish and many marine ambush feeders swim up to see what is going on. When the retrieve is started again, instinct takes over and they have already eaten your lure whether they really wanted it or not. This trick also works if you can feel a fish nudging or bumping your lure during the retrieve. A slight pause often gets a hookup.

Golden perch, in particular, often follow lures up to the surface. I have had 10 kilogram plus goldens stick their heads out of the water trying unsuccessfully to eat my lure. Unlike most trout, a native that follows to the boat can still be caught with perseverance.

Just leave a metre or so of line off the rod tip when you finish each cast. If you get a follow, stick your rod under the water and make an exaggerated figure of eight. Keep your drag light and hang on, because with this method about half the goldens which follow to where you can see them clearly will strike. Other species like barracuda and some trevally will also hit frequently in this way.

TROLLING SINKERS & LEAD CORE

If you do not own a downrigger, trolling sinkers represent the best method of getting lures deeper without giving up too much of the fish's fight.

Lead core line is a very successful way of getting lures deeper. However, it creates significant drag in the water and can dramatically sandbag the fight of the fish. Lead core responds very slowly to turns when trolling and is likely to 'slide' into other lines, especially if they are unweighted, resulting in tangles.

There are only a few situations where lead core would be my first preference in attaining greater depth, and they are mainly when trolling flies. Even when trolling these flies very slowly for trout a small sinker provides another option and you will definitely know when you have a fish on.

Stainless steel trolling line, which we have used in previous tests, was better than lead core but is not widely available. It cut through the water more efficiently and gave better feel to the lure and to any fish. It has a few practical applications, but has the potential to kink and is expensive.

The only real drawback to trolling sinkers is in recovering snagged lures. The trolling sinker itself stops most lure retrievers and makes it hard to free the lure. You can modify your lure retriever to climb over the sinker to get to the lure, or you can use a lighter trace to the lure. If the sinker gets caught up, the lure will float free.

However, the advantages of trolling sinkers are great. You can easily pick up a couple of metres of depth. It is therefore possible to get lures like the McGrath diver or a Tasmanian Devil to the same depth as a Mann's 30+, with the bonus of having it appeal to a wider size range of fish.

You can improve the appeal of your lure and, in the long run, your catches will improve SO DAM HOT. Trolling sinkers should definitely be put into the 'why didn't I try it before' category.

For greater depth with small lures you cannot go past downriggers. Tests on downriggers are really beyond the scope of both the flume tank and previous tests with divers as they would require depths of up to about 40 metres and decompression tables.

Downriggers are terrific, and are being increasingly recognised for a variety of fresh and saltwater situations. They work for trout on those lazy days of summer when the fish are below a very deep thermocline and beyond the reach of standard techniques, as well as for Spanish mackerel or tuna when they are feeding on mid-water bait schools. The other big advantage of downriggers is that you fight the fish directly, without the interference of the weights.

Paravanes, dipsy divers and diving boards can also get you down to great depths, but the toughest thing with many of them is working out whether you have a fish on. Some of these devices have a trip mechanism or release clip that reduces resistance when fighting a fish.

CONCLUSIONS

Good luck with your fishing. Take a kid fishing and help to keep our aquatic environment clean and healthy for the next generation.

There is much more to lure fishing than just tying on a lure and chucking and winding. By using the copious information in this book, you should be able to better select what fish to target and where to make your cast. You should be better able to select a lure to do the job and know what it will be doing when you are casting or trolling with different sized lines or at different distances behind the boat.

And you should be able to select new lures that give you new features, depths, actions or other attributes to cover a wider range of situations while you are fishing.

When you have caught your first fish with lures your addiction will increase. And with your 100,000th fish you will continue to experience the excitement and thrill of catching fish on lures.

I only ask you to take only as many fish as you need and to return the fish that you don't need in good condition. Consider flattening the barbs on your hooks. It not only helps in the release of the fish, it also makes it much easier to get a hook back out of you!

Presentation and perseverance are two extremely important factors if you want to land a magnificent Murray cod like this one.

No.	Lure	Manufacturer	Action	Depth	No.	Lure	Manufacturer	Action	Depth
131	Wobbler 10 g Sparkler	Halco	Med. wobble	0.3	825	Bunyip	Predatek	Med. wide wide	4.3
135	Tasmanian Devil 13.5g	Wigston's	Med. wobble	0.35	838	Bell Buster	Taylor Made	Med. sway	4.4
202	Inkoo 26g	Blue Fox	Med. wobble	0.85	840	Hydro Squirt	Yo-Zuri Lures	Med wobble, tight roll	4.4
220	Jointed Swim Wizz	Homer Le Blanc Tackle	Wide sway, wide roll	0.95	844	Bandit 400 Series	Bandit Lures	Med. med pictch	4.4
238	Salty Tasmanian Devil 40g	Wigston's	Wide wobble, wide pitch	1.1	846	Barra 120	Clasic Lures	Tight sway Tight Pitch	4.4
294	Spoon 14g	Wonder Fishing Tackle	Med. wobble	1.5	849	HotLips Express ¼ oz	Lurhr Jensen	Med. sway	4.45
296	Mirror Spoon 4	Tackle Master	Wide wobble	1.5	851	Combat	Halco	Med. sway	4.5
309	Husky Jerk HJ8	Rapala	Tight Roll, med. Pitch	1.5	856	Magnum CD-11	Rapala	Med. sway	4.5
331	Aile Killifish	Yo-Zuri Lures	Shimmy	1.65	861	Codger 85	Goulburn Lures	Wide sway	4.55
351	Tasmanian Devil Dual Depth Deep	Wigston's	Wide wobble	1.85	874	Invincible DR 12cm	Nilsmaster	Med. sway, med pitch	4.6
370	Blade Runner	Tackle Master	Tight wobble	2.05	878	Shrimp	Deception Lures	Med sway	4.65
371	Murray Cod Spinnerbait 1¼	Legend Lures	Blade wobble	2.05	879	Magnum wiggle wart (old)	Storm	Medium sway. tight pitch	4.65
392	Hot Shot 60	Luhr Jensen	Med Sway	2.2	882	Hard At It	Hard At It Lures	Med. wide sway	4.7
402	Attack Lure	Attack Lures	Shimmy, med. pitch	2.25	884	Deep Wart	Storm	Med. sway	4.7
406	Master Shad	Bagley	Very wide sway med. pitch	2.25	895	Probe	Rabble Rouser Lures	Med. sway, tight pitch	4.75
422	Shad Rap Jointed JSR4	Rapala	Med. sway	2.35	899	Merlin	Bennet Lures	Very wide sway	4.75
430	Baby Extractor - Shallow	Custom Crafted Lures	Shimmy	2.4	903	Wiggle wart	Storm	Med sway	4.8
449	Shallow Thunder 15	Storm	Med sway, med roll	2.45	909	Viper 150	Predatek	Tight sway, tight roll	4.85
453	Mini Z Shallow	The Producers	Tight roll, tight pitch	2.5	921	Original B-52	Bo-Bo Lures	Med sway	4.9
456	Burmek B1 Pike Jointed	Uncle Josh	Med. Sway	2.5	923	Mulgar 80	Majik Lures	Med wide sway	4.9
457	Palaemon	Deception Lures	Tight sway, tight pitch	2.55	925	Deep Z	The Producers	Tight sway, tight pitch	4.9
467	Dinkum Yabby-Small	Kokoda	Tight sway	2.6	931	Boomerang 65	Predatek	Tight sway, med. pitch	4.95
473	Shakespear Minnow	Shakespear Lues	Med. Sway, med. roll	2.6	937	Magnum CD-9	Rapala	Tight sway	5
492	Barra	Lenny's Lures	Med. roll	2.7	938	Scale Raza 20 +	DK Lures	Med. sway, tight pitch	5
529	Spence Scout	Stike King Lure Company	Tight sway	2.85	941	Codger	Goulbourne Lures	Med. sway	5.05
541	Hijaker 5+	Majik Lures	Med wide sway	2.95	948	Boney	Peter Newell Lures	Med sway	5.05
552	Super Spot	Cotton Cordell	Tight sway, vibrate	2.95	949	Tempest TT 70	Kingfisher Lures	Med. sway, tight roll	5.05
555	RMG Scorpion 52 DD	Halco	Tight sway, tight rool	3	964	Double Downer #3	The Producers	Med. sway	5.2
567	Newell 3	Peter Newell Lures	Medium roll	3.1	975	Jumbo DD	Nilsmaster	Med sway, med pitch	5.3
575	MinMin Deep	Predateck	Tight sway	3.1	981	KK Large	Custom Crafted Lures	Slow medium roll	5.35
591	Honey B	Bagley	Tight sway	3.2	986	Wedgetail - Deep 16	Illusion Lures	Med. slow sway, med roll	5.4
597	TD Hyper Shad Ti60	Team Daiwa	Med. sway	3.2	988	Spoonbill	Predatek	Med sway, med roll	5.45
618	Bream Bandit	Kokoda	Tight sway, tight pitch	3.35	1003	Heavy Duty Stretch 12 +	Mann's Lures	Tight sway	5.55
634	Stretch 5 +	Mann's Lures	Tight sway	3.45	1006	Tempest TT85	Kingfisher Lures	Med. sway	5.65
682	Tail Dancer TD9	Rapala	Med. sway med. roll	3.6	1008	Hellbender - Magnum	Pradco	Med wide sway	5.65
686	Silver Jointed 13	Rapala	Tight sway med. roll	3.6	1009	Prime DD Crankbait 25	Spro	Med sway, tight roll	5.7
719	Shad Rap Jointed JSR5	Rapala	Fast sway, tight pitch	3.75	1013	AC Minnow 60 mm	AC Lures	Med. sway	5.85
723	The Outback	Legend Lures	Med. Sway	3.8	1026	Hot'N Tot Magnum (old)	Storm	Med. sway	6.05
724	Super Shad Rap 14	Rapala	Tight sway, med roll	3.8	1029	Stumpjumper 1 deep bib	JJ's Lures	Med. wide sway	6.15
772	Old Faithful Deep	Tinaroo Lures	Med. sway Med roll	4	1032	Cudgeeshrimp 2	Cudgeefish	Med wide sway	6.15
777	Larrikin LKI30	Larrikin Lures	Tight sway, med. roll/pitch	4.05	1034	TD Hyper Crank Ti65	Team Daiwa	Wide sway	6.15
778	Newell M6	Peter Newell Lures	Tight sway, med. roll	4.05	1036	Fat Bob Deep	Cudgeefish	Med sway	6.3
781	Invincible 25	Nilsmaster	Med roll	4.1	1040	River King	Lawson Lures	Med sway, med roll	6.35
782	Kanga	Kanga Lures	Med. sway, Med. roll	4.1	1043	Reef Runner Deep Diver	Reef Runner Tackle Co	wide sway	6.45
789	Wiggle Wart	Storm	Med. sway	4.15	1044	Hydro Magnum 95g	Yo-Zuri Lures	Slow med sway	6.45
794	Deep Crawfish	Rebel	Tight sway	4.15	1048	Scal Raza 12 +	DK Lures	Med. sway	6.5
798	A & B Barra Blaster	JAR Lures	Med sway, tight roll	4.15	1054	Kadaitcha	Perter Newell Lures	Wide sway	6.85
799	Bevy Shad 75	Lucky Craft Lures	Tight sway, tight pitch	4.15	1055	Long A-H Duty	Bomber	Wide sway	6.9
809	Baby Scud	Custom Craft Lures	Tight sway, tight pitch	4.3	1058	RMG Scorpion 150 XDD	Halco	wide sway, tight roll	7.05
817	Dytiscus	Hydroburg Lures	Med sway, med. roll	4.3	1063	Hotlips Express ¾ oz	Luhr Jensen	Wide sway	7.6

THE AUSTRALIAN FISHING ENCYCLOPEDIA *LURE TEST RESULTS*

No.	Lure	Depth Test	Maker's Depth	Action	Comments	Buoyancy	Body Material	Bib Material	Bib Width mm	Tow Point	Weight g	Body Length mm	Actual Length with Bib	Depth on 6.9m at 1.5 knots
1	Hawg Stopper #1 F	0		Chugger		Floating	Plastic	Bibless	22.5	Nose	8.2	39.4	57.4	
2	Hopper Popper HP04	0		Chugger		Floating	Plastic	Bibless	9.1	Nose	2	42.6	45.1	
3	Crickhopper PopR	0		Chugger		Floating	Plastic	Bibless	16.4	Nose	4	44.3	53	
4	Hula Popper RT	0		Chugger		Floating	Plastic	Bibless	21.8	Nose	11.2	47.8	60	
5	Teeny Pop R	0		Chugger		Floating	Plastic	Bibless	12.6	Nose	3.7	48.8	51.3	
6	Cyber Laser S-Probe #33	0		Chugger		Floating	Plastic	Bibless	20.5	Nose	7.5	49.5	55.3	
7	Cane Toad	0		Chugger		Floating	Plastic	Bibless	22.9	Nose	9.1	58.3	63.3	
8	Popper 5/8oz F	0		Chugger		Floating	Plastic	Bibless	19	Nose	11.3	58.4	62.3	
9	Skitter Pop SP-5 SB	0		Chugger		Floating	Wood	Bibless	11.9	Nose	6.2	58.5	64.1	
10	Crazy Popper #14	0		Chugger		Floating	Plastic	Bibless	19.5	Nose	12.5	59.3	63.6	
11	Chug Bug 6 cm	0		Chugger		Floating	Plastic	Bibless	14.8	Nose	7.5	61.4	65.2	
12	Pop-R Excalibur	0		Chugger		Floating	Plastic	Bibless	18.6	Nose	11.5	62.5	76.6	
13	Bubble Pop 65	0		Chugger		Floating	Plastic	Bibless	15.4	Nose	7.1	64.8	68.5	
14	Frenzy Surface	0		Chugger		Floating	Plastic	Bibless	14.5	Nose	8.9	66	73.5	
15	Splash Pop 65	0		Chugger		Floating	Plastic	Bibless	16.1	Nose	9.8	66.1	69.2	
16	Lazerlite Junior Popper	0		Chugger		Floating	Plastic	Bibless	14.5	Nose	5.8	66.1	70	
17	Super Bass SB 70z	0		Chugger		Floating	Plastic	Bibless	19.3	Nose	10.3	68	70.5	
18	Skitter Pop SP-7 FT	0		Chugger		Floating	Plastic	Bibless	13.8	Nose	7.3	70.4	78.4	
19	Intruder Cruiser	0		Chugger		Floating	Plastic	Bibless	14.5	Nose	8.7	70.5	70.5	
20	Kingfisher Pop'r	0		Chugger			Plastic	Bibless	16.6	Nose	11.6	82.9	88.8	
21	Saltwater Chug Bug 8 cm	0		Chugger		Floating	Plastic	Bibless	16.4	Nose	10.7	84.1	87.4	
22	Rattlin' Chug Bug	0		Chugger			Plastic	Bibless	16.5	Nose	10.9	84.1	88	
23	Lucky 13	0		Chugger		Floating	Plastic	Bibless	21.7	Nose	17.6	88.8	98.6	
24	Skitter Pop SP-9 HCL	0		Chugger		Floating	Plastic	Bibless	16.4	Nose	14.3	89	99	
25	Teeny Torpedo	0		Fizzer		Floating	Plastic	Bibless	18.7	1 prop	2.8	34.6	43.3	
26	Mice 40	0		Fizzer		Floating	Plastic	Bibless	30.6	2 prop	5	40.2	80.6	
27	Cricket 50	0		Fizzer		Floating	Plastic	Bibless	25	1 prop	5.2	46.7	61.5	
28	Tiny Torpedo	0		Fizzer		Floating	Plastic	Bibless	24.5	1 prop	5.7	47.6	59.6	
29	Turbo #1	0		Fizzer		Floating	Plastic	Bibless	22.5	1 prop	6.2	48	59.5	
30	Sky Turbo #04	0		Fizzer		Floating	Plastic	Bibless	23.2	1 prop	6.3	49.5	60.7	
31	Mice 50	0		Fizzer		Floating	Plastic	Bibless	36	2 prop	11.2	52.3	95	
32	Sputterbuzz	0		Fizzer			Plastic	Bibless	31.6	1 prop	10.2	58	105.9	
33	Baby Torpedo	0		Fizzer		Floating	Plastic	Bibless	33.4	1 prop	8.2	61.2	73.4	

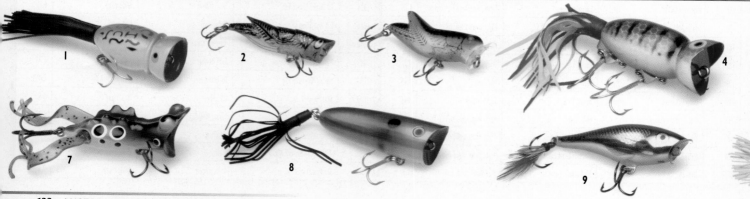

Depth on 6.9m at 2.5 knots	Manufacturer	Country of Manufacture
	The Producers	China
	Storm	Estonia
	Rebel	USA
	Fred Arbogast	El Salvador
	Rebel	USA
	The Prince	China
	Bounty Hunter Lures	Aust—NSW
	The Producers	China
	Rapala	Ireland
	The Prince	
	Storm	Estonia
	Rebel	USA
	River 2 Sea	
	Berkley	USA
	Surebite Lures—SureCatch	
	McLaughlin's Lures	Taiwan
	Surebite Lures—SureCatch	China
	Rapala	Ireland
	Jarvis Walker	Vietnam
	Lively Lures	Aust—Qld
	Storm	Estonia
	Storm	Estonia
	Heddon	El Salvador
	Rapala	Ireland
	Heddon	Mexico
	Bill's Bugs	Aust—NSW
	Bill's Bugs	Aust—NSW
	Heddon	El Salvador
	The Producers	China
	The Prince	
	Bill's Bugs	Aust—NSW
	Fred Arbogast	El Salvador
	Heddon	Mexico

No.	Lure	Depth Test	Maker's Depth	Action	Comments	Buoyancy	Body Material	Bib Material	Bib Width mm	Tow Point	Weight g	Body Length mm	Actual Length with Bib	Depth on 6.9m at 1.5 knots
34	Woodchopper 3/8oz	0		Fizzer		Floating	Wood	Bibless	34.3	2 prop	12.1	61.8	86.2	
35	Turbo #2	0		Fizzer		Floating	Plastic	Bibless	31.3	1 prop	9.7	62.7	73.4	
36	Cricket 65	0		Fizzer		Floating	Plastic	Bibless	28.8	1 prop	11.6	70.5	87.7	
37	Fuzz Bug 75	0		Fizzer		Floating	Plastic	Bibless	36	2 prop	11.8	72.5	123.6	
38	Mice 75	0		Fizzer		Floating	Plastic	Bibless	42.4	2 prop	17.5	73.7	131.4	
39	Tommy 70	0		Fizzer		Floating	Plastic	Bibless	24.3	1 prop	8.6	79.7	76.2	
40	Woodchopper 1/2oz	0		Fizzer		Floating	Wood	Bibless	43	2 prop	19.8	80.4	109.1	
41	Skitter Prop SPR-7 FT	0		Fizzer		Floating	Plastic	Bibless	33.9	1 prop	8.6	80.5	89.5	
42	Fuzz Bug 100	0		Fizzer		Floating	Plastic	Bibless	44.8	2 prop	20.9	92.9	152.6	
43	Dying Flutter	0		Fizzer		Floating	Plastic	Bibless	31.9	2 prop	10.8	94.1	109.2	
44	Double Ender	0		Fizzer		Floating	Plastic	Bibless	34.5	2 prop	14.5	95.7	109.2	
45	Woodchopper	0		Fizzer		Floating	Wood	Bibless	54.9	2 prop	26.1	103.4	135	
46	Devil's Horse AF100	0		Fizzer		Floating	Plastic	Bibless	26.6	2 prop	11.9	106.1	121.5	
47	Rat 120	0		Fizzer		Floating	Plastic	Bibless	53.5	2 prop	55.5	113.8	119.9	
48	Jitterbug 1/8 oz	0		Paddler		Floating	Plastic	Metal	34.2	Nose	4.4	37	46	
49	Jitterbug Clicker 1/4oz	0		Paddler		Floating	Plastic	Metal	36.5	Nose	6.8	43	53.6	
50	Jitterbug 1/4oz	0		Paddler		Floating	Plastic	Metal	36.3	Nose	6.3	43.5	54.5	
51	Jitter Mouse 1/8oz	0		Paddler		Floating	Plastic	Metal	34.5	Nose	4.2	44.3	51.4	
52	Tiny Crazy Crawler	0		Paddler		Floating	Plastic	Bibless, metal ,wings	60.2	Nose	7.2	45.3	54.1	
53	Bugger Chug	0		Paddler		Floating	Plastic	Plastic	18.2	Nose	7.3	45.4	47.4	
54	Basscada	0		Paddler		Floating	Wood	Plastic	61.4	Nose	6.1	47.8	51.4	
55	Flutterbug 50	0		Paddler		Floating	Plastic	Bibless, metal ,wings	35.7	Nose	6.4	49.9	58.3	
56	Cicada Pop 55	0				Floating	Plastic	Plastic	41.5	Nose		53.4	55.9	
57	Depthcharge Small	0		Paddler		Floating	Plastic	Metal	40.2	Nose	9	55.5	71	
58	Jitterbug Clicker	0		Paddler		Floating	Plastic	Metal	38.8	Nose	9.8	56.3	62.5	
59	Bass-A-Rooney	0		Paddler		Floating	Plastic	Metal	48.5	Nose	9.4	56.3	65.7	
60	Jitter #03	0		Paddler		Floating	Plastic	Metal	40	Nose	9.6	57	65.8	
61	Jitterbug JTD 3/8oz	0		Paddler		Floating	Plastic	Metal	38.7	Nose	9.7	60.4	69.3	
62	Crazy Crawler	0		Paddler		Floating	Plastic	Bibless,metal ,wings	92.3	Nose	15.4	62.4	67	
63	Night Walker	0		Paddler		Floating	Plastic	Plastic	52.5	Nose	11.7	65	67	
64	Jitterbug 5/8oz	0		Paddler		Floating	Plastic	Metal	42.9	Nose	13.5	66.5	73	
65	Cicada Pop 70	0				Floating	Plastic	Plastic	53.7	Nose		69.5	72.1	
66	Flutter Bug 75	0		Paddler		Floating	Plastic	Bibless,metal ,wings	43	Nose	14.4	70	80.8	

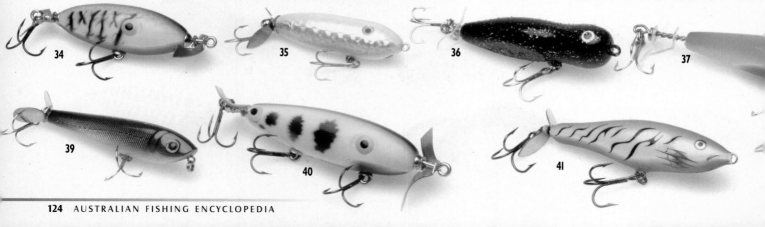

	Depth on 6.9m at 2.5 knots	Manufacturer	Country of Manufacture
		Luhr Jensen	Mexico
		The Producers	China
		Bill's Bugs	Aust—NSW
		Bill's Bugs	Aust—NSW
		Bill's Bugs	Aust—NSW
		Surebite Lures—SureCatch	
		Luhr Jensen	Mexico
		Rapala	Ireland
		Bill's Bugs	Aust—NSW
		Heddon	Mexico
		The Producers	China
		Luhr Jensen	Mexico
		Smithwick	Mexico
		Bill's Bugs	Aust—NSW
		Fred Arbogast	Guatemala
		Fred Arbogast	El Salvador
		Fred Arbogast	El Salvador
		Fred Arbogast	El Salvador
		Heddon	Mexico
		Kokoda	China
		Taylor Made	Austw—NSW
		Bill's Bugs	Aust—NSW
		River 2 Sea	Japan
		Mudeye Lures	Aust—NSW
		Fred Arbogast	El Salvador
		The Producers	China
		The Prince	China
		Fred Arbogast	El Salvador
		Heddon	Mexico
		Halco	Aust—WA
		Fred Arbogast	El Salvador
		River 2 Sea	Japan
		Bill's Bugs	Aust—NSW

No.	Lure	Depth Test	Maker's Depth	Action	Comments	Buoyancy	Body Material	Bib Material	Bib Width mm	Tow Point	Weight g	Body Length mm	Actual Length with Bib
67	Depthcharge Large	0		Paddler		Floating	Plastic	Metal	51.8	Nose	21.3	74.8	98.9
68	Jitterbug JTD 5/8oz	0		Paddler		Floating	Plastic	Metal	42.9	Nose	17.1	77	88
69	Flutterbug 100	0		Paddler		Floating	Plastic	Bibless, metal, wings	54.6	Nose	23.6	91.7	103.4
70	XL Jitterbug	0		Paddler		Floating	Plastic	Metal	64.8	Nose	31.2	113.7	124.4
71	Kingfisher Bass Bug	0		Popper		Floating	Plastic	Bibless	21.5	Nose	8.3	48.6	53.3
72	Kingfisher Poppit	0		Popper			Plastic	Bibless	18.3	Nose	11.4	60.4	66.8
73	Kingfisher Barra	0		Popper			Plastic	Bibless	15.7	Nose	13.2	85.5	90.4
74	Kingfisher Mini Turbo	0		Popper			Plastic	Bibless	18.5	Nose	13.8	87	92
75	Ranger 90 R10	0		Popper			Plastic	Bibless	17.3	Nose	14.5	89.4	93.5
76	Pop Cruiser PC 90 TW	0		Popper			Plastic	Bibless	13.3	Nose	13.6	90.3	95.1
77	Pop Tiger PT 90	0		Popper			Plastic	Bibless	19.3	Nose	24.3	91.5	97.8
78	K9 Popper	0		Popper			Plastic	Bibless	26.9	Nose	22	93.7	98
79	Kingfisher Supa Bloopa	0		Popper			Plastic	Bibless	25.4	Nose	28.3	98	103.7
80	Roger 10	0		Popper		Sinking	Plastic	Bibless	19	Nose	27.8	101.9	109.9
81	Monster Popper F	0		Popper			Plastic	Bibless	23	Nose	23.2	108.4	113.5
82	Pop Cruiser PC 110 TW	0		Popper			Plastic	Bibless	16.1	Nose	22.4	109.9	114.5
83	Saltwater Chug Bug	0		Popper			Plastic	Bibless	23.5	Nose	25.7	112	116.8
84	Pop Tiger PT 110	0		Popper			Plastic	Bibless	23.8	Nose	40.7	112.5	115.5
85	Kingfisher Fat R's	0		Popper		Sinking	Plastic	Bibless	15.8	Nose	56.4	115.4	123.4
86	Mal Florence's Masta Poppa	0		Popper			Plastic	Bibless	21.3	Nose	29	118.3	131.3
87	K12 Pencil Popper	0		Popper			Plastic	Bibless	19.7	Nose	29.8	124.1	127.9
88	Skitter Pop SSP 12	0		Popper		Floating	Plastic	Bibless	22.7	Nose	38.3	129.2	146.2
89	Lazerlite Popper	0		Popper			Plastic	Bibless	17.2	Nose	37.9	129.6	136.7
90	Pop Cruiser PC 130 TW	0		Popper			Plastic	Bibless	19.2	Nose	35.1	131	135.1
91	Pop Tiger PT 130	0		Popper		Sinking	Plastic	Bibless	27.8	Nose	63.3	132.4	137.9
92	Pencil Popper Small	0		Popper			Plastic	Bibless	13.9	Nose	32.2	146.3	152
93	Roger 15	0		Popper		Sinking	Plastic	Bibless	28.9	Nose	88.4	150.7	158
94	Kingfisher Steely	0		Popper		Sinking	Plastic	Bibless	16.9	Nose	62.4	157.2	154.4
95	Pencil Popper Large	0		Popper		Sinking	Plastic	Bibless	17.5	Nose	47.3	165.6	172.6
96	Mini-Me Ghost F	0		Stick bait		Floating	Plastic	Bibless		Nose	10	62.2	65.9
97	Spit'n Image Jr	0		Stick bait		Floating	Plastic	Bibless		Nose	10	73.5	78.8
98	Spit'n Image	0		Stick bait		Floating	Plastic	Bibless		Nose	13.6	82.9	89
99	Floating Mullet BM7	0		Stick bait		Floating	Plastic	Bibless		Body	12.4	93	93

67 68 69 70

72 73 74 75

at 2 knots	Depth on 6.9m at 2.5 knots	Manufacturer	Country of Manufacture
		Mudeye Lures	Aust—NSW
		Fred Arbogast	El Salvador
		Bill's Bugs	Aust—NSW
		Fred Arbogast	El Salvador
		Lively Lures	Aust—Qld
		Lively Lures	Aust—Qld
		Lively Lures	Aust—Qld
		Lively Lures	Aust—Qld
		Ambush Lures	Aust—Qld
		Surebite Lures—SureCatch	China
		Surebite Lures—SureCatch	China
		Killalure	Aust—Qld
		Lively Lures	Aust—Qld
		Kokoda	China
		The Producers	China
		Surebite Lures—SureCatch	China
		Storm	Estonia
		Surebite Lures—SureCatch	China
		Lively Lures	Aust—Qld
		Refined Lure Technology	Aust—Vic
		Killalure	Aust—Qld
		Rapala	Ireland
		McLaughlin's Lures	Taiwan
		Surebite Lures—SureCatch	China
		Surebite Lures—SureCatch	China
		Cotton Cordell	USA
		Kokoda	China
		Lively Lures	Aust—Qld
		Cotton Cordell	El Salvador
		The Producers	China
		Excalibur	El Salvador
		Excalibur	El Salvador
		Bomber	El Salvador

No.	Lure	Depth Test	Maker's Depth	Action	Comments	Buoyancy	Body Material	Bib Material	Bib Width mm	Tow Point	Weight g	Body Length mm
100	Intruder Fugitive	0		Stick bait		Floating	Plastic	Bibless		Nose	14.4	99.4
101	Bubble 100	0		Stick bait			Plastic	Bibless		Nose	13	99.8
102	Ghost F	0		Stick bait		Floating	Plastic	Bibless		Nose	19.7	108.2
103	Thunder Dog	0		Stick bait		Floating	Plastic	Bibless		Nose	19.3	110.1
104	Jumpin' Minnow	0		Stick bait		Floating	Plastic	Bibless		Nose	21.9	113.1
105	Mega Ghost	0		Stick bait		Floating	Plastic	Bibless		Nose	29.6	130.9
106	Mustang	0		Stick bait		Floating	Plastic	Bibless		Nose	20.2	132.8
107	Little Tease 7 g	0.1		Medium roll		Sinking	Metal	Bibless	1.3	Nose	5.6	59.8
108	Elver 10 g	0.1		Tight roll		Sinking	Metal	Bibless		Nose	8.3	57.3
109	Wobbler 7 g	0.1		Medium wobble		Sinking	Metal	Bibless	2	Nose	8.5	47.8
110	Wobbler fish Chrome 7g	0.1		Medium wobble		Sinking	Metal	Bibless	1.5	Nose	6.7	48
111	Aglia Size 1	0.1		Spinner		Sinking	Metal			Nose		33.3
112	Bait School lure pair	0.1		Vibrate	Better at 1.5 knots or slower.	Sinking	Metal	Bibless		Nose	5	
113	Twisty 5 g	0.15		Tight roll		Sinking	Metal	Bibless	4.1	Body	5.8	48
114	Rio's Prawn 5 g	0.15		No action, not for trolling	Little action but looks life-like.	Sinking	Plastic	Bibless		Nose	5.4	66
115	Rio's Prawn 13 g	0.15		Tight sway		Sinking	Plastic	Bibless	3.3	Nose	11.4	84.5
116	Hopper Spinner 3 g	0.15		Spinner		Sinking	Metal	Bibless			2.7	
117	Live Chrome 10 g	0.2		Shimmy	Little action.	Sinking	Metal	Bibless	3.3	Nose	11.8	43.3
118	Hogback Fly	0.2		Spinner		Sinking	Metal	Bibless	7.8	Nose	9	55
119	Wobbler 20 g Sparkler	0.2		Medium wobble		Sinking	Metal	Bibless	2.2	Nose	23.3	67.1
120	Power Prawn Small	0.2		No action, not for trolling		Sinking	Rubber	Bibless		Nose	3.8	60.2
121	Super Prawn PR 105	0.2		Very slow medium wobble		Sinking	Plastic	Bibless	15.2	Body	23.5	106.3
122	Aglia TW 1 Streamer	0.2		Spinner		Sinking	Metal	Bibless			3.8	
123	S H Wobbler 7 g	0.25		Medium wobble, tight pinch	Good action.	Sinking	Metal	Bibless	6.3	Nose	6.9	47.5
124	Bang-O-Lure #5	0.25		Tight sway, medium roll		Floating	Wood	Plastic	12.6	Nose	11.6	131.2
125	Killer Spinner 2 g	0.25		Spinner	Spinner only fair.	Sinking	Metal	Bibless			2.1	
126	Hopper 5 g	0.25		Spinner		Sinking	Metal	Bibless			3.2	
127	Little Tasmanian Devil	0.3		Medium wobble		Sinking	Plastic	Bibless	6	Nose	7	38.5
128	Wonder Pilchard 15g	0.3		Medium sway	Good action at 2.5 knots.	Sinking	Metal	Bibless	2.2	Nose	13.7	56.5
129	Wobler fish shape 42g	0.3		Medium wobble		Sinking	Metal	Bibless	4.1	Nose	39.4	68.3
130	Hexagon Sparkler 10 g	0.3		Tight wobble		Sinking	Metal	Bibless	6.5	Nose	10.2	43
131	Wobbler 10 g Sparkler	0.3		Medium wobble	Great action.	Sinking	Metal	Bibless	2	Nose	9.4	47.5
132	Wobbler fish shape 10 g	0.3		Medium wobble		Sinking	Metal	Bibless	2.2	Nose	8.6	48.3
133	Kelta 3 g	0.3		Spinner		Sinking	Metal	Bibless			3	

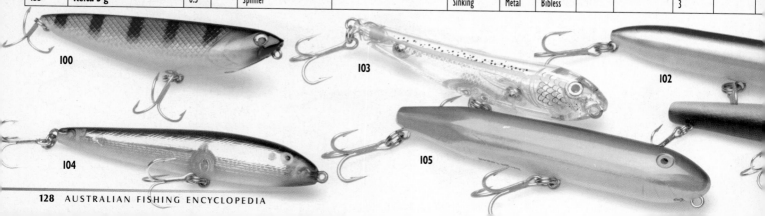

100

103

102

104

105

Depth on 6.9m at 1.5 knots	Depth on 6.9m at 2 knots	Depth on 6.9m at 2.5 knots	Manufacturer	Country of Manufacture
	0		Jarvis Walker	Vietnam
	0		River 2 Sea	
	0		The Producers	China
	0		Storm	Estonia
	0		Rebel	Mexico
	0		The Producers	China
	0		Bo-Bo Lures	Aust—NSW
	0.05		Juro	Taiwan
	0.05		Fishfighter Lures	NZ
	0.05		Wonder Fishing Tackle	Aust—Vic
	0.05		Hawk Fishing Tackle	China
	0.05		Mepps Lures	France
	0.05		Tackle Master	Aust—Qld
	0.05		Halco	Aust—WA
	0.1		Rio's Lures	Aust—Qld
	0.05		Rio's Lures	Aust—Qld
	0.1		Gillies	
	0.1		Rio's Lures	Aust—Qld
	0.1		Gillies	
	0.1		Halco	Aust—WA
	0.1		Kokoda	China
	0.1		Surebite Lures—SureCatch	China
	0.1		Mepps Lures	France
	0.1		Gillies	
	0.1		Bagley	Dominican Rep
	0.15		Gillies	
	0.15		Gillies	
	0.15		Wigston's	Aust—Tas
	0.15		Wonder Fishing Tackle	Aust—Vic
	0.15		Hawk Fishing Tackle	Korea
	0.15		Halco	Aust—WA
	0.15		Halco	Aust—WA
	0.15		Hawk Fishing Tackle	China
	0.15		Juro	Taiwan

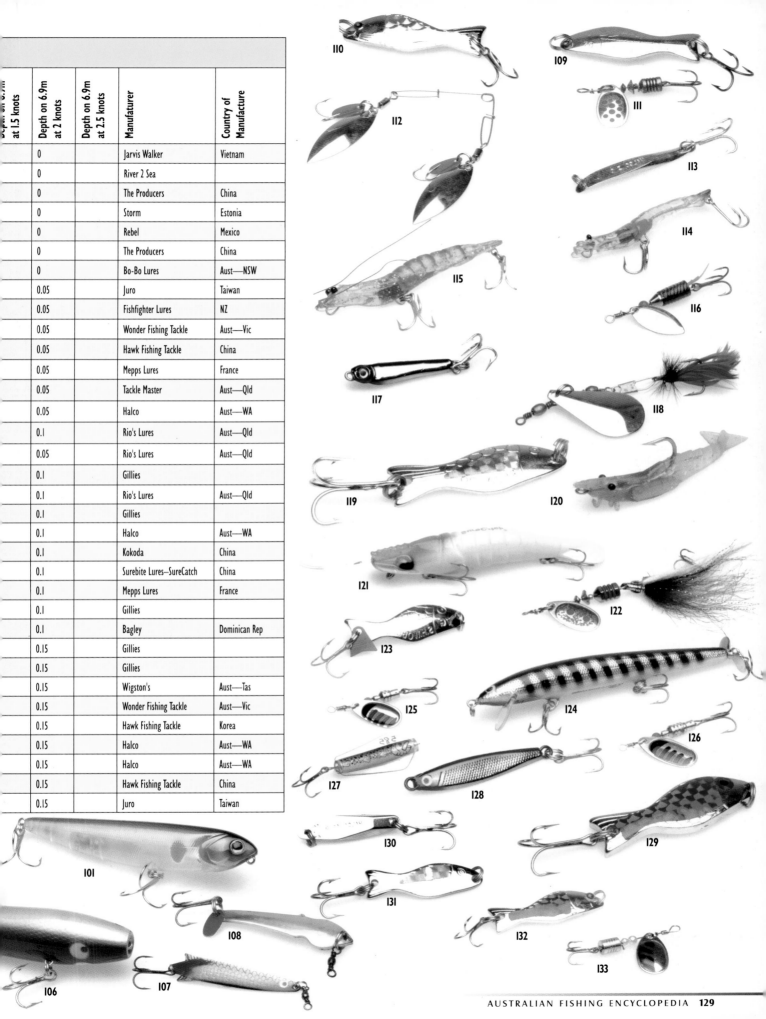

No.	Lure	Depth Test	Maker's Depth	Action	Comments	Buoyancy	Body Material	Bib Material	Bib Width mm	Tow Point	Weight g	Body Length mm
134	Tasmanian Devil 7 g	0.3		Medium wobble		Sinking	Plastic	Bibless		Nose	6.9	
135	Tasmanian Devil 13.5 g	0.35		Medium wobble	Great action.	Sinking	Plastic	Bibless	6	Nose	13.4	52.5
136	Pilchard 40 g	0.35		Medium roll		Sinking	Metal	Bibless	3.9	Nose	41.4	82.8
137	Streaker 10 g	0.35		Tight wobble, tight pinch		Sinking	Metal	Bibless	8.2	Nose	10.5	44.5
138	Kwikfish K9	0.35		Wide sway			Plastic	Plastic	18.9	Body	6.6	49.9
139	Harasser Minnow	0.4		Tight roll		Sinking	Metal	Bibless		Nose	10.2	42
140	Baitfish Flash 10 g	0.4		Shimmy wobble	Little action.	Sinking	Metal	Bibless	2.5	Nose	12.2	53.1
141	Flash Shad 6	0.4		Tail wiggle		Sinking	Rubber	Bibless	4	Nose	5.3	56.7
142	Krocodile 10 g	0.4		Medium wide wobble	Good action.	Sinking	Metal	Bibless	2.2	Nose	11.8	54.4
143	Wobbler fish shape 30 g	0.4		Medium wobble		Sinking	Metal	Bibless	4.2	Nose	39.2	67.8
144	Glimmy 7 g	0.4		Tight wobble		Sinking	Metal	Bibless	5	Nose	6.9	44
145	Wobbler 40 g Sparkler	0.4		Medium wobble		Sinking	Metal	Bibless	2.8	Nose	31	67.5
146	Power Prawn Large	0.4		No action, not for trolling		Sinking	Rubber	Bibless	4.8	Nose	18.2	112
147	Hot Shot 5 g	0.4		Spinner		Sinking	Metal	Bibless			4.5	
148	Killer Spinner 3.5 g	0.4		Spinner		Sinking	Metal	Bibless				
149	Raptor 20 g	0.45		Little action, needs speed		Sinking	Metal	Bibless	3	Nose	15.8	49.5
150	Wobbler 30 g Sparkler	0.45		Medium wobble		Sinking	Metal	Bibless	2.8	Nose	27.1	68.5
151	Big Ant	0.45	0.6	Fast sway		Floating	Plastic	Plastic	14.1	Bib	2.5	31.6
152	Bang-O-Lure #4	0.45		Medium roll	Good action. Prop turns well.	Floating	Wood	Plastic	12.6	Nose	9.7	106.
153	Eucumbene Spinner 1	0.45		Spinner		Sinking	Metal	Bibless		Nose	5.4	
154	Bait School lure pair large	0.45		Vibrate		Sinking	Metal	Bibless			6.9	
155	Marble Spinner 7 g	0.45		Spinner		Sinking	Metal	Bibless			7.4	
156	Pilchard 8 g	0.5		Vibrate	Better at 2.5 knots.	Sinking	Metal	Bibless	3	Nose	7.3	38.4
157	Twisty 15 g	0.5		Tight wobble		Sinking	Metal	Bibless	5.1	Nose	14.3	56.5
158	Devon 1"	0.5		Tight spin		Sinking	Metal	Plastic		Nose		25.6
159	Super Vibrax 0	0.5		Spinner	Works well at 2 knots.	Sinking	Metal	Bibless			3.2	
160	Mini Whacker 1/6oz	0.5		Blade	Needs 1.5 knots or slower.	Sinking	Metal	Bibless			6.5	
161	Krocodile	0.5		Medium wobble, medium pitch	Good action.	Sinking	Metal	Bibless			7.2	
162	Kwikfish K4	0.55		Wide sway	Better at 1.5 knots.		Plastic	Bibless	10	Body	1.2	37.3
163	Super Prawn PR 85	0.55		Very slow medium wobble		Sinking	Plastic	Bibless	11.8	Body	11.7	86
164	Kiwi Lure	0.6		Wide wobble		Sinking	Plastic	Bibless		Nose	13.4	52.4
165	Minnow Spin Super Vibrax 2	0.6		Spinner, slow roll		Sinking		Bibless		Nose	11.7	83.
166	Wonder Wobbler 30 g	0.6		Slow medium wobble	Slower wobble than Halco.	Sinking	Metal	Bibless	3	Nose	33.6	68

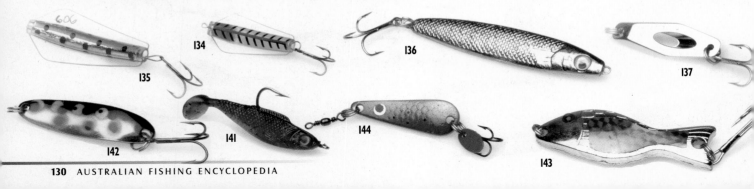

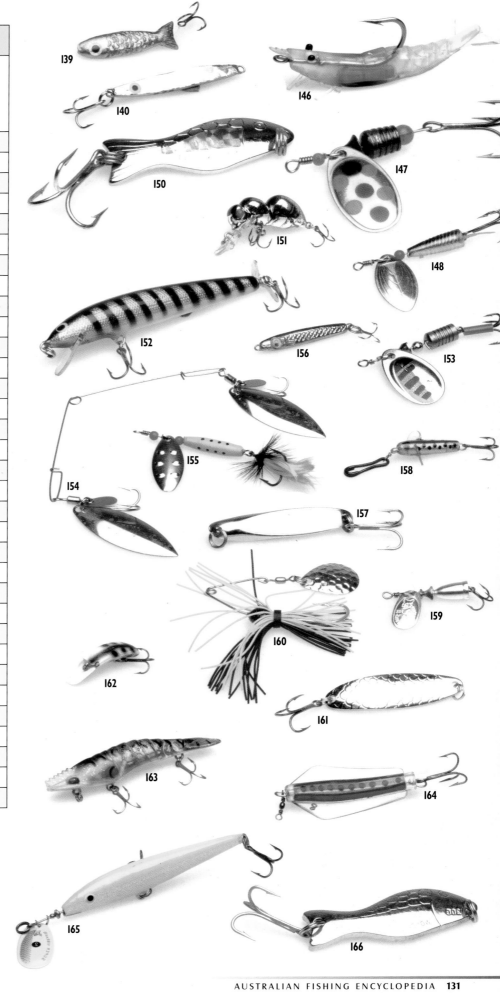

Depth on 6.9m at 2 knots	Depth on 6.9m at 2.5 knots	Manufacturer	Country of Manufacture
0.15		Wigston's	Aust—Tas
0.2		Wigston's	Aust—Tas
0.15		Hawk Fishing Tackle	Korea
0.15		Halco	Aust—WA
0.15		Luhr Jensen	USA
0.2		Hirst Lures	Aust
0.2		Hawk Fishing Tackle	China
0.2		Kokoda	China
0.2		Wonder Fishing Tackle	Aust—Vic
0.2		Hawk Fishing Tackle	China
0.2		Fishfighter Lures	NZ
0.2		Halco	Aust—WA
0.2		Kokoda	China
0.2		Wonder Fishing Tackle	Aust—Vic
0.2		Gillies	
	0.25	Kokoda	China
0.15		Halco	Aust—WA
0.2		Rebel	USA
0.2		Bagley	Dominican Rep
0.25		Hawk Fishing Tackle	Korea
0.25		Tackle Master	Aust—Qld
0.25		Gillies	
0.25	0.25	Hawk Fishing Tackle	Korea
0.25		Halco	Aust—WA
0.25		Tillins Lures	Aust—Tas
0.25		Blue Fox	Finland
0.25		Bomber	El Salvador
0.25		Gillies	
0.25		Luhr Jensen	USA
0.25		Surebite Lures–SureCatch	China
0.3		Kiwi Lures	NZ
0.3		Blue Fox	Finland
0.3		Wonder Fishing Tackle	Aust—Vic

No.	Lure	Depth Test	Maker's Depth	Action	Comments	Buoyancy	Body Material	Bib Material	Bib Width mm	Tow Point	Weight g	Body Length mm	Actual Length with Bib	Depth on 6.9m at 1.5 knots
167	Oxboro Ox Spoon	0.6		Wide wobble		Sinking	Metal	Bibless		Nose	23.5	90.5	90.5	
168	Finlandia S	0.6		Shimmy	Swivel affects action.		Wood	Plastic	8.4	Nose	1.8	27	30.7	
169	Eucumbene Spinner 1/8oz	0.6		Spinner	Blade only working intermittently.	Sinking	Metal	Bibless		Nose	4.1			
170	Live Chrome 20 g	0.65		Vibrate	Little action.	Sinking	Metal	Bibless	4.2	Nose	18.6	62.2	69.5	
171	Baitfish Flash 16 g	0.65		Tight wobble		Sinking	Metal	Bibless	2.5	Nose	19.7	67.7	73.5	
172	Super Duper 8 g	0.65		Medium wobble		Sinking	Metal	Bibless	1	Nose	8.5	43.6	45.8	0.2
173	Surf Rider 35 g	0.65		Tight roll	Better at 2.5 knots.	Sinking	Metal	Bibless		Nose	35.2	109.7	109.7	
174	Fintastic	0.65		Medium wobble	Good action.	Sinking	Metal			Nose		54.6	58	
175	Rooster Tail 1/8oz	0.65		Spinner	Good action.	Sinking	Metal	Bibless			3.6			
176	Super Vibrax 1	0.65		Spinner		Sinking	Metal	Bibless			3.9			
177	Rooster Tail Spinner 1/8oz	0.65		Spinner		Sinking	Metal	Bibless		Nose	5.3			
178	Streaker 20 g	0.7		Tight wobble, tight pitch		Sinking	Metal	Bibless	8	Nose	20.4	61.1	61.1	
179	Froggy 15 g	0.7		Tight wobble	Average.	Sinking	Metal	Bibless	10	Nose	14.6	82	82	
180	Toby 14 g	0.7		Medium wobble	Good at 2 knots.	Sinking	Metal	Bibless	5.6	Nose	12.1	61.1	61.1	
181	Crawdaddy #0	0.7		Wide pitch		Floating	Plastic	Plastic	10.6	Nose	2.7	39.4	46.5	
182	Super Vibrax Minnow Spin 2	0.75		Spinner		Sinking	Metal	Bibless		Nose		50	74	
183	Tasmanian Devil 13.5 g	0.75		Medium wobble		Sinking	Plastic	Bibless	6.3	Nose	13.4	50.5	59.1	
184	Enticer 15 g	0.75		Shimmy	Little action.	Sinking	Metal	Bibless	3.2	Nose	17.3	52.1	63	
185	Vector 30 g	0.75		Slow roll	Little action.	Sinking	Metal	Bibless	3.9	Nose	24.4	65.5	75	
186	Streaker 40 g	0.75		Medium wobble		Sinking	Metal	Bibless	9.8	Nose	42	78.1	78.1	
187	Streaker 30 g	0.75		Medium wobble		Sinking	Metal	Bibless	10.3	Nose	31.1	67	67	
188	Nature Hopper 1/8oz	0.75		Spinner		Sinking	Metal	Bibless		Nose	3.2	16.2	38.6	
189	Abanka Lure	0.75		Tight sway	Needs at least 2.5 knots.	Sinking	Plastic	Bibless		Nose	14.1	59.2	61.6	
190	Bang Tail 2 1/8oz	0.75		Spinner		Sinking	Metal	Bibless			6			
191	Hogback 8 g	0.75		Medium wobble		Sinking	Metal	Bibless			8.9			
192	Big Tasmanian Devil	0.8		Medium wide sway		Sinking	Plastic	Bibless	7.7	Nose	26.1	76.4	85	0.35
193	Turbular 28 g	0.8		Medium roll	Good action.	Sinking	Metal	Bibless	10	Nose	35	64.5	64.5	
194	Rio's Prawn 19 g	0.8		Very slow wobble		Sinking	Plastic	Bibless	17.2	Nose	18.4	104.1	104.1	
195	Kwikfish K5	0.8		Wide sway			Plastic	Bibless	11.6	Body	1.9	31.6	43.5	
196	1/4oz Tandem Spinnerbait	0.8		Blade wobble		Sinking	Metal	Bibless			14			
197	True Trac Classic 3/8oz	0.8		Blade wobble		Sinking	Metal	Bibless			17.5			
198	Harasser Baltic	0.85		Tight wobble	Good erratic action.	Sinking	Metal	Bibless		Nose	13	39.8	39.8	
199	Pilchard 20 g	0.85		Tight roll		Sinking	Metal	Bibless	3.9	Nose	21.5	52.4	59.7	
200	Enticer 28 g	0.85		Shimmy		Sinking	Metal	Bibless	3.5	Nose	29.4	65.4	75.3	

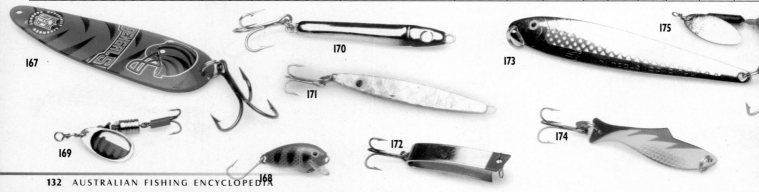

167   169   168   170   171   172   173   174   175

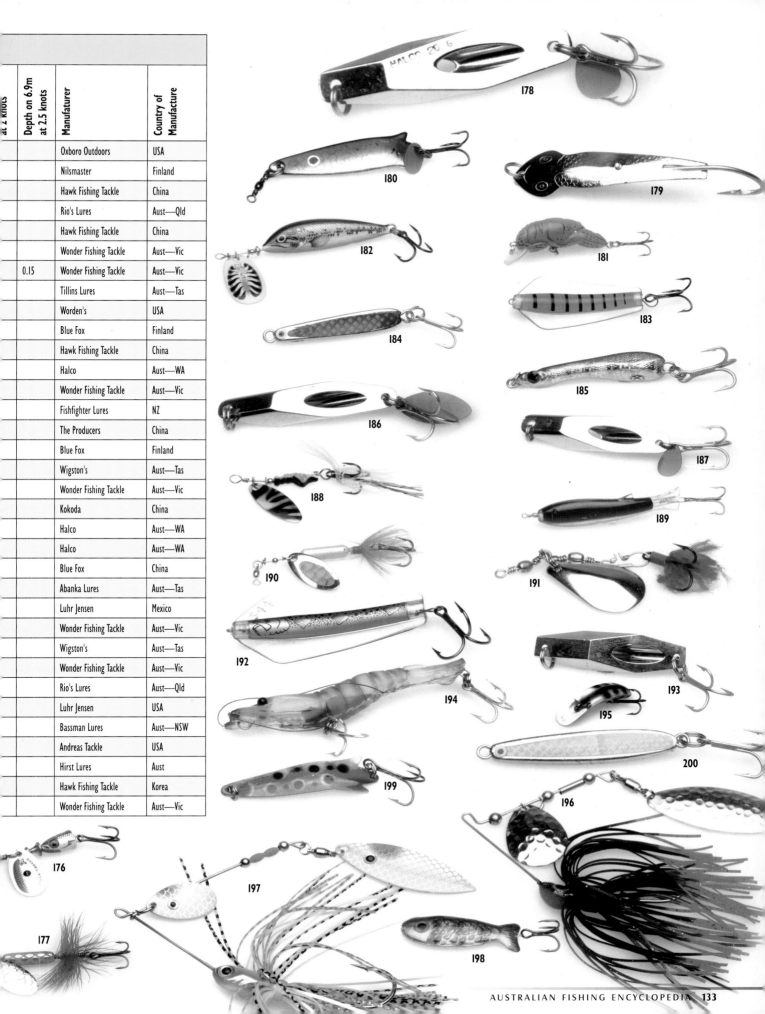

at 2 knots	Depth on 6.9m at 2.5 knots	Manufaturer	Country of Manufacture
		Oxboro Outdoors	USA
		Nilsmaster	Finland
		Hawk Fishing Tackle	China
		Rio's Lures	Aust—Qld
		Hawk Fishing Tackle	China
		Wonder Fishing Tackle	Aust—Vic
	0.15	Wonder Fishing Tackle	Aust—Vic
		Tillins Lures	Aust—Tas
		Worden's	USA
		Blue Fox	Finland
		Hawk Fishing Tackle	China
		Halco	Aust—WA
		Wonder Fishing Tackle	Aust—Vic
		Fishfighter Lures	NZ
		The Producers	China
		Blue Fox	Finland
		Wigston's	Aust—Tas
		Wonder Fishing Tackle	Aust—Vic
		Kokoda	China
		Halco	Aust—WA
		Halco	Aust—WA
		Blue Fox	China
		Abanka Lures	Aust—Tas
		Luhr Jensen	Mexico
		Wonder Fishing Tackle	Aust—Vic
		Wigston's	Aust—Tas
		Wonder Fishing Tackle	Aust—Vic
		Rio's Lures	Aust—Qld
		Luhr Jensen	USA
		Bassman Lures	Aust—NSW
		Andreas Tackle	USA
		Hirst Lures	Aust
		Hawk Fishing Tackle	Korea
		Wonder Fishing Tackle	Aust—Vic

No.	Lure	Depth Test	Maker's Depth	Action	Comments	Buoyancy	Body Material	Bib Material	Bib Width mm	Tow Point	Weight g
201	Pilchard 30 g	0.85		Medium wobble		Sinking	Metal	Bibless	3	Nose	31
202	Inkoo 26 g	0.85		Medium	Great action.	Sinking	Metal	Bibless		Nose	25.6
203	Fishfighter Minnow 10 g	0.85		Medium wobble,	Good action.	Sinking	Metal	Bibless tight pitch	6.3	Nose	10.6
204	Twisty 20 g	0.85		Tight wobble		Sinking	Metal	Bibless	8.4	Nose	20.3
205	Hexagon Sparkler 20 g	0.85		Tight wobble	Good action.	Sinking	Metal	Bibless	8.1	Nose	19.3
206	Wide Wing Deep Diving Cobra	0.85	2.1	Wide wobble,	Good action.	Sinking	Metal	Plastic medium pitch		Nose	
207	Super Vibrax 2	0.85		Spinner		Sinking	Metal	Bibless			5.7
208	Rooster Tail 1/6oz	0.85		Spinner		Sinking	Metal	Bibless			6.4
209	Firetail Lure Multi	0.85		Spinner		Sinking	Metal	Bibless			6.6
210	Super Vibrax 4	0.85		Spinner		Sinking	Metal	Bibless			10.1
211	Bushwacker 1/4oz	0.85		Blade wobble		Sinking	Metal	Bibless			13.5
212	Raptor 40 g	0.9		Little action,needs speed	Little action, needs more than 2.5kn.	Sinking	Metal	Bibless	4.3	Nose	36.9
213	Hexagon Sparkler 30 g	0.9		Tight wobble		Sinking	Metal	Bibless	9.9	Nose	30.9
214	Sub Wart 5 cm	0.9	0–0.3	Medium sway			Plastic	Plastic	15	Nose	8.5
215	Lofty's Cobra	0.9	1.4	Wide wobble		Sinking	Metal	Plastic		Nose	
216	Super Vibrax 6	0.9		Spinner		Sinking	Metal	Bibless			18
217	Minnow Spin Super Vibrax 1	0.95		Spinner	Better at 1.5 knots.	Sinking	Metal	Bibless		Nose	4.3
218	Vibrax Minnow Chaser 2	0.95		Spinner		Sinking	Metal	Bibless		Nose	16.5
219	Super Champ 28 g	0.95		Medium roll	Good action.	Sinking	Metal	Bibless	6	Nose	31.9
220	Jointed Swim Whizz	0.95		Wide sway, wide roll	Great action. Used bottom line attachment.	Floating	Plastic	Plastic	28.4	Bib	53.2
221	King Cobra	0.95		Wide wobble, tight pitch	Good action.	Sinking	Metal	Plastic		Nose	
222	Strike Pro Double Bladed Spinnerbait	0.95		Blade wobble		Sinking	Metal	Bibless			12.4
223	Pilchard 15 g	1		Med roll	Good at 2 knots.	Sinking	Metal	Bibless	3.5	Nose	16.1
224	Live Chrome 35 g	1		Tight roll		Sinking	Metal	Bibless	4.2	Nose	33.1
225	Baitfish Flash 40 g	1		Shimmy		Sinking	Metal	Bibless	2.5	Nose	41.1
226	Z Spinner 8 g	1		Medium wobble		Sinking	Metal	Bibless	11.6	Nose	6.8
227	Prince Minnow PM50F	1		Tight roll		Floating	Plastic	Plastic	6.1	Nose	2.3
228	Prince Minnow PM105F	1		Slow roll		Floating	Plastic	Plastic	12.1	Nose	16.2
229	Devon	1		Tight spin		Sinking	Metal	Plastic		Nose	
230	Devon 2"	1		Tight spin		Sinking	Metal	Plastic		Nose	

with Bib	Depth on 6.9m at 1.5 knots	Depth on 6.9m at 2 knots	Depth on 6.9m at 2.5 knots	Manufacturer	Country of Manufacture
		0.35		Hawk Fishing Tackle	China
		0.4		Blue Fox	Finland
		0.4		Fishfighter Lures	NZ
		0.35		Halco	Aust—WA
		0.35		Halco	Aust—WA
		0.4		Lofty's Lures	Aust—Tas
		0.4		Blue Fox	Finland
		0.4		Worden's	Mexico
		0.4		Juro	Taiwan
		0.4		Blue Fox	Finland
		0.4		Bomber	El Salvador
			0.4	Kokoda	China
		0.4		Halco	Aust—WA
		0.4		Storm	Estonia
		0.45		Lofty's Lures	Aust—Tas
		0.45		Blue Fox	Finland
	0.5	0.2		Blue Fox	Finland
		0.45		Blue Fox	Finland
		0.45		Wonder Fishing Tackle	Aust—Vic
		0.45		Homer Le Blanc Tackle	USA
		0.45		Tillins Lures	Aust—Tas
		0.45		McLaughlin's Lures	Taiwan
		0.4		Hawk Fishing Tackle	China
		0.4		Rio's Lures	Aust—Qld
		0.4		Hawk Fishing Tackle	China
		0.4		Fishfighter Lures	NZ
		0.4		SureBite Lures—SureCatch	China
		0.4		SureBite Lures—SureCatch	China
		0.4		Abanka Lures	Aust—Tas
		0.4		Tillins Lures	Aust—Tas

212

217

216

218

219

220

223

221

222

224

225

227

226

230

215

213

229

228

214

No.	Lure	Depth Test	Maker's Depth	Action	Comments	Buoyancy	Body Material	Bib Material	Bib Width mm	Tow Point	Weight g	Body Length mm	Actual Length
231	Teeny Wee Frog	1.05	0.9	Medium sway	Better at 1.5 knots.	Floating	Plastic	Plastic	10.5	Nose	2.7	38.1	4
232	Mystic Ghost Minnow	1.05		Tight roll, tight pitch		Floating	Plastic	Plastic	8.3	Nose	2.9	57.2	62
233	Intruder Poddy Minnow	1.05		Medium sway, wide roll			Plastic	Plastic	10	Nose	11.3	90.6	9
234	Super Vibrax 3	1.05		Spinner		Sinking	Metal	Bibless			8		
235	1/4oz Trifecta	1.05		Blade wobble		Sinking	Metal	Bibless			14.7		
236	Wonder Pilchard 45 g	1.1		Medium wobble		Sinking	Metal	Bibless	2.3	Nose	46.1	87.4	9
237	Baitfish Flash 60 g	1.1		Med roll		Sinking	Metal	Bibless	3	Nose	59.5	107.7	1
238	Salty Tasmanian Devil 40 g	1.1		Wide wobble, wide pitch	Great action at 2.5 knots.		Plastic	Bibless	4	Nose	41.5	54.8	54
239	Pin's Minnow	1.1		Shimmy		Floating	Plastic	Plastic	6.9	Nose	1.8	54	6
240	Legend Spinnerbait 1/4oz	1.1		Blade wobble		Sinking	Metal	Bibless			11.3		
241	Tiger Minnow	1.15		Medium wobble, med pitch	Very good action. Better at 2 knots.	Sinking	Metal	Bibless	1.5	Nose	11.2	63.4	63
242	Jointed Minnow J-5	1.15		Shimmy, tight pitch		Floating	Wood	Plastic	8.3	Nose	3.5	55.8	63
243	Sub Wart	1.15	0–0.3	Wide sway			Plastic	Plastic	11.9	Nose	5.4	41.3	48
244	Humbug Min 45S	1.15		Tight sway	Better at 1.5 knots.	Sinking	Plastic	Plastic	10	Nose	4.7	44	4
245	Super Vibrax 5	1.15		Spinner		Sinking	Metal	Bibless			12.2		
246	3/8oz Double Colorado Spinnerbait	1.15		Blade wobble		Sinking	Metal	Bibless			17.2		
247	Spinnerbait Barra Lure 3/8oz	1.15		Blade wobble		Sinking	Metal	Bibless			18		
248	Bushwacker 3/8oz	1.15		Blade wobble	Lots of blade action.	Sinking	Metal	Bibless					
249	Sting 12	1.2		Medium wobble	Good action.		Plastic	Bibless		Nose		58.8	58
250	Mirror Spoon 6	1.2		Wide wobble	Better at 2.5 knots.	Sinking	Metal	Bibless		Nose	46.9	157.2	15
251	Kwikfish K7	1.2		Wide sway	Better slower at 1.5 knots.		Plastic	Plastic	14.5	Body	3.1	42.6	58
252	Extra Shallow Diver 90	1.2		Medium roll			Plastic	Plastic	18	Nose	16.5	92.3	97
253	Tumbleweed Charlie's Spinnerbait 3/8oz	1.2		Blade wobble		Sinking	Metal	Bibless			18.5		
254	3/8 Double Willow Spinnerbait	1.2		Blade wobble		Sinking	Metal	Bibless			21.1		
255	Vector 50 g	1.25		Slow roll		Sinking	Metal	Bibless	2.5	Nose	38.7	79	9
256	Baitfish Flash 30 g	1.25		Shimmy		Sinking	Metal	Bibless	2.7	Nose	29.5	80.2	8
257	Pilchard 70 g	1.25		Medium roll		Sinking	Metal	Bibless	5.3	Nose	66.6	97.2	9
258	Flash Shad 13	1.25		Tight wobble	Much better than expected.		Rubber	Bibless	6.3	Nose	32.2	123.5	12
259	Flashback Treble	1.25		Medium wobble		Sinking	Metal	Bibless		Nose	37.7	76.5	76
260	Chrome Dancer 20 g	1.25		Tight wobble		Sinking	Metal	Bibless	9	Nose	18.6	53.2	53

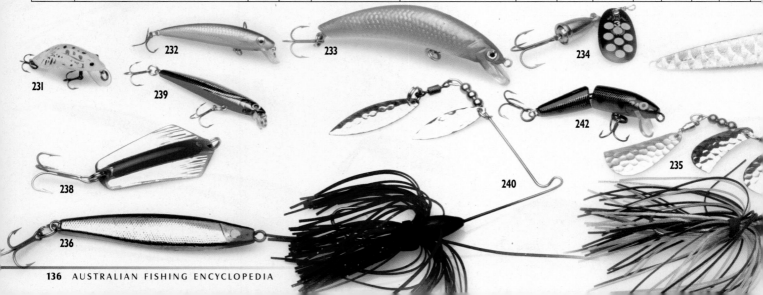

231 232 233 234

239

238 242 235

240

236

at 1.5 knots	Depth on 6.9m at 2 knots	Depth on 6.9m at 2.5 knots	Manufacturer	Country of Manufacture
0.45			Rebel	Mexico
0.5			Rebel	Mexico
0.5			Jarvis Walker	Vietnam
0.5			Blue Fox	Finland
0.5			Bassman Lures	Aust—NSW
0.45			Wonder Fishing Tackle	Aust—Vic
0.45			Hawk Fishing Tackle	China
0.45			Wigston's	Aust—Tas
0.45			Yo-Zuri Lures	Japan
0.45			Legend Lures	Aust—NSW
0.35			Pegron	Aust—NSW
0.55			Rapala	Ireland
0.55			Storm	Estonia
0.55			River 2 Sea	
0.55			Blue Fox	Finland
0.55			Bassman Lures	Aust—NSW
0.55			Bassman Lures	Aust—NSW
0.55			Bomber	El Salvador
0.5			Sting Lures	Aust—Tas
0.6			Tackle Master	Aust—Qld
0.55			Luhr Jensen	USA
0.55			Bill's Bugs	Aust—NSW
0.6			The Producers	China
0.6			Bassman Lures	Aust—NSW
0.5			Kokoda	China
0.5			Hawk Fishing Tackle	China
0.5			Hawk Fishing Tackle	Korea
0.5			Kokoda	China
0.55			Tackle Master	Aust—Qld
0.5			Juro	China

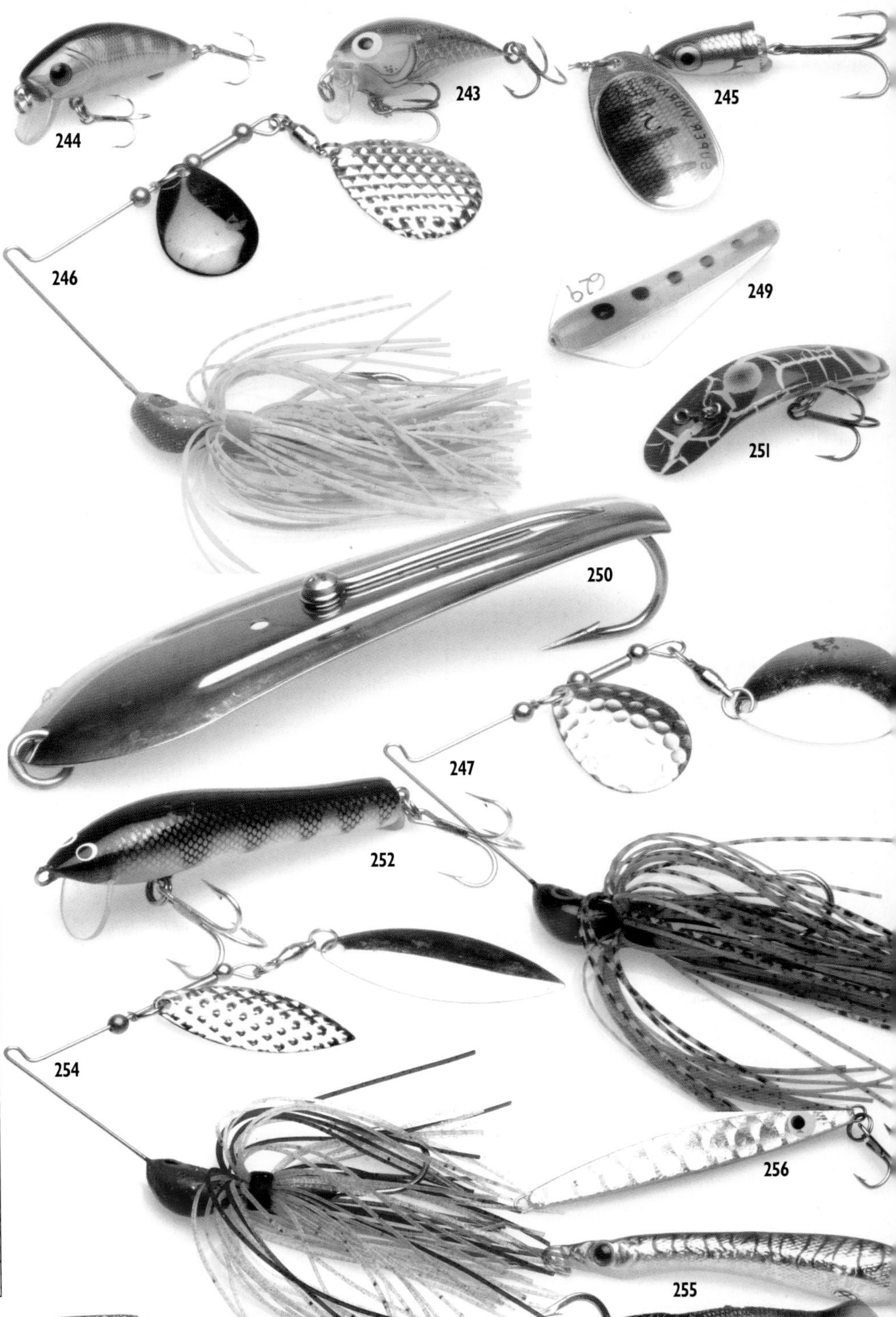

244

243

245

246

249

251

250

247

252

254

256

255

258

257

237

253

248

260

259

241

No.	Lure	Depth Test	Maker's Depth	Action	Comments	Buoyancy	Body Material	Bib Material	Bib Width mm	Tow Point	W...
261	Lancaster	1.25		Medium sway, tight roll	Better slower.		Plastic	Plastic	10	Nose	6
262	Ace Minnow AM60F	1.25		Little action	Poor action.	Floating	Plastic	Plastic	6.7	Nose	3
263	Jointed Minnow J-7	1.25		Shimmy	Good action for jointed lure.	Floating	Wood	Plastic	10.6	Nose	4
264	Ashley Devon	1.25		Tight spin		Sinking	Metal	Plastic		Nose	
265	Rooster Tail Spinner 1/4oz	1.25		Spinner		Sinking	Metal	Bibless		Nose	9
266	Flashback Single	1.3		Medium wobble		Sinking	Metal	Bibless	10.7	Nose	3
267	Bardi Grub	1.3		Tight roll, med pitch			Wood	Plastic	18	Nose	7.
268	Humbug Min 45F	1.3		Tight sway	Very good action. Better at 1.5 kn. Some lateral action.	Floating	Plastic	Plastic	10.3	Nose	3.
269	Roscoe's Shiner 5	1.3		Med roll		Floating	Plastic	Plastic	18.8	Nose	1
270	Shallow A	1.3		Tight sway			Plastic	Plastic	17.3	Nose	9.
271	Jet Spinner Bass	1.3		Spinner	Can take more speed.	Sinking	Metal	Bibless		Nose	15
272	Jet Spinner Minnow	1.3		Spinner		Sinking	Metal	Bibless		Nose	11
273	Vibrax Minnow Chaser 1	1.35		Spinner	Better at 2 knots.	Sinking	Wood	Bibless		Nose	12
274	Hexagon Sparkler 55 g	1.35		Medium wobble		Sinking	Metal	Bibless	12.8	Nose	55
275	AC Minnow 45	1.35		Tight sway			Wood	Plastic	11.6	Bib	3.
276	Gobimaru 70	1.35		Med roll		Floating	Plastic	Plastic	9.4	Nose	5.
277	Humbug Min 65F	1.35		Tight sway, tight roll		Floating	Plastic	Plastic	10	Nose	8.
278	Nymph	1.35	1.2	Med pitch			Plastic	Plastic	12.2	Bib	3.
279	Sting	1.35	2	Medium, wobble med pitch	Tighter action than other lures of this style.	Sinking	Metal	Plastic		Nose	
280	Bang Tail 4	1.35		Spinner	Good action.	Sinking	Metal	Bibless			9
281	Jig Spinner	1.35		Blade wobble	Good combination.	Sinking	Rubber	Bibless			17.
282	Kill'r B-II Super Shallow	1.4	0–0.3	Tight sway		Floating	Wood	Plastic	16.9	Nose	10.
283	Fat Bob	1.4	1	Med sway, tight roll		Sinking	Wood	Plastic	22.3	Bib	13.
284	Murray Cod Spinnerbait 3/4	1.4		Blade wobble	Nice configuration.	Sinking	Metal	Bibless			28.
285	True Trac Pro 3/4oz	1.4		Blade wobble		Sinking	Metal	Bibless			30
286	Original Minnow 3	1.45		Fast tight sway, tight roll		Floating	Plastic	Plastic	10.2	Nose	1.8
287	Suicide Original BalsaMinnow	1.45		Med roll	Needs to be slower.	Sinking	Wood	Plastic	9.8	Nose	2.7
288	Crickhopper	1.45	0–0.9	Tight roll	Needs 1.5 knots or slower.	Floating	Plastic	Plastic	14.4	Bib	3.9
289	Elmo's Zipfish #2	1.45		Medium sway	Works well at 2 knots.	Floating	Plastic	Bibless	13.3	Body	2.5
290	Just Under	1.45	0.3	Med roll, tight pitch		Floating	Plastic	Plastic	16	Nose	8.1

261 262 263 264 267 268 269 270 271 272

Actual Length with Bib	Depth on 6.9m at 1.5 knots	Depth on 6.9m at 2 knots	Depth on 6.9m at 2.5 knots	Manufacturer	Country of Manufacture
100.8		0.5		Deception Lures	Aust—NSW
67.3		0.5		SureBite Lures—SureCatch	Japan
77		0.55		Rapala	Ireland
52.8		0.5		Ashley Lure	Aust—Tas
		0.5		Hawk Fishing Tackle	China
74.2		0.5		Tackle Master	Aust—Qld
83		0.6		Huey's Lures	Aust—Tas
48.8	0.6	0.6		River 2 Sea	
116.1		0.6		The Producers	China
56.7		0.6		Bomber	USA
63.6		0.55		Jack's Fishing	Thailand
58		0.65		Jack's Fishing	Thailand
99.2	0.85	0.55		Blue Fox	Finland
77		0.55		Halco	Aust—WA
61.1		0.55		AC Lures	Aust—NSW
75.5		0.55		Surebite Lures—SureCatch	Japan
72		0.55		River 2 Sea	
58.2		0.55		S K Lures	Aust—Qld
58.5		0.55		Sting Lures	Aust—Tas
		0.55		Luhr Jensen	Mexico
		0.55		Horsey's Lures	Aust—Qld
70		0.65		Bagley	Dominican Rep
88.2		0.65		Cudgeefish	Aust—NSW
		0.7		Legend Lures	Aust—NSW
		0.7		Andreas Tackle	USA
43.8		0.6		Rapala	Ireland
56.8		0.7		Juro	Taiwan
56.5	0.7	0.65		Rebel	USA
51.6		0.7		The Producers	China
86.8		0.7		Classic Lures	Aust

No.	Lure	Depth Test	Maker's Depth	Action	Comments	Buoyancy	Body Material	Bib Material	Bib Width mm	Tow Point	Weight g	Body Length mm	Actual Length with Bib	Depth on 6.9m at 1.5 knots
291	Stretch 1 Minus	1.45		Slow roll		Floating	Plastic	Plastic	18.9	Nose	18.6	112.4	119.7	
292	Blade Runner Mini	1.45		Tight wobble	Good action.	Sinking	Metal	Bibless		Nose	13.7	52.5	52.5	
293	Enticer 55 g	1.5		Shimmy		Sinking	Metal	Bibless	4	Nose	48	73.5	83.8	
294	Spoon 14 g	1.5		Medium wobble	Great erratic action.	Sinking	Metal	Bibless	1.3	Nose	11.1	58.5	58.5	
295	Snap Shad super small	1.5		Shimmy			Plastic	Plastic	11.7	Bib	2.5	39.8	56.5	
296	Mirror Spoon 4	1.5		Wide wobble	Great erratic action.	Sinking	Metal	Bibless	15.8	Nose	20.8	99.1	99.1	
297	Pro's Choice Minnow	1.5		Tight roll			Plastic	Plastic	8.9	Nose	5.5	79.8	84.7	
298	MMLS Crankbait	1.5		Tight sway			Plastic	Metal	8	Bib	2.1	40.3	52.7	
299	Super Lucky SL33	1.5		Tight sway		Sinking	Plastic	Plastic	9	Nose	3.4	35.2	42.6	
300	McGrath Minnow Shallow	1.5	1	Tight roll		Floating	Wood	Plastic	12	Nose	4.3	63.3	65.6	
301	McGrath Minnow Mini	1.5	1–1.5	Shimmy		Floating	Wood	Plastic	11.7	Nose	3.3	52.8	63.2	
302	Ace Minnow AM80F	1.5		Tight sway, tight roll		Floating	Plastic	Plastic	9.1	Nose	5.9	79.7	86.8	
303	Countdown Minnow CD3	1.5		Shimmy		Sinking	Wood	Plastic	10.6	Nose	3.1	38.3	44.1	
304	Original Minnow 5	1.5		Shimmy		Floating	Wood	Plastic	10	Nose	2.3	51.6	57	
305	3-D Fingerling Suspending	1.5	1.8	Tight roll		Suspend.	Plastic	Plastic	9.1	Bib	7.2	69.9	81	
306	Golden Hunter Minnow	1.5	1	Tight sway, tight roll		Floating	Plastic	Plastic	7.9	Nose	5.4	70	75.8	
307	Humbug Min 65S	1.5		Tight sway, tight roll		Sinking	Plastic	Plastic	10	Nose	8.9	66	72.5	
308	TD Hyper Minnow	1.5	2	Med roll		Suspend.	Plastic	Metal	12.1	Bib	6	69.4	91.2	
309	Husky Jerk HJ8	1.5		Tight roll, med pitch	Great action.	Suspend.	Plastic	Plastic	11.1	Nose	6.1	71.7	78.4	
310	TD Hyper Minnow	1.5	2	Med sway. med pitch	Very good action.	Floating	Plastic	Metal	12.1	Bib	5.6	68.8	92	
311	Finn Mann	1.5		Vibrate			Plastic	Bibless	9.5	Body	5	37.1	37.1	
312	1/2oz Copperblade Tandem	1.5		Blade wobble		Sinking	Metal	Bibless			19.1			
313	Jointed Minnow J-11	1.55		Tight sway		Floating	Wood	Plastic	14.8	Nose	8.2	107.5	114	
314	Super Hopper SH48	1.55		Tight sway, med pitch	Needs 1.5 knots or slower.	Sinking	Plastic	Plastic	17.8	Nose	5	46.6	55.9	
315	Original Minnow 13	1.55		Tight sway, med roll		Floating	Wood	Plastic	11.1	Nose		126	133.8	
316	Aeroplane Spinner #1	1.55		Spinner	Hook spinning.	Sinking	Metal	Bibless		Nose	96.4			
317	Tasmanian Devil Dual Depth	1.6		Medium wobble		Sinking	Plastic	Bibless		Nose		56.2	56.2	
318	Flash Shad 10	1.6		Shimmy	Good action from tail.	Sinking	Rubber	Bibless		Nose	19.1	96.6	101.4	
319	Pilchard 90 g	1.6		Tight roll		Sinking	Metal	Bibless	6.1	Nose	88.6	102.5	110	
320	Roscoe's Shiner 4	1.6		Tight roll			Plastic	Plastic	13.9	Nose	6.1	82.5	88.2	

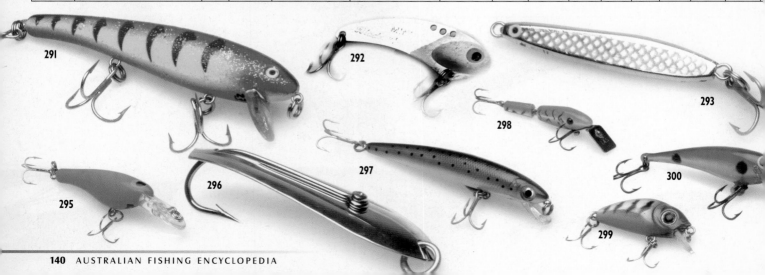

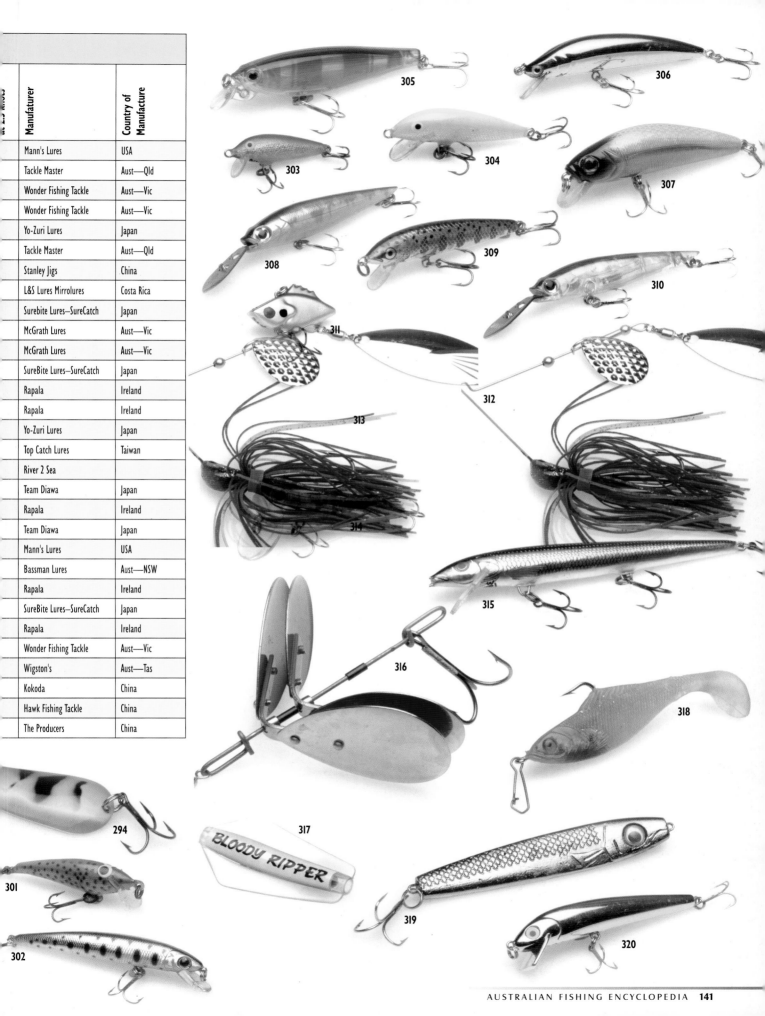

Manufacturer	Country of Manufacture
Mann's Lures	USA
Tackle Master	Aust—Qld
Wonder Fishing Tackle	Aust—Vic
Wonder Fishing Tackle	Aust—Vic
Yo-Zuri Lures	Japan
Tackle Master	Aust—Qld
Stanley Jigs	China
L&S Lures Mirrolures	Costa Rica
Surebite Lures—SureCatch	Japan
McGrath Lures	Aust—Vic
McGrath Lures	Aust—Vic
SureBite Lures—SureCatch	Japan
Rapala	Ireland
Rapala	Ireland
Yo-Zuri Lures	Japan
Top Catch Lures	Taiwan
River 2 Sea	
Team Diawa	Japan
Rapala	Ireland
Team Diawa	Japan
Mann's Lures	USA
Bassman Lures	Aust—NSW
Rapala	Ireland
SureBite Lures—SureCatch	Japan
Rapala	Ireland
Wonder Fishing Tackle	Aust—Vic
Wigston's	Aust—Tas
Kokoda	China
Hawk Fishing Tackle	China
The Producers	China

No.	Lure	Depth Test	Maker's Depth	Action	Comments	Buoyancy	Body Material	Bib Material	Bib Width mm	Tow Point	Weight g
321	LK 080	1.6		Tight sway				Plastic	16	Nose	3
322	Teeny Crawfish	1.6	0.9–1.2	Tight sway		Floating	Plastic	Plastic	13.2	Bib	2.5
323	Finnigan's Minnow #4	1.6		Shimmy, tight pitch			Plastic	Plastic	13.1	Nose	6.4
324	Bijou Lure	1.6		Slow med roll		Floating	Plastic	Plastic	11.4	Nose	4.5
325	Super Minnow SM60	1.6		Slow roll		Floating	Plastic	Plastic	9.9	Bib	5.5
326	Husky Jerk HJ6	1.6		Tight sway, tight roll		Suspend.	Wood	Plastic	9.8	Nose	3.3
327	Original Minnow 9	1.6		Med roll		Floating	Wood	Plastic	10.3	Nose	4.2
328	Original Minnow 7	1.6		Tight sway, tight roll		Floating	Plastic	Plastic	10.2	Nose	3.5
329	Bushwacker 1/2oz	1.6		Blade wobble		Sinking	Metal	Bibless			22.5
330	Walure	1.65		Shimmy	Good action.	Floating	Wood	Plastic	8.2	Nose	
331	Aile Killifish	1.65	0.3–0.4	Shimmy	Great action. Better at 1.5 knots.	Floating	Plastic	Plastic	11.6	Nose	1.5
332	Prince Minnow PM130F	1.65		Slow roll		Floating	Plastic	Plastic	14.1	Nose	27.5
333	Gobimaru 130	1.65		Slow wide roll		Floating	Plastic	Plastic	12.5	Nose	29.8
334	Finnigan's Minnow #5	1.65		Med roll			Plastic	Plastic	19.6	Nose	13.8
335	Big Mouth	1.65	Cast 1.0 Troll 2.0	Tight sway, tight roll			Plastic	Bibless	17.3	Nose	6
336	LK 090	1.7		Tight sway				Plastic	16.1	Nose	2.8
337	Twisty 55 g	1.7		Medium wobble,		Sinking	Metal	Bibless tight pitch	10.1	Nose	58.2
338	RMG Sneaky Bream Scorpion 35	1.7	1.4			Suspend.	Plastic	Plastic	12.2	Bib	2.6
339	True Trac Spin 1/2oz	1.7		Blade wobble	Good spinner blade action.	Sinking	Metal	Bibless			22.9
340	Invincible 8	1.75	2	Med roll		Floating	Wood	Plastic	12.8	Nose	5.9
341	Craw Fish #21	1.75		Medium sway	Needs 1.5 knots or slower.	Floating	Plastic	Plastic	11.1	Nose	3
342	Prince Minnow PM90F	1.75		Slow roll		Floating	Plastic	Plastic	10.4	Nose	11.1
343	RMG Scorpion 35 STD	1.75	1	Tight sway	Much better slower.		Plastic	Plastic	12.4	Bib	2.9
344	Gobimaru 90	1.75		Slow wide roll		Floating	Plastic	Plastic	10.3	Nose	9.6
345	The Bandit	1.75		Slow roll			Plastic	Plastic	13.9	Nose	23.1
346	Shallow Thunder II	1.75	0.9–1.8	Slow med roll			Plastic	Plastic	17.8	Nose	22
347	Live Chrome 50 g	1.8		Tight roll	Needs at least 2.5 knots.	Sinking	Metal	Bibless	4.8	Nose	51.1
348	Jointed Minnow J-9	1.8		Med pitch		Floating	Wood	Plastic	15	Nose	7.2
349	Cudgeeshrimp 2 1+	1.8	1	Med roll		Floating	Wood	Plastic	22.1	Bib	14.3
350	Elmo's Zipfish #3	1.8		Wide sway	Better at 1.5 knots.	Floating	Plastic	Plastic	17.6	Body	5.3

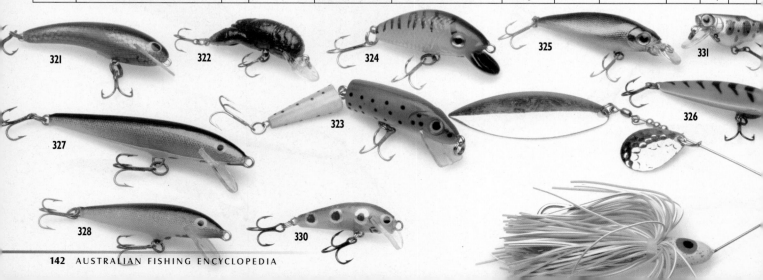

Depth on 6.9m at 1.5 knots	Depth on 6.9m at 2 knots	Depth on 6.9m at 2.5 knots	Manufacturer	Country of Manufacture
	0.65		Larrikin Lures	Aust—Vic
	0.65		Rebel	Mexico
	0.65		The Producers	China
	0.65		Hawk Fishing Tackle	China
	0.65		Surebite Lures—SureCatch	Japan
	0.65		Rapala	Ireland
	0.65		Rapala	Ireland
	0.65		Rapala	Ireland
	0.65		Bomber	El Salvador
	0.7		Walures	Aust—Tas
0.7	0.8		Yo-Zuri Lures	Japan
	0.65		SureBite Lures—SureCatch	China
	0.8		Surebite Lures—SureCatch	China
	0.8		The Producers	China
	0.65		Nilsmaster	Finland
	0.7		Larrikin Lures	Aust—Vic
	0.7		Halco	Aust—WA
	0.7		Halco	Aust—WA
	0.7		Andreas Tackle	USA
	0.7		Nilsmaster	Finland
	0.7		The Prince	
	0.7		SureBite Lures—SureCatch	China
0.75	0.7		Halco	Aust—WA
	0.7		Surebite Lures—SureCatch	Japan
	0.7		McLaughlin's Lures	Taiwan
	0.7		Storm	Estonia
		0.75	Rio's Lures	Aust—Qld
	0.85		Rapala	Ireland
	0.85		Cudgeefish	Aust—NSW
1.1	0.85		The Producers	China

No.	Lure	Depth Test	Maker's Depth	Action	Comments	Buoyancy	Body Material	Bib Material	Bib Width mm	Tow Point	Weight g	Body Length mm
351	Tasmanian Devil Dual Depth Deep	1.85		Wide wobble	Great erratic action.	Sinking	Plastic	Bibless		Nose		56.2
352	Salty Tasmanian Devil 70 g	1.85		Wide wobble, tight pitch	Needs at least 2.5 knots.	Sinking	Plastic	Bibless	13	Nose	76.6	74.8
353	Lil' Ripper	1.85	1.2	Fast tight sway			Wood	Plastic	10.9	Nose	3.2	45.8
354	Mini Fat Rap	1.85		Shimmy		Sinking	Wood	Plastic	11.7	Nose	4.2	34.2
355	Gobimaru 105	1.85		Slow wide roll		Floating	Plastic	Plastic	10.9	Nose	17.2	105.6
356	Lightning Minnow #1	1.85		Slow roll, med pitch		Floating	Plastic	Plastic	12	Bib	3.5	52.1
357	Spinnerbait Classic 3/4oz	1.85		Blade wobble	Good blade action.	Sinking	Metal	Bibless			31.3	
358	True Trac Classic 1oz	1.85		Blade wobble	Good blade action.	Sinking	Metal	Bibless			37	
359	Super Crawfish SCF40F	1.9		Med sway, tight pitch		Floating	Plastic	Plastic	18.7	Bib	5.7	51.6
360	Intruder Ko-Jack	1.9		Huge pitch (out of tune)	Extremely difficult to tune.			Metal	11.9	Nose	8.9	69.8
361	Kwikfish K8	1.9		Wide sway	Needs 1.5 knots or slower.		Plastic	Plastic	17.6	Body	5.5	45.3
362	Team Esko TE7	1.95		Med roll		Floating	Wood	Plastic	13.7	Nose	5.9	65.2
363	Long Cast Minnow LC12	1.95	0.3–1.2	Slow roll			Wood	Plastic	13.1	Nose	21.4	129.1
364	AC Minnow 45	1.95		Tight sway			Wood	Plastic	13	Bib	3.8	44.5
365	Classic 65	2	2	Tight roll			Plastic	Plastic	18.1	Nose	7.5	62.6
366	Countdown Minnow CD5	2		Fast shimmy		Sinking	Wood	Plastic	11	Nose	4.8	51.6
367	Super Skippy	2		Vibrate		Sinking	Plastic	Bibless	10.1	Body	6.7	55.2
368	Baby Shad BS50P	2		Tight sway	Good action.	Suspend.	Plastic	Plastic	9.1	Bib	3.6	52.8
369	Rattlin' Rapala RNR-4	2		Vibrate		Sinking	Plastic	Bibless	9.6	Body	5.3	48.3
370	Blade Runner	2.05		Tight wobble	Great action.	Sinking	Metal	Bibless	9.5	Body	16.8	73
371	Murray Cod Spinnerbait 1 1/4	2.05		Blade wobble	Great blade action.	Sinking	Metal	Bibless			41.4	
372	Shad Rap Shallow 7	2.1		Slow roll		Floating	Wood	Plastic	14.5	Nose	6.5	70.8
373	Wee Frog	2.1	1.5–2.1	Med sway, tight pitch	Good action but better slower.	Floating	Plastic	Plastic	18.1	Bib	7.2	55.5
374	Wedgetail - Shallow 6	2.1		Medsway			Wood	Plastic	13.3	Nose	6.5	60.1
375	Honey B Super Shallow	2.1	0–0.3	Shimmy		Floating	Wood	Plastic	12.9	Nose	5.1	37.2
376	Crickhopper	2.1	0–0.9	Tight sway		Floating	Plastic	Plastic	14.1	Bib		37.2
377	Nose Systems Small	2.1		Tight sway			Plastic	Plastic	9.7	Nose	4.4	49.8
378	Laser Pro 190 STD	2.1	1	Med sway, med roll	Better at 2.5 knots.		Plastic	Plastic	18.5	Nose	45	178
379	Slap-Stick	2.1		Med sway, med roll	Loud rattle.	Floating	Plastic	Plastic	12.1	Nose	11.2	111.8
380	Elmo's Zipfish #8	2.1		Wide sway	Better at 1.5 knots.		Plastic	Plastic	35.5	Body	33.3	99.4

351

353   352

357   353   354

Depth on 6.9m at 1.5 knots	Depth on 6.9m at 2 knots	Depth on 6.9m at 2.5 knots	Manufacturer	Country of Manufacture
	0.75	0.65	Wigston's	Aust—Tas
	0.75		Wigston's	Aust—Tas
	0.75		Oar-Gee Lures	Aust—NSW
	0.75		Rapala	Ireland
	0.75		Surebite Lures—SureCatch	Japan
	0.7		The Producers	China
	0.75		Bassman Lures	Aust—NSW
	0.75		Andreas Tackle	USA
	0.75		Surebite Lures—SureCatch	China
	0.75		Jarvis Walker	Vietnam
	0.9		Luhr Jensen	USA
	0.8		Rapala	Ireland
	0.8		Rapala	Estonia
	0.8		AC Lures	Aust—NSW
	0.8		Classic Lures	Aust
	0.85		Rapala	Ireland
	0.75		Surebite Lures—SureCatch	China
	0.75		SureBite Lures—SureCatch	Japan
	0.8		Rapala	Ireland
	0.7		Tackle Master	Aust—Qld
	0.85		Legend Lures	Aust—NSW
	0.85		Rapala	Ireland
	0.85		Rebel	Mexico
	0.85		Illusion Lures	Aust—NSW
	0.85		Bagley	Dominican Rep
	0.85		Rebel	USA
	0.85		Transkei Lures	
	0.7	1.1	Halco	Aust—WA
	0.85		Bill Lewis Lures	USA
	1		The Producers	China

362

363

364

365

366

367

369

368

371

370

373

374

372

375

376

377

378

380

356

360

361

379

No.	Lure	Depth Test	Maker's Depth	Action	Comments	Buoyancy	Body Material	Bib Material	Bib Width mm	Tow Point
381	MinMin Shallow	2.15	1.5	Tight sway		Floating	Plastic	Plastic	12.3	Nose
382	Newell 1/2	2.15		Tight sway, tight pitch	Much better at 1.5 knots.	Floating	Wood	Plastic	11.5	Nose
383	Original Minnow II	2.15		Slow roll		Floating	Wood	Plastic	11.2	Nose
384	Baby Shad BS65P	2.15		Shimmy, med pitch	Better slower. Unstable at 2 knots.	Suspend.	Plastic	Plastic	13.9	Bib
385	Jigger 3	2.15		No action, not for trolling		Sinking	Metal	Bibless		Body
386	Big Bud (Coors)	2.15		Med wide sway		Floating	Plastic	Plastic	23.4	Nose
387	Legend Spinnerbait 3 1/4oz	2.15		Blade wobble		Sinking	Metal	Bibless		
388	LK 020	2.2		Shimmy	Good action.			Plastic	16	Nose
389	LK 010	2.2		Shimmy			Plastic	Plastic	16.1	Nose
390	Shad Rap Shallow 5	2.2		Shimmy		Floating	Wood	Plastic	13.3	Nose
391	Laser Pro 45	2.2	1	Fast roll		Floating	Plastic	Plastic	12.3	Bib
392	Hot Shot 60	2.2		Med. sway	Great action at 1.5 knots.	Floating	Plastic	Plastic	11.1	Body
393	Silver Hunter	2.2	1.5	Med. pitch		Sinking	Plastic	Plastic	10.1	Nose
394	Thunderstick 6	2.2	0.3–1.5	Tight sway			Plastic	Plastic	12.7	Nose
395	Nitro Express 9 cm	2.2		Med. roll			Plastic	Plastic	13.3	Nose
396	Humbug Min 90S	2.2		Tight roll		Sinking	Plastic	Plastic	9	Nose
397	Invincible 5	2.2	1	Tight roll		Floating	Wood	Plastic	13.1	Nose
398	Golden Hunter	2.2	1	Med. sway	Better at 2 knots.	Floating	Plastic	Plastic	10.9	Nose
399	Rattlin' Rogue ARB1200	2.2	0.6	Tight sway, med. roll		Floating	Plastic	Plastic	11.6	Nose
400	Super Spot	2.2		Vibrate	Rattle.	Sinking	Plastic	Bibless	7.2	Body
401	Mad Mullet 2.5" Shallow	2.25	1	Very slow roll	Needs more speed. Very slight action at 2 knots.		Plastic	Plastic	17.9	Nose
402	Attack Lure	2.25		Shimmy, med. pitch	Excellent action, much better at 1.5 knots.	Floating	Wood	Plastic	13.1	Nose
403	Shallow Diver 135	2.25		Med. sway, med. roll			Plastic	Plastic	21	Nose
404	Rat-L-Trap Tiny Trap	2.25		Vibrate		Sinking	Plastic	Bibless	12.9	Body
405	Vibration #16	2.25		Shimmy		Sinking	Plastic	Bibless	11.7	Body
406	Master Shad	2.25	3.7	Very wide sway, med. pitch	Excellent erratic action. Extremely erratic but stable at 1.5 and 2 knots.	Sinking	Wood	Plastic	33.2	Bib
407	Invincible Jointed 8	2.3	2	Shimmy		Floating	Wood	Plastic	12.9	Nose
408	Big O	2.3		Tight sway		Floating	Plastic	Plastic	10.8	Nose
409	Deep Teeny Craw	2.3	0.9–1.2	Tight sway	Much better at 1.5 knots.	Floating	Plastic	Plastic	14.1	Bib
410	Bayou Boogie	2.3		Vibrate			Plastic	Bibless	12.1	Body

Actual Length with Bib	Depth on 6.9m at 1.5 knots	Depth on 6.9m at 2 knots	Depth on 6.9m at 2.5 knots	Manufacturer	Country of Manufacture
60.9		0.8		Predatek	Aust—NSW
60	0.85	0.95		Peter Newell Lures	Aust—NSW
112.2		0.9		Rapala	Ireland
84.5		0.8		Surebite Lures—SureCatch	Japan
64.1		0.85		Nilsmaster	Finland
95.3		0.95		Heddon	USA
		0.8		Legend Lures	Aust—NSW
59.7		0.9		Larrikin Lures	Aust—Vic
54.7		0.9		Larrikin Lures	Aust—Vic
69.2		0.9		Rapala	Ireland
66.1		0.9		Halco	Aust—WA
46.7	1.05	0.9		Luhr Jensen	USA
97.2		0.9		Top Catch Lures	Taiwan
71.6		0.9		Storm	Estonia
11.5		0.9		Jarvis Walker	Vietnam
97.5		0.9		River 2 Sea	
57.8		0.9		Nilsmaster	Finland
119.7		0.9	0.75	Top Catch Lures	Taiwan
122.1		0.9		Smithwick	Mexico
53.6		0.9		Cotton Cordell	USA
84.6		0.85		Lively Lures	Aust—Qld
61	1.1	0.8		Attack Lures	Aust—Vic
144.3		0.9		Bill's Bugs	Aust—NSW
44		0.95		Bill Lewis Lures	USA
68.9		0.9		The Prince	
156	0.9	1.05		Bagley	Dominican Rep
87.3		0.95		Nilsmaster	Finland
52.9		0.95		Cotton Cordell	El Salvador
58.9	1	0.6		Rebel	USA
56.3		1		Heddon	USA

391

392

394

393

395

396

397

400

399

398

401

402

403

404

405

408

409

406

383

384

388

390

410

407

No.	Lure	Depth Test	Maker's Depth	Action	Comments	Buoyancy	Body Material	Bib Material	Bib Width mm	Tow Point	Weight g	Body Length mm	Actual Length
411	Laser Pro 160 STD	2.3	1	Med. sway, tight roll	Better at 2.5 knots.		Plastic	Bibless	164.5	Nose	27.2	151.8	162.
412	Nippy Nymph	2.35	2	Tight sway			Wood	Plastic	14.4	Bib	3.4	46.5	61.5
413	Native Minnow	2.35		Tight sway, tight pitch			Plastic	Plastic	13.9	Nose	4.4	55.1	68.9
414	A & B Barra Blaster 2"	2.35		Tight sway, tight roll	Good action.		Plastic	Plastic	14.1	Nose	4.4	51.6	63.5
415	Classic Barra	2.35		Tight sway		Floating	Plastic	Plastic	18.3	Bib	12.6	97.5	107.
416	Tiny N	2.35	0.6–1.2	Tight sway			Plastic	Plastic	12.9	Nose	4.4	41.5	52.7
417	Magnum Mag-7	2.35		Tight roll		Floating	Wood	Plastic	12.9	Nose	7.1	73.2	89
418	Explosion Minnow EXM 120F	2.35		Slow roll		Floating	Plastic	Plastic	11.7	Nose	16.9	120.3	131.7
419	Swim'n Image Shallow Runner	2.35		Tight sway, med. roll			Plastic	Plastic	15.7	Nose	12.4	73.2	84.1
420	Magnum Mag-9	2.35		Med. roll		Floating	Wood	Plastic	14.6	Nose	12.8	93.5	108.2
421	Sunshine Minnow #13B PI2	2.35		Slow wide roll			Plastic	Plastic	12.5	Nose	14.5	114.4	125.
422	Shad Rap Jointed JSR4	2.35	1.2–1.8	Med. sway	Excellent action, best of Jointed lures.		Plastic	Plastic	13.6	Bib	5.4	50.2	75.2
423	Intruder Nitro Express	2.35	2	Slow roll			Plastic	Plastic	11.4	Nose	23.1	115	125
424	Triho Min 120F	2.35		Tight roll		Floating	Plastic	Plastic	13.5	Nose	15.1	118.8	126
425	Hookers Rattling	2.35		Slow roll		Floating	Plastic	Plastic	13.7	Nose	13	118.7	127.9
426	Countdown Minnow CD7	2.35		Fast shimmy		Sinking	Wood	Plastic	14.8	Nose	7	64.7	72
427	Long A Minnow 1/2oz	2.35		Tight sway, med. roll	Good action.		Plastic	Plastic	14	Nose	11.9	117.8	127.3
428	The Original Pig	2.4	0.9–1.8	Very slow wide sway	Average.		Wood	Bibless		Nose	101.1	178.7	197.6
429	Ambush Cray	2.4	2	Tight sway, tight pitch			Plastic	Plastic	11.6	Nose	4.7	47.4	53.1
430	Baby Extractor - Shallow	2.4	1.2	Shimmy	Great action at 1.5 knots.	Floating	Wood	Plastic	17.2	Nose	4.5	49.4	56.4
431	Shallow Sand Viper	2.4		Med. sway, tight roll			Plastic	Plastic	23	Nose	27.5	139	155
432	Roscoe's Shiner 7	2.4		Med. sway, med. roll	Better at 2.5 knots.		Plastic	Plastic	15.2	Nose	22.2	150.1	160.2
433	Zero #2	2.4		Vibrate		Sinking	Plastic	Bibless		Body	9.3	63	63
434	Rattlin' Rapala RNR5	2.4		Vibrate		Sinking	Plastic	Bibless	10.2	Body	10.6	61.1	64.4
435	LK 100	2.45		Tight sway, tight roll			Plastic		20	Nose	5.1	83.1	91.1
436	Klawbaby	2.45		Shimmy		Floating	Plastic	Plastic	15.6	Bib	3.2	34.2	46.1
437	Lil' Fergo	2.45	1.2	Fast tight roll			Plastic	Plastic	14.4	Nose	4.1	56.6	57.8
438	A & B Barra Blaster 1"	2.45		Tight sway, med pitch	Better at 1.5 knots.		Plastic	Plastic	14.2	Nose	4.4	53.5	63.7
439	Shad Rap Shallow 8	2.45		Med. sway		Floating	Wood	Plastic	14.4	Nose	8.6	81.4	93.4
440	Runt	2.45		Shimmy		Floating	Plastic	Plastic	12.6	Nose	3	43.7	56.5

at 1.5 knots	Depth on 6.9m at 2 knots	Depth on 6.9m at 2.5 knots	Manufacturer	Country of Manufacture
0.95	1		Halco	Aust—WA
0.95			Taylor Made	Aust—NSW
0.95			Knol's Lures	Malaysia
0.95			JAR Lures	Aust—Qld
0.95			Classic Lures	Aust
0.95			Norman Lures	USA
0.95			Rapala	Ireland
0.95			Surebite Lures—SureCatch	China
0.95			Excalibur	El Salvador
0.95			Rapala	Ireland
0.95			The Prince	
0.95			Rapala	Estonia
0.95			Jarvis Walker	Vietnam
0.95			River 2 Sea	
0.95			Top Catch Lures	Taiwan
0.95			Rapala	Ireland
0.95			Bomber	Mexico
1.15	0.95		Odyssey Lures	USA
	1		Ambush Lures	Aust—Qld
5	0.85		Custom Crafted Lures	Aust—NSW
0.95			Predatek	Aust—NSW
0.95			The Producers	China
1			The Producers	China
0.95			Rapala	Ireland
1			Larrikin Lures	Aust—Vic
1			Luhr Jensen	Mexico
1			Willo Lures	Aust—Qld
1			JAR Lures	Aust
1			Rapala	Ireland
1			JP Lures	Aust—NSW

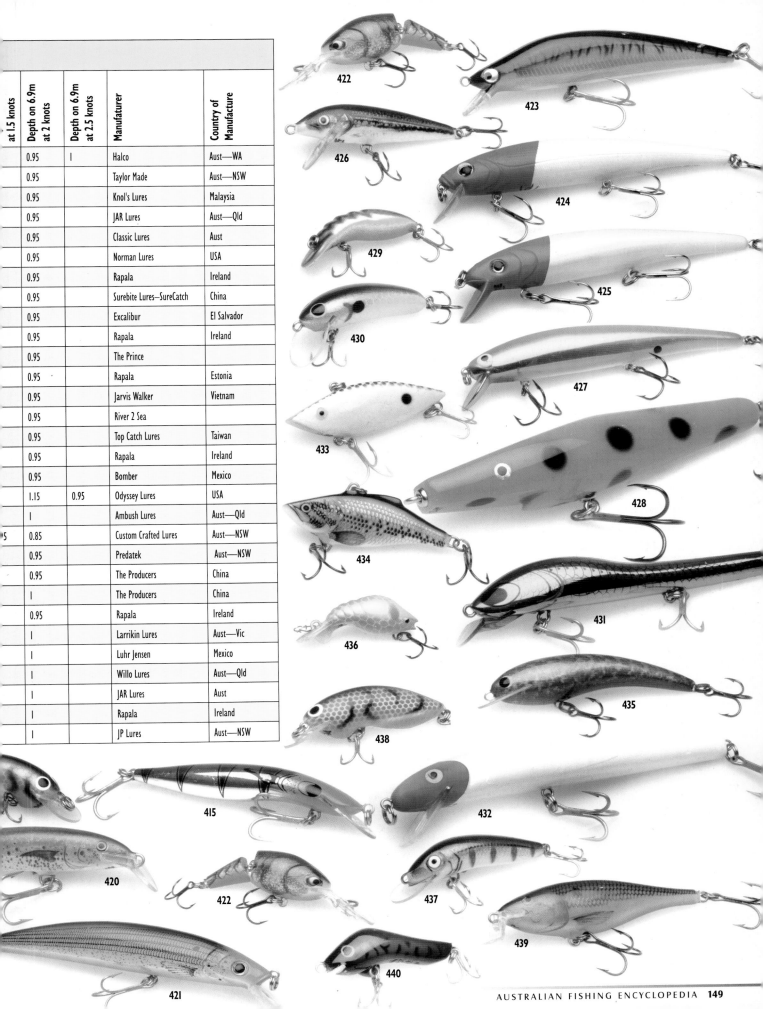

422

423

426

424

429

425

430

427

433

428

434

431

436

435

438

415

432

420

422

437

421

440

439

No.	Lure	Depth Test	Maker's Depth	Action	Comments	Buoyancy	Body Material	Bib Material	Bib Width mm	Tow Point	Weight g	Body Length mm	Actual Length with Bib	Depth on 6.9m
441	Mirashad Fry Size MS50SP	2.45		Tight sway, tight pitch		Suspending	Plastic	Plastic	13.2	Bib	4.5	49.1	67.1	
442	Long A 3/8oz	2.45		Med. pitch	This lure is difficult to tune.		Plastic	Plastic	12.3	Nose	9.3	84	96.1	
443	Jointed Long A	2.45		Med. sway	Good action for jointed lure, rattle.		Plastic	Plastic	13.7	Nose	16.3	117.2	126	
444	Classic Barra +3	2.45		Tight sway, tight roll			Plastic	Plastic	22.6	Nose	21.8	121.2	134.8	
445	Wee Pee Shallow	2.45	1.2	Wide sway			Wood	Plastic	20.1	Bib	7.6	43.9	72	
446	Laser Pro 120 STD	2.45	1	Wide roll	Better faster.		Plastic	Plastic	15.2	Nose	16.6	117	123.3	
447	Killalure Tiger 4BB	2.45	3	Med. roll, tight pitch		Floating	Plastic	Plastic	17.5	Nose	15.7	99.1	105.3	
448	Stanley Minnow	2.45		Med. sway, tight roll			Plastic	Plastic	14.4	Nose	15.6	115.9	125.4	
449	Shallow Thunder 15	2.45	1 to 2	Med. sway, med. roll	Great action.		Plastic	Plastic	21.3	Bib		150.7	167.5	
450	Long A Select Series	2.45		Med. sway, tight roll			Plastic	Plastic	14.4	Nose	13.3	117.9	127.7	
451	Shallow Thunder 15	2.45	1–2	Tight sway, slow med. roll	Better at 2.5 knots.		Plastic	Plastic	21.4	Nose	42.8	151.1	167.5	
452	Balsa B-I	2.45	1–1.2	Tight sway, tight pitch	Better at 1.5 knots.	Floating	Wood	Plastic	23.4	Nose	13	53.1	67.8	1.0
453	Mini Z Shallow	2.5		Tight roll, tight pitch	Excellent action.	Floating	Plastic	Plastic	15.9	Nose	10.6	60.6	63.3	
454	Balsa B-III	2.5	0–1.2	Med sway, tight roll		Floating	Wood	Plastic	23.6	Nose	22	78.8	90.5	
455	Rat-L-Trap Mini Trap	2.5		Vibrate		Sinking	Plastic	Bibless	10	Body	12.6	62.9	62.9	
456	Burmek B1 Pike Jointed	2.5		Med. sway	Great action. Extra kick on tail section.		Plastic	Plastic	31.6	Bib	63.9	187.5	214	
457	Palaemon	2.55		Tight sway, tight pitch	Great action at both speeds.		Wood	Plastic	15	Nose	3.1	47.5	60.3	1.1
458	Trout Masta	2.55		Tight sway			Plastic	Plastic	15.3	Bib	4.5	52.8	75.2	
459	Super Spot	2.55		Tight sway, vibrate	Loud rattle.	Sinking	Plastic	Bibless	9.8	Body	9.2	63.2	63.2	
460	Aeroplane Spinner #4	2.55		Spinner		Sinking	Metal	Bibless		Nose	51.4			
461	Invincible DR5	2.6	2	Tight roll			Wood	Plastic	16.9	Nose	5	53.2	60.3	
462	LK 050	2.6		Shimmy				Plastic	17.5	Nose	3.6	51.2	64.9	
463	Evolver 3BB	2.6	1.2	Slow roll	Nice finish.	Sinking	Plastic	Plastic	17.7	Nose	9.9	76.9	84.5	
464	MicroMin - Shallow	2.6	1.5	Tight sway		Sinking	Plastic	Plastic	7.8	Nose	3	40	50	
465	Wee Crawfish	2.6	1.2–1.8	Med. sway		Floating	Plastic	Plastic	18.1	Bib	5.8	51.6	64.2	
466	AC Minnow 80	2.6		Tight roll			Wood	Plastic	17.7	Bib	9.2	80.3	97.5	
467	Dinkum Yabby - Small	2.6	1.2	Tight sway	Great action. Arms move well.	Floating	Plastic	Plastic	10.4	Nose	6.6	49.8	64.4	
468	Bumble Bug	2.6	0.6	Tight sway	Good action.	Floating	Plastic	Plastic	14	Nose	2.9	36	46.2	1.1
469	Shallow Diver 90	2.6		Med. roll			Plastic	Plastic	22.1	Nose	14.8	95.2	109.4	
470	Husky Jerk HJ12	2.6		Slow roll		Suspend.	Plastic	Plastic	14.1	Nose	12.7	116.2	125.1	

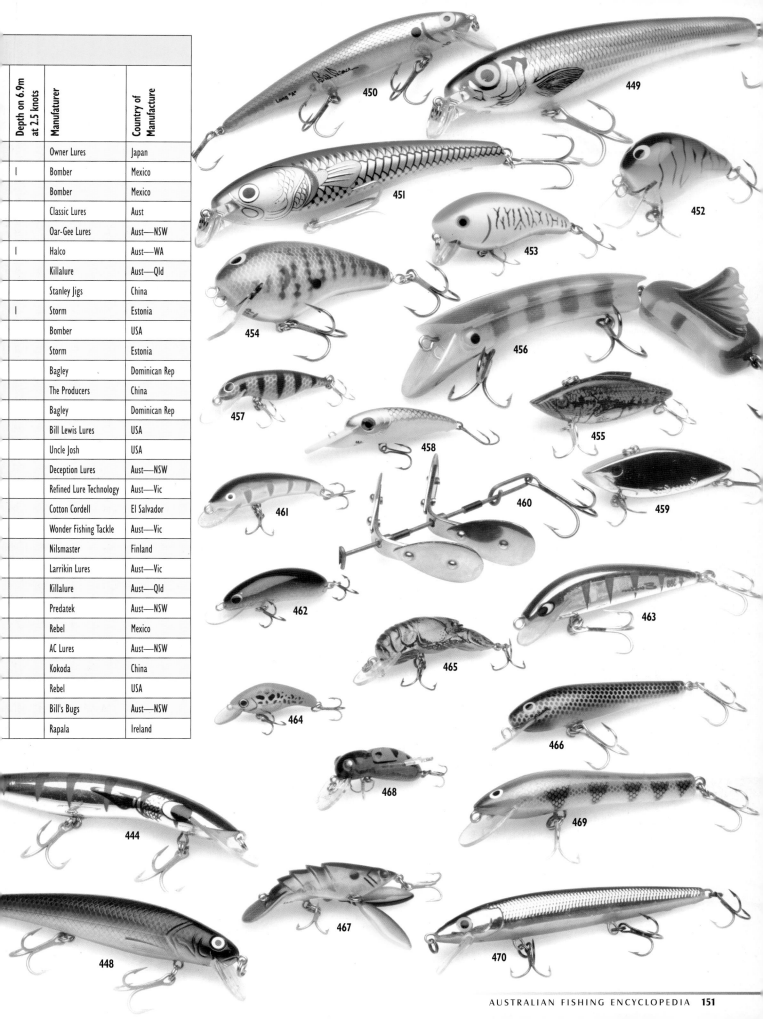

Depth on 6.9m at 2.5 knots	Manufacturer	Country of Manufacture
	Owner Lures	Japan
1	Bomber	Mexico
	Bomber	Mexico
	Classic Lures	Aust
	Oar-Gee Lures	Aust—NSW
1	Halco	Aust—WA
	Killalure	Aust—Qld
	Stanley Jigs	China
1	Storm	Estonia
	Bomber	USA
	Storm	Estonia
	Bagley	Dominican Rep
	The Producers	China
	Bagley	Dominican Rep
	Bill Lewis Lures	USA
	Uncle Josh	USA
	Deception Lures	Aust—NSW
	Refined Lure Technology	Aust—Vic
	Cotton Cordell	El Salvador
	Wonder Fishing Tackle	Aust—Vic
	Nilsmaster	Finland
	Larrikin Lures	Aust—Vic
	Killalure	Aust—Qld
	Predatek	Aust—NSW
	Rebel	Mexico
	AC Lures	Aust—NSW
	Kokoda	China
	Rebel	USA
	Bill's Bugs	Aust—NSW
	Rapala	Ireland

No.	Lure	Depth Test	Maker's Depth	Action	Comments	Buoyancy	Body Material	Bib Material	Bib Width mm	Tow Point	Weight g	Body Length mm	Actual Length
471	Explosion Minnow EXM 150F	2.6		Very slow roll		Floating	Plastic	Plastic	14.4	Nose	32.2	149.6	165.5
472	A-Salt	2.6		Slow roll	Much better faster.		Plastic	Plastic	15.2	Nose	26.3	145.2	161
473	Shakespeare Minnow	2.6		Med. sway, med. roll	Great action.		Plastic	Plastic	12.2	Nose	36.4	129	140.3
474	Thunderstick	2.6	0.3–1.5	Slow shim.			Plastic	Plastic	14.4	Nose	8	90.4	96.7
475	Thunderstick II	2.6	0.6–1.5	Slow sway			Plastic	Plastic	14.9	Nose	14.8	115	123.4
476	Saltwater Thunderstick	2.6	0.9–1.8	Tight sway, me.d roll			Plastic	Plastic	14.6	Nose	16.4	115.6	120.4
477	Long A H-Duty 7/8oz	2.6		Tight roll			Plastic	Plastic	14.8	Nose	33.6	151.5	162.3
478	Hookers Rattling M16	2.6		Med. roll			Plastic	Plastic	16	Nose	29.9	153.6	168.5
479	Prospector 3"	2.6		Tight sway	Good action.		Rubber	Plastic	14.5	Nose	13.5	71.2	76.6
480	Long A Magnum 1 1/2oz	2.6		Med. roll			Plastic	Plastic	16	Nose	41.6	177.2	192.4
481	Vibra Max VM70	2.6		Vibrate		Sinking	Plastic	Bibless	11.4	Body	9.7	71.3	71.3
482	Piglet	2.65	0.3–1.2	Slow wide sway	Little action.	Floating	Wood	Bibless		Nose	31.2	120	133
483	Jerky Min 100F	2.65		Tight sway		Floating	Plastic	Plastic	9.5	Nose	12.7	102.5	111
484	Balsa B-11	2.65	0–1.2	Med. wide sway, tight pitch		Floating	Wood	Plastic	23.8	Nose	17.4	63.4	78
485	Jew Lure 126	2.65		Slow wide sway, med. roll			Plastic	Plastic	36	Nose	57.7	161.2	181.1
486	Aeroplane Spinner #2	2.65		Spinner	Hook design fault.	Sinking	Metal	Bibless		Nose	79		
487	Mad Mullet 3" Shallow	2.7		Slow roll	Much better at 2.5 knots.		Plastic	Plastic	18	Nose	10.1	85	99.1
488	RMG Scorpion 125 SR	2.7	0.8–1	Med. sway, tight roll	Good action.		Plastic	Plastic	23.2	Bib	23.6	124	143
489	Shallow Diver 75	2.7		Fast, med. roll			Plastic	Plastic	19.7	Nose	8.2	73.9	84.5
490	Power Minnow	2.7	1.5–2.1	Slow roll		Floating	Plastic	Plastic	18.8	Nose	7.3	80.1	87.6
491	Spitfire	2.7		Med. sway, slow roll			Plastic	Plastic	19.2	Bib	6.2	83	103.5
492	Barra	2.7		Med. roll	Great action.	Floating	Wood	Plastic	23.6	Nose	17	109.7	128.6
493	Small Fry Bass	2.7	0–2.1	Med. sway, tight roll		Floating	Wood	Plastic	20.6	Bib	7.7	60.4	81.9
494	Wee Whop	2.7	1	Shimmy		Floating	Plastic	Plastic	15.3	Nose	6.7	51	61.9
495	Crawdaddy #1	2.7		Tight sway	Slightly unstable at 2 knots.	Floating	Plastic	Plastic	18.3	Nose	6.6	50.4	63.9
496	Stumpjumper 3 shallow bib	2.7		Tight sway, med. roll		Floating	Plastic	Plastic	15.4	Bib	6.3	58.8	71.5
497	Husky Jerk HJ14	2.7		Slow roll	Better at 2.5 knots.	Suspend.	Plastic	Plastic	14.5	Nose	18.9	136.1	145.2
498	Baby Shad BS50F	2.7		Tight sway		Floating	Plastic	Plastic	12.2	Bib	3.5	52.5	69.8
499	Barra King Shallow	2.7		Tight roll			Wood	Metal	20.2	Nose	14.1	85.4	98
500	Pro Long 15A	2.7		Med. roll		Suspend.	Plastic	Plastic	14.4	Nose	16.5	119.2	127.4

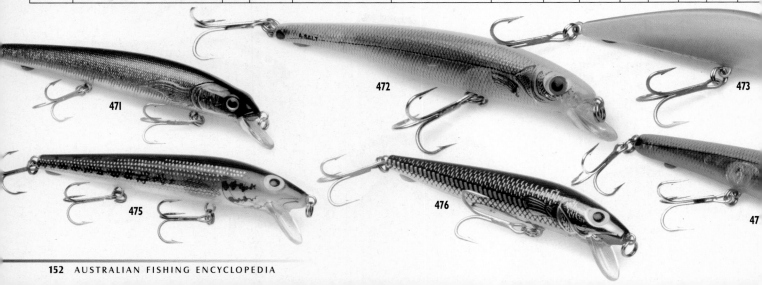

471   472   473   475   476

47

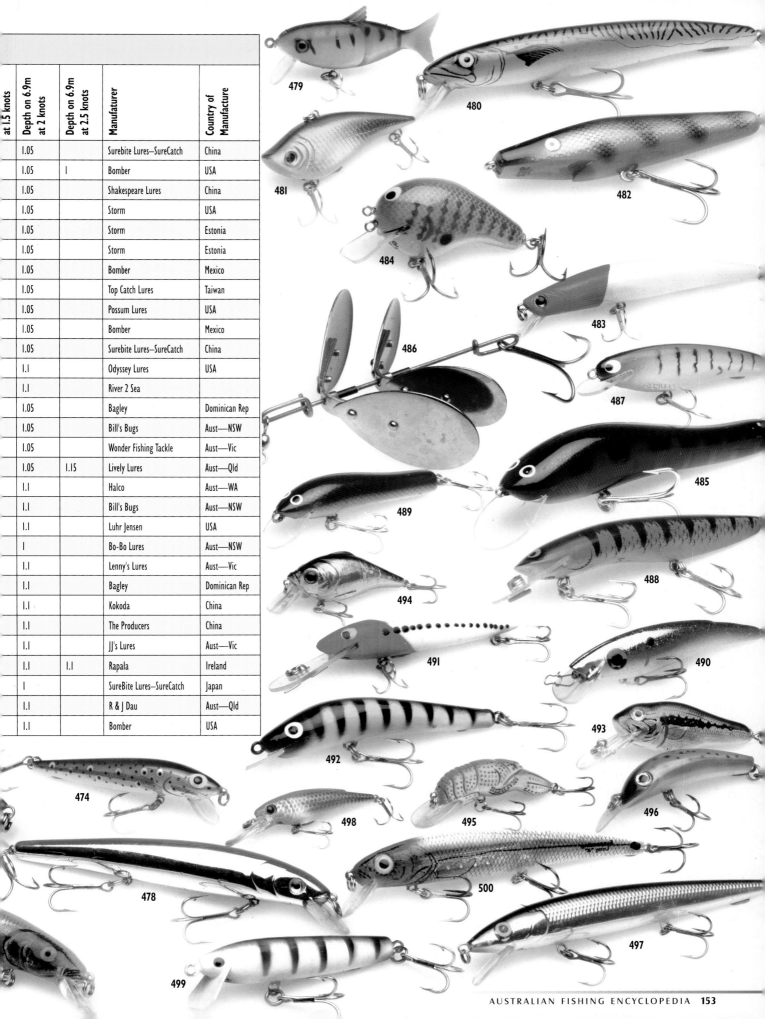

at 1.5 knots	Depth on 6.9m at 2 knots	Depth on 6.9m at 2.5 knots	Manufacturer	Country of Manufacture
1.05			Surebite Lures—SureCatch	China
1.05	1		Bomber	USA
1.05			Shakespeare Lures	China
1.05			Storm	USA
1.05			Storm	Estonia
1.05			Storm	Estonia
1.05			Bomber	Mexico
1.05			Top Catch Lures	Taiwan
1.05			Possum Lures	USA
1.05			Bomber	Mexico
1.05			Surebite Lures—SureCatch	China
1.1			Odyssey Lures	USA
1.1			River 2 Sea	
1.05			Bagley	Dominican Rep
1.05			Bill's Bugs	Aust—NSW
1.05			Wonder Fishing Tackle	Aust—Vic
1.05	1.15		Lively Lures	Aust—Qld
1.1			Halco	Aust—WA
1.1			Bill's Bugs	Aust—NSW
1.1			Luhr Jensen	USA
1			Bo-Bo Lures	Aust—NSW
1.1			Lenny's Lures	Aust—Vic
1.1			Bagley	Dominican Rep
1.1			Kokoda	China
1.1			The Producers	China
1.1			JJ's Lures	Aust—Vic
1.1	1.1		Rapala	Ireland
1			SureBite Lures—SureCatch	Japan
1.1			R & J Dau	Aust—Qld
1.1			Bomber	USA

479
480
481
482
484
483
486
487
485
489
488
494
491
490
492
493
498
495
496
474
500
478
499
497

No.	Lure	Depth Test	Maker's Depth	Action	Comments	Buoyancy	Body Material	Bib Material	Bib Width mm	Tow Point	Weight g	Body Length mm
501	Suspending Thunder Stick	2.7	0.6–1.5	Slow roll		Suspend.	Plastic	Plastic	14.1	Nose	17.7	115.3
502	Stalwart 8	2.7	2.5	Shimmy		Floating	Wood	Plastic	16.9	Nose	8.8	76.1
503	Intruder Creek Monster	2.7	2	Slow shimmy			Plastic	Plastic	16.9	Nose	13.3	75.2
504	Countdown Minnow CD9	2.7		Tight roll		Sinking	Wood	Plastic	15.4	Nose	11.6	83.2
505	Sea Min 120 F	2.7		Tight roll		Floating	Plastic	Plastic	12.2	Nose		114.5
506	Prism Shad	2.7		Vibrate	Loud rattle.	Sinking	Plastic	Bibless	11.7	Body	11.9	68.2
507	Baby Merlin	2.75		Tight sway, tight pitch	Very good action.		Wood	Plastic	13.2	Nose	3.1	48.3
508	Hot Shot 50	2.75		Med. sway	Slightly better faster but deeper slower.	Floating	Plastic	Plastic	11.2	Bib		31.4
509	Barra King Shallow Diver	2.75		Med. roll			Wood	Metal	24.7	Nose	20	98.7
510	Barra King Shallow	2.75		Wide roll		Floating	Wood	Metal	24.5	Nose	26.7	139.8
511	Nose Systems Medium	2.75		Tight sway			Plastic	Plastic	18	Nose	12.6	80.1
512	Wedgetail	2.75		Slow wide roll	Better faster.		Wood	Plastic	25.8	Nose	32.6	120.3
513	Aeroplane Spinner #3	2.75		Spinner		Sinking	Metal	Bibless		Nose	62.9	
514	Hellmax 70 Shallow	2.8	1.8–3.6	Med. sway		Floating	Plastic	Plastic	17.4	Nose	5.6	67
515	Micro Mauler	2.8	1.8	Shimmy			Plastic	Plastic	11	Bib	2.2	43.1
516	Super Minnow SM70	2.8		Tight sway		Floating	Plastic	Plastic	12.2	Bib	9.7	74.5
517	Baby Shad BS65F	2.8		Shimmy		Floating	Plastic	Plastic	13.9	Bib	5.9	66.4
518	Clancy's Dancer No. 4	2.8		Tight sway			Plastic	Plastic	15.5	Bib	7.4	84.7
519	Barra Pro Mini	2.8		Med. sway, tight roll			Wood	Plastic	22.5	Bib	11.1	68.3
520	X 4 Flatfish	2.8		Wide sway	Better at 1.5 knots.	Floating	Plastic	Plastic	17.5	Body	6	47.4
521	Mad N	2.85	1.2	Tight sway			Plastic	Plastic	20.2	Bib	9.7	51.5
522	Mad Mullet 4" Shallow	2.85	2	Slow roll			Plastic	Plastic	20	Nose	17.2	105.1
523	Jester	2.85		Med. roll	Much better at 2.5 knots.		Wood	Plastic	25.7	Nose	40	122.8
524	Shad Rap Shallow 9	2.85		Shimmy			Wood	Plastic	17.9	Nose	11.8	94.4
525	Invincible 12	2.85	2	Slow med.roll		Floating	Wood	Plastic	16.9	Nose	22.3	115.6
526	Husky Jerk 10 Suspending	2.85	1.2–2.4	Tight sway, tight roll		Suspend.	Plastic	Plastic	14.2	Nose	9.5	94.5
527	Spearhead 8	2.85	2.5	Tight sway			Wood	Plastic	17	Nose	11.6	73.7
528	Husky Jerk Susp 14	2.85		Slow roll		Suspend.	Plastic	Plastic	14.5	Nose	19.7	136.3
529	Spence Scout	2.85		Tight sway	Great action.	Floating	Plastic	Metal	17.9	Nose	14.6	61.5
530	Nose System Large	2.85		Med. sway			Plastic	Plastic	16.1	Nose	14.2	99.9

at 1.5 knots	Depth on 6.9m at 2 knots	Depth on 6.9m at 2.5 knots	Manufacturer	Country of Manufacture
1.1			Storm	Estonia
1.1			Nilsmaster	Finland
1.1			Jarvis Walker	Aust
1.1			Rapala	Ireland
1.1			River 2 Sea	
1.1			The Producers	China
1.05			Bennett Lures	Aust—NSW
0.85			Luhr Jensen	USA
1.1			R & J Dau	Aust—Qld
1.1			R & J Dau	Aust—Qld
1.1			Transkei Lures	
1.1	1.3		Illusion Lures	Aust—NSW
1.15			Wonder Fishing Tackle	Aust—Vic
1.05			Legend Lures	Aust—NSW
1.05			Mac's Maulers	Aust—Qld
1.05			Surebite Lures—SureCatch	Japan
1.05			Surebite Lures—SureCatch	Japan
1.05			The Producers	China
1.05			C Lures	Aust—Qld
1.1			Worden's	USA
1.15			Norman Lures	USA
1.15			Lively Lures	Aust—Qld
1.1	1.15		Illusion Lures	Aust—NSW
1.15	1.15		Rapala	Finland
1.15			Nilsmaster	Finland
1.15	1.15		Rapala	Ireland
1.15			Nilsmaster	Finland
1.15			Rapala	Ireland
1.15			Strike King Lure Company	Costa Rica
1.15			Transkei Lures	

511

512

513

514

516

515

518

517

520

519

522

521

524

523

525

526

504

527

510

528

529

530

No.	Lure	Depth Test	Maker's Depth	Action	Comments	Buoyancy	Body Material	Bib Material	Bib Width mm	Tow Point	Weight g
531	Mal Florence's Masta Casta	2.85		Needs speed	Must be at least 3 knots.	Sinking	Plastic	Bibless	11.8	Body	43.4
532	Surfi Vib 80	2.85		Vibrate		Sinking	Plastic	Bibless		Body	
533	Invincible 12J	2.9	2	Shimmy, tight pitch		Floating	Wood	Plastic	16.9	Nose	22
534	Big Z	2.9		Tight sway, slow roll		Floating	Plastic	Plastic	21.6	Nose	18.9
535	Cudgeeshrimp 3 1 m	2.9	1	Med. sway, med. roll			Wood	Plastic	23	Bib	24.3
536	Floating Diver Minnow LK 080	2.95		Tight sway		Floating	Wood	Plastic	16.1	Nose	1.9
537	AC Minnow 60	2.95		Tight sway, med. roll		Floating	Wood	Plastic	17.8	Bib	6.2
538	Shallow Rattler	2.95	1.5	Tight sway			Plastic	Plastic	21.6	Nose	7.8
539	Phoenix	2.95		Tight sway			Wood	Plastic	17	Bib	4.9
540	Millennium Bug	2.95	1.5	Tight sway			Plastic	Plastic	20.5	Nose	7.7
541	Hijacker 5+	2.95		Med. wide sway	Excellent action.	Floating	Plastic	Plastic	28.8	Bib	11
542	Dinkum Yabby - Medium	2.95	1.5	Med. sway	Loud rattle.	Floating	Plastic	Plastic	20.1	Bib	9.6
543	Midive Min 80F	2.95		Med. sway, tight roll		Floating	Plastic	Plastic	14	Bib	8.8
544	Shad	2.95	1.2	Med. sway			Wood	Plastic	20.2	Bib	9.1
545	Craw Fish #22	2.95		Unstable pitch	Difficult to tune.	Floating	Plastic	Plastic	18.5	Nose	6.3
546	Pee Wee Rattle	2.95	3.1	Fast sway	Loud rattle, better slower.	Floating	Plastic	Plastic	22.7	Bib	10.6
547	Little Lucifer	2.95	2.5	Med. sway, med. roll		Floating	Plastic	Plastic	17	Bib	
548	Wedgetail Rattle	2.95		Slow wide roll		Floating	Wood	Plastic	25.9	Nose	35.8
549	Suspending Super Rogue	2.95	1.5	Tight pitch	Slightly better at 2.5 knots.	Suspend.	Plastic	Plastic	16.4	Nose	15.3
550	Terminator 2	2.95	2.4	Tight sway, tight pitch			Plastic	Plastic	16.5	Nose	13.5
551	Diver Vib 65	2.95		Needs speed	Needs at least 2.5 knots.	Sinking	Plastic	Bibless		Body	23.9
552	Super Spot	2.95		Tight sway, vibrate	Great action. Best action of rattling type lures. Better at 2 knots.	Sinking	Plastic	Bibless		Body	13.7
553	Trembler 70	3	0.7	Vibrate	Much better faster but this Trembler can work at slow speeds.	Sinking	Plastic	Bibless	12.6	Body	16.6
554	Elmo's Zipfish #6	3		Wide sway	Needs 1.5 knots or slower.		Plastic	Plastic	26.9	Body	17.1
555	RMG Scorpion 52 DD	3	2.5	Tight sway, tight roll	Great action.		Plastic	Plastic	16.8	Bib	5.9
556	Klawdad	3.05		Shimmy		Floating	Plastic	Plastic	17.5	Bib	6.4
557	RMG Scorpion 52 STD	3.05	1.6	Tight roll			Plastic	Plastic	15.9	Nose	5.4
558	Cyber Laser Shad	3.05		Vibrate		Floating	Plastic	Plastic	12.8	Bib	3.8
559	Hypa-Active	3.1		Tight sway			Plastic	Plastic	20	Bib	4.2
560	Baby 4	3.1	1.2	Med. sway,			Plastic	Plastic	22.1	Nose	11.4

with Bib	Depth on 6.9m at 1.5 knots	Depth on 6.9m at 2 knots	Depth on 6.9m at 2.5 knots	Manufacturer	Country of Manufacture
			1.15	Refined Lure Technology	Aust—Vic
		1.15		River 2 Sea	
		1.2		Nilsmaster	Finland
		1.15		The Producers	China
		1.15		Cudgeefish	Aust—NSW
		1.1		Larrikin Lures	Aust—Vic
		1.1		AC Lures	Aust—NSW
		1.2		Top Catch Lures	Taiwan
		1.1		Illusion Lures	Aust—NSW
		1.2		Ambush Lures	Aust—Qld
		1.2		Majik Lures	Aust—Qld
		1.2		Kokoda	China
		1.1		River 2 Sea	
		1.2		Oar-Gee Lures	Aust—NSW
		1.1		The Prince	
	1.1	1.2		Oar-Gee Lures	Aust—NSW
		1.1		Reidy's	Aust
		1.2		Illusion Lures	Aust—NSW
		1.1	1.2	Smithwick	Mexico
		1.2		Killalure	Aust—Qld
			1.2	River 2 Sea	
		1.2	1.15	Cotton Cordell	El Salvador
		1.15	1.1	Halco	Aust—WA
		1.2		The Producers	China
		1.1		Halco	Aust—WA
		1.25		Luhr Jensen	Mexico
		1.15		Halco	Aust—WA
		1.15		The Prince	
		1.15		Top End Imports	Aust—NT
		1.25		Mann's Lures	USA

541

540

542

543

544

545

547

548

550

551

549

553

552

554

555

534

556

557

539

559

558

560

No.	Lure	Depth Test	Maker's Depth	Action	Comments	Buoyancy	Body Material	Bib Material	Bib Width mm	Tow Point	Weight g	Body Length mm	Actual Length with Bib
561	Tail Dancer TD7	3.1		Tight sway, tight roll			Wood	Plastic	17.1	Bib	8.5	72.7	101.4
562	Premier Pro-Model Series 1	3.1	0.6–1.5	Med. sway		Floating	Plastic	Plastic	20.8	Nose	9.6	51.9	65.4
563	Deep Tiny N	3.1	1.2–1.8	Tight sway			Plastic	Plastic	15.1	Bib	4.8	42.5	62.3
564	Model 2A	3.1		Tight sway, tight pitch			Plastic	Plastic	18.4	Bib	8.8	54.3	67.5
565	Tom Thumb	3.1		Med. sway			Plastic	Plastic	18	Bib	5.5	56.8	81.9
566	Super Crank SK45	3.1		Shimmy		Floating	Plastic	Plastic	15	Bib	4.9	46.3	68.8
567	Newell 3	3.1	3.6	Med. roll	Great action.	Floating	Wood	Plastic	23.8	Bib	17.3	111	136.1
568	Hurricane	3.1	3	Tight sway, med. roll			Plastic	Plastic	21.9	Bib	9.9	54.5	78.3
569	Clatter Tadpolly	3.1		Med. sway	Loud rattle.	Floating	Plastic	Plastic	19.1	Bib	9.1	48.5	77.4
570	Small Fry Crayfish	3.1		Med. sway, tight roll		Floating	Wood	Plastic	20.7	Bib	7.5	52.6	78.3
571	Static Shad 70 Su	3.1		Tight sway		Suspend.	Plastic	Plastic	15.3	Bib	9.9	72.7	92.8
572	River Minnow	3.1		Med. sway			Plastic	Metal	20	Nose	8	56.3	66.3
573	AC Minnow 80	3.1		Tight sway, med. roll		Floating	Wood	Plastic	18.2	Bib	10.3	80.3	114.8
574	Mini Buster	3.1	3	Med. sway, tight roll			Plastic	Plastic	17.8	Bib		49.1	76.5
575	MinMin Deep	3.1	2.5	Tight sway	Great action.	Floating	Plastic	Plastic	16.8	Bib	3.4	50.4	78.6
576	Countdown Minnow CDII	3.1		Slow roll		Sinking	Wood	Plastic	17.7	Nose	16.4	104.7	112.5
577	Mal Florence's Masta Blasta	3.1		Vibrate	Must be at least 3 knots.	Sinking	Plastic	Bibless	11.7	Body	58.9	172.2	180.4
578	Tiger Prawn	3.15	4.5	Tight sway			Wood	Plastic	27.6	Bib	16.4	112.1	145
579	Original Minnow 18	3.15		Tight roll		Floating	Plastic	Plastic	15	Nose	22	165.7	175
580	Barramundi Mauler 9	3.15		Tight sway, wide roll			Plastic	Plastic	28.8	Bib	47	177	226.5
581	Bullet 65	3.2		Tight sway, tight roll			Plastic	Plastic	20	Bib	6.8	64.1	88.8
582	Nomad	3.2		Tight sway, tight pitch			Plastic	Plastic	19.6	Bib	5.8	77.5	96.1
583	Sprat	3.2	1.5	Tight sway, tight roll		Floating	Plastic	Plastic	17.9	Bib	4.9	47	70
584	Mauler Shallow Runner	3.2	1.8	Tight sway			Plastic	Plastic	19.1	Bib	5.6	65.1	88.2
585	Invader 40	3.2		Tight sway			Wood	Plastic	18	Bib	4.8	41.6	66.4
586	Willo Minnow	3.2		Tight sway			Plastic	Plastic	18.3	Bib	5.9	56.5	76.8
587	Obese Crank 45	3.2		Tight sway	Better at 1.5 knots.	Floating	Plastic	Plastic	18.5	Nose	10	45.6	57
588	Mini Micro	3.2	2	Shimmy			Plastic	Plastic	14.8	Bib	2.7	41	63.7
589	Poddy	3.2	1.8	Shimmy		Floating	Wood	Plastic	14.3	Nose	4.7	55.5	68.8
590	Hornet 50	3.2		Tight sway,			Plastic	Plastic	20	Bib	6.1	56.1	82.8

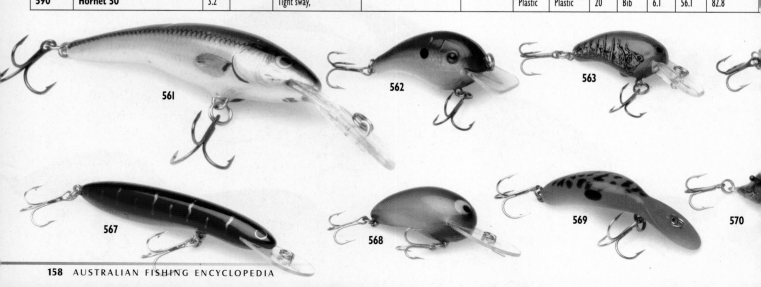

561   562   563

567   568   569   570

Depth on 6.9m at 2.5 knots	Manufacturer	Country of Manufacture
	Rapala	Ireland
	Strike King Lure Company	Mexico
	Norman Lures	USA
	Bomber	Mexico
	Horsey's Lures	Aust—Qld
	Surebite Lures—SureCatch	China
	Peter Newell Lures	Aust—NSW
	Bo-Bo Lures	Aust—NSW
	Heddon	USA
	Bagley	Dominican Rep
	River 2 Sea	
	The Producers	China
	AC Lures	Aust—NSW
	Eddy Lures	Aust—Qld
	Predatek	Aust—NSW
	Rapala	Ireland
1.15	Refined Lure Technology	Aust—Vic
	Taylor Made	Aust—NSW
	Rapala	Ireland
	The Producers	China
	Ambush Lures	Aust—Qld
	Mudeye Lures	Aust—NSW
	Majik Lures	Aust—Qld
	Mac's Maulers	Aust—Qld
	AC Lures	Aust—NSW
	Willo Lures	Aust—Qld
	River 2 Sea	
	Lively Lures	Aust—Qld
	Peter Newell Lures	Aust—NSW
	JP Lures	Aust—NSW

No.	Lure	Depth Test	Maker's Depth	Action	Comments	Buoyancy	Body Material	Bib Material	Bib Width mm	Tow Point	Weight g	Body Length mm	Actual Length with Bib	Depth on 6.9m at 1.5 knots
591	Honey B	3.2	0–2.1	Tight sway	Great action.	Floating	Wood	Plastic	20.7	Bib	5.8	39.4	63.9	
592	Old Faithful Shallow	3.2		Tight sway, tight roll			Plastic	Plastic	19.1	Nose	15.2	102.7	123	
593	Adrenalin Minnow	3.2		Shimmy, tight pitch		Sinking	Plastic	Metal	14.4	Bib	9.4	71.1	97	
594	Little Z	3.2		Tight sway		Floating	Plastic	Plastic	16.6	Nose	12.8	67.3	83	
595	Super Crawfish SC60	3.2		Med. sway, tight pitch		Floating	Plastic	Plastic	23	Bib	8.5	58.5	88.9	
596	MicroMin - Deep	3.2	2.5	Tight sway		Sinking	Plastic	Plastic	16.8	Bib	2.8	40.2	67.8	
597	TD Hyper Shad Ti60	3.2		Med. sway	Great action.	Floating	Plastic	Metal	18.5	Bib	10.9	66	97.9	
598	Magnum Mag-II	3.2		Tight sway		Floating	Wood	Plastic	17.4	Nose	13.6	111.6	130.9	
599	Jointed Minnow J-13	3.2		Tight sway, tight pitch		Floating	Plastic	Plastic	17	Nose	19.2	128	149.3	
600	TD Hyper Minnow 90	3.2		Med. roll		Floating	Plastic	Metal	18.7	Bib	10.2	90	122	
601	Rat-L-Trap Rattletrap	3.2		Tight sway		Sinking	Plastic	Bibless	9.7	Body	17	75.2	75.2	
602	Zero #3	3.2		Vibrate		Sinking	Plastic	Bibless	10.3	Body	16.1	75.8	75.8	
603	Rattlin' Rapala RNR7	3.2		Shimmy		Sinking	Plastic	Bibless	12.2	Body	15.9	73.8	77.4	
604	Legend Minnow - Shallow	3.25	1.5–3	Tight shimmy		Floating	Plastic	Plastic	17.3	Nose	5.2	55.4	68.5	
605	Big O	3.25		Tight sway			Plastic	Plastic	15.5	Nose	7.8	50.3	63.7	
606	Hooker Rattling L19	3.25		Slow med. sway			Plastic	Plastic	18	Nose	43.5	177.9	194	
607	Classic 160	3.25	3.1	Tight sway, tight pitch			Plastic	Plastic	28.5	Nose	27.2	160.1	180.8	
608	Growler Intruder	3.25		Vibrate		Sinking	Plastic	Bibless	12.6	Body	16.1	73.9	73.9	
609	The One	3.3		Tight sway			Plastic	Plastic	20	Bib	3.8	48.7	70.8	
610	Grumble Bum	3.3	2	Tight sway, tight roll	Good at both speeds.	Floating	Wood	Plastic	19.4	Bib	7.6	48.8	79.1	1.25
611	Tempest 70	3.35		Med. sway, tight roll			Plastic	Plastic	21.9	Bib	14.3	69.7	92.6	
612	RMG Scorpion 68 STD	3.35	2.5	Tight sway			Plastic	Plastic	21.9	Bib	8.2	69.2	88.4	
613	Tiny Nugget	3.35	3	Tight sway,			Wood	Plastic	21.9	Bib	4.5	46.6	68.8	
614	Jindivik	3.35		Tight sway, med. roll		Floating	Plastic	Plastic	28.9	Bib	18	82.1	107.8	
615	Deep Herring 50	3.35		Shimmy		Sinking	Plastic	Plastic	18.3	Bib	5.3	50	73	
616	Snag Master 6	3.35	1.9	Tight sway, tight roll			Plastic	Plastic	18.1	Nose	10	75.2	89.6	
617	Yeah Yeah	3.35	2.5	Med. sway			Wood	Plastic	19.6	Bib	8.5	60.3	94	
618	Bream Bandit	3.35		Tight sway, tight pitch	Excellent action.	Floating	Plastic	Plastic	17.5	Bib	6.6	56	76.1	
619	Shad Rap Deep SR5	3.35		Fast sway		Floating	Wood	Plastic	15.4	Bib	5.3	56.1	78.5	
620	Stinger	3.35		Med. sway,	Eye moves nicely.		Plastic	Metal	22	Nose		87.5	108.8	

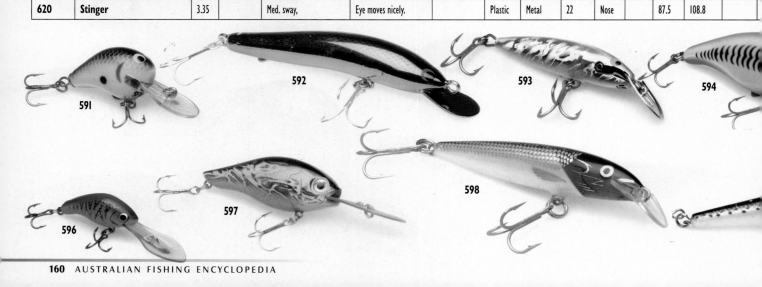

591   592   593   594   596   597   598

at 2.5 knots	Manufacturer	Country of Manufacture
	Bagley	Dominican Rep
	Tinaroo Lures	Aust—Qld
	McLaughlin's Lures	Taiwan
	The Producers	China
	Surebite Lures—SureCatch	China
	Predatek	Aust—NSW
	Team Diawa	Japan
	Rapala	Ireland
	Rapala	Ireland
	Team Diawa	Japan
	Bill Lewis Lures	USA
	The Producers	China
	Rapala	Ireland
	Legend Lures	Aust—NSW
	Cotton Cordell	El Salvador
	Top Catch Lures	Taiwan
	Classic Lures	Aust
	Jarvis Walker	Vietnam
	Mudeye Lures	Aust—NSW
	Cudgeefish	Aust—NSW
	Kingfisher Lures	Aust—NSW
	Halco	Aust—WA
	Taylor Made	Aust—NSW
	Predatek	Aust—NSW
	Bill's Bugs	Aust—NSW
	DK Lures	Aust—Qld
	Cudgeefish	Aust—NSW
	Kokoda	China
	Rapala	Ireland
	Eddy Lures	Aust—Qld

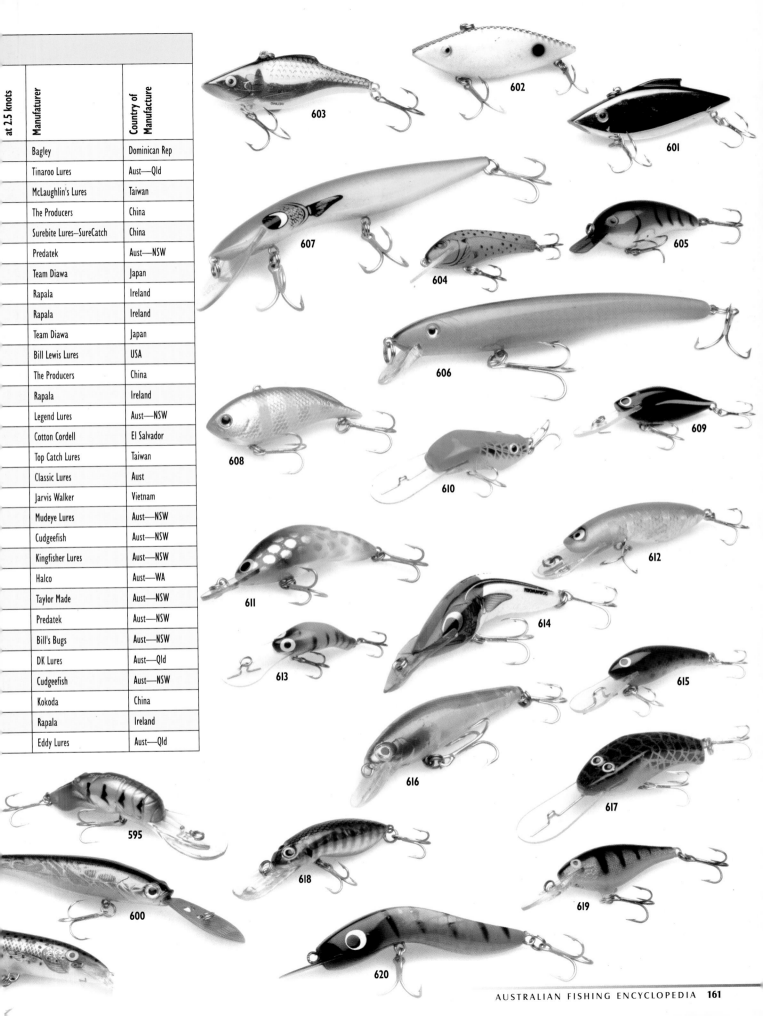

595

600

601

602

603

604

605

606

607

608

609

610

611

612

613

614

615

616

617

618

619

620

No.	Lure	Depth Test	Maker's Depth	Action	Comments	Buoyancy	Body Material	Bib Material	Bib Width mm	Tow Point	Weight g	Body Length mm
621	Wasp 12+	3.35	3.6	Med. sway		Floating	Plastic	Plastic	17.8	Bib		62.3
622	Salty	3.35		Med. sway				Plastic	19.8	Bib	9.6	64
623	Premier Pro-Model Series 4S	3.35	0.6–1.2	Med. sway, tight roll				Plastic	22.9	Nose	17.2	63.8
624	Slavko Bug	3.35	1.5	Tight sway		Floating	Plastic	Plastic	16.2	Bib	4.4	52.6
625	Thunder Killer 19B	3.35		Tight sway		Floating	Plastic	Plastic	21.5	Bib	14.9	122
626	Extractor - Shallow	3.35		Med. sway		Floating	Wood	Plastic	25.5	Nose		67.3
627	Invincible DR8	3.4	3	Tight roll			Wood	Plastic	16.7	Nose	6.2	73.9
628	Avoidance Behaviour Lure - Eel	3.4		Med. wide sway	Excellent action but must be at 1.5 knots.	Floating	Plastic	Plastic	21.9	Bib	11.7	50.1
629	Tempest SR85	3.4		Tight sway, tight pitch	Loud rattle.		Plastic	Plastic	30	Bib	21.2	84.5
630	Clancy's Dancer No 5	3.4		Med. roll			Plastic	Plastic	22.2	Bib	14.4	110.7
631	Mid Wart	3.45	2.5–3	Med. sway			Plastic	Plastic	20.2	Bib	9.4	51.2
632	Kill'r B-1	3.45	0–2.1	Tight sway		Floating	Wood	Plastic	20.6	Bib	8.4	46.8
633	Whitmore's Minnow	3.45		Tight sway	Better at 1.5 knots.		Plastic	Plastic	21	Bib	5.2	54
634	Stretch 5+	3.45	1.5	Tight sway	Great action.		Plastic	Plastic	19.6	Bib	6.5	64.7
635	Blue Pilly Shallow	3.45		Slow roll			Plastic	Plastic	28.3	Nose	44.1	172
636	Barra Bug Shallow 155	3.45		Tight sway, med. roll	Good action.		Plastic	Plastic	31	Nose	34.5	153.3
637	Jewie 150	3.45	0.9	Wide sway, med. roll	Good erratic action.		Plastic	Plastic	30.8	Nose	56.6	150.2
638	Rattlin' Rapala RNR8	3.45		Vibrate		Sinking	Plastic	Bibless	13	Body	22.6	84.7
639	Baby Extractor - Deep	3.5	3	Tight sway		Floating	Wood	Plastic	19.3	Bib	4.4	49.5
640	Grinner	3.5		Tight sway			Wood	Plastic	17	Bib	5.5	42.1
641	Nipper	3.5		Tight sway, med. pitch	Different, stable bouncing action.		Wood	Plastic	24	Bib	4.6	51.5
642	Mustang	3.5		Med. roll	Good action.		Plastic	Plastic	22.7	Bib	17.6	107.9
643	Demon	3.5	2.5	Med. sway, tight roll			Wood	Plastic	19.3	Bib	8.2	54.5
644	Tadpolly	3.5		Med. sway		Floating	Plastic	Plastic	19.1	Bib	8.8	49.1
645	Hellmax 70 Deep	3.5		Tight sway		Floating	Plastic	Plastic	18	Bib	6.2	67.5
646	Micro Mullet	3.5	2+	Tight sway			Plastic	Plastic	17.8	Bib	3.6	47.3
647	Invader 50	3.5		Tight sway			Wood	Plastic	18.4	Bib	7.6	52.7
648	Hornet 60	3.5		Tight sway			Plastic	Plastic	23.7	Bib	8.4	65
649	5+	3.5	1.5	Tight sway	Much better at 1.5 knots.		Plastic	Plastic	20.3	Bib	5.7	39.7
650	Clawdaddy #2	3.5		Med. sway		Floating	Plastic	Plastic	22.9	Bib	8.7	58.1

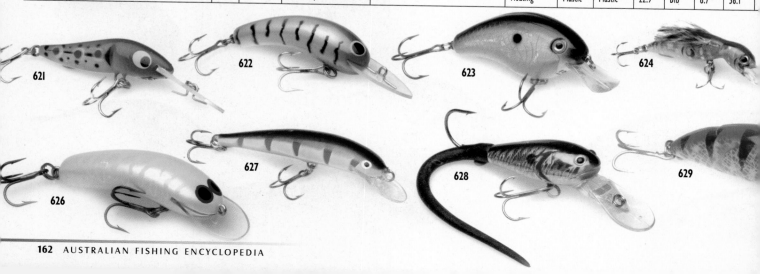

621 622 623 624

626 627 628 629

Depth on 6.9m at 1.5 knots	Depth on 6.9m at 2 knots	Depth on 6.9m at 2.5 knots	Manufacturer	Country of Manufacture
1.25			Eddy Lures	Aust—Qld
1.25			Oar-Gee Lures	Aust—NSW
1.35			Strike King Lure Company	Mexico
1.25			Yo-Zuri Lures	Japan
1.25			The Prince	
1.3			Custom Crafted Lures	Aust—NSW
1.3			Nilsmaster	Finland
			Bass Pro Shops	China
1.35			Kingfisher Lures	Aust—NSW
1.35			The Producers	China
1.3			Storm	Estonia
1.35			Bagley	Dominican Rep
1.25			Whitmore	Aust—NSW
1.3			Mann's Lures	USA
1.4			Lively Lures	Aust—Qld
1.4			Bill's Bugs	Aust—NSW
1.4			Killalure	Aust—Qld
1.3			Rapala	Ireland
1.3			Custom Crafted Lures	Aust—NSW
1.3			Illusion Lures	Aust—NSW
1.3			Deception Lures	Aust—NSW
1.3			Horsey's Lures	Aust—Qld
1.3			Cudgeefish	Aust—NSW
1.3			Heddon	USA
1.3			Legend Lures	Aust—NSW
1.3			Lively Lures	Aust—Qld
1.3			AC Lures	Aust—NSW
1.3			JP Lures	Aust—NSW
1.3			Mann's Lures	USA
1.3			The Producers	China

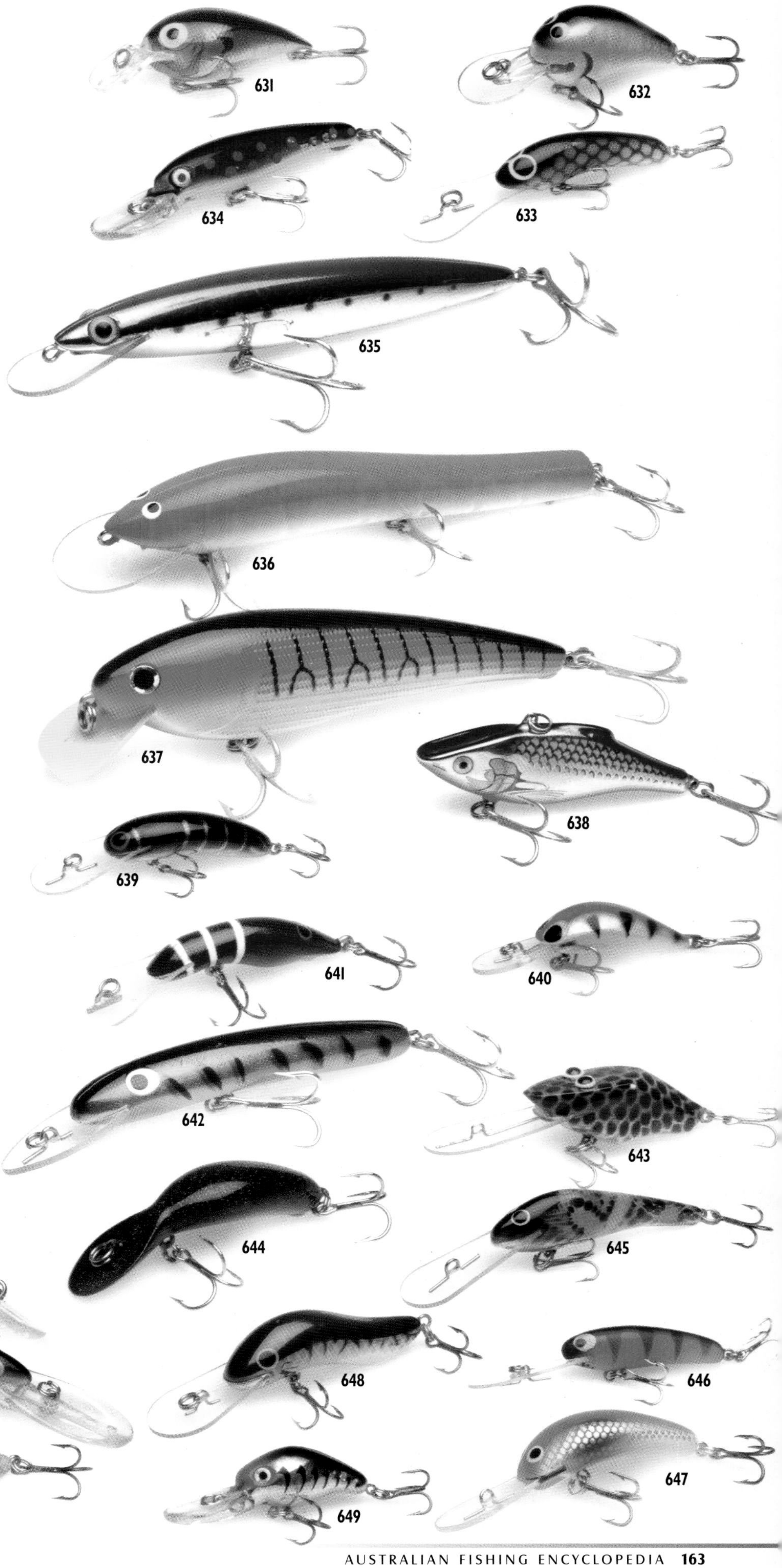

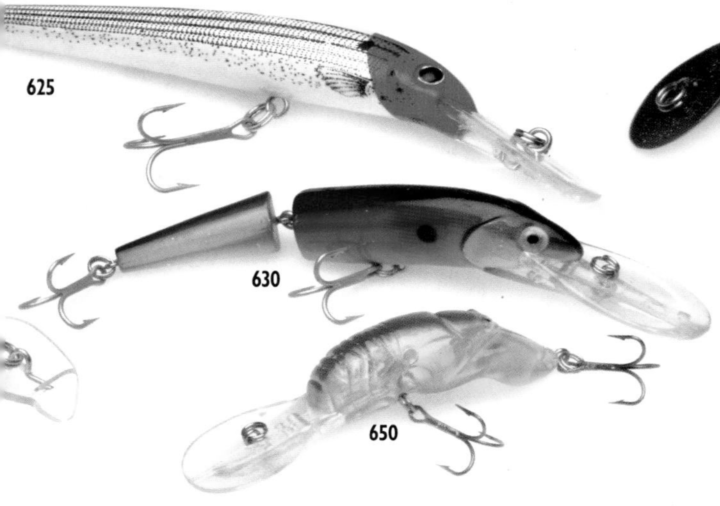

631

632

634

633

635

636

637

638

639

641

640

642

643

644

645

625

630

648

646

647

650

649

THE AUSTRALIAN FISHING ENCYCLOPEDIA *LURE TEST RESULTS*

No.	Lure	Depth Test	Maker's Depth	Action	Comments	Buoyancy	Body Material	Bib Material	Bib Width mm	Tow Point	Weight g	Body Length mm	Actual Length
651	Rocket Diver RD80	3.5		Med. sway	Difficult to tune.	Floating	Plastic	Plastic	24.4	Bib	7.9	79.8	110
652	Mimic series 80	3.5		No action, not for trolling	No action.		Plastic	Plastic	16.1	Nose	15.4	80.5	95.
653	Aqua-rat	3.5	2	Med. sway, med. roll		Floating	Plastic	Plastic	20.9	Nose		110	129
654	Bass Masta	3.5		Tight sway			Plastic	Plastic	18.2	Bib	7	62.2	88.
655	Whitmore	3.5		Med. sway	Good action. Horizontal position.		Plastic	Plastic	25.5	Bib	9.4	61.2	97.
656	Wide Body McGrath Minnow	3.5	5	Tight sway, med. pitch		Floating	Wood	Plastic	22.3	Bib	6.8	66.6	91.
657	Laser Pro 120 DD	3.5	2	Med. sway			Plastic	Plastic	18.6	Nose	17	116.1	137
658	Deep ThunderStick	3.5	2.4–3.6	Med. sway, med. roll	Good action.		Plastic	Plastic	17.5	Bib	8.7	89.6	118
659	Prism Shad #3S	3.5		Vibrate			Plastic	Bibless	11.6	Body	20.8	85.1	85.
660	Mudeye 40 mm	3.55		Tight sway	Stable lateral movement.		Plastic	Plastic	19.8	Bib	4.9	42.2	66.
661	Mud Bug 1/4oz	3.55		Med. sway	Erratic lateral movement, but stable.	Floating	Plastic	Metal	23.4	Bib	10.5	52.2	75.
662	Mad Mullet 6" Shallow	3.55	2.5	Tight sway, tight roll	Much better at 2.5 knots.		Plastic	Plastic	24	Nose	28.8	140	162
663	Mulgar 10+	3.55	3	Med. sway			Plastic	Plastic	26.2	Bib	20.8	103.2	137
664	Dusky Diver	3.55	2.1	Tight sway, tight roll		Suspend.	Plastic	Plastic	17.5	Bib	12.9	85	113
665	Diver Vib 80	3.55		Needs speed	Needs at least 2.5 knots.	Sinking	Plastic	Bibless		Body	42.2	80	83
666	Cherabin	3.6		Med. sway, tight roll			Plastic	Plastic	25.5	Bib	10.8	87.3	117
667	AC Minnow 45	3.6		Tight sway			Wood	Plastic	22.7	Bib	4.3	45.1	72.
668	Baby Bass Pig	3.6		Tight sway, tight roll			Plastic	Plastic	19.7	Bib	4.2	52.5	73.
669	Mohican Dart	3.6		Tight sway			Wood	Metal	18	Bib	8.5	59.1	83
670	Fastrac Jointed FTJ20	3.6	3.5	Tight sway		Floating	Plastic	Plastic	19.2	Bib	12.8	116.1	139
671	Midi S	3.6		Med. sway			Plastic	Plastic	19.5	Nose	12.7	60.5	76.
672	Viper Lure	3.6	3.6–4.2	Tight sway, tight roll		Floating	Plastic	Plastic	25.7	Bib		54.4	80.
673	Legend Minnow 60	3.6	3	Tight sway, med. roll			Plastic	Plastic	18.3	Bib	5.8	56.5	85
674	Lenny's Barra	3.6		Tight sway, med. roll	Good action.		Wood	Plastic	30.2	Nose	27	150.4	171
675	RMG Scorpion 68 DD	3.6	3.1	Tight sway, slow roll			Plastic	Plastic	22.3	Bib	8.6	68.8	98.
676	Wee Pee	3.6	3.6	Tight sway				Plastic	22.7	Bib	8.1	44	76.
677	Cranky Franky	3.6	5	Med. sway, med. roll			Wood	Plastic	38.2	Bib	30.8	94.7	130
678	Model 5A	3.6		Tight sway	Lateral movement.		Plastic	Plastic	17.7	Bib	7.7	45.7	67.
679	Magnum CD-7	3.6		Med. roll	Better faster.	Sinking	Wood	Metal	15	Bib	11	74	95.
680	Invincible 18	3.6		Med. roll	Better at 2.5 knots.		Wood	Plastic	22.5	Nose	44.5	180.7	193

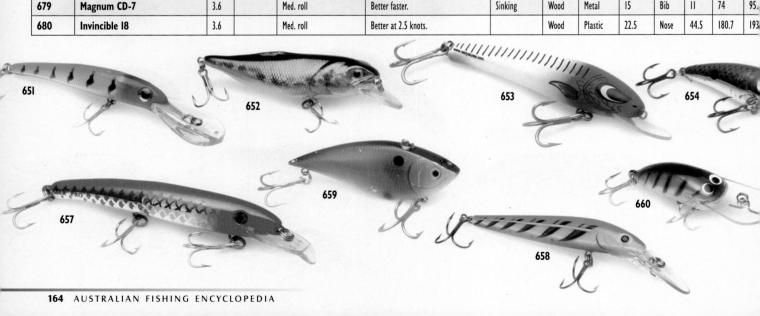

Depth on 6.9m at 2 knots	Depth on 6.9m at 2.5 knots	Manufacturer	Country of Manufacture
1.2		SureBite Lures—SureCatch	China
1.3		Saiko Lures	China
1.3		Reidy's	Aust
1.3		Refined Lure Technology	Aust—Vic
1.3		Whitmore	Aust—NSW
1.3		McGrath Lures	Aust—Vic
1.3		Halco	Aust—WA
1.3		Storm	Estonia
1.3		The Producers	China
1.35		Mudeye Lures	Aust—NSW
1.35		Fred Arbogast	El Salvador
1.4	1.35	Lively Lures	Aust—Qld
1.3		Majik Lures	Aust—Qld
1.2		Kokoda	China
	1.4	River 2 Sea	
1.35		Mudeye Lures	Aust—NSW
1.35		AC Lures	Aust—NSW
1.35		Spawn Lures	Aust
1.35		Dream Catcher Lures	USA
1.35		Rebel	USA
1.35		Shakespeare Lures	
1.35		Viper Lures	Aust
1.35		Legend Lures	Aust—NSW
1.35		Lenny's Lures	Aust—Vic
1.35		Halco	Aust—WA
1.35		Oar-Gee Lures	Aust—NSW
1.45		Cudgeefish	Aust—NSW
1.35		Bomber	Mexico
1.35	1.3	Rapala	Estonia
1.35	1.4	Nilsmaster	Finland

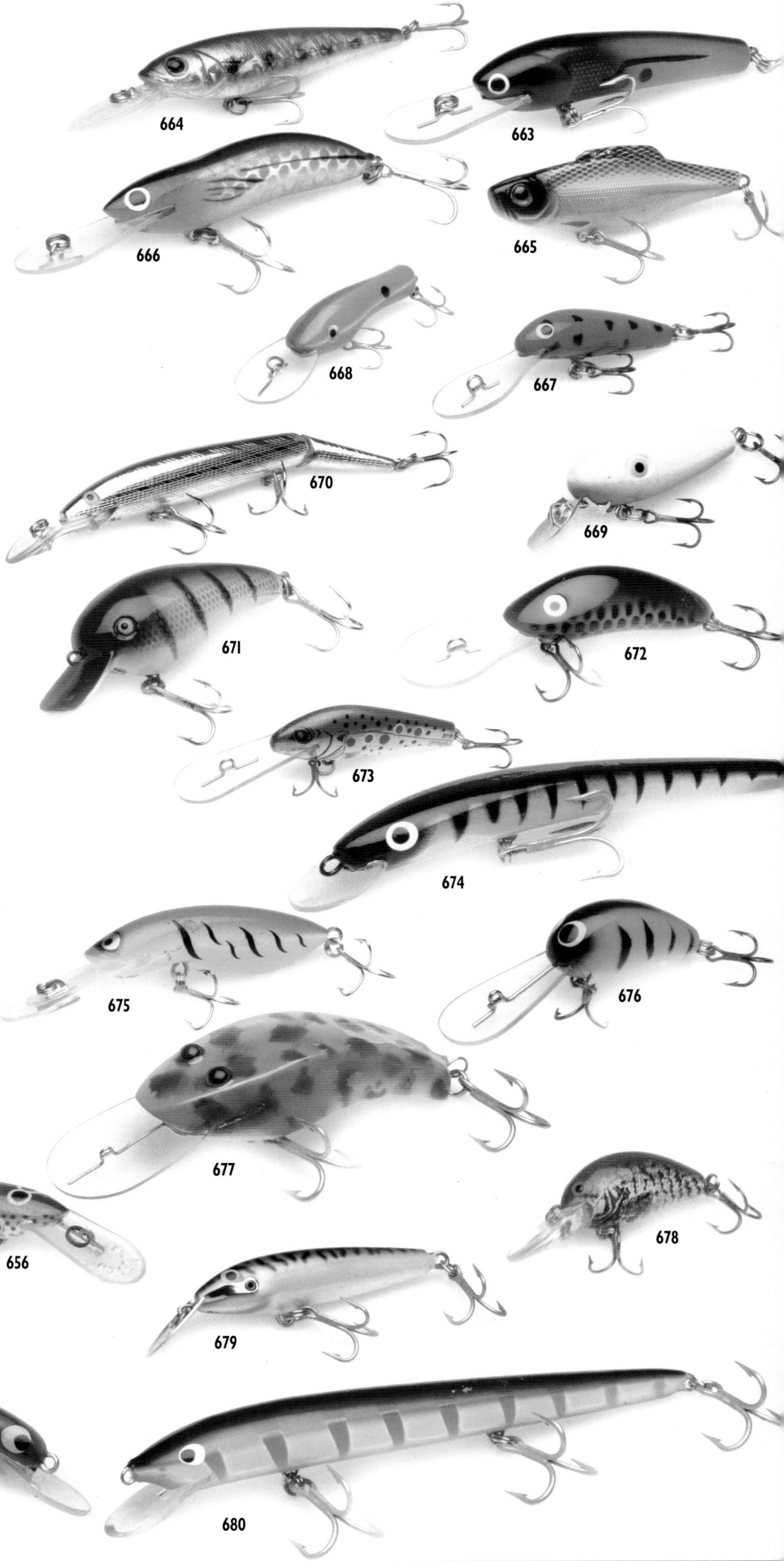

663

664

665

666

667

668

669

670

671

672

673

674

675

676

677

678

679

680

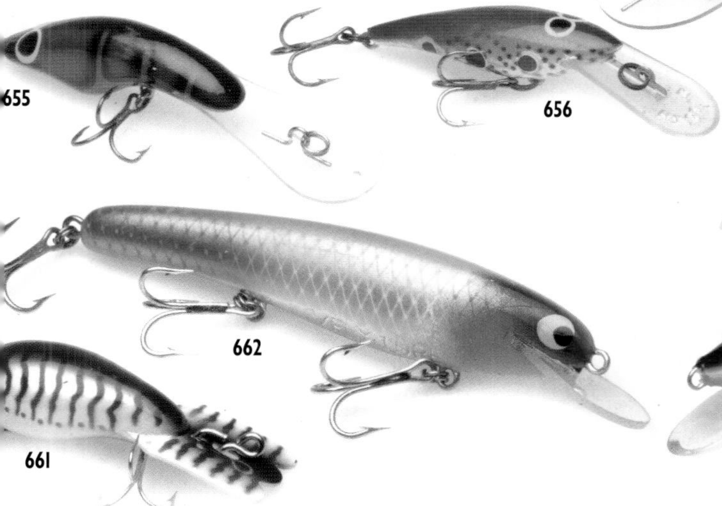

655

656

661

662

No.	Lure	Depth Test	Maker's Depth	Action	Comments	Buoyancy	Body Material	Bib Material	Bib Width mm	Tow Point	Weight g
681	Static Shad 60 Su	3.6		Tight sway, tight pitch		Suspend.	Plastic	Plastic	15	Bib	5.
682	Tail Dancer TD9	3.6	1.9–3.5	Med. sway, med. roll	Great action.		Wood	Plastic	19.4	Bib	14
683	Codger 55	3.6	3	Med. wide sway, tight pitch	Rattle.		Plastic	Plastic	26.2	Bib	9.
684	John's Spirit 10B	3.6		Med. roll		Floating	Plastic	Plastic	21.8	Bib	15
685	Super Bug BU60	3.6		Tight sway, med. pitch		Floating	Plastic	Plastic	14.2	Nose	8.
686	Sliver Jointed 13	3.6		Tight sway, med. roll	Great action at 2.5 knots.		Plastic	Metal	14	Bib	
687	Bullet 75	3.6		Med. sway, med. roll				Plastic	18.6	Bib	9.
688	Pegron Diver	3.6		Med. sway, tight roll			Plastic	Plastic	27.3	Bib	15
689	Fat Rap FR5	3.65		Fast sway		Floating	Wood	Plastic	18	Bib	10
690	Double Downer #2	3.65		Med. sway	Better at 1.5 knots.		Plastic	Metal	22.1	Bib	7
691	Crawdad	3.65	2.1	Med. sway, tight roll	Loud rattle.		Plastic	Plastic	19.8	Bib	10
692	Wedgetail - Shallow 16	3.65		Very slow sway	Much better at 2.5 knots.		Wood	Plastic	25.3	Nose	5
693	Jointed Pikie 3000	3.65	1.2–2.1 casting, trolling	Tight sway	Little action.	Sinking	Plastic	Metal	27	Bib	42
694	Intruder Ko-Jack 130 mm	3.65		Tight roll	Better at 2.5 knots.		Plastic	Metal	17	Bib	31
695	Magnum Stretch 8+	3.65	2.44	Med. sway, wide roll	Better at 2.5 knots.		Plastic	Plastic	36.7	Bib	10
696	Trembler 110	3.65	1	Vibrate	Needs at least 2 knots.	Sinking	Plastic	Bibless	15.8	Body	42
697	Mud Bug 1/8oz	3.7		Med. sway, tight pitch		Floating	Plastic	Metal	20.1	Bib	7
698	AC Minnow 60	3.7		Fast tight roll			Wood	Plastic	18.3	Bib	7.
699	Tilsan Minnow	3.7	2.5	Tight roll		Floating	Wood	Plastic	16.9	Bib	4.
700	Barramundi Mauler 4	3.7		Tight shimmy			Plastic	Plastic	17.3	Bib	7.
701	Nomad 120	3.75		Tight sway, med. roll				Plastic	30.4	Bib	17
702	Fergo	3.75	1.8	Tight roll			Plastic	Plastic	21	Nose	14
703	Larrikin LK110	3.75		Tight sway, tight roll			Wood	Plastic	22.3	Nose	6.
704	Tini Titan	3.75		Med. sway			Plastic	Plastic	20	Bib	7.
705	RMG Scorpion 125 STD	3.75	3	Tight sway, tight roll			Plastic	Plastic	27.8	Bib	24
706	Power Minnow Suspending	3.75	1.5–2.1	Slow roll		Suspend.	Plastic	Plastic	23.6	Nose	15
707	Bass Pig	3.75	4.8	Med. sway, tight roll	Good at both speeds.		Plastic	Plastic	25.9	Bib	10
708	Crank Fighter #15	3.75		Tight sway		Floating	Plastic	Plastic	18.1	Bib	10
709	Intruder Gutter Boss	3.75		Med. sway, tight roll			Plastic	Plastic	27.8	Bib	18
710	Deep Herring 65	3.75		Med. sway	Good action.		Plastic	Plastic	25	Bib	10

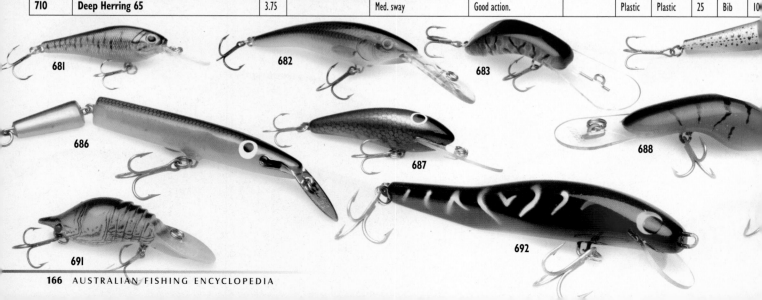

681 682 683

686 687 688

691 692

Depth on 6.9m at 1.5 knots	Depth on 6.9m at 2 knots	Depth on 6.9m at 2.5 knots	Manufacturer	Country of Manufacture
	1.35		River 2 Sea	
	1.35		Rapala	Ireland
	1.35		Goulburn Lures	Aust—Vic
	1.35		The Prince	
	1.35		SureBite Lures—SureCatch	China
	1.35	1.35	Rapala	Ireland
	1.35		Ambush Lures	Aust—Qld
	1.35		Pegron	Aust—NSW
	1.4		Rapala	Ireland
1.4	1.35		The Producers	China
	1.4		Mann's Lures	USA
	1.15	1.45	Illusion Lures	Aust—NSW
	1.45		Creek Chub	El Salvador
	1.45	1.35	Jarvis Walker	Vietnam
	1.45	1.5	Mann's Lures	USA
	1.45	1.35	Halco	Aust—WA
	1.4		Fred Arbogast	USA
	1.25		AC Lures	Aust—NSW
	1.25		Halco	Aust—WA
	1.25		The Producers	China
	1.4		Mudeye Lures	Aust—NSW
	1.4		Willo Lures	Aust—Qld
	1.4		Larrikin Lures	Aust—Vic
	1.4		Horsey's Lures	Aust—Qld
	1.4		Halco	Aust—WA
	1.4		Luhr Jensen	USA
1.4	1.4		Spawn Lures	Aust
	1.4		The Prince	
	1.4		Jarvis Walker	Vietnam
	1.4		Bill's Bugs	Aust—NSW

694

695

696 TREMBLER

697

699

700

701

702

703

704

705

706

707

708

709

710

685

689

690

693

No.	Lure	Depth Test	Maker's Depth	Action	Comments	Buoyancy	Body Material	Bib Material	Bib Width mm	Tow Point	Weight g	Body Length mm
711	Old Man	3.75		Med. sway			Plastic	Plastic	30	Bib	10.9	73.9
712	Skinny Bob	3.75	2	Slow med.sway	Works well at 2 knots.		Wood	Plastic	22.3	Bib	9.7	79.2
713	Cudgeeshrimp 1	3.75	3	Tight sway, tight roll		Sinking	Wood	Plastic	22.2	Bib		67.4
714	Sardinops Shallow	3.75		Med. sway, slow roll	Very good action and appearance.	Floating	Wood	Plastic	24.4	Nose	15.4	92.3
715	Deep Baby N	3.75	1.8–2.4	Tight sway	Works well at 1.5 and 2 knots.		Plastic	Plastic	17.9	Bib	9.7	50.9
716	RMG Rellik Doc	3.75	2.5	Med. sway, tight roll			Plastic	Plastic	26.9	Bib	16.2	74.8
717	Wee Willy	3.75	2.4	Tight roll			Plastic	Plastic	20.9	Bib	6.2	48.1
718	Triho Min 180F	3.75		Med. roll		Floating	Plastic	Plastic	23.5	Nose	41.6	177.6
719	Shad Rap Jointed JSR5	3.75	1.8–2.4	Fast sway, tight pitch	Great action.	Suspend.	Plastic	Plastic	17.9	Bib	8.4	61.1
720	Intruder	3.75		Med. sway			Plastic	Plastic	23	Bib	15.7	74.2
721	Super Bug BU75	3.75		Tight sway, tight pitch		Floating	Plastic	Plastic	17.2	Nose	12.8	75
722	Stumpjumper 3 deep straight bib	3.8		Tight sway, shimmy		Floating	Plastic	Plastic	20	Nose	6	58
723	The Outback	3.8		Med. sway	Great action 2 knots.		Plastic	Plastic	29.3	Bib	28.3	80.8
724	Super Shad Rap 14	3.8	1.5–2.7	Tight sway, med. roll	Great action.		Plastic	Plastic	27.5	Nose	46.6	144.2
725	Barramundi Mauler	3.8		Med. sway			Plastic	Plastic	22.5	Bib	18.7	112.5
726	Barramundi Mauler 6	3.8		Med. sway			Plastic	Plastic	24.1	Bib	26.7	132.5
727	Rat-L-Trap Magnum Force	3.8		Tight sway		Sinking	Plastic	Bibless	12.9	Body	33.5	101.7
728	Willy's Worm No 1	3.85		Shimmy			Plastic	Plastic	16.3	Bib	4.7	40
729	Wedgetail - Deep 6	3.85		Tight sway			Wood	Plastic	20.1	Bib	8.8	60
730	Sonar Mac	3.85		Med. sway, tight roll			Plastic	Plastic	20.2	Bib	11.9	70
731	Throbber	3.85		Tight sway, slow roll			Plastic	Plastic	20	Bib	11.5	69.7
732	Mudeye 80	3.85		Wide sway, tight pitch			Plastic	Plastic	36.1	Bib	17.7	75.1
733	Baby Shad BS80F	3.85		Slow med. roll			Plastic	Plastic	18.7	Bib	12.2	80.2
734	Kwikfish K12	3.85		Wide sway	Works well at 2 knots.		Plastic	Plastic	22.1	Body	10.1	68.7
735	LK 160	3.85		Tight sway, tight pitch			Wood	Plastic	37	Nose	24.9	122.7
736	Kwikfish K15	3.85		Wide sway			Plastic	Plastic	28	Body	28.2	92.6
737	RMG Scorpion 90 STD	3.9	3	Med. sway, tight roll	Rattle.		Plastic	Plastic	27.4	Bib	15.3	86.7
738	Klawdad	3.9		Tight sway		Floating	Plastic	Plastic	23.4	Bib	11	75.8
739	McGrath Minnow Deep Diver	3.9	3.5	Shimmy	Very stable action.	Floating	Wood	Plastic	15.6	Bib	5.1	61
740	Porky's Diver Small	3.9		Med. sway			Plastic	Plastic	21.9	Bib	5.6	50.6

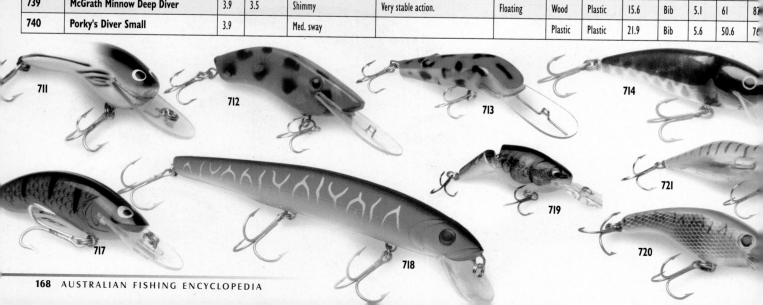

Depth on 6.9m at 1.5 knots	Depth on 6.9m at 2 knots	Depth on 6.9m at 2.5 knots	Manufaturer	Country of Manufacture
1.4			Mudeye Lures	Aust—NSW
1.4			Cudgeefish	Aust—NSW
1.4			Cudgeefish	Aust—NSW
1.4			Deception Lures	Aust—NSW
1.4			Norman Lures	USA
1.4			Halco	Aust—WA
1.4			S K Lures	Aust—Qld
1.4			River 2 Sea	
1.4			Rapala	Ireland
1.4			Jarvis Walker	
1.4			SureBite Lures–	China
1.4			JJ's Lures	Aust—Vic
1.4			Legend Lures	Aust—NSW
1.3	1.5		Rapala	Ireland
1.4			The Producers	China
1.4			The Producers	China
1.45			Bill Lewis Lures	USA
1.3			The Producers	China
1.3			Illusion Lures	Aust—NSW
1.3			McLaughlin's Lures	Taiwan
1.3			Jarvis Walker	Vietnam
1.55			Mudeye Lures	Aust—NSW
1.3			Surebite Lures–	Japan
1.55			Luhr Jensen	USA
1.55			Larrikin Lures	Aust—Vic
1.55			Luhr Jensen	USA
1.45			Halco	Aust—WA
1.45			Luhr Jensen	Mexico
1.35			McGrath Lures	Aust—Vic
1.45			Porky's Lures	Aust

723

724

725

726

727

728

729

730

731

732

733

734

735

716

722

736

737

738

739

740

No.	Lure	Depth Test	Maker's Depth	Action	Comments	Buoyancy	Body Material	Bib Material	Bib Width mm	Tow Point	Weight g	Body Length mm
741	Your Bass Lure	3.9	3.6–4.2	Med. sway			Plastic	Plastic	25.6	Bib	7	54.9
742	Super Crawfish SCF40SF	3.9		Shimmy	Unstable even at slow speed.	Floating	Plastic	Plastic	21.2	Bib	3.4	40.5
743	Rattlin' Fat Rap RFR-5	3.9		Med. sway, tight roll		Floating	Wood	Plastic	18.2	Bib	11.1	51.8
744	Bandit 200 Series	3.9	1.2–2.4	Tight sway, tight roll			Plastic	Plastic	20.1	Bib	8.4	52.4
745	Deep Rattler	3.9	3	Tight sway		Floating	Plastic	Plastic	20.2	Bib	7.9	51.7
746	Jewel	3.9		Tight sway, slow wide roll			Wood	Plastic	28.1	Nose	48.5	122
747	Shad 3.6 m	3.9	3.6	Med. sway, tight roll	Good action.			Plastic	22.7	Bib	9.3	64
748	TD Hyper Crank	3.9		Med. sway			Plastic	Metal	17	Bib	7.8	49.7
749	Tempest TT55	3.9		Med. sway			Plastic	Plastic	26	Bib	8.8	55.9
750	Mac Magic +8	3.9	2.4	Med. sway, tight roll			Plastic	Plastic	25	Nose	29.8	141
751	Invincible F15	3.9	3	Wide roll		Floating	Wood	Plastic	23.7	Nose	29.3	154
752	Barra Bait +8	3.9	2.4	Med. roll			Plastic	Plastic	25	Nose	28.9	141
753	Barra Lure	3.9	3	Med. sway, med. roll			Plastic	Plastic	22	Bib	23.5	117.6
754	Predator Prawn	3.95	3	Tight sway			Wood	Plastic	21.9	Bib	6	65.6
755	Dam Buster	3.95	4.5	Wide sway, tight pitch	Very good action.		Plastic	Metal	29.9	Bib		80
756	Laser Pro 160 DD	3.95	2	Slow tight sway	Rattle.		Plastic	Plastic	21	Nose	29	157
757	Magnum Mag-18	3.95		Slow med. sway		Floating	Plastic	Plastic	22.5	Nose		178.5
758	Power Minnow	4	1.5–2.1	Tight roll		Floating	Plastic	Plastic	23.9	Nose	13.5	103.9
759	Lenny's Diver	4		Tight sway, med. roll		Floating	Wood	Plastic	31.8	Bib	18.5	87.4
760	Merlin - Deep	4		Tight sway		Floating	Plastic	Plastic	18.2	Bib	6.5	59.2
761	Psycho baitfish	4		Med. roll	Very good action.		Plastic	Plastic	21.3	Bib	10.4	90
762	Wee Whop Deep	4	2.4	Med. sway		Floating	Plastic	Plastic	18.3	Bib	7	50.8
763	Thunder Crank 6	4	1.2–2.4	Shimmy			Plastic	Plastic	18.6	Bib	9.5	63
764	Billy Crank #29	4		Tight sway		Floating	Plastic	Plastic	18.1	Bib	8.2	49.7
765	Woomera	4		Med. sway, tight pitch	Loud rattle.		Plastic	Plastic	26.8	Nose	14.3	86.4
766	Hot'N Tot 5	4	1.5–2.4	Tight sway			Plastic	Plastic	24.6	Bib	5.6	51.7
767	KK Medium shallow	4	1.5	Tight sway, med. roll		Floating	Wood	Plastic	21.1	Nose	16.3	97.8
768	Pee Wee 15ft	4	4.5	Wide sway	Good action at 2 knots and slower. Very stable action.		Wood	Plastic	28.4	Bib	12.1	54.1
769	Spoonbill Super Rogue	4	3.6	Med. sway, tight roll	Good action.	Suspend.	Plastic	Plastic	24.9	Bib	18.3	127
770	Barra King Deep Diver	4		Med. roll			Wood	Metal	22.6	Nose	17.2	100.1

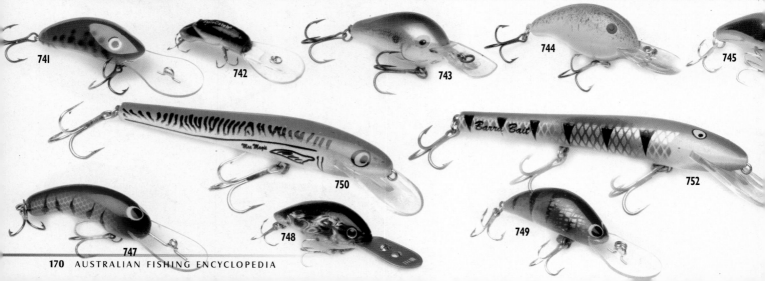

with Bib	Depth on 6.9m at 1.5 knots	Depth on 6.9m at 2 knots	Depth on 6.9m at 2.5 knots	Manufacturer	Country of Manufacture
		1.45		Viper Lures	Aust—Qld
	1.45	1.45		Surebite Lures—SureCatch	China
		1.45		Rapala	Ireland
		1.45		Bandit Lures	USA
		1.45		Top Catch Lures	Taiwan
		1.45		Illusion Lures	Aust—NSW
		1.45		Oar-Gee Lures	Aust—NSW
		1.45		Team Diawa	Japan
		1.45		Kingfisher Lures	Aust—NSW
		1.45		Killalure	Aust—Qld
		1.45		Nilsmaster	Finland
		1.45		Killalure	Aust—Qld
		1.45		S K Lures	Aust—Qld
		1.35		Taylor Made	Aust—NSW
		1.45		Eddy Lures	Aust—Qld
		1.45		Halco	Aust—WA
		1.45		Rapala	Ireland
		1.5		Luhr Jensen	USA
		1.5		Lenny's Lures	Aust—Vic
		1.35		Bennett Lures	Aust—NSW
		1.35		McLaughlin's Lures	Taiwan
		1.35		Kokoda	China
		1.35		Storm	Estonia
		1.35		The Prince	
		1.45		Predatek	Aust—NSW
		1.5		Storm	Estonia
		1.5		Custom Crafted Lures	Aust—NSW
	1.5	1.5		Oar-Gee Lures	Aust—NSW
		1.5		Smithwick	USA
		1.5		R & J Dau	Aust—Qld

756

754

755

757

758

759

760

761

762

763

764

765

766

767

768

769

770

746

751

No.	Lure	Depth Test	Maker's Depth	Action	Comments	Buoyancy	Body Material	Bib Material	Bib Width mm	Tow Point	Weight g	Body Length mm
771	Magnum Mag-14	4		Med. sway		Floating	Plastic	Plastic	19.2	Nose	24.9	139.2
772	Old Faithful Deep	4	2.5–3	Med. sway, med. roll	Great action and colour.		Plastic	Plastic	22.5	Nose	15.5	101.7
773	Fat Bob	4	3	Med. sway			Wood	Plastic	23.4	Bib	13.2	79
774	Rat-L-Trap Magnum Trap	4		Tight sway		Sinking	Plastic	Bibless	11.4	Body	25.4	87.6
775	Shad Rap Deep SR7	4.05		Tight sway		Floating	Wood	Plastic	18.3	Bib	8.3	69.8
776	Stumpjumper 1 shallow bib	4.05		Med. sway, med. roll		Floating	Plastic	Plastic	28.2	Nose	37.8	113
777	Larrikin LK130	4.05		Needs 1.5 knots	Great action but only at 1.5 knots.		Wood	Plastic	32.5	Nose	11.1	99.4
778	Newell M6	4.05		Tight sway, med. roll	Great action.	Floating	Wood	Plastic	28.5	Nose		143.9
779	Stuckey's Small	4.1		Shimmy			Wood	Plastic	22.4	Bib	3.5	50.2
780	Shad Rap Deep SR8	4.1	3–3.6	Med. sway		Floating	Wood	Plastic	19.7	Bib	10.5	80.7
781	Invincible 25	4.1		Med. roll	Great colour.		Wood	Plastic	42.6	Nose	102.2	244
782	Kanga	4.1		Med. sway, med. roll	Great action.		Wood	Plastic	42.8	Nose	220.1	257
783	Invader 40 Deep	4.15		Fast sway, tight pitch			Wood	Plastic	27.4	Bib	5.7	42.9
784	Boomerang 65 Shallow	4.45		Tight sway	Very horizontal presentation.	Floating	Plastic	Plastic	21.7	Bib	9.1	65
785	Poltergeist 50	4.15	3	Tight sway			Plastic	Plastic	26.7	Bib	7.1	50.8
786	Spider 45	4.15	3	Med. sway, tight pitch			Plastic	Plastic	24.3	Bib	6	49
787	Deep Wee R	4.15	2.4–3	Med. sway, tight pitch	Good action.	Floating	Plastic	Plastic	21	Bib	10.8	51.8
788	Pizzcutter	4.15	6	Medium strong sway			Plastic	Plastic	34.4	Bib	15	68.5
789	Wiggle Wart	4.15	2–3.6	Med. sway	Great action. Exaggerated action at slower speed.		Plastic	Plastic	21.7	Bib	11.6	50.7
790	Pegron Diver 65	4.25	3	Med. sway			Plastic	Plastic	22.5	Bib	9.2	65.5
791	Mad Mullet 2.5" Deep	4.15	2	Med. sway, slow roll			Plastic	Plastic	20.5	Bib	8.7	72
792	Invader 60	4.15		Med. sway		Floating	Wood	Plastic	32.7	Bib	12.2	60.1
793	Intruder Depth 10' plus	4.15		Tight sway, tight roll			Plastic	Plastic	24.4	Bib	12.1	82.7
794	Deep Crawfish	4.15	2.1–2.7	Tight sway	Great action.		Plastic	Plastic	22.4	Bib	9.2	58.6
795	Rattlin' Fat Rap RFR-7	4.15		Med. sway		Floating	Wood	Plastic	19.9	Bib	17.3	71.6
796	Chaser	4.15		Med. sway, tight pitch	Loud rattle.		Plastic	Plastic	23.8	Bib	11.9	66.6
797	Smokin Bandit	4.15		Tight sway		Floating	Plastic	Plastic	22.5	Bib	9.8	73.7
798	A & B Barra Blaster	4.15		Med. sway, tight roll	Great action.		Plastic	Plastic	27.2	Nose	28.7	130.2
799	Bevy Shad 75	4.15		Tight sway, tight roll	Great action.	Suspend.	Plastic	Plastic	17.2	Bib	10.4	74.6
800	Arafura Barra	4.15		Tight sway, tight roll			Plastic	Plastic	27.8	Nose	31.2	147

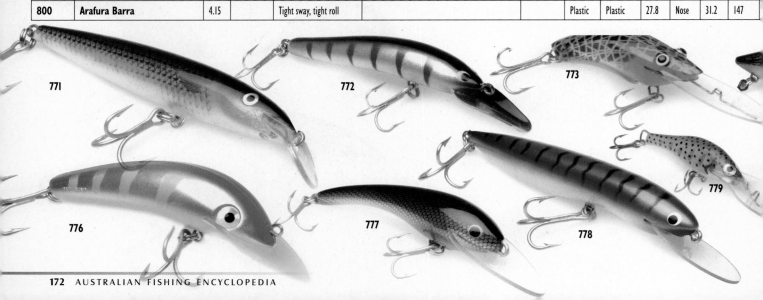

771 772 773

776 777 778 779

Depth on 6.9m at 2 knots	Depth on 6.9m at 2.5 knots	Manufacturer	Country of Manufacture
1.5		Rapala	Ireland
1.5		Tinaroo Lures	Aust—Qld
1.5		Cudgeefish	Aust—NSW
1.35		Bill Lewis Lures	USA
1.4		Rapala	Ireland
1.5		JJ's Lures	Aust—Vic
		Larrikin Lures	Aust—Vic
1.5		Peter Newell Lures	Aust—NSW
1.4		Stuckey's Lures	Aust—NSW
1.45		Rapala	Ireland
1.65		Nilsmaster	Finland
1.65		Kanga Lures	Aust
1.55		AC Lures	Aust—NSW
1.5		Predatek	Aust—NSW
1.55		Halco	Aust—WA
1.55		Majik Lures	Aust—Qld
1.55		Rebel	USA
1.55		S K Lures	Aust—Qld
1.55		Storm	Estonia
1.45		Pegron	Aust—NSW
1.4		Lively Lures	Aust—Qld
1.55		AC Lures	Aust—NSW
1.4		Jarvis Walker	Vietnam
1.55		Rebel	Mexico
1.55		Rapala	Ireland
1.55		Hydrobug Lures	Aust
1.55		Kokoda	China
1.55		JAR Lures	Aust—Qld
1.4		Lucky Craft Lures	Japan
1.55		Lively Lures	Aust—Qld

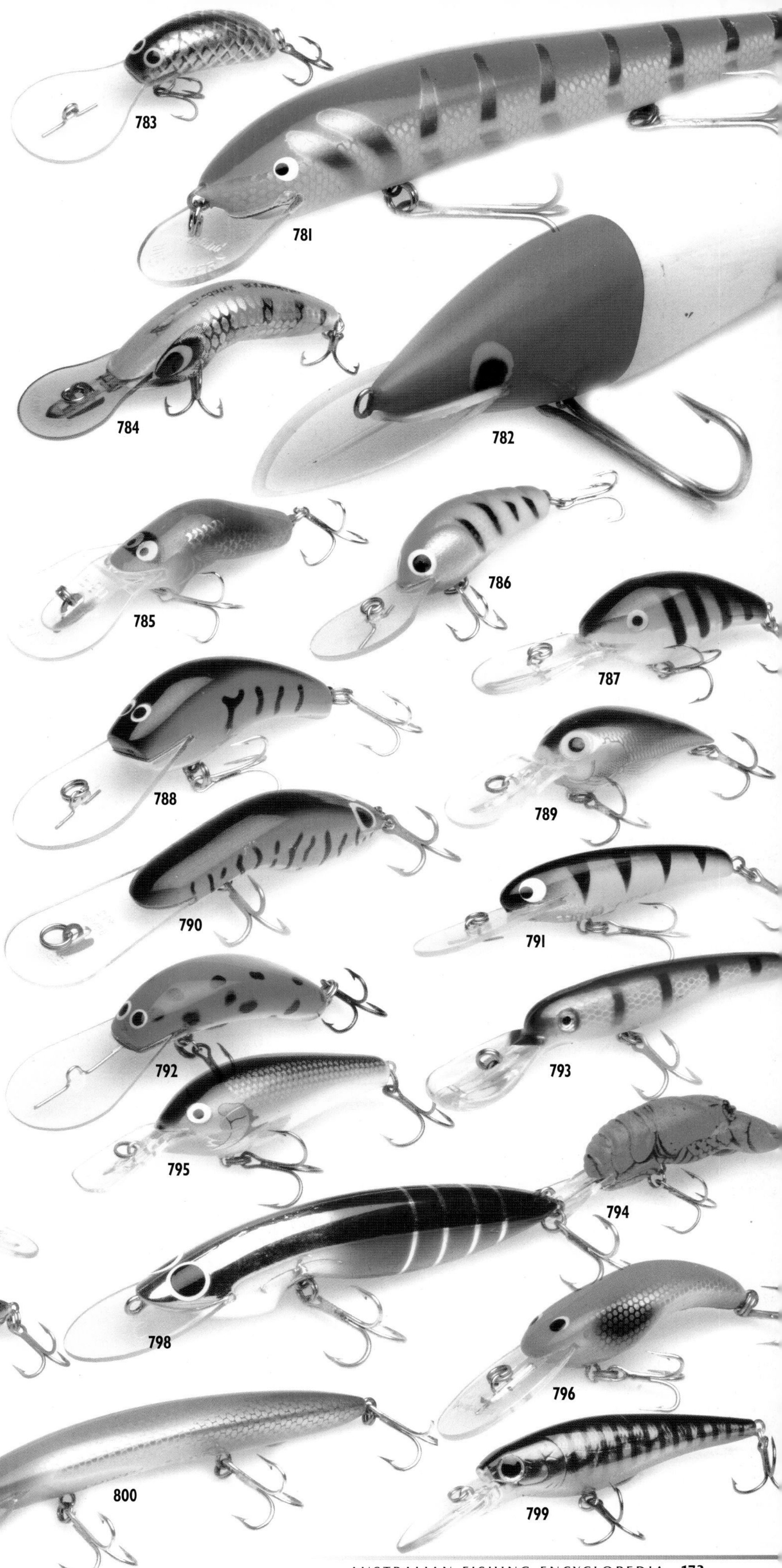

783

781

784

782

785

786

787

788

789

790

791

792

793

795

794

796

774

775

797

780

798

800

799

No.	Lure	Depth Test	Maker's Depth	Action	Comments	Buoyancy	Body Material	Bib Material	Bib Width mm	Tow Point	Weight g
801	RMG Scorpion 125 DD	4.15	4	Tight sway			Plastic	Plastic	31	Bib	24.
802	Cudgeeshrimp 2 Shallow	4.15	2	Tight sway, tight roll			Wood	Plastic	23.4	Bib	16.
803	Laser Pro 190 DD	4.15		Tight sway, tight roll	Better at 2.5 knots.		Plastic	Plastic	23.3	Nose	45.
804	Stumpjumper 2 shallow bib	4.2		Med. sway, tight roll		Floating	Plastic	Plastic	21	Nose	15
805	Cudgeeshrimp 3 5 m	4.2	5	Med. wide sway			Wood	Plastic	37	Bib	27.
806	Callop 1	4.25		Tight sway		Floating	Wood	Plastic	24.4	Bib	6.7
807	Pegron Diver Large	4.15	3.7	Med. wide sway	Loud rattle.		Plastic	Plastic	18.1	Nose	16.
808	Fat Rap FR7	4.25		Fast sway		Floating	Wood	Plastic	20	Bib	
809	Baby Scud	4.3	3	Tight sway, tight roll	Great action at both speeds. Great colour.	Floating	Wood	Plastic	14.3	Bib	5
810	Slim Invader 50 mm Low Buoyancy	4.3	5.4	Med. sway		Floating	Wood	Plastic	27.3	Bib	
811	Water Dragon	4.3		Shimmy		Floating	Plastic	Plastic	24	Bib	12.
812	Jack Snack Deep	4.3		Med. sway			Wood	Plastic	23.3	Bib	9
813	Mulgar 60	4.3	3	Tight sway, tight roll			Plastic	Plastic	23.7	Bib	6.4
814	Porky's Diver Medium	4.3		Med. sway, med. roll			Plastic	Plastic	27.8	Bib	8.8
815	Tempest SC 70	4.3		Med. sway			Plastic	Plastic	28.4	Bib	14.
816	Willy's Worm No 2	4.3		Med. sway			Plastic	Plastic	24.9	Bib	8.4
817	Dytiscus	4.3		Med. sway, med. roll	Great action.		Plastic	Plastic	29	Bib	10.
818	Willy's Worm No 3	4.3		Med. sway			Plastic	Plastic	22	Bib	13
819	The Billabong	4.3		Med. sway			Wood	Plastic	26	Bib	17.
820	Tilsan Barra	4.3	3.5	Tight sway, tight roll		Floating	Wood	Plastic	20.4	Bib	11.
821	Hot'N Tot 7	4.3	2.1–3	Med. sway			Plastic	Plastic	31.6	Bib	12
822	Classic Barra Rattler +10	4.3	3	Med. sway	Rattle.		Plastic	Plastic	27.7	Nose	22.
823	Barra King Deep Diver	4.3		Med. sway, med. pitch		Floating	Wood	Metal	22.7	Nose	24
824	Sonic Mac GM	4.3		Tight sway		Sinking	Plastic	Plastic	24	Bib	18.
825	Bunyip	4.3	3.9–4.5	Med. wide sway	Great action.		Plastic	Plastic	25.9	Bib	15.
826	Hydro Magnum	4.3		Slow med. sway	Much better at 2.5 knots.	Sinking	Plastic	Plastic	18	Bib	32.
827	Midive Min 140S	4.3		Slow tight sway, tight roll		Sinking	Plastic	Plastic	21.5	Bib	49.
828	Hellbender Baby	4.35		Med. sway, tight roll		Floating	Plastic	Metal	22.2	Bib	7.7
829	Big Jaws	4.35	4.5	Med. sway, tight pitch	Very good erratic action.		Plastic	Plastic	28	Bib	18.
830	Mud Bug 5/8oz	4.35		Med. roll		Floating	Plastic	Metal	26.4	Bib	13.

Actual Length with Bib	Depth on 6.9m at 1.5 knots	Depth on 6.9m at 2 knots	Depth on 6.9m at 2.5 knots	Manufaturer	Country of Manufacture
156.3		1.55		Halco	Aust—WA
138		1.4		Cudgeefish	Aust—NSW
207.6		1.55		Halco	Aust—WA
100.3		1.55		JJ's Lures	Aust—Vic
185		1.55		Cudgeefish	Aust—NSW
79.5		1.6		Peter Newell Lures	Aust—NSW
124.2		1.55		Pegron	Aust—NSW
100.1		1.55		Rapala	Ireland
82.1	1.5	1.45		Custom Crafted Lures	Aust—NSW
86.3		1.6		AC Lures	Aust—NSW
143		1.45		Peter Newell Lures	Aust—NSW
95.4		1.45		C Lures	Aust—Qld
89.3		1.45		Majik Lures	Aust—Qld
100.8		1.6		Porky's Lures	Aust
102.5		1.6		Kingfisher Lures	Aust—NSW
77.3		1.6		The Producers	China
79.2		1.6		Hydrobug Lures	Aust
91.7		1.6		The Producers	China
105		1.6		Legend Lures	Aust—NSW
115.5		1.45		Halco	Aust—WA
96.3		1.6		Storm	Estonia
142.6		1.6		Classic Lures	Aust
166		1.6		R & J Dau	Aust—Qld
133.2		1.45		McLaughlin's Lures	Taiwan
118.1		1.6		Predatek	Aust—NSW
159.5		1.45	1.45	Yo-Zuri Lures	Japan
181		1.45	1.45	River 2 Sea	
78.5		1.5		Pradco Lures	USA
96.7		1.65		Willo Lures	Aust—Qld
89.3		1.6		Fred Arbogast	USA

No.	Lure	Depth Test	Maker's Depth	Action	Comments	Buoyancy	Body Material	Bib Material	Bib Width mm	Tow Point
831	Extractor	4.35	4.8	Fast tight sway		Floating	Wood	Plastic	30.9	Bib
832	Scout	4.35		Med. sway, tight pitch	Lateral movement.		Plastic	Plastic	36	Bib
833	Shad #18	4.35		Tight sway, tight roll		Floating	Plastic	Plastic	16.8	Bib
834	Porky's Diver Large	4.35		Med. sway, tight roll	Better at 1.5 knots.		Plastic	Plastic	33.8	Bib
835	Frenzy Diving Minnow	4.35	3	Med. roll		Floating	Plastic	Plastic	22.9	Bib
836	Fishstik - Small	4.4	3	Tight sway, tight pitch			Plastic	Plastic	20.3	Bib
837	RMG Scorpion 150 STD	4.4	3.5	Med. roll		Floating	Plastic	Plastic	27.4	Nose
838	Belly Buster	4.4	5.5	Med. sway	Excellent action both speeds.		Wood	Plastic	33.5	Bib
839	Fishstik - Medium	4.4	5.4	Tight sway, med. roll		Floating	Wood	Plastic	30.9	Bib
840	Hydro Squirt	4.4		Medium wobble, tight roll	Excellent action. Skirt looks great. One of top lures.	Floating	Plastic	Plastic	23.3	Bib
841	Invader 70	4.4		Med. sway			Wood	Plastic	31.8	Bib
842	Stumpjumper 2 round bib	4.4		Med. sway, tight roll	Good action.	Floating	Plastic	Plastic	23.5	Nose
843	Kill'r B-II	4.4	0–4.2	Med. sway, tight pitch		Floating	Wood	Plastic	28.7	Bib
844	Bandit 400 Series	4.4	3.6–4.8	Med. sway, med. pitch	Great action. Lateral movement.		Plastic	Plastic	28.3	Bib
845	Goodoo	4.4	4	Med. strong sway			Plastic	Plastic	31.9	Bib
846	Barra 120	4.4	5	Tight sway, tight pitch	Great action. Lateral movement. Rattle.		Plastic	Plastic	30.8	Bib
847	Boomerang 65 Medium	4.45		Med. sway		Floating	Plastic	Plastic	23.7	Bib
848	Mini Boggle Eyes	4.45		Med. sway			Plastic	Plastic	29.8	Bib
849	Hot Lips Express 1/4oz	4.45	3.6–4.8	Med. sway	Great action.		Plastic	Plastic	30.3	Bib
850	Barra Bug Deep 155	4.45		Med. sway, tight roll			Plastic	Plastic	31	Nose
851	Combat	4.5	2.5–3	Med. sway	Great action and lateral movement at slower speed.	Floating	Plastic	Plastic	20	Bib
852	Hardcore SH-60SP	4.5		Tight sway		Suspend.	Plastic	Plastic	16.6	Bib
853	Lightning Minnow #2	4.5		Shimmy			Plastic	Plastic	16.7	Bib
854	Lb Minnow LBM65P	4.5		Tight sway		Suspend.	Plastic	Plastic	16.3	Bib
855	Headmaster Deep	4.5		Tight sway, med. roll			Wood	Plastic	22.7	Bib
856	Magnum CD-11	4.5		Med. sway	Great action at 2.5 knots.	Sinking	Plastic	Metal	19.2	Bib
857	10+	4.55	3	Tight sway, tight roll			Plastic	Plastic	24.3	Bib
858	Mini Wild	4.55	3.6	Med. sway			Plastic	Plastic	29.8	Bib
859	Bass	4.55	3	Med. sway	Better at 1.5 knots. Slightly unstable lateral movement at 2 knots.		Plastic	Plastic	23.6	Bib
860	Pro's Choice Lil Lonnie	4.55	3.6	Tight sway			Plastic	Plastic	24.6	Bib

Actual Length with Bib	Depth on 6.9m at 1.5 knots	Depth on 6.9m at 2 knots	Depth on 6.9m at 2.5 knots	Manufacturer	Country of Manufacture
97.3		1.6		Custom Crafted Lures	Aust—NSW
107.3		1.6		Mudeye Lures	Aust—NSW
91		1.35		The Prince	
116.1	1.6	1.65		Porky's Lures	Aust
133.1		1.65		Berkley	USA
72.8		1.5		Custom Crafted Lures	Aust—NSW
172		1.65		Halco	Aust—WA
97.4	1.65	1.65		Taylor Made	Aust—NSW
112.2		1.65		Custom Crafted Lures	Aust—NSW
143.2		1.65		Yo-Zuri Lures	Japan
116.3		1.65		AC Lures	Aust—NSW
97		1.65		JJ's Lures	Aust—Vic
98.3		1.55		Bagley	Dominican Rep
110.1		1.65		Bandit Lures	USA
122.7		1.65		Classic Lures	Aust
149.5		1.65		Classic Lures	Aust
91.3		1.5		Predatek	Aust—NSW
89.3		1.65		Horsey's Lures	Aust—Qld
88.6		1.65		Luhr Jensen	USA
192.1		1.65		Bill's Bugs	Aust—NSW
73.9	1.55	1.55		Halco	Aust—WA
91		1.4		Duel	Japan
91.7		1.4		The Producers	China
92.8		1.4		Surebite Lures—SureCatch	Japan
117.5		1.5		C Lures	Aust—Qld
144.7		1.5	1.5	Rapala	Finland
79.8		1.7		Mann's Lures	USA
83.1		1.7		S K Lures	Aust—Qld
95	1.7	1.7		Classic Lures	Aust
104.1		1.7		Stanley Jigs	China

841

842

843

844

845

846

847

848

849

850

851

852

853

854

855

856

857

858

859

860

835

840

No.	Lure	Depth Test	Maker's Depth	Action	Comments	Buoyancy	Body Material	Bib Material	Bib Width mm	Tow Point
861	Codger 85	4.55	7.5	Wide sway	Great action.		Plastic	Plastic	39.9	Bib
862	Dusky	4.6	3	Tight sway		Floating	Wood	Plastic	23.8	Bib
863	King Predator	4.6	3.5	Tight sway, tight roll			Wood	Plastic	23	Bib
864	Fergo 12+	4.6	3.6	Tight sway				Plastic	27.9	Bib
865	Voodoo Lure	4.6	4.5	Tight sway, tight roll	Good lateral action.	Floating	Plastic	Plastic	30.2	Bib
866	Mad Mullet 3" Deep	4.6		Med. sway			Foam	Plastic	26.1	Bib
867	Shad Rap Suspending RS5	4.6		Tight sway		Suspend.	Plastic	Plastic	18.7	Bib
868	Deep Flat A	4.6		Tight sway, tight roll			Plastic	Plastic	21.1	Bib
869	Model 6A	4.6		Tight sway			Plastic	Plastic	20.8	Bib
870	The Codfather - Suicide	4.6		Med. sway			Plastic	Plastic	24.9	Bib
871	Jaberoo BR-15	4.6	0.9	Slow tight roll	Better at 2.5 knots.	Floating	Plastic	Plastic	19.7	Nose
872	McDiver	4.6	1.8–2.4	Med. sway		Suspend.	Plastic	Plastic	20	Bib
873	Stumpjumper 2 deep bib	4.6		Med. sway, tight roll	Good action. More exaggerated at slower speed.	Floating	Plastic	Plastic	24.7	Nose
874	Invincible DR 12 cm	4.6	7	Med. sway, med. pitch	Great action.	Sinking	Wood	Plastic	24	Nose
875	Galaxia	4.65		Tight sway		Floating	Wood	Plastic	24.4	Bib
876	Hot'N Tot (old)	4.65		Med. wide sway	Excellent action. Lateral movement. Better at 1.5 knots.	Floating	Plastic	Plastic	28	Body
877	Baby Shad BS80P	4.65		Tight roll		Suspend.	Plastic	Plastic	18.3	Bib
878	Shrimp	4.65		Med. sway	Great action at both speeds.		Wood	Plastic	28.9	Bib
879	Magnum wiggle wart (old)	4.65		Med. sway, tight pitch	Excellent action both speeds. Loud rattle. Trailing hook stable.	Floating	Plastic	Plastic	25.6	Bib
880	Hellbender Midget	4.7		Med. sway, tight pitch	Good action. Lateral movement.	Floating	Plastic	Metal	24.7	Bib
881	RMG Scorpion 90 DD	4.7	4	Tight roll		Floating	Plastic	Plastic	34.6	Bib
882	Hard At It	4.7		Med. wide sway	Great action.		Wood	Metal	27.8	Bib
883	Plow 60	4.7	3.6	Fast med. sway		Floating	Plastic	Plastic	29.5	Bib
884	Deep Wart	4.7		Med. sway	Great action. Some lateral movement.		Plastic	Plastic	23.4	Bib
885	Aust Record Lure Small	4.7		Tight sway			Plastic	Plastic	31.1	Bib
886	Long Bob 3 m	4.7	3	Med. sway			Wood	Plastic	38	Bib
887	Avoidance Behaviour Lure	4.7		Tight sway, med. pitch	Good erratic action caused by blade.	Floating	Plastic	Plastic	28.8	Bib
888	Hot Rod	4.7	4.5	Wide sway		Floating	Wood	Plastic	36.7	Bib
889	Plow 75	4.7	4.5	Med. sway		Sinking	Plastic	Plastic	34	Bib
890	Long Bob 5 m	4.7	5	Med. sway, tight roll, tight pitch			Wood	Plastic	37	Bib

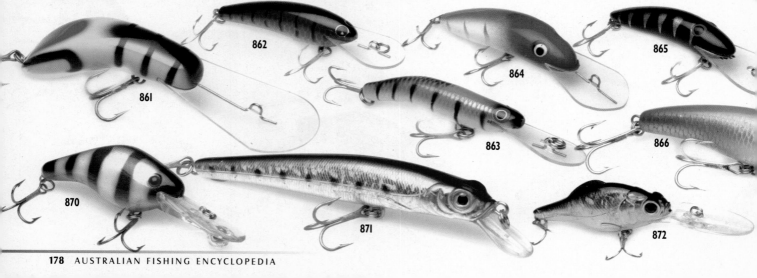

Actual Length with Bib	Depth on 6.9m at 1.5 knots	Depth on 6.9m at 2 knots	Depth on 6.9m at 2.5 knots	Manufacturer	Country of Manufacture
141.5		1.7		Goulburn Lures	Aust—Vic
102.2		1.55		Peter Newell Lures	Aust—NSW
112.4		1.55		Taylor Made	Aust—NSW
112		1.55		Willo Lures	Aust—Qld
100.1		1.55		Voodoo Lures	Aust—Qld
122.8		1.55		Lively Lures	Aust—Qld
89.9		1.55		Rapala	Ireland
90.6		1.55		Bomber	USA
82.1		1.55		Bomber	Mexico
104.6		1.7		Juro	Taiwan
172.5		1.55	1.55	Kokoda	China
101.6		1.55		Kokoda	China
103.1	1.6	1.7		JJ's Lures	Aust—Vic
150		1.65		Nilsmaster	Finland
84.2		1.45		Deception Lures	Aust—NSW
94.2	1.75	1.8		Storm	USA
104.4		1.45		SureBite Lures—SureCatch	Japan
102.7	1.6	1.55		Deception Lures	Aust—NSW
94.7	1.6	1.7		Storm	USA
95.7		1.65		Pradco Lures	USA
114.3		1.75		Halco	Aust—WA
81.4	1.7	1.75		Hard At It Lures	Aust
99.9		1.75		Oar-Gee Lures	Aust—NSW
83.3	1.75	1.75		Storm	Estonia
93.2		1.75		Knol's Lures	Malaysia
171.6		1.75		Cudgeefish	Aust—NSW
111.3		1.75		Bass Pro Shops	China
127		1.75		Custom Crafted Lures	Aust—NSW
116.5		1.75		Oar-Gee Lures	Aust—NSW
189.2		1.75		Cudgeefish	Aust—NSW

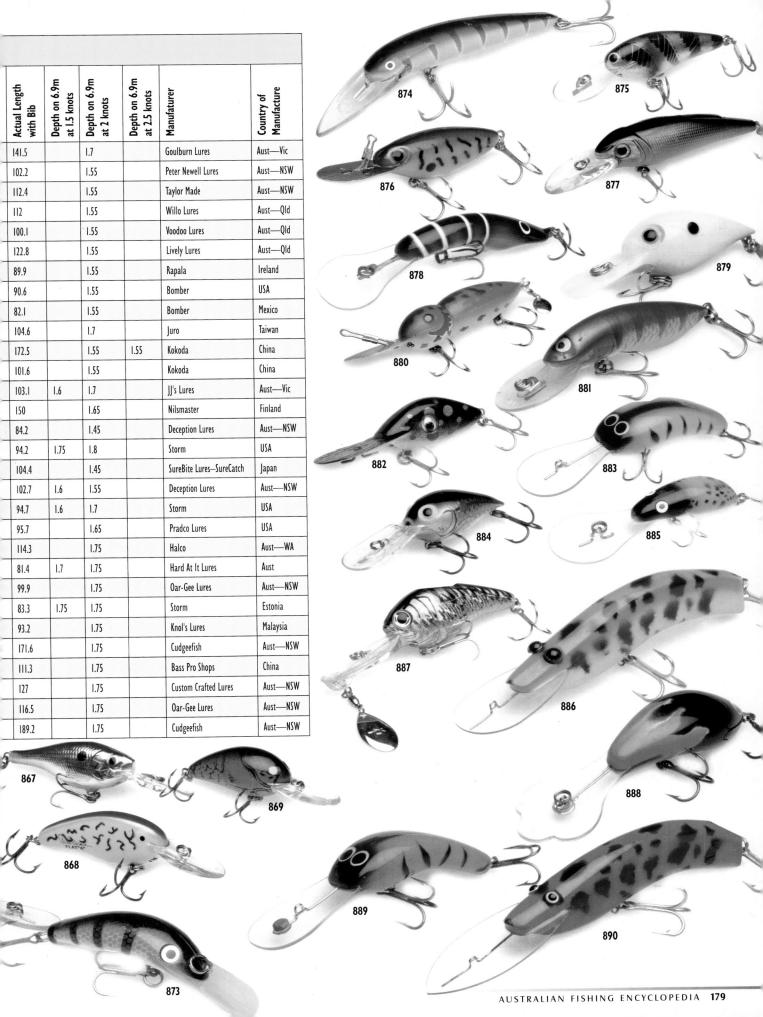

No.	Lure	Depth Test	Maker's Depth	Action	Comments	Buoyancy	Body Material	Bib Material	Bib Width mm	Tow Point	
891	River King - Bass	4.75		Tight sway, tight roll			Plastic	Plastic	25.7	Bib	8
892	Haka Down Deep	4.75		Tight sway	Looks good both speeds.		Wood	Plastic	22.7	Bib	8
893	Phantom	4.75		Med. sway, slow roll			Plastic	Plastic	30	Bib	
894	Sardinops Deep	4.75		Tight sway,tight roll			Wood	Plastic	28.8	Bib	
895	Probe	4.75		Med. sway, tight pitch	Great action.	Floating	Plastic	Plastic	30.6	Bib	
896	Super Crank SK65	4.75		Tight sway	Extremely difficult to tune.	Floating	Plastic	Plastic	20.1	Bib	1.
897	A & B Tiny Boy	4.75		Med. sway	Erratic lateral movement, but stable.		Plastic	Plastic	32	Bib	1
898	Frenzy	4.75	3	Med. sway		Floating	Plastic	Plastic	22.6	Bib	
899	Merlin	4.75		Very wide sway	Great action at both speeds. Bit more exaggerated at 1.5 knots.	Sinking	Wood	Plastic	39.9	Bib	5
900	Husky Jerk Deep DHJ-12	4.75		Med. sway, slow roll		Suspend.	Plastic	Plastic	22.2	Bib	1.
901	Adrenalin Minnow 9	4.75		Med. pitch	Poor action	Sinking	Plastic	Metal	19	Bib	17
902	Yarrum	4.8	4.2	Med. sway	Better slower.		Plastic	Plastic	38.3	Bib	2.
903	Wiggle Wart	4.8	3.6–5.4	Med. sway	Great action at both speeds.		Plastic	Plastic	26.1	Bib	19
904	Long A Minnow	4.8		Med. sway			Plastic	Plastic	26	Bib	20
905	Tilsan Bass	4.85	4.5	Tight sway,tight pitch		Sinking	Wood	Plastic	23.7	Bib	7.
906	Wiggle 'O'	4.85	4.2–5.4	Med. wide sway	Better slower. Great colour.		Plastic	Plastic	21.6	Bib	11
907	Barra Pro Deep	4.85		Med. sway	Better slower.		Wood	Plastic	23.4	Bib	15
908	All Rounder	4.85	3	Tight sway, tight roll	Slightly deeper at slower speed.		Plastic	Plastic	26.2	Bib	9.
909	Viper 150	4.85		Tight sway, tight roll	Excellent action at 2.5 knots.		Plastic	Plastic	27.3	Nose	28
910	Deep Stalker	4.9	4.8	Med. sway			Plastic	Plastic	25.8	Bib	12
911	Cudgeeshrimp 3	4.9	3	Med. sway, tight roll		Sinking	Wood	Plastic	38	Bib	29
912	Cherax	4.9		Wide sway, tight roll			Wood	Plastic	35.6	Bib	17
913	Shad Deep	4.9		Fast tight sway		Wood	Plastic	29.8	Bib	9.8	63
914	Flatz Rat 2	4.9	10	Med. sway			Plastic	Plastic	25.1	Bib	10
915	Hard At It	4.9		Wide sway			Wood	Plastic	29	Bib	10.
916	Big Willy	4.9	3.6	Wide sway	Action exaggerated at slower speed.		Plastic	Plastic	27.7	Bib	10.
917	Boomerang 80M	4.9		Tight sway, tight roll			Plastic	Plastic	26.7	Bib	18.
918	Mad Mullet 4" Deep	4.9	4	Tight sway, slow roll			Plastic	Plastic	27.2	Bib	18.
919	Stretch 10+	4.9	3	Med. sway	Works well both speeds.		Plastic	Plastic	24.4	Bib	13.
920	Premier Pro-Model Series 5	4.9	3–3.6	Med. sway med. roll			Plastic	Plastic	28	Bib	19.

891 892 893 894
897 898 899

Actual Length with Bib	Depth on 6.9m at 1.5 knots	Depth on 6.9m at 2 knots	Depth on 6.9m at 2.5 knots	Manufacturer	Country of Manufacture
89.2		1.6		Lawson Lures	Aust—NSW
96.4	1.6	1.6		Nilsmaster	Finland
148.7		1.6		Horsey's Lures	Aust—Qld
129.4		1.6		Deception Lures	Aust—NSW
86.6	1.7	1.7		Rabble Rouser Lures	USA
92.2		1.6		Surebite Lures—SureCatch	China
96.9		1.75		JAR Lures	Aust—Qld
104		1.6		Berkley	USA
177.4	1.7	1.8		Bennett Lures	Aust—NSW
161		1.6		Rapala	Ireland
128.3		1.6		McLaughlin's Lures	Taiwan
131.2	1.8	1.8		Legend Lures	Aust—NSW
96.2	1.7	1.8		Storm	Estonia
156.8		1.8		Bomber	Mexico
88		1.5		Halco	Aust—WA
77.2	1.65	1.55		Cotton Cordell	USA
118.7	1.8	1.35		C Lures	Aust—Qld
109.3	1.7	1.6		Classic Lures	Aust
166		1.7	1.6	Predatek	Aust—NSW
101.3		1.65		Spawn Lures	Aust
177.6		1.65		Cudgeefish	Aust—NSW
114.2	1.75	1.65		Deception Lures	Aust—NSW
42.5	1.65			Oar-Gee Lures	Aust—NSW
106.1		1.65		Killalure	Aust—Qld
100.9	1.65	1.65		Hard At It Lures	Aust
95.2	1.6	1.65		S K Lures	Aust—Qld
111.1		1.65		Predatek	Aust—NSW
141.2		1.65		Lively Lures	Aust—Qld
114.1		1.55	1.6	Mann's Lures	USA
114.6		1.65		Strike King Lure Company	Mexico

No.	Lure	Depth Test	Maker's Depth	Action	Comments	Buoyancy	Body Material	Bib Material	Bib Width mm
921	Original B-52	4.9	3	Med. sway	Very good action. Better at 2.5 knots.	Sinking	Plastic	Plastic	34.3
922	Deep Diver 75	4.9		Tight sway, tight roll		Sinking	Plastic	Plastic	26.7
923	Mulgar 80	4.9	5	Medium wide sway	Great action. Great colour.		Plastic	Plastic	30.3
924	Model 7A	4.9		Tight sway, tight pitch			Plastic	Plastic	21.8
925	Deep Z	4.9		Tight sway,tight pitch	Great colour.	Floating	Plastic	Plastic	24.4
926	Baby Bandit	4.9	4.5	Fast sway			Plastic	Plastic	26.1
927	Adrenalin Minnow II	4.9		Wide pitch,poor action	Poor action.	Sinking	Plastic	Metal	19.4
928	Invincible DRI5	4.9	4	Med. roll			Wood	Metal	22.2
929	Deep ThunderStick	4.9	3–4.2	Med. sway, tight roll		Sinking	Plastic	Bibless	22.3
930	Hydro Magnum 140 mm	4.9		Med. sway, med. roll		Sinking	Plastic	Plastic	20.5
931	Boomerang 65	4.95		Tight sway, med. pitch	Great kicking action both speeds.	Floating	Plastic	Plastic	32.2
932	Sliver Jointed 20	4.95		Tight sway, med. roll	Much better at 2.5 knots.		Plastic	Metal	18.8
933	Stuckey's Medium	5		Med. sway			Wood	Plastic	27.3
934	Mudeye 60	5		Tight sway, tight roll			Plastic	Plastic	30
935	Lb Minnow LB85P	5		Med. roll		Suspend.	Plastic	Plastic	21.1
936	Aust Record Lure Large	5		Med. sway			Plastic	Plastic	39
937	Magnum CD-9	5		Tight sway	Excellent action at 2.5 knots.	Sinking	Wood	Metal	19.4
938	Scale Raza 20+	5	6	Med. sway, tight pitch	Great action. Unique erratic movement. Best lure of tests.		Plastic	Plastic	35
939	Hammerhead - Small	5.05	3.6	Med. sway, tight roll	Loud rattle.		Plastic	Plastic	27.7
940	Mauler Jack Hammer	5.05	5.4	Med. sway, tight roll			Plastic	Plastic	30.4
941	Codger	5.05	4.5	Med. sway	Great exaggerated action at 1.5 knots.		Plastic	Plastic	28.8
942	Snag Master 10+	5.05	3	Med. sway, tight roll	Stable lateral movement.		Plastic	Plastic	25.3
943	KK Medium	5.05	5.4	Med. sway,tight roll		Floating	Wood	Plastic	30.2
944	Boomerang 65	5.05		Fast sway	Colours look great.	Floating	Plastic	Plastic	26.8
945	Spider 58	5.05	6	Wide sway			Plastic	Plastic	30.5
946	Shad Rap Suspending RS7	5.05		Tight sway		Suspend.	Wood	Plastic	21.7
947	Radar Ratz	5.05		Tight sway,tight roll	Good action.	Sinking	Plastic	Plastic	26.1
948	Boney	5.05	6	Med. sway	Great action.	Floating	Wood	Plastic	32.5
949	Tempest TT 70	5.05		Med. sway, tight roll	Great action.		Plastic	Plastic	31.5
950	Moonsault CB-350	5.05		Med. sway		Floating	Plastic	Plastic	20.7

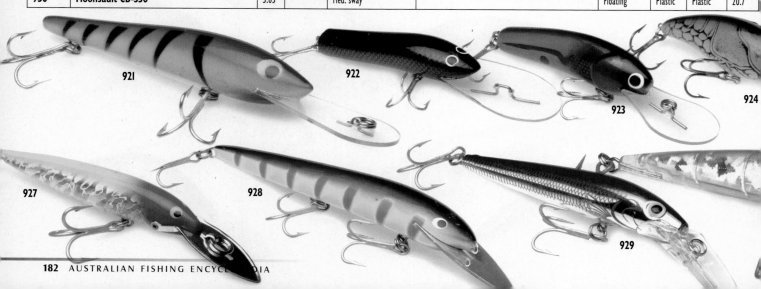

Body Length mm	Actual Length with Bib	Depth on 6.9m at 1.5 knots	Depth on 6.9m at 2 knots	Depth on 6.9m at 2.5 knots	Manufacturer	Country of Manufacture
155.6	200.2		1.65	1.65	Bo-Bo Lures	Aust—NSW
77.1	115.3		1.65		Bill's Bugs	Aust—NSW
83	117.6		1.65		Majik Lures	Aust—Qld
65.9	93.9		1.65		Bomber	Mexico
69.2	106.5		1.65		The Producers	China
65.6	115.9		1.65		Horsey's Lures	Aust—Qld
106.2	145.5		1.65		McLaughlin's Lures	Taiwan
152.3	182.5		1.65		Nilsmaster	Finland
115	152.8		1.65		Storm	Estonia
139.2	186.5		1.65		Yo-Zuri Lures	Japan
65.2	108.3	1.85	1.85		Predatek	Aust—NSW
203	239		1.6	1.7	Rapala	Ireland
61.4	93.6		1.7		Stuckey's Lures	Aust—NSW
58	85		1.7		Mudeye Lures	Aust—NSW
85	121.1		1.55		Surebite Lures—SureCatch	Japan
75.2	121.6		1.85		Knol's Lures	Malaysia
92.7	126.5		1.65	1.6	Rapala	Ireland
116.7	160.4	1.9	1.8		DK Lures	Aust—Qld
68.7	94.5		1.7		Custom Crafted Lures	Aust—NSW
86.5	120.9		1.7		Mac's Maulers	Aust—Qld
54.4	92.5	1.7	1.7		Goulburn Lures	Aust—Vic
75.4	130		1.7		DK Lures	Aust—Qld
97	134.7		1.7		Custom Crafted Lures	Aust—NSW
65.3	99.2		1.7		Predatek	Aust—NSW
61.4	99.4		1.7		Majik Lures	Aust—Qld
74.9	111.2		1.7		Rapala	Ireland
64.7	102.3		1.7		McLaughlin's Lures	Taiwan
98.9	134.7		1.7		Peter Newell Lures	Aust—NSW
70	106.2		1.7		Kingfisher Lures	Aust—NSW
62.6	97.4		1.7		Lucky Craft Lures	Japan

No.	Lure	Depth Test	Maker's Depth	Action	Comments	Buoyancy	Body Material	Bib Material
951	Risto Rap RR-8	5.05		Med. sway, tight roll		Floating	Wood	Plastic
952	Barra Bait +12	5.05	3.7	Med. sway, tight roll			Plastic	Plastic
953	River Rat 130 mm	5.05	3.7	Med. wide sway		Sinking	Plastic	Plastic
954	Shad Rap Deep SR9	5.1	3.6–4.2	Med. sway, tight roll		Floating	Wood	Plastic
955	Invader 90	5.1		Wide sway	Good action.	Floating	Wood	Plastic
956	RMG Poltergeist 80	5.1	5	Med.sway		Sinking	Plastic	Plastic
957	Wild Willy	5.15	6	Med. sway	Better slow.		Plastic	Plastic
958	Suspending Fat Free Fry	5.15		Tight sway		Suspend.	Plastic	Plastic
959	Fat Free Fry	5.15		Tight sway			Plastic	Plastic
960	Nose Systems Deep	5.15		Tight sway	Needs 1.5 knots or slower.		Plastic	Plastic
961	Giant Trembler	5.15	2	Tight sway	Better at 2.5 knots. Really stable.needs more speed	Sinking	Plastic	Bibless
962	Elton	5.2		Shimmy			Plastic	Plastic
963	KK Small	5.2	4.2	Tight sway,tight roll		Floating	Wood	Plastic
964	Double Downer #3	5.2		Med. sway	Great action. Lateral movement.		Plastic	Metal
965	Grave Digger	5.2		Med. wide sway			Plastic	Plastic
966	Blue Pilly Jnr Deep	5.2	3	Tight sway, tight roll	Better faster.		Plastic	Plastic
967	Power Dive Minnow 1/2oz	5.2	6	Fast tight sway			Plastic	Plastic
968	Deep Diver 90	5.2		Med. sway			Plastic	Plastic
969	Rattlin' Rogue ASSRB1200	5.25	3	Med. sway		Suspend.	Plastic	Plastic
970	Thunder Crank	5.25	2.4–4.5	Med. sway			Plastic	Plastic
971	Deep Husky Jerk DHJ-10	5.25		Med. sway		Suspend.		Plastic
972	River Rat +12	5.25	3.7	Med. sway	Better at 2.5 knots.	Sinking	Plastic	Plastic
973	15+	5.3	4.5	Med. sway		Floating	Plastic	Plastic
974	Mack Bait	5.3		Vibrate		Sinking	Plastic	Bibless
975	Jumbo DD	5.3		Med. sway, med. pitch	Great erratic action. A real winner. Better at 2.5 knots.	Floating	Wood	Plastic
976	Rocket Diver 120	5.35		Med. sway		Floating	Plastic	Plastic
977	Goulburn Jack	5.35	5	Med. sway, tight roll		Floating	Plastic	Plastic
978	Deep Stinger	5.35	5.4	Med. sway, tight roll	Eyes prominent.		Plastic	Plastic
979	Ferret 10+	5.35	3.1	Tight sway			Plastic	Plastic
980	Tempest 85	5.35		Med. sway	Loud rattle.		Plastic	Plastic

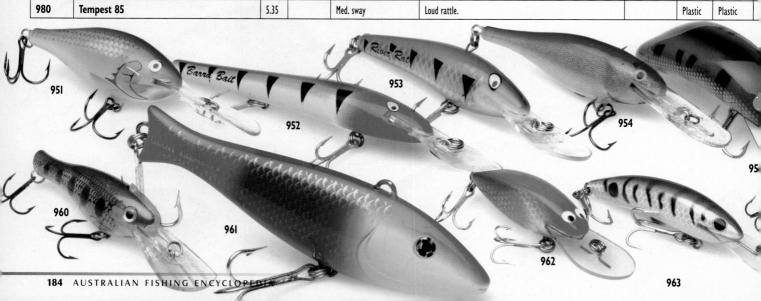

Weight g	Body Length mm	Actual Length with Bib	Depth on 6.9m at 1.5 knots	Depth on 6.9m at 2 knots	Depth on 6.9m at 2.5 knots	Manufacturer	Country of Manufacture
	77.6	123.9		1.7		Rapala	Ireland
30.1	140.5	181		1.7		Killalure	Aust—Qld
19.9	102.3	140.5		1.7		Killalure	Aust—Qld
14.6	92.6	129.2		1.6		Rapala	Ireland
30.8	91.6	152		1.9		AC Lures	Aust—NSW
19.4	78	121.2		1.9		Halco	Aust—WA
13.2	61.1	90.8	1.75	1.85		S K Lures	Aust—Qld
9.9	51.6	82		1.6		Excalibur	USA
9.4	51.9	82		1.6		Excalibur	USA
11.5	69	98.2	1.65			Transkei Lures	
128.4	176.3	176.3		1.9	1.75	Halco	Aust—WA
8.3	60.3	86.2		1.75		Hypa Active	Aust
12	81.1	102.6		1.6		Custom Crafted Lures	Aust—NSW
12.7	62.7	97.6		1.75		The Producers	China
10.3	58.3	95.2		1.75		Bounty Hunter Lures	Aust—NSW
21.4	115	155.8		1.6		Lively Lures	Aust—Qld
9.7	81.4	116.7		1.75		Luhr Jensen	USA
17.6	92.6	135.3		1.75		Bill's Bugs	Aust—NSW
13.7	113.7	155.9		1.65		Smithwick	Mexico
12.3	77.4	112.6		1.65		Storm	Estonia
11.8	96.7	132.3		1.65		Rapala	Ireland
29.9	141	180.7		1.65	1.75	Killalure	Aust—Qld
13.8	57	96.6		1.75		Mann's Lures	USA
47.8	107.5	107.5		1.65		Lively Lures	Aust—Qld
	114.8	141.1		1.8	1.85	Nilsmaster	Finland
19.1	119	157.9		1.65		Surebite Lures—SureCatch	China
	86.9	127.6		1.65		Reidy's	Aust
	88.5	136.1		1.65		Eddy Lures	Aust—Qld
11.1	80.3	112.7		1.65		DK Lures	Aust—Qld
22.3	84.6	124.5		1.8		Kingfisher Lures	Aust—NSW

969

968

970

972

971

973

974

975

976

977

978

979

980

956

957

959

958

964

965

966

967

No.	Lure	Depth Test	Maker's Depth	Action	Comments	Buoyancy	Body Material	Bib Material	
981	KK Large	5.35	6.6	Slow med. roll	Excellent action at 2 knots.	Floating	Wood	Plastic	3
982	Crank'n Shad	5.35	2.4	Tight sway		Floating	Plastic	Plastic	2
983	Codzilla	5.35		Wide sway	Nice erratic action.		Plastic	Plastic	2
984	Down Deep Husky Jerk 12	5.35		Med. wide sway, tight		Suspend.	Plastic	Plastic	2
985	Hammerhead - Medium	5.4	6	Wide sway		Floating	Wood	Plastic	3
986	Wedgetail - Deep 16	5.4		Med. slow sway, med. roll	Excellent action at 2.5 knots.		Wood	Plastic	2
987	Wally Minnow CS8	5.45	6.3	Med. wide sway	Good action.	Suspend.	Plastic	Plastic	2
988	Spoonbill	5.45		Med. sway, med. roll	Great action.		Plastic	Plastic	2
989	RMG Scorpion 150 DD	5.45	5	Tight sway, tight roll			Plastic	Plastic	3
990	Merlin - Ultra Deep	5.5		Med. sway		Floating	Plastic	Plastic	3
991	Agro	5.5	6	Med. sway, tight pitch			Plastic	Plastic	3
992	Invader 50 Deep	5.5		Fast tight sway	Better slower.		Wood	Plastic	3
993	Rocket Diver RD100	5.5		Med. sway, tight roll		Floating	Plastic	Plastic	3
994	Mud Bug	5.5		Med. wide sway		Floating	Plastic	Metal	3
995	Magnum Wasp	5.5	4.8	Med. sway, tight roll			Plastic	Plastic	3
996	Wedgetail - Deep 12	5.5		Med. sway, tight roll	Better at 2 knots.		Wood	Plastic	2
997	Mac Magic 29 g	5.5	3.7	Med. sway	Better at 2.5 knots.	Sinking	Plastic	Plastic	2
998	Rocket Diver 140	5.5		Med. sway, med. roll			Plastic	Plastic	2
999	Deep Diver 135	5.5		Tight sway, tight roll		Sinking	Plastic	Plastic	2
1000	Magnum CD-14	5.5		Med. sway, tight roll	Better at 2.5 knots.	Sinking	Plastic	Metal	2
1001	Hookers Rattling S12	5.5	3	Tight sway, tight pitch		Floating	Plastic	Plastic	2
1002	Cisco Kid 1800	5.55		Wide sway, tight roll			Plastic	Metal	4
1003	Heavy Duty Stretch 12+	5.55		Tight sway	Great action and sound. Would be even better at 3 knots or above.		Plastic	Plastic	3
1004	Borer - Xtra deep	5.6		Med. wide sway	Lateral movement but stable at 2 knots.		Wood	Plastic	3
1005	Suspend DD-22	5.65	4.5–5.4	Med. sway		Suspend.	Plastic	Plastic	3

Weight g	Body Length mm	Actual Length with Bib	Depth on 6.9m at 1.5 knots	Depth on 6.9m at 2 knots	Depth on 6.9m at 2.5 knots	Manufacturer	Country of Manufacture
26.7	107.8	151		1.8		Custom Crafted Lures	Aust—NSW
10.7	73.2	110.7		1.65		Yo-Zuri Lures	Japan
24.8	78.2	129.6		1.8		McLaughlin's Lures	Taiwan
16.2	116.4	160.4		1.65		Rapala	Ireland
32.3	92.8	134.5		1.85		Custom Crafted Lures	Aust—NSW
53.2	160	203		1.75	1.8	Illusion Lures	Aust—NSW
15	102.2	138.9		1.7		Cotton Cordell	USA
14	84.2	115.9		1.7		Predatek	Aust—NSW
32.6	148.4	179.5		1.8		Halco	Aust—WA
6.8	58.1	87.2		1.85		Bennett Lures	Aust—NSW
15.5	78.3	110.5		1.85		S K Lures	Aust—Qld
8.9	51.6	97.8	1.85	1.85		AC Lures	Aust—NSW
14.4	100.1	139		1.7		Surebite Lures—SureCatch	Japan
	77.7	108.6		1.7		Fred Arbogast	USA
	142.7	187		1.7		Eddy Lures	Aust—Qld
26.1	119.7	167	1.8	1.7		Illusion Lures	Aust—NSW
28.7	141	180.8		1.7	1.7	Killalure	Aust—Qld
34.7	139.5	187.3		1.7		Surebite Lures—SureCatch	China
25.4	130.5	169		1.85		Bill's Bugs	Aust—NSW
38.8	133	175		1.7	1.7	Rapala	Ireland
22.4	118	164.5		1.85		Top Catch Lures	Taiwan
87.1	194	236		1.85		Suick Lures	USA
47.2	150.2	199.2		1.7		Mann's Lures	USA
11.3	60.9	101.7		1.9		C Lures	Aust—Qld
30.2	75.9	130.7		1.9		Norman Lures	USA

994

993

995

996

997

998

999

1001

1000

1002

1003

1004

991

990

992

989

1005

No.	Lure	Depth Test	Maker's Depth	Action	Comments	Buoyancy	Body Material	Bib Material	Bib Width mm	Tow Point	Weight g	Body Length mm
1006	Tempest TT85	5.65		Med. sway	Great action.		Plastic	Plastic	37.7	Bib	23	84
1007	Power Dive Minnow	5.65	9	Med. sway, tight roll	Strong lateral movement.		Plastic	Plastic	38.3	Bib		10
1008	Hellbender - Magnum	5.65		Med. wide sway	Excellent action. Lateral movement. One of best lures.	Floating	Plastic	Metal	34.4	Bib		88
1009	Prime DD Crankbait 25	5.7	3–4.5	Med. sway, tight roll	Excellent action—steep dive. Rattle.		Plastic	Plastic	24.2	Bib	13.3	63
1010	Blue Pilly Deep	5.7	4	Med. roll		Sinking	Plastic	Plastic	34	Bib		14
1011	Boof Bait	5.8	3.6	Med. sway			Plastic	Plastic	30.1	Bib	22.1	1
1012	DD-22	5.8	4.5–5.4	Med. sway			Plastic	Plastic	30.9	Bib	28.3	75
1013	AC Minnow 60	5.85		Med. sway	Great action.		Wood	Plastic	34.3	Bib	7.8	62
1014	Whitmore's Deep Diver	5.85		Med. sway	Much better at 1.5 knots. Great colour.	Plastic	Plastic	Bib	39.7	9.2	62.1	10
1015	Long A	5.85		Med. sway			Plastic	Plastic	23.9	Bib	12	87
1016	Lb Minnow LBM110P	5.85		Slow sway, med. roll		Suspend.	Plastic	Plastic	27.5	Bib	31.7	1
1017	Intruder Ko-Jack 150 mm	5.85		Tight sway, med. roll	Would be better at 3 knots.		Plastic	Metal	18	Nose	46.3	14
1018	Ferret 15+	5.9	4.5	Med. sway			Plastic	Plastic	28.7	Bib	11.4	8
1019	Scud - Medium	5.9	6.6	Med. sway, med. pitch	Slightly better action at 1.5 knots.	Floating	Wood	Plastic	36.7	Bib	15.6	66
1020	Boomerang 80	5.9		Med. sway	Much better at 1.5 knots.	Floating	Plastic	Plastic	35.8	Bib	20.1	82
1021	Mac Magic +20	5.9	6.1	Med. sway			Plastic	Plastic	35.2	Bib	29.8	14
1022	Suspending Fat Free Shad	5.95		Med. sway		Suspend.	Plastic	Plastic	27.9	Bib	19	65
1023	Grave Digger Deep 8	6		Wide sway			Wood	Plastic	37.3	Bib	18.9	71
1024	Stretch 20+	6	6.1	Med.sway	Better at 2 knots.		Plastic	Plastic	35.5	Bib	24.4	1
1025	Premier Pro-Model Series 6	6	4.8	Med. sway			Plastic	Plastic	30.6	Bib	27.6	78
1026	Hot'N Tot Magnum (old)	6.05		Med. sway	Great action. Some lateral movement.	Floating	Plastic	Metal	33.2	Bib	20.5	74
1027	Mad Mullet 6" Deep	6.05	5	Med. sway			Plastic	Plastic	36.5	Bib	33.2	14
1028	Lumo Diver	6.1	8.1	Med. sway		Floating	Wood	Plastic	37.1	Bib	26	77
1029	Stumpjumper 1 deep bib	6.1		Med. wide sway	Great action.	Floating	Plastic	Plastic	35.2	Nose	38.8	1
1030	Magnum Stretch 18+	6.1	5.5	Wide sway, med. roll	Better at 2.5 knots.		Plastic	Plastic	44	Bib	110	2
1031	Chaser - Deep	6.15		Med. sway			Plastic	Plastic	30.7	Bib	12.5	67
1032	Cudgeeshrimp 2	6.15	4.5	Med. wide sway	Great action.		Wood	Plastic	38.3	Bib	15.7	93
1033	Flatz Rat	6.15	4.5	Med sway		Floating		Plastic	30.1	Bib	11.8	72
1034	TD Hyper Crank Ti65	6.15		Wide sway	Great action at this speed and slower. Huge rattles.		Plastic	Metal	30	Bib	16.8	64
1035	Hornet 70	6.2		Med.sway			Plastic	Plastic	35.8	Bib	17.2	80

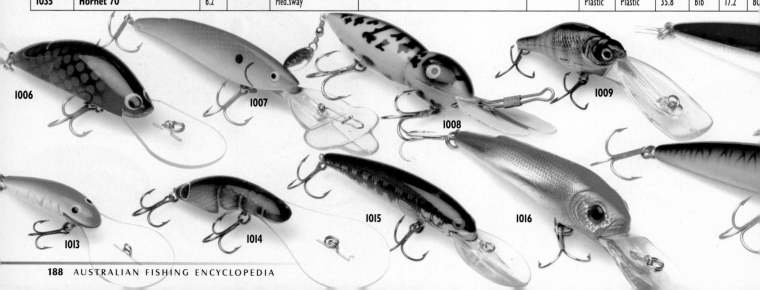

1006 1007 1008 1009
1013 1014 1015 1016

Depth on 6.9m at 1.5 knots	Depth on 6.9m at 2 knots	Depth on 6.9m at 2.5 knots	Manufacturer	Country of Manufacture
	1.9		Kingfisher Lures	Aust—NSW
	1.9		Luhr Jensen	USA
	1.9		Pradco Lures	USA
	1.75		Spro	China
	1.75		Lively Lures	Aust—Qld
	1.8		Mann's Lures	USA
	1.9		Norman Lures	USA
	1.8		AC Lures	Aust—NSW
1.7			Whitmore	Aust—NSW
	1.8		Bomber	Mexico
	1.8		Surebite Lures—SureCatch	China
	1.8		Jarvis Walker	Vietnam
	1.8		DK Lures	Aust—Qld
1.9	1.85		Custom Crafted Lures	Aust—NSW
1.9	1.85		Predatek	Aust—NSW
	1.8		Killalure	Aust—Qld
	1.85		Excalibur	USA
	1.85		Bounty Hunter Lures	Aust—NSW
1.95	1.85		Mann's Lures	USA
	1.85		Strike King Lure Company	Mexico
	1.95		Storm	USA
	1.85		Lively Lures	Aust—Qld
	1.95		Custom Crafted Lures	Aust—NSW
1.8	1.9		JJ's Lures	Aust—Vic
	1.9	1.95	Mann's Lures	USA
	1.9		Hydrobug Lures	Aust
	1.9		Cudgeefish	Aust—NSW
	1.9		Killalure	Aust—Qld
1.95	1.9		Team Diawa	Japan
	1.9		JP Lures	Aust—NSW

1012
1020
1021
1022
1023
1025
1024
1027
1026
1028
1029
1031
1030
1032
1033
1035
1034
1010
1011
1018
1019

No.	Lure	Depth Test	Maker's Depth	Action	Comments	Buoyancy	Body Material	Bib Material
1036	Fat Bob Deep	6.3	4	Med. sway	Great action. Lateral movement.		Wood	Plastic
1037	Lew's Speed Lure Crank	6.3		Med. sway, tight roll	Rattle.		Plastic	Plastic
1038	Daly Devil	6.35		Med. sway			Plastic	Plastic
1039	Rocket Diver RD120F	6.35		Med. sway		Floating	Plastic	Plastic
1040	River King	6.35		Med. sway, med. roll	Excellent action.		Plastic	Metal
1041	Suspending Fat Free Shad - Large	6.35		Med. wide sway, tight		Suspend.	Plastic	Plastic
1042	Magnum CD-26	6.4		Med. sway	Better at 2.5 knots.	Sinking	Plastic	Metal
1043	Reef Runner Deep Diver	6.45	8.4	Wide sway	Great action. Lateral movement. Better at 2 knots. One of best lures.		Plastic	Plastic
1044	Hydro Magnum 95 g	6.45		Slow med. sway	Great action at 2.5 knots.	Sinking	Plastic	Plastic
1045	Hammerhead - Large	6.5	9	Very wide	Very good action at both speeds. sway	Floating	Wood	Plastic
1046	Plow Deep 75	6.5	7.6	Med. wide	Good at both speeds. sway		Plastic	Plastic
1047	River Rat 20	6.5	6.1	Med. sway			Plastic	Plastic
1048	Scale Raza 12+	6.5	3.7	Med. sway	Great action.		Plastic	Plastic
1049	Hot Lips Express 1/2oz	6.5	4.5–5.4	Med. sway			Plastic	Plastic
1050	Hookers Deep Diver 3 m+	6.5	3	Med. sway, tight roll	Loud sound on retrieve.		Plastic	Plastic
1051	111MR Deep Diver	6.55	7.6	Med. sway, tight roll		Sinking	Plastic	Plastic
1052	Rocket Diver 180	6.65		Med. sway, med. roll	Good action. Would be better at 2.5 knots.	Floating	Plastic	Plastic

Weight g	Body Length mm	Actual Length with Bib	Depth on 6.9m at 1.5 knots	Depth on 6.9m at 2 knots	Depth on 6.9m at 2.5 knots	Manufaturer	Country of Manufacture
14.4	79.1	112.6		1.95		Cudgeefish	Aust—NSW
22.4	77.8	123.7		1.95		Bass Pro Shops	China
26.6	114.1	157.6		1.95		Reidy's	China
24.8	118.5	160.3		1.95		Surebite Lures—SureCatch	Japan
18.5	86.1	131.9		1.95		Lawson Lures	Aust—NSW
31.7	78.3	121.8		1.95		Excalibur	El Salvador
126.7	258	318.5		1.95	1.95	Rapala	Ireland
18.9	119.8	157.6		2	1.9	Reef Runner Tackle Co	USA
98	180	239.5		2.05	1.95	Yo-Zuri Lures	Japan
46.7	118.5	174.5	2	2		Custom Crafted Lures	Aust—NSW
	75	127.2	2	2		Oar-Gee Lures	Aust—NSW
20.8	102.2	145.8		2		Killalure	Aust—Qld
19.3	116.3	154.5		2		DK Lures	Aust—Qld
19.6	67.7	113.2		2		Luhr Jensen	USA
43.4	149.4	207.5		2		Top Catch Lures	Taiwan
63.8	174.9	220		2		L&S Lures Mirrolures	
68.1	179	247.5		2		Surebite Lures—SureCatch	China

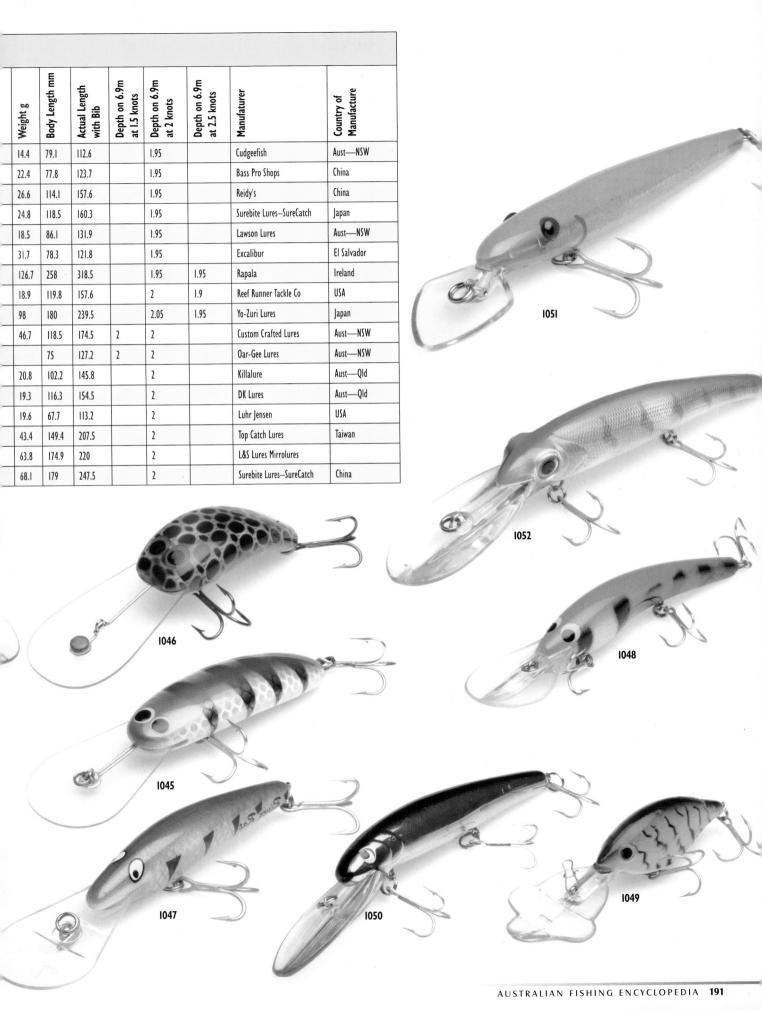

1051

1052

1048

1046

1045

1047

1050

1049

No.	Lure	Depth Test	Maker's Depth	Action	Comments	Buoyancy	Body Material	Bib Material
1053	Deep Thunder 15	6.8	6 to 10	Med. sway, med. roll			Plastic	Plastic
1054	Kadaitcha	6.85		Wide sway	Great action. True Australian legend.	Floating	Wood	Metal
1055	Long A H-Duty	6.9		Wide sway	Great action.		Plastic	Plastic
1056	Magnum CD-18	6.95		Med. sway, med. roll	Better at 2.5 knots.	Sinking	Wood	Metal
1057	Hookers Deep Diver 3 m+ L19	7		Med. wide sway	Loud rattle.		Plastic	Plastic
1058	RMG Scorpion 150 XDD	7.05	8	Wide sway, tight roll	Great action. Better at 2.5 knots.	Sinking	Plastic	Plastic
1059	Deep Thunder 15	7.15		Med. sway, tight roll			Plastic	Plastic
1060	Boomerang Ultra-Deep 80	7.2	8	Med. sway	Better slow. Very deep Australian classic.	Floating	Plastic	Plastic
1061	Heavy Duty Stretch 25+	7.3	7.6	Med. sway			Plastic	Plastic
1062	Magnum CD-22	7.4		Med. sway, tight roll	Better at 2.5 knots.	Sinking	Plastic	Metal
1063	Hot Lips Express 3/4oz	7.6	5.4–7.2	Wide sway	Great action at both speeds. Still wants to go deeper.		Plastic	Plastic
1064	Magnum Stretch 30+	7.9	9.15	Med. sway			Plastic	Plastic
1065	Gigantus 50+	8.4	15.25	Wide sway, wide roll		Sinking	Plastic	Plastic

1053

1054

1055

1056

1057

1062

Weight g	Body Length mm	Actual Length with Bib	Depth on 6.9m at 1.5 knots	Depth on 6.9m at 2 knots	Depth on 6.9m at 2.5 knots	Manufacturer	Country of Manufacture
	152	213.5		2.05		Storm	Estonia
45.6	120	163.8	1.95	2.05		Peter Newell Lures	Aust—NSW
41	152.7	212		1.95	2.05	Bomber	Mexico
74.9	178.5	234		2.05	2.05	Rapala	Ireland
66.7	178.5	249		2.05		Top Catch Lures	Aust
33	149	183		2	2.05	Halco	Aust—WA
58	151.1	213		2.1		Storm	Estonia
	82.1	136.5	2.1	2		Predatek	Aust—NSW
50.9	148.9	203.1		2.1		Mann's Lures	USA
89.5	217.5	274.5		2.1	2.15	Rapala	Ireland
26.9	82.4	135.5	2.1	2.15		Luhr Jensen	USA
	204	279.5		2.25		Mann's Lures	USA
391.2	294	402		2.25		Mann's Lures	USA

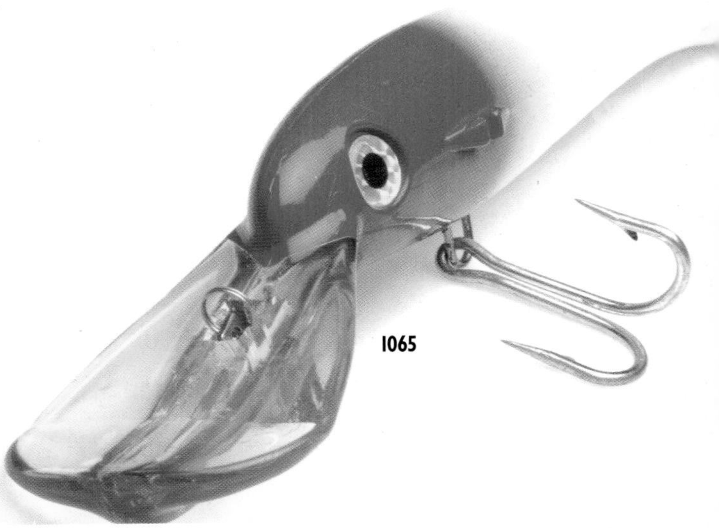

1065

1060

1061

1058

1059

1063

1064

CHAPTER FIVE

BEST LURES FOR OUR
POPULAR FISH
CATCHING AUSTRALIAN SPECIES

With hundreds of thousands, perhaps millions, of Australians fishing at least once a year the number of species of fish that are caught annually in Australia's productive waters is very large, however the list of species that is actively sought by anglers is considerably more manageable. The most frequently targeted species are presented in this chapter along with identifying marks, feeding notes, distribution, and the gear, methods, techniques and rigs that are most frequently used and are most effective to catch them. This comprehensive species summary is designed to quickly ensure that any angler is successful, whatever method they choose to use.

BAIT

Baitfishing is the technique that is practised by the vast majority of Australian anglers because it requires very little expertise or experience, and the gear required to get started is relatively inexpensive. Techniques have been developed and, with improvements in tackle, have been refined over the years—these methods are all proven fish catchers.

For each of the commonly targeted species we detail where to find them, the gear required and the techniques, rigs and baits that work, taking into account the feeding locations, times and conditions that the species prefers. The rigging diagrams are easy to understand and duplicate, even for the beginner.

LURES

There are so many choices with lures and all of them work for some people and on some species. The market place is simply too tough for lures that don't or won't work to last long. Anglers talk about what works and quickly fill their tackle boxes with the latest gun lure.

However, there are a few tried and true performers for the major lure munching species. It is also a minefield, for instance, for someone planning their first trip for barramundi to work out what to buy to make a trip truly memorable. To help the beginner, and even the experienced angler, for each species that are ready lure eaters in Australia I have prepared a ready reckoner that includes what and how they eat and a few

Redfin are a frequent target with lures as this fine specimen taken by Frank Prokop shows.

tips for catching them on lures. I have also gone out on a limb and nominated 'the' definitive lure for each species (or group of species) and the ten lures that I would carry to catch them. This is sure to evoke comment and even criticism from specialists for each species. The lures that you and your mates use to catch fish will continue to catch fish and should be used by those who feel confident with them. Within this section what I have tried to do is provide a different perspective on lure fishing for Australian fish and the lures that provide a good option.

The lures that are included, especially as the definitive lures, were the ones that were sent for testing and which are included and reviewed in this book. Other lures, such as large metal slices for fishing in 50–80 metres of water for kingfish or Samson fish are not included in the definitive lure list but are included in the applicable rigs. Similarly, there is a wide range of poppers available, many of them made locally in small quantities that would work well.

Archer fish

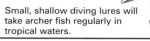

Where: Tropical freshwater rivers and estuaries.
When: All year.
Gear: Light spinning tackle, small lures, fish bait, prawns, flies.
Technique: Cast toward banks and structure.

Small, shallow diving lures will take archer fish regularly in tropical waters.

Bass, Australian

Where: East Coast freshwater streams and dams, from Tin Can Bay, Queensland, to Lakes Entrance, Victoria.
When: Year round, peaks in summer.
Gear: Spin, baitcast and fly tackle, surface and diving lures, soft plastics, live shrimp baits.
Technique: Cast to snags, troll along riverbanks and dam shorelines, deep jig over structure.
Feeding notes: The Australian bass is a classic cover oriented ambush feeder and it will stay very close to bankside snags or rock bars and will frequently move only very short distances to take a lure. The Australian bass and the closely related estuary perch are more active from dusk until just after dawn. Both species will move down the estuaries in winter to spawn and may form large aggregations in the middle reaches of estuaries at this time.
Diet: The Australian bass and estuary perch will consume a wide variety of foods including fish, shrimps, prawns, insects, mice, lizards and worms.
Fishing notes: The Australian bass takes a wide variety of lures ranging from crashing surface lures to deeper diving lures. Australian bass can be extremely aggressive and will hit lures very hard and then try to bury an unsuspecting angler in the nearby snag.
Lure fishing: One of the most important factors in bass fishing is to be able to consistently place the lure within 30 centimetres of the bank or snag. For this reason, baitcasting tackle is preferred. Letting the lure sit on the surface for a few seconds before starting the retrieve can bring greatly improved results. With the exception of surface lures, a lure that dives reasonably quickly will bring more strikes.
Action type: Action types vary from surface lures to diving lures. The paddlers and fizzers seem to be the most popular for surface lures, with medium wobble and sway most prevalent in the popular bass lures. Suspending lures are increasing in popularity due to their capacity to be worked slowly in the strike zone near snags, while spinnerbaits are being used to work close to bankside cover with plenty of flash.
Profile type: The most common profile is a medium profile, which imitates prey fish, shrimps and insects such as cicadas.
Lure sizes: Most common lure size would be 4–7 centimetres, although on occasion bass can be taken on very large lures. Very small bass are often taken on lures that are nearly the same size as the fish.
The top ten lures: Arbogast Jitterbug, Mann's 5+, Rapala Fat Rap FR5, Storm Wiggle Wart, Yo-Zuri Slavko Bug, Heddon Tiny Torpedo, Deception Nipper, Tilsan Bass, 7 gram spinnerbaits, Rebel Crawdad.

THE DEFINITIVE LURE

NO. 50 ARBOGAST JITTERBUG

Live shrimp rig. Hook the shrimp lightly through the tail to keep it active. Fish unweighted or with a small running sinker.

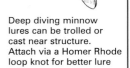

Deep diving minnow lures can be trolled or cast near structure. Attach via a Homer Rhode loop knot for better lure action.

Black drummer

Where: East Coast ocean rocks.
When: Year round, peaks autumn - winter, best on tide changes.
Gear: Strong rods, sidecast or spin tackle, 1/0 to 2/0 hooks, bread, cunjevoi, abalone and cabbage baits.
Technique: Float fish or use lightly weighted bottom baits. Cast into white water and hang on!

Running sinker rig. Use minimal weight with the sinker running right to the hook for the best presentation.

Crabs should be hooked through the carapace with the hook point well exposed for better hook ups.

Soft baits such as cunjevoi and abalone gut are bound to the hook with elastic.

Barracouta

NO. 178: HALCO STREAKER 20 GRAM.

Where: Warm temperate to tropical waters from Sydney across the Top End to at least Carnarvon.

When: All year.

Gear: Medium spinning and baitcasting tackle, small to large lures, fish bait.

Technique: Troll, cast or fish baits around prominent drop offs and areas of current flow.

Feeding notes: The barracouta is highly prized as a food and sportfish from the waters of Tasmania and Victoria. The 'couta is poorly regarded as a 'pick-handle' in warmer NSW waters because its presence heralds cold water that shuts down many species and the flesh is often worm riddled. The barracouta is a pelagic species that cruises looking for food. It has sharp teeth that can tear wooden lures to shreds in quick time.

Diet: Barracouta feed mainly on fish but they will also take squid and cuttlefish.

Fishing notes: Large barracouta are very highly regarded for their fight and for food, especially in Tasmania. They will take live and dead baits or hit lures.

Lure fishing: Barracouta are taken by trolling chrome, Christmas tree or minnow lures along the cold water edge of currents, around feeding fish indicated by birds or around deeper water at the back of a bombora.

Action type: Chrome lures with a narrow wobble that gives off plenty of flash catch the most fish.

Profile type: A narrow or medium profile best imitates the baitfish that these species feed upon.

Lure sizes: Lures of 4–8 centimetres work best.

The top ten lures: Halco Streaker 20 grams, Fishfighter Toby 10 grams, Halco Wobbler 10 grams, Halco Twisty 20 grams, Wonder Spoon 14 grams, Wonder Tubular 28 grams, Halco Hexagon Sparkler 10 grams, Rapala Countdown CD9, RMG Scorpion 68 STD, Bomber Long A Minnow, Pegron Minnow.

Trolling rig. Secure about a metre of single strand wire trace with haywire twists to a gang of 3x 4/0 4202 Mustad hooks at one end and a plain black swivel at the other.

In this rig a bobby cork is added, with a ball sinker for casting weight.

Barracouta will also take lead slug type lures. Note the need for wire trace.

Barramundi

NO. 527: NILSMASTER SPEARHEAD

Where: Tropical freshwater rivers and estuaries, inshore reefs, tropical freshwater dams.

When: Year round, peaks around change over between wet and dry seasons.

Gear: Spin and baitcast tackle, minnows, poppers, spinnerbaits, soft plastics, flies, prawn and fish baits.

Technique: Cast to pocket water and snags, trolling, live baiting.interest.

Feeding notes: Barramundi are generally an ambush feeder, but can be an opportunistic feeder depending upon the state of the tide, the season or the time of day, with fish cruising more widely during the night.

Diet: Barramundi will take a wide range of foods including small fish, cherabin, shrimps, crabs, frogs, snakes, worms, birds and small mammals.

Fishing notes: Barramundi are regarded by many as the archetypal tropical species, ranging from freshwater billabongs to tidal rivers or even open ocean waters or beaches. The barramundi's high flying, gill flaring jumps, large size and the exotic locations make this species a fantasy target for many anglers.

Lure fishing: Barramundi will take an enormous range of lures and flies—adding to the challenge of selecting the lures which work the best for any given season, day or even time of the tide.Barramundi will take surface lures, shallow running lures, rattlin' spot type lures, spinnerbaits, spoons and deep divers. Within each of these categories there are a range of styles, sizes and action types that will take barra.

Action type: Barramundi prefer a narrow wobble and a narrow sway. Spinnerbaits and surface lures, especially fizzers and paddlers, take many fish. The shimmy of rattlin' spot lures also takes barramundi.

The top ten lures: Nilsmaster Spearhead, DK Scale Raza 20+, Mann's Boof Bait, Tilsan Barra, Nilsmaster Invincible series, Cotton Cordell Rattlin' Spot, Rapala Shad Rap, Classic Barra, RMG Scorpion 125, Lively Lures Arafura Barra.

Minnow lure, attached to heavy monofilament leader with Homer Rhode loop knot to allow better action.

Bait fishing rig, utilising a heavy ball sinker and swivel above the trace and a large (5/0 to 7/0) hook.

Live banana prawn rig. Note that the prawn is hooked lightly through the tail to keep it active.

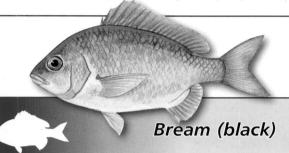

Bonefish

Where: Mostly remote tropical inshore sandflats and cays, rarely enters some southern estuaries.
When: Spring through summer
Gear: Light to medium spinning rods and reels, saltwater fly tackle (8-weight to 10-weight)
Technique: Usually sight fished with polarising sunglasses, by casting small light jigs or weighted flies.

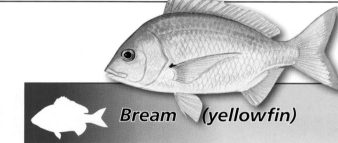

Bream (black)

Where: Estuaries, rocks, breakwalls, surf beaches and inshore reefs, Sydney south to Victoria, Tasmania, South Australia, Western Australia up to Shark Bay.
When: Year round, peaks in summer and autumn
Gear: Light spin rods and reels, live nippers, bloodworms, crabs, prawns, fish baits, small lures and flies.
Technique: In estuaries, cast toward holding areas such as sandy river margins, snags, oyster leases, rock bars and weed beds. From the rocks and around islands, work the washes and on beaches cast into clear water alongside foam patches.corks.baits down to them.

Bream (yellowfin)

Where: Estuaries, rocks, breakwalls, surf beaches and inshore reefs, Lakes Entrance Victoria, north to Townsville, Queensland.
When: Year round, peaks (Queensland) in winter and spring, (NSW and Victoria) spring to autumn
Gear: Light spin rods and reels, live nippers, bloodworms, crabs, prawns, fish baits, small lures and flies.
Technique: In estuaries, cast toward holding areas such as sandy river margins, snags, oyster leases, rock bars and weed beds. From the rocks and around islands, work the washes. On beaches cast into clear water alongside foam patches.

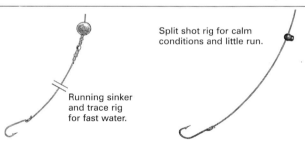

Split shot rig for calm conditions and little run.

Running sinker and trace rig for fast water.

Live crab rig, note one leg has been removed to provide entry point for hook.

Running sinker to hook rig for rough water.

Feeding notes: Fishing for black bream and the yellowfin bream has seen the greatest recent expansion in lure fishing in Australia. The black bream is found from Shark Bay in WA to Mallacoota in Victoria as well as Tasmania, and the yellowfin bream is found from Lakes Entrance to Townsville on the E. Coast.Bream can be opportunistic or ambush feeders depending upon the season, location in the river or even time of the tide. Bream can associate with cover such as bridges, drop-offs or oyster leases or can cruise the tidal flats looking for food. Diet: Bream will consume everything from oysters to small fish. They will eat shrimps and prawns, cockles, mussels and pipis, nippers, worms, small fish and other food that they happen across.

NO.353: OAR-GEE LILRIPPER

Fishing notes: For all their wide diet, they can be quite selective when it comes to lures and a good cast and careful presentation is important. A relatively tentative strike can be made up for with a surging run to get back to oyster encrusted cover and to bust off an unwary angler. On other occasions, bream will savagely strike a lure, almost ripping the rod from the hand of the angler. Even small bream give an excellent account of themselves on lures and at certain times of the year, especially autumn, schools of spawning bream can provide excellent sport.

Lure fishing: Lure fishing for bream is almost equally divided into fishing with soft plastic jigs and the hard bodied lures covered by this book. Hard bodied lures work better around woody snags , rock ledges or where bream eat more minnows. A good cast close to cover or a drop-off is necessary. Suspending lures are a distinct advantage to work the strike zone and entice strikes from wary bream. A pause and rip retrieve can be more successful than a straight retrieve and it pays to explore and try different lures, colours, sizes or different areas as things can change quite quickly when bream fishing.

Action type: A medium wobble and tight or medium sway works best but experimentation can pay off.
Profile type: A narrow or medium profile is recommended.
Lure sizes: Lures of 2.5–6.5 centimetres work well.
The top ten lures: Oar-Gee Lil Ripper, Halco Laser Pro 45, Deception Palaemon, Taylor Made Nippy Nymph, Attack Lure, RMG Sneaky Bream Suspending, Mirashad Fry, RMG Scorpion 52, Yo-Zuri Slavko Bug, Custom Crafted Shallow Extractor.

Fork-tail catfish

Where: Estuaries and freshwater rivers and billabongs of tropical Australia.
When: Year round.
Gear: Casting tackle, small lures, baits of any fish flesh or shrimp.
Technique: Trolling, bottom fishing, casting to structure and lily pads.

Running sinker rig for catfish. Use dead or live bait.

Calamari

Where: Around Australia (various species) ocean rocks, inshore re[...]
large estuarine bays near weed.
When: Northern areas autumn to spring, southern areas spring to
summer, best on rising to full tide.
Gear: Squid jigs, handlines or spin rods and reels.
Technique: Cast jigs and allow to sink nearly to the bottom, then
draw them back with slow lifts

Cobia

Where: Inshore reefs Cape Naturaliste Western Australia to Northern Territory, Queensland,
NSW as far south as Jervis Bay.
When: Year round, peaks in southern waters from late summer to autumn.
Gear: Strong overhead, spin or saltwater fly gear, minnows, poppers, streamer flies, live baits.
Technique: Jigging, trolling, spinning, drifting with baits out. Cast near manta rays or
navigation buoys.

Surface lures cast near manta rays work well.

Lures for trolling or casting for cobia need to be robust.

Live fish fished unweighted while on the drift.

Cod

Feeding notes: This wide range of marine cod species includes the estuary cod, black cod, greasy cod and
Queensland groper. These are generally ambush feeders, closely associated with reefs or snags. They are some of the
largest fish in the ocean and are capable of taking other fish, which have been hooked and are played to the boat.
Diet: The cods generally prefer fish but will also eat squid, cuttlefish, octopus, lobsters and sea urchins.
Fishing notes: The cods are extremely strong, large fish which will try to bury an unwary angler in their pet snag
or reef outcrop. Frequently, when the largest cod is removed from an area, the next largest fish moves into the
prime ambush or feeding position.
Lure fishing: All of the cods have extremely large mouths and can take virtually any lure or indeed the largest specimens can take a
hooked fish of up to 10 kilograms. The cod stay close to their preferred lie, or in the case of estuary cod, their favourite deep hole. Lures
need to be close enough to evoke a strike, but far enough away to avoid snagging and give some hope of stopping the fish running back
into cover. Consequently, heavier lines and a well tuned drag as well as extra strong hooks are important.Some cods can be cast to in
the channels between reefs or around favoured snags. Small estuary cod or juvenile Queensland groper are often taken from rivers and
estuaries when fishing for barramundi.
Action type: Medium and wide sway and wobble will work, but large spoons and casting lures fished near cover will also take cod.
Profile type: Medium and robust profiles will take these fish.
Lure sizes: Small lures can tempt very large fish, but changing to extra strong hooks can affect the action of smaller lures. Most cod
lures are of 9–25 centimetres.
The top ten lures: Rapala Magnum CD14, Halco Laser Pro 160 DD, Storm Deep Thunderstick, DK Scale Raza 20+, Mann's Stretch
20+, Mann's Stretch 18+, Rapala Magnum CD22, Reef Runner Deep Diver, RMG Scorpion 150XDD (Crazy Deep), Yo-Zuri Hydro
Magnum.

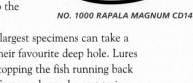

THE DEFINITIVE LURE

NO. 1000 RAPALA MAGNUM CD14

Cod, Estuary

Where: Tropical Australia as far south as Rottnest Island in Western Australia and Port Stephens in NSW.

When: Year round peaks in southern waters in summer

Gear: Casting tackle, minnow lures, poppers, soft plastics, saltwater flies.

Technique: Cast towards structure, work tidal change periods and mangrove banks.

Live prawns rigged so they stay alive are excellent bait for estuary cod.

Minnow lures rigged with a heavy leader can be cast into mangrove stands for estuary cod.

Cod, Murray

THE DEFINITIVE LURE

NO. 1054: NEWELL KADAITCHA

Where: Throughout several rivers in the greater Murray-Darling drainage basin, from central Queensland, through NSW and Victoria to South Australia. Murray cod have also been stocked into several large freshwater impoundments in NSW and Victoria. Three related species, the trout cod, Mary River cod and Eastern cod are endangered species and must be returned to the water if caught.

When: Year round with definite peaks at the onset of the first frosts of winter and again in high summer. Closed seasons apply to the taking of Murray cod, so consult local Fisheries regulations.

Gear: Medium spin and baitcast gear, large bibbed lures, spinnerbaits and big bushy flies. Baits include bardi grubs, crayfish and scrub worms.

Technique: Trolling and casting with lures around snag piles, sunken trees and drowned creek beds in reservoirs. Rocky cliffs and midstream boulders also provide cover for these fish as do dense rush and weed stands. All of these places should be tried and persistence will pay off as Murray cod may take some agitation before striking.

Feeding notes: The Murray cod is a classic ambush feeder, holding close to cover and attacking food that comes near. Murray cod are opportunistic feeders and will take very large food items into their large mouths. At night Murray cod will move around and may be taken in shallow waters.

Diet: Murray cod will take just about anything that they can fit into their mouths. Their feeding preference is for fish and crustaceans, with bony bream, carp, redfin and small native fish being popular and yabbies and Murray crayfish also being sought after food. Murray cod will also readily take bardi grubs, shrimp and worms. Some of the more unusual items that Murray cod will take include ducklings and other hatchlings, moorhens, snakes, lizards, frogs and old timers tell of using a scorched starling as a bait to take large Murray cod.

Fishing notes: Murray cod will take a wide variety of lures and lure types, with the key factors being to persevere and work likely looking snags or holes as a cod can often be enticed to strike and to use a large lure wherever possible.

Lure fishing: Deep diving lures either cast or trolled to snags or drop-offs where a cod can move the least distance for the most food are the best. Cod are territorial and the best snag will usually hold the best fish. If the largest fish is taken from the snag the second largest fish will often move in. This means that conservation by skilled anglers is extremely important. You must work the strike zone carefully and slowly as Murray cod will often follow a lure and will frequently just give a tiny bump. If a bump is felt, a pause in the retrieve will often result in a more solid strike. Spinnerbaits as well as the old favourite aeroplane spinner also work very well.

Action type: A wide sway is the classic Murray cod lure, but other lures with a more modest action can also work well. Larger spinnerbaits and surface lures have their place. After the war, aeroplane spinners were considered so deadly that there were moves to have them banned.

Profile type: Most cod lures have a medium profile, although a robust profile is also successful.

Lure sizes: It is unlikely that a commercially produced lure could be too big for a Murray cod of over 20 kilograms. Even modest cod to 5 kilograms will take lures in the 20 centimetre range. In contrast, really big cod will occasionally monster a smaller lure, but their bony and strong jaws can mangle lower grade or smaller hooks leaving a shaking angler with an unusual souvenir.

The top ten lures: Newell Kadaitcha, Magnum Hellbender, Custom Crafted Hammerhead, Mann's 30+, T50 Flatfish, Predatek 80 mm Boomerang Deep, 42 gram spinnerbait, StumpJumper 1 Deep, Oar-Gee Plow Deep 75, RMG Poltergeist.

Bardi grub bait attached to hook with Bait Mate.

Running sinker rig for bobbing or drifting in open water.

Deep running bibbed minnow rig – large bib of lure makes it dive deep.

Fixed sinker rig.

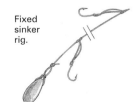

Crabs, Mud

Where: Mud-bottomed estuaries and mangrove forests, from Exmouth Western Australia, throughout the tropics and down as far as Bega in southern NSW.

When: In NSW and southern Queensland, late spring to summer. In Northern Wesern Australia and the Northern Territory, they are available all year, but are mostly gathered during the dry season when access to backwaters and secluded creeks is easier.

Gear: Dilly traps, wire mesh cages and witch's hats, baited with fish flesh, or a stout wire crook that is inserted into burrows and hooked over a leg or claw to draw the crab out. In some extremely remote areas, they are so plentiful they can be scoop-netted by hand in shallow open water.

Technique: Set pots and traps in bankside channels or drainage gutters on a rising tide. Wire hooking can only be done at

Dart, Swallowtail

Feeding notes: The dart is found in temperate and tropical waters foraging in shallow waters on tidal flats or in the surf zone. They are active cruisers and can form schools at times.

Diet: The dart feeds heavily on pipis, oysters, nippers, prawns, worms and shrimps. They will also take octopus, fish and crabs.

NO. 123: GILLIES SH WOBBLER 7 GRAM

Fishing notes: Many anglers do not target dart with lures, but they can be enthusiastic lure takers and provide excellent sport, especially on light line. Fishing the surf zone or drop-offs on a dropping tide can produce a mixed bag of flathead, trevally, bream and dart and make a memorable fishing experience.

Lure fishing: Jigs and small chrome lures work best for dart.

Action type: Lures with plenty of flash and a wide action are favoured. They can also be cast further and cover more ground until individuals or a school of dart are located. Tasmanian Devil type lures are successful and often overlooked for this type of flats fishing.

Profile type: Narrow or medium profile lures work best, but the wobbler type chrome lures also work well.

Lure sizes: Dart have a relatively small mouth, so lures of 3-6 centimetres are more likely to take these fish.

The top ten lures: Gillies SH Wobbler 7 g, Halco Twisty 5 gram, Gillies Krocodile, Tasmanian Devil 13.5 gram, Rio's Prawn, Pegron Tiger Minnow, Halco Hexagon Sparkler 10 gram, Horsey's Jig Spinner, Wonder spoon 10 gram, AC Minnow 45.

Dart, Spotted

Where: Tropical fish that ranges southward on both east and west coasts into temperate areas. It is also known as the black-spotted dart. It is similar to and related to the swallowtail dart and common dart. All three fish forage in the surf zone of ocean beaches, around islands and sometimes over reef. Will enter large estuaries and bays in dense shoals to feed savagely on small bait fish schools.

When: Year round, best in spring through summer.

Gear: Light threadline and sidecast gear on rods suitable for terrain. Baits of pipi, beach worm, fish strip, peeled prawn and nippers. Will take small chrome lures, rubber tail jigs and surf candy flies.

Technique: Cast baits into shallows of surf zone, keep bait moving and strike against sudden rattling bite. Cast lures and flies into deep holes where current scours through estuaries.

Light Paternoster rig for targeting dart in the surf.

Emperor, Long-nosed

Where: Tropical coral reef areas.

When: Year round.

Gear: Heavy handlines, baited with squid or fish strips, robust rod and reel tackle with lead head jigs.

Technique: Jigs can be fished without bait or tipped with a strip of fish or squid, then dropped down and bounced just off the bottom until a fish takes.

Running sinker rig with heavy monofilament leader.

Fixed sinker Paternoster rig for reef fishing.

Emperor, Spangled

Feeding notes: The spangled emperor is an opportunistic feeder that can also be found in schools. The spangled emperor is highly prized throughout northern waters. There are many closely related Lethrinus species known as north-west snappers or by names such as red-throat, black snapper or tricky snapper. Spangled emperor form quite large schools of similar sized fish, with larger fish forming smaller schools and taking the best positions relative to cover such as reefs.

Diet: Spangled emperor take a wide range of foods, including fish, squid, cuttlefish, crabs, prawns, shellfish, worms and sea urchins.

Fishing notes: Spangled emperor are most often taken with bait fishing methods. The use of Japanese style rigs with Flashabou is increasing. Spangled emperor prefer reefs or cover near reefs. The closely related black snapper can be found on weed areas near reefs.

Lure fishing: In shallow water, or when actively feeding, spangled emperor can be reasonably enthusiastic lure takers. While most spangled emperor are taken on white bucktail or soft plastic tipped jigs, tipping the jigs or even lures with bait, such as a squid tentacle, helps greatly. As with the southern snapper, the spangled emperor can be taken with vertical jigs. At the backs of breaking reefs in areas such as those frequented by coral trout and the various cod species, spangled emperor will take lures trolled or cast for these species. Using a slightly smaller lure will increase the strike rate with the spangled emperor.

Action type: A narrow or medium wobble and tight sway works well.

Profile type: Narrow or medium profiles are recommended.

Lure sizes: The best sizes are 4–10 centimetres, although larger lures take fish as well.

The top ten lures: Rapala Magnum CD9, Lively Lures Mad Mullet 4" Deep, Kokoda Vector 30 gram, Rio's Live Chrome 20 gram, Intruder Ko-Jack, RMG Scorpion 68DD, Mann's Stretch 10+, River 2 Sea Diver Vib65, Reidy's Little Lucifer, Tilsan Barra.

NO. 937 RAPALA MAGNUM CD9

Fingermark

Feeding notes: Fingermark are a classic ambush feeder, hanging near cover and rushing out to smack a lure and then diving back into their home cover.

Diet: Fingermark feed mainly on fish but also eat squid, octopus and crabs.

Fishing notes: Fingermark are aggressive feeders and highly prized by anglers in North Queensland and the Northern Territory.

Lure fishing: Fingermark are most frequently taken by trolling or casting diving lures to rock bars or rocky reef edges near the mouths of estuaries.

Action type: A medium or tight wobble and medium sway works best.

Profile type: A medium profile is most popular.

Lure sizes: Lures of 6–12 centimetres.

The top ten lures: Predatek Boomerang 65 Deep, Rapala Countdown CD9, Halco Laser Pro 100 DD, Storm Deep Thunderstick, DK Scale Raza 20+, Mann's Boof Bait 12+, Custom Crafted Lumo Diver, Predatek Jindivik, Nilsmaster Jumbo DD, C Lures Jack Snack Deep.

NO. 931: PREDATEK BOOMERANG 65 DEEP

Flounder

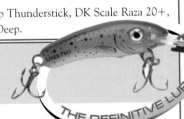

Feeding notes: Flounder are ambush feeders, waiting partially buried in sandy or light gravel bottom before exploding out to eat a hapless fish, prawn or lure. Flounder are considered exceptional eating.

Diet: Flounders eat small fish, prawns, shrimps, crabs, nippers, or worms.

Fishing notes: Flounder are often found in similar areas to flathead. A dropping tide concentrates food at the edge of drop-offs or channels. Flounders will also wait on the edges of drop-offs or on sand near rocky reef. While there are a number of locations that fish well on the rising tide, such as near the base of rock walls, most flounder fishing in the estuaries is better on a dropping tide. Flounder can be finicky lure takers and often follow a lure or jig to your feet.

Lure fishing: Flounder can be taken from a boat by trolling drop-offs, although they prefer a smaller lure and a slightly slower trolling speed than commonly used for flathead. Many flounder are also taken casting to the shallows or by wading the shallows and casting to drop-offs. Smaller, quick diving lures that just bump the bottom and kick up a small puff of sand are particularly effective

Action type: Lures with a medium sway and medium wobble are often the most successful.

Profile type: Medium profile lures are frequently used.

Lure sizes: Lures of 3–7 centimetres work best.

The top ten lures: Halco Laser Pro 45, Mann's Stretch 5+, RMG Scorpion 52, Rapala Jointed Shad Rap 4, Yo-Zuri Aile Killifish, Rebel Crawdad, Oar-Gee Lil Ripper, Taylor Made Nippy Nymph, Predatek MinMin Deep, Mac's Micro Mauler.

NO. 391: HALCO LASER PRO 45.

Flathead (dusky)

Where: Estuaries, inshore reef areas, Mackay, Queensland, throughout NSW to Wilson's Promontory, Victoria.
When: Year round, best from spring through summer
Gear: Casting tackle, handlines, saltwater fly gear, minnow lures, soft plastics saltwater flies, fish strips, live nippers, live poddy mullet.
Technique: Troll and cast around channels and weedy sand flats, bottom fish near inshore reef.

Flathead (sand)

Where: Inshore sandy areas, some bay entrances, Moreton Bay, Queensland, all of NSW, to Lakes Entrance, Victoria.
When: Spring through summer.
Gear: Handlines, rods and reels, heavy sinkers and Paternoster rigs with cut fish baits.
Technique: Drift fish over mixed sand and inshore reef in 20-30 metres.

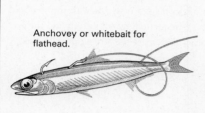

Anchovey or whitebait for flathead.

Lures for flathead, Mr Twister and Wonder Wobbler or similar.

Paternoster 'outside' drifting rig flathead. Additional droppers can be incorporated.

Estuary bait drifting rig for flathead.

Live mullet drift rig for flathead. Alternatively, bait can be lip hooked for drifting in fast current.

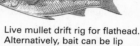

THE DEFINITIVE LURE

NO. 634 MANN'S STRETCH 5+

Feeding notes: The dusky and bar-tail flathead are the two most important lure taking species, although the southern blue spot is also popular. Sand flathead are frequently taken, but it is a small species. The majestic dusky flathead is found from Mackay in Queensland to Wilson's Promontory and eastern Bass Strait, and can grow to 10 kilograms. The smaller bar-tail flathead is found from Fremantle in Western Australia all around the top end and as far as Port Hacking in NSW, and is seldom seen bigger than 60 centimetres. All flathead are classic ambush feeders, waiting partially buried in a sand or light gravel bottom before exploding out to eat a hapless fish, prawn or lure. The largest flathead are female. Flathead have surprisingly sharp teeth and can cut through line if they swallow a lure. Their gill covers have extremely sharp spines, which can make releasing the 5 or 6 hooks on a large lure quite a challenge. Turning the fish onto its back helps and a pair of pliers and a filleting glove can be very useful in unhooking flathead.

Diet: Flathead eat small fish, prawns, crabs, nippers, or worms.

Fishing notes: A dropping tide concentrates food at the edge of drop-offs or channels. Flathead will sit on the edges of drop-offs, on sand near rocky reef or along weed lines waiting for hapless prey to wander close enough to be engulfed. While there are a number of locations that fish well on the rising tide, most flathead fishing in the estuaries is better on a dropping tide. Flathead, with mulloway, are the most highly prized lure targets in estuaries. Flathead will often hit a lure hard and have a dogged fight. On other occasions, they will lazily follow a lure right to your feet before either shooting off to the depths or settling into the sand right next to you.

Lure fishing: Flathead can be taken from a boat by trolling drop-offs and casting to the shallows or by wading the shallows and casting to drop-offs. As flathead lie on the bottom, lures that just bump the bottom and kick up a small puff of sand are particularly effective.

Action type: Lures with a medium sway and medium wobble are often the most successful.

Profile type: Medium profile lures are frequently used.

Lure sizes: Lures of 4–10 centimetres can take flathead.

The top ten lures: Mann's Stretch 5+, RMG Scorpion 68, Rapala Jointed Shad Rap, Fat Rap 7, Kokoda Dinkum Yabby, Rebel Crawdad, Majik lures Mulgar, Team Daiwa Hyper Minnow, Storm Deep Thunder Stick, Luhr Jensen Power Minnow.

Gemfish

Where: Deep ocean waters beyond the Continental Shelf south from Sydney to the western edge of the Great Australian Bight.
When: All year.
Gear: Heavy handlines, deck winches, deep water rigs, flesh baits, heavy sinkers.
Technique: Find concentrations of fish over deep sea mounts and fish baits down to them. Fish small dams with handlines and meat.

Paternoster rig for deep or rough water.

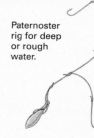

Garfish

Where: Estuaries, freshwater lakes, oceans around the entire coast.
When: All year.
Gear: Light threadline outfit, berley, dough bait, maggots, flesh baits.
Technique: Berley to attract garfish and fish lightly weighted or unweighted bait freely or under floats in berley stream on small hooks.

Berley float and waggler combination for garfish.

Quill float rig for garfish. Note two hooks and split shot used to ballast float.

Grenadier, Blue

Where: Deep ocean waters beyond the Continental Shelf south from Sydney around the bottom of Australia to Perth.
When: All year.
Gear: Heavy handlines, deck winches, deep water rigs, flesh baits, heavy sinkers.
Technique: Find concentrations of fish over deep sea mounts and fish baits down to them.

Paternoster rig for deep or rough water.

Groper

Where: Tropical and semi-tropical waters of Australia.
When: All year.
Gear: Heavy handline or stout threadline and baitcasting outfits, flesh baits, live baits.
Technique: Cast offerings towards reef edges, holes and gutters. Groper are big, strong fish that demand heavy-handed tactics.

Soft bait rig for groper, using baits like abalone gut and cray tail. Bait is bound to hook with hosiery elastic (Bait Mate).

Bobby cork rig for rough water fishing with crab baits.

Unweighted rig for calm conditions and clear water.

Hapuku

Where: Deep ocean waters beyond the Continental Shelf south from Sydney around the bottom of Australia to Perth.
When: All year.
Gear: Heavy handlines, deck winches, deep water rigs, flesh baits, large, heavy sinkers.
Technique: Find concentrations of fish over sea mounts and fish baits down to them.

Paternoster rig for deep or rough water.

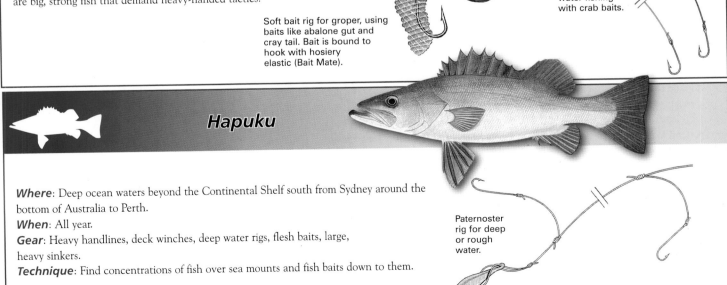

Herring, Australian

Feeding notes: The Australian herring is a common schooling inshore or embayment species from southern waters that feeds opportunistically. Herring can be found in the surf, off breakwalls or around shallow reefs or weedbeds.

Diet: Herring feed on small fish, the leftovers of tailor and other larger species, prawns, shrimps, mussels, cockles, pipis, sea urchins and other available food. They will also feed heavily on maggots, which flourish in winter washed weed on shorelines and may be washed back into the water.

THE DEFINITIVE LURE

NO. 113: HALCO TWISTY 5 GRAM

Fishing notes: Herring, or Tommy rough, feed best at dusk and dawn but can be enticed to bite at any time with the use of fish oil based berley. Schools are often mixed with garfish and small trevally may be under the herring schools.

Lure fishing: Herring are very much underrated, but they are frequently enthusiastic lure takers. On lures, herring cartwheel and go on strong runs. Many fish are lost on the jump, but there is usually another fish to grab the lure as soon as it hits the water. Up to three or four fish can be hooked and lost on a single cast. While not necessarily the best way to fill the boat with herring, it is certainly the most fun. Small, flashy lures work best for herring and a splash of red seems to greatly increase their effectiveness.

Action type: Lures with a wide, exaggerated action do well, but a piece of green drinking straw on an otherwise plain hook is regarded as the original herring 'lure'. When berleyed up, herring are not too selective about action type.

Profile type: Spoons, spinners and narrow profile lures should be the first choice.

Lure sizes: Lures of 2.5–4 centimetres are recommended for this small species.

The top ten lures: Halco Twisty 5 gram, Gillies Wobbler 7 gram with red tag on hook, small Tasmanian Devil, Size 2 Blue Fox spinner, 1/16oz Bang Tail Spinner, Gillies Hogback Fly, Fishfighter Glimmy, Yo-Zuri Aile Killifish, Tillins 2" Devon, Wonder Wobbler 7

Kingfish

THE DEFINITIVE LURE

NO. 212 KOKODA RAPTOR 40 GRAMS.

Where: Reefs and headlands and some large coastal bays, from around Rockhampton, Queensland, throughout NSW and Victoria, northern Tasmania, South Australia and in Western Australia as far north as Shark Bay.

When: Year round, smaller fish common in summer, with larger fish usually encountered in winter.

Gear: Strong overhead, threadline and gamefishing tackle, minnow lures, metal jigs, soft plastics and saltwater flies. Cut fish baits, squid strips and live baits are also taken.

Technique: Trolling lures and live baits, drifting with livebaits and jigs, casting lures from ocean rocks and some deepwater jetties.

Feeding notes: Yellowtail kingfish are a schooling pelagic species. While they can be closely associated with prime habitat such as at the edge of reefs or cover like FADS or channel markers, they will act co-operatively on most occasions to round up and feed on baitfish. Small kingfish, also known as rats, form much larger schools and can be found in harbours or embayments. Larger kingfish prefer near shore or offshore reefs. Very large kingfish can be found close to shore where deep water is nearby such as in prime land-based gamefishing locations.

Diet: Yellowtail kingfish feed mainly on fish, but they also love squid and cuttlefish. In some areas, they will feed on crabs or lobsters.

Fishing notes: Yellowtail kingfish are one of the most powerful and dirtiest fighters in the ocean. Even small kingfish will do everything possible to reach the nearest cover and bury the angler. There are two main schools of thought when taking kingfish. The first is to lock the drag and bulldog the fish away from cover. This tactic requires stout tackle and a strong back, and may not work for larger specimens. The second tactic is to put only minimum pressure on the hooked fish, including only setting the hook lightly. Many kingfish can be steered to the boat in reasonably quick time and many do not even try to strongly run back to cover. One disadvantage of this method is that it is possible to get an extremely 'green' or underplayed kingfish to the boat, which presents some danger to a net or gaff man when the fish finally decides to go ballistic.

Lure fishing: Yellowtail kingfish are a challenge for lure fishers as they can test the skill of the angler and the quality of their tackle very quickly. It certainly pays to replace the hooks and split rings of all imported lures and even some of the Australian offerings. Many kingfish are taken on heavy vertical jigs, where the jig is dropped to the bottom and then retrieved with very fast rips. The trick is to pretend to get the jig back to the surface without being hit. If the fish are there—it won't! When kingfish are closer to the surface they can be taken by casting or trolling chrome and minnow lures. Soft plastics are increasing in popularity.

Action type: Most of the deep water jigs (the new Japanese-style jigs were not tested for this book) have little innate action and rely on speed and a some fluttering on the drop to attract strikes. Chrome wobblers and standard minnow lures also catch kingfish.

Profile type: Narrow profile.

Lure sizes: Lures of 7-15 centimetres generally work best.

The top ten lures: Kokoda Raptor 40 gram, Hawk Pilchard 90 gram, Halco Wobbler 30 gram, Kokoda Vector 50 gram, Wonder Pilchard 45 gram, Legend Murray Cod Spinnerbait, Halco Crazy Deep 150 DD, Rapala Magnum CD14, Halco Twisty 30 gram, Mann's Heavy Duty Stretch 25.

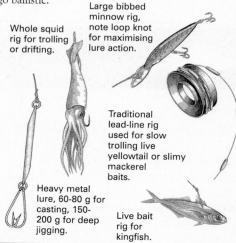

Whole squid rig for trolling or drifting.

Large bibbed minnow rig, note loop knot for maximising lure action.

Traditional lead-line rig used for slow trolling live yellowtail or slimy mackerel baits.

Heavy metal lure, 60-80 g for casting, 150-200 g for deep jigging.

Live bait rig for kingfish.

Leather Jacket

Where: Reef areas with kelp and weed both inshore and within estuaries and bays, mostly distributed below 29 degrees South, i.e. from the Houtman Abrolhos in Western Australia round the southern states and up into southern Queensland. Leatherjackets generally dislike rough water and strong currents.

When: Year round, peak activity within estuaries during summer and within inshore ocean waters from autumn

Gear: Light handlines, or spin tackle, long shank hooks to protect line against their chisel-like teeth, baits of peeled prawn, small cut fish baits or squid.

Technique: Moor near suitable structure and berley before casting small, lightly weighted baits into berley zone.

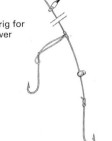

Paternoster rig for deep or rough water.

Running waggler float rig for calm water and shallower presentations.

Ling

Where: Deep ocean waters beyond the Continental Shelf south from Newcastle around the bottom of Australia to Busselton, Western Australia.

When: All year.

Gear: Heavy handlines, deck winches, deep water rigs, flesh baits, heavy sinkers.

Technique: Find concentrations of fish over deep sea mounts and fish baits down to them.

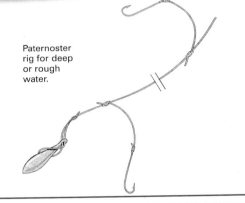

Paternoster rig for deep or rough water.

Luderick

Where: Around deepwater tide-washed weedbeds and rock faces in estuaries and from ocean rocks and inshore islands. Found from Noosa in Queensland throughout the NSW coast, into Victoria, northern Tasmania and Gulf St Vincent in South Australia.

When: Year round, peaks in winter and again in summer. Large northward migrations can be seen along the coast during autumn.

Gear: Long, supple rods with either threadline or centrepin reels, floats are used and can be slender stem types or small round bobby corks. Hooks are small sizes 6 to 10 to suit the luderick's small mouth and baits can be green weed, live nippers and squirt worms in estuaries, or green weed and sea lettuce from the ocean rocks. Will occasionally take small lures intended for bream.

Technique: Float fishing with particular attention paid to depth settings, which can be critical. Floats are ballasted so they slip under at the slightest touch and drifted with moving currents through an area that has been berleyed with chopped weed or bread.

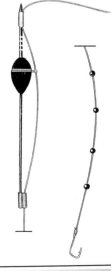

Fixed stem float rig. Note evenly spaced split shot to keep bait and trace in feeding zone. Floats can also be rigged as running floats, or substituted with small bobby corks.

Mackerel, Spanish

Feeding notes: Spanish mackerel are a mobile, largely tropical or sub-tropical pelagic species, which may feed in schools to attack bait species. The larger the fish, the smaller the number of fish in the school. While Spanish mackerel may travel widely for food, other larger fish can be relatively residential near prime feeding stations. Consequently, large Spanish mackerel in Queensland can be a moderate ciguatera risk and only small meals should be consumed initially.

Diet: Spanish mackerel feed on fish species, on residential reef fish and can feed on squid, especially spawning aggregations.

Fishing notes: The Spanish mackerel takes a wide range of lures including diving minnows, spoons, bibless minnows or resin headed pusher-type lures intended for marlin or sailfish.

NO. 756: HALCO LASER PRO DD

Lure fishing: Most Spanish mackerel are taken by trolling near current lines, reef drop-offs, around bait schools or while travelling to wide fishing grounds. Spanish mackerel will take lures trolled from 2–10 knots, although they will occasionally take large lures trolled faster for large pelagics. The sharp teeth of the Spanish mackerel makes a wire trace necessary and can wreck havoc with expensive skirted pusher lures and rigged hooks. Excellent fishing can be had by casting metal spoons to boiling fish and retrieving fast. This is particularly successful with the smaller but closely related broad-barred (or grey) mackerel. Anglers can take Spanish mackerel by casting lures from headlands with deep water nearby such as Steep Point in Western Australia. Here, heavy minnows work well. These may be weighted with a roll of lead on the line to increase casting distance.

Action type: With faster trolling being successful, a narrow wobble, narrow sway or a shimmy with bibless minnows and a wider wobble with spoons works well..

Profile type: Generally use a narrow profile to imitate bait species such as pilchards. However, bibless minnows with a broader profile can work well.

Lure sizes: Lures of 12–25 cm will work for the majority of mackerel fishing.

The top ten lures: Halco Laser Pro 160 DD, Rapala Magnum CD14, Halco 125 STD, Nilsmaster Invincible 15, Halco Giant Trembler, Rapala Magnum CD18, Halco Laser Pro 160 STD, Bomber Long A Magnum, Storm Saltwater Thunderstick.

Mahi-mahi (Dolphinfish)

Where: All tropical offshore waters, as far south as the Recherche Archipelago in Western Australia and Narooma in NSW. Will often be found around floating objects, like ropes, sheets of plywood, fish trap buoys and other specially-placed FAD (Fish Aggregating Devices).

When: Year round, best in southern states during summer

Gear: Light to medium threadline, fly fishing and overhead tackle, will take skirted trolling lures, small bright minnows, saltwater flies, poppers and fish baits.

Technique: Trolling or drifting and casting around flotsam or along current lines. Drifting and berleying is effective providing the current is not too fast.

Popper for casting towards FADs and floating debris.

NO.446 HALCO LASER PRO 120 STD

Feeding notes: Mahi mahi is a blue water pelagic species rarely encountered in inshore waters. The mahi mahi or dolphinfish is arguably the most beautiful fish in the ocean. Mahi mahi love floating debris and large numbers can be found sheltering or feeding under floating logs, sea containers or fish attracting devices (FADs). Schools are usually of similar sized fish. Mahi mahi can also be found cruising along current lines. There are often larger fish such as tuna below the mahi mahi. The mahi mahi is one of the fastest growing fish in the ocean, growing up to 1 cm in a day if food is plentiful. While this means that they are voracious feeders, they are surprisingly finicky when taking lures, especially if they are being heavily fished such as around FADs.

Metal slug for distance casting and for jigging.

Diet: Mahi mahi feed almost exclusively on a variety of fish and on squid.

Fishing notes: Mahi mahi take a wide range of lures including diving minnows, slice lures, bibless minnows or resin headed pusher type lures with the smaller sizes being particularly successful for smaller mahi mahi.

Deep diving minnow for trolling.

Lure fishing: Mahi mahi are either taken by casting chrome or minnow lures to FADs or surface debris or trolling near current lines, around bait schools or around FADs. When trolling blue water or near current lines, mahi mahi will often dash up in a flash of yellow and blue to investigate large pusher lures intended for marlin or large tuna. Putting a small lure in the troll pattern will pick up mahi mahi. They will take lures trolled 2–8 kn, with a distinct preference for speeds around 3–5 kn.

Feathered and skirted trolling lures for searching the water.

Action type: Trolled lures work best at 3–5 kn. Generally, minnows with a narrow wobble, narrow sway work best. A shimmy from smaller bibless minnows and sliced lures will also take fish.

Profile type: A narrow or very narrow profile to imitate bait species such as pilchards is recommended.

Lure sizes: A wide range of sizes will work with size selection determined to the size of the most common forage species in the vicinity. Lures of 5–20 cm will take mahi mahi and other pelagic species that are likely to be found with them.

The top ten lures: Halco Laser Pro 120 STD, Rapala Magnum CD11, Halco Laser Pro 120 DD, Halco Trembler 110, Yo-Zuri Hydro Magnum, Storm Thunderstick 11, Hawk Pilchard 40 gram, Halco Laser Pro 160 STD, Bomber Long A Magnum, Wonder Pilchard 45 gram.

Troll bait for mahi-mahi.

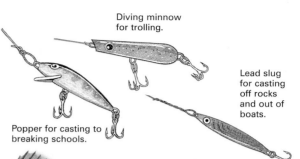

Mackerel, Shark

Where: Reef and islands in tropical waters, south to Geographe Bay in Western Australia and Coffs Harbour in NSW. The range of related species such as Spanish mackerel and spotted mackerel extends further southward in NSW to Montague Island and Wollongong respectively.

When: Year round in tropics, best months November through April elsewhere. Spotted mackerel peak around South West Rocks in NSW around Easter. Gear: Spin baitcast and fly tackle for smaller fish, heavier overhead tackle for bigger Spanish mackerel. Wire traces are essential for these species to withstand their fearsome teeth and ganged hook bait rigs are popular for the same reason. Metal jigs, poppers, bibbed minnows and skirted trolling lures will all take these fish as will strip baits, live baits and trolled whole fish baits.

Technique: Trolling, jigging spinning, bait drifting. Berley is not as widely used as it should be for these fish.

Diving minnow for trolling.

Popper for casting to breaking schools.

Lead slug for casting off rocks and out of boats.

Mangrove jack

THE DEFINITIVE LURE

NO. 820: TILSAN BARRA

Where: Estuaries and inshore reefs from the tropical north, down the Western Australia coast as far as Shark Bay and down the East Coast as far as Wollongong, NSW.

When: Year round in tropics, most likely in Northern NSW and southern Queensland from spring through summer.

Gear: Baitcast and spin gear, strong line, heavy leader, bibbed minnows, flies, soft plastics and live baits.

Technique: Cast lures and flies close to bankside cover and snags, be ready to strike hard and pull fish away from trouble. Drift live mullet or similar baitfish past snags and rock bars with the tide.

Feeding notes: Mangrove jacks are one of the toughest ambush feeders in Australian waters. Mangrove jacks are closely associated with rock bars, snags, mangrove roots or deep holes in tropical estuarine or tidal rivers. Interestingly, the mangrove jacks most frequently encountered by lure fishers in inshore waters are juveniles or young adults. Large mangrove jacks move onto offshore reefs where they can reach much larger size and may live to 50 years.

Diet: Mangrove jacks feed aggressively on small fish, crabs, prawns, shrimp, octopus, shellfish and other food that happens by.

Fishing notes: Mangrove jacks have enormous torque and power. They will dash out from their home snag, smash a lure and head back as quickly and strongly as possible. This means that tackle must be of high quality and most foreign lures need to have stronger hooks added or a decent sized jack will mangle them.

Lure fishing: A large snag could hold as many as twenty mangrove jacks and it pays to work quality cover. Casts need to be close up to cover to entice a strike except at the right time of the tide, which can vary from place to place. At night mangrove jacks will roam further from their snags. Leaving the lure on the surface for a few seconds before commencing the retrieve is recommended and an erratic retrieve is usually more successful than a constant speed.

Action type: Mangrove jacks will hit lures with a wide range of action when in the mood, varying from medium wobble and sway to the shimmy of rattlin' spot type lures to spinnerbaits.

Profile type: Narrow or medium profile lures work best.

Lure sizes: Mangrove jacks have little fear, with tiny jacks frequently hitting lures that are the same size. Many jacks hit larger lures intended for barramundi and I have seen a 2 kg mangrove jack mistaken for a 10 kg barramundi during the fight. The standard mangrove jack lure is 5–12cm.

The top ten lures: Tilsan Barra, C Lures Jack Snack Deep, Lively Lures Mad Mullet Deep, DK Lures Snag Master 6, Predatek Jindivik, Eddy Lures Wasp, RMG Scorpion 68 DD, Deception Shrimp, StumpJumper 2 Deep, Classic Lures All Rounder.

Live bait rig for baits like mullet, herring, yellowtail and whiting. Note trace is heavy monofilament.

Large dead prawn rig. Use king prawns, royal reds, or banana prawns.

Marlin, Black

Where: Right around Australia, inshore waters to Continental Shelf.

When: Summer through autumn south of Brisbane, spring through summer northward.

Gear: Strong overhead rods and reels, 15 kg line upwards, skirted lures, live baits, rigged dead baits. Technique: Trolling current lines, reef areas, around bait schools. Live baiting from ocean rocks.

Technique: Trolling current lines, reef areas, around bait schools. Live baiting from rocks.

Trolled squid rig with one or two hooks depending on squid size. Troll slowly for best results.

Live baits hooked lightly near the tail are effective from the rocks or fished out on the Continental Shelf.

Mulloway

NO. 367: KILLALURE JEWIE 150

Where: Estuaries, inshore reefs, surf beaches and rocky coastal areas from Bundaberg in Queensland right throughout NSW to the Victorian border and northern Tasmania. They are somewhat discontinuous in their distribution between southern NSW and Melbourne, but west of here again, they become plentiful once more, continuing throughout South Australia and into Western Australia as far north as North West Cape. From here to around Gladstone in northern Queensland, a related species known as 'black' jewfish take over.

When: In some southern parts of their range, catches peak in winter, while in the north, summer can often be better. There are countless theories about which phase of the moon is best for mulloway, but general agreement is the week either side of a full moon is productive. In many estuaries, they seem to bite best as the tide slows to dead low or full.

Gear: Handlines are used extensively in reef fishing, but robust rods and reels and heavy line are used from the rocks in the surf and for most estuary fishing. Mulloway will also take lures, mostly Japanese feathers, large poppers and minnows and even big saltwater flies and large soft plastics.

Technique: When bait fishing from a boat, drop baits down and set them a metre or so above the bottom. For rock and surf fishing, cast baits into areas where water movement will carry the bait around and when lure fishing wind slowly and be ready to set the hook when a fish takes. Feeding notes: A big mulloway is the Holy Grail of southern estuarine anglers. Mulloway are opportunistic feeders and will school up with small mulloway or 'soapies' forming large schools. Fish over 10 kg or so generally travel alone or with two or three mates. Until recently, lure fishing for mulloway was confined to casting a red feather jig into muddy floodwaters at the mouth of one of the larger east coast rivers. Since that time, dedicated anglers have worked out that those who are willing to put in the effort can take mulloway on lures and even flies. Mulloway are much more active at night and around deep holes on beaches or in estuaries.

Diet: Mulloway feed on small and medium sized fish, squid, cuttlefish, octopus, crabs, beach worms and pipis.

Fishing notes: Mulloway are renowned for displaying two powerful runs and then almost giving up. Large mulloway are quite difficult to revive and release. Old timers claim that you can hear mulloway croaking in estuaries, especially through the hulls of aluminium boats. They also claim that rubbing the bait or lure on the side of the first fish caught to impart the distinctive cucumber smell will attract the mate of that fish.

Lure fishing: An increasing number of mulloway are being taken as a bonus by anglers fishing for bream and flathead. The majority of mulloway are being taken by slow trolling through deep holes or around obvious structure such as bridge pylons. Most anglers troll into the tide so that the lure is in the most attractive area for as long as possible. Working the rod to impart an erratic action seems to increase strikes. Other anglers pick up fish by casting large heavy lures from breakwalls.

Action type: A medium sway and wobble works best.   Profile type: Medium profiles catch good mulloway.

Lure sizes: While soapies can be taken on small bream lures, those intended specifically for mulloway are 8–18 cm.

The top ten lures: Killalure Jewie 150, Bill's Bugs Jew Lure 126, Predatek Viper 150, Mann's 12+ Boof Bait, Illusion Lures Wedgetail Deep 12, Illusion Lures Jester, Majik Lures Mulgar 10+, Mudeye Lures Nomad, Larrikin Lures LK 160, RMG Scorpion 125 DD.

Mark Shean's 'half a squid' rig. Excellent around inshore reefs and islands.

Gang hooked baits with minimal weight can be very effective at night.

Surf rig, using two hooks and pyramid sinker attached above trace and swivel.

Mullet

Where: Right around Australia in estuaries, coastal saltwater lakes, and annually, along inshore coastal waters when they are on annual spawning migrations. Some species are purely freshwater dwellers, while others spend their juvenile stages in freshwater and run to sea when mature.

When: Year round, best in summer.

Gear: Light spin tackle and line, flyfishing gear, quill floats, small hooks split shot and baits of bread, peeled prawn or dough.

Technique: Berley them into shallows and along deepwater channel edges with bread. Rig baits under floats or use fly tackle and small white flies. Baiting clear plastic cylinder traps with bread can trap small 'poddy' mullet.

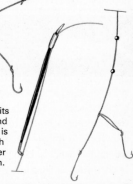

Clip-on bob-float rig for mullet. Red and white float provides good visibility in rough conditions or poor light.

Berley sinker rig with two droppers above sinker. Berley is crammed into the spiral cage of the berley sinker and attracts fish into the vicinity of the baits above it.

Quill float rig. Suits mullet, garfish and yellowtail. Note float is rigged as running, with slide on rubber stopper set to desired depth.

Perch, Golden

NO. 944: PREDATEK 65 MM BOOMERANG

Where: Freshwater streams and dams in Central NSW, southern Queensland, northern Victoria.
When: Year round spring and summer to autumn best.
Gear: Spin and baitcast tackle, fly tackle. Bibbed lures, spinnerbaits, soft plastics, flies, worms, crayfish.
Technique: Troll bibbed lures past points and along contour lines. Cast to snags and tree-lines, jig and bob over submerged structure.
Feeding notes: The golden perch is generally an ambush feeder on drop-offs or around snags and weed lines. In rivers this fish prefers moderately sluggish water. The golden perch can be an opportunistic feeder and can cruise for food, especially at dusk and dawn. They can form spawning aggregations in rivers especially before floods and can aggregate in spring near warmer water inflows in dams.
Diet: Golden perch feed on a variety of foods including yabbies, shrimps, fish, worms, and frogs. They will take terrestrial animals including mice and grasshoppers when available.
Fishing notes: Golden perch will take a variety of lures and action types, Golden perch will often follow lures to a boat or shore. Making a figure-of-eight with the rod tip, which is put under the water, with about 45 centimetres of line out will often take followers. It is worth persevering with repeated casts or a change in lure size and type as interested fish can usually be teased into a strike. Another important trick when casting is to pause in the retrieve at the point near the end of the cast when the lure starts to rise towards the surface. This pause will often incite a following fish to strike.
Lure fishing: Deep diving lures either cast or trolled near likely cover work best, although sight fishing to cruising fish on weed edges can take many fish. Lures with relatively large bibs and quick diving capacity work best in most circumstances.
Action type: Slow, wide sway and medium wobble works best, but some of the tighter action lures and spinnerbaits are becoming increasingly popular and successful.
Profile type: Robust lures that imitate food such as yabbies or small carp work very well. Some medium profile lures are successful.
Lure sizes: Golden perch can be taken on anything from small spinners to large lures intended for cod, such as the magnum Hellbender. Golden perch have a large mouth and when in the mood can take lures larger than 10 centimetres, but the best lures are 5–8 centimetres.
The top ten lures: Predatek 65 mm Boomerang Deep, Rapala Fat Rap FR7, Storm Hot'N Tot large, Arbogast Mud Bug 1/2oz, Mann's 15+, Eddy Lures Dam Buster, Majik Lures Mulgar, Deception Cherax, Custom Crafted Small Hammerhead, 14 gram spinnerbait.

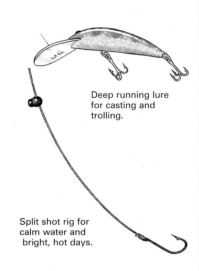

Deep running lure for casting and trolling.

Split shot rig for calm water and bright, hot days.

Running sinker rig for 'bobbing' crays and shrimp.

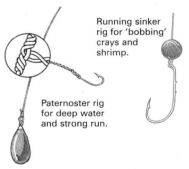

Paternoster rig for deep water and strong run.

Perch, Jungle

Feeding notes: The jungle perch is a relatively small and aggressive fish of the tropical north-east. It takes up residence in clear and pristine tropical streams. There is a distinctive hierarchy in each hole, with larger fish taking the prime feeding positions near snags or where the most food passes closely.
Diet: The jungle perch is an opportunistic feeder, taking shrimps, terrestrial and aquatic insects, frogs, small lizards and insect larvae.
Fishing notes: Jungle perch are a fantasy capture for many anglers from southern climes. It is not their size that is most important as a fish over a half kilogram is these days considered large, but the spectacular scenery and pristine locations that are as important as the fish, which are now released by all conservation-minded anglers. Jungle perch are actually very aggressive, provided a stealthy approach is made and can be seriously overfished. Casts need to be accurate to take the best fish and overhanging vegetation impedes many back casts.
Lure fishing: Jungle perch take a variety of small lures, including spinners, small minnow or frog imitations and small surface lures.
Action type: Lures with a medium wobble and spinners seem to work best. Paddlers or fizzers are recommended.
Profile type: A narrow or medium profile is the most versatile.
Lure sizes: Small lures of 2–5 centimetres work best.
The top ten lures: Nilsmaster Invincible 5, Rapala Mini Fat Rap, Predatek Micro Min, Halco Laser Pro 45, Blue Fox 2 Spinner, Heddon Teeny Torpedo, Deception Palaemon, Oar-Gee Lil Ripper, Bill's Bugs Mice 40, Rebel Wee Frog.

NO. 397: NILSMASTER INVINCIBLE 5

Perch, Macquarie

Feeding notes: Macquarie perch are opportunistic feeders. They can form schools with smaller fish forming larger schools and trophy sized fish in pairs or alone. They prefer gravel areas near standing timber or rock walls and feed better at dusk, dawn and through the night.

Diet: Macquarie perch feed mainly on insect larvae, worms, shrimps and rarely small fish.

Fishing notes: Macquarie perch are not a renowned lure taker as they have a relatively small mouth, but they are a very welcome bonus. They are most commonly taken on worms, live shrimp or mudeyes. They can be timid biters and will frequently follow a lure repeatedly without showing much interest in actually striking. A change to a smaller lure or a jerky retrieve may bring that elusive hit.

Lure fishing: Macquarie perch are most commonly taken on lures intended for trout or silver perch. They are totally protected throughout their range, except in Lake Dartmouth, the Yarra River and the Upper Coliban Reservoir and their tributaries, and should be returned to the water unharmed.

Action type: Spinners or narrow wobble lures work best for Macquarie perch.

Profile type: A medium profile covers most bases.

Lure sizes: Small lures to 4.5 centimetres work best for these timid lure takers.

The top ten lures: Blue Fox 2 Spinner, Nilsmaster Invincible 5, Rapala Mini Fat Rap, Predatek Micro Min, Halco Laser Pro 45, Dan McGrath Attack Lure, Deception Palaemon, Oar-Gee Lil Ripper, Mann's 5+, Rapala Countdown CD3.

NO.207: BLUE FOX 2 SPINNER

Pipis

Where: The intertidal zone of ocean beaches.

When: Best on a falling tide, least effective in a southerly wind.

Gear: Bucket or similar container.

Technique: Look for pipis breathing holes in sand or 'V' wakes as waves recede. If pipis are not visible at surface, twist your feet back and forth as the waves wash around them and you will feel the shells underfoot.

Perch, Redfin

Where: Both alpine and semi-lowland streams and dams throughout NSW, Victoria, South Australia and Tasmania.

When: Year round, but when fishing in declared trout waters, seasonal closures apply.

Gear: Light spin and baitcast tackle, metal jigs, soft plastics, spinnerbaits, bladed lures, bibbed minnows, baits of shrimp, worms or crayfish tail.

Technique: Cast, troll or jig in same places as for trout, though especially where water deepens suddenly.

Feeding notes: Redfin can be an ambush feeder or can cruise wider areas searching for food. Redfin form schools, with smaller fish forming larger schools and the bigger fish of over a kilogram becoming increasingly solitary. Redfin can be voracious feeders and can stunt out, with hordes of mature fish at only 15–20 centimetres, too small to eat. Importantly, redfin do not feed after dark.

Diet: Redfin take a wide variety of food including minnows and other small fish, yabbies, shrimp, worms, grubs, insects and their larvae, water fleas, fish eggs, snails and nearly everything edible they can fit in their prodigious mouths. While redfin can impact native fish in some waters, they do make excellent eating themselves but they must be skinned, as the scales are akin to armour plating.

Fishing notes: Redfin can be very easy to catch and a school can be worked with a hooked fish being kept in the water at all times. Redfin school to spawn, usually in spring, and large catches are possible if a spawning school is found. Interestingly, water that is full of tiny redfin by day can also yield large trout or natives by night, often fat from eating small redfin.

Lure fishing: Bobbing for redfin with special jigs is extremely popular. Fish are either found in a school on a depth sounder or by exploring—usually at the base of standing trees or a rock drop-off. The lure is dropped to the bottom and jigged up 1-2 metres then fluttered back to the bottom. Redfin will take the lure either on the rise or the drop. If there is no bite after a couple of minutes, move to another spot or try another lure. Redfin will take cast or trolled lures. Spinners are also successful. Lures with some red or orange seem to incite a strike.

Action type: Nearly every action type will take feeding redfin. The largest specimens prefer jigs, spinners, small spinnerbaits or medium sway lures.

Profile type: Medium profile lures, spinners or spinnerbaits and jigs work best.

Lure sizes: While tiny redfin can attack huge lures, the standard redfin lures are 3–7 centimetres.

The top ten lures: Hirst's Harasser Baltic, Rapala Fat Rap 5, Storm Hot'N Tot, No 3 Mepps or Blue Fox, Nilsmaster jig, 4 gram spinnerbait, Ashley Probe, Deception Nipper, Kokoda Yabby, Oar-Gee Lil Ripper.

NO. 198 HIRST'S HARASSER BALTIC

Paternoster rig for redfin, use shrimp or worms for bait.

Running ball sinker to swivel and trace rig. Suits bobbing with crayfish or shrimp.

Vibrax bladed spinner. This axis-type spinner is very effective for redfin in streams.

Pink nippers

Where: Estuary sand flats.
When: Low tide.
Gear: Nipper pumps, sieve, bucket.
Technique: Look for burrow holes and insert pump barrel as the handle is withdrawn to suck liquified sand into pump. Discharge pump contents into floating sieve or onto ground and pick out nippers, placing them in a bucket of water. Nippers are best used live, so water changes may be necessary every hour or so.

Prawns

Where: Shallow weedbeds, sandflats and deep channels in estuaries and coastal lakes with significant tidal exchange.
When: Best in summer, during 'dark' periods of the lunar cycle as this is when prawns 'run' to the ocean.
Gear: Gas or kerosene lanterns, scoop nets, drag nets and buckets, strong garden rakes, submersible lights and battery packs.
Technique: Scoop netting is usually done at night from a boat, using lanterns to illuminate the prawns' eyes as they float by on the tide. You can also walk sand flats at night with a headlamp or submersible prawning light on a pole. The lamp is powered by a small battery pack carried on a belt. Where drag netting is allowed (check local regulations) two people take a drag pole each and walk slowly through the shallow margins of lakes and bays, periodically stopping to check and empty the net's contents. In some southern estuaries, such as Bemm River in Victoria, prawns can be raked from weed beds during the day and scooped as they dart from cover.

 ## Queenfish

NO. 81: PRODUCERS MONSTER POPPER F
(YOU MAY NEED TO CHANGE SPLIT RINGS)

Where: Tropical Australia, in estuaries, bays and inshore reef waters.
When: Year round, best from May through November. Tide changes are less important than the presence of strong tidal of coastal currents and large baitfish schools. In spring and summer, when squid spawn inshore, queenfish can target these schools almost obsessively around inshore reefs and bommies.
Gear: Threadline fly and baitcast tackle, 4 to 8 kg line, with 20 kg leaders. Poppers, fizzers, metal jigs, soft plastics, saltwater flies, bibbed minnows, pilchards, cut fish baits and squid.
Technique: Lures are cast or trolled around surface feeding schools, close to near-surface reef or rocky shores, island corners and estuary mouths or creeks. Baits can be fished into deep tidal holes and creek and river junctions or from jetties or rock walls.
Feeding notes: The queenfish is a top ambush predator. It behaves like a pelagic species but is most often found close to breaking reefs, at the edge of sand bars or near islands where they lie in wait for small baitfish. Queenfish can form schools and slash through baitfish schools. Queenfish are quite light in weight for their size, often called skinnyfish. However, when they turn side on to the fight, they can provide exceptional power and resistance.
Diet: Queenfish primarily feed on fish but will also take squid, prawns and crabs.
Fishing notes: Queenfish are often found at the edge of white water around reefs or islands. They aren't usually found in the strongest tidal flows, preferring to sit at the edges or eddies waiting for bait. They will also patrol beaches and sandbars, staying just at the edge of the surge zone. Their feeding and behaviour is often dictated by the state of the tide and they can go from feeding freely to disappearing, or vice versa, within minutes. The queenfish has a huge mouth, which can take large baits but they can be finicky and require size specific food such as small whitebait.
Lure fishing: Queenfish are excellent sportfish with strong powerful runs. They can also jump or porpoise spectacularly, with silver flanks showering spray. They are powerful enough to decimate poor quality hooks and even straighten spilt rings. Queenfish are enthusiastic takers of poppers, but they can also be frustrating on occasions, boiling repeatedly just behind the lure or screaming up behind a lure to turn away at the last possible instant. The key is to cast close to likely looking washes and retrieve quickly, evoking a predatory response.
Action type: Poppers, spoon type lures and minnows with a medium wobble all work well.
Profile type: Narrow lures that imitate common baitfish.
Lure sizes: Queenfish lures are most commonly from 4–12 centimetres.
The top ten lures: Producers Monster Popper F, Lively Lures Kingfisher Super Blooper, Kokoda Roger 10, Cotton Cordell Pencil Popper, Halco Wobbler 30 gram, Halco Twisty 30 gram, Fishfighter Toby 20 gram, Rio's Live Chrome 20 gram, Storm Suspending Thunderstick, Lively Lures Blue Pilly.

Fat-tail popper – retrieve this popper type at top speed with the rod tip held high.

Bibbed minnow lure for queenfish. Note strong hooks and rings and loop knot attachment

Salmon, Atlantic

NO. 131: HALCO WOBBLER 10 GRAM

Feeding notes: Atlantic salmon fishing in Australia falls into two categories. There is some fishing in Lake Jindabyne and, even more sporadically, in Burrinjuck Dam and Lake Bullen Merri where Atlantic salmon that are often identified as under-nourished brown trout. There is a small but increasing fishery for escaped Atlantic salmon from the aquaculture farms in Tasmania. These fish are larger but have been fed on pellets all their lives.

Diet: Atlantic salmon prefer fish, especially in estuarine waters. They will also take shrimp, insects, worms, snails and insect larvae.

Lure fishing: In NSW, these fish are taken when trolling for other species and standard trout lures work well. In Tasmania, flashy spoons or metal lures cast or trolled around current edges, or as close to salmon pens as you are allowed, work best.

Action type: Spoons or Tasmanian Devil type lures work well. Standard trout lures can be effective as well.

Profile type: Medium profile lures with flash are successful, while narrow smelt imitations can take fish in season.

Lure sizes: Lures of 3–7 centimetres work best. Large Rapala Minnows can take large estuarine salmon on occasions.

The top ten lures: Halco Wobbler 10 grams, Big Tasmanian Devil, Halco Twisty 10 grams, #2 Blue Fox, Countdown Rapala CD5, Helin Flatfish X4, Fish Fighter Minnow 10 g, Tillins King Cobra, Rebel Crawfish, Worden's Rooster Tail.

Salmon, Australian

NO. 79 LIVELY LURES KINGFISHER SUPER BLOOPER

Where: From Brisbane south to Kalbarri (Western Australia), including Tasmania.

When: All year.

Gear: Medium threadline and baitcasting tackle from boats and in inlets. Mid-range surf fishing tackle for beaches wand rocks.

Technique: Cast lures and baits out into prominent gutters and holes on beaches. Keep baits and lures on the move to attract the salmon's interest.

Feeding notes: The Australian Salmon is a schooling pelagic species, which frequents beaches and inshore waters. The Australian salmon is not related to the trout-like salmon and is actually closely related to the mullets. Australian salmon undertake spawning migrations along the East and West Coast and this is an important sport fish throughout the southern half of Australia. The western species gets to 10 kilograms, with 5–7 kilograms being average, while the eastern species averages from 2.5–5 kilograms.

Diet: Australian salmon feed mainly on fish and will round up schools of whitebait, bluebait and even herring and feed strongly. Salmon also eat squid, cuttlefish, beach worms, pipis and crabs.

Fishing notes: Australian salmon are a very highly regarded sportfish. They fight strongly and can jump spectacularly. During the spawning season, salmon form large schools and fishing can be very poor until a huge black school moves onto the beach or near shore. When a school is in the area, salmon are generally easy to catch, but on occasions can be frustrating and not interested in food.There are often residential fish within the main range of the Australian salmon. These fish often frequent the deepest holes on beaches or a patch of reef at the ends of long beaches and respond well to lures or bait.

Lure fishing: Australian salmon are underrated as a lure target. They will hit poppers, chrome and minnow lures. Salmon taken on lures fight even more strongly than those taken on bait and aerial displays are common. Australian salmon have a distinct preference for light coloured lures.

Action type: Poppers, spoon type lures and minnows with a medium wobble all work well.

Profile type: Narrow or nearly narrow lures that imitate pilchards, whitebait or herring work best.

Lure sizes: Salmon lures are 4–12 centimetres.

The top ten lures: Lively Lures Kingfisher Super Blooper, Rapala Skitter Pop 12, Kokoda Roger 10, Halco Wobbler 30 gram, Halco Twisty 30 gram, Rapala Magnum Mag-11, RMG Scorpion, Storm Suspending Thunderstick, Mauler Shallow Runner, Mann's Stretch 1 Minus.

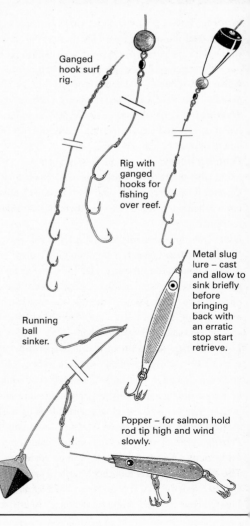

Ganged hook surf rig.

Rig with ganged hooks for fishing over reef.

Running ball sinker.

Multi dropper surf rig.

Metal slug lure – cast and allow to sink briefly before bringing back with an erratic stop start retrieve.

Popper – for salmon hold rod tip high and wind slowly.

Salmon, Chinook

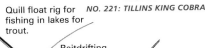

NO. 221: TILLINS KING COBRA

Where: Western lakes in Victoria.

When: Year round — check for season closures.

Gear: Light spin tackle, small minnows, whitebait, live galaxias fished under floats.

Technique: Spin from boats or bank, troll or drift with whitebait.

Feeding notes: The chinook salmon is really only found in Lake Purrumbete and Bullen Merri in Victoria where they produce good sport, especially in spring. They prefer fish for food and are taken by trolling on flatlines or with downriggers.

Diet: Chinook prefer galaxiid minnows and other fish food. They will also feed on shrimp and more traditional trout fare of insect larvae, worms and snails on occasion.

Fishing notes: Chinook salmon are often well over 4.5 kg and reach as much as 9 kg in these waters, but they are unable to breed and must be stocked. They can gorge themselves on schools of baitfish and provide excellent sport for those who put in the time and target this excellent sport fish.

Lure fishing: Chinook can be found crashing into bait schools in the shallows on occasion. They are also caught by downrigging at the thermocline where bait schools show up on the sounder.

Action type: Wide sway from lures, like Tasmanian Devil Lures, and tight wobble lures that imitate baitfish work well.

Profile type: A narrow profile that imitates smelt or gudgeon is generally recommended.

Lure sizes: Best lures are 3–7 centimetres, although larger minnow lures can trigger strikes.

The top ten lures: Tillins King Cobra, Duel Depth Tasmanian Devil, Countdown Rapala CD7, Halco Wobbler 10 gram, Rapala Original Minnow 11, Countdown Rapala CD5, Tilsan Minnow, McGrath Diver, Trout Masta, Predatek Micro Min.

Quill float rig for fishing in lakes for trout.

Baitdrifting rig for live grasshoppers and crickets.

Small diving plugs are best rigged with a loop knot.

Bubble float rig for fishing mudeyes for trout.

Paravane rig for trolling lures such as Cobras and Tassie Devils.

Salmon, Threadfin

NO. 204: HALCO TWISTY 20 GRAM IN GOLD.

Where: Tropical estuarine waters from The Kimberly in Western Australia throughout the Northern Territory and down to about Cardwell in north Queensland. There are several species of threadfin salmon, the 'blue' salmon, the 'king' or 'Burnett' salmon, the 'seven-fingers' threadfin and the 'striped' threadfin, also known as the 'putty-nosed perch'.

When: Year round with peaks in activity either end of the dry season. Very much a fish that feeds according to tides and moon phases, timing of threadfin trips can be critical to get the best fishing on offer.

Gear: Most commonly, baitcasting or spin tackle is used, but fly anglers are increasingly discovering the virtues of this species as a fly fishing target. Four to 8 kg main lines with 20 kg leaders are common. Bibbed minnows, poppers, fizzers, spinnerbaits, soft plastics and flies are taken with equal gusto. The threadfin will also take metal spoons, baits of fish strip or whole live prawns and small crabs.

Technique: Trolling past snags or points of land, casting to bankside structure or fish that can be seen 'working' the surface.

Feeding notes: The threadfin salmon is an opportunistic feeder in some circumstances, but can also act as an ambush feeder, especially in tidal creeks. Threadfin salmon cruise the shallows looking for food, especially on a dropping tide.

Diet: Threadfin salmon eat fish, crabs, octopus and prawns.

Fishing notes: Threadfin salmon are extremely good sportfish, undertaking strong runs with spectacular jumps. They cruise at current eddies especially on a dropping tide, or in the active tidal zone on a rising tide in the northern areas where the tidal range is very large. Most northern local anglers rate threadfin salmon as a superior eating fish to the barramundi.

Lure fishing: Threadfin salmon have a distinct preference for light coloured or shiny baits. Therefore, gold or silver lures are the most popular. In WA metal lures are much more successful while in the NT and QLD, gold minnow lures are more frequently used. Threadfin salmon are a welcome bonus when fishing for barramundi or mangrove jacks.

Action type: Metal lures with a bright finish, especially in gold, and a narrow sway work best. Minnow lures generally have a metallic finish and a narrow wobble or sway.

Profile type: Narrow profile lures.

Lure sizes: Lures of 4–7.5 centimetres are most commonly used.

The top ten lures: Halco Twisty 20 gram, Halco Hex Sparkler 20 gram, Fishfighter Toby 14 gram, Wonder Enticer 28 gram, Halco Wobbler 20 gram,

Live prawn hooked lightly through tail to allow bait to move freely.

Running sinker rig for fishing live prawns and small baitfish.

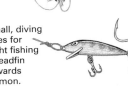

Small, diving lures for sight fishing threadfin towards salmon.

Samson, Fish

NO.255: KOKODA VECTOR 50 GRAM

Feeding notes: The samson fish is a large species, which is powerful but not as dirty a fighter as the related yellowtail kingfish. The samson fish is more closely associated with bottom cover such as reefs or weedbeds and are rarely enticed to the surface. Samson fish will school to spawn, and extremely large catches have been taken from the aggregations from October to March near Perth. However, at other times of the year, samson fish are found either singly or in small groups and can range from inshore to 150 metres.

Diet: Samson fish feed mainly on fish but they love squid, cuttlefish and lobsters. They will also feed on crabs or shellfish.

Fishing notes: Samson fish are extremely powerful, making strong runs and a very dogged fight. However, when a samson fish reaches the bottom, they will generally run along the bottom rather than seeking out reefs or cover to bury an angler. However, even when taken out of deep water, a samson fish will fight all the way to the boat, making them a real test of stamina.

Lure fishing: Samson fish are a challenge for lure fishers as they can test the skill of the angler and the quality of their tackle very quickly. It is essential to replace the hooks and split rings of all imported lures. Most samson fish are taken on heavy vertical jigs. These jigs are rigged with the hook at the top of the jig, and are dropped to the bottom and then retrieved with very fast rips or with a slow bouncing retrieve. These lures have revolutionised fishing for samson fish, with fish up to 55 kilograms being taken. Soft plastics rigged on large lead head jigs are increasing in popularity. While samson fish do not often patrol at the surface, they will follow up hooked fish and can be more easily taken by casting chrome and minnow lures.

Action type: The deep water jigs (the new Japanese style jigs were not tested for this book) have little innate action and rely on speed and a some fluttering on the drop to attract strikes. Chrome wobblers and standard minnow lures work on occasions.

Profile type: Narrow profile.

Lure sizes: Lures of 7–20 centimetres generally work best.

The top ten lures: Kokoda Vector 50 gram, Kokoda Raptor 40 gram, Hawk Pilchard 90 gram, Wonder Pilchard 45 gram, Legend Murray Cod Spinnerbait, Hawk Pilchard 40 gram, Rapala CD-14, Halco Twisty 30 gram, Mann's Heavy Duty Stretch 25, Halco Wobbler 30 gram.

Saratoga

NO. 62 : HEDDON CRAZY CRAWLER
Bibbed minnow type lure, troll or cast and wind slowly and erratically past structure.

Where: Natural distribution is in tropical north of Queensland from Bundaberg upward to Cape York and across to Northern Territory, and adjacent islands with enough freshwater to carry them. There have also been successful artificial stockings of saratoga in various Queensland dams south of the Fitzroy/Dawson catchment, including Borumba Dam near Imbil, and Cania Dam near Monto.

When: Year round, best from spring to autumn.

Gear: Spin, baitcast and fly fishing gear, lines 4 to 6 kg with heavier leader. Bibbed minnows, poppers, flies, spinnerbaits and soft plastics.

Float rig for bait-fishing to saratoga

Technique: Cast to fringing pandanus along edges of water courses, weedbeds, lily pads and under bankside trees.

Feeding notes: There are two species, with the gulf saratoga being larger and being stocked into impoundments for fantastic recreational fishing. Saratoga are opportunistic feeders, usually cruising near the surface around cover looking for food. The straight dorsal profile gives a clue that saratoga are largely surface feeders.

Diet: Saratoga cruise looking for food such as terrestrial insects, frogs, lizards, shrimps, small fish and insect larvae.

Popper – retrieve with short stabs of rod tip and frequent pauses.

Fishing notes: Surface or shallow running lures work best for saratoga. A crashing surface strike or strong boil signifies a hit. Casting to fringing vegetation along weed edges or into pockets among lilies is the preferred method. Many fish can be sight targeted. Accuracy can be important, and making the lure look like an insect that has fallen onto the water via a slow and irregular retrieve can be best.

Lure fishing: Saratoga are highly respected lure and fly targets. They are basically inedible and this, coupled with their low egg production, means that each fish should be released as soon as possible in good condition to allow others to enjoy future sport. Surface lures should be left on the surface for a few seconds before commencing a slow, irregular retrieve. Saratoga can be teased into striking with a well-timed twitch when a fish is right below the lure.

Action type: Surface paddlers, fizzers and chuggers work well. A medium or narrow wobble and a suspending lure that can be worked slowly are recommended.

Profile type: Medium profile lures or those that imitate specific insects are best.

Lure sizes: Lures of 3–7 centimetres are most commonly used. Saratoga have an impressive mouth and can be occasionally taken on large surface lures intended for barramundi.

The top ten lures: Heddon Crazy Crawler, Arbogast Jitterbug, Bill's Bugs Mice 40 or 50, River 2 Sea Cicada Pop, Rapala Shad Rap Suspending, Heddon Tiny Torpedo, Rapala Skitter Pop, Bassman Spinnerbait Classic 1/4oz, Bagley's Bang-O-Lure #4, Halco Night Walker.

Snapper

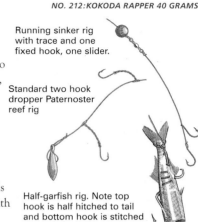

NO. 212: KOKODA RAPPER 40 GRAMS

Running sinker rig with trace and one fixed hook, one slider.

Standard two hook dropper Paternoster reef rig

Half-garfish rig. Note top hook is half hitched to tail and bottom hook is stitched through the bait.

Where: Ranges from deep offshore water to inshore shallows around reef. Seasonally enters large bays and estuaries. Distributed from Capricorn region of Queensland throughout NSW, Victorian and South Australian coastal waters. In Tasmania snapper are more plentiful in the north of the island's waters while in Western Australia they extend as far north as Coral Bay. Exceptional fisheries exist in the Gulf of St Vincent South Australia, and in the Shark Bay region of Western Australia.

When: Year round, although spring through summer are peak periods in most places. Seasonal closures apply to parts of the Western Australia fishery, notably Shark Bay area. Consult local fisheries regulations. Tide changes, dawn and dusk and throughout the night are all good periods to fish for snapper.

Gear: Threadline through baitcast to heavy overhead tackle, depending on fish size and terrain in which they are found. Snapper will occasionally take lures such as bibbed minnows, metal jigs and soft plastics but are essentially a bait species, taking squid, prawns, cut fish baits, live baits and various 'rock' baits such as cunjevoi and abalone gut.

Technique: Berley heavily and fish baits down on the bottom on Paternoster rigs over deep reef, or lightly weighted or unweighted 'floaters' in shallow water. Experts disagree on best hooking methods, some setting reels out of gear with the ratchet on, others, fishing rods hand held and reels in free spool, still others setting rods with the reels on full drag and in gear. Different fish in different locations appear to take baits differently too.

Feeding notes: The snapper is a schooling, opportunistic feeder. The pink snapper is one of the most desirable fish species as it can grow to around 20 kilograms, is excellent eating and ranges throughout the lower two thirds of Australia. They form large schools of similar sized fish, with larger fish becoming increasingly solitary, although even they form large schools to spawn. Juveniles are found in estuaries or rivers and sub-adults move to inshore reefs. The larger fish generally move into deeper water.

Diet: Snapper take a wide range of foods, including fish, squid, cuttlefish, crabs, prawns, mussels, cockles, worms and sea urchins.

Fishing notes: Snapper are most often taken with bait fishing methods and standard paternoster rigs in deeper water. The use of Japanese style rigs with Flashabou is increasing. Snapper prefer reefs or gravel patches near reefs and can be found in depths to 150 metres. Snapper respond extremely well to berley. On near-shore reefs they can be coaxed up from the bottom to mid-water or close to the surface.

Lure fishing: Whilst snapper are not highly regarded as lure takers, more fish are being taken this way. The most common lures are bucktail or soft plastic tipped jigs. Juvenile snapper in estuaries have a distinct preference for jigs and are often taken while fishing for bream. Tipping the jigs with bait such as a squid tentacle greatly increases the strike rate. Snapper can be taken with vertical jigs, and on occasion on wobblers or minnow lures. An erratic retrieve increases strikes. Snapper hooked on lures fight particularly hard and make the effort worthwhile.

Action type: A variety of actions work on snapper and it pays to experiment.

Profile type: Narrow or medium profiles take the most fish.

Lure sizes: The best lures are 4–10 centimetres.

The top ten lures: Kokoda Raptor 40 grams, Kokoda Vector 30 grams, Rio's Live Chrome 20 grams, Intruder Ko-Jack, Halco Wobbler 30 grams, Rapala Magnum CD9, RMG Scorpion 68 DD, Rattlin' Rapala RNR7, River 2 Sea Diver Vib 65, Rapala Sliver 13.

Sooty Grunter

NO. 555: RMG SCORPION 52

Feeding notes: Sooty grunter take a similar niche in tropical waters to rainbow trout in colder climes. They prefer faster running water in rivers and will occupy prime feeding stations at the head of pools or along weed lines. In tropical impoundments, sooty grunter will take up ambush positions near good cover, on weed edges or along drop-offs.

Diet: Sooty grunters take a wide range of foods including shrimps and cherabin, small fish, insects and frogs.

Fishing notes: Sooty grunters are an underrated sport species in tropical fresh water. They take a range of lures readily and fight tenaciously. Sooty grunter do not jump and are only moderate eating, which detract from what should be much wider recognition. It is sad that the giant sooty grunter of Tinaroo have fallen away, although East Coast sooty grunters are larger than their West Coast brethren.

Lure fishing: Sooty grunter will rush out from cover and smack a well presented lure then attempt to duck back to their preferred lie. While they lack the true power of a mangrove jack, they are quality sport. Sooty grunter will take most minnow style lures, small spinnerbaits and spoons.

Action type: A medium wobble, medium sway lure works well, but a good presentation to cover or eddies in current is at least as important as action.

Profile type: Medium profile is a good all-rounder for sooty grunter.

Lure sizes: Medium sized lures of 5–7 centimetres are most successful, although sooty grunter will occasionally take a larger lure intended for barramundi.

The top ten lures: RMG Scorpion 52, Rapala Fat Rap 5, Halco Combat, RMG Scorpion 68, Nilsmaster Invincibles, Storm Hot'N Tot 5, Majik Sprat, Deception Nipper, Mann's 5+, Bennett Baby Merlin.

Snook

Where: Southern ocean waters.

When: All year, better in autumn and early summer.

Gear: Light to medium threadline and baitcasting tackle, small diving lures, pilchard or flesh baits in berley.

Technique: Berley around rocky point and headlands where weed beds are present. Cast lures and lightly weighted baits into the berley stream and retrieve slowly. Troll deep lures off a weighted handline near reef edges.

Feeding notes: Pike and snook are often confused. Snook is the larger species and prefers weedy areas including those further offshore, while pike are often caught from rocks or quite close to shore. Both are pelagic predators, moving through their home ranges feeding mainly on fish. While not a true schooling fish, snook in particular can be taken in reasonable numbers from productive areas and these areas will consistently produce fish.

Diet: Snook and pike mainly feed on fish but they will also take squid, cuttlefish, octopus and crabs.

Fishing notes: Large snook are very highly regarded for its fight and for food, especially in South Australia. The smaller striped pike is often used as live bait for larger predators, while the long-finned pike makes reasonable eating, but is highly regarded as a cut bait. All species have prominent teeth, but a wire trace is rarely used when fishing with lures.

Lure fishing: Pike, and especially snook, are taken by trolling chrome or minnow lures over weedbeds. Areas where weed is near a bombora can be particularly productive. Areas where snook have been taken in the past are always worth a future visit, as they will consistently hold fish. Pike are often taken by casting chrome lures to the back of white water from rocks. Good tailor are often mixed with the pike.

Action type: Flashy spoons and lures with an exaggerated wobble that gives off plenty of flash catch the most fish.

Profile type: A narrow or medium profile best imitates the baitfish that these species feed upon.

Lure sizes: Lures of 4–8 centimetres work best.

The top ten lures: Fishfighter Toby 14 gram, Halco Wobbler 10 gram, Halco Twisty 20 gram, Wonder Spoon 14 gram,Wonder Tubular 28 gram, Halco Hexagon Sparkler 10 gram, Rapala Magnum Mag-9, Rapala Sliver 13, Rapala Shad Rap Shallow 8, Pegron Minnow.

NO. 180 : THE FISHFIGHTER TOBY 14 GRAM

Hand spool and heavy cord lead-line. Note sinkers crimped onto line at intervals.

Minnow type lure.

Pilchard on ganged hooks for snook.

Tarpon

Where: This tropical freshwater fish, also ranges into saline water around estuaries and coastal bays. Look for them wherever rivers deepen off shallow sand or mud banks, where lily pads and bankside grasses encroach on the water and around corners and eddies where currents strike trees and rock bars. They are also available over shallow coastal flats, where they tend to stick close to mangrove fringes, drainage points and rubble and marl bottom.

When: Year round with peaks in activity around spring to summer Gear: Light to moderate spin, baitcast and fly tackle, bibbed minnows, poppers, rubber tail jigs, saltwater flies and baits of whitebait, whole or peeled prawns, shiny fish strips or tiny live baitfish rigged on appropriately small hooks.

Technique: In freshwater lagoons and billabongs, look for surface rings indicating fish coming up to gulp air. Do not fish for them on the surface in this situation though, use small white rubber tail jigs and drop them to the bottom and retrieve with a short jerking motion. Cast poppers and bibbed minnows toward river corners and snags, and cast flies in and around shallow mangrove-lined coastal flats.

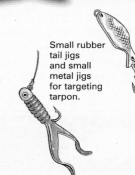

Small rubber tail jigs and small metal jigs for targeting tarpon.

Tusk fish

Where: Tropical reef and inshore waters.

When: Year round.

Gear: Handlines for bait fishing, medium spin and baitcast outfits for lure casting or trolling. Will take lures such as bibbed minnows, leadhead jigs tipped with bait, soft plastics and metal jigs. Baits can be any cut fish strips, or even some shellfish.

Technique: Troll over reef edges, alongside drop offs, or near coral bommies. Bait fish over same country or where a lagoon or cay deepens into the ocean proper.

Heavy duty lure for trolling along reef edges.

Running sinker rig for fishing near bommies and reefs.

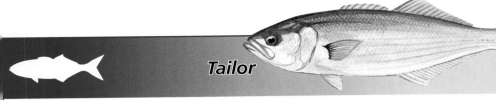

Tailor

Where: Principally a fish of the east and west coast in the southern half of Australia, tailor occur in Victoria, South Australia and Tasmania but in nowhere near the numbers, or reaching the same sizes as east and west coast fish. They favour inshore reefs, wash areas of offshore islands, bomboras, headlands and rocky coastlines. They also enter and feed in the surf, will prowl through estuaries and bays and, on occasion, can intrude into estuaries as far as the brackish water interchange area.

When: Year round but peak along the NSW coast from Easter to late winter with a run of smaller fish throughout summer. In southern Queensland, the run peaks with a renowned spawning aggregation off Fraser Island from about August through November. There is a closed season around this time on Fraser Island and you should check for exact dates before fishing. Similar seasonal timing applies to west coast areas at similar latitudes.

Gear: Spin, baitcast and sidecast tackle. Flyfishing gear is adequate for most fish but terrain and conditions can make it difficult to fish fly land-based. Overhead tackle is really overkill on these fish, except when they get up into their optimum sizes, which can exceed 5 kg and even top 10 kg in some quarters, such as the Steep Point region of Western Australia. Wire traces are advisable if not essential on small tailor but the bigger fish demand the same respect as mackerel, being capable of shearing through the heaviest nylon with ease. For the same reason, whole fish baits rigged on ganged hooks are the usual approach. Tailor take almost any lure you can imagine, and are hard on them too, often stripping paint, shredding tails and even biting clean through some lightly built models.

Technique: Cast from ocean rocks and surf beaches, or from boats toward breaking water or surface feeding fish. Troll past reefs and bomboras, drop jigs down to them in deep water and fish baits as floaters or on the bottom. Tailor are very willing and cooperative biters.

Feeding notes: A voracious schooling pelagic species, the tailor is named after its capacity to cut through a bait like a tailor's shears. Tailor are well known for their capacity to gorge themselves to the point of regurgitating before continuing to feed. Juveniles are found in estuaries, adults are found along beaches or around white water on inshore bomboras or reefs. The largest tailor are found at Fraser Island in Queensland and Shark Bay in WA.

Diet: Tailor feed almost exclusively on fish but will also take squid and have been taken on prawns or pipi baits.

Fishing notes: The larger the tailor, the smaller the school and it is possible to work a school of tailor by keeping a hooked fish in the water at all times. Berley helps to keep tailor in a feeding mood and to remain in the vicinity. Tailor bite best at dusk and dawn, with some excellent fish being taken at night, when they are more likely to be deep and can be taken on baits and lures intended for mulloway.

Lure fishing: Lures that are cast or trolled into white water at the edges of gutters on beaches, rock washes or near shore bomboras take by far the most tailor. In recent years poppers have come into their own, replacing traditional slice type lures such as the Tailor 'Ticer as the prime tailor lure. Poppers should be cast and retrieved as quickly as possible to entice a strike. Tailor are aggressive and will take large lures. The sharp teeth of a tailor can make short work of wooden lures and plastic is therefore more durable and popular.

Action type: Poppers, metal wobbling lures and tight and medium wobble lures are successful.

Profile type: Narrow or near narrow profiles best imitate the prime baitfish which are the prey of tailor.

Lure sizes: Best lures are 4–15 centimetres.

The top ten lures: Kingfisher Mini Turbo, Killalure K9 Popper, Lively Lures Kingfisher Super Blooper, Mustang Lures Bo-Bo, Cotton Cordell Pencil Popper, Halco Wobbler 30 gram, Halco Twisty 30 gram, Fishfighter Toby 14 gram, Wonder Pilchard 15 gram, Lively Lures Blue Pilly.

Metal 'slug' type lure for tailor rigged on a wire trace.

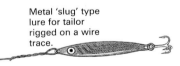

Pilchard on three ganged hooks for tailor.

Tailor surf rig with three ganged hooks on heat-weld wire trace.

Trevalla, Deep sea

Where: Deep ocean waters beyond the Continental Shelf south from Sydney around the bottom of Australia to Perth.

When: All year.

Gear: Heavy handlines, deck winches, deep water rigs, flesh baits, heavy sinkers.

Technique: Find concentrations of fish over deep sea mounts and fish baits down to them.

Paternoster rig for deep or rough water.

Trevally, Golden

Where: Estuaries, tidal flats and beaches of northern Australia, occasionally caught from ocean rocks as far south as Wollongong on the east Coast and Denmark in Western Australia.

When: Year round, rarely found southward of Brisbane except in summer.

Gear: Spin, baitcast and fly tackle, bibbed lures, metal jigs, soft plastics, flies, baits of prawn and fish.

Technique: Cast to schooling fish over shallow sand flats, spin off ocean rocks, fly fish to flats feeders.

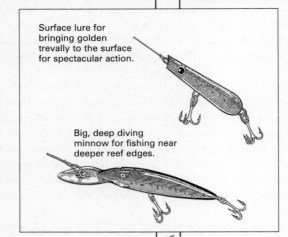

Surface lure for bringing golden trevally to the surface for spectacular action.

Big, deep diving minnow for fishing near deeper reef edges.

Trevally, Giant

Where: Reefs, ocean rocks and estuaries from tropical Australia south to Rottnest Island in Western Australia and Wollongong in NSW.

When: Year round, peak in summer in southern waters.

Gear: Strong spin and casting tackle, minnows, jigs, poppers, live baits, cut fish baits.

Technique: Troll reef and bommies, cast to (or from) coastal rocks, troll or cast near estuary breakwalls.

Trevally, Silver

Where: East coast, extending south to the west coast

When: All year

Gear: Light to medium threadline tackle and baitcasting outfits, flesh baits, small lures

Technique: Fish baits and lures close to structure such as bridges, rocky outcrops and weed beds.

THE DEFINITIVE LURE

NO. 86 : MAL FLORENCE'S MASTA POPPER

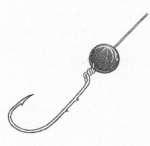

Running sinker rig – suits silver trevally in estuaries and bays and over shallow reef.

Feeding notes: The trevally category covers a huge range of lure munching and very hard fighting species including giant trevally, silver, golden, brassy, and bigeye trevally. Trevally are either ambush feeders or opportunistic feeders. The trevally that are ambush feeders frequently use the location relative to the tide to bring food to them. They will hang behind a rock or at the edge of a drop-off. This circumstance and location can vary depending upon the state of the tide. If the tide is wrong, trevally can sometimes be seen in large numbers but refuse to respond to even the best presented lure. Silver and golden trevally can be more opportunistic, cruising a home range picking up food. Most trevally are schooling fish, and competition within the school means that several fish will shoulder each other out of the way to get the lure. Similarly, other trevally will follow a hooked fish, often trying to eat the lure from the fish you have on. This frequently leads to multiple hook-ups or two fish on the same lure. Many species can be found at the edge of very strong tidal currents or at the edge of white water on bomboras or shore breaks.

Diet: Trevally eat a variety of foods and species can vary in their preferences. Most trevally eat fish, prawns, shrimp, crabs, squid and shellfish. Golden and silver trevally eat more crustaceans, while giant trevally, brassy and bigeye trevally eat more fish.

Fishing notes: Pound for pound, trevally are amongst the strongest fighters. However, most trevally do not fight as dirty as kingfish, or as close to cover as mangrove jacks so they aren't the top of the sportfishing totem. However, a 30 kilogram giant trevally is one of the toughest propositions on a lure, irrespective of the tackle. Trevally take poppers and chrome wobbler lures particularly well, but can also be enticed on spinnerbaits and minnow lures. Many lures, especially those from North America, will need to have stronger hooks and split rings fitted.

Lure fishing: Silver trevally can be taken by berleying up near an inshore reef, or as juveniles in harbours or estuaries. They will take jigs and chrome lures when in the mood. Other trevally are much more consistent lure takers. Most trevally do not have huge mouths, so smaller lures take smaller fish, while larger lures, especially poppers can evoke a strike in larger trevally.

Action type: Poppers and bright flashy wobbling spoons work well. Profile type: Narrow and medium profiles are recommended. Lure sizes: Tailor the size of the lure to the expected size of the fish, 4–13 centimetre lures work best.

The top ten lures: Mal Florence's Masta Popper, Kingfisher Mini Turbo, Ambush Lures Ranger 90, Lively Lures Kingfisher Barra, Halco Wobbler 30 gram, Halco Twisty 30 gram, Fishfighter Toby 20 gram, Wonder Pilchard 15 gram, Halco Sparkler 40 gram, Rapala Magnum CD11.

Trout, Coral

NO. 856 : RAPALA MAGNUM CD11.

Feeding notes: Coral trout are ambush feeders. As their name suggests, they have a close association with coral reefs and may inhabit a cave or have a small range around prime habitat where food comes to them. It is hard to envisage a fish that better embodies the characteristics of prestige, fight and eating qualities than the coral trout. Coral trout are generally loners. Although a number of coral trout may be found in a small area, there is usually a well defined pecking order. Coral trout, especially large specimens, have been implicated in ciguatera poisoning in Queensland. Coral trout are susceptible to overfishing, with spear fishing and the live fish trade in Queensland being implicated.

Diet: Coral trout primarily eat fish, but they will also take prawns, shrimp, crabs, squid, lobsters and shellfish.

Fishing notes: Coral trout are closely associated with reef cover and it is important to fish closely enough to the reef to get a strike but not so close that you snag on the sharp reef or that the fish has an easy run to snag up the unwary. Coral trout are strong and perfectly capable of diving back into the reef.

Lure fishing: While a few coral trout are taken on poppers, the majority are taken on diving lures. The most popular method is to troll deep divers near reefs or especially in the channels between reefs. Casting to reef edges is also successful.

Action type: A tight or medium wobble and sway works best.

Profile type: Most coral trout lures are narrow minnow imitations.

Lure sizes: Lures of 7–15 centimetres get results.

The top ten lures: Rapala Magnum CD11, Halco Laser Pro 125 DD, Rapala Magnum CD14, Halco 150 XDD Crazy Deep, Nilsmaster Invincible 15, Nomad 120, Bomber Long A Magnum, Storm Saltwater Thunderstick, Predatek Viper 150, Yo-Zuri Hydro Squirt.

Trout, Brown

NO. 366: RAPALA COUNTDOWN CD5

Where: Alpine streams and dams in NSW, Victoria, Tasmania, South Australia and Lower Western Australia. Look for places in streams where current is deflected and depth changes occur. In lakes, work shallow margins, points, weed beds and around drowned tree-lines.

When: Year round, check season closures for each state. Fish sometimes feed vigorously at dawn and dusk or when insect hatches occur.

Gear: Light spin tackle, fly fishing gear, lures, flies and baits such as worms, mudeyes, crickets and grasshoppers.

Technique: Wade or bank cast streams. In dams, troll or fish from bank.

Feeding notes: Brown trout are frequently closely cover-associated during the day, with larger specimens taking the preferred lies. When feeding from dusk to dawn, brown trout are cruising opportunistic feeders.

Diet: Brown trout take a wide range of food items. However, brown trout will selectively feed on yabbies, shrimp, mudeyes or terrestrial insects. Large brown trout may target larger minnows, redfin or juvenile trout. They will also take worms, grubs, snails and in spite of their reputation for dietary discernment, many are taken on maggots or corn by anglers using coarse angling techniques.

Quill float rig for fishing in lakes for trout.

Bubble float rig for fishing mudeyes for trout.

Bladed spinners work by sonic and visual attraction.

Baitdrifting rig for live grasshoppers and crickets.

Small diving plugs are best rigged with a loop knot.

Fishing notes: Brown trout have a reputation as being harder to catch than rainbow trout and fight more doggedly. Brown trout generally prefer deeper, slower water or deep holes.

Lure fishing: A wide range of lures and styles attracts brown trout. They prefer more subdued lures and placement and depth are extremely important, especially to take large fish.

Action type: Brown trout can be taken on spinners, or lures with a shimmy or wide wobble. Ironically, lures with a medium sway and/or wobble seem to be less successful.

Profile type: The majority of the most popular trout lures have a narrow profile. However, Flatfish and Kwikfish type lures have a broader profile and an exaggerated action.

Lure sizes: Small to medium sized lures work best for brown trout. Most lures up to 7 centimetres will work well. Large brown trout can be tempted with larger sizes of popular lures, although many anglers are afraid to deviate from those popular lures.

The top ten lures: Rapala Countdown CD5, Mepps or Blue Fox #2, X4 Flatfish, Rebel Crawfish, Rapala Husky Jerk 6, McGrath Minnow, Tillins Cobra, Pegron Minnow, Worden's Rooster Tail, Tasmanian Devil 13 gram.

Trout, Brook

Feeding notes: The brook trout traditionally favours small pristine streams where they hold tight to woody cover or undercut banks in holes. In Australia, brook trout are only caught in Lake Jindabyne in a few places and must be viewed as an expensive novelty to produce.

Diet: Brook trout feed mainly on terrestrial insects and their aquatic larvae. They will also take frogs, shrimp, small minnows and worms.

Fishing notes: Brook trout are either taken while trolling, mainly for brown trout, or in the Thredbo River, and by casting small lures. Brook trout are the most beautiful of the trout species found in Australia.

Lure fishing: Brook trout are generally an incidental capture and methods for rainbow and brown trout, especially the use of downriggers, work well.

Action type: Spinners and narrow wobble lures are most highly regarded.

Profile type: Narrow profile lures work best.

Lure sizes: Small to medium sized lures work best for rainbow trout. Most lures up to 7 centimetres will work well, although many lures of 5 centimetres or less are among the top 10. There are occasions when a CD11 or Rapala Original Minnow 11 will work for larger fish.

The top ten lures: Size 2 Blue Fox, small Tasmanian Devil, Rapala Countdown CD5, Predatek Micro Min, Kwikfish K7, Halco Laser Pro 45, Rapala Countdown CD3, Tillins King Cobra, Rebel Crawfish, Worden's Rooster Tail.

NO.207: BLUE FOX SIZE 2

Trout, Rainbow

NO.234: SIZE 3 BLUE FOX:

Where: Alpine freshwater streams and lakes from New England, Central Tablelands and Snowy Mountains in NSW, various highland rivers and lakes in Victoria, some streams in South Australia and southwest Western Australia. Widely distributed throughout Tasmania. Look for places in streams where current is deflected and depth changes occur. In lakes, work shallow margins, points, weed beds and around drowned tree-lines.

When: Most lakes are open year round but seasonal closures affect streams. Check local fishing regulations.

Gear: Light spin tackle, fly fishing gear, lures, flies and baits such as worms, mudeyes, crickets and grasshoppers.

Technique: Wade or bank cast streams. In dams, troll or fish from bank.

Feeding notes: Rainbow trout are cruising, opportunistic feeders and may tend to concentrate in numbers near identified food sources. They may patrol and feed in a set beat. Rainbow trout prefer faster water in riffles or at the heads of pools in rivers.

Diet: They eat a wide range of food items including minnows, insects and their aquatic larvae, worms, snails, water fleas, and yabbies. Stocked fish can often be taken on corn, maggots or dog food.

Fishing notes: Rainbow trout are more aggressive than brown trout and so widely considered easier to catch. However, they fight more spectacularly with jumps and stronger runs.

Lure fishing: A wide range of lures and styles attracts rainbow trout. Rainbows can prefer some flash or bright colour with fluorescent orange or red being popular especially close to spawning season.

Action type: Rainbow trout can be taken on spinners or lures with a shimmy or wide wobble. Surface lures are rarely successful. This diversity means that a wide range of lures is suitable for rainbow trout.

Profile type: The majority of trout lures have a narrow profile. Flatfish and Kwikfish type lures that are also successful have a broader profile. In a number of dams where there are large numbers of goldfish, a more robust profile in smaller sized lures can work well.

Lure sizes: Small to medium sized lures work best for rainbow trout. Most lures up to 7 centimetres will work well, although many lures of 5 centimetres or less are among the top 10. There are occasions when a Rapala Countdown CD11 or Rapala Original Minnow 11 will work for larger fish.

The top ten lures: Size 3 Blue Fox spinner, small Tasmanian Devil, Rapala Countdown CD5, X4 Flatfish, Tilsan Minnow, Halco Laser Pro 45, Rapala Countdown CD3, Tillins Cobra, Pegron Minnow, Worden's Rooster tail.

Quill float rig for fishing in lakes for trout.

Baitdrifting rig for live grasshoppers and crickets.

Bubble float rig for fishing mudeyes for trout.

Bladed spinners work by sonic and visual attraction.

Small diving plugs are best rigged with a loop knot.

Where: Inshore coastal waters and reef areas, as well as close in to ocean rock platforms, throughout the tropics and as far south as Geographe Bay in Western Australia and Eden in NSW.

When: Year round in the north and principally spring through autumn in the southern states. Often bites around tide changes.

Gear: Overhead tackle from ocean rocks, heavy spin tackle or saltwater fly gear from boats. Metal slug lures, poppers, saltwater flies, occasionally takes strip baits, often takes live baits fished from the rocks.

Technique: Surface feeding schools are targeted with spinning or saltwater fly tackle and usually from boats in large bays. Larger, less obvious fish are live baited from the rocks or trolled for from gamefishing boats.

Where: In shore reefs, headlands and large estuarine bays in south of range (Cape Leeuwin Western Australia and Merimbula in NSW) but will also shoal in large numbers around coral reefs and islands some distance offshore in Queensland and northern Western Australia.

When: Year round in the north, southern Queensland and Western Australia and NSW see semi-regular appearances of shoals of mackerel tuna in winter and spring.

Gear: Light overhead and light to medium spin and fly tackle. Small metal slugs are used to imitate the usually small baitfish prey and squid, larger minnows and poppers are used when they are feeding on larger prey. They will also take live baits from boats or the ocean rocks.

Technique: Cast to surface shoaling fish with slugs, poppers or saltwater flies, drop jigs down to fish on sounder or troll minnows and plastic squid around headlands, reefs and islands.

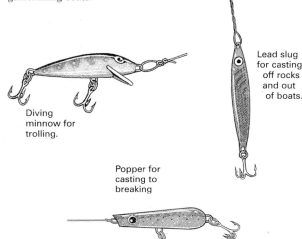

Diving minnow for trolling.

Lead slug for casting off rocks and out of boats.

Popper for casting to breaking

Diving minnow for trolling.

Lead slug for casting off rocks and out of boats.

Popper for casting to breaking schools.

NO. 1000: RAPALA MAGNUM CD14

Feeding notes: The variety of tuna species are pelagic and cruise widely in search of food. This category covers a range of species from yellowfin tuna, bigeye and southern bluefin tuna to the smaller mackerel tuna, frigate tuna and bonito. Many tuna species form schools and can work co-operatively to herd up baitfish before predating upon them. The schools are usually of similar sized fish, but there can be larger fish below the smaller tuna. When on the surface, tuna will attract large numbers of feeding birds, which can be seen from quite a distance. Other tuna just cruise the blue waters, hold above underwater features or near FADs. Bonito in particular can be caught close inshore, although rock fishing with lures or live baits for larger tuna is a tough challenge.

Diet: Tuna mainly feed on fish but also feed on squid and cuttlefish.

Fishing notes: Tuna take a wide range of lures including diving minnows, slice lures, bibless minnows or resin headed pusher type lures in the smaller sizes. The lack of teeth in tuna (except the dogtooth, which is a true bluewater or offshore species) makes the use of wooden lures much more acceptable.

Lure fishing: Tuna are either taken by trolling near current lines, reef drop-offs or around bait schools or by casting chrome lures to surface feeding fish. When trolling blue water or near current lines, tuna will frequently be caught with marlin, mahi mahi, wahoo or Spanish mackerel. Tuna will take lures trolled at 2–10 knots, with a distinct preference for speeds around 4–5 knots. Anglers can take bonito casting minnow lures from shore and boat or by casting chrome lures to feeding schools of tuna. On occasions, frigate and mackerel tuna can be extremely size selective and will only take very small bullet type lures. On other occasions, they will only take Christmas tree style lures (not reviewed for this book).

Action type: Lures must be able to tolerate troll speeds of 3–7 knots. Quality lures will hold together at this speed. Generally, minnows with a narrow wobble, narrow sway work best. In addition, a shimmy from bibless minnows and sliced lures is a first rate choice.

Profile type: A narrow or very narrow profile to imitate bait species such as pilchards is recommended. However, bibless minnows with a broader profile also work well, especially for larger tuna.

Lure sizes: Lures of 3–25 centimetres will cover the wide range of tuna species.

The top ten lures: Rapala Countdown CD14, Halco Laser Pro 160 DD, Halco Trembler 110, Rapala Countdown CD18, Yo-Zuri Hydro Magnum, Storm Deep Thunderstick, Hawk Pilchard 30 gram, Halco Laser Pro 160 STD, Bomber Long A Magnum, Halco Wobbler 30 gram.

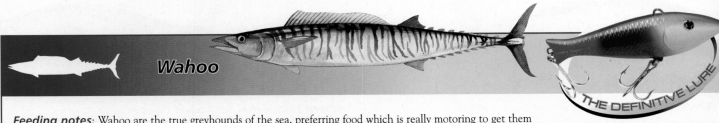

Wahoo

NO. 961: HALCO GIANT TREMBLER

Feeding notes: Wahoo are the true greyhounds of the sea, preferring food which is really motoring to get them excited. They are a true pelagic species that will chase down baitfish and use their razor sharp teeth to good effect. Wahoo have a bad reputation with marlin fishers for biting through skip baits, taking the skirts off pusher lures or simply biting through a monofilament trace intended for beaked species.

Diet: Wahoo feed on a variety of fish species and will also feed on squid.

Fishing notes: The wahoo takes a wide range of lures including diving minnows, slice lures, bibless minnows or resin headed pusher type lures intended for marlin or sailfish.

Lure fishing: Most wahoo are taken by trolling near current lines, reef drop-offs or around bait schools. Wahoo are generally not common enough to be specifically targeted, but are frequently encountered when trolling for marlin, mahi mahi or Spanish mackerel. They will take lures trolled at 2–10 knots, with a distinct preference for speeds above 5 knots. The sharp teeth of the wahoo make a wire trace essential when they are around. Trolling sliced lures can produce excellent fishing, especially if small wahoo are around. The teeth can also damage expensive wooden lures. Anglers rarely take wahoo by casting lures from headlands with deep water nearby, such as Steep Point in Western Australia.

Action type: Lures must be able to tolerate troll speeds from 3–10 knots. At this speed, minnows with a narrow wobble, narrow sway work best. In addition, a shimmy from bibless minnows and sliced lures is a first rate choice.

Profile type: Generally use a narrow profile to imitate bait species such as pilchards however, bibless minnows with a broader profile can work well.

Lure sizes: A wide range of sizes will work with size selection determined by the size of the predominate forage species in the vicinity. As a good rule of thumb, lures of 12–25 centimetres will cover a range of species and options, including wahoo.

The top ten lures: Halco Giant Trembler, Halco Trembler 110, Halco Laser Pro 160 DD, Mal Florence Masta Blasta, Rapala Magnum CD18, Yo-Zuri Hydro Magnum, Rapala Magnum CD22, Halco Laser Pro 160 STD, Bomber Long A Magnum, Halco Hex Sparkler 60 gram.

Whiting (sand)   (school)

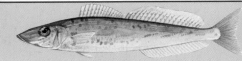

Where: Cape York in Queensland, through NSW and to Lakes Entrance in Victoria. Some parts of eastern Tasmania. One of seven species of whiting commonly caught by anglers, the sand whiting prefers clean sandy bottom, interspersed with weed and occasional low rubble and reef. It enters the surf freely and is a mainstay of summer beach anglers.

When: Year round, with definite peaks in summer through to Easter. Usually bites best when the tide is running either way. Is best fished over shallow and flats early to mid-morning and mid afternoon to nightfall.

Gear: Light handlines or rod and reel combos. Threadline tackle suits the light casting weights best. Fly tackle will work but approaches and getting the fish to bite are critical and demanding. Best baits are live nippers, tiny crabs, squirt worms, blood worms, beach worms and pipis, peeled prawn segments, very thin strips of fish flesh with the skin attached and skinned, tenderised squid strips. Running sinker rigs are popular, as are Paternoster rigs in southern states. Hooks should be small gaped and long shanked and lead should be just enough to get the baits down into the feeding zone, which is a few centimetres above the bottom. Whiting will also take small bibbed minnow lures, tiny rubber tail jigs and short, sparsely dressed weighted flies.

Technique: Cast and retrieve baits or lures over sand flats and through deeper holes. Anchor and feed long trace baits out in tidal runs of estuary channels, or drift over mixed sand and weed bottom with baits out on a weighted rig.

Where: Offshore areas in Moreton Bay Queensland, throughout NSW and Victoria to Western Port Bay, northern Tasmania (eastern school whiting). A similar species, (the western school whiting) in restricted in its distribution between Geographe Bay and Coral Bay Western Australia. Various other deep sea whiting are of less interest to anglers, but the highly regarded and much larger King George whiting is found from Jervis Bay in NSW, throughout Victoria and north-east Tasmania, South Australia and in Western Australia as far north as Jurien Bay.

When: Year round to some degree, but best in spring and summer.

Gear: Handlines or threadline and centrepin reels on short stout rods. Heavy sinkers rigged as Paternosters with several droppers and cut fish baits.

Technique: Same drifting technique as for sand flathead and often caught as bycatch when doing so.

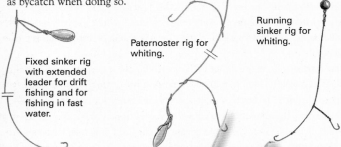

Fixed sinker rig with extended leader for drift fishing and for fishing in fast water.

Paternoster rig for whiting.

Running sinker rig for whiting.

Yabby, Freshwater

Where: Freshwater rivers and dams from coastal plains to alpine areas. Australia wide, various species.

When: Best spring through to autumn.

Gear: Yabby traps, wire scoops, short handlines tied to pieces of meat

Technique: Bait traps set in slow-flow areas or narrow lake bays. Fish small dams with handlines and meat.

CHAPTER SIX

HANDY GUIDES

BASIC HOOK GUIDE

The following are some suggested hook sizes for species. Hook size is governed by bait size, not by the size of the fish you are after. You may want to adjust the size or type of hook being used depending on bait. For live baiting the thickness of the shank is important, which is why Tuna Circles are not recommended, however they have a growing following among anglers fishing fillets and those trolling skip baits.

Species	Hook Size	Hook Style	Bait
Whiting	No. 6–8	long shank hooks	squid, pippies
Snapper	3/0–6/0	Suicide or Octopus	pilchards, squid
Flathead	1/0–3/0	Suicide or Octopus	whitebait, squid
Salmon	2/0–4/0	Suicide or long shank	whitebait, pippies
Mulloway	4/0 –6/0	Suicide or Octopus	
Tailor	2/0 –4/0	long shanked and ganged	
Estuary perch	No. 4 No. 10 No. 6 – 8	Baitholder Baitholder Baitholder	shrimp, bass yabbies; smelt/minnow; worms
Trout	No. 14 No. 10	Suicide or long shank Suicide or long shank	mudeyes; straight shanked smelt and minnow;
Murray cod	No. 4 – 2/0	long shank	bardi grubs, worms and yabbies
Yellowbelly	No. 4 – 2/0	long shank	bardi grubs, worms and yabbies
Tuna	6/0 to 9/0	Suicide or Octopus	
Sharks	2X strong; 4/0–8/0 small sharks; 14/0 for big denizens.		
Barracouta	3/0 to 4/0	long shank	
Barramundi	2/0 to 6/0	Suicide or Octopus	
Carp	No. 4 – 6 No. 10 as big as No. 2		corn, worms, shrimp; maggots; dough baits and cheese.
Bream	No. 4– 8	Baitholder pattern	
Elephant fish	2/0–4/0	Suicide or Octopus pattern	
Yellowtail kingfish	6/0–8/0		depending on bait size

WEIGH YOUR FISH WITH A RULER

Fish Biologists have collected vast quantities of length and weight data from a variety of fish species. This has enabled length and weight relationships to be calculated for some fish species which can be used to estimate weight of a fish by measuring its length. Please note that these figures are estimates only and individual fish weight will vary depending on age, sex, season and recent feeding activity.

MEASURING LENGTH

In some of the conversion tables, fork length measurements have been used. Fork length is measured from the snout to the fork of the tail. Total length is measured from the snout to the tip of the tail.

Remember: Legal lengths (total lengths) are measured from the point of the snout to the tip of the tail.

The data was sourced from: *http://www.fisheries.nsw.gov.au/rec/gen/weigh.htm* and is subject to their copyright.

SPECIES: **MURRAY COD**
Maccullochella peelii peelii

Total Length (cm)	Weight (kg)	Total Length (cm)	Weight (kg)
40	1.1	72	7.6
42	1.3	74	8.3
44	1.5	76	9
46	1.8	78	9.8
48	2	80	10.7
50	2.3	82	11.6
52	2.6	84	12.5
54	3	86	13.5
56	3.3	88	14.6
58	3.7	90	15.7
60	4.2	92	16.8
62	4.6	94	18
64	5.2	96	19.3
66	5.7	98	20.7
68	6.3	100	22.1
70	6.9		

SPECIES: **AUSTRALIAN BASS**
Macquaria novemaculeata

Please note: The following table has fork length measurements. Legal lengths are total lengths and are measured from the point of the snout to the tip of the tail.

Fork Length (cm)	Weight (kg)	Fork Length (cm)	Weight (kg)
25	0.3	43	1.6
26	0.3	44	1.7
27	0.4	45	1.8
28	0.4	46	1.9
29	0.5	47	2
30	0.5	48	2.2
31	0.6	49	2.3
32	0.6	50	2.5
33	0.7	51	2.6
34	0.8	52	2.8
35	0.8	53	2.9
36	0.9	54	3.1
37	1	55	3.3
38	1.1	56	3.5
39	1.2	57	3.7
40	1.3	58	3.9
41	1.3	59	4.1

Reference: Harris, J. H. 1987. Growth of Australian bass, Macquaria novemaculeata (Perciformes, Perchthyidae), in the Sydney basin. Australian Journal of Marine and Freshwater Research 38:351-361.

Courtesy of U.S. Fish & Wildlife Service

Species: **TROUT**
Salmo trutta, Oncorhynchus mykiss, Salvelinus fontinalis

Total Length (inches)	Brown Weight (pounds)	Rainbow Weight (pounds)	Brook Weight (pounds)
7	0.14	0.15	0.13
8	0.22	0.22	0.21
9	0.29	0.29	0.29
10	0.40	0.38	0.39
11	0.52	0.51	0.53
12	0.67	0.65	0.69
13	0.83	0.88	1.00
14	1.06	1.11	1.33
15	1.33	1.31	1.87
16	1.65	1.62	2.14
17	1.94	1.90	2.59
18	2.35	2.13	3.19
19	2.83	2.60	
20	3.39	3.45	
21	3.94	3.63	
22	4.26	3.80	
23	4.92		
24	5.70		
25	5.73		
26	5.95		
27	6.19		

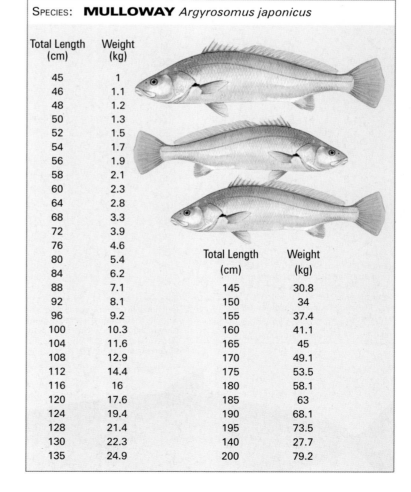

Species: **MULLOWAY** *Argyrosomus japonicus*

Total Length (cm)	Weight (kg)
45	1
46	1.1
48	1.2
50	1.3
52	1.5
54	1.7
56	1.9
58	2.1
60	2.3
64	2.8
68	3.3
72	3.9
76	4.6
80	5.4
84	6.2
88	7.1
92	8.1
96	9.2
100	10.3
104	11.6
108	12.9
112	14.4
116	16
120	17.6
124	19.4
128	21.4
130	22.3
135	24.9

Total Length (cm)	Weight (kg)
145	30.8
150	34
155	37.4
160	41.1
165	45
170	49.1
175	53.5
180	58.1
185	63
190	68.1
195	73.5
140	27.7
200	79.2

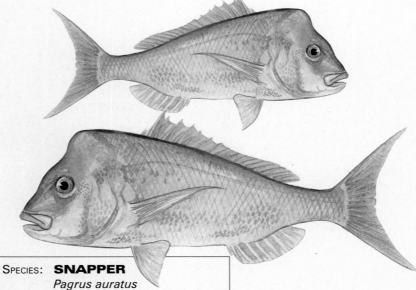

SPECIES: **YELLOWFIN BREAM**
Acanthopagrus australis

Please note: The following table has fork length measurements. Legal lengths are total lengths and are measured from the point of the snout to the tip of the tail.

Fork Length (cm)	Weight (kg)	Fork Length (cm)	Weight (kg)
25	0.4	48	2.7
26	0.4	49	2.9
27	0.5	50	3.1
28	0.5	51	3.2
29	0.6	52	3.4
30	0.7	53	3.6
31	0.7	54	3.8
32	0.8	55	4.1
33	0.9	56	4.3
34	1	57	4.5
35	1	58	4.8
36	1.1	59	5.1
37	1.2	60	5.3
38	1.3	61	5.5
39	1.5	62	5.8
40	1.6	63	6.1
41	1.7	64	6.4
42	1.8	65	6.7
43	1.9	66	7.1
44	2.1	67	7.3
45	2.2	68	7.7
46	2.4	69	8
47	2.5	70	8.4

Reference: Steffe, A.S., Murphy, J.J., Chapman, D.J., Tarlinton, B.E. and Grinberg, A.? 1996. An assessment of the impact of offshore recreational fishing in NSW? waters on the management of commercial fisheries. FRDC Project no. 94/053.? Publishers, Fisheries Research Institute, NSW Fisheries. 139pp.

SPECIES: **SNAPPER**
Pagrus auratus

Please note: The following table has fork length measurements. Legal lengths are total lengths and are measured from the point of the snout to the tip of the tail.

Fork Length (cm)	Weight (kg)	Fork Length (cm)	Weight (kg)
30	0.6	62	4.5
31	0.7	64	4.9
32	0.7	66	5.4
33	0.8	68	5.8
34	0.9	70	6.3
35	0.9	72	6.9
36	1	74	7.4
37	1.1	76	8
38	1.2	78	8.6
39	1.3	80	9.2
40	1.3	82	9.8
42	1.5	84	10.5
44	1.7	86	11.2
46	2	88	12
48	2.2	90	12.7
50	2.5	92	13.5
52	2.8	94	14.4
54	3.1	96	15.2
56	3.4	98	16.1
58	3.8	100	17.1
60	4.1		

Reference: Moran M. J. and C. Burton. 1990. Relationships among partial and whole lengths and weights for Western Australian pink snapper Chrysophys auratus (Sparidae). Fisheries Department of Western Australia, Fisheries Research Report No. 89.

SPECIES: **YELLOWTAIL KINGFISH**
Seriola lalandi

Please note: The following table has fork length measurements. Legal lengths are total lengths and are measured from the point of the snout to the tip of the tail.

Fork Length (cm)	Weight (kg)	Fork Length (cm)	Weight (kg)
60	2.8	94	10.6
61	2.9	96	11.3
62	3	98	12
63	3.2	100	12.8
64	3.4	105	14.8
65	3.5	110	17
66	3.7	115	19.4
67	3.8	120	22
68	4	125	24.9
69	4.2	130	28
70	4.4	135	31.4
71	4.6	140	35
72	4.8	145	38.9
73	5	150	43
74	5.2	155	47.5
76	5.6	160	52
78	6.1	165	57.3
80	6.5	170	62.6
82	7	175	68.3
84	7.6	180	74.3
86	8.1	185	80.7
88	8.7	190	87.4
90	9.3	195	94.5
92	9.9	200	101.9

Reference: Stewart, J., D. J. Ferrell, B. van der Walt, D. Johnson,and M. Lowry. 2002.? Assessment of length and age composition of commercial kingfish landings. Final report to the Fisheries Research and Development Corporation, Project No. 97/126. NSW Fisheries, Cronulla.

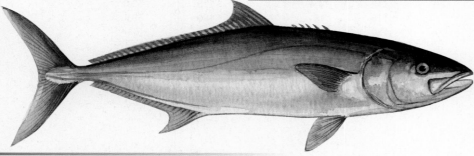

FRESHWATER FISH

NATIVE FISH	RANGE C	RANGE F	MOST ACTIVE C	MOST ACTIVE F	SPAWNING C	SPAWNING F
Australian Bass	2–36	36–97	15–25	60–78	14–20	58–69
Barramundi	20–40	69–105	24–29	77–85	25–30	78–86
Estuary Perch	10–25	50–78	15–22	60–72	14.5–16	58–61
Clarence River Cod	Assumed to be the same as Murray Cod					
Golden Perch	4–37	40–100	14–27	58–82	23–26	74–79
Gulf Saratoga	7–40	45–105	24–29	77–85	30	86
Macquarie Perch	4–28	40–83	10–17	50–63	14–20	58–69
Murray Cod	2–34	36–94	16–25	61–78	17–22	63–72
River Blackfish	0–28	32–83	15–23	60–74	16	61
Southern Saratoga	7–40	45–105	25–31	20–88	20–23	63–74
Silver Perch	4–38	40–101	14–26	58–79	24–27	77–82
2-Spined Blackfish	0–25	32–78	15–23	60–74	16	61
Trout Cod	4–28	40–83	13–19	56–67	15–21	60–70
INTRODUCED SPECIES						
Atlantic Salmon	3–25	37–78	10–18	50–65	7–10	45–50
Brook Trout	0–25	32–78	10–15	50–60	7–12	45–55
Brown Trout	3–25	37–78	13–20	56–69	7–10	45–50
Chinook Salmon	3–25	37–78	10–18	50–65	7–10	45–50
European Carp	0–41	32–106	15–32	60–90		
Redfin	0–36	32–98	8–27	47–82	10–20	50–69
Rainbow Trout	3–25	37–78	10–18	50–65	7–10	45–50
Roach	0–38	32–101	8–25	47–78	15	60
Tench	0–39	32–102	20–26	69–79	16	61

SALTWATER FISH

Water temperature has less of an effect on saltwater fish, but is still worth looking at.

	C	F
Atlantic Salmon	10–18	50–85
Barramundi	24–29	77–85
Black Marlin	19–26	67–79
Bonito	16–24	61–77
Cobia	19–29	67–85
Dolphinfish	24–30	77–86
Frigate Mackerel	19–24	67–77
SHARKS		
–Black Whaler	11–31	51–87
–Bronze Whaler	11–31	51–87
–Tiger	17–31	63–87
–Mako	15–31	60–87
–Hammerhead	15–31	60–87
–Blue	15–26	60–79
–Thresher	15–24	60–77
Snapper	12–16	55–61
Spanish Mackerel	23–30	74–86
TUNA		
–Big-eye	15–29	60–85
–Longtail	18–21	65–70
–Mackerel	15–29	60–85
–Southern Bluefin	11–25	51–78
–Striped Tuna	15–27	60–82
–Yellofin	15–29	60–85
Wahoo	23–30	74–86
Yellowtail Kingfish	13–25	56–78

BASIC GUIDE TO WIND SPEED

When most people hear the weather forecast and it is for moderate to fresh winds, not too many would know how fast the wind speed will be.

The Beaufort Wind Scale is the standard measure and gives you some idea of what conditions will be like on the water.

	Units in km/h	Units in knots	Description on Land.	Description at Sea
CALM	0	0	Smoke rises vertically.	Sea like a mirror.
LIGHT WINDS	19 km/h or less	10 knots or less	Wind felt on face; leaves rustle; ordinary vanes moved by wind.	Small wavelets, ripples formed but do not break: A glassy appearance maintained.
MODERATE WINDS	20–29 km/h	11–16 knots	Raises dust and loose paper; small branches are moved.	Small waves - becoming longer; fairly frequent white horses.
FRESH WINDS	30–39 km/h	17–21 knots	Small trees in leaf begin to sway; crested waveless form on inland water.	Moderate waves, taking a more pronounced long form; many white horses are formed—a chance of some spray.
STRONG WINDS	40–50 km/h	22–27 knots	Large branches in motion; whistling heard in telephone wires; umbrellas used with difficulty.	Large waves begin to form; the white foam crests are more extensive with probably some spray.
	51–62 km/h	28–33 knots	Whole trees in motion; inconvenience felt when walking against wind.	Sea heaps up and white foam from breaking waves begins to be blown in streaks along direction of wind.
GALE	63–75 km/h	34–40 knots	Twigs break off trees; progress generally impeded.	Moderately high waves of greater length; edges of crests begin to break into spindrift; foam is blown in well-marked streaks along the direction of the wind.
	76–87 km/h	41–47 knots	Slight structural damage occurs—roofing dislodged; larger branches break off.	High waves; dense streaks of foam; crests of waves begin to topple, tumble and roll over; spray may affect visibility.
STORM	88–102 km/h	48–55 knots	Seldom experienced inland; trees uprooted; considerable structural damage.	Very high waves with long overhanging crests; the resulting foam in great patches is blown in dense white streaks; the surface of the sea takes on a white appearance; the tumbling of the sea becomes heavy with visibility affected.
	103 km/h or more	56 knots plus	Very rarely experienced—widespread damage.	Exceptionally high waves; small and medium sized ships occasionally lost from view behind waves; the sea is completely covered with long white patches of foam; the edges of wave crests are blown into froth.

The following are suggested line options based on scenario.

SPECIES	SCENARIO	METHOD	LINE
Whiting/flathead	Beach/bay	Bait	Mono 3–5 kg
	Deep water/current	Bait	Braid 10 kg
Snapper	Beach/bay	Bait	Mono 8 kg
	Deep water/current	Bait	Braid 15 kg
Mulloway	Estuary/surf	Bait	Braid 15 kg
			Mono 10 kg
Australian Bass Estuary perch	River	Bait	Mono 3 kg
		Spin/troll	Braid 10 kg
Salmon/tailor	Beach/bay	Bait	Mono 3–5 kg
		Spin/troll	Braid 10 kg
Murray cod Yellowbelly	Lakes/rivers	Trolling	Braid 10–15 kg
		Spinning	Braid 10 kg
		Bait	Mono 8–10 kg
Trout	Lakes	Trolling	Braid 5 kg
		Bait	Mono 3 kg
	Rivers	Bait	Mono 3 kg
	Lakes/rivers	Spin	Mono 2–3 kg
Barramundi	Beach/estuary	Troll	Braid 10 kg
		Spin	Braid 10 kg
		Bait	Mono/Braid 8–10 kg
Mangrove jack	Estuary	Spin	Braid 10 kg
		Bait	Mono 8 kg
	Offshore reefs	Bait	Braid 15 kg
Small tuna	Offshore/Landbased Game	Trolling	Mono 5–10 kg
		Spin	
		Bait	
Big tuna	Offshore	Trolling	Mono 10–15 kg
		Cubing	Braid 15 kg
	Landbased Game	Live bait	Mono 15 kg
		Spinning	Mono 10 kg
Marlin	Landbased Game	Live bait	Mono 15–24 kg
			Braid 24 kg
	Offshore	Trolling	Mono/braid 15–6 kg
Sharks	Offshore	Bait	Braid/Mono 15–24 kg
	Landbased Game	Bait	Braid/Mono 15–24 kg

It is very easy to own a boat in Australia, but with ownership comes the responsilbility for the safety of your passengers and equipment. It is also vital that you know all the boating regulations in the areas that you will be using your boat. While there are many regulations that are similar if not the same for each state, it is still up to you as skipper to know or find out the specific regulations for the areas you intend to go boating.

Remember that you must have a current boating licence.

GETTING STARTED

Before you purchase a boat, go out on the water with other boat owners. Try to go boating in as many different types, shapes and sizes and brands of boats as possible. You might want the boat primarily for fishing, but what type of fishing? Open sea, bay, river, dam—the style of fishing you want to do will dictate what type of boat you will need.

Once you have settled on the boat type, the next major purchases will be the motor and the trailer. It is important that you have the right power to suit your boat choice. Boating Industry Association dealers will advise you an a range of power to suit your boat and what you may require it to do.

If you are purchasing a used boat, you will have less legal safeguards than when buying from a registered dealer. You will need to take extra care in assessing the condition of the boat and the motor. As with buying a used car, it will pay to have an expert look at it for you. Even if the motor is a write off, the boat itself may still be worth purchasing.

HOUSING YOUR BOAT

You must also consider where you will keep your boat. How much space you have will determine where it is kept, and where it is kept will determine how often you use it. It's not much use having to plan weeks ahead to get to your boat—you might as well not have it.

PLANNING YOUR TRIP

The safety and success or any boating trip depends on the amount of preparation before venturing out on the water.

- Get up-to-date nautical charts and study them closely. They will accurately display information about ocean depths, coastal features, lights, piles, beacons and navigation hazards.

- Make sure that your boat is suitable for where you plan to go

- Make sure it is seaworthy when fully loaded

- Check the motor is in good condition

- Check that you have enough fuel for the trip and any unforeseen changes in plans

- Check that you have all the safety equipment required and that it is in good condition

- Make sure that you know how to use the safety equipment

- Make sure that the weather forecast is the most up-to-date that you can get.

- Make sure that you carry the right gear other than what the law insists on. eg: chart, compass, water, food, extra clothing, tools, extra line for the anchor and sun protection.

- Before you take to the water, leave your trip intentions with someone. Make sure that they know when you are leaving, where you are going, when you are returning, vessel details and a contact number.

LOADING THE BOAT

The boat you have might be the best model, well constructed with the highest safety standards, well powered by the motor, and be properly equipped, but still have a poor ride and even at times be dangerous. In the end it all comes down to how well the skipper handles the boat, where the passengers are positioned, and how many of them there are. The boat's seaworthiness depends on the complete load it carries and where and how it is placed. Remember that if it looks and feels wrong it is wrong.

GETTING INTO THE WATER

Before getting anywhere near the water at the end of the ramp, make sure that the trailer lighting is disconnected and the boat is firmly attached to the trailer. Treat all other boat owners with respect, you never know when you might need their help. Make sure the bung is in.

Make sure that there are no hazards on the ramp or in the surrounding water area. Line up your car and trailer so that you can keep your backing down the ramp as straight and as short as possible.

When actually launching the boat, keep hold of the bow line, so the boat doesn't float off without you. It is better to get your passengers on board after the boat is launched and the engine started. Park your trailer sensibly, and not in anyone else's way.

OUT ON THE WATER

The rules and regulations of the road which apply to waters in most states are so long and intricate they are a complete book in themselves. The following points cover most of the encounters you might have with other vessels.

- The whole time you are on the water, you must keep extremely alert and be ready to give way to any other vessels.

- If you are the vessel that must give way, do it in good time. When you make your move, make it so that it will be obvious to the other vessel

- Generally power boats have to keep out of the way of sailing and fishing vessels, and any other vessels that are hampered by dredging, cable laying, etc.

BASIC BOATING MANOEUVRES

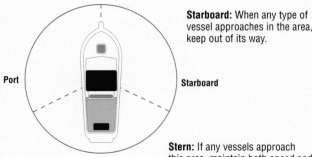

Port: If a power driven vessel approaches in this area, procede with caution, maintaining both course and speed.

Starboard: When any type of vessel approaches in the area, keep out of its way.

Port

Starboard

Stern: If any vessels approach this area, maintain both speed and course with caution.

Stern

- Always keep to the right in channels. Remember when on the water, look to the right, give way to the right, turn to the right and stay to the right.

⎈ CROSSING A BAR

Conditions on a bar change suddenly without warning. No amount of experience or boat type makes crossing a bar safe when the conditions are adverse or at least marginal. No situation can warrant taking the risk of trying to cross when conditions are questionable.

Once started, you are committed to crossing the bar, so if in any doubt do not even try to cross.

Here are some pointers for going out to sea over a bar:

- Craft not capable of standing up to adverse sea conditions outside the bar should not leave port

- Ensure that there is reserve fuel and provisions if conditions prevent returning over the bar when it is time to go back to port

- Get a weather report for the time of your crossing out to sea and also one for when you are going to return

- Do not venture out if you are in any doubt of your ability to return

- Cross on an incoming tide —vessels are more likely to experience adverse conditions at or near low tide.

- Watch where other vessels are crossing—this will be the most likely spot where you should cross

- Make sure that the vessels ahead are well clear before attempting your own crossing

- Approach at moderate speed, watching for the spot where the waves break least or at best not at all. Wait for a flatter than usual stretch of water and motor through.

- If at all possible, it is best to have the waves slightly on the bow so that your boat gently rolls over the crest of each wave.

Here are some pointers for coming in to shore over a bar:

- Coming in from the open sea, increase the power of your vessel to catch up with the ingoing waves.

- Position your vessel on the back of the wave. **Definitely do not surf down the face of the wave.**

- Match your vessel's speed to that of the waves **but do not try to overtake the waves.**

⎈ GETTING OUT OF THE WATER

Centre your boat to the centre of your trailer and carefully take your boat up to the trailer until the winch or safety chain can be secured.

If you do not have the confidence to drive your boat on to the trailer, secure a line to the bow and stern to control the boat as you use the winch.

Get your trailer and boat off the ramp as quickly as possible to allow other boats to get access to the ramp. Park in the appropriate area and finish securing the boat ready for towing.

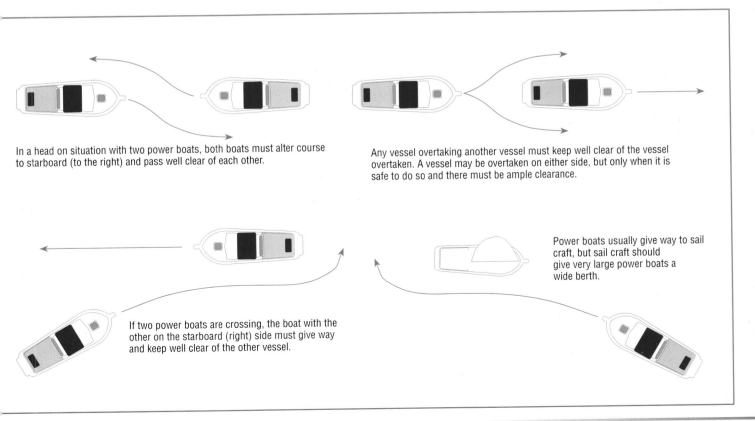

In a head on situation with two power boats, both boats must alter course to starboard (to the right) and pass well clear of each other.

Any vessel overtaking another vessel must keep well clear of the vessel overtaken. A vessel may be overtaken on either side, but only when it is safe to do so and there must be ample clearance.

If two power boats are crossing, the boat with the other on the starboard (right) side must give way and keep well clear of the other vessel.

Power boats usually give way to sail craft, but sail craft should give very large power boats a wide berth.

ANCHOR BEND

An Anchor Bend is the knot most commonly used to connect a line to an anchor.

1. Make two turns around the shackle, leaving turns open.
Take a half turn around the standing line and thenfeed the free end through the turns and pull tight.

2. Tie a half hitch around the standing part and pull tight.

3. Sieze the free end or tie a backup knot with the free end around the standing part.

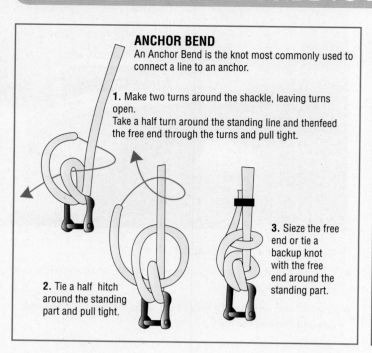

BOWLINE

One of the most useful knots. It forms a secure loop, is easy to tie and untie and won't jam.

1. Form an eye in the rope with the standing part of the rope running underneath. Run the free end up through the eye making a loop below the eye.

2. Take a turn around the standing part and feed the free end back down into the eye and hold there.

3. Pull standing part to tighten down the knot.

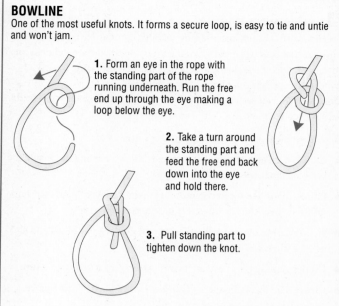

CLEAT HITCH

Take a turn around the base of the cleat and bring the line over the front face of the cleat, below each of the horns in turn in a figure 8 pattern. Then back and underneath the crossing turn as shown in step 4.

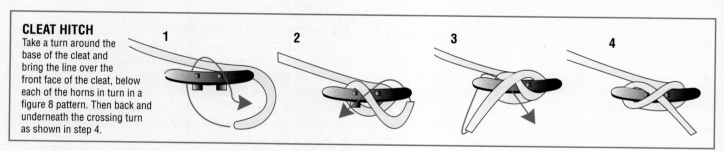

CLOVE HITCH

A simple hitch, it holds firmly but is not totally secure.

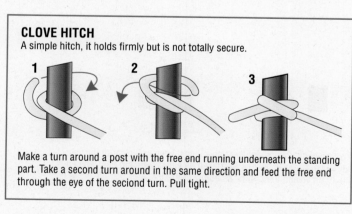

Make a turn around a post with the free end running underneath the standing part. Take a second turn around in the same direction and feed the free end through the eye of the seciond turn. Pull tight.

MOORING HITCH

A knot which holds fast while under tension, yet can be quickly released by a tug on the free end. It is only a temporary knot though, and not to be used to moor a boat.

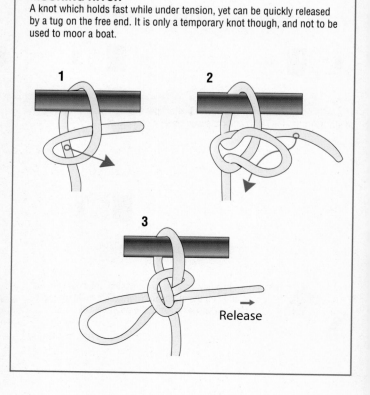

Release

SHEET BEND

Very good for tying two lines together, especially lines of different sizes. This knot will also hold slippery nylon rope in it's doubled form, but not well enough for climbers.

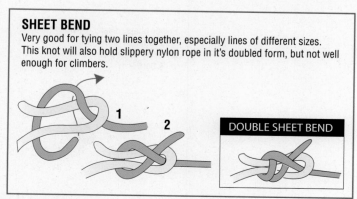

DOUBLE SHEET BEND

CHAPTER SEVEN

GUIDE TO
FISH ID

FRESHWATER SPORTFISH

ARCHER FISH

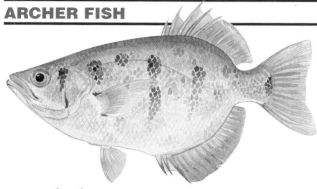

Scientific name *Toxotes chatareus*. Also known as Rifle fish.

Range The archer fish is found from the northern end of 80-Mile beach south of Broome around the top end to the Townsville area. The similar Gulf archer fish *Toxote jaculatrix* is found in streams of the Gulf of Carpentaria.

Description A deep bodied fish of tropical freshwater regions. The dorsal fin is set well back, which enables the fish to sit parallel to the surface where it watches for insect life in overhanging branches which it shoots down with a spurt of water from its mouth. They have several large spots on the body and a large, upturned mouth which makes identification relatively easy. While the archer fish may grow to around a kilogram and 30 cm, they are commonly encountered at much smaller sizes.

Fishing Archer fish are avid takers of lures and flies, often hitting large lures intended for barramundi. They are good fun on light spinning or fly tackle and will take all standard trout flies or lures in larger sizes. Small archer fish make good live baits for barramundi but they are more attractive as aquarium fish, where their water spouting habits make them immensely popular with local kids. Fair eating quality.

Rigs and Tactics

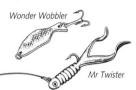

Wonder Wobbler

Mr Twister

24 kg trace

Minnow Lure

Fly fishing is successful

BASS, AUSTRALIAN

Scientific name *Macquaria novemaculeata*. Also known as Bass, Australian perch.

Range From Fraser Island and the Mary River and coastal drainages as far as the Gippsland lakes system in Victoria. The range of Australian bass has been considerably expanded through stockings and the fish can be found in a number of impoundments in Queensland, NSW and Victoria.

Description The Australian bass is a handsome fish which can reach more than 4 kg in impoundments, but any fish from the rivers over 2.4 kg is an extremely noteworthy capture. Males are smaller than females and a large male will be up to 1.5 kilograms. The Australian bass is easily confused with the similar estuary perch. Even experts can confuse the two species, but they can be most easily separated by the forehead profile which is straight or slightly rounded in the bass and is concave or slightly indented in the estuary perch. Estuary perch prefer tidal waters or the lower reaches of coastal rivers. Australian bass are more common in the northern part of the range with estuary perch becoming increasingly common in southern NSW and Victoria. Australian bass must have salt water to breed and the increased construction of weirs and dams on coastal streams has had a significant impact on bass numbers.

Fishing The Australian bass is arguably the best light tackle sportfish of temperate waters in Australia. They have a close affinity for structure and will dash out from their snag to grab a lure, bait or fly and madly dash back into cover, busting off the unwary. While not as powerful as mangrove jacks of tropical waters, they are spectacular sport in their own right. Australian bass can be extremely aggressive, feeding on fish, shrimps, prawns, insects, lizards and small snakes that may fall into the water. Australian bass are more active at dusk, dawn or at night. Fishing on a summer's evening is almost unbeatable, with surface lures or popping bugs on a fly rod producing spectacular strikes at dusk and well into the night. Many lures work well and bass anglers are have massive collections of surface lures, shallow divers, deep divers, soft plastics, spinnerbaits and special lures in every conceivable pattern and colour. Bass can also be taken trolling in dams very close to cover or in rivers along rock walls or under overhanging branches where casting is very difficult. In many instances, casts with lure or fly have to be within 30 cm of cover to get a strike.

Very slowly working the lure near cover will bring a bass out for a look and when the retrieve is commenced, a slashing strike can result. Many baits work well for bass, with live baits being best. A live shrimp or prawn drifted under a quill float will almost guarantee a response from any bass, but this includes very small fish which may be gut hooked if the hook is set too late. Live fish such as poddy mullet also work well, as do grasshoppers, worms and live cicadas during summer. Although Australian bass make excellent eating, almost all fish are now returned by increasingly enlightened anglers, but it must be stressed that fish in dams will not breed, even if they have very full ovaries.

Rigs and Tactics

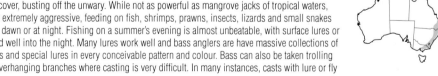

Balance with lead shot

2–3 metres

Stopper

Float

No. 6 to 4 fly hook

No. 00 to 1 ball sinker

No. 6 to 4 light gauge fly hook

Pistol shrimp No. 6 to 2 hook

Estuary shrimp No. 10 to 6 hook

No. 0 to 2 ball sinker

Deep Diving Minnow

Freshwater popper

Fly fishing is also successful.

CARP

Scientific name *Cyprinus carpio*. Also known as European carp, Euro, common carp, koi, blubber lips, mud sucker. Lightly scaled individuals known as mirror carp and those with no or very few scales are known as leather carp.

Range Introduced into Australia in 1872, the carp did not have a significant impact until the so-called Boolara strain escaped into Lake Hawthorn near Mildura in 1964. Since then the carp has spread widely throughout the Murray-Darling drainage and coastal systems along the east coast and recently Tasmanaia. A recent report from the Peel-Harvey system near Mandurah Western Australia indicates that the spread may not yet be complete. Introductions are likely to continue through escaped koi carp from farm dams or poorly designed garden ponds. Carp are also introduced by foolish but well intentioned people who release their pets into waterways when they grow too large or the family goes on holidays.

Description The carp has a relatively small, downward pointing mouth surrounded by two pairs of barbels, with the second pair more prominent. The first spines in the dorsal and anal fins are strongly serrated. Scales may be present, in rows and of a larger size, or almost entirely absent. The decorative koi is a variety of carp and, if released, can breed to wild strain fish capable of much more rapid growth and reproduction. Carp can hybridise with common goldfish (*Carassius auratus*).

Fishing Although much maligned, the carp is a powerful fighting fish, especially on light line. Carp are here to stay and in many urban areas provide fishing where little or none was previously available. They can reach 10 kg or more but are more common at 2 – 5 kilograms. Carp can be taken on a wide variety of bait rigs, but coarse fishing techniques elevate carp to a much higher level. The use of coarse fishing gear, rigs and baits such as corn kernels and maggots can account for big bags of carp. Carp take wet flies well and occasionally take lures intended for trout. Carp should not be returned to the water but should not just be left on the banks to rot. Carp are poor eating, although some people do enjoy them, in spite of their frequent muddy taste and large number of Y shaped bones.

Rigs and Tactics

No. 00 to 1 ball sinker

No. 6 to 4 light gauge fly hook

No. 6 to 4 Baitholder hook

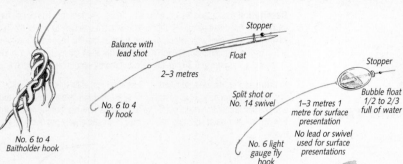

Balance with lead shot

2–3 metres

No. 6 to 4 fly hook

Stopper

Float

Split shot or No. 14 swivel

No. 6 light gauge fly hook

Stopper

1–3 metres 1 metre for surface presentation

No lead or swivel used for surface presentations

Bubble float 1/2 to 2/3 full of water

CATFISH, EEL-TAILED

Scientific name *Tandanus tandanus*. Also known as Tandan, freshwater jewfish, dewfish, freshwater catfish, kenaru, cattie, tandan catfish.

Range Widespread throughout the Murray-Darling drainage system, but significantly reduced in areas of high carp infestation and/or intensive agricultural spraying. Also found in fresh waters of coastal drainages from south of Sydney NSW to north of Cairns, Queensland. A similar but more slender species (*Tandanus bostocki*) is found in south-west Western Australia and a number of eel-tailed catfishes are found in tropical Australia.

Description A fascinating largely nocturnal species with smooth skin and a robust eel-like tail. The eel-tailed catfishes' intimidating looks mask a terrific eating and hard fighting fish. The eel-tailed catfish possesses stout and poisonous spines on the dorsal and pectoral fins. The poison is stronger in juvenile catfish for, as the fish grows, the channel along the spine where the poison passes grows over and the spikes become less dangerous in animals over about 20 centimetres. However, the small fish hide in weeds during the day and can spike unwary waders. Immerse the wound in hot water and seek medical advice if swelling or persistent pain cause continued discomfort. These catfish do not possess a true stomach, merely a modification of the intestine. The testes look like fancy scalloping edging and catfish mate in large excavated nests of up to a metre in diameter which they aggressively defend.

Fishing The eel-tailed catfish is a nocturnal feeder, so fishing after dark is by far the best. These catfish take worms, shrimps, yabbies, prawns and insect larvae. A small running sinker rig will produce the best results and, as the fish roam widely after dark, fishing in shallow water near the edge of drop-offs can be extremely productive. A berley of crushed garden snails laid out on dusk can attract large numbers of catfish. Fish with snails or worms for best results. Eel-tailed catfish will occasionally take lures during nesting and invariably fool the angler into thinking they have hooked a large cod. Catfish fight hard but dirty and will dive into nearby sticks or rocks to break you off. Excellent eating.

Rigs and Tactics

No. 00 to 2 ball sinker

No. 4 to 1 Suicide or baitholder hook

No. 00 to 1 ball sinker

No. 6 to 4 light gauge fly hook

No. 6 to 4 Baitholder hook

Attach grub to hook with hosiery elastic (bait mate)

No. 6 to 8 Long shank baitholder

COD, EASTERN FRESHWATER

Scientific name *Maccullochella ikei*. Also known as Clarence River cod, Eastern cod, East coast cod, cod.

Range Richmond and Clarence River systems. Stocked fish replaced extinction in Richmond system in recent years. Endangered species. The recovery of Eastern Freshwater cod is largely due to Dr Stuart Rowland.

Description Closely related to the Murray cod but distinguished by range and Eastern Freshwater cod possess long leading filaments on ventral fin. Eastern Freshwater cod are more lightly built than Murray cod, especially near the tail and have heavier mottling patterns.

Fishing Classic ambush feeder living near cover in deep holes in beautiful clear streams. Takes diving and surface lures and large live baits. The fight is strong and there is inevitably a surge when the boat or angler is first sighted and the danger realised. This species is totally protected and if accidently taken must be returned immediately to the water.

Rigs and Tactics
Not applicable as Eastern Freshwater Cod are a protected species.

COD, MURRAY

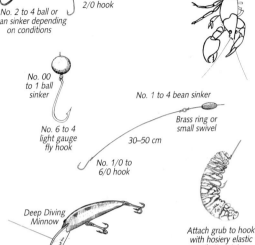

Rigs and Tactics

No. 4 to 2/0 hook

3 kg

No. 2 to 3 ball

No. 4 to 4/0 (depending on bait size) Kendall Kirby hook

No. 4 to 2/0 hook

No. 2 to 4 ball or bean sinker depending on conditions

No. 00 to 1 ball sinker

No. 6 to 4 light gauge fly hook

No. 1 to 4 bean sinker

Brass ring or small swivel

30–50 cm

No. 1/0 to 6/0 hook

Deep Diving Minnow

Attach grub to hook with hosiery elastic (bait mate)

Scientific name *Maccullochella peelii peelii*. Also known as Cod, goodoo, green fish, codfish, ponde.

Range Once common throughout the Murray-Darling basin except for at high altitude, numbers have become progressively reduced. Recent closed seasons, bag limits and further controls on set lines coupled with increased community and public stockings have seen cod fishing improve in a number of areas in recent years. Murray cod have been introduced into other waters including Lake Grassmere in Western Australia.

Description The Murray cod is the largest Australian freshwater fish, reaching 1.8 m and 113 kilograms. Cod grow an average of 1 kg per year in rivers and 2 kg per year in larger dams. Has prominent mottling on body, reducing towards a white or cream belly. Fin borders except pectoral fins are white. Differs from similar trout cod in having lower jaw equal or longer than upper jaw , more prominent mottling and heavier tail wrist. Murray cod also prefer more sluggish water than trout cod.

Fishing Murray cod are the largest predator in many inland waters. They take large lures, especially deep divers cast to snags or drop-offs in larger, slower rivers or dams. Murray cod are now a legitimate target for keen fly fishers. Murray cod reward patience, as a lure repeatedly cast to cod holding cover, or to a following fish will often eventually evoke a strike. As Murray cod are ambush feeders, large or flashy lures often work best. Murray cod are best known for taking a wide range of baits including live fish (where permitted), bardi grubs, yabbies, worms, ox heart and even scorched starlings. Murray cod are very good eating, especially under 10 kilograms. Anglers should only take as many cod as they need.

COD, MARY RIVER

Scientific name *Maccullochella peeli mariensis*. Also known as Cod, Queensland freshwater cod.

Range The Mary River cod is considered to found only in the Mary River system, but the status of the now extinct Brisbane River cod is unknown. Has now been stocked into several Queensland impoundments.

Description Similar to Eastern Freshwater cod, but more closely related to the Murray cod. Easily separated by the limited range.

Fishing Takes lures and baits within its limited range. This species is at risk and should be returned regardless of the prevailing regulations.

Rigs and Tactics

Not applicable as Mary River Cod are a protected species.

COD, TROUT

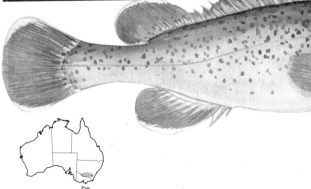

Rigs and Tactics

Not applicable as Mary River Cod are a protected species.

Scientific name *Maccullochella macquariensis*. Also known as Blue nose cod, bluenose, rock cod, blue cod.

Range The trout cod was originally widespread throughout the Murray-Darling basin, but the range and abundance has been reduced to the extent that they have been considered endangered since 1971. Work at Narrandera and Snobs Creek has expanded the range to include the Abercrombie River and Talbingo Dam. Although totally protected in NSW, Victoria and ACT, it can be found in reasonable numbers in the Murrumbidgee River downstream of Gundagai, Seven Creeks, Upper Murray River and downstream of Yarrawonga Weir and several other smaller waters in NSW and Victoria.

Description The trout cod is capable of reaching 16 kg and 800 mm but much more common at 1 – 2 kilograms. A handsome aggressive fish which puts up a terrific fight for its size, the trout cod has a slate grey to greenish blue colour and dashed markings. Trout cod, particularly juveniles have a prominent stripe through the eye and an overhanging upper jaw. The tail wrist is much narrower than in Murray cod.

Fishing Trout cod are aggressive and feed on yabbies, bardi grubs and scrub worms. They will also take a wide variety of lures and seem to

EEL, LONG FINNED

Scientific name *Anguilla reinhardtii*. Also known as Freshwater eel, eel, spotted eel.

Range From Cape York south to Melbourne Victoria and northern and eastern Tasmania. These eels now use the Snowy Mountains scheme to be recorded from the Murray and Murrumbidgee Rivers.

Description Eels are fascinating animals which are often loathed but play an important part in culling older or sick fish, birds or anything else they can catch. Australian eels are thought to spawn in the Coral Sea. Juvenile eels as elvers migrate great distances up rivers and can travel overland over wet grass and can negotiate large dams walls. Long-finned eels can spend more than 10 years in fresh waters until the urge to move downstream takes the adult eels. The long-finned eel is much larger than the short-finned eel (*Anguilla australis*) and has the dorsal fin extending well forward of the anal fin. The head is broad and the lips fleshy. Colour varies with the environment but, except when migrating to the sea, is brown or olive-green with a lighter belly.

Fishing The long-finned eel is often taken while fishing for other fish. They fight extremely hard and can be mean enough to try to bite the hand which tries to unhook it. The long-finned eel can demonstrate knot tying tricks when hooked. These eels are opportunistic feeders and can take live baits larger than the 10% of the body length which legend believes applies. Worms, grubs, live fish or cut baits will take eels, but liver and beef heart are irresistible. Long-finned eels can reach over 2 m and 20 kg, although divers claim much larger sizes in some dams. Eels make good eating, especially when smoked, although many Australians are strongly prejudiced against them. Large eels gain a top price in China, whereas smaller eels are more popular in Japan.

Rigs and Tactics

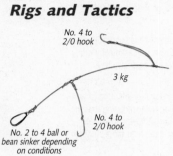

No. 4 to 2/0 hook

3 kg

No. 4 to 2/0 hook

No. 2 to 4 ball or bean sinker depending on conditions

Attach grub to hook with hosiery elastic (bait mate)

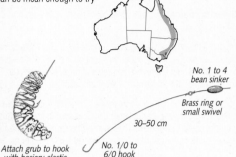

No. 1 to 4 bean sinker

Brass ring or small swivel

30–50 cm

No. 1/0 to 6/0 hook

No. 2 to 3 ball

No. 4 to 4/0 (depending on bait size) Kendall Kirby hook

GRUNTER, SOOTY

Scientific name *Hephaestus fuliginosus*. Also known as Black bream, purple grunter, sooty.

Range From the Kimberley region of Western Australia around the top end to central Queensland. This species has been stocked into a number of Queensland impoundments where they have demonstrated exceptional growth and provide quality sport.

Description In the wild, sooty grunter can reach 4 kg and 50 cm, but in stocked impoundments such as Tinaroo Dam they can be considerably larger than this. This species has a reasonably large mouth and the lips may be blubbery in some specimens. Colour can be extremely variable, from light brown to black. Sooty grunter can be omnivorous and will on occasion eat green algae.

Fishing The sooty grunter prefers faster water in rivers and can inhabit mid-stream snags in riffles. In dams these fish are found around cover, especially fallen timber. Sooty grunter will readily take live shrimp or cherabin, worms or grubs. They will readily take a variety of lures including diving lures, spinner baits, bladed spinners, jigs, soft plastics and flies. Sooty grunter fight well without jumping and are undervalued as a sport fish by many anglers, partly because they are reasonably common in many areas. Sooty grunter are a fair to poor food fish which can be weedy tasting. Species such as barramundi which occur in the same areas are much better fare.

Rigs and Tactics

Minnow Lure

24 kg trace

No. 1/0 to 6/0 hook

No. 1 to 4 bean sinker

Brass ring or small swivel

30–50 cm

Fly fishing can also be successful.

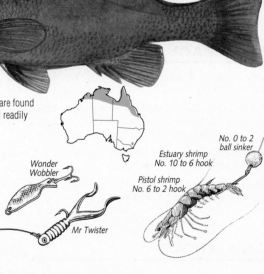

Wonder Wobbler

Mr Twister

Estuary shrimp No. 10 to 6 hook

Pistol shrimp No. 6 to 2 hook

No. 0 to 2 ball sinker

PERCH, JUNGLE

Scientific name *Kuhlia rupestris*. Also known as Rock flagtail.

Range Burdekin River and other eastern Cape York streams down to Fraser Island in Queensland.

Description A handsome fish which can be distinguished by its preference for clean clear freshwater coastal streams. The body and base of the caudal fin is liberally speckled with dark spots. The lobes of the tail fin are generally white. The mouth is large and can take large baits and lures. This species has been severely reduced in range and number due to decreasing water quality in its streams. The jungle perch is a relatively small species, reaching 2.4 kg but frequently caught above 0.5 kilograms.

Fishing A true recreational fishing prize, the jungle perch takes a variety of small lures readily. They can also be taken on fly, but the remote nature and often overgrown of their preferred habitat makes fly presentation difficult. Baits such as frogs, grasshoppers and worms also work well. While this species is reputed to be good eating, the jungle perch is vulnerable to overfishing and all fish should be carefully released.

Rigs and Tactics

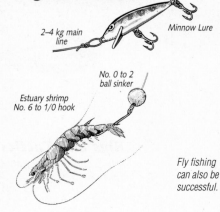

2–4 kg main line

Minnow Lure

No. 0 to 2 ball sinker

Estuary shrimp No. 6 to 1/0 hook

Fly fishing can also be successful.

PERCH, GOLDEN

Scientific name *Macquaria ambigua*. Also known as Golden, callop, yellowbelly, Murray perch.

Range Wide distribution throughout the Murray-Darling basin. Separate genetic stocks are thought to be found in the Dawson-Fitzroy system and the Bulloo and Lake Eyre internal drainage systems. Golden perch have had their range substantially increased through stockings into areas outside its normal range. These stockings have been spectacularly successful. They have also been introduced into Western Australia, central Queensland and western South Australia. Golden perch cannot reproduce in farm dams or impoundments.

Description The golden perch is a deep bodied fish which becomes more heavily set as it gets larger. Fish over 5 kg resemble a football, with a tail and a small moderately tapered head with a distinctly concave forehead. The lower jaw extends slightly beyond the upper jaw. The colour varies with the water quality, ranging from pale green to almost cream out of very muddy western waters to deep green and with obvious golden overtones, particularly in the throat and belly region. There are two distinctive extended filaments on the ventral fins. Golden perch are most commonly encountered in the 1 – 2 kg range especially in rivers. However, the extremely successful stocking in Queensland, New South Wales and to a lesser extent Victorian impoundments has seen a huge increase in the number of 5 – 10 kg fish being caught with the odd fish to 15 kg being reported.

Fishing The natural rivers where golden perch were once extremely common no longer ever run clear through poor land use and de-snagging. In these rivers, golden perch are almost exclusively a bait proposition, except in the upper reaches or near barrages where lures can be used. Baits include worms, yabbies, shrimps, bardi and wood grubs, frogs (where legal) and less common baits such as kangaroo meat or liver. However, fishing for golden perch has exploded in popularity in impoundments. Bait fishing includes bobbing with yabbies near drowned timber or sight fishing with shrimps or live fish to cruising fish on the edge of weed beds, along rock walls or on drop-offs near points where this species positions itself to ambush prey. Lure fishing is now the most popular method of fishing for golden perch. Golden perch often follow lures, so a slight pause near the end of the retrieve will often entice a strike and working the rod while trolling is similarly more successful.

Rigs and Tactics

No. 1 to 4 bean sinker

Brass ring or small swivel

30–50 cm

No. 4/0 to 3/0 hook

Deep Diving Minnow

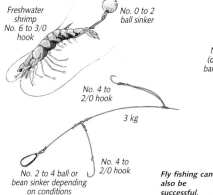

Freshwater shrimp
No. 6 to 3/0 hook

No. 0 to 2 ball sinker

No. 4 to 2/0 hook

3 kg

No. 2 to 4 ball or bean sinker depending on conditions

No. 4 to 2/0 hook

Fly fishing can also be successful.

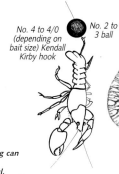

No. 4 to 4/0 (depending on bait size) Kendall Kirby hook

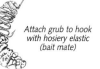

No. 2 to 3 ball

Attach grub to hook with hosiery elastic (bait mate)

PERCH, MACQUARIE

Scientific name *Macquaria australasica*. Also known as Mountain perch, white eye perch, silvereye, macca, mountain perch, Murray bream, black perch, Macquaries.

Range Increasingly restricted due to decreasing water quality and competition with species such as redfin, the Macquarie perch is now found only in the cooler upper reaches of streams in the Murray-Darling system. It is likely that there is a separate and smaller sub-species found in coastal streams from the Sydney water supply south to the Shoalhaven system plus the Yarra system in Victoria. Macquarie perch can do well in dams such as Dartmouth, Wyangala, Burrinjuck, Tallowa and Cataract.

Description Macquarie perch are a distinctly perch-like fish reaching 3.5 kg but are commonly caught at half a kilogram. The Tallowa Dam and Kangaroo River population is rarely seen at even this size and many fish are around 15 to 20 centimetres. Although colouration can vary from black to blue-grey to light grey and piebald, the Macquarie perch has a distinctive white iris around the eye in all but black specimens. The mouth is relatively small and the lips are fairly obvious without being blubbery. The pectoral fins have two extended white filaments which readily separates them from Australian bass in Tallowa Dam.

Fishing The Macquarie perch is a somewhat timid biter and is extremely curious, often repeatedly following small minnow lures, spinners or flies. They can be taken by lure or fly, but most Macquarie perch are taken on worms, with mudeyes, yabbies and wood grubs also working. In some streams Macquarie perch will be caught on crickets and grasshoppers. A lightly weighted bottom rig or a vertical jigging bait rig in impoundments will take the most fish. In dams, fish around the base of drowned timber, especially if there is a gravel bottom (such as a drowned road) nearby, while in rivers, the edges of drop-offs or near deep snags or rock walls are best. Macquarie perch are more active at night or at dusk and dawn. Macquarie perch are excellent eating but they are totally protected in many areas and care should be taken to preserve these magnificent fish.

Rigs and Tactics

No. 6 to 1/0 hook

No. 0 to 4 ball or bean sinker depending on conditions

3 kg

2/0 hook

No. 6 to 4 Baitholder hook

No. 00 or 2 bean sinker

No. 2 to 3 ball

No. 6 to 8 Long shank baitholder

Brass ring or small swivel

30–50 cm

No. 1/0 to 6/0 hook

No. 4 to 1 (depending on bait size) Kendall Kirby hook

PERCH, SILVER

Scientific name *Bidyanus bidyanus*. Also known as grunter, black bream, bidyan, Murray perch, tcheri, freshwater bream, silver.

Range Widespread but patchy distribution throughout the Murray-Darling basin except the cooler headwaters of streams. The silver perch has suffered a significant decline in number and range. Silver perch are now considered threatened in many Murray-Darling basin rivers where they were once as common as carp are now. The range is being extended by aquaculture ventures, escapees and stocking in Queensland Dams. Silver perch are common in Cataract Dam near Sydney which is unfortunately closed to angling. Silver perch breed in Cataract Dam and Burrinjuck Dam.

Description The silver perch is a fine freshwater fish species, reaching 8 kg but most frequently encountered at between 0.3 kg and 1 kg, especially in impoundments. Larger silver perch frequently become omnivorous or almost entirely vegetarian, full of the green slimy weed which can seriously affect lure and bait fishing at some times of the year. The silver perch has a small head and small mouth, but they take large lures on occasions. As the fish grows, its head appears smaller than its body, especially in dams where fast growth rates leave a heavier body in larger fish. The rear margin of the small scales is dark grey or deep brown which gives a cross hatched appearance. The fish may grunt on capture but this is not as loud or as common as in other species. In dams especially, silver perch form schools of similar sized fish, with smaller schools of large fish.

Fishing Silver perch are becoming increasingly rare in rivers. Silver perch are totally protected in SA, and in NSW they may only be taken from stocked impoundments. Quite easy to breed in hatcheries, large numbers have been stocked into dams throughout south-eastern Australia. Silver perch prefer faster water and can be taken in or downstream of rapids or broken water. Best baits are worms, peeled yabby tail, shrimps and a variety of smaller grubs. More exotic baits like snails, ox heart and chicken breast will also take fish on occasion. Silver perch can sometimes be found schooled near sunken timber where bobbing with worm or small yabby baits will pick up silvers and other species. Silver perch will take lures, but their small mouth means that small lures are best. In rivers or shallow waters silver perch love Celta or other spinner type lures, while small minnows like the Mann's 5+, McGrath minnow, small Legend Lure and small Halco Laser lures work well. Silver perch fight well and are a good eating fish, although larger specimens can be dry and may have a slight weed taint.

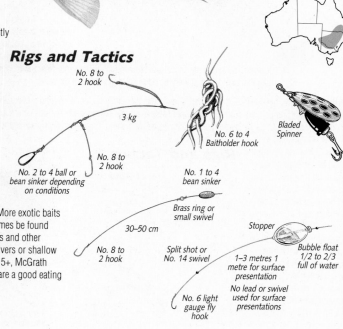

Rigs and Tactics

No. 8 to 2 hook

3 kg

No. 8 to 2 hook

No. 2 to 4 ball or bean sinker depending on conditions

No. 6 to 4 Baitholder hook

Bladed Spinner

No. 1 to 4 bean sinker

Brass ring or small swivel

30–50 cm

No. 8 to 2 hook

Split shot or No. 14 swivel

No. 6 light gauge fly hook

Stopper

1–3 metres 1 metre for surface presentation

No lead or swivel used for surface presentations

Bubble float 1/2 to 2/3 full of water

REDFIN

Scientific name *Perca fluviatilis* Also known as English perch, European perch, redfin perch, reddie.

Range An introduced species with a wide distribution in temperate waters ranging from around Pindari Dam in northern NSW, throughout southern NSW and Victoria, Tasmania, southern South Australia and the south-west of Western Australia. Redfin are found in some coastal drainages in a few dams.

Description The redfin has prominent scales and five to six prominent vertical stripes which may extend nearly to the belly. These stripes are less prominent in larger fish. The dorsal fin is set well forward and when erect, resembles a small 'sail'. The ventral and anal fins are often very bright red or orange, often with a tinge of white at the ends. The tail fin can also be bright orange, or orange-yellow. Redfin are often found around drowned timber, at drop-offs near points, or on submerged islands. Redfin prefer cooler water and in summer, the largest fish are almost always below the thermocline in dams or large river holes. Redfin are aggressive and prolific breeders. In impoundments they can stunt out, producing thousands of mature fish as small as 15 cm who consume everything and continue to reproduce. In other areas, they can reach 3 kg and provide excellent sport with a variety of techniques.

Fishing In dams, one of the most successful techniques is to anchor among drowned timber and bob with bait or lures. With bait, a small ball sinker runs to the top of the hook which is baited with yabby, worm, cricket, grub or shrimp. Lures like the Baltic Bobber or the Buzz Bomb also work well. In any case, the bait is lowered to the bottom and vertically jigged between 30 cm and a metre or so before being dropped to the bottom. Drifting baits near drowned timber in large holes in rivers or near drop-offs in rivers or dams is very succesful. Redfin are aggressive lure takers, with bladed, Celta type lures, diving lures and small Rapala minnows taking many fish.

Rigs and Tactics

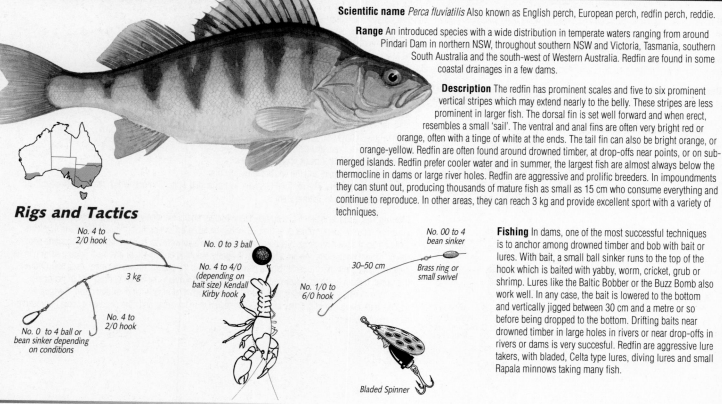

No. 4 to 2/0 hook

3 kg

No. 0 to 4 ball or bean sinker depending on conditions

No. 4 to 2/0 hook

No. 0 to 3 ball

No. 4 to 4/0 (depending on bait size) Kendall Kirby hook

No. 1/0 to 6/0 hook

No. 00 to 4 bean sinker

30–50 cm

Brass ring or small swivel

Bladed Spinner

RIVER BLACKFISH

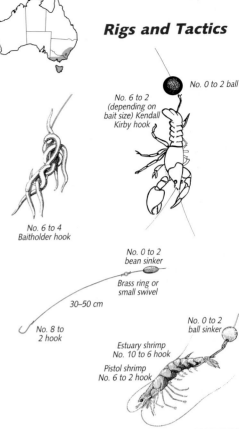

Rigs and Tactics

No. 0 to 2 ball

No. 6 to 2
(depending on
bait size) Kendall
Kirby hook

No. 6 to 4
Baitholder hook

No. 0 to 2
bean sinker

Brass ring or
small swivel

30–50 cm

No. 8 to
2 hook

No. 0 to 2
ball sinker

Estuary shrimp
No. 10 to 6 hook

Pistol shrimp
No. 6 to 2 hook

Scientific name *Gadopsis marmoratus*. Also known as Blackfish, marble cod, slippery, slimy.

Range There are now several species of river blackfish recognised including a larger species Gadopsis bispinosis, the two spined river blackfish. The distribution of the river blackfish is patchy and becoming increasingly rare in many areas. River blackfish exist in a variety of locations including in the Abercrombie River, lower Murrumbidgee River and are relatively common in Dunn's Swamp near Rylestone in NSW with a wider distribution in Victoria.

Description The river blackfish is a small elongated native freshwater fish species which is easily identified by the pelvic fins which are reduced to two rays, each of which is divided and finger-like near the end. The dorsal fin is very long and the tail fin is obviously rounded. The mouth is fairly large and the lower jaw is shorter than the upper jaw. This species has a distinctive marbled colouring and fish may vary in colour from almost black, to olive or light brown and there may be obvious purple overtones. The scales are small and the body feels very slimy, giving rise to several alternate common names. River blackfish do not appear to cohabit well with trout and prefer very snaggy waters. They are mainly nocturnal, laying up during the day in cover like hollow logs, which they also use to lay their eggs. The river blackfish can reach over 35 cm, although the two-spined species (which has obvious golden overtones) can reach nearly 5 kg in remote areas.

Fishing River blackfish are much more active at night and are a bait fishing proposition, although they have been taken on wet flies and nymphs on occasion. River blackfish are fished with lightly weighted or unweighted rigs, but the line needs to be strong enough for the snaggy country these fish prefer. Coarse fishermen often take river blackfish from waters where they are not commonly encountered. The best bait by far is worms, with shrimps, maggots and mudeyes taking fish. This species will frequently swallow the hook, so setting the hook quickly, or leaving the hook in gut hooked fish is recommended. River blackfish are quite rare so if possible, they should be returned to the water. River blackfish are quite small but have been regarded as a quality food fish in past times.

SALMON, ATLANTIC

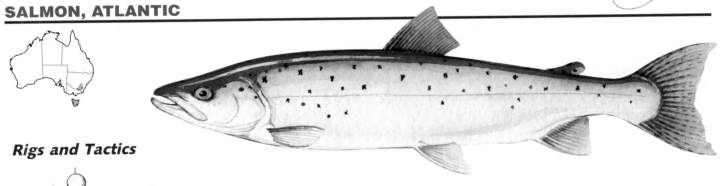

Rigs and Tactics

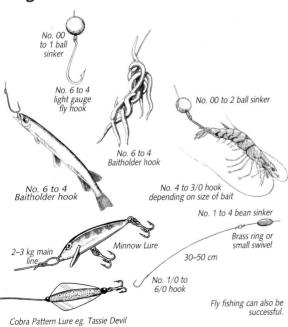

No. 00
to 1 ball
sinker

No. 6 to 4
light gauge
fly hook

No. 00 to 2 ball sinker

No. 6 to 4
Baitholder hook

No. 6 to 4
Baitholder hook

No. 4 to 3/0 hook
depending on size of bait

No. 1 to 4 bean sinker

Brass ring or
small swivel

30–50 cm

2–3 kg main
line

Minnow Lure

No. 1/0 to
6/0 hook

Cobra Pattern Lure eg. Tassie Devil

Fly fishing can also be
successful.

Scientific name *Salmo salar*. Also known as Salmon.

Range The Atlantic salmon has a very restricted range in the wild in Australia, limited to areas where they are regularly stocked. In NSW Atlantic salmon are found in Jindabyne and Burrinjuck Dams. Experimental stockings below Hume, Burrinjuck and Wyangala Dams have failed. They are caught in reasonable numbers in Tasmania as escapees from the increasing aquaculture industry.

Description The Atlantic salmon is a generally silvery fish that can have relatively few spots on its body and is often confused even by experienced anglers with silvery, lake coloured brown trout. The most obvious difference (other than location) is that the Atlantic salmon has a tail that while not clearly forked, is obviously indented. The brown trout is frequently called square tail and has a straight tail profile. The caudal peduncle (wrist of tail) is longer than for the similar brown trout. Atlantic salmon need very cold clean water which is basically unavailable in Australia. In Europe and North America they are the prince of fish but here they are quite slender, with a tendency towards being decidedly skinny and undernourished in NSW, while some smelt feeders in Tasmania can be more robust. In NSW fish over a kilogram, other than released broodfish are rare, while in Tasmania the size is frequently determined by the size at escape from fish farms.

Fishing Heralded by Donald Francois of NSW Fisheries on its introduction as the saviour of freshwater fishing, the Atlantic salmon has been a disastrous experiment for recreational anglers, although it has created a sizeable aquaculture industry in Tasmania. It is only a matter of time before NSW Fisheries stops stocking this species which provides its best fishing in Lake Jindabyne for a few days after older broodstock are released. Atlantic salmon are taken on standard trout lures and flies while fishing for other species. They prefer fish as food and smelt or gudgeon patterns work best in Tasmania. Atlantic salmon from sea cages taste devine, but specimens from Burrinjuck Dam taste very ordinary.

SALMON, CHINOOK

Rigs and Tactics

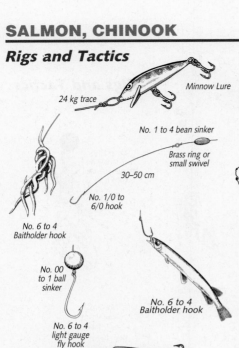

Minnow Lure

24 kg trace

No. 1 to 4 bean sinker

Brass ring or small swivel

30–50 cm

No. 1/0 to 6/0 hook

No. 6 to 4 Baitholder hook

No. 00 to 1 ball sinker

No. 6 to 4 Baitholder hook

No. 6 to 4 light gauge fly hook

Cobra Pattern Lure eg Tassie Devil

Scientific name *Oncorhynchus tshawytscha*. Also known as Quinnat salmon, king salmon.

Range Chinook salmon are produced in Victoria for stocking into waters there. The best fisheries are in Lakes Purrumbete and Bullen Merri. They are also released into Toolondo Reservoir and Albert Lakes in Victoria. The Chinook salmon in Australia does not reproduce naturally and must be stocked.

Description The chinook salmon is a handsome fish with silver sides and a rather more pointed head than other trout and salmon species, with mature males developing a distinctive hooked jaw. The mouth around the teeth in the lower jaw is distinctly grey-black which clearly identifies this species. Chinook salmon can reach 9 kg, but growth and survival is dependent upon water conditions and availability of forage species like galaxiids and pygmy perch.

Fishing Controversy dogs the stocking program for this important species due to stocking rates, size and times. Chinook salmon feed mainly on fish and can be taken by casting or trolling classical trout lures, or with live minnows or even dead smelt or whitebait. Fishing is best in spring when the fish are found in shallower water and accessible with a broader range of methods. Later in the season, trolling with lead lines or downriggers or vertical jigging around baitfish which show on a depth sounder produces fish. A very good fighting fish and excellent eating

SARATOGA, GULF

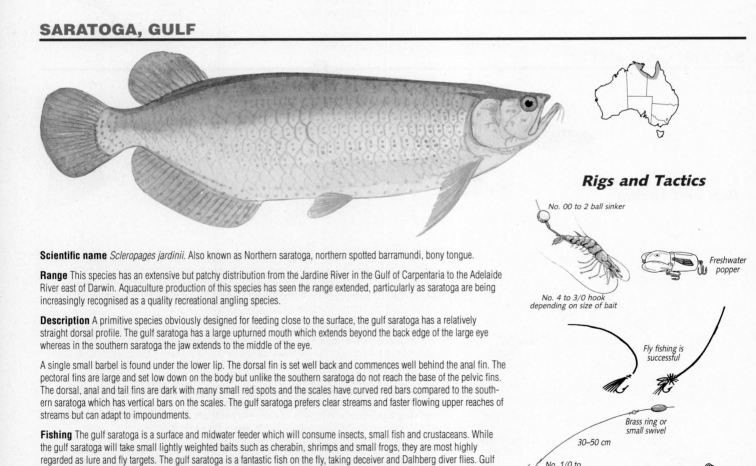

Rigs and Tactics

No. 00 to 2 ball sinker

No. 4 to 3/0 hook depending on size of bait

Freshwater popper

Fly fishing is successful

Brass ring or small swivel

30–50 cm

No. 1/0 to 6/0 hook

24 kg trace

Minnow Lure

Scientific name *Scleropages jardinii*. Also known as Northern saratoga, northern spotted barramundi, bony tongue.

Range This species has an extensive but patchy distribution from the Jardine River in the Gulf of Carpentaria to the Adelaide River east of Darwin. Aquaculture production of this species has seen the range extended, particularly as saratoga are being increasingly recognised as a quality recreational angling species.

Description A primitive species obviously designed for feeding close to the surface, the gulf saratoga has a relatively straight dorsal profile. The gulf saratoga has a large upturned mouth which extends beyond the back edge of the large eye whereas in the southern saratoga the jaw extends to the middle of the eye.

A single small barbel is found under the lower lip. The dorsal fin is set well back and commences well behind the anal fin. The pectoral fins are large and set low down on the body but unlike the southern saratoga do not reach the base of the pelvic fins. The dorsal, anal and tail fins are dark with many small red spots and the scales have curved red bars compared to the southern saratoga which have vertical bars on the scales. The gulf saratoga prefers clear streams and faster flowing upper reaches of streams but can adapt to impoundments.

Fishing The gulf saratoga is a surface and midwater feeder which will consume insects, small fish and crustaceans. While the gulf saratoga will take small lightly weighted baits such as cherabin, shrimps and small frogs, they are most highly regarded as lure and fly targets. The gulf saratoga is a fantastic fish on the fly, taking deceiver and Dalhberg diver flies. Gulf saratoga will also take minnow and spinner lures. Surface lures such as jerk baits, prop lures and chuggers work very well. The bony mouth can make setting the hook difficult and many lures are thrown on the jump. As saratoga are mouth breeders, there will be times in the spring/early summer when the females who carry the eggs will not feed. The gulf saratoga can reach 90 cm and more than 17 kg, but most fish caught are between 50 and 65 cm in length. The saratoga is a very poor table fish and should be released to provide sport for the future.

SARATOGA, SOUTHERN

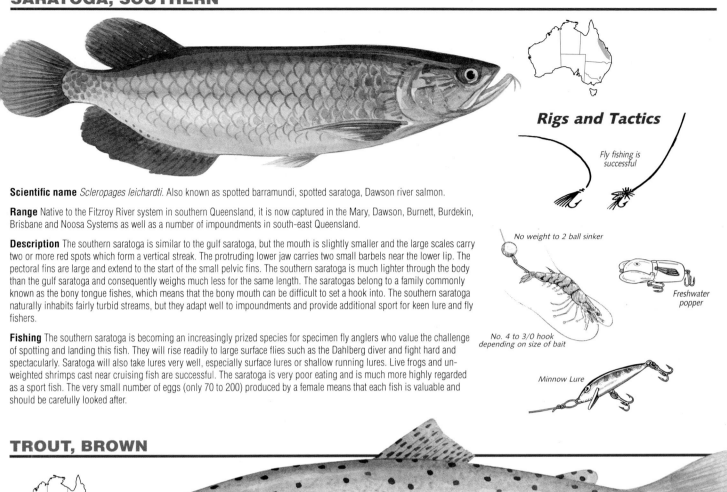

Scientific name *Scleropages leichardti*. Also known as spotted barramundi, spotted saratoga, Dawson river salmon.

Range Native to the Fitzroy River system in southern Queensland, it is now captured in the Mary, Dawson, Burnett, Burdekin, Brisbane and Noosa Systems as well as a number of impoundments in south-east Queensland.

Description The southern saratoga is similar to the gulf saratoga, but the mouth is slightly smaller and the large scales carry two or more red spots which form a vertical streak. The protruding lower jaw carries two small barbels near the lower lip. The pectoral fins are large and extend to the start of the small pelvic fins. The southern saratoga is much lighter through the body than the gulf saratoga and consequently weighs much less for the same length. The saratogas belong to a family commonly known as the bony tongue fishes, which means that the bony mouth can be difficult to set a hook into. The southern saratoga naturally inhabits fairly turbid streams, but they adapt well to impoundments and provide additional sport for keen lure and fly fishers.

Fishing The southern saratoga is becoming an increasingly prized species for specimen fly anglers who value the challenge of spotting and landing this fish. They will rise readily to large surface flies such as the Dahlberg diver and fight hard and spectacularly. Saratoga will also take lures very well, especially surface lures or shallow running lures. Live frogs and un-weighted shrimps cast near cruising fish are successful. The saratoga is very poor eating and is much more highly regarded as a sport fish. The very small number of eggs (only 70 to 200) produced by a female means that each fish is valuable and should be carefully looked after.

Rigs and Tactics

Fly fishing is successful

No weight to 2 ball sinker

Freshwater popper

No. 4 to 3/0 hook depending on size of bait

Minnow Lure

TROUT, BROWN

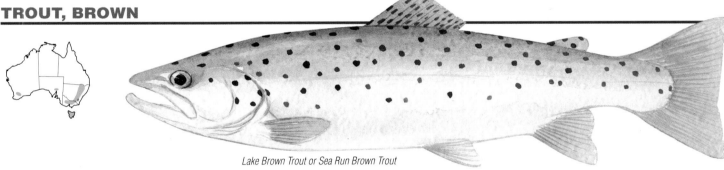

Lake Brown Trout or Sea Run Brown Trout

Scientific name *Salmo trutta*. Also known as Brownie, sea trout, Loch Leven trout.

Range This European native has a wide distribution in cooler waters in Australia. Brown trout are found in upper and occasionally mid reaches of streams in NSW, Victoria, Tasmania, South Australia and south-west Western Australia. There is an increasing fishery for sea run brown trout in Tasmania, although they are also occasionally taken in Victorian coastal streams and the Blackwood estuary in Western Australia.

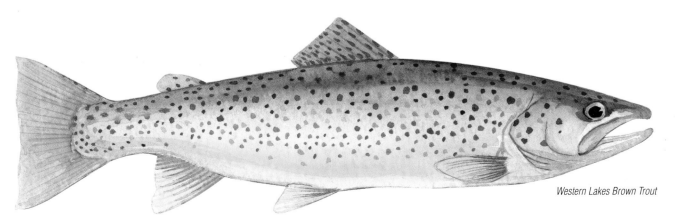

Western Lakes Brown Trout

River Brown Trout

Rigs and Tactics

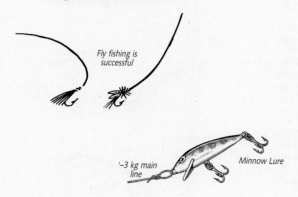

Fly fishing is successful

Minnow Lure

'-3 kg main line

No. 6 to 4 Baitholder hook

Cobra Pattern Lure eg Tassie Devil

No. 6 to 8 Long shank baitholder

Bladed Spinner

Description The brown trout is a handsome fish which can exhibit wide colour variations, partly dependent upon the environment in which the fish is found. Sea run fish and some lake dwelling fish are silver in colour with a few spots on the body. River fish in particular can have a beautiful golden sheen and large black spots on the upper body. There are frequently beautiful red spots, surrounded by a white halo below the lateral line which may be mixed with black spots. In all fish, the dorsal fins has some spots but the tail fin has none or a few very faint spots. The tail fin is either square or very slightly indented, whereas the Atlantic salmon has an obvious indent or fork to the tail. The adipose fin is obvious and may be lobe-like in larger fish. The mouth is large and the jaws become hooked to a degree in males during spawning. Brown trout can grow quickly, especially where food is plentiful such as in dams when new ground is being inundated, or for sea run fish feeding on whitebait or other fish. The brown trout can reach 25 kg overseas, but in Australia they have been recorded to 14 kilograms.

Fishing Many books have been specifically written about fishing for this challenging and rewarding species. Brown trout are generally the most highly regarded Australian trout species, due to their large size and the skill which is needed to entice these fish to strike. Brown trout take a variety of foods which may include other trout, minnows, insect larvae, terrestrial insects, snails and worms. Brown trout are specifically targeted by a huge number of recreational fishers, wherever they occur. Brown trout can be taken throughout the day, but the best times are dawn, dusk and at night. Night time is often the best in heavily fished waters, where a few wily, large, and often cannibalistic specimens can often be found. Many brown trout are taken on fly, with nymphs, streamers, wet flies and dry flies all taking fish. Many brown trout feed heavily on yabbies or snails and imitations of these can be very productive. Brown trout generally prefer the slower waters of pools or the tails of pools in streams or deeper waters of lakes, moving into feeding stations during peak periods. Brown trout are more difficult to entice to take flies than rainbow trout and their strong dogged fight makes them a rewarding capture. Brown trout are also taken on a wide variety of lures, with favourites including lead head jigs, spoons, bladed lures like the Celta, and minnow or yabby lures. Large brown trout can become cannibalistic, so the spotted dog colour pattern in a 5 – 7 cm minnow lure works well. As brown trout are often tight to cover, accurate casting is required and may result in lost lures. It is important to work the lure or fly close to cover, or near the bottom where many brown trout take the majority of their food. Trolling lures by themselves or with cowbells or lead lines can cover lots of territory and pick up active fish. Lures should work near the thermocline, along drop-offs or close to other cover. When fish are found at a certain depth, different lures should be tried to maximise catches. Brown trout take a variety of baits, with mudeyes, yabbies, minnows, grubs and worms being most successful. Brown trout will also take maggots, garden snails, corn, cheese, marshmallows and dog food on at least some occasions. There are two basic bait rigs. The first is the classic bubble float (or quill) rig which is used mainly with mudeye or where legal, live minnow baits. However, worms and even yabbies fished under a float close to the bottom can do well especially if there are also carp or other bottom feeders in the area. The other bait rig is the bottom rig, with the least amount of weight you can use being favoured. A long trace and a sliding sinker works well as does a paternoster rig in rivers with a moderate flow. If possible, brown trout should be allowed to move a short distance with the bait before setting the hook. Brown trout are very good eating although like all trout there are some fine bones to be navigated. The general rule with brown trout is that they taste better out of colder and cleaner water.

No. 6 to 4 Baitholder hook

No. 00 to 1 ball sinker

No. 6 to 4 light gauge fly hook

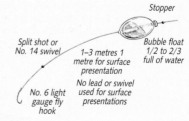

Stopper

Split shot or No. 14 swivel

1–3 metres 1 metre for surface presentation

Bubble float 1/2 to 2/3 full of water

No. 6 light gauge fly hook

No lead or swivel used for surface presentations

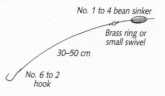

No. 1 to 4 bean sinker

Brass ring or small swivel

30–50 cm

No. 6 to 2 hook

TROUT, BROOK

Scientific name *Salvelinus fontinalis*. Also known as Brookie, brook char, char.

Range A species of char with a very strong preference for clear cold water which severely limits the available waters in Australia. The brook trout is found in Lake Jindabyne, Three Mile Dam and a few small creeks around Jindabyne and the Upper Snowy Mountains. They are found in a few locations in Tasmania, notably Clarence Lagoon and had been introduced with minimal success in a few streams in South Australia.

Description The brook trout is a stunningly attractive species. The ventral and anal fins are bright orange with a black line and then a white leading edge. The markings on the dark upper body are either dots or irregular small lines of cream or off white. The dorsal fin has wavy colouration. The males in spawning condition develop a markedly hooked jaw and even brighter colours. The mouth is large, extending well behind the back edge of the eye. The tail is large and moderately indented or lightly forked. The brook trout can reach around 4 kg in Australia, but the largest fish are generally released brood stock from the hatcheries. These fish do extremely well in hatcheries but do not adapt nearly as well to the wild where they are generally out-competed by other trout species. Any wild caught brook trout is a prize in Australia.

Fishing The brook trout will feed on minnows, flies and insects and may be taken with natural baits and artificials of all these. Dry flies, wet flies and nymphs work best and these hard fighting fish are a real challenge on the fly. Brook trout will take lead head jigs and small minnow lures. Brook trout prefer small and pristine streams and presentation is important due partly to the nature of the lies in these streams. In impoundments, brook trout favour creek or river mouths and may be taken with standard casting or trolling methods. The brook trout is excellent eating, frequently having bright orange flesh, but due to their rarity, most anglers release these fish after a photograph is taken. The long term future for the brook trout in Australia is not good and they may ultimately disappear from wild waters.

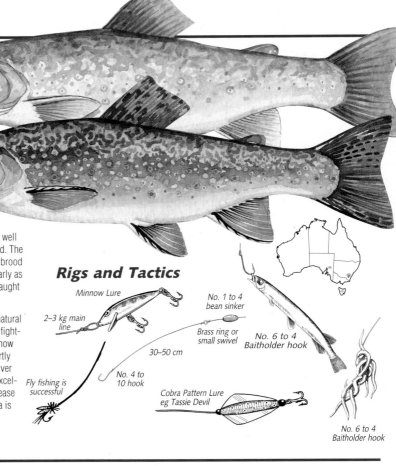

Rigs and Tactics

Minnow Lure

2–3 kg main line

No. 1 to 4 bean sinker

Brass ring or small swivel

30–50 cm

No. 6 to 4 Baitholder hook

Fly fishing is successful

No. 4 to 10 hook

Cobra Pattern Lure eg Tassie Devil

No. 6 to 4 Baitholder hook

TROUT, RAINBOW

Scientific name *Oncorhynchus mykiss*. (formerly *Salmo gairdnerii*) Also known as rainbow, 'bow, Steelhead.

Range Rainbow trout are found from Spring Creek in southern Queensland, through cooler waters at higher elevation across NSW and Victoria. Rainbow trout are found in Tasmania, in the hills of South Australia and south-western Western Australia as far north as Lake Leschenaultia east of Perth. Australia does not possess the prolific runs of 'Steelhead' rainbow trout found in the species' native North America, but some sea run fish are taken in Tasmanian estuaries. Rainbow trout have recently been reclassified in recognition to its relationship with the Pacific salmon such as the Chinook or Quinnat salmon.

Description Rainbow trout possess the fleshy adipose fin of all salmonids behind the dorsal fin. The tail may be slightly forked but characteristically rainbow trout have spots over the entire tail and all of the body except the belly. A pink stripe along the body ranges from very pale in sea run and lake fish to crimson in river fish and those on their spawning run. Male rainbows develop a hooked lower jaw as spawning approaches. Females retain a more rounded head.

Fishing Rainbow trout are generally easier to catch than brown trout but usually fight harder and often jump spectacularly. Rainbow trout are more mobile and will feed more freely in mid to shallow depths. This means that methods such as trolling are more successful, but rainbow trout can selectively feed on daphnia (water fleas) which can make them more difficult to catch. Rainbow trout prefer faster water in streams than brown trout and will often take up station at the head of pools. Rainbow trout can be taken on fly, lure or bait. They take dry flies, wets, nymphs and streamer flies. Rainbow trout can be taken on bright colours and gaudy streamer flies can work well. All standard trout lures work well for rainbow trout, with spinner blade lures like the Celta, Tasmanian devil type lures, leadhead jigs and small minnow lures like the Rapala CD5 and Halco Laser Pro 45 among the most consistent producers. Rainbow trout take all baits. A lightly weighted worm in streams or fairly close to the bank takes fish as do mudeyes fished under a bubble float or trolled with Cowbell trolling blades. Yabbies, grubs and live fish (where legal) take good catches. Rainbow trout make good or excellent eating, especially when taken from cold water and the flesh is bright orange. There are a wide variety of excellent recipes for rainbow trout, but a freshly caught fish wrapped in foil with the gut cavity filled with onion, tomato, butter and lemon pepper certainly takes some beating.

Rigs and Tactics

No lead or swivel used for surface presentations

Stopper

Split shot or No. 14 swivel

1–3 metres 1 metre for surface presentation

Bubble float 1/2 to 2/3 full of water

Bladed Spinner

No. 6 light gauge fly hook

Minnow Lure

Fly fishing is successful

2–3 kg main line

No. 1 to 4 bean sinker

No. 6 to 4 Baitholder hook

Brass ring or small swivel

30–50 cm

No. 4 to 10 hook

Cobra Pattern Lure eg Tassie Devil

SHARK/RAY SPECIES

ELEPHANT FISH

Scientific name *Callorhynchus milii*. Also known as Elephant shark, ghost shark, whitefish, plownose chimera.

Range A cool water fish found from Esperance in Western Australia to Jervis Bay in NSW. It can be found in deeper water most of the year, with females entering shallow bays in summer to lay their eggs.

Description The elephant fish is a unique species easily recognised by the fleshy nose which is used to find food in sandy or lightly silted bottoms. The pectoral fins are large and used like a ray for navigation. The eggs are spindle shaped, about 20 cm long and take 8 months to hatch. Unlike most sharks, the elephant fish has a single gill slit. It has a prominent dorsal spine like a Port Jackson shark and can inflict a painful wound if not handled carefully.

Fishing Until recently, these fish were shunned due to their ugly appearance. However, the flesh is white and firm and good eating and they are being increasingly targeted in southern bays and inlets in summer. Light bottom rigs get maximum sport from these fish. However it is important to realise that the summer fishery targets spawning fish and the take of these fish should be limited to ensure that they are not over-exploited.

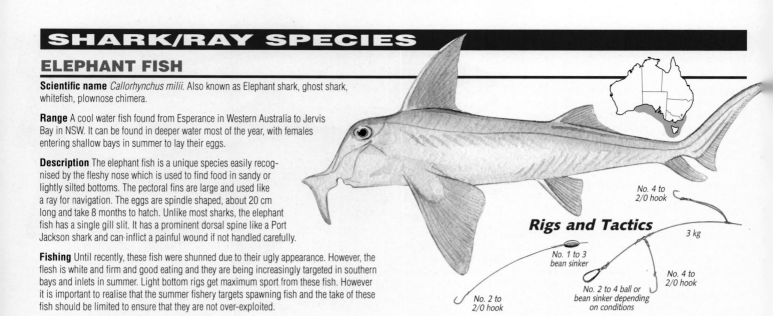

Rigs and Tactics

No. 4 to 2/0 hook
3 kg
No. 1 to 3 bean sinker
No. 4 to 2/0 hook
No. 2 to 2/0 hook
No. 2 to 4 ball or bean sinker depending on conditions

RAY, EAGLE

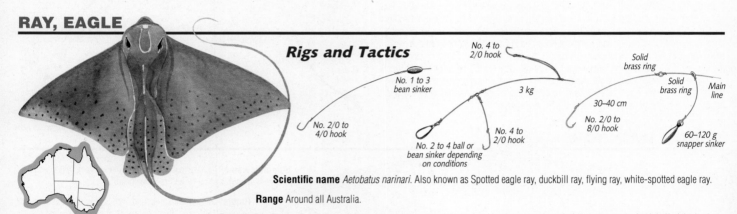

Rigs and Tactics

No. 4 to 2/0 hook
No. 1 to 3 bean sinker
3 kg
Solid brass ring
Solid brass ring
Main line
No. 2/0 to 4/0 hook
30–40 cm
No. 2/0 to 8/0 hook
No. 4 to 2/0 hook
No. 2 to 4 ball or bean sinker depending on conditions
60–120 g snapper sinker

Scientific name *Aetobatus narinari*. Also known as Spotted eagle ray, duckbill ray, flying ray, white-spotted eagle ray.

Range Around all Australia.

Description The eagle ray has a shining brown-black top of the body with a large number of white spots on the back half of the body. The eagle ray has an unusual bulging head with a long and tapering snout which is flattened rather like a duck's bill. The teeth are shaped like a chevron and are used for crushing oysters, pipis and other molluscs. The tail is very long and thin and is around 4 times the width of the body. The eagle ray has 2 – 6 barbed spines at the base of the tail. The eagle ray is a very large species, reaching a width of around 3.5 m, but it is commonly seen at around 1.8 metres.

Fishing The eagle ray is commonly seen jumping or cruising in shallow water or near the surface in ocean waters. The flaps often break the water as the eagle ray moves along, giving the impression of two sharks travelling together. Like most stingrays, the eagle ray is not specifically targeted by recreational anglers. The eagle ray's ability to swerve and rapidly change direction makes the fight of the eagle ray more interesting than the usual dour, physical slog of most other rays. The eagle ray bites best on mollusc baits including pipi, cockle or mussel. They are also taken on squid and cuttlefish baits. Like all rays, the mouth is under the body and the bait should be right on the bottom. As the barbs are close to the body, and the spiracles are large for gripping the eagle ray, this is one of the less dangerous rays. The flesh is of good quality and is under-rated as a food fish.

SHARK, BLUE

Scientific name *Prionace glauca*. Also known as Blue whaler, great blue shark.

Range Circum-Australia but rarely seen in tropical waters or close to land.

Description The blue shark is a striking blue colour which inhabits oceanic waters. Similar in appearance to the mako but the blue shark has much larger pectoral fins which are floppy and scythe-like, smaller gill slits and the teeth are triangular and serrated. When at the surface, both the dorsal fin and top lobe of the tail of the blue shark breaks the surface, but the blue shark can also be caught at great depth. The blue shark can grow to 3.8 m and nearly 200 kilograms.

Fishing Being an oceanic species, the blue shark is most commonly encountered by game fishermen. The blue shark is also commonly caught on long lines by commercial fishermen. The blue shark can be taken on live baits, whole fish, cut baits or squid and at a wide variety of depths. The blue shark can be annoying for those specialist anglers who fish for the ultimate prize, broadbill swordfish, taking deeply fished cyalume lit baits. The blue shark will not jump and though regarded as dangerous, is not often encountered by divers and swimmers.

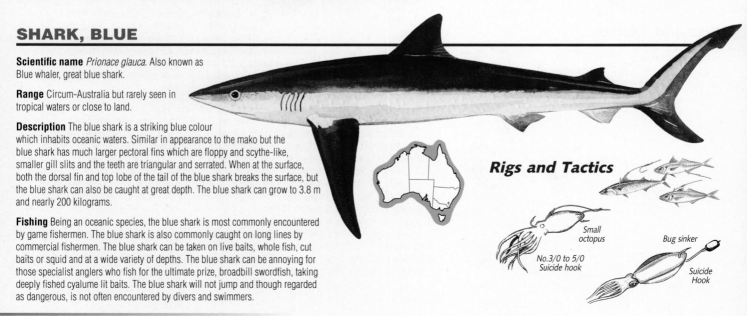

Rigs and Tactics

Small octopus
No.3/0 to 5/0 Suicide hook
Bug sinker
Suicide Hook

SHARK, BRONZE WHALER

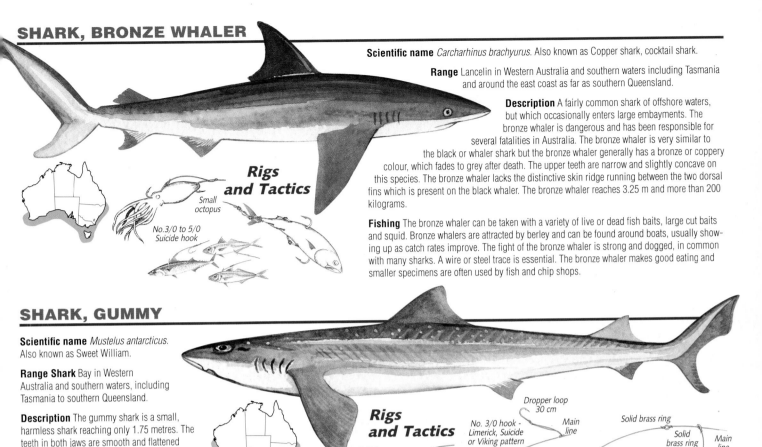

Scientific name *Carcharhinus brachyurus*. Also known as Copper shark, cocktail shark.

Range Lancelin in Western Australia and southern waters including Tasmania and around the east coast as far as southern Queensland.

Description A fairly common shark of offshore waters, but which occasionally enters large embayments. The bronze whaler is dangerous and has been responsible for several fatalities in Australia. The bronze whaler is very similar to the black or whaler shark but the bronze whaler generally has a bronze or coppery colour, which fades to grey after death. The upper teeth are narrow and slightly concave on this species. The bronze whaler lacks the distinctive skin ridge running between the two dorsal fins which is present on the black whaler. The bronze whaler reaches 3.25 m and more than 200 kilograms.

Fishing The bronze whaler can be taken with a variety of live or dead fish baits, large cut baits and squid. Bronze whalers are attracted by berley and can be found around boats, usually showing up as catch rates improve. The fight of the bronze whaler is strong and dogged, in common with many sharks. A wire or steel trace is essential. The bronze whaler makes good eating and smaller specimens are often used by fish and chip shops.

Rigs and Tactics

Small octopus

No.3/0 to 5/0 Suicide hook

SHARK, GUMMY

Scientific name *Mustelus antarcticus*. Also known as Sweet William.

Range Shark Bay in Western Australia and southern waters, including Tasmania to southern Queensland.

Description The gummy shark is a small, harmless shark reaching only 1.75 metres. The teeth in both jaws are smooth and flattened and arranged in a flat pavement-like pattern. The gummy shark looks similar to the school shark, but the school shark's teeth are sharp and triangular and the tail fin has a broad and deeply notched upper lobe, giving a double tail appearance. The upper body of the gummy shark is covered with small white spots which are less apparent in larger fish.

Rigs and Tactics

Solid brass ring

Barrel sinker

30–50 kg trace

1 metre

50 cm

1/2 kg snapper sinker

No. 3/0 hook - Limerick, Suicide or Viking pattern

Dropper loop 30 cm

Dropper loop 15 cm

Main line

50 cm

No. 3/0 hook

Solid brass ring

Solid brass ring

30–40 cm

No. 2/0 to 8/0 hook

Main line

60–120 g snapper sinker

Fishing The gummy shark is frequently taken by anglers on deeper water snapper grounds with standard snapper baits and rigs. The gummy shark is more common on deeper water grounds and is a commercial fishing target which has been seriously overfished in many southern waters. The gummy shark can move into shallow water on occasion. The best baits for gummy shark are squid, cuttlefish, octopus, pilchard and any fresh fish baits. They are most often taken on the bottom hook of a snapper paternoster rig. The gummy shark makes excellent eating and is highly regarded.

SHARK, MAKO

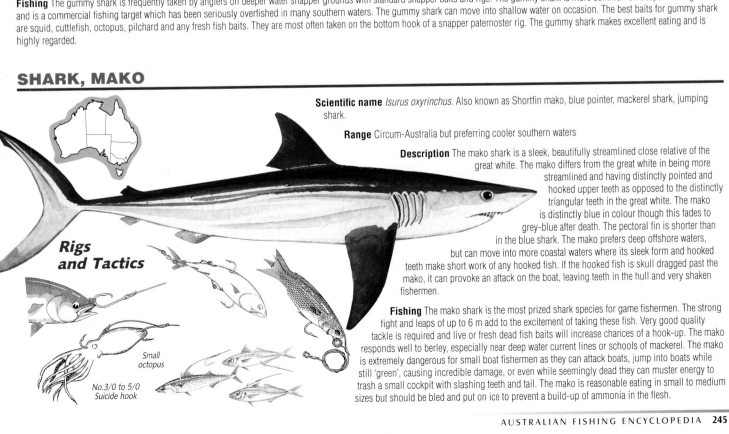

Scientific name *Isurus oxyrinchus*. Also known as Shortfin mako, blue pointer, mackerel shark, jumping shark.

Range Circum-Australia but preferring cooler southern waters

Description The mako shark is a sleek, beautifully streamlined close relative of the great white. The mako differs from the great white in being more streamlined and having distinctly pointed and hooked upper teeth as opposed to the distinctly triangular teeth in the great white. The mako is distinctly blue in colour though this fades to grey-blue after death. The pectoral fin is shorter than in the blue shark. The mako prefers deep offshore waters, but can move into more coastal waters where its sleek form and hooked teeth make short work of any hooked fish. If the hooked fish is skull dragged past the mako, it can provoke an attack on the boat, leaving teeth in the hull and very shaken fishermen.

Fishing The mako shark is the most prized shark species for game fishermen. The strong fight and leaps of up to 6 m add to the excitement of taking these fish. Very good quality tackle is required and live or fresh dead fish baits will increase chances of a hook-up. The mako responds well to berley, especially near deep water current lines or schools of mackerel. The mako is extremely dangerous for small boat fishermen as they can attack boats, jump into boats while still 'green', causing incredible damage, or even while seemingly dead they can muster energy to trash a small cockpit with slashing teeth and tail. The mako is reasonable eating in small to medium sizes but should be bled and put on ice to prevent a build-up of ammonia in the flesh.

Rigs and Tactics

Small octopus

No.3/0 to 5/0 Suicide hook

SHARK, SCHOOL

Scientific name *Galeorhinus galeus*. Also known as Snapper shark, eastern school shark, greyboy, grey shark, soupfin shark, tope.

Range Rottnest Island in Western Australia and southern waters including Tasmania and around the east coast as far as southern Queensland.

Description The school shark is a very slow growing, small and harmless species which is common in cool southern waters. It is more common in offshore areas, where it forms the basis of a substantial, but overfished commercial fishery. Juveniles may occasionally be found in coastal bays. This species is readily identified by the tail fin shape, which has the upper lobe broad and deeply notched, giving the appearance of a double tail. The dorsal fin is set well forward and is closer to the commencement of the pectoral than the ventral fins. Both jaws carry sharp, triangular teeth of similar size which immediately separates the school shark from the gummy shark with its smooth and flattened teeth. The school shark can reach 2 m and 60 kg but is commonly much smaller. School sharks can live more than 40 years and a tagged fish had grown only 18 cm in over 35 years at liberty.

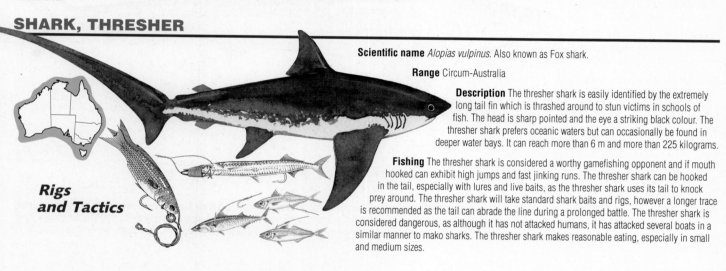

Rigs and Tactics

Fishing The school shark is frequently taken with gummy sharks and other cool water reef species on the deeper reefs of southern waters. Standard snapper rigs and baits of fish flesh, squid and cuttlefish will take the majority of school sharks. A trace is recommended as the school shark can easily bite through monofilament lines. Smaller specimens can be taken on similar shallower reefs in larger bays and estuaries. The school shark is excellent eating but should be kept cool as, like all sharks, a build up of ammonia can accumulate in the flesh if the fish is not well handled.

SHARK, THRESHER

Scientific name *Alopias vulpinus*. Also known as Fox shark.

Range Circum-Australia

Description The thresher shark is easily identified by the extremely long tail fin which is thrashed around to stun victims in schools of fish. The head is sharp pointed and the eye a striking black colour. The thresher shark prefers oceanic waters but can occasionally be found in deeper water bays. It can reach more than 6 m and more than 225 kilograms.

Rigs and Tactics

Fishing The thresher shark is considered a worthy gamefishing opponent and if mouth hooked can exhibit high jumps and fast jinking runs. The thresher shark can be hooked in the tail, especially with lures and live baits, as the thresher shark uses its tail to knock prey around. The thresher shark will take standard shark baits and rigs, however a longer trace is recommended as the tail can abrade the line during a prolonged battle. The thresher shark is considered dangerous, as although it has not attacked humans, it has attacked several boats in a similar manner to mako sharks. The thresher shark makes reasonable eating, especially in small and medium sizes.

STINGAREE, COMMON

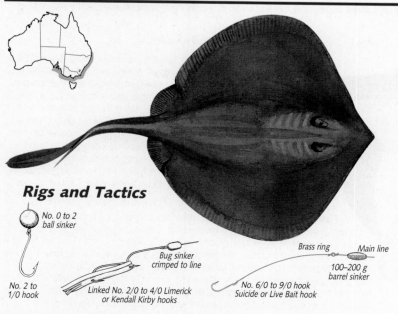

Rigs and Tactics

No. 0 to 2 ball sinker

No. 2 to 1/0 hook

Bug sinker crimped to line

Linked No. 2/0 to 4/0 Limerick or Kendall Kirby hooks

No. 6/0 to 9/0 hook Suicide or Live Bait hook

Brass ring

Main line

100–200 g barrel sinker

Scientific name *Trygonoptera testaceous*

Range Around the Gulf of St Vincent in South Australia and east including the east coast to Brisbane in Queensland.

Description The stingarees are easily separated from the stingrays by having a tail fin on a relatively short tail rather than a whip like tail ending in a point. The common stingaree reaches 75 cm which makes it a real challenge on bream gear. It is found in coastal waters or estuaries where it favours areas of sand and reef. It is most common in NSW waters. The common stingaree has no spots or bands on its dorsal surface which is sandy-brown to a deep chocolate brown. The bottom or ventral surface is white or creamy white and has a brown margin. There are one or two spines which are serrated and venomous. A sting requires medical attention and is very prone to deep infection.

Fishing The common stingaree is not a target species but is taken in reasonable numbers by anglers fishing for bream, flathead or mulloway. The common stingaree is most active at night and can move into quite shallow water. Like all the ray species, the common stingaree puts up an extremely strong, dogged and unspectacular fight. They may burrow into the sand and not be able to be dislodged, especially if the angler is using light line. The common stingaree is an opportunistic feeder and can be taken on most baits if presented on the bottom. The common stingaree is not generally regarded as a food fish.

BARRAMUNDI

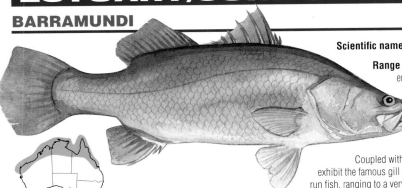

Scientific name *Lates calcarifer*. Also known as Barra, giant perch.

Range The barramundi range extends from the Mary River in Queensland around the top end to Shark Bay in Western Australia, although the barramundi is most famous as a northern Australia species.

Description The barramundi is a special fish which is as beautiful in reality as it is in the dreams of so many anglers. It has a small head with a large mouth and large eyes which glow bright red in torch light or at certain angles in daylight. Barramundi have large scales and a particularly powerful tail. Coupled with their thick shoulders, barramundi can put up a good fight although not all fish will exhibit the famous gill arching leaps when hooked. The barramundi can be a brilliant silver colour for sea run fish, ranging to a very dark, chocolate brown colour for fish in billabongs at the end of the dry season or those grown in aquaculture facilities. Small barra and those in aquaria exhibit a characteristic light stripe down the forehead between the eyes which becomes more pronounced when the fish is excited. Barramundi in Australia change sex as they grow older (interestingly barramundi in Thailand do not change sex). All fish start out as males and, after spawning once or twice, become female for the rest of their lives. It is therefore impossible to catch a granddaddy barra as it would certainly be female. This sex change is more related to age than size, but barramundi over 8 kg are almost certainly all female. This fact, coupled with the need to spawn in estuaries, makes barramundi vulnerable to overfishing and makes management of the species particularly difficult.

Fishing There are few thrills in fishing in Australia to match the thumping strike of a large saltwater barramundi on a well cast lure or fly. Barramundi are taken in some of the most beautiful country in Australia and, as top predators which are susceptible to commercial and recreational overfishing, the more remote the area, the better your chances of really large specimens. Barramundi are classical ambush feeders and require some stream craft to be most successful. In tidal reaches, look for places which congregate food, especially on a dropping tide such as eddies or draining creek mouths. In freshwater, look for cover and cast close to or beyond likely looking snags, drop-offs or rock bars. Baitcast or trolled diving minnow lures have been the most successful for barramundi for many years, but a supply of rattling spot lures, soft plastic jigs and spinnerbaits can be deadly. Even when there is little or no surface activity, barramundi can make a spectacular slashing strike at a surface lure. With many American made lures, change the hooks, as a large barramundi can be lost through straightening light gauge hooks designed for smaller fish. More and more anglers are fishing for barramundi with the fly. Flies such as Dahlberg Divers and Deceiver patterns work very well and have the advantage of being able to be repeatedly placed very near to cover while drifting along a shore, teasing barra to strike. Many barramundi are taken on live bait. A common rig is to fish a live fish on the bottom of a large hole. However, a live cherabin or fish under a float and drifted past a likely snag can entice even the most reluctant fish to strike. The Northern Territory and Western Australia have strict rules for the taking of barramundi. The only way that quality fishing can be maintained is to increase commercial closed waters and recreational fishers should take only the fish which are absolutely necessary.

Rigs and Tactics

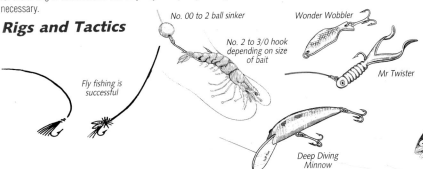

Fly fishing is successful

No. 00 to 2 ball sinker

No. 2 to 3/0 hook depending on size of bait

Wonder Wobbler

Mr Twister

Deep Diving Minnow

No. 1 to 3 bean sinker

No. 2 to 2/0 hook

24 kg trace

Live bait

Minnow Lure

BREAM, BLACK

Scientific name *Acanthopagrus butcheri*. Also known as Bream, blue nosed bream and southern black bream.

Range From Shark Bay in Western Australia and around southern and western coasts to Mallacoota in Victoria and Tasmania.

Description The black bream is a very highly sought after angling species of the estuaries of the southern parts of Australia. It can be found in oceanic waters in the gulf regions of South Australia but not in Western Australia. A recently discovered population in Lake Clifton near Perth can tolerate salinity over double that of sea water. The black bream looks very similar to the yellowfin bream and hybrids have been recorded from the Gippsland lakes in Victoria. The major difference is in fin colour, with the black bream possessing brownish or dusky ventral and anal fins. The mouth is fairly small with rows of peg like teeth and crushing plates on the palate. It reaches a maximum size of around 3.5 kg, but a specimen over 1 kg is highly regarded.

Fishing This is one of the most sought after species in Australia. They are most commonly fished with a light line of 3 – 5 kilograms. Alvey reels on long slow action rods were the most popular but bait running reels on shorter rods are mounting a serious challenge. Bream generally bite best on a rising tide and after dark but many quality fish, including on lures, are taken during the day and in ambush sites on the bottom half of the tide. Bream can be timid biters so as little weight as possible should be used and any sinker must run freely. Best baits are prawn and yabby, although beach, blood and squirt worms, pipi, anchovy or blue sardine and flesh baits also work extremely well. Some anglers make their own special dough baits out of flour and water with added meat, cheese, sugar, fish oils or other secret ingredients. When bream bite, it is important to let them run up to a metre before setting the hook. The bream will then run strongly for the nearest cover and many fish are lost on this initial surge. Many bream are now being taken on lures and is one of the fastest growing forms of lure fishing. Small minnow lures or soft plastics fished close to cover, drop offs or oyster leases can provide fantastic fishing. The black bream makes excellent eating.

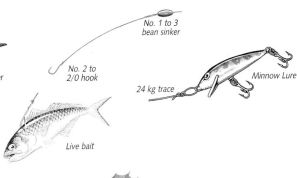

Rigs and Tactics

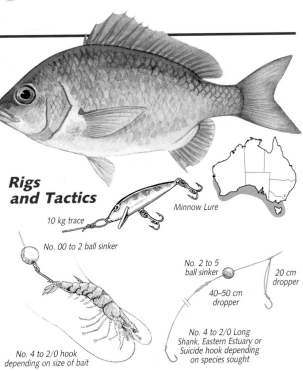

Minnow Lure

10 kg trace

No. 00 to 2 ball sinker

No. 2 to 5 ball sinker

20 cm dropper

40–50 cm dropper

No. 4 to 2/0 hook depending on size of bait

No. 4 to 2/0 Long Shank, Eastern Estuary or Suicide hook depending on species sought

BREAM, PIKEY

Scientific name *Acanthopagrus berda* Also known as Bream.

Range Onslow in Western Australia around the northern coast to central Queensland.

Description The pikey bream is very similar to the black bream, but with more pointed snout and very stout second anal spine. The pikey bream overlaps in range with the western and eastern yellowfin bream, both of which possess yellow anal and caudal fins. The pikey bream also lacks the characteristic black spot at the base of the pectoral fin of the yellowfin bream. Attains a maximum size of 55 centimetres.

Fishing Similar methods as for the black bream, but more common around jetties, pylons and creek mouths. The pikey bream makes excellent eating but should be bled and chilled after catpure.

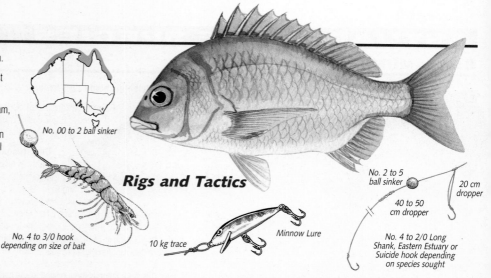

Rigs and Tactics

No. 00 to 2 ball sinker

No. 4 to 3/0 hook depending on size of bait

10 kg trace

Minnow Lure

No. 2 to 5 ball sinker

40 to 50 cm dropper

20 cm dropper

No. 4 to 2/0 Long Shank, Eastern Estuary or Suicide hook depending on species sought

BREAM, YELLOWFIN

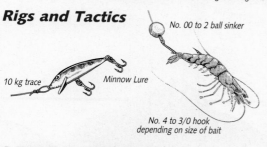

Scientific name *Acanthopagrus australis*. Also known as Silver bream, sea bream, surf bream, Eastern black bream.

Range Townsville in Queensland to Lakes Entrance in Victoria.

Description The yellowfin bream is similar to other bream, but with a black spot at the base of the pectoral fin. Also has yellow or yellowish anal and ventral fins. Frequently taken from inshore oceanic waters where the colour is frequently silver, varying to dark olive from estuaries. Lacks the brown horizontal stripes and black stomach cavity lining of the similar tarwhine. Attains a maximum size of 66 cm and 4.4 kg but fish over a kilogram are noteworthy.

Fishing Fantastic fishing for yellowfin bream can be had near the mouths of estuaries in winter when the fish moves downstream to spawn. Estuarine fish can be taken as described for black bream, with oyster leases, rock walls and edges of drop offs being prime spots. Berley works very well when fish are finicky. In ocean waters, bream can be occasionally taken on cabbage weed while fishing for luderick. They are also a prime target when using cunjevoi, often inhabiting the same white water washes as drummer, but often a little further out. Yellowfin bream can be targeted with lightly weighted blue sardines, anchovies or half a pilchard cast into the edge of a good wash. When tailor are feeding, a bait which sinks through the tailor can take some thumping bream. In the surf, pilchards which repeatedly come back with the gut area eaten out by small bites is a sign that bream may be present, especially if fishing the edges of gutters. A half a pilchard rigged on smaller hooks, a pipi or beach worm bait can take these fish. Yellowfin bream are excellent eating although fish taken on weed can have an iodine taint.

Rigs and Tactics

10 kg trace

Minnow Lure

No. 00 to 2 ball sinker

No. 4 to 3/0 hook depending on size of bait

No. 4 to 2/0 hook

3 kg

No. 2 to 4 ball or bean sinker depending on conditions

No. 4 to 2/0 hook

No. 1 to 4 bean sinker

Brass ring or small swivel

30–50 cm

No. 1/0 to 6/0 hook

No. 2 to 5 ball sinker

40–50 cm dropper

20 cm dropper

No. 4 to 2/0 Long Shank, Eastern Estuary or Suicide hook depending on species sought

CATFISH, FORKTAIL

Scientific name *Cnidoglanis macrocephalus*. Also known as Cobbler.

Range Estuarine and coastal waters from southern Queensland to eastern Victoria and northern Tasmania. Also from western South Australia around to the Abrolhos Islands in Western Australia.

Description A very long eel-tailed species found in muddy or weedy estuaries. They are most commonly caught near washed up weeds or near weed patches. When spawning, cobbler form balls of fish which can be spotted by the muddy water which surrounds them. They make nests in weed and may be significantly affected by weed removal activities. The pectoral and dorsal fins possess a large spine which contains a poison gland. A puncture wound causes a great deal of pain. Treatment is with hot water or compresses to cook the protein. The wound may require hospitalisation or painkilling injections.

Fishing Cobbler are actively fished for in many areas with light bottom rigs and baits of prawn or worms. They are good fighters but must be handled carefully when being unhooked. In some areas, estuary catfish are taken by gidgee or spear in the shallows at night but this method is illegal in many areas and at the very least is not conducive to catch and release fishing. In spite of their appearance, estuary catfish are excellent eating and are highly prized, especially in Western Australia.

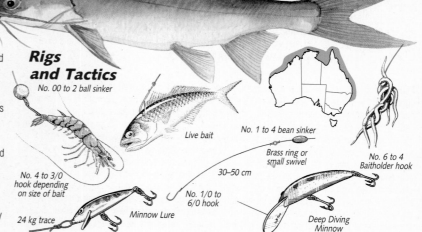

Rigs and Tactics

No. 00 to 2 ball sinker

Live bait

No. 1 to 4 bean sinker

Brass ring or small swivel

No. 6 to 4 Baitholder hook

No. 4 to 3/0 hook depending on size of bait

30–50 cm

No. 1/0 to 6/0 hook

24 kg trace

Minnow Lure

Deep Diving Minnow

DART, SNUBNOSE

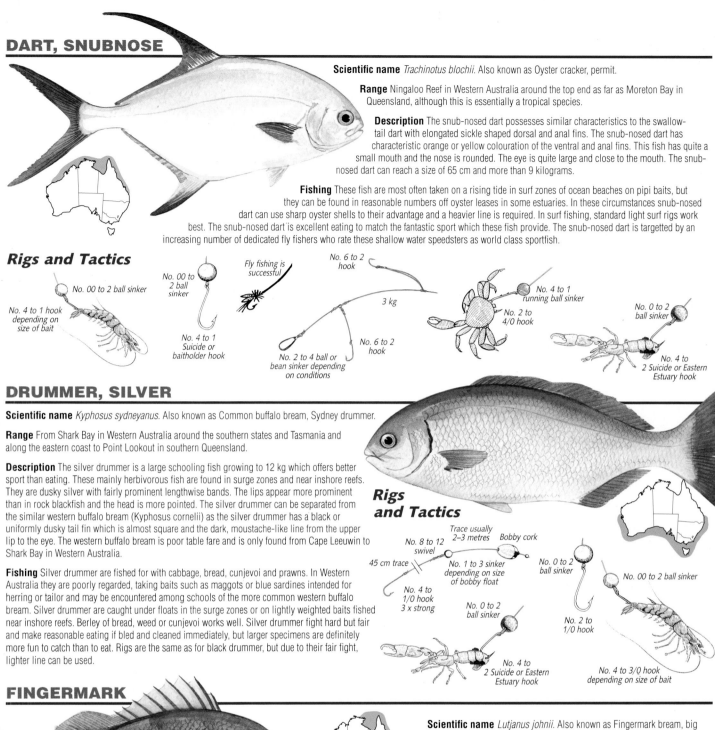

Scientific name *Trachinotus blochii*. Also known as Oyster cracker, permit.

Range Ningaloo Reef in Western Australia around the top end as far as Moreton Bay in Queensland, although this is essentially a tropical species.

Description The snub-nosed dart possesses similar characteristics to the swallow-tail dart with elongated sickle shaped dorsal and anal fins. The snub-nosed dart has characteristic orange or yellow colouration of the ventral and anal fins. This fish has quite a small mouth and the nose is rounded. The eye is quite large and close to the mouth. The snub-nosed dart can reach a size of 65 cm and more than 9 kilograms.

Fishing These fish are most often taken on a rising tide in surf zones of ocean beaches on pipi baits, but they can be found in reasonable numbers off oyster leases in some estuaries. In these circumstances snub-nosed dart can use sharp oyster shells to their advantage and a heavier line is required. In surf fishing, standard light surf rigs work best. The snub-nosed dart is excellent eating to match the fantastic sport which these fish provide. The snub-nosed dart is targetted by an increasing number of dedicated fly fishers who rate these shallow water speedsters as world class sportfish.

Rigs and Tactics

No. 00 to 2 ball sinker

No. 4 to 1 hook depending on size of bait

No. 00 to 2 ball sinker

No. 4 to 1 Suicide or baitholder hook

Fly fishing is successful

No. 6 to 2 hook

3 kg

No. 2 to 4 ball or bean sinker depending on conditions

No. 6 to 2 hook

No. 4 to 1 running ball sinker

No. 2 to 4/0 hook

No. 0 to 2 ball sinker

No. 4 to 2 Suicide or Eastern Estuary hook

DRUMMER, SILVER

Scientific name *Kyphosus sydneyanus*. Also known as Common buffalo bream, Sydney drummer.

Range From Shark Bay in Western Australia around the southern states and Tasmania and along the eastern coast to Point Lookout in southern Queensland.

Description The silver drummer is a large schooling fish growing to 12 kg which offers better sport than eating. These mainly herbivorous fish are found in surge zones and near inshore reefs. They are dusky silver with fairly prominent lengthwise bands. The lips appear more prominent than in rock blackfish and the head is more pointed. The silver drummer can be separated from the similar western buffalo bream (Kyphosus cornelii) as the silver drummer has a black or uniformly dusky tail fin which is almost square and the dark, moustache-like line from the upper lip to the eye. The western buffalo bream is poor table fare and is only found from Cape Leeuwin to Shark Bay in Western Australia.

Fishing Silver drummer are fished for with cabbage, bread, cunjevoi and prawns. In Western Australia they are poorly regarded, taking baits such as maggots or blue sardines intended for herring or tailor and may be encountered among schools of the more common western buffalo bream. Silver drummer are caught under floats in the surge zones or on lightly weighted baits fished near inshore reefs. Berley of bread, weed or cunjevoi works well. Silver drummer fight hard but fair and make reasonable eating if bled and cleaned immediately, but larger specimens are definitely more fun to catch than to eat. Rigs are the same as for black drummer, but due to their fair fight, lighter line can be used.

Rigs and Tactics

Trace usually 2–3 metres   Bobby cork

No. 8 to 12 swivel

45 cm trace

No. 4 to 1/0 hook 3 x strong

No. 1 to 3 sinker depending on size of bobby float

No. 0 to 2 ball sinker

No. 4 to 2 Suicide or Eastern Estuary hook

No. 0 to 2 ball sinker

No. 00 to 2 ball sinker

No. 2 to 1/0 hook

No. 4 to 3/0 hook depending on size of bait

FINGERMARK

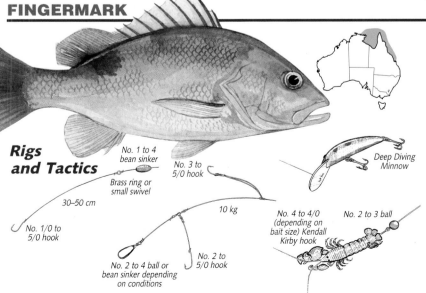

Rigs and Tactics

No. 1 to 4 bean sinker

No. 3 to 5/0 hook

Brass ring or small swivel

30–50 cm

No. 1/0 to 5/0 hook

10 kg

No. 2 to 4 ball or bean sinker depending on conditions

No. 2 to 5/0 hook

Deep Diving Minnow

No. 4 to 4/0 (depending on bait size) Kendall Kirby hook

No. 2 to 3 ball

Scientific name *Lutjanus johnii*. Also known as Fingermark bream, big scale red, golden snapper.

Range This species is found in northern waters, from the Territory to central Queensland. This fish should not be confused with another species also called Fingermark (Lutjanus russelli) which is found over a wider range including Western Australia which is more correctly known as the Moses perch.

Description The fingermark is a large sea-perch commonly taken from northern inshore and reef waters and estuaries. It has a speckled appearance because of a dark spot on each scale, which gives the appearance of parallel fine stripes. A large black blotch which varies in colour and intensity is located below the soft dorsal rays. Grows to 90 cm and more than 10 kilograms.

Fishing This species has become a renowned deep diving lure taker through the writing of the great Vic McCristal. It can be taken on lures near the mouths of estuaries or rocky outcrops. They also take cut and whole fish baits well and provide excellent sport. Small schools of similar sized fish are frequently encountered. Fingermark are considered excellent eating.

FLATHEAD, DUSKY

Scientific name *Platycephalus fuscus.* Also known as Estuary flathead, mud flathead, black flathead, flattie, frog and lizard (especially large specimens).

Range Mackay in Queensland to Wilson's Promontory and eastern Bass Strait in Victoria.

Description The dusky flathead is the largest of the 30 species of flathead in Australia, reaching 10 kg and 150 centimetres. Any fish above 5 kg is certainly worth boasting about. The flathead shape is unmistakable, and the dusky flathead also has the sharp opercular (cheek) spines to spike the unwary. The colouration is highly variable from light fawn to black depending on the type of bottom they are found on. The belly ranges from creamy yellow to white. The tail fin features a characteristic dark spot in the top end corner and a patch of blue on the lower half. This is an estuarine or inshore species. This feature plus its large size and good eating make it the ultimate prize for many weekend anglers.

Fishing These are magic fish to target, being common enough to reward the beginner but challenging for the specialist or dedicated angler. Big dusky flathead leave a tell tale indentation in estuarine sand or soft substrate at low tide. They are ambush feeders best fished on a dropping tide in areas where food is concentrated. This includes creek mouths, drop-offs, the sandy side of weed edges and gutters in the surf zone. Dusky flathead can be caught on a rising tide but they can be more finicky and spread out. Trolling the deep edges of drop-offs or flicking baits into these areas works well. Dusky flathead love lures, where the active approach generally brings better results. Diving lures, wobblers and lead head jigs work very well. Trolling diving lures along channel edges takes good numbers of sometimes very large fish and the lure, if weed is not too prevalent, should occasionally touch bottom, putting up a puff of sand. Dusky flathead cannot resist a live poddy mullet or prawn, while cut fish baits, pilchards, whitebait, bluebait, anchovies and prawns all take many fish. It is best to drift or keep the bait moving as they are ambush feeders waiting for the food to come to them. Dusky flathead are very good eating.

Rigs and Tactics

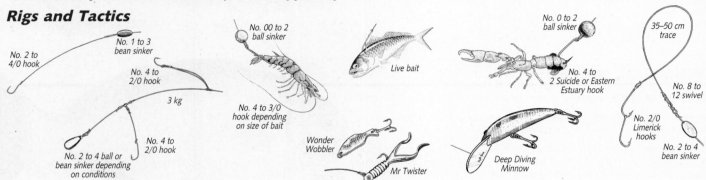

No. 2 to 4/0 hook

No. 1 to 3 bean sinker

No. 4 to 2/0 hook

3 kg

No. 2 to 4 ball or bean sinker depending on conditions

No. 4 to 2/0 hook

No. 00 to 2 ball sinker

No. 4 to 3/0 hook depending on size of bait

Live bait

Wonder Wobbler

Mr Twister

No. 0 to 2 ball sinker

No. 4 to 2 Suicide or Eastern Estuary hook

Deep Diving Minnow

35–50 cm trace

No. 8 to 12 swivel

No. 2/0 Limerick hooks

No. 2 to 4 bean sinker

FLATHEAD, SAND

Scientific name *Platycephalus arenarius* (Northern sand flathead), *Platycephalus bassensis* (Southern sand flathead) Also known as Northern-flag tailed flathead; Souther–slimy flathead, bay flathead, common flathead, sandy flathead.

Range The northern sand flathead is found from the Northern Territory part of the Gulf of Carpentaria to northern NSW, but can be found as far south as the Central Coast on occasions. The southern sand flathead is found from around Port Macquarie in NSW, but is more common from the NSW south coast to Tasmania and to South Australia. A similar species, the Western sand flathead (*Platycephalus longispinis*) is found from Cape Leeuwin to Carnarvon in Western Australia.

Description The various sand flatheads are generally smaller than the blue-spotted or dusky flathead. The northern sand flathead can reach 45 cm but is more commonly encountered in large numbers at around 30 cm in estuaries or on adjacent beaches. They can be found to a depth of 30 fathoms. They have a distinctive pattern of long, horizontal black stripes on its tail. The southern sand flathead has two or sometimes three squared off black patches on the lower part of the tail fin. This species is reputed to reach over 3 kg but is rarely found over a kilogram.

Fishing These fish are taken with similar methods for other flathead. The northern sand flathead will move upwards a greater distance to take a lure than the other flathead. These fish can be found with other flathead species and can be a pest at smaller sizes, seemingly being all mouth and spines and picking apart baits intended for tailor, bream or large dusky flathead that can all be found in similar areas. They are good eating and are undervalued.

Rigs and Tactics

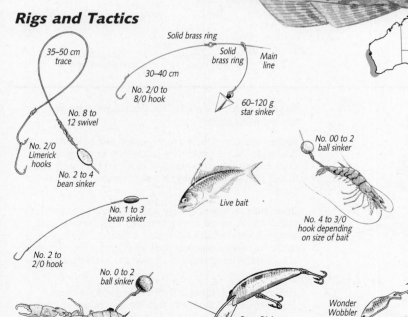

35–50 cm trace

Solid brass ring

Solid brass ring

30–40 cm

Main line

No. 2/0 to 8/0 hook

60–120 g star sinker

No. 8 to 12 swivel

No. 2/0 Limerick hooks

No. 2 to 4 bean sinker

No. 1 to 3 bean sinker

No. 2 to 2/0 hook

Live bait

No. 00 to 2 ball sinker

No. 4 to 3/0 hook depending on size of bait

No. 0 to 2 ball sinker

No. 4 to 2 Suicide or Eastern Estuary hook

Deep Diving Minnow

Wonder Wobbler

Mr Twister

FLATHEAD, SOUTHERN BLUE-SPOTTED

Scientific name *Platycephalus speculator*. Also known as Southern flathead, yank flathead, Castelnau's flathead, southern dusky flathead, bluespot flathead, long nose flathead, shovelnose flathead.

Range From Kalbarri in Western Australia and around the southern part of Australia and Tasmania to the southernmost NSW waters.

Description This flathead can be distinguished on the basis of grey-green spots on the top half of the tail and 3 to 5 large black spots on the lower portion, surrounded by white or off-white. This species also has only one dorsal spine compared with two for many other flathead. The southern blue-spotted flathead can reach a maximum size of nearly 8 kg, although any fish of 3 kg is rare and it is much more common at around a kilogram.

Fishing The southern blue-spot flathead can be found in similar areas to other flatheads, ambushing prey wherever possible. This species can occasionally be found over weed patches or around the edges of weeds. It is not as commonly taken on lures and can be a welcome bonus when fishing for King George whiting or when baits sink through berley fishing for herring and garfish. Like all the flathead, the southern blue-spotted is good eating.

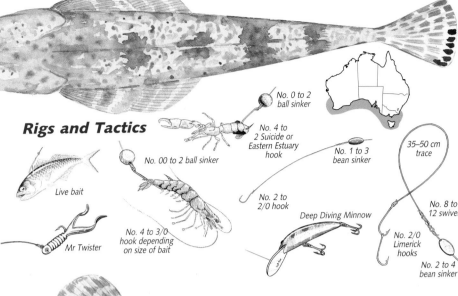

Rigs and Tactics

Live bait

Mr Twister

No. 00 to 2 ball sinker

No. 4 to 3/0 hook depending on size of bait

No. 0 to 2 ball sinker

No. 4 to 2 Suicide or Eastern Estuary hook

No. 1 to 3 bean sinker

No. 2 to 2/0 hook

Deep Diving Minnow

35–50 cm trace

No. 8 to 12 swivel

No. 2/0 Limerick hooks

No. 2 to 4 bean sinker

FLATHEAD, TIGER

Scientific name *Neoplatycephalus richardsoni*. Also known as Trawl flathead, king flathead, spiky flathead, toothy flathead.

Range Found from around Sydney in NSW south into Victorian and Tasmanian waters, but they are not found from Western Victoria.

Description Tiger flathead have a somewhat more cylindrical body compared to the obviously compressed form of the other flathead. Tiger flathead colour varies but generally has a reddish-orange or reddish-brown base colour but with brighter orange spots which extend to the tail. The tiger flathead has large teeth on the roof of the mouth. The maximum size is 2.5 kg but they are most often encountered from 0.5 to 1.5 kilograms.

Fishing Tiger flathead are a common trawl species in the south-eastern waters to a depth of 80 fathoms. However, in parts of Victoria and Tasmania they can enter bays, harbours and estuaries. As they are often taken from deep water, heavy handlines or boat rods and typical paternoster rigs with up to four droppers are used. Baits of fish flesh, pilchards, squid or prawns take most fish. In shallower water, live baits prove deadly. Tiger flathead are a highly regarded food fish

Rigs and Tactics

No. 1 to 5 bean sinker

No. 2 to 2/0 hook

No. 3/0 hook - Limerick, Suicide or Viking pattern

Dropper loop 30 cm

Main line

50 cm

50 cm

Dropper loop 15 cm

1/2 kg snapper sinker

No. 3/0 hook

No. 2 to 5 ball sinker

20 cm dropper

40–50 cm dropper

No. 4 to 2/0 Long Shank, Eastern Estuary or Suicide hook depending on species sought

FLOUNDER, LARGE TOOTHED

Scientific name *Pseudorhombus arsius*. Also known as Flounder.

Range Found in varying numbers throughout Australia, but rare in South Australia and south of Cockburn Sound in Western Australia.

Description The large toothed flounder is a left eyed flounder, i.e. both eyes are on the left side after the right eye migrates around the head during juvenile development. This species has highly variable colouration which can change rapidly, depending on the bottom where it is found. It ranges from the shallow mud and sand banks of estuaries to depths of 35 fathoms. The large toothed flounded possesses large front teeth in its upper and lower jaws. Reaches 50 cm and more than 1 kg but is most common at 30 to 35 centimetres. Flounders have a separate tail which easily distinguishes them from the sole which is another flat fish.

Fishing These flounder are most often a pleasant addition to catches of flathead, bream and whiting. They can take a reasonably large bait and fish flesh, small whole fish and prawns most often successful. As with other ambush feeders, a more mobile approach and lighter line increases catches. Flounders take small lures readily, with lead head jigs, small minnow lures, wobblers and flies providing great sport. Flounders make excellent eating.

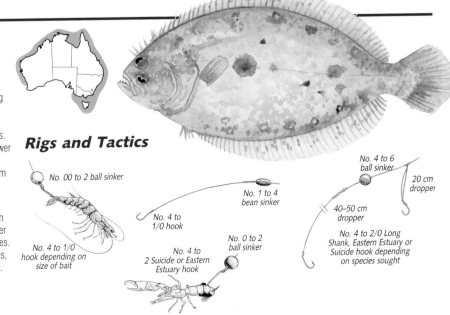

Rigs and Tactics

No. 00 to 2 ball sinker

No. 4 to 1/0 hook depending on size of bait

No. 4 to 1/0 hook

No. 4 to 2 Suicide or Eastern Estuary hook

No. 0 to 2 ball sinker

No. 1 to 4 bean sinker

No. 4 to 6 ball sinker

20 cm dropper

40–50 cm dropper

No. 4 to 2/0 Long Shank, Eastern Estuary or Suicide hook depending on species sought

FLOUNDER, SMALL TOOTHED

Scientific name *Pseudorhombus jenynsii*.

Range A generally cooler water species but found from Exmouth Gulf in Western Australia around the southern states but rarely from Tasmania to central Queensland.

Description The small toothed flounder is also left-eyed and similar to the large toothed flounder but does not possess large teeth in the jaws. This species also has five or six prominent eye spots on the body which are an aggregation of small brown spots surrounded by white. Grows to 36 centimetres.

Fishing The small toothed flounder is taken from similar habitats as the other flounders and with similar baits. Flounder can often be taken by drifting or casting to the deeper edges of drop-offs or near the edges of gravel, mud and sand where these fish often lie in wait. Small toothed flounder can also be taken on jigs. Although not a large species, the shape and bone structure lends itself to a tasty and attractive plate presentation.

Rigs and Tactics

Wonder Wobbler

Mr Twister

No. 00 to 2 ball sinker

No. 6 to 2 hook depending on size of bait

No. 1 to 3 bean sinker

No. 6 to 2 hook

No. 4 to 2 Suicide or Eastern Estuary hook

No. 0 to 2 ball sinker

No. 2 to 5 ball sinker

40–50 cm dropper

20 cm dropper

No. 4 to 6 hook

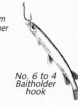

No. 6 to 4 Baitholder hook

HAIRTAIL

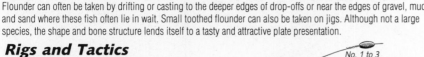

Scientific name *Trichiurus lepturus*. Also known as Ribbonfish, Australian hairtail, largehead hairtail, cutlassfish.

Range Found with a disjointed distribution in deeper estuaries or harbours from Shark Bay in Western Australia to Victoria and South Australia and as far as southern Queensland.

Description The hairtail is a brilliantly silver fish which is strongly compressed and elongated, growing to 2.35 m and a weight of 6 kg, although it is frequently encountered at around 1.5 to 1.8 metres. The hairtail has fearsome fangs which also possess an anti-coagulant, making any cuts bleed profusely. The hairtail has no tail, whereas the similar frostfish (*Lepidopus caudatus*) has a tiny forked tail. The hairtail has no scales, but the brilliant silver skin can be removed by rubbing with a rough cloth. They appear in some estuaries sporadically and in large numbers, but then may not be seen for several more years. The best bets for these fish are in Coal and Candle and Cowan Creeks in the Hawkesbury system and Port Kembla and Newcastle harbours in NSW during autumn and especially winter months, but commercial fishing has had an impact.

Fishing The vast majority of fish are taken at night. The hairtail is a predator which prefers live bait, with yellowtail and slimy mackerel favoured. Hairtail are often taken on dead fish such as garfish, pilchards or fresh cut flesh. Hairtail will strike lures including diving lures and vertically jigged lures or jigs when feeding well but hook-ups are difficult through the teeth. Wire traces or ganged hooks are essential and some anglers use light sticks to assist hairtail finding the bait. As the fish are found in deep holes, setting baits at different depths until fish are found will rapidly locate the optimum depth so all baits can be moved to the same level. The hairtail is excellent to eat with delicate flesh which cooks very quickly.

Rigs and Tactics

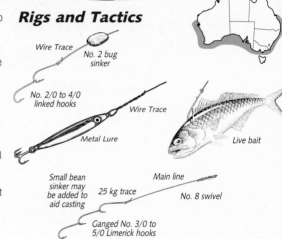

Wire Trace

No. 2 bug sinker

No. 2/0 to 4/0 linked hooks

Metal Lure

Wire Trace

Live bait

Small bean sinker may be added to aid casting

25 kg trace

Main line

No. 8 swivel

Ganged No. 3/0 to 5/0 Limerick hooks

HERRING, AUSTRALIAN

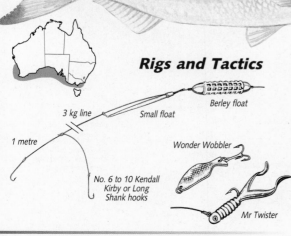

Scientific name *Arripis georgiana*. Also known as Tommy rough, tommy, ruff, bull herring, Western herring.

Range Taken from Shark Bay in Western Australia along the south coast to the far south coast of NSW but more commonly south of Gippsland Lakes in Victoria and Geraldton in Western Australia.

Description A pretty and highly sought after species, especially in South Australia and Western Australia, the Australian herring is not a 'true' herring from the family Clupidae. Although the Australian herring can reach 40 cm, they are commonly caught at between 22 and 28 centimetres. The herring is similar to the closely related juvenile Australian salmon, but the herring has a larger eye, black tips on the ends of the tail fin lobes and no black blotch at the base of the pectoral fin. The herring's scales feel rough when rubbed towards the head which gives rise to the common name 'ruff', whereas an Australian salmon feels smooth.

Fishing Australian herring specialists can turn angling for these scrappy little fighters to an art form. Standard rigs include a wooden blob (float) whose hole is filled with pollard and pilchard oil, a reasonably long trace and a bait of maggot, prawn, squid or blue bait. When biting freely, Australian herring are taken on pieces of green drinking straw as bait. Herring are an inshore schooling fish which is commonly taken from rock groynes and beaches and are attracted to berley slicks when boat angling, especially inshore around shallow sea grass beds. Best berley includes bread, pollard, finely chopped fish scraps and chip pieces leftover from the local fish and chip shop. Herring are also taken on lures, with Halco wobblers and Tassie Devils or any small lure with red working well. On lures, herring jump as well as their cousins the salmon and although some throw the hooks, they are terrific fun. Herring are also very good eating and far superior to Australian salmon.

Rigs and Tactics

3 kg line

Small float

Berley float

1 metre

Wonder Wobbler

No. 6 to 10 Kendall Kirby or Long Shank hooks

Mr Twister

HERRING, GIANT

Scientific name *Elops machnata*. Also known as Pincushion-fish.

Range A mainly tropical species, the general range is from Albany in Western Australia around the top end and throughout Queensland to Nowra in NSW, although giant herring have been recorded from South Australia.

Description The giant herring is a beautiful, streamlined fish covered in small scales which are easily dislodged. This species is the largest of the true herrings (Family Clupidae), reaching 1.2 m and 11 kg, although it is frequently encountered at 1 – 4 kilograms. The giant herring has a single dorsal fin with a tiny trailing last ray compared to the tarpon (page 138) which has a prominent trailing filament and a much larger eye. The giant herring has a very large upper jaw. The giant herring moves southward with warm currents and is found more commonly in summer and early autumn in more southern areas.

Fishing The giant herring is attracting increasing attention as its qualities as a sports fish are being recognised. Giant herring take trolled or cast lures such as wobblers, spoons and small minnow lures readily and are a challenging proposition on the fly. Giant herring will also take live or fresh fish and prawns. Their spectacular leaps enhance their fight. The giant herring is full of fine bones which make them a very poor table fish. Their loose scales means that they need to be carefully handled to survive release.

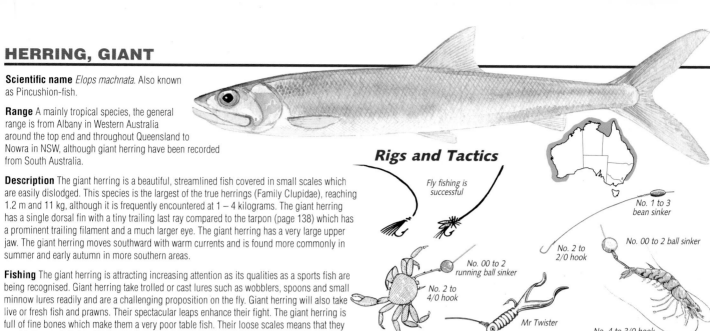

Rigs and Tactics

Fly fishing is successful

No. 1 to 3 bean sinker

No. 00 to 2 ball sinker

No. 2 to 2/0 hook

No. 00 to 2 running ball sinker

No. 2 to 4/0 hook

Mr Twister

No. 4 to 3/0 hook depending on size of bait

JEWFISH, BLACK

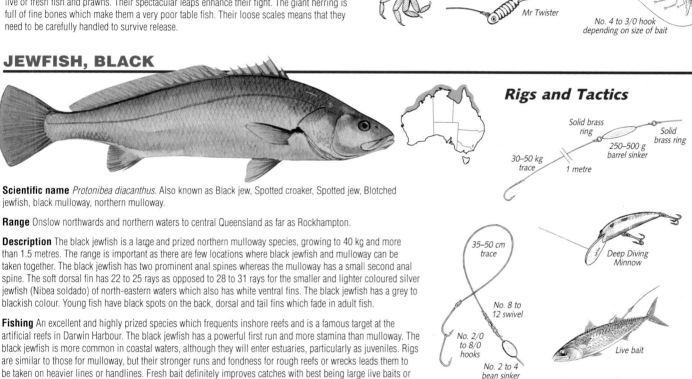

Rigs and Tactics

Solid brass ring

Solid brass ring

250–500 g barrel sinker

30–50 kg trace

1 metre

35–50 cm trace

No. 8 to 12 swivel

No. 2/0 to 8/0 hooks

No. 2 to 4 bean sinker

Deep Diving Minnow

Live bait

Scientific name *Protonibea diacanthus*. Also known as Black jew, Spotted croaker, Spotted jew, Blotched jewfish, black mulloway, northern mulloway.

Range Onslow northwards and northern waters to central Queensland as far as Rockhampton.

Description The black jewfish is a large and prized northern mulloway species, growing to 40 kg and more than 1.5 metres. The range is important as there are few locations where black jewfish and mulloway can be taken together. The black jewfish has two prominent anal spines whereas the mulloway has a small second anal spine. The soft dorsal fin has 22 to 25 rays as opposed to 28 to 31 rays for the smaller and lighter coloured silver jewfish (Nibea soldado) of north-eastern waters which also has white ventral fins. The black jewfish has a grey to blackish colour. Young fish have black spots on the back, dorsal and tail fins which fade in adult fish.

Fishing An excellent and highly prized species which frequents inshore reefs and is a famous target at the artificial reefs in Darwin Harbour. The black jewfish has a powerful first run and more stamina than mulloway. The black jewfish is more common in coastal waters, although they will enter estuaries, particularly as juveniles. Rigs are similar to those for mulloway, but their stronger runs and fondness for rough reefs or wrecks leads them to be taken on heavier lines or handlines. Fresh bait definitely improves catches with best being large live baits or fresh cut or whole fish, squid or fresh large prawns. The black jewfish is a prized for its size, tenacity and eating qualities which are excellent.

LONGTOM, STOUT

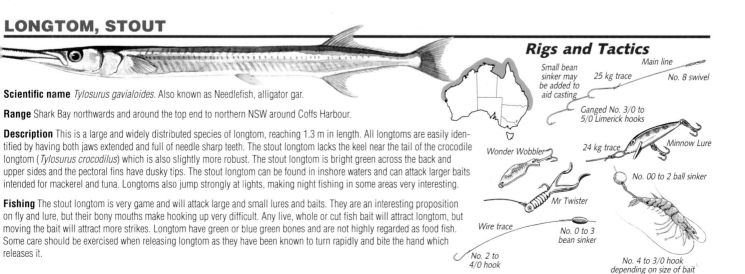

Rigs and Tactics

Main line

Small bean sinker may be added to aid casting

25 kg trace

No. 8 swivel

Ganged No. 3/0 to 5/0 Limerick hooks

24 kg trace

Minnow Lure

Wonder Wobbler

No. 00 to 2 ball sinker

Mr Twister

Wire trace

No. 0 to 3 bean sinker

No. 2 to 4/0 hook

No. 4 to 3/0 hook depending on size of bait

Scientific name *Tylosurus gavialoides*. Also known as Needlefish, alligator gar.

Range Shark Bay northwards and around the top end to northern NSW around Coffs Harbour.

Description This is a large and widely distributed species of longtom, reaching 1.3 m in length. All longtoms are easily identified by having both jaws extended and full of needle sharp teeth. The stout longtom lacks the keel near the tail of the crocodile longtom (*Tylosurus crocodilus*) which is also slightly more robust. The stout longtom is bright green across the back and upper sides and the pectoral fins have dusky tips. The stout longtom can be found in inshore waters and can attack larger baits intended for mackerel and tuna. Longtoms also jump strongly at lights, making night fishing in some areas very interesting.

Fishing The stout longtom is very game and will attack large and small lures and baits. They are an interesting proposition on fly and lure, but their bony mouths make hooking up very difficult. Any live, whole or cut fish bait will attract longtom, but moving the bait will attract more strikes. Longtom have green or blue green bones and are not highly regarded as food fish. Some care should be exercised when releasing longtom as they have been known to turn rapidly and bite the hand which releases it.

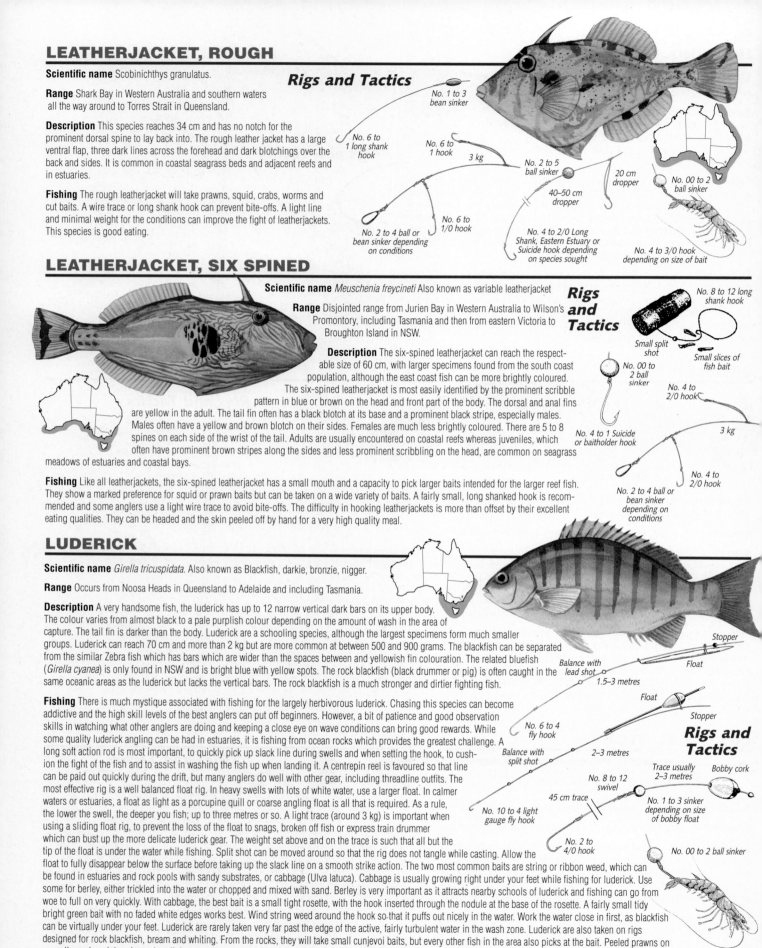

LEATHERJACKET, ROUGH

Scientific name *Scobinichthys granulatus*.

Range Shark Bay in Western Australia and southern waters all the way around to Torres Strait in Queensland.

Description This species reaches 34 cm and has no notch for the prominent dorsal spine to lay back into. The rough leather jacket has a large ventral flap, three dark lines across the forehead and dark blotchings over the back and sides. It is common in coastal seagrass beds and adjacent reefs and in estuaries.

Fishing The rough leatherjacket will take prawns, squid, crabs, worms and cut baits. A wire trace or long shank hook can prevent bite-offs. A light line and minimal weight for the conditions can improve the fight of leatherjackets. This species is good eating.

Rigs and Tactics

No. 1 to 3 bean sinker

No. 6 to 1 long shank hook

No. 6 to 1 hook

3 kg

No. 2 to 5 ball sinker

20 cm dropper

40–50 cm dropper

No. 00 to 2 ball sinker

No. 2 to 4 ball or bean sinker depending on conditions

No. 6 to 1/0 hook

No. 4 to 2/0 Long Shank, Eastern Estuary or Suicide hook depending on species sought

No. 4 to 3/0 hook depending on size of bait

LEATHERJACKET, SIX SPINED

Scientific name *Meuschenia freycineti* Also known as variable leatherjacket

Range Disjointed range from Jurien Bay in Western Australia to Wilson's Promontory, including Tasmania and then from eastern Victoria to Broughton Island in NSW.

Description The six-spined leatherjacket can reach the respectable size of 60 cm, with larger specimens found from the south coast population, although the east coast fish can be more brightly coloured. The six-spined leatherjacket is most easily identified by the prominent scribble pattern in blue or brown on the head and front part of the body. The dorsal and anal fins are yellow in the adult. The tail fin often has a black blotch at its base and a prominent black stripe, especially males. Males often have a yellow and brown blotch on their sides. Females are much less brightly coloured. There are 5 to 8 spines on each side of the wrist of the tail. Adults are usually encountered on coastal reefs whereas juveniles, which often have more prominent brown stripes along the sides and less prominent scribbling on the head, are common on seagrass meadows of estuaries and coastal bays.

Fishing Like all leatherjackets, the six-spined leatherjacket has a small mouth and a capacity to pick larger baits intended for the larger reef fish. They show a marked preference for squid or prawn baits but can be taken on a wide variety of baits. A fairly small, long shanked hook is recommended and some anglers use a light wire trace to avoid bite-offs. The difficulty in hooking leatherjackets is more than offset by their excellent eating qualities. They can be headed and the skin peeled off by hand for a very high quality meal.

Rigs and Tactics

No. 8 to 12 long shank hook

Small split shot

Small slices of fish bait

No. 00 to 2 ball sinker

No. 4 to 2/0 hook

No. 4 to 1 Suicide or baitholder hook

3 kg

No. 4 to 2/0 hook

No. 2 to 4 ball or bean sinker depending on conditions

LUDERICK

Scientific name *Girella tricuspidata*. Also known as Blackfish, darkie, bronzie, nigger.

Range Occurs from Noosa Heads in Queensland to Adelaide and including Tasmania.

Description A very handsome fish, the luderick has up to 12 narrow vertical dark bars on its upper body. The colour varies from almost black to a pale purplish colour depending on the amount of wash in the area of capture. The tail fin is darker than the body. Luderick are a schooling species, although the largest specimens form much smaller groups. Luderick can reach 70 cm and more than 2 kg but are more common at between 500 and 900 grams. The blackfish can be separated from the similar Zebra fish which has bars which are wider than the spaces between and yellowish fin colouration. The related bluefish (*Girella cyanea*) is only found in NSW and is bright blue with yellow spots. The rock blackfish (black drummer or pig) is often caught in the same oceanic areas as the luderick but lacks the vertical bars. The rock blackfish is a much stronger and dirtier fighting fish.

Fishing There is much mystique associated with fishing for the largely herbivorous luderick. Chasing this species can become addictive and the high skill levels of the best anglers can put off beginners. However, a bit of patience and good observation skills in watching what other anglers are doing and keeping a close eye on wave conditions can bring good rewards. While some quality luderick angling can be had in estuaries, it is fishing from ocean rocks which provides the greatest challenge. A long soft action rod is most important, to quickly pick up slack line during swells and when setting the hook, to cushion the fight of the fish and to assist in washing the fish up when landing it. A centrepin reel is favoured so that line can be paid out quickly during the drift, but many anglers do well with other gear, including threadline outfits. The most effective rig is a well balanced float rig. In heavy swells with lots of white water, use a larger float. In calmer waters or estuaries, a float as light as a porcupine quill or coarse angling float is all that is required. As a rule, the lower the swell, the deeper you fish; up to three metres or so. A light trace (around 3 kg) is important when using a sliding float rig, to prevent the loss of the float to snags, broken off fish or express train drummer which can bust up the more delicate luderick gear. The weight set above and on the trace is such that all but the tip of the float is under the water while fishing. Split shot can be moved around so that the rig does not tangle while casting. Allow the float to fully disappear below the surface before taking up the slack line on a smooth strike action. The two most common baits are string or ribbon weed, which can be found in estuaries and rock pools with sandy substrates, or cabbage (*Ulva latuca*). Cabbage is usually growing right under your feet while fishing for luderick. Use some for berley, either trickled into the water or chopped and mixed with sand. Berley is very important as it attracts nearby schools of luderick and fishing can go from woe to full on very quickly. With cabbage, the best bait is a small tight rosette, with the hook inserted through the nodule at the base of the rosette. A fairly small tidy bright green bait with no faded white edges works best. Wind string weed around the hook so that it puffs out nicely in the water. Work the water close in first, as blackfish can be virtually under your feet. Luderick are rarely taken very far past the edge of the active, fairly turbulent water in the wash zone. Luderick are also taken on rigs designed for rock blackfish, bream and whiting. From the rocks, they will take small cunjevoi baits, but every other fish in the area also picks at the bait. Peeled prawns on a small running sinker rig work well. In estuaries, prawns, worms and nippers (bass yabbies) collect a mixed bag including any luderick in the area. Luderick make good eating if bled and cleaned soon after killing. It is important to gut the fish quickly or the flesh can take on a weed or iodine taint.

Stopper

Balance with lead shot

Float

1.5–3 metres

Float

Stopper

No. 6 to 4 fly hook

Balance with split shot

2–3 metres

Rigs and Tactics

Trace usually 2–3 metres

Bobby cork

No. 8 to 12 swivel

No. 1 to 3 sinker depending on size of bobby float

45 cm trace

No. 10 to 4 light gauge fly hook

No. 2 to 4/0 hook

No. 00 to 2 ball sinker

No. 4 to 3/0 hook depending on size of bait

MANGROVE JACK

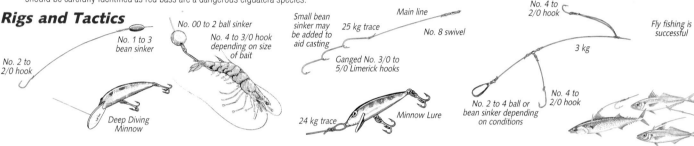

Scientific name *Lutjanus argentimaculatus*. Also known as Jacks, red bream, dog bream, red perch, reef red bream, purple sea perch, creek red bream.

Range Exmouth Gulf and tropical waters to around Coffs Harbour in northern NSW.

Description The mangrove jack is best known for its destruction of fishing tackle in tidal creeks, but these tend to be juvenile or small adult fish. The largest specimens are taken on offshore reefs to a depth of 100 metres. Mangrove jack can reach more than 1.2 m and a weight of 15 kg but fish in inshore waters are a real handful at 1 – 3 kilograms. The mangrove jack is often confused with the red bass, which is a much more notorious ciguatera species, especially if caught on reefs. The mangrove jack has a taller dorsal fin, a lack of lengthwise stripes on its side and the absence of black on the fins. Mangrove jacks lack the distinctive pit before the eye of the red bass which is predominantly a coral reef species.

Fishing Mangrove jack are arguably the toughest and dirtiest fighters (pound for pound) in Australian waters. They will dash out and engulf a lure or bait and break off an unwary angler on the nearest snag before they realise the strike has been made. As a result, mangrove jacks require quality, well maintained gear and tight drags. They can destroy cheap equipment as they dive into snags. Mangrove jacks like tough dirty cover although they can be found in deeper holes in tidal waters where they are a bit easier to handle. Diving lures, spinner baits, jigs and flies work well for jacks. They will take cut or whole fish baits, prawns, crabs and especially live baits. The strike is savage and a prelude to the action to come. Mangrove jacks taken on offshore reefs put up a strong fight, and the heavier gear usually used for tropical reef fishing gives a better chance of landing these fish. Mangrove jacks should be handled carefully as their dorsal and opercular spines can create a nasty wound, especially on water softened hands. Jacks can also take a nip at fingers while being unhooked, but they are a hardy fish which survives handling well. The mangrove jack is good eating but in offshore waters should be carefully identified as red bass are a dangerous ciguatera species.

Rigs and Tactics

No. 2 to 2/0 hook

No. 1 to 3 bean sinker

Deep Diving Minnow

No. 00 to 2 ball sinker

No. 4 to 3/0 hook depending on size of bait

Small bean sinker may be added to aid casting

25 kg trace

Main line

No. 8 swivel

Ganged No. 3/0 to 5/0 Limerick hooks

24 kg trace

Minnow Lure

No. 4 to 2/0 hook

3 kg

No. 2 to 4 ball or bean sinker depending on conditions

No. 4 to 2/0 hook

Fly fishing is successful

MORWONG, DUSKY

Scientific name *Dactylophora nigricans* Also known as Strongfish, butterfish, tillywurti.

Range Lancelin in Western Australia and southern waters including Tasmania to Wilson's Promontory.

Description A large and handsome fish which is easily separated from the other morwongs by longer and more slender body. The dusky morwong can reach 1.2 metres and has the typical morwong mouth with the larger lips and down turned aspect. The pectoral fins have extended rays and the tail fin is prominently forked. Although the dusky morwong is often a slate grey colour, they can be almost silver when on sand and can be mistaken for mulloway from the shore, causing much excitement but no return.

Fishing The dusky morwong is almost never taken by line fishermen as they eat small items and rarely take bait. They are occasionally accidentally hooked on prawn, pipi, squid or worm baits intended for whiting or other species. This species will frequently rest on the bottom and is not easily spooked, making them an easy target for spearfishing. Poor eating.

Rigs and Tactics

Rarely taken by line fishing.

MULLET, SAND

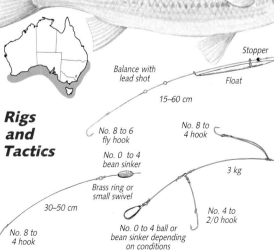

Scientific name *Myxus elongatus*. Also known as Tallegalane, black spot mullet, lano.

Range From Cape Naturaliste in Western Australia around southern waters including Tasmania to south Queensland around the Gold Coast. Rare in Western Australia.

Description The sand mullet is a moderately small mullet reaching 41 cm and nudging a kilogram but most commonly encountered around 25 – 30 centimetres. This species has a straight upper profile and pointed head which differs from the sea mullet which has a more rounded snout. The sand mullet generally has a black blotch at the top of the base of the pectoral fin and lacks the obvious fatty eyelid (adipose eyelid) of the sea mullet. The eye colour is yellow-brown or light brown as opposed to the bright yellow of the yellow-eye mullet, but the most obvious difference is that the sand mullet has 9 rays in the anal fin and the yellow-eye mullet 12 rays. The sand mullet is found in bays, lower estuaries and ocean beaches in schools, usually of similar sized fish. They have a strong preference for sandy bottoms.

Fishing The sand mullet will take bread and is particularly susceptible if berleyed up with bread and fished near the surface with a small pinch of dough or bread which is squeezed on the hook. Sand mullet will also take prawns, beach and blood worms, nippers, maggots and occasionally small pieces of skinned squid. The sand mullet will rise to baits so small float rigs work well. A good trick in tidal areas is to use a small float of quill or even cork held against the current with small split shot to a size 12 long shank hook with the bread or dough bait. In estuaries, keep the bait in the finely ground berley trail and allow the fish to hook themselves against the current. Where there is a sandy bottom, very light bottom rigs can produce good mixed bags including mullet. Small prawn pieces can improve your scope for other species, but a smaller hook is recommended for sand mullet. Keeping the bait moving attracts bites and helps to work out when a bread bait may have washed off the hook. Sand mullet are good eating and their slightly oily flesh is ideal for nearly every fish recipe. Mullet also make ideal live, dead or cut bait.

Rigs and Tactics

Balance with lead shot

15–60 cm

Float

Stopper

No. 8 to 6 fly hook

No. 8 to 4 hook

No. 0 to 4 bean sinker

Brass ring or small swivel

3 kg

30–50 cm

No. 8 to 4 hook

No. 0 to 4 ball or bean sinker depending on conditions

No. 4 to 2/0 hook

MULLET, SEA

Scientific name *Mugil cephalus*. Also known as Bully mullet, bully, mullet, hard-gut mullet, river mullet. Juveniles referred to as poddy mullet or poddies.

Range Circum-Australia, but sea mullet are most common from southern Queensland to southern NSW, where large schools migrate along the coast in autumn and early winter.

Description The sea mullet is a cylindrical barrel of muscle which is readily identified by the thick, transparent, gelatinous covering over all but the centre of the eyes. They often have several diffuse lateral stripes on the side, but the colour and intensity can vary with the environment. Sea mullet have a distinguishing enlarged and pointed scale behind the top of the pectoral fin. Sea mullet are found from far above the tidal reaches of coastal rivers to reasonable distances offshore, but they are best known for the vast shoals they can form at spawning time on east coast beaches. They are a very large species, reaching 80 cm and over 5 kg, but sea mullet are most commonly encountered at 1 – 2 kilograms.

Fishing Sea mullet are almost exclusively vegetarian and as a result have to be enticed to be taken by recreational anglers, but they are worth the effort. There are few better fighters pound for pound in Australia and on light line, they really sizzle. Sea mullet can be taken on flies and very rarely on accident with small lures but these are challenges beyond all but the most dedicated angler. Sea mullet are best targeted where effluent such as from fruit or vegetable factories, bakeries or flour mills enter the water. Here mullet are trained to take foods such as corn, pineapple or peas and are much easier to catch. In other areas, it may take several days of berley in the same area and tide before sea mullet begin to bite freely. Best baits are dough or bread, prawn or worm pieces, generally fished on or just under the surface. Methods described for sand mullet work well. Patience is required, but well rewarded although in WA they remain almost impossible to catch. Sea mullet are much better eating if taken from ocean beaches where they become hard-gut mullet, not eating but preparing for spawning. Unfortunately in the ocean larger fish are only taken through accidental foul hooking by recreational anglers. Estuarine fish (soft-gut mullet) can taste muddy or weedy and should be cleaned quickly. This poorer taste along with the high by-catch is another reason why commercial gill netting for mullet should be stopped in estuaries.

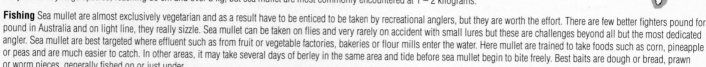

Rigs and Tactics

No. 12 to 8 hook

No. 1 to 3 bean sinker

No. 12 to 8 hook

3 kg

No. 4 to 2/0 hook

No. 2 to 4 ball or bean sinker depending on conditions

Balance with lead shot

20–30 cm

Stopper

Float

No. 6 to 4 fly hook

MULLET, YELLOW-EYE

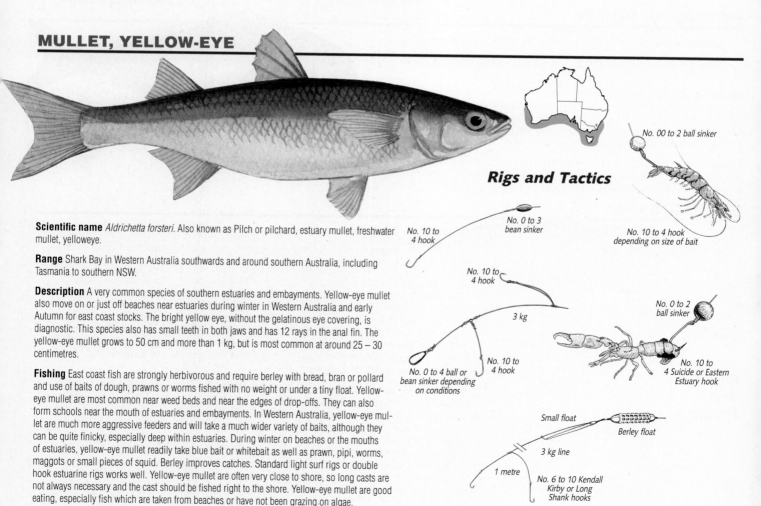

Rigs and Tactics

No. 00 to 2 ball sinker

No. 10 to 4 hook depending on size of bait

No. 10 to 4 hook

No. 0 to 3 bean sinker

No. 10 to 4 hook

3 kg

No. 0 to 4 ball or bean sinker depending on conditions

No. 10 to 4 hook

No. 0 to 2 ball sinker

No. 10 to 4 Suicide or Eastern Estuary hook

Small float

Berley float

3 kg line

1 metre

No. 6 to 10 Kendall Kirby or Long Shank hooks

Scientific name *Aldrichetta forsteri*. Also known as Pilch or pilchard, estuary mullet, freshwater mullet, yelloweye.

Range Shark Bay in Western Australia southwards and around southern Australia, including Tasmania to southern NSW.

Description A very common species of southern estuaries and embayments. Yellow-eye mullet also move on or just off beaches near estuaries during winter in Western Australia and early Autumn for east coast stocks. The bright yellow eye, without the gelatinous eye covering, is diagnostic. This species also has small teeth in both jaws and has 12 rays in the anal fin. The yellow-eye mullet grows to 50 cm and more than 1 kg, but is most common at around 25 – 30 centimetres.

Fishing East coast fish are strongly herbivorous and require berley with bread, bran or pollard and use of baits of dough, prawns or worms fished with no weight or under a tiny float. Yellow-eye mullet are most common near weed beds and near the edges of drop-offs. They can also form schools near the mouth of estuaries and embayments. In Western Australia, yellow-eye mullet are much more aggressive feeders and will take a much wider variety of baits, although they can be quite finicky, especially deep within estuaries. During winter on beaches or the mouths of estuaries, yellow-eye mullet readily take blue bait or whitebait as well as prawn, pipi, worms, maggots or small pieces of squid. Berley improves catches. Standard light surf rigs or double hook estuarine rigs works well. Yellow-eye mullet are often very close to shore, so long casts are not always necessary and the cast should be fished right to the shore. Yellow-eye mullet are good eating, especially fish which are taken from beaches or have not been grazing on algae.

MULLOWAY

Scientific name *Argyrosomus japonicus*. Also known as Jewfish, jew, jewie, butterfish, river kingfish, silver kingfish. Small fish to around 3 kg are generally referred to as soapies due to their rather bland or soapy taste. Fish from 3 – 8 kg are frequently known as Schoolies as they are often encountered in schools which decrease in number as the size increases.

Range Exmouth Gulf in Western Australia around southern waters but extremely rare in Tasmania and along the east coast as far north as Rockhampton.

Description Mulloway are a large and highly prized species found in estuaries, embayments and inshore ocean waters throughout its range. The mulloway can vary in colour from dark bronze to silver and there may be red or purple tinges, but a silver ocean mulloway is a stunning fish. The mulloway has large scales and a generous mouth. A line of silvery spots follows the lateral line in live fish which glows under artificial lights as do the eyes which shine a bright red. A conspicuous black spot is just above the pectoral fin. The tail fin is convex (rounded outwards) and this characteristic differentiates them from the smaller teraglin which has a concave tail and a yellow inside of the mouth. Mulloway differ from the black jewfish which is generally darker with black blotches on the back and has a prominent second anal spine which is short in the mulloway. Mulloway can reach 1.8 m and more than 60 kg, but any fish over 25 kg is worth long term boasting rights for the angler. Mulloway are most commonly caught at 3 – 10 kilograms.

Fishing The mulloway is the largest and most prized species for estuarine and beach fishermen where it is found. A large specimen is generally a test of endurance for the angler with long nights without even a mulloway run, but there is no greater thrill than a large mulloway caught by a dedicated angler. The mulloway can be difficult to hook as they can run reasonable distances before spitting out the bait, just as the angler is preparing to strike. Removing prawn trawling from some NSW estuaries is already paying dividends in better recruitment. The best mulloway fishing is at night although opinions vary on the best moon phases, with many shunning the full moon, while others prefer this time. However, with large mulloway, any night spent using a large, very fresh or live bait gives an advantage for these challenging fish. Soapy or school mulloway can be found in large schools, so if mulloway are located, the action can be quite frantic for a time. A trick of the old time beach fishermen is to rub the next bait on the first mulloway, as they have a distinctive kerosene or faintly cucumber odour and even the largest mulloway often travel in pairs. The theory is that the mulloway scent attracts other fish to the bait which they consume. Mulloway fishing is best near the mouth of tidal rivers or estuaries after heavy rain and on nearby ocean beaches, especially those adjacent to coastal lakes when they break through to the sea. At these times, live mullet or yellowtail, or the famous red and white feather jigs work well. Increasing numbers of fish are being taken on larger diving lures such as Halco Lasers and Mann's Stretch series trolled around bridge pylons, through deep and renowned mulloway holes, or along current lines. A few very dedicated anglers have taken mulloway on flies. Many anglers are disappointed with the fight of mulloway. There is a strong and promising first run followed by a shorter second run. Generally there is a greater chance of losing the fish in a surf zone, to a poor gaff shot or to a lightly hooked fish. Mulloway destined for release need to be quickly returned as they do not handle well. However, the almost legendary status of a large mulloway more than compensates for any disappointment in the fight. Mulloway take baits ranging from fresh fish, especially those with oily flesh, beach worms, live baits, pipi, squid, cuttlefish and less frequently pilchards. The most important attribute of mulloway bait is that it must be very fresh. Best fishing times are from dusk to dawn, although good catches can be made during floods during the day and at some inshore reefs. Rigs should be as light as possible to fit the depth of water or current conditions. A running sinker is essential as mulloway run a long distance before swallowing a bait. Mulloway larger than 3 kg are very good eating and all but the largest fish are very tasty but they can have worms in the flesh. Mulloway are a fast growing species and smaller returned fish will rapidly reach boasting size if handled carefully.

Rigs and Tactics

No. 1 to 4/0 hook

3 kg

No. 2 to 4 ball or bean sinker depending on conditions

No. 1 to 4/0 hook

Deep Diving Minnow

Minnow Lure

24 kg trace

Solid brass ring

Solid brass ring

250–500 g barrel sinker

30–50 kg trace

1 metre

Brass ring

Main line

100–200 g barrel sinker

No. 6/0 to 9/0 hook Suicide or Live Bait hook

PERCH, MOSES

Scientific name *Lutjanus russelli*. Also known as One spot sea perch, finger-mark (WA).

Range From Shark Bay in Western Australia and tropical waters and as far south as Coffs Harbour in northern NSW.

Description Has a general reddish or pinkish hue, a large mouth with discernible canine teeth and 14 or 15 rays in the dorsal fin. The Moses perch has a distinctive black spot which can be quite pale, below the start of the soft dorsal rays. Most of the black spot is above the obvious lateral line, while the similar black-spot sea perch (*Lutjanus fulviflamma*) has a small black spot, most of which is below the lateral line. The lateral yellow stripes of the black-spot sea perch are not present on the Moses perch. The Moses perch often forms schools of similar sized fish, hanging near coral outcrops and in eddies near reefs. They can be found near drop-offs, on reefs or in depths of up to 80 m, with larger specimens frequently captured from deeper water. The Moses perch reaches 50 cm and nearly 3 kg but is commonly caught at between 25 and 30 centimetres.

Fishing Like many species in this group, the Moses perch can be an aggressive feeder, rising well to minnow lures, feather jigs and even surface poppers cast or trolled to the downstream side of coral outcrops. The school can jostle to be the first to take the lure or bait. Baits include whole or cut fish baits, squid, octopus or prawns. Weights should be kept to a minimum depending on the depth and mood of the fish, as Moses perch will rise to a bait which also puts them further from dangerous coral which they will try to use. In deeper water, lighter weights allow the fish to fight better and keeping the bait just above the bottom will deter some pickers but not Moses perch. The Moses perch is a good eating fish.

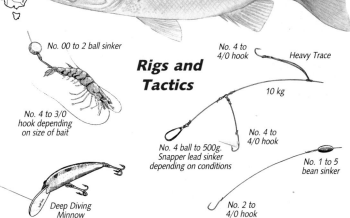

Rigs and Tactics

No. 00 to 2 ball sinker

No. 4 to 3/0 hook depending on size of bait

No. 4 to 4/0 hook

Heavy Trace

10 kg

No. 4 to 4/0 hook

No. 4 ball to 500g. Snapper lead sinker depending on conditions

No. 1 to 5 bean sinker

No. 2 to 4/0 hook

Deep Diving Minnow

PERCH, ESTUARY

Scientific name *Macquaria colonorum*. Also known as Perch.

Range From the Mary River on Fraser Island in Queensland around the east coast and to the Murray mouth in South Australia. Populations of the Estuary perch have recently been discovered from the lower reaches of some northern Tasmanian streams.

Description The estuary perch is easily confused with Australian bass which can be found in the same areas. Even experienced anglers have difficulty telling the two species apart. The most obvious distinguishing feature is the head profile which is indented or concave in estuary perch and rounded in bass. Estuary perch are very rarely found above the tidal influence of rivers. Estuary perch are also increasingly common in southern waters. Like bass, larger specimens are all female and they must have access to salt water to breed.

Fishing Estuary perch are an excellent fighting and eating fish, but like their cousin the bass, most are returned unhurt today. They are aggressive and can be over-fished by skilled fishers. Estuary perch take surface and deep diving lures and larger flies well, fishing very close to snags and bank-side cover in tidal areas. Accurate casts, within 30 cm of the snag and patience at the beginning of the retrieve gets the best results. Estuary perch are also caught with bait in deep holes in lower tidal reaches during winter spawning aggregations. Estuary perch are particularly partial to a live prawn fished under a float near snags or drop-offs near cumbungi beds. Other popular baits, fished under a float or with minimal weight include live fish, crickets, worms and crabs.

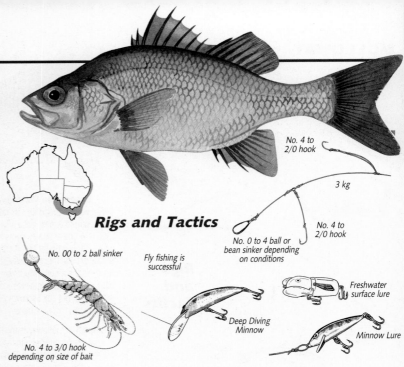

Rigs and Tactics

No. 4 to 2/0 hook

3 kg

No. 4 to 2/0 hook

No. 0 to 4 ball or bean sinker depending on conditions

No. 00 to 2 ball sinker

Fly fishing is successful

Deep Diving Minnow

Freshwater surface lure

Minnow Lure

No. 4 to 3/0 hook depending on size of bait

PIKE, LONGFINNED

Scientific name *Dinolestes lewini*. Also known as Pike, jack pike, skipjack pike.

Range A coldwater species found from Rottnest Island in Western Australia, but more common south of Geographe Bay and southern waters including Tasmania and along the east coast as far north as Taree.

Description The lonfinned pike is a long slender fish with a large head, large mouth and an underslung jaw extending almost to the front edge of the large eye. This species has two distinct dorsal fins. A prominent and extended anal fin separates this species from the similar striped seapike which also has 2 – 3 brown lateral stripes along its side. The tail and wrist of the tail of the long finned pike are yellow or golden whereas in the striped seapike the tail has a yellow hue, especially near the back edge. The longfinned pike can be confused with the snook, which has the two dorsal fins widely separated and the ventral fin is set well behind the pectoral fin. The snook is a much larger species, reaching more than a metre and over 5 kilograms. The longfinned pike can reach more than 2 kg and 90 cm but is most often encountered at between 40 and 50 centimetres.

Fishing The longfinned pike can form small groups or large schools and in a range of habitats from seagrass meadows to reefs in medium depths but they are most common near shallow reefs or seagrass and near cover such as jetties in shallow water. Longfinned pike take trolled lures such as chrome spoons, small minnows and jigs. They will also take baits such as fresh cut baits, or whole fish such as pilchards, whitebait or anchovies. Longfinned pike feed better closer to the surface or in midwater, so rigs which use little or no weight or a water filled plastic bubble to aid casting distance will bring the best results. Longfinned pike can be taken from rocks or boat and when a school is located good numbers can be taken. Longfinned pike are not highly regarded as a food fish. Smaller specimens can be used as a live bait for samson fish, kingfish, mulloway or other large predators but must be handled carefully as the scales can shed and the fish do not last as long. Pike makes a good cut bait.

Rigs and Tactics

Stopper

No. 10 swivel

Bobby float

No. 2 to 4 ball or bean sinker

No. 3/0 to 5/0 hook gang

Wire Trace

Metal Lure

Bug sinker crimped to line

Linked No. 2/0 to 4/0 suicide or Kendall Kirby hooks

Small bean sinker may be added to aid casting

25 kg trace

Main line

No. 8 swivel

Ganged No. 3/0 to 5/0 hooks

PORCUPINE FISH ☠

Scientific name Family *Diodontidae*. Also known as Burr fish, prickle fish, globe fish.

Range A variety of species are found in inshore areas of Australia, reaching a maximum of 43 cm, but commonly seen at around 20 – 25 centimetres.

Description A very easy group to identify, distinguished by the prominent spines set into the skin and the ability to inflate their bodies with air or water. The spines distinguish porcupine fish from the smooth skinned puffer fish. The similar globe fish group can be distinguished by having the ability to erect their much longer body spines while the body is inflated. The mouth is small but the teeth are fused into two plates which can be capable of cutting fine hooks and easily through line. The dorsal and anal fins are set well back on the body.

Fishing Porcupine fish are not a target fish. They are often taken while fishing for other species in estuaries, bays and in shallow waters such as near sea grass meadows. They can also be a by-catch in prawn dray nets. Porcupine fish will take a wide variety of baits intended for other species, with a special liking for prawns, squid, octopus, nippers and worms. Care should be taken when handling these fish as they can rapidly inflate their bodies and the spines can inflict painful wounds. Porcupine fish are toxic and should never, ever be consumed. The toxins are strongest in the skin, liver and other internal organs but even carefully prepared flesh can result in death.

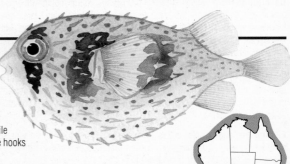

Rigs and Tactics

Not applicable as Porcupine Fish are not recommended as an angling species.

PUFFERFISH (see also Toadfish) ☠

Scientific name Family *Tetraodontidae* Also known as Toadfish, toad, toado, blowfish, blowie.

Range Circum-Australia, with various species common in inshore waters in different locations.

Description Pufferfish are a group of generally small, smooth skinned species with the ability to inflate their bodies with water or air on capture. The mouth is small and the teeth are fused into plates and separated in the front. Colours vary, with several species brightly coloured. These fish prefer inshore waters where they frequently form large schools. All species are poisonous and should never be consumed or fed to animals. The silver pufferfish, or nor-west blowie (Lagocephalus sceleratus) is of particular interest as it can reach a length of nearly a metre. This species can attack divers for no apparent reason and it is capable of biting through hooks or even bones.

Fishing Pufferfish can form vast hordes in shallow water, swarming over any bait and pecking it until it is gone. While pufferfish are almost never targeted, they are frequently captured by young or very inexperienced anglers, some of whom want to keep them. All pufferfish species are highly toxic and should never be consumed, no matter how well they are cleaned. Many pets die after being fed unwanted specimens. Although these fish are not desired and can be despised when schools steal every bait, codes of practice dictate that these fish should either be returned to the water or killed quickly. The only way to avoid pufferfish when they are in plague proportions is to move, fish with a large bait in the hopes that something will remain for more desirable fish, use a large weight to get to the bottom quickly, or use lures, although pufferfish will attack soft plastic and leadhead jigs.

Rigs and Tactics Not applicable as Pufferfish are not recommended as an angling species.

QUEENFISH

Scientific name *Scomberoides commersonnianus*. Also known as Giant leatherskin, leatherskin, queenie, talang queenfish, skinny, skinnyfish.

Range Exmouth Gulf in Western Australia and through tropical northern waters to Moreton Bay in southern Queensland, but primarily a tropical species.

Description The queenfish is a large, long and laterally (side to side) compressed species which leads to the common name of skinny and a light weight for the length. The mouth is large and extends mouth well beyond the back of the eye whereas other smaller queenfish species have smaller mouths. A series of 5 to 8 oval shaped blotches are found on the sides above the lateral line. The similar but smaller double spotted queenfish (Scomberoides lysan) has a double row of spots above and below the lateral line. The queenfish also has a prominent, high and light coloured front part of the dorsal and anal fins. These fish have lance shaped scales which are deeply embedded in a leathery skin. The queenfish can reach 120 cm and more than 11 kilograms. This light weight for the length indicates how skinny the queenfish is when viewed head on.

Fishing Queenfish are found from the upper tidal reaches of tropical rivers to inshore reefs and occasionally near outer reefs which have shallow breaks. Queenfish prefer slightly turbid water with plenty of flow. They are ambush feeders and will lurk near cover such as eddies, rock bars, wharves and creek mouths, especially on a falling tide. Queenfish are spectacular and exciting sportfish, with their slashing strikes and blistering runs, often with aerial displays. Queenfish will take dead baits such as mullet, pilchard, garfish, mudskippers, whiting or fresh prawns and squid. They are also partial to live bait. Queenfish are renowned lure takers, with cast or trolled lures such as sliced chrome lures, spoons, shallow and deep diving minnows, spinner baits and surface lures. Queenfish are excited by escaping baitfish, so a fast, erratic retrieve is most successful. Fly enthusiasts are increasingly targeting queenfish as they are an exciting challenge on light fly gear. Large minnow type flies retrieved through current eddies on a fast strip works best. A heavy monofilament leader is recommended when fishing for queenfish as their jaws and small teeth can damage light traces. The queenfish is an under-rated food fish, mainly because they are often caught in conjunction with barramundi and threadfin salmon which are excellent food fish. Like all tropical fish, the quality of queenfish is improved with immediate bleeding and placing in an ice brine slurry.

Rigs and Tactics

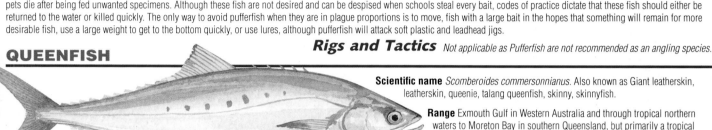

Deep Diving Minnow

Minnow Lure

24 kg trace

Fly fishing is successful

Live bait

No. 3/0 to 5/0 hook gang

No. 10 swivel

1–2 m

Stopper

Bobby float

No. 2 to 4 ball or bean sinker

No. 2/0 linked Limerick hook

No. 2 bug sinker

SALMON, THREADFIN

Scientific name *Polydactylus sheridani*. Also known as Blue threadfin, blue salmon, Burnett salmon, king salmon.

Range From the Kimberley region in Western Australia around the top end to around Hervey Bay in Queensland. Some reports have been received that this fish is occasionally taken as far south as Karratha.

Description The threadfin salmon is similar to the Cooktown salmon, but possesses 5 long, distinctive fingers on the lower edge of the pectoral fin. This species has a more pronounced blue colour and a long and relatively narrow caudal wrist. The threadfin salmon is common between 0.5 and around 3 kg with occasional specimens slightly larger. Another similar species, the Northern or striped threadfin salmon (Polydactylus plebius) is separated by its more prominent stripes and overall golden colour and five free filaments, of which the two uppermost are longest.

Fishing The threadfin salmon is a more common lure target, taking small barra lures, bright spoons, spinnerbaits and shiny minnow lures and saltwater flies. This species also prefers fresh bait with a white or silver sheen as well as prawns or crab baits. Although smaller, the threadfin salmon is a better target species as it is a more reliable bait or lure taker. The threadfin salmon is an excellent eating species which should be cleaned quickly and eaten fresh.

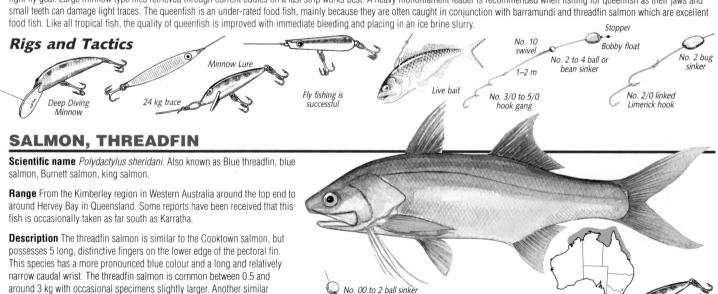

No. 00 to 2 ball sinker

No. 4 to 3/0 hook depending on size of bait

Fly fishing is successful

No. 4 to 2/0 hook

3–10 kg

No. 2 to 4 ball or bean sinker depending on conditions

No. 4 to 2/0 hook

Small bean sinker may be added to aid casting

No. 2 to 4/0 hook

Ganged No. 3/0 to 5/0 Limerick hooks

25 kg trace

Main line

No. 8 swivel

Rigs and Tactics

Minnow Lure

24 kg trace

No. 1 to 3 bean sinker

SALMON, AUSTRALIAN

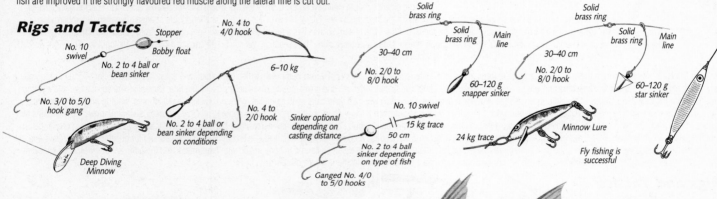

Scientific name *Arripis trutta* (Eastern species), *Arripis truttacea* (Western species) Also known as Salmon, black back, cocky salmon, colonial salmon, kahawai. Salmon trout and bay trout, (juveniles).

Range There are now generally accepted to be two different species. The eastern species extends from Tweed Heads to Port Phillip Bay and including Tasmania, but is not common north of Sydney. The Western species extends from Kalbarri in Western Australia around the south coast to Lakes Entrance in Victoria, but is rare north of Yanchep lagoon. The range and abundance is linked to commercial netting and current strength on the east and west coast with strong southerly currents keeping the stocks further south. In some years, few salmon make it to the west coast or into NSW waters.

Description These 'salmon' species are not related to true trout and salmon in the family Salmonidae and are more closely related to the mullets. Both Australian salmon species are very similar, with the only difference being that the western species has fewer gill rakers and reaches a larger maximum size, 9 kg for western fish and 7 kg for eastern fish. In both cases, the larger fish are more commonly found at the northern end of the range as the fish undergo spawning migrations, reaching their northernmost points in late winter on the east coast and around Easter on the west coast. Very small salmon are often confused with Australian herring (tommy rough) but juvenile herring have black tips to the caudal fin and the body feels rough to a finger slid along the body, while the salmon feels smooth. The forked tail of adult salmon is dark, and the eye is generally yellow. The body is classically torpedo shaped and full of power. The head is quite large, and the mouth moderately large. There are distinctive brown dots or dashes along the dorsal surface although the larger specimens become dark across the back. The belly is silvery to white.

Fishing The Australian salmon is one of the best light tackle sportsfish in Australia. They are the best fighting fish taken from the beach, where their strong runs and spectacular leaps more than compensate for the average eating quality. Australian salmon form large schools as they move around the coasts, making them vulnerable to commercial fishing. There is little doubt that commercial fishing can affect local abundance and recreational fishing quality. These schools can provide spectacular fishing, but on occasions these schooling fish will not feed. Australian salmon are frequently caught on pilchards and cut baits, with belly fillets or baits with white skin attached doing better. Pipis, cockles and beach worms take many fish and can really surprise an unsuspecting whiting fisherman. In estuaries, salmon trout are often taken on whitebait, blue bait, prawns or squid. When Australian salmon are heavily fished, live bait will entice a strike when the freshest baits fail. The bite of the salmon is frequently quite fumbling and some patience is required before setting the hook. Australian salmon bite well on cast or trolled lures. Chrome spoons or slices, feather lures, surface poppers and minnow lures work well and are underutilised. Australian salmon will also take flies such as deceiver patterns for those who want real arm stretching action on light fly gear. Australian salmon are poorly regarded as food fish, with larger specimens becoming decidedly tough. The western species is better eating but all fish are improved if the strongly flavoured red muscle along the lateral line is cut out.

Rigs and Tactics

No. 10 swivel
Stopper
Bobby float
No. 2 to 4 ball or bean sinker
No. 3/0 to 5/0 hook gang
Deep Diving Minnow

No. 4 to 4/0 hook
6–10 kg
No. 2 to 4 ball or bean sinker depending on conditions
No. 4 to 2/0 hook

Sinker optional depending on casting distance
No. 10 swivel
15 kg trace
50 cm
No. 2 to 4 ball sinker depending on type of fish
Ganged No. 4/0 to 5/0 hooks

Solid brass ring
Solid brass ring
Main line
30–40 cm
No. 2/0 to 8/0 hook
60–120 g snapper sinker
24 kg trace
Minnow Lure

Solid brass ring
Solid brass ring
Main line
30–40 cm
No. 2/0 to 8/0 hook
60–120 g star sinker
Minnow Lure
Fly fishing is successful

SALMON, COOKTOWN

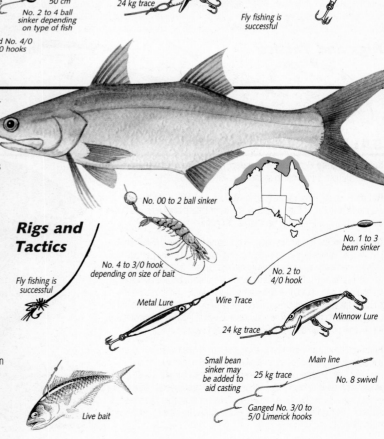

Scientific name *Eleutheronema tetradactylum*. Also known as Threadfin, giant thread-fin, blue salmon, Rockhampton kingfish.

Range Port Hedland northwards and through tropical waters to around Hervey Bay in Queensland, although they are very rare this far south.

Description Even reliable reference books provide confusing information on the status of the various threadfin salmon species. The Cooktown salmon is the largest of these distinctive species which are easily identified by the unusual overshot upper jaw and absence of lips around a large mouth. The threadfin salmon species have an unusual body shape as the body is thickest through the second dorsal fin. The most obvious diagnostic feature is the divided pectoral fin with its separate, finger-like filaments. The Cooktown salmon has four separate, and shorter pectoral filaments as opposed to five in the threadfin salmon (see below). These fish are commonly found in estuaries, where they can range up to the tidal limit in creeks and rivers. They are also found close to shore, near jetties, in harbours or over coastal tidal mud or sand flats. The Cooktown salmon can reach 1.2 m and up to 18 kilograms.

Fishing The Cooktown salmon is often encountered while fishing for other tropical species such as barramundi or mangrove jacks as they frequent similar areas, although salmon are often found in turbid waters. The Cooktown salmon is less commonly taken on lures, although they will sometimes take bright lures. They prefer live or very fresh baits of prawn, crab, mullet or other fish, especially those with bright silver colour. When hooked, the Cooktown salmon is a spectacular aerialist, especially in shallow water and is highly regarded as a sportfish. Best fishing is at the edges of current lines, on the outside edges of mangroves or channels draining with the tide. Cooktown salmon are excellent eating and are regarded by many locals as being superior to barramundi. The flesh bruises easily and does not freeze well, but is superb fresh.

Rigs and Tactics

No. 00 to 2 ball sinker
No. 4 to 3/0 hook depending on size of bait
Fly fishing is successful
Metal Lure
Wire Trace
24 kg trace

No. 1 to 3 bean sinker
No. 2 to 4/0 hook
Minnow Lure

Small bean sinker may be added to aid casting
25 kg trace
Main line
No. 8 swivel
Ganged No. 3/0 to 5/0 Limerick hooks
Live bait

STONEFISH ☠

Scientific name *Synanceja horrida*. Also known as Estuarine stonefish, reef stonefish.

Range Shark Bay in Western Australia and tropical northern waters as far south as Moreton Bay in Southern Queensland.

Description Several authors describe two separate species, the estuarine stonefish and the reef stonefish (*Synanceja verrucosa*). These extremely well camouflaged species are separated by the habitat preference and the number of pectoral rays which is 16 in the estuarine species 18 or 19 for the reef stonefish. The estuarine stonefish reaches 47 cm and the reef species 35 centimetres. However, for all but taxonomists, counting stonefish pectoral rays is dangerous and highly unlikely. The stonefish has 13 extremely poisonous dorsal spines which can inject poison deeply into a wound and can lead to death.

Fishing The stonefish is never a target species and is rightly avoided at all costs. It is however, an effective ambush feeder of inshore reef or estuarine waters, often lying in extremely shallow water, where they can be trodden on. Sandshoes should be worn when walking on tropical reef tops or in tropical estuarine waters to provide some protection from stonefish, coral cuts and stingrays. Stonefish are particularly partial to small live baits, but they will also take prawns, crabs, and fish baits. They can also take slowly worked lures and flies. With stonefish, always cut off the hook and release the animal with no handling. If stung, immerse the wound in hot, but not scalding water. Seek hospitalisation immediately as morphine and medical supervision is likely to be required.

Rigs and Tactics

Not applicable as Stonefish are not recommended as an angling species.

TAILOR

Scientific name *Pomatomus saltatrix*. Also known as Tailer, chopper, bluefish (USA), elf (South Africa), skipjack.

Range Point Quobba in Western Australia and southern waters including Tasmania and as far north as Fraser Island in Queensland. Tailor are however, very rare along most of the south coast and Tasmania.

Description The tailor is a renowned predatory species best known for its relatively small but extremely sharp teeth. The tailor has a moderately forked tail, and a bluish to blue-green back which changes to more silvery and white on the belly. The eye can be yellow. The fins vary in colour but the tail fin is usually darker than the others. Juvenile tailor are found in estuaries and embayments. Larger tailor move to the beaches and inshore reefs at between 25 – 35 centimetres. Tailor undergo a spawning migration, finishing at Fraser Island in Queensland and possibly the Abrolhos Islands in Western Australia, although the largest fish are most commonly found in Shark Bay. Tailor can reach 10 kg with any fish over 5 kg being rightly claimed as a prize and fish over 1.5 kg being large. Tailor are voracious feeders, with individual fish gorging themselves before regurgitating to continue in a feeding frenzy.

Fishing Tailor are a highly prized species which readily takes a bait, fights hard and, if bled immediately after capture make fine eating. Tailor can be taken from boat or shore, on lure, fly or bait and by anglers of any skill level. The most common bait and rig would be a whole pilchard bait on a gang hook rig. In the surf and where casting distance is required, a sliding sinker rig works best, with a star or spoon sinker on a dropper trace doing well. In estuaries, from a boat, or in calmer surf, an unweighted or minimally weighted bait provides by far the best results. Tailor readily feed high in the water column and avidly attack a floating bait. Another rig which works well is to use a nearly filled plastic bubble to gain casting distance without rapidly sinking the bait. Tailor also bite well on whitebait, bluebait and cut flesh baits but they will also take prawn, squid, cuttlefish, mince, heart and other red meats. If using live baits, a small stinger hook near the tail will prevent the loss of successive baits to tailor. A wire trace is required with single hook rigs and small lures, but tailor almost always attack the offering from the back and bite offs are not that common with ganged hook rigs and minnow type lures. Tailor love chrome lures, jigs, spoons and minnow lures which are cast or trolled, especially into white water near rocks, reefs or bommies where tailor aggregate. Tailor will also take flies but their teeth badly knock around feathers. Tailor bite best at dusk and dawn. Tailor smoke very well and are fair eating when fresh which is improved if fish are immediately bled. The flesh of the tailor is fairly oily and bruises easily. Tailor makes a quality cut bait.

Rigs and Tactics

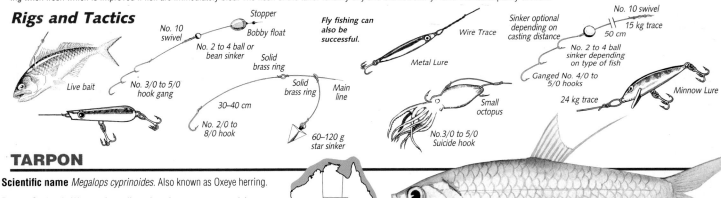

Live bait

Stopper

No. 10 swivel

Bobby float

No. 2 to 4 ball or bean sinker

No. 3/0 to 5/0 hook gang

Solid brass ring

30–40 cm

No. 2/0 to 8/0 hook

Solid brass ring

Main line

60–120 g star sinker

Fly fishing can also be successful.

Metal Lure

Wire Trace

Small octopus

No.3/0 to 5/0 Suicide hook

Sinker optional depending on casting distance

No. 10 swivel

15 kg trace

50 cm

No. 2 to 4 ball sinker depending on type of fish

Ganged No. 4/0 to 5/0 hooks

24 kg trace

Minnow Lure

TARPON

Scientific name *Megalops cyprinoides*. Also known as Oxeye herring.

Range Onslow in Western Australia and northern waters around the east coast as far south as Sydney NSW.

Description The tarpon is most easily identified by the long trailing filament at the rear of the single dorsal fin. The eye is also very large as are the upper jaw bones. The tail is deeply forked and powerful. The scales are very large. Tarpon are commonly found in mangrove creeks, larger estuaries and bays. The tarpon can grow to 1.5 m and around 3.5 kilograms.

Fishing The tarpon will take dead fish bait but can be very finicky. They can sometimes be taken on small live baits. However, tarpon are a fantastic fighting fish and are a target species for lure and fly fishers. Most fish are taken on small white jigs or small chrome lures. They are also avid fly takers. The mouth of the tarpon is bony and hooks should be at their absolute sharpest to get a solid hookup that can survive the strong fight and aerial display of the tarpon. Tarpon are extremely bony and are considered poor eating. Care should be taken with handling to reduce scale loss and long term mortality of released fish.

Rigs and Tactics

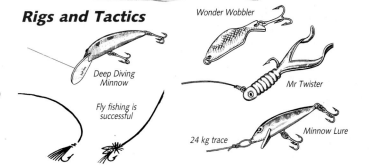

Deep Diving Minnow

Wonder Wobbler

Mr Twister

Fly fishing is successful

24 kg trace

Minnow Lure

TARWHINE

Scientific name *Rhabdosargus sarba*. Also known as Silver bream.

Range The tarwhine has a broken distribution, from Esperance to Shark Bay in Western Australia and from the Great Barrier Reef in northern Queensland to the Gippsland Lakes in Victoria.

Description The tarwhine is similar to the various bream species but differs in a few key areas. The tarwhine has a number of thin golden or brown stripes running the length of the otherwise silver body. The nose of the tarwhine is blunt and there are 11 or 12 anal rays whereas bream have 9 or fewer. The fins other than the dorsal fin are generally bright yellow or yellow-orange and the tarwhine has a black lining to its gut cavity. Tarwhine are common in inshore and estuarine areas and may be found on offshore reefs on occasions. Tarwhine form schools, especially in smaller sizes. Tarwhine can reach 80 cm and more than 3 kg but they are most commonly caught at a few hundred grams.

Fishing Tarwhine can be voracious feeders, taking a wide variety of foods. Tarwhine readily take cut flesh, bluebait, whitebait and parts of pilchard but many more are caught on prawn, pipi, worm, nipper or squid baits. Tarwhine are also occasionally taken on cabbage baits by luderick and drummer fishermen in NSW. While tarwhine bite very hard, their relatively small mouth and frequent small size makes them nuisance bait pickers in many instances. Use a smaller hook for better results, but don't let the fish run with the bait too far as they can easily become gut hooked. In estuaries or shallow waters, a light running ball sinker rig works best while off the rocks or in deeper water, use as little weight and as light a rig as you can get away with. Tarwhine fight well for their size. They also make very good eating although they can have an iodine taste if not bled immediately and the guts and black stomach lining removed as soon as possible.

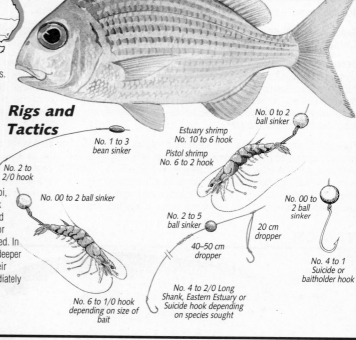

Rigs and Tactics

No. 1 to 3 bean sinker

No. 2 to 2/0 hook

No. 00 to 2 ball sinker

No. 6 to 1/0 hook depending on size of bait

Estuary shrimp No. 10 to 6 hook
Pistol shrimp No. 6 to 2 hook

No. 0 to 2 ball sinker

No. 2 to 5 ball sinker

40–50 cm dropper

No. 4 to 2/0 Long Shank, Eastern Estuary or Suicide hook depending on species sought

20 cm dropper

No. 00 to 2 ball sinker

No. 4 to 1 Suicide or baitholder hook

TOADFISH, COMMON ☠

Scientific name *Tetractenos hamiltoni* Also known as blowie, toado

Range Townsville in Queensland and southwards to Merimbula in southern NSW.

Description A small species of the toadfish reaching only 15 centimetes. The body is fairly slender and there are several vertical stripes on the lower sides of the body. There is no long stripe along the body as in the banded toadfish. The common toadfish also has small prickles over its skin whereas the smooth toadfish has smooth skin. Like all the toadfish, the common toadfish will inflate its body with air or water upon capture which makes the prickles stand up. Although much despised, the toadfish are one of the most advanced groups of fish from an evolutionary standpoint, a feature which is generally lost on those who catch them regularly.

Fishing This small species is a well known bait stealer. Travelling in schools, the fused teeth enable any bait no matter how robust to be stripped. There are no specialist rigs for this species and only luderick anglers using green weed seem to be immune from their attentions when they are in the area. The common toadfish is highly toxic and must not be consumed or fed to pets under any circumstance. Because of this all toadfish should not be left anywhere where pets or wild animals can consume them as they will kill if not treated by trained professionals.

Rigs and Tactics
Not applicable as Toadfish are not recommended as an angling species.

TREVALLY, BLUEFIN

Scientific name *Caranx melampygus* Also known as blue-finned trevally, spotted trevally

Range Exmouth Gulf in Western Australia and northwards through tropical waters and then as far south as Sydney in NSW.

Description Differentiating the various trevally species can be difficult even for trained taxonomists. However, the bluefin trevally exhibits several features that are readily identifiable to the average angler. The common name gives a clue to a diagnostic feature, with the prominent blue tail fin. The soft dorsal fin and anal fins as well as along the scutes which form along the tail end of the lateral line are also blue or bright blue. The transparent pectoral fin is elongated and extends to the commencement of the tail scutes. There are a number of small blue or dark spots on the upper body which may extend onto the head, but these spots are more numerous and never golden as in the thicklip trevally. The bluefin trevally is found on coastal reefs although larger specimens can be found along deeper reefs or adjacent slopes. The bluefin trevally can reach 1 metre which makes it a challenge on lighter gear near reefs.

Fishing The bluefin trevally is a typically hard fighting fish, turning side on and using all its resistance to get to some reef to break off the unwary angler. The bluefin trevally is taken on a variety of rigs, ranging from lures such as poppers, wobblers, minnow lures, soft plastics and fly gear to shallow, lightly rigged baits and standard reef bouncing paternoster rigs. The bluefin trevally will take a variety of baits including cut baits, whole fish, squid, prawns and live bait. The bluefin trevally is considered to be among the better trevally species to eat.

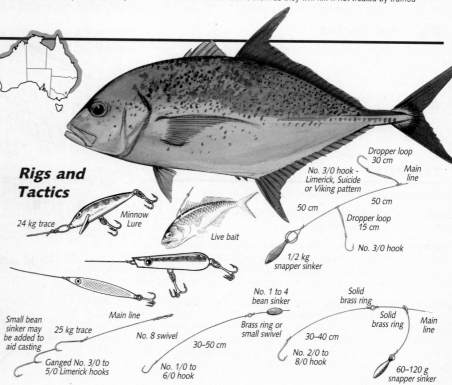

Rigs and Tactics

24 kg trace

Minnow Lure

Live bait

Main line

25 kg trace

Small bean sinker may be added to aid casting

Ganged No. 3/0 to 5/0 Limerick hooks

No. 8 swivel

30–50 cm

No. 1/0 to 6/0 hook

No. 3/0 hook - Limerick, Suicide or Viking pattern

Dropper loop 30 cm

Main line

50 cm

Dropper loop 15 cm

50 cm

No. 3/0 hook

1/2 kg snapper sinker

No. 1 to 4 bean sinker

Brass ring or small swivel

No. 2/0 to 8/0 hook

30–40 cm

Solid brass ring

Solid brass ring

Main line

60–120 g snapper sinker

TREVALLY, GIANT

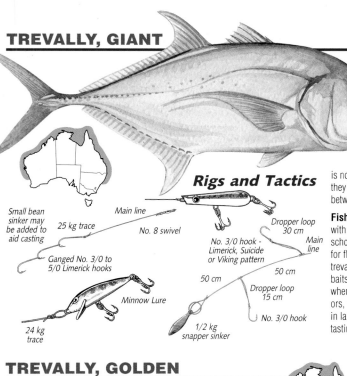

Scientific name *Caranx ignobilis*. Also known as Lowly trevally, barrier trevally.

Range Rottnest Island in Western Australia northwards including tropical waters and as far south as Sydney on the east coast.

Description The giant trevally is the largest of the trevally reaching 1.7 m in length and 60 kg which would be almost unstoppable on stand up fishing tackle. The steep profile of the head is typical of the giant trevally. There is also a small scale-less area on the ventral surface immediately in front of the ventral fins. A small patch of scales is generally found in the middle of this otherwise scale-less patch. There is no opercular (cheek) spot which is present on the bigeye trevally. As giant trevally increase in size, they form smaller schools with the largest fish frequently loners. Large fish also prefer deeper channels between large reefs while smaller fish are found on tidal flats or on the edges of shallower reefs.

Fishing Small giant trevally are one of the most challenging species for lure fishers in the tropics, with spinning near the edges of reefs, on drop-offs on tidal flats or sight fishing to individuals or small schools working well. Poppers are particularly attractive to these fish and can also be used as a teaser for fly fishers. Giant trevally also take minnow lures, large spoons and lead-headed jigs. Large giant trevally are most frequently taken on live baits. They will also take dead baits, including fresh dead baits, cut baits, pilchards or less frequently squid or large prawn baits. Giant trevally can be hooked when bottom bouncing with standard reef rigs for other species such as coral trout or various emperors, with arm stretching and tackle testing results. Top quality gear and gel spun lines are an advantage in landing these challenging fish. Small giant trevally are good eating but fish over 10 – 12 kg are poor tasting and are better released after a photograph to record the encounter.

Rigs and Tactics

Small bean sinker may be added to aid casting
25 kg trace
Main line
No. 8 swivel
Dropper loop 30 cm
Main line
No. 3/0 hook - Limerick, Suicide or Viking pattern
50 cm
50 cm
Dropper loop 15 cm
Ganged No. 3/0 to 5/0 Limerick hooks
Minnow Lure
1/2 kg snapper sinker
No. 3/0 hook
24 kg trace

TREVALLY, GOLDEN

Scientific name *Gnathanodon speciosus*.

Range A wide ranging species from Denmark on the south coast of Western Australia and the entire west coast, northern waters and as far south as Wollongong in NSW but most common in tropical waters.

Description The golden trevally is also a large species reaching 1.2 m and 37 kilograms. Juvenile golden trevally are striking and are often associated with large fish or sharks. They are a bright gold with vertical black stripes the first of which passes through the eye. Larger fish lose the distinctive stripes and the eye is quite small. These fish are often quite silvery when caught but flash yellow as they die and then are golden coloured, especially on the belly. A number of black spots are often present on the side, commonly near the tail but the number and size varies and they may not be present. The most obvious feature of this species is that they lack teeth.

Fishing Like many trevally, golden trevally form schools of similar sized fish, with smaller schools of larger fish. Large golden trevally are often taken trolling minnow lures in the vicinity of offshore reefs. Smaller fish are taken by shore based or small boat anglers either with lures including poppers, slices, spoons or minnow lures or less commonly on fly. Golden trevally take baits well, with prawns, pilchard, small fish or cut baits working well. Over sand, the baits can be weighted, but near reefs, lightly weighted or floating baits work better as the further any trevally moves from a reef to take a bait, the better the chances of landing it, as they fight very strongly and make use of any rocky outcrop. Golden trevally make very good eating, especially if bled and chilled immediately on capture.

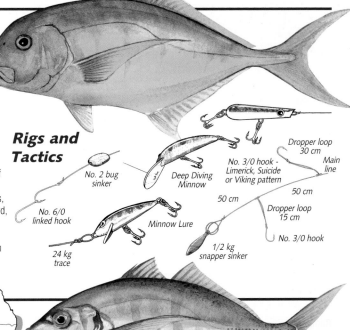

Rigs and Tactics

No. 2 bug sinker
Deep Diving Minnow
Dropper loop 30 cm
Main line
No. 3/0 hook - Limerick, Suicide or Viking pattern
No. 6/0 linked hook
Minnow Lure
50 cm
50 cm
Dropper loop 15 cm
24 kg trace
1/2 kg snapper sinker
No. 3/0 hook

TREVALLY, SILVER

Scientific name *Pseudocaranx dentex*. Also known as White trevally, skipjack trevally, skippy, trevally, blurter.

Range North-west Cape in Western Australia and southwards, along the entire south coast and Tasmania and as far north as south Queensland.

Description A common schooling fish of cooler waters, the silver trevally is found in inshore areas but may be found near offshore cover. Juveniles are often encountered in estuaries and bays but larger fish can also be found in these areas on occasions. The fins may be yellow and a narrow yellow stripe is often found on these fish but most fish are silver with a blue-green or darker blue, and dark bands may be present. The very similar sand trevally (*Pseudocaranx wrighti*) of central Western Australia only grows to around 800 g and has more prominent dark bands. The silver trevally can reach 1 m and more than 10 kg but fish of 2 kg are much more common and in most areas, a fish of 5 kg is noteworthy. The mouth is relatively small, finishing well in front of the start of the eye and the lips are rubbery. There is an obvious black spot on the rear edge of the opercular (cheek) bone.

Fishing The silver trevally can be present in almost plague proportions with areas like Port Stephens NSW famous for its 'blurter' runs. Like all trevally, they can be good sport, especially on light line. Silver trevally can be taken on small lures such as small spoons, leadhead jigs and small minnow lures. They can be coaxed to take flies, particularly when berley is used with a school of fish. While silver trevally can feed on the surface, they prefer to feed on or near sandy or gravel bottoms and lures presented close to the bottom do best. Silver trevally are a better bait proposition, taking baits such as half pilchard, bluebait, whitebait, cut fish baits, squid, prawn, crab, pipi, nipper or cunjevoi depending on the food found in the area fished. Silver trevally respond well to berley. Silver trevally can be taken on lines of 3 – 8 kg where they provide excellent sport. As they are a schooling fish which are not too prone to disperse if one fish escapes, persistence pays off with light line. Small silver trevally make excellent live baits, but size and bag limits must be followed. Silver trevally are fair eating, and must be bled on capture.

Rigs and Tactics

No. 4 to 3/0 hook
No. 00 to 2 ball sinker
3–8 kg
No. 4 to 3/0 hook
No. 2 to 4 ball or bean sinker depending on conditions
No. 4 to 3/0 hook depending on size of bait
Solid brass ring
barrel sinker
Solid brass ring
30–50 kg trace
1 metre
No. 2 bug sinker
No. 2/0 linked hook

TRUMPETER

Scientific name *Pelates quadrilineatus* Also known as four-lined trumpeter

Range Shark Bay in Western Australia and northwards through tropical waters and as far south as Narooma in NSW

Description A common bait stealing species of the estuaries and coastal bays. While it has a wide range, it is best known from NSW where it forms schools over weed and sand areas from the Sydney region northwards and disrupt bream, whiting and flathead fishing. The trumpeter has a more elongated nose than the striped trumpeter and there are four or five prominent stripes which run the length of the body. The mouth is relatively small, and as it only grows to 20 cm, this species is difficult to hook. A dark blotch behind the head and under the start of the dorsal fin is usually present.

Fishing The trumpeter is not generally targeted and isn't even highly regarded as a live bait. The trumpeter will take almost all baits but is more commonly associated with the picking of baits such as worm, pipi, prawn or mullet gut intended for other species. They are attracted to berley intended for bream and they can also be taken on bait jigs. While the trumpeter makes a good cut bait, their small size means that they are not targeted as a food fish.

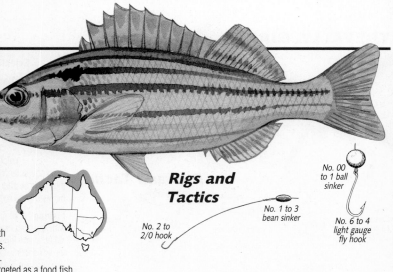

Rigs and Tactics

No. 2 to 2/0 hook

No. 1 to 3 bean sinker

No. 00 to 1 ball sinker

No. 6 to 4 light gauge fly hook

TRUMPETER, STRIPED

Scientific name *Pelates sexlineatus*. Also known as Striped perch, striped grunter, trump.

Range Shark Bay in Western Australia southwards as far as Kangaroo Island in South Australia.

Description A small species reaching 32 cm and around 500 g, but more common at a bait stealing 25 centimetres. The striped trumpeter forms schools in coastal bays and estuaries over sand or weed bottom or near broken ground. The small mouth makes hooking difficult. The short head is quite rounded and there are around 5 – 6 lines running through the head and along the body. There may be a number of vertical blotches with one most prominent behind the head overlaying the stripes. The top stripes may be wavy.

Fishing While frequently considered a pest species, the striped trumpeter is a frequent early encounter for young anglers. The striped trumpeter will take most baits, but the small mouth and darting bites of a school means that a small long-shanked hook will improve catches. Baits of peeled prawns, cut flesh, blue bait, pipi, worms, or squid work well, with more robust baits such as squid recommended. Striped trumpeter make hardy and quality live baits. Striped trumpeter are not highly regarded as food fish but are often served to the family by proud young fishermen.

Rigs and Tactics

No. 0 to 4 bean sinker

Brass ring or small swivel

30–50 cm

No. 8 to 1 hook

No. 6 to 4 Baitholder hook

No. 00 to 2 ball sinker

No. 6 to 1 hook depending on size of bait

No. 8 to 2 hook

3 kg

No. 8 to 2 hook

No. 2 to 4 ball or bean sinker depending on conditions

TURRUM

Scientific name *Carangoides fulvoguttatus*. Also known as Gold spotted trevally, yellow spotted trevally.

Range Augusta in Western Australia and northwards including tropical waters and as far south as Maroochydore in Queensland.

Description The turrum is a largely tropical species that may move further south during summer. It is found in inshore waters and around shallow and occasionally mid water reefs. A number of species are known as turrum, especially in Queensland, but the true turrum can be identified by a number of features. These include the complete lack of scales up to the base of the pectoral fin whereas the giant trevally has a small oval shaped patch of tiny scales in an otherwise large scaleless area of the breast. The second dorsal fin of the turrum has between 25 – 30 rays while the giant trevally has 18 – 21. The turrum differs from many other trevally in only having a band of fine teeth in each jaw. The turrum can reach 1.3 m and a weight of around 12 kilograms.

Fishing Many turrum are taken while trolling minnow lures near the edges of reefs, reef channels or other drop-offs. They will also rise to pusher type lures, slices, feathers and larger flies. Cast lures will also take fish. Turrum readily take live baits and are also taken on fresh whole fish, squid or cut-baits. Tackle needs to be strong. Small turrum are fair eating but larger fish are better returned to fight another day.

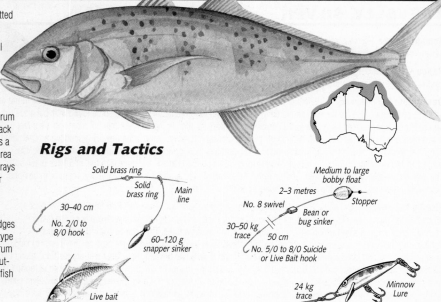

Rigs and Tactics

Solid brass ring

Solid brass ring

Main line

30–40 cm

No. 2/0 to 8/0 hook

60–120 g snapper sinker

Live bait

Medium to large bobby float

2–3 metres

No. 8 swivel

Bean or bug sinker

Stopper

30–50 kg trace

50 cm

No. 5/0 to 8/0 Suicide or Live Bait hook

24 kg trace

Minnow Lure

WHITING, KING GEORGE

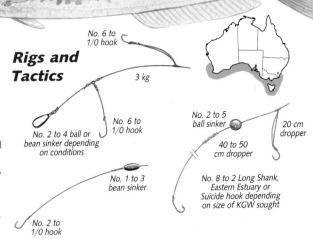

Scientific name *Sillaginodes punctata*. Also known as Spotted whiting, KG, KGW.

Range Dongara in Western Australia and southern waters, although rarely in eastern Tasmania and as far north as Jervis Bay but reasonably uncommon in NSW.

Description The King George whiting is the largest and most sought after whiting species in Australia reaching 67 cm and more than 2 kg, with the largest specimens found in oceanic waters. Juveniles spend time near sea grass beds inshore or in estuaries before moving to more open waters. King George whiting prefer sand patches near weed beds, gravel or broken reef country with water up to 10 m in depth being the most productive. King George whiting are readily identified by the typical whiting down-turned mouth and the distinctive dark brown or red-brown spots and broken dashes along the body.

Fishing The King George whiting is a magnificent and hard fighting whiting species. Smaller fish succumb most readily to baits of prawn, pipi, mussel, crab, nippers and worms. These baits are fished on light line with minimal weight near the edges of drop-offs or sand patches in sea grass beds or reef areas. Larger specimens, or fish taken in Western Australia are most frequently caught on blue sardines, whitebait or small cut baits. The largest King George whiting from South Australia and Western Australia are taken on reef fishing rigs intended for snapper or other species near reefs in depths up to 30 metres. Berley can work well, but can also attract bait pickers such as toads which are a nuisance. The best King George whiting experts adopt a mobile approach, fishing sometimes tiny sand patches near heavy cover and moving on if there are no bites in a few minutes. King George whiting are rarely taken on jigs, flies or other small lures generally intended for flathead or flounder. The King George whiting is magnificent eating, combining the meat quality of all whiting in a size large enough that generous boneless fillets can be obtained.

Rigs and Tactics

No. 6 to 1/0 hook — 3 kg
No. 2 to 4 ball or bean sinker depending on conditions — No. 6 to 1/0 hook
No. 1 to 3 bean sinker
No. 2 to 1/0 hook
No. 2 to 5 ball sinker — 20 cm dropper — 40 to 50 cm dropper — No. 8 to 2 Long Shank, Eastern Estuary or Suicide hook depending on size of KGW sought

WHITING, SAND

Scientific name *Sillago ciliata*. Also known as Silver whiting, summer whiting, blue nose whiting.

Range Cape York in Queensland and along the east coast as far south as eastern Tasmania and Lakes Entrance in Victoria.

Description The sand whiting is a common species of inshore and tidal sandy areas. The sand whiting can reach 47 cm and around a kilogram. It is readily identified by the lack of a silver stripe along the side and the dusky blotch at the base of the pectoral fin. Large sand whiting are sometimes confused with bonefish, but all whitings have two dorsal fins while the bonefish has one. A similar species, the yellow-finned whiting (also known as the Western sand whiting) (Sillago schomburgkii) reaches 42 cm but is only found from the Gulf of St Vincent in South Australia to Shark Bay in Western Australia. The yellow-finned whiting species lacks the dusky blotch at the base of the pectoral fin and is commonly taken on blue sardines, whitebait or small cut baits.

Fishing A scrappy little fighter which gives a good account of itself for its size. The sand whiting is a terrific light line quarry and fine tackle will greatly increase the number of strikes. Use the absolute minimum weight to either reach the bottom or to keep the bait from swinging wildly in current or wave wash. Sand whiting will take a moving bait and a slow retrieve will attract fish. A long trace behind a small ball sinker is the preferred rig. As whiting have a small mouth, a long shank hook around size 6 – 2 is recommended. Either putting red tubing or a few red beads above the hook works very well. The sand whiting feeds on nippers, pipis, prawns and especially beach, squirt or blood worms and all these make terrific baits. On a rising tide, sand whiting can be caught in very shallow water of only a few centimetres, while on a falling tide, fish the deeper edges of gutters or drop-offs but success is less assured. Sand whiting are a delicate, sweet flavoured fish often highly priced in restaurants but there can be a number of fine bones.

Rigs and Tactics

No. 1 to 3 bean sinker
No. 8 to 4 long shank hook
No. 2 to 5 ball sinker — 20 cm dropper — 40–50 cm dropper — No. 8 to 2 Long Shank, Eastern Estuary or Suicide hook depending on species sought
No. 4 to 2/0 hook — 3 kg — No. 8 to 4 hook
No. 0 to 4 ball or bean sinker depending on conditions

WHITING, YELLOWFIN

Scientific name *Sillago schombergkii* Also known as western sand whiting, yellow-finned whiting

Range Shark Bay in Western Australia and southwards to the Gulf of St Vincent in South Australia

Description A similar species to the sand whiting but lacks the black spot at the base of the pectoral fin. The characteristic yellow to orange ventral and anal fins become less apparent in larger individuals. There is no obvious silver strip along the sides or any markings on the dorsal surface. Although the yellowfin whiting is found in South Australian waters it is most common on the west coast of Western Australia. It is found foraging in the estuaries and surf areas and can reach the most respectable size for a whiting of 42 centimetres. It is not uncommon at around 33 – 35 centimetres.

Fishing The excellent eating which this species provides makes it a worthwhile target for anglers. While they may be found in the estuaries, with the exception of the Peel-Harvey estuary, the best specimens are taken from ocean beaches. A light ball sinker and a bluebait or whitebait on small ganged hooks fished on a flick rod are highly recommended. When fishing for whiting, fishing at your feet first is good advice as many anglers cast way out behind the active feeding zone of this fish. They fish much better on a rising tide and can be in the sand wash area in only a few centimetres of water. Indeed, places where other anglers wade out to cast can help to attract yellowfin whiting. A slow retrieve works best.

Rigs and Tactics

No. 1 to 3 bean sinker
No. 4 to 1 hook
No. 2 bug sinker
No. 6 to 2 linked Limerick hook
No. 00 to 1 ball sinker
No. 6 to 4 light gauge fly hook

BASS, SAND

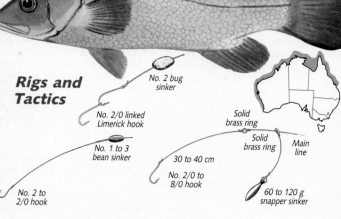

Scientific name *Psammoperca waigiensis* Also known as Glass-eyed perch, jewel eye, dwarf palmer perch, reef barramundi.

Range Fremantle northwards through tropical waters to central Queensland.

Description The sand bass has one large flat spine at rear angle of preoperculum. Colour varies from light silvery grey to dark brown; eyes reddish. The lateral line extends onto the caudal fin. Inhabits rocky or coral reefs, frequently in weedy areas, usually in holes and crevices by day. This species can enter estuaries where it can be confused with juvenile barramundi. It can be separated from the barramundi in that the sand bass has granular teeth on the tongue, has a prominent lateral line and only reaches 47 cm but is more common at 30–35 centimetres. The sand bass forages on fishes and crustaceans at night.

Fishing The sand bass makes good eating, but does not reach the size of its more illustrious cousin the barramundi. Fishing for this species is best adjacent to rocky reefs. The large mouth of the sand bass means that it can be taken on baits intended for other species. The sand bass will take lures or jigs on occasion but they are more widely regarded as a bait species, with cut baits, squid and pilchards.

Rigs and Tactics

No. 2 bug sinker

No. 2/0 linked Limerick hook

No. 1 to 3 bean sinker

No. 2 to 2/0 hook

Solid brass ring

Solid brass ring

Main line

30 to 40 cm

No. 2/0 to 8/0 hook

60 to 120 g snapper sinker

COD, BLACK

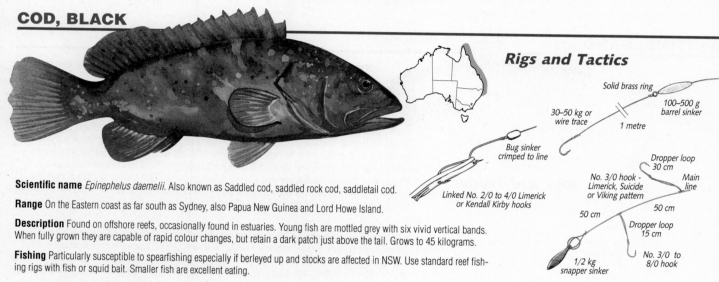

Scientific name *Epinephelus daemelii*. Also known as Saddled cod, saddled rock cod, saddletail cod.

Range On the Eastern coast as far south as Sydney, also Papua New Guinea and Lord Howe Island.

Description Found on offshore reefs, occasionally found in estuaries. Young fish are mottled grey with six vivid vertical bands. When fully grown they are capable of rapid colour changes, but retain a dark patch just above the tail. Grows to 45 kilograms.

Fishing Particularly susceptible to spearfishing especially if berleyed up and stocks are affected in NSW. Use standard reef fishing rigs with fish or squid bait. Smaller fish are excellent eating.

Rigs and Tactics

Solid brass ring

100–500 g barrel sinker

30–50 kg or wire trace

1 metre

Bug sinker crimped to line

Linked No. 2/0 to 4/0 Limerick or Kendall Kirby hooks

Dropper loop 30 cm

No. 3/0 hook - Limerick, Suicide or Viking pattern

Main line

50 cm

50 cm

Dropper loop 15 cm

1/2 kg snapper sinker

No. 3/0 to 8/0 hook

COD, FLOWERY

Scientific name *Epinephelus fuscoguttatus* Also known as carpet cod, black rock-cod.

Range Dampier archipelago in Western Australia and northwards through tropical waters to northern NSW around South West Rocks.

Description A heavy bodied cod species, the flowery cod generally has a fairly pale brown colour with darker chocolate brown 'flower' blotches on the sides. There are also numerous smaller spots over the body, including the stomach and the fins. The tail fin is heavily spotted and rounded while the spots on the ventral fins are an unusual feature of several closely related species. Juvenile flowery cod up to around 4 kg are often found in northern mangrove creeks. Adults are found on offshore reefs or on broken ground near reefs. This species can reach 90 cm while the small toothed cod reaches 63 centimetres.

Fishing In estuaries, juvenile flowery cod take a wide variety of baits and will take lures which are presented near them. They will take live or dead baits and provide good sport. On offshore reefs, larger specimens are taken on heavier, bottom reef fishing rigs. The flowery cod is highly regarded as a table fish presenting a thick fillet of white meat. Even large fish retain a high quality.

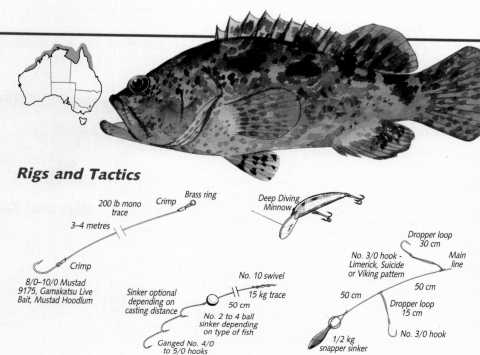

Rigs and Tactics

200 lb mono trace

Crimp

Brass ring

Deep Diving Minnow

3–4 metres

Crimp

8/0–10/0 Mustad 9175, Gamakatsu Live Bait, Mustad Hoodlum

No. 10 swivel

15 kg trace

50 cm

Sinker optional depending on casting distance

No. 2 to 4 ball sinker depending on type of fish

Ganged No. 4/0 to 5/0 hooks

Dropper loop 30 cm

No. 3/0 hook - Limerick, Suicide or Viking pattern

Main line

50 cm

50 cm

Dropper loop 15 cm

1/2 kg snapper sinker

No. 3/0 hook

DORY, JOHN

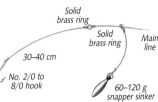

Scientific name *Zeus faber*. Also known as St Peter's fish, doorkeeper's fish, dory keparu (NZ).

Range From Cape Cuvier in Western Australia, around the southern part of the country, including Tasmania, to Bundaberg in southern Queensland.

Description An unusual fish with a large, upward pointing mouth which can be extended the length of its head. The John dory has a distinctive, prominent mark on each side, said to be made by the fingers of St Peter when he picked up this fish. The John dory has very fine scales compared with the mirror dory which has no scales. The elongated dorsal rays give a distinctive appearance. John dory are most common near mid to deepwater reefs from 10 to 80 m but can be found in deeper estuaries like the Hawkesbury River and Sydney Harbour in NSW. The John dory can reach 75 cm and 4 kg although they are commonly taken at around a kilogram.

Fishing The John dory is a poor fighter but it is absolutely delicious. The John dory is a common deep water trawl species in temperate waters but can be taken by anglers near deep reefs, wrecks and in deep estuaries such as the Hawkesbury. John dory greatly prefer live fish such as yellowtail for bait but can be caught on very fresh fillets.

Rigs and Tactics

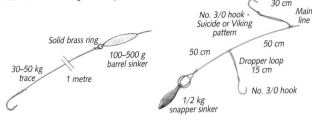

Live bait

Solid brass ring / Solid brass ring / Main line / 30–40 cm / No. 2/0 to 8/0 hook / 60–120 g snapper sinker

Solid brass ring / 100–500 g barrel sinker / 30–50 kg trace / 1 metre

Dropper loop 30 cm / Main line / No. 3/0 hook - Suicide or Viking pattern / 50 cm / 50 cm / Dropper loop 15 cm / No. 3/0 hook / 1/2 kg snapper sinker

DORY, MIRROR

Scientific name *Zenopsis nebulosus*. Also known as Trawl dory, deepwater dory, deepsea dory.

Range From the Pilbara in Western Australia around the southern part of Australia, including Tasmania to Southern Queensland.

Description The mirror dory is smaller than John dory, reaching 58 cm and 2.4 kilograms. The mirror dory is almost exclusively a deep water trawl species. It possesses a fainter fingerprint on its side. The forehead is distinctly convex and the anal fin has three spines as opposed to four in the John dory.

Fishing This excellent eating species is rarely taken by anglers as it prefers the deep waters of the Continental shelf. Occasionally encountered, the mirror dory also prefers live or extremely fresh baits and can be found near wrecks or deeper reefs.

Rigs and Tactics

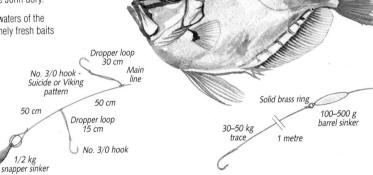

Solid brass ring / Solid brass ring / Main line / 30–40 cm / No. 2/0 to 8/0 hook / 60–120 g snapper sinker

Live bait

Dropper loop 30 cm / Main line / No. 3/0 hook - Suicide or Viking pattern / 50 cm / 50 cm / Dropper loop 15 cm / No. 3/0 hook / 1/2 kg snapper sinker

Solid brass ring / 100–500 g barrel sinker / 30–50 kg trace / 1 metre

EMPEROR, RED

Scientific name *Lutjanus sebae*. Also known as Government bream, red kelp.

Range From Shark Bay northwards and around to Moreton Bay in southern Queensland, although specimens are occasionally taken further south.

Description A striking and highly prized reef fish. The red emperor is a schooling fish which means that fishing can be fast and furious, but this valuable species can be taken in large numbers in commercial fish traps and trawls. The red emperor changes appearance as it grows. Juveniles are known as Government bream as the three striking bands resemble a convict's broad arrow. This pattern fades with age and fish over 13 kg become a uniform scarlet or salmon pink. The reddish fins are narrowly edged with white. The cheeks are scaled and there is a deep notch in the lower edge of the pre-operculum (inner cheekbone).

Fishing Red emperor fight extremely well, even when taken from deeper waters where they are increasingly taken. The red emperor can reach 22 kg and more than a metre in length which increases their allure. Red emperor prefer moving water in channels near deeper reefs. As a result, they can be taken on drifts between reef patches in seemingly open ground. They tend to form schools of similar sized fish and are partial to cut fish baits, octopus, squid or pilchards. The red emperor is excellent eating even in the larger sizes and is considered safe from ciguatera.

Rigs and Tactics

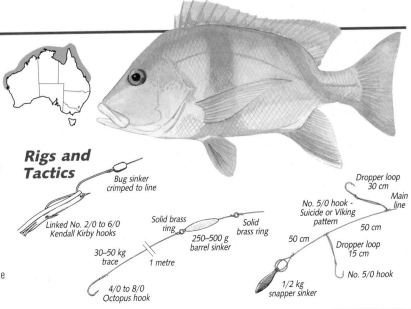

Bug sinker crimped to line / Linked No. 2/0 to 6/0 Kendall Kirby hooks / 30–50 kg trace / 1 metre / 4/0 to 8/0 Octopus hook

Solid brass ring / Solid brass ring / 250–500 g barrel sinker

Dropper loop 30 cm / Main line / No. 5/0 hook - Suicide or Viking pattern / 50 cm / 50 cm / Dropper loop 15 cm / No. 5/0 hook / 1/2 kg snapper sinker

EMPEROR, SPANGLED

Scientific name *Lethrinus nebulosus*. Also known as Nor-west snapper, Nor'wester, yellow sweetlip, sand snapper, sand bream.

Range Rottnest Island north and around the top end to Coffs Harbour in northern NSW.

Description A striking member of the sweetlip group. This species is easily identified by the blue spots on each scale and the blue bars on the cheek. This species can reach 86 cm and 6.5 kg and is considered very good eating.

Fishing The spangled emperor is generally taken adjacent to coral or rock reefs over gravel or sand bottoms. They frequent lagoons and coral cays and can be taken from the beach in Western Australia where there are reef patches nearby. They are particularly active at night. The spangled emperor can be taken with standard reef rigs, but as they are most common in water under 15 metres deep, lighter rigs and berley can bring these fish up into the open. Use cut fish, pilchards, squid, octopus, crab or prawn baits. Spangled emperor will take jigs or minnow lures either trolled or cast in areas near reefs where spangled emperor feed.

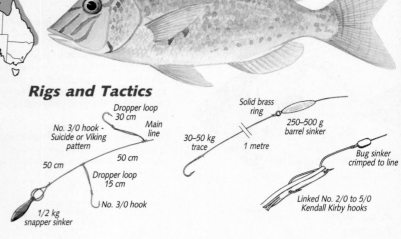

Rigs and Tactics

EMPEROR, SWEETLIP

Rigs and Tactics

Scientific name *Lethrinus miniatus*. (formerly *Lethrinus chrysostomus*) Also known as Sweetlip, lipper, red-throat, trumpeter (Norfolk Island).

Range Abrolhos Islands around the top end to northern NSW around Evan Head but found as far south as Perth or Sydney on occasions.

Description The sweetlip emperor is the most common of the emperor species, especially in Queensland. This species is identified by orange areas around the eyes, a bright red dorsal fin, and a red patch at the base of the pectoral fins. The inside of the mouth is red. Some fish have a series of brown vertical bands but many fish are a uniform colour. This species reaches a metre and 9 kg but is more common from 1 to 2.5 kilograms.

Fishing Found in reef country, but frequently taken from areas between reefs, the sweetlip emperor can be berleyed up and large catches taken from the feeding school. The sweetlip emperor fights well and is able to dive to the bottom and break off an unwary angler. These fish respond well to oily fleshed baits such as pilchard or mackerel, but when feeding can be caught on most baits including cut baits, squid, octopus, prawn and crab. Sweetlip emperor are highly regarded food fish.

GROPER, EASTERN BLUE AND WESTERN BLUE

Scientific name *Achoerodus viridis* (Eastern blue groper) *Achoerodus gouldii* (Western blue groper) Also known as Red groper, brown groper (Actually female colouration of the Eastern blue groper), giant pigfish, blue tank.

Range The Eastern blue is found from Harvey Bay in southern Queensland to Wilson's Promontory in Victoria, while the Western Blue groper can be found from the Abrolhos Islands off Geraldton in Western Australia to west of Melbourne.

Description The second largest wrasse species (behind the hump-headed Maori wrasse), the Western blue groper is capable of reaching 1.6 m and 40 kilograms. The eastern blue groper can reach 20 kg but has been seriously over fished in many areas and fish of 2 to 10 kg are much more likely. The blue gropers are easily identified by their size, often brilliant colours, their fleshy lips, heavy scales and peg like teeth. Eastern blue groper prefer turbulent rocky shorelines or inshore bomboras. Western blue groper are found in similar areas, but the largest fish come off deep reefs of the south coast, or near remote islands of the Recherché Archipelago. Both species are curious and extremely susceptible to spearfishing. Female eastern blue groper are red or dirty brown and if the largest (blue) male from a group is taken, the largest female becomes a blue male and begins to grow larger. This phenomenon has not been recorded for the Western blue groper where most specimens are blue-green to a brilliant cobalt blue.

Fishing Blue groper present a real test for shore based anglers. They can be taken on cunjevoi, prawns and squid, fresh crabs, and especially the red crabs found in the intertidal areas of the east coast. Crabs are easily the best bait. Heavy rods and line and extra strong hooks are required for these hard, dirty fighters. A groper should not be given its head as it will bury you in the nearest cave or under any rock ledge. Western blue groper are more frequently taken by fishing the white water of offshore reefs with a boat. Small to medium blue groper are good eating, but large ones are dry and the flesh coarse. These are hardy fish which many anglers choose to return to the water, as their fight is their best and most memorable feature.

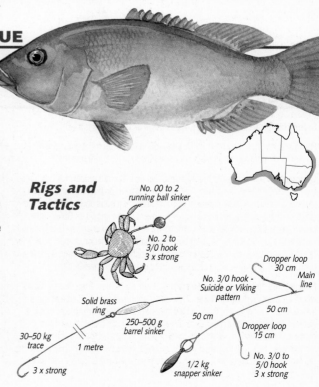

Rigs and Tactics

GROPER, QUEENSLAND

Rigs and Tactics

Bug sinker crimped to line

Linked No. 4/0 to 10/0 Kendall Kirby hooks

Solid brass ring

wire

1 metre

250–500 g barrel sinker

Dropper loop 30 cm

No. 8/0 hook - Suicide or Viking pattern

Main line

50 cm

50 cm

Dropper loop 15 cm

1/2 kg snapper sinker

No. 8/0 hook

Scientific name *Epinephelus lanceolatus*. Also known as groper, giant groper, grouper.

Range Rottnest Island in Western Australia and northwards around the top end as far as Broughton Island in central NSW, with occasional specimens outside this range and larger specimens most common in northern Western Australia to the Great Barrier Reef.

Description A massive cod species, capable of reaching 2.7 m in length and nearly 300 kg in weight, if not taken by line fishing or spearfishing. The Queensland groper is one of the largest of all bony fishes. The Queensland groper prefers to live near coral reefs and rocky areas and can take up residence in large caves. This species can occasionally move into large estuaries and can be found near jetties or other cover. They can move south in summer on currents, sometimes surprising divers when they first encounter these fish. The size of the Queensland groper makes large specimens easy to identify. The tail is huge, rounded and powerful. The colour is dark grey or black and may have lighter coloured patches or blotches. The eye is relatively small, but the mouth is very large. The Queensland groper can be confused with the greasy or estuary cod, (Epinephelus suillus) when small, but the pre-operculum (first cheekbone) of the Queensland groper is rounded while in the greasy cod it is angular. The three spines near the back edge of the gill cover are obvious in the Queensland groper and the middle spine is closer to the lower spine.

Fishing The Queensland groper is an extremely strong fighter, which coupled with its large size makes them difficult to land in their larger sizes. The Queensland groper can be curious and is vulnerable to spearfishing. Given the size of the fish and its mouth, few baits were too large for a big Queensland groper, with large live baits working best. The Queensland groper is edible in smaller sizes up to around 25 kg, but the flesh is strongly flavoured. Above this size the fish is almost inedible. In many areas Queensland groper are rightly protected and they should be released immediately or left alone. They become important tourist attractions, although they have been known to help themselves to other line or spear caught fish.

GURNARD, RED

Scientific name *Chelidonichthys kumu*. Also known as Gurnard, flying gurnard, latchet, kumu gurnard, kumukumu.

Range From Shark Bay in Western Australia, through southern waters including Tasmania and around the east coast as far north as the southern extremity of the Great Barrier Reef.

Description The red gurnard is a beautiful species with its large pectoral fins and brightly patterned ventral fins which are bright blue with a large black spot and scattered paler spots. The first three rays of the pectoral fin are free and act as 'fingers' for the detection of food in the sand. While the head is bony, it is smooth and the red gurnard lacks the bony horns of some other species. The red gurnard can reach 60 cm and more than 2 kg but is more common at 40 – 45 centimetres. It is commonly found from 80 m to the continental shelf but can be taken from shallower waters at times.

Fishing The red gurnard feeds on crabs, worms, molluscs and small fish and all these work for this species. The red gurnard is taken when fishing deeper waters for other species, being most prevalent on sand or broken ground near reefs and is generally taken on the bottom hook of a standard bottom drift rig. The fight is limited due to the depth which requires heavy lines and sinkers. The red gurnard is a highly regarded food fish.

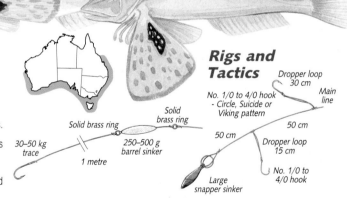

Rigs and Tactics

Dropper loop 30 cm

No. 1/0 to 4/0 hook - Circle, Suicide or Viking pattern

Main line

50 cm

50 cm

Dropper loop 15 cm

Solid brass ring

Solid brass ring

30–50 kg trace

1 metre

250–500 g barrel sinker

Large snapper sinker

No. 1/0 to 4/0 hook

HAPUKU

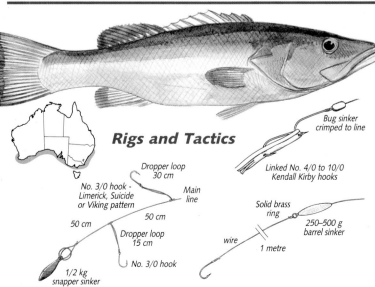

Rigs and Tactics

Dropper loop 30 cm

No. 3/0 hook - Limerick, Suicide or Viking pattern

Main line

50 cm

50 cm

Dropper loop 15 cm

1/2 kg snapper sinker

No. 3/0 hook

Bug sinker crimped to line

Linked No. 4/0 to 10/0 Kendall Kirby hooks

Solid brass ring

wire

1 metre

250–500 g barrel sinker

Scientific name *Polyprion oxygeneios*.

Range Lancelin in Western Australia and southern waters to around Port Macquarie in NSW.

Description A very large species reaching 1.8 cm and 70 kilograms. It can be found occasionally in waters as shallow as 15 metres, and from 50 to 400 metres but is most common in 150 - 350 metre depths. This attractive fish is frequently slate grey to blue-grey and may tend towards dusky grey. The head and mouth is large and can take very big baits. The lower jaw is undershot which is diagnostic. The gill cover has a horizontal ridge which ends in a modest spine.

Fishing It is only in the last decade or so that anglers have been willing to chase hapuku in private boats as the depths they are found in involves considerable travel, favourable weather and specialised deep water gear. The use of braid line has made the task of getting a kilogram or more of weight and large hapuku back to the surface more realistic. Due to the extreme depths, most fish show considerable signs of barotrauma including popped eyes and protruding stomachs. Some charter boats are now targeting this species with some concern that they are vulnerable to over-exploitation at even modest fishing levels. Hapuku are frequently caught with other large species such as the bar cod and bass groper. Caught in shallow water, the hapuku puts up a strong fight. The fight in deeper water is sandbagged by the huge weights and heavy gear often used. The hapuku is caught by many commercial fishers and is considered to be one of the best cooler water fish to eat.

LEATHERJACKET, CHINAMAN

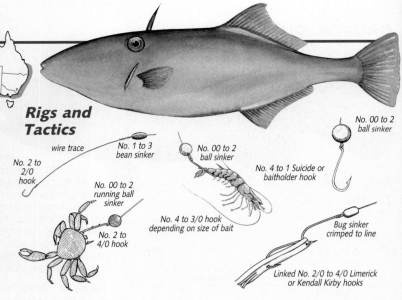

Scientific name *Nelusetta ayraudi*. Also known as Yellow leatherjacket.

Range North West Cape in Western Australia around southern water but excluding Tasmania to southern Queensland.

Description The extremely long head and long first dorsal and anal rays are diagnostic of the Chinaman leatherjacket. Females and juveniles are bright orange with red-orange fins, the males yellow or yellow-brown with yellow fins. This species can be found to depths of over 350 m but juveniles school seasonally in estuaries and coastal embayments. The Chinaman leatherjacket can reach over 70 cm and 3.5 kg making it one of the world's largets leatherjackets. It is often caught in inshore waters at 25 – 35 centimetres.

Fishing When schooling Chinaman leatherjacket can feed on almost anything. They will take prawns, squid, crabs, worms and cut baits. A wire trace or long shank hook can prevent bite-offs from the strong teeth. This species can move close to the surface and bite through lines fishing deeply, especially if a small bit of slime or weed catches on the line. This species is good eating when the skin is removed which is quite simple with the leatherjackets.

Rigs and Tactics

No. 2 to 2/0 hook
wire trace
No. 1 to 3 bean sinker
No. 00 to 2 ball sinker
No. 00 to 2 ball sinker
No. 4 to 1 Suicide or baitholder hook
No. 00 to 2 running ball sinker
No. 2 to 4/0 hook
No. 4 to 3/0 hook depending on size of bait
Bug sinker crimped to line
Linked No. 2/0 to 4/0 Limerick or Kendall Kirby hooks

LING, ROCK

Scientific name *Genypterus tigerinus*. Also known as Tiger ling.

Range Albany in Western Australia and southern waters including Tasmania to southern NSW.

Description The body of the rock ling is pale grey to white and densely patterned in black. The dorsal and anal fins lack black bars which are found on the similar pink ling. The 'beard' is actually a modified ventral fin which is positioned under the chin. Easily separated from the beardie as the rock ling does not have a tail and the dorsal and anal fins meet at the end of the body. This species can be found to depths of 60 m and adults are found on rocky reefs and broken ground while juveniles are found inshore and in bays and estuaries.

Fishing Taken as part of mixed reef catches in cooler waters with standard reef paternoster rigs. The rock ling prefers fresh baits of cut and whole fish, squid and cuttlefish baits. This is an excellent food fish and a welcome bonus in a mixed bag.

Rigs and Tactics

Dropper loop 30 cm
Main line
No. 2 to 2/0 hook - Suicide or Viking pattern
50 cm
50 cm
Dropper loop 15 cm
Ball sinker
1/2 kg snapper sinker
No.2 to 2/0 hook
No. 2 to 2/0 linked Limerick hook
Solid brass ring
250–500 g barrel sinker
Solid brass ring
30–50 kg trace
1 metre

MORWONG

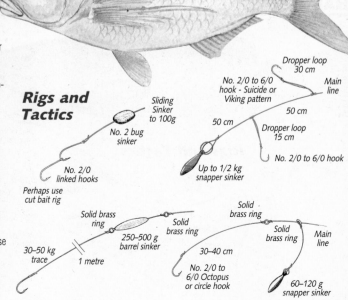

Scientific name *Nemadactylus douglasii*. Also known as Grey morwong, silver morwong, blue morwong, common morwong, rubberlip, blubberlip, jackass, mowie, sea bream, porae (New Zealand).

Range Southern Queensland around Bundaberg southwards along the east coast to Melbourne and eastern Bass Strait and north-east Tasmania.

Description The morwong is a deep bodied fish with a relatively small mouth and prominent fleshy lips. The colour ranges from a pale grey to silver and to silvery blue. In common with other morwong, this species has several extended rays in each pectoral fin. Morwong can reach 70 cm and more than 4 kg, but is commonly caught at 1 – 2 kilograms. The morwong can be separated from the banded morwong and red morwong by their distinctive colourations and the queen snapper has distinctive gold lines on the head in large adults and gold stripes on smaller fish.

Fishing The morwong was once considered a poor second alternative to snapper, particularly in NSW, but increasingly scarce snapper numbers have elevated morwong as a more desirable species. Morwong feed on prawns, worms, squid, molluscs, fish flesh and other food which they encounter opportunistically. Best baits include fish flesh, prawns, squid and octopus tentacles. Baits are best presented on a traditional two hook paternoster rig, with sufficient weight to reach the bottom and bounce along the bottom on a slow drift. Morwong are often found in small loose schools so once fish are encountered, repeated drifts over the same area should continue to produce fish. If the current or wind is strong, a drogue or drift anchor will slow the drift and keep the baits in productive water which includes the edges of deep water reefs and drop-offs, with broken rock and gravel being particularly important. On occasions morwong can be taken over sand or mud bottoms, but a depth sounder is important to save time as fish feed more infrequently in these areas. Morwong are most commonly encountered from 30 to 200 m, but they are occasionally taken from shallower waters. They are an easy target for spearfishermen. The morwong is fair to good eating but can have a slight iodine taste, especially if fish have been grazing on weed which they occasionally do. Filleting helps improve the quality of the flesh.

Rigs and Tactics

Dropper loop 30 cm
Main line
No. 2/0 to 6/0 hook - Suicide or Viking pattern
50 cm
50 cm
Dropper loop 15 cm
Sliding Sinker to 100g
No. 2 bug sinker
Up to 1/2 kg snapper sinker
No. 2/0 to 6/0 hook
No. 2/0 linked hooks
Perhaps use cut bait rig
Solid brass ring
250–500 g barrel sinker
Solid brass ring
Solid brass ring
Solid brass ring
Main line
30–50 kg trace
1 metre
30–40 cm
No. 2/0 to 6/0 Octopus or circle hook
60–120 g snapper sinker

NANNYGAI

Scientific name *Centroberyx affinis*. Also known as Eastern nannygai, redfish.

Range A prolific east coast species ranging as far north as Moreton Bay in Queensland, but the nannygai is much more common from the Mid-North coast of NSW around to western Melbourne in Victoria including north-east Tasmania.

Description A pink to bright red or orange coloured fish, with large eyes, a large upturned mouth, a rounded snout and no pale fin margins. The nannygai is separated from other similar species such as the red snapper as it has 7 as opposed to 6 dorsal spines. The similar western nannygai is separated by its range (which commences around the South Australian/Victorian border to Shark Bay in Western Australia) and the western species has a yellow eye. While juveniles can school in estuaries and on inshore reefs, larger fish are found in larger schools in waters deeper than 25 m and out towards the edge of the continental shelf where they are a common trawl species. The nannygai is not a large fish, reaching around 45 centimetres.

Fishing The nannygai is often encountered when fishing deeper reefs for snapper and other deep water species. The large weights and relatively small size of nannygai means that they are less highly regarded than many other species. The large mouth and schooling nature of the nannygai means that large numbers can be caught, and on large baits. Standard snapper paternoster rigs with sufficient weight to drag bottom on a drift will take nannygai. Nannygai can be found near offshore reefs or near drop-offs over gravel or silt bottoms. Nannygai will take baits of fish, squid, octopus, crab, prawn and pilchard. When nannygai are biting freely, a fish can be caught on each hook on each drop and will often beat any snapper or other target species to the hook. Nannygai make good eating with firm white fillets. They are taken by trawlers in large quantities which are marketed as redfish.

Rigs and Tactics

No. 3/0 hook - Limerick, Suicide or Viking pattern

Dropper loop 30 cm

Main line

50 cm

50 cm

Dropper loop 15 cm

1/2 kg snapper sinker

No. 3/0 hook

Solid brass ring

Solid brass ring

Main line

30–40 cm

No. 2/0 to 8/0 hook

60 –120 g snapper sinker

Solid brass ring

100–500 g barrel sinker

30–50 kg trace

1 metre

PARROTFISH

Scientific name *Family Scaridae*.

Range A group of generally tropical species which are rarely found south of Shark Bay in Western Australia or the NSW-Queensland border, due in part to their close association with coral which they actively consume.

Description Closely related to the similarly colourful wrasses, but parrotfish have their teeth fused into strong beak-like plates. Sexes can have different colours and juveniles often have very different colours from adults. Some parrotfish can change sex when the largest male in a group is removed. Many parrotfish sleep in reef caves at night and can secrete a mucous envelope around their bodies while they rest. Sizes of parrotfish can range from the humphead parrotfish which can be up to 1.2 m to the more common green finned parrotfish which reaches 30 centimetres.

Fishing Parrotfish are almost never taken by line fishermen, but some species can be important spearfishing targets. The surf parrotfish can be herded into shallows and captured by hand in some Queensland reefs. The few parrotfish that are taken by line bite on prawn or worm baits intended for other species. Once hooked, the beak-like teeth can bite through lines and hooks. Parrotfish graze on live or dead corals or algae and can be important in the overall evolution of coral reefs. Parrotfish are highly regarded food fish but the bones are pale green which some find off-putting.

No. 1 to 3 bean sinker

No. 8 to 4 hook

No. 00 to 2 ball sinker

Rigs and Tactics

No. 8 to 4 long shank hook depending on size of bait

PERCH, PEARL

Scientific name *Glaucosoma scapulare*. Also known as Pearly, nannygai (Qld.).

Range Southern Queensland to NSW as far south as Newcastle but now very rare south of South West Rocks.

Description This is a handsome fish with a large eye and a large mouth. There is a small black spot at the base of the pectoral fin and a distinctive black flap of skin and bone near the top back edge of the gill cover. A similar species, the deepsea or northern dhufish (*Glaucosoma burgeri*) is found from Onslow north and lacks the distinctive flap on the gill cover, has a bright silvery appearance and can reach 2.5 kilograms. The pearl perch can reach 5 kg, but a fish over 3 kg is a quality fish.

Fishing This is widely regarded as one of the best, if not the best eating fish on the east coast. It was once found on mid depth reefs as far south as Newcastle, but commercial and recreational overfishing has pushed these fish further north and onto less heavily fished deep reefs in more than 50 m of water. Pearl perch are frequently taken in conjunction with snapper and other deep water reef species, although they bite most freely at dusk and dawn with early night being the next most productive time. Heavy weights are necessary to reach bottom where pearl perch are found. Best baits are fresh cut baits, squid or cuttlefish with pilchards being a reliable standby.

Rigs and Tactics

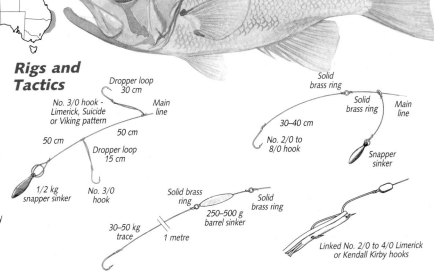

Dropper loop 30 cm

No. 3/0 hook - Limerick, Suicide or Viking pattern

Main line

50 cm

50 cm

Dropper loop 15 cm

1/2 kg snapper sinker

No. 3/0 hook

Solid brass ring

Solid brass ring

Main line

30–40 cm

No. 2/0 to 8/0 hook

Snapper sinker

Solid brass ring

250–500 g barrel sinker

Solid brass ring

30–50 kg trace

1 metre

Linked No. 2/0 to 4/0 Limerick or Kendall Kirby hooks

SERGEANT BAKER

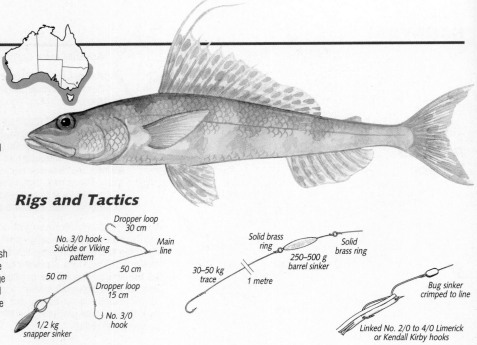

Scientific name *Aulopus purpurissatus.*

Range Coral Bay in Western Australia southwards including Tasmania and around to southern Queensland.

Description A reasonably common fish of deeper coastal reefs and adjacent sandy patches, but can move into larger bays on occasion. Sergeant baker have a red, ruddy or rusty brown colour and a small adipose-like second dorsal fin. The longer first dorsal fin unusually does not have any spines, only soft rays and the second and third ray is elongated in male fish. The caudal fin is forked and the pectoral fins are large but the sergeant baker lacks the distinctive 'fingers' or bony head ridges of the gurnards. The sergeant baker reaches 70 cm in length and around 3 kg, but is more common at around 45 to 50 centimetres.

Fishing Sergeant baker are taken on standard bottom bouncing rigs adjacent to mid to deep water reefs. Sergeant baker prefer fresh fish fillets, pilchards, squid, octopus, prawn, or crab baits, but the large mouth does not prevent them from being taken on quite large live or dead baits. Sergeant baker can also be taken on bait tipped jigs. The flesh is white but only fair compared to other species like snapper or morwong taken from the same areas and can have a muddy taste.

Rigs and Tactics

Dropper loop 30 cm
No. 3/0 hook - Suicide or Viking pattern
Main line
50 cm
50 cm
Dropper loop 15 cm
1/2 kg snapper sinker
No. 3/0 hook

Solid brass ring
Solid brass ring
30–50 kg trace
250–500 g barrel sinker
1 metre

Bug sinker crimped to line
Linked No. 2/0 to 4/0 Limerick or Kendall Kirby hooks

SNAPPER

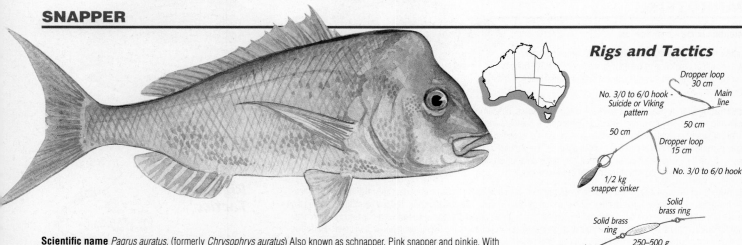

Rigs and Tactics

Dropper loop 30 cm
No. 3/0 to 6/0 hook - Suicide or Viking pattern
Main line
50 cm
50 cm
Dropper loop 15 cm
1/2 kg snapper sinker
No. 3/0 to 6/0 hook

Solid brass ring
Solid brass ring
30–50 kg trace
250–500 g barrel sinker
1 metre

Solid brass ring
Solid brass ring
Main line
30–40 cm
No. 2/0 to 8/0 hook
60–120 g snapper sinker

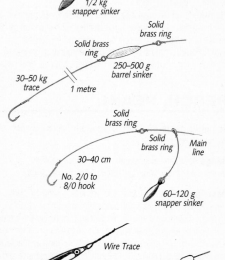

Scientific name *Pagrus auratus.* (formerly *Chrysophrys auratus*) Also known as schnapper, Pink snapper and pinkie. With increasing size known as Cockney bream, red bream, squire, snapper and ultimately 'old man snapper' with the characteristic hump.

Range Snapper are common in southern waters and range from Coral Bay in Western Australia to the Capricorn Group in Queensland.

Description A truly stunning and highly sought after species, the snapper can have iridescent pink to burnished copper colouration with bright blue spots from the lateral line upwards which are brightest in younger fish. A hump on the head and nose area develops in some fish and is more likely in male fish. Snapper are relatively slow growing and mature at 29 to 35 cm and four to five years of age. Snapper numbers have been affected by both commercial and recreational overfishing. Prawn trawl by-catch and anglers gut hooking juvenile snapper in places like Botany Bay in NSW have contributed to the reduction in quality snapper fishing on the east coast in recent years. Recreational over-fishing in the eastern gulf of Shark Bay has affected one of the best snapper fisheries in Australia.

Fishing Snapper are traditionally taken on bottom paternoster rigs with the famous snapper lead. Snapper prefer the edges of reefs or broken ground and can be taken from the shore or as deep as 50 fathoms. Drifting over broken ground or drop-offs at the edges of reefs with just enough weight to bounce bottom will find fish and repeated drifts will pick up more fish. Like many reef species, snapper form schools of similar sized fish, with the size of the school decreasing with larger fish. In late winter on the east coast, snapper move inshore to feed on spawning cuttlefish and large fish can be taken from the rocks on cuttlefish baits. In Western Australia, snapper form large schools in winter in Shark Bay and around October in Cockburn Sound. Quality snapper can be taken by sinking a bait under a feeding school of tailor, salmon or small mackerel, feeding on uneaten baitfish. Good catches can also be made fishing washes at the backs of breaking reefs, frequently mixed with tailor, bream and other fish. Best baits for snapper are pilchard, bonito, squid, cuttlefish, octopus and yellowtail. Snapper respond well to berley and will rise in a berley trail to take lightly weighted or unweighted baits. In shallow waters, snapper are a magnificent fighting fish. Recent tagging research indicates that many snapper are residential, so letting fish go, or moving on to take other species means that the fish you leave are likely to be there at a later date. Snapper are also taken on leadhead or vertical jigs, especially tipped with a piece of fish or octopus. Snapper are taken while trolling, particularly around bommies or reef with minnow and feather lures working well. Like bream, snapper are being incresingly recognised as a lure taker. Snapper can be excellent eating, but do not freeze particularly well.

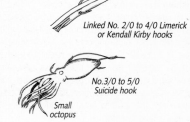

Metal Lure
Wire Trace
Bug sinker crimped to line
Linked No. 2/0 to 4/0 Limerick or Kendall Kirby hooks

No.3/0 to 5/0 Suicide hook
Small octopus

SNOOK

Scientific name *Sphyraena novaehollandiae.* Also known as Short finned sea pike, sea pike, short finned barracuda.

Range Jurien Bay in Western Australia and southern waters, including Tasmania and around the east coast as far north as southern Queensland.

Description The snook is a very long and skinny southern relative of the barracuda. It is easily separated from the barracuda by its southern range and the first dorsal fin which commences well behind the end of the pectoral fin, while the first dorsal commences at the tip of the pectoral fin in barracuda. The snook is similar to the long finned sea pike but most easily separated by the snook's shorter anal fin, and its ventral fins which are set well behind the pectoral fin. The snook reaches 1.1 m and 5 kilograms.

Fishing The snook is relatively common in inshore cooler waters with a distinct preference for areas of weed or sand areas adjacent to weed or slight drop offs. The snook is an ambush feeder which may hunt in small packs, providing exciting fishing at times. Snook also favour regular haunts and may be found in identified hot-spots on a regular basis. Snook will take baits of whitebait, pilchard, bluebait, cut flesh or squid. Over shallow weed beds, lightly weighted or unweighted baits on single hooks or gang hook rigs work best and a gentle jigging action attracts additional strikes. Over deeper waters, or where snook may be holed up a small running sinker with a short trace to defend against the teeth will work well. Snook take lures and flies well. Best bets are silver or chrome spoons such as Tobys, or Wonder Wobblers. Feather jigs and small minnow lures also work well but the toothy mouth of the snook means that some fish can be lost to short strikes and lures and flies damaged. The snook makes good to excellent eating although the flesh is little soft and may bruise unless handled well.

Rigs and Tactics

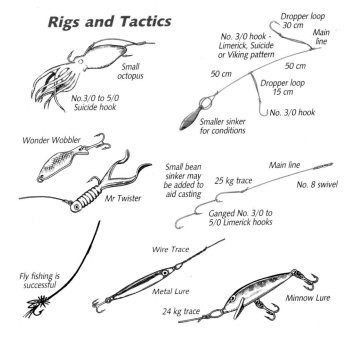

SWEEP, SEA

Scientific name *Scorpis aequipinnis.* Also known as Sweep.

Range Shark Bay in Western Australia and southern waters including Tasmania and the east coast as far north as Jervis Bay.

Description The sea sweep is a deep bodied fish quite common on deeper reefs of the south coast and south-west of Australia, but which can also be found inshore, especially in schools when young. The sea sweep is generally slate grey in colour. It may have two darker grey patches on the upper body above the back edge of the pectoral fin and also the back part of the dorsal fin. This species has a prominent lobe to the first dorsal ray whereas the similar silver sweep (Scorpis lineolatus) has a flat dorsal fin profile. The mouth extends to the middle of the eye in the sea sweep and only to the front edge of the eye in the silver sweep. The banded sweep (Scorpis georgianus) has prominent black bands, a lightly forked tail and is only found from Kangaroo Island in South Australia to Shark Bay in Western Australia. The sea sweep can reach 61 cm and more than 3.5 kilograms.

Fishing In its smaller sizes, the sweep is frequently considered a pest. Its small mouth, schooling nature and fondness for picking baits intended for larger species has earned the sea sweep a poor reputation in some areas. However, in larger sizes sea sweep make good eating and are a welcome addition to mixed bags. As a rule, the larger fish are found in smaller groups and further offshore, with bait picking juveniles inshore. Sea sweep will take a variety of baits, with prawns, squid, cuttlefish and fresh cut fish baits working best. Smaller, long shank hooks will improve your hookup rate. If pickers are prominent, putting a smaller hook on a dropper above your standard snapper rigs will tell you the nature of the bait stealers. Small sea sweep make a hardy live bait for fish like kingfish or samsonfish.

Rigs and Tactics

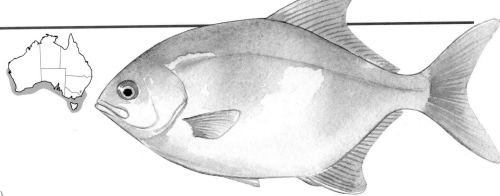

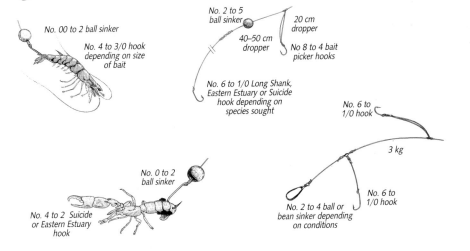

TERAGLIN

Scientific name *Atractoscion aequidens.* Also known as Trag, trag-jew.

Range Double Island Point in Queensland to Montague Island in NSW.

Description The teraglin is very similar to the mulloway but can be separated by the shape of the tail, which is slightly concave (inwards curving) in the teraglin and convex (outward curving) in the mulloway. The inside of the teraglin's mouth is yellow or orange and this extends to the inside of the gill covers and occasionally to the lips. The anal fin is closer to the tail fin in the teraglin but this is only obvious when the two are seen together. The teraglin reaches a smaller size than mulloway, growing to up to a metre and 10 kg but any fish over 5 – 6 kg is considered large. The teraglin is found on offshore reefs and commonly forms schools which are smaller in number for larger fish.

Fishing The teraglin is commonly caught in depths of 20 to 80 m and over broken reef, although they can be found on the edge of larger deep reefs or on gravel bottom. Unlike mulloway, teraglin are rarely found inshore and not in estuaries. Teraglin are most common on the bottom but can be found in mid-water, especially when berley is used. Teraglin feed much more strongly at night and an area that produces nothing during the day can produce large catches of trag after dark. Teraglin bite best on small live baits or large strip baits with squid, cuttlefish, pilchard and large prawns also producing fish. Teraglin bite strongly and heavy lines are frequently used so that the fish are brought to boat quickly as a lost fish can often take the school with them. The school will often rise with hooked fish, enabling them to be taken in mid water. Common two hook snapper rigs are most commonly used for teraglin. As teraglin frequently school in the same areas, they are susceptible to over-fishing and only as many as are needed should be taken. Teraglin are excellent eating, with many rating them better quality than mulloway.

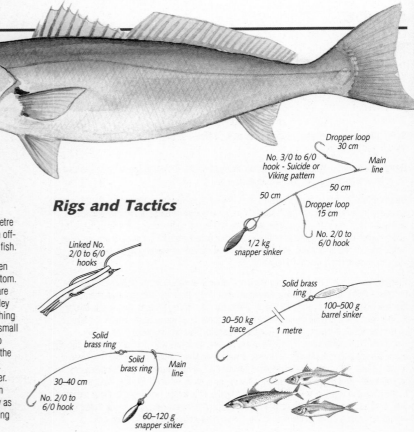

Rigs and Tactics

Linked No. 2/0 to 6/0 hooks

Dropper loop 30 cm
No. 3/0 to 6/0 hook - Suicide or Viking pattern
Main line
50 cm
50 cm
Dropper loop 15 cm
No. 2/0 to 6/0 hook
1/2 kg snapper sinker

Solid brass ring
Solid brass ring
Main line
30–40 cm
No. 2/0 to 6/0 hook
60–120 g snapper sinker

Solid brass ring
30–50 kg trace
1 metre
100–500 g barrel sinker

TROUT, CORAL

Scientific name *Plectropomus leopardus.* Also known as Leopard cod, leopard trout, trout, blue-spot trout.

Range Dongara in Western Australia northwards around the top end to the southern extent of Queensland reefs.

Description The coral trout is frequently confused with other similar species, but the coral trout has numerous small and always round spots on the head and body. The colour varies but can be a brilliant red or red-orange or a brick red. The soft dorsal fin is rounded and the tail square cut which may have a blue edge. It has a large mouth and sharp but widely spaced canine teeth. The coral trout grows to over a metre and 20 kg, but can be over fished and is generally taken at a smaller size. Irresponsible overfishing for the live fish export trade in Queensland has had a big impact on coral trout numbers there.

Fishing This is undoubtedly one of the premier reef fish due to its brilliant appearance, hard fight near coral outcrops and excellent eating. Coral trout can be taken on bait, lure and fly but fishing is typified by a short battle of strength and will between the angler and the coral trout. Best lures include minnow lures which dive to different depths, as coral trout will readily move upwards to slam a lure. Poppers can take some large fish. Coral trout, like many of the cod which are found in similar areas, can take large baits, with live baits being best, followed by whole dead fish, fresh fillets, pilchards, prawns and squid. A trace can offer some protection during the fight. The frequent presence of numerous sharp coral outcrops in many locations and a strong fish like the coral trout means that if the fish is given his head a break-off is certain. Some of the largest coral trout are taken in deeper waters near less obvious cover, providing a welcome surprise for the lucky angler. Large coral trout have been implicated with ciguatera and some caution should be exercised with the largest fish, consuming a small portion initially otherwise this species provides a culinary delight.

Rigs and Tactics

Dropper loop 30 cm
No. 3/0 hook - Limerick, Suicide or Viking pattern
Main line
50 cm
50 cm
Dropper loop 15 cm
No. 3/0 hook
1/2 kg snapper sinker

Solid brass ring
250–500 g barrel sinker
Solid brass ring
30–50 kg trace
1 metre

Bug sinker crimped to line
Linked No. 2/0 to 4/0 Limerick or Kendall Kirby hooks

No. 2 to 3 ball
No. 4 to 4/0 (depending on bait size) Kendall Kirby hook

Minnow Lure
24 kg trace

TRUMPETER, TASMANIAN

Scientific name *Latris lineata*. Also known as Striped trumpeter, common trumpeter, stripey, real trumpeter.

Range Albany in Western Australia and eastwards along the south coast ncluding Tasmania and as far north as Montague Island in NSW and rarely as far north as Sydney.

Description The Tamanian trumpeter is is a medium to large species reaching 1.2 m and up to 25 kg, although the largest fish are found in deep waters. Overfishing has depleted stocks of the Tasmanian trumpeter on inshore reefs, where mainly juveniles are now found. The Tasmanian trumpeter has three distinctive brownish stripes along the sides. The Tasmanian trumpeter is easily separated from the similar morwongs as it lacks the extended 'fingers' on the pectoral fins. The fins are dusky and may have a yellow or reddish tinge. The mouth is large and the lips quite blubbery.

Fishing Fishing is with standard deep reef fishing rigs, with sufficient weight to get the bait to the bottom. Best baits are squid, prawns, octopus or cut fish baits. Pilchards and other small whole fish or live baits will also work well. Tasmanian trumpeter are occasionally taken on large lead head or vertical jigs, but tipping with squid increases strike rates. Smaller fish are likely to be encountered on inshore reefs and like many reef species, the smaller the size of the fish, the larger the school is likely to be. Working the edges of reefs when a school is located will bring good catches. The Tasmanian trumpeter is excellent eating and is rated as one of the best cool water reef species.

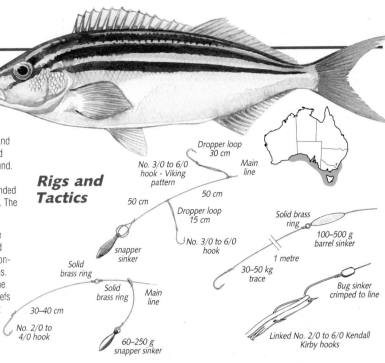

Rigs and Tactics

TUSKFISH, VENUS

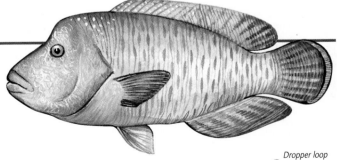

Scientific name *Choerodon venustus*. Also known as Cockie.

Range Found only on the east coast from the northern Great Barrier reef as far south as northern NSW although occasional juveniles have been recorded as far south as Sydney.

Description The venus tuskfish is a fairly small species, reaching 5 kg but most commonly seen at around a kilogram. They are generally bright pink along the flanks, being darker above and paler on the belly. There are numerous small white or blue spots on the body and the fins and tail are splashed with blue as are the lips and chin. The venus tuskfish prefers shallow to mid depth reef country and is found very close to reefs where it feeds.

Fishing Venus tuskfish are generally taken while fishing for other reef species and can be taken on a variety of baits including prawns, crabs, whitebait, fresh cut baits and squid. Tackle needs to be fairly robust as even small fish can bury the angler in any nearby coral outcrops. The fight is strong and the first run needs to be stopped to avert a break-off. The venus tuskfish makes excellent eating and should be more highly regarded as a food fish than it is currently.

Rigs and Tactics

WRASSE, HUMP HEADED MAORI

Scientific name *Cheilinus undulatus*. Also known as Maori wrasse, giant Maori wrasse, double-headed maori wrasse, Napoleon wrasse.

Range Shark Bay in Western Australia and tropical waters and to central Queensland but this is essentially a tropical species.

Description The hump-headed Maori wrasse is the giant of the wrasses, capable of reaching 2.3 m and nearly 200 kilograms. The scales are extremely large and can be used as drink coasters from large fish. The scales are edged with cream which forms a series of wavy lines down the body. These lines match the wavy lines on the snout and the dorsal, anal and tail fins. Smaller fish can move in groups of 4 – 10 into coral reef bays to crush dead coral for the shellfish or worms which it contains with their peg-like teeth. Large fish develop a fleshy hump above and between the eyes.

Fishing The hump-headed Maori wrasse is totally protected in Western Australia and these magnificent animals should be released wherever possible. They are particularly prone to spearfishing. On a line, the hump-headed Maori wrasse pulls extremely strongly and will break off the unwary on nearby coral. Best baits are large prawns, crabs, mussels or squid. Due to the extremely large size of this fish, very heavy handlines, gloves and a strong back are most often used.

Rigs and Tactics

PELAGIC SPECIES

ALBACORE

Rigs and Tactics

Scientific name *Thunnus alalunga*. Also known as Tuna (Chicken of the sea).

Range Circum-Australia but common in waters well offshore of Australia's southern half, usually in schools.

Description A common species of offshore waters. Average size is 2 to 5 kg but can attain a weight of 30 kilograms. Adults are easily identified by the largest pectoral fin of all tunas, extending well behind the commencement of the second dorsal fin. Juveniles have smaller pectoral fins but the distinctive white rear border of the tail fin differentiates albacore from juvenile yellowfin or bigeye tuna.

Fishing A good light game fish which fights strongly and requires quality tackle. The albacore readily takes lures such as a feather, minnow or Konahead type lure trolled at around 6 knots. Albacore also take live bait drifted or fished under a bobby cork at a depth of 2.5 to 3 metres. The albacore is excellent eating, with firm white flesh and a delicate texture.

AMBRERJACK

Rigs and Tactics

35–50 cm trace

No. 8 to 12 swivel

No. 2/0 to 6/0 hooks

No. 2 to 4 bean sinker

30–50 kg trace

2/0 to 6/0 hook

Solid brass ring

250–500 g barrel sinker

1 metre

Solid brass ring

Deep Diving Minnow

Small octopus

No.3/0 to 5/0 Suicide hook

24 kg trace

Minnow Lure

Scientific name *Seriola dumerili*.

Range A temperate and tropical species found from Albany in Western Australia around the northern part of Australia to Wollongong in NSW.

Description A relatively large, fast swimming species mainly found in offshore waters in the vicinity of reefs or drop-offs. Sometimes confused with yellowtail kingfish, the amberjack has a dark blue to olive tail fin whereas the kingfish has a yellow tail fin. The anal fin of the amberjack is darker in colour with a characteristic white edging. Differs from similar samson fish in having more rays in the dorsal fin (32 – 33) versus 23 – 25 for the samson fish. The samson fish also appears to have red teeth, due to blood engorged gums. The amberjack attains a weight of 36 kilograms.

Fishing A hard fighting fish which takes feather or minnow lures trolled near reefs and drop offs. Amberjacks will also take both live and dead bait fished in the vicinity of offshore reefs. The amberjack makes good eating, although larger specimens tend to be dry and coarse textured.

BARRACOUTA

Scientific name *Thyrsites atun*. Also known as 'Couta, pickhandle, axehandle, occasionally by its South African name snoek.

Range Found from Shark Bay in Western Australia around the entire southern part of the country to northern NSW. Barracouta are a cold water species which are most common in waters of Tasmania, southern Victoria and South Australia to Cape Leeuwin in Western Australia. Barracouta are a good indicator of the presence of a cold water current. They are regarded as a pest in the northern part of their range due to significant parasitic infestation in the flesh which renders them inedible and the cold currents in which they are found put warmer water fish off the bite.

Description The barracouta is a member of the same family as gemfish (hake) which is a much deeper bodied fish. There is no resemblance to the more tropical barracuda. The barracouta has a very long first dorsal with a distinctive black patch near the leading edge and around 5 finlets on the caudal peduncle (the gemfish has 2 finlets). The colour is steely grey and the small scales are easily shed. The barracouta has three large teeth on its upper jaw. Grows to 4.5 kg and 1.3 m but commonly caught at 1 – 2 kilograms.

Fishing Barracouta can take a variety of baits and lures. They are frequently taken on chrome spoons or casting lures. Barracouta will also take minnow lures and feathers and soft plastics, but their teeth make short work of all but the most robust lures. A wire trace will help prevent bite offs of expensive lures and increase the catch rates with baits. Barracouta will take fish flesh, garfish or pilchard baits readily and while partial to live baits are difficult to hook due to a bony mouth and a habit of running with the bait across their jaws. Barracouta should be handled carefully due to their sharp teeth which also have an anticoagulant which makes any cuts bleed profusely. Barracouta are considered good eating from cooler water in the southern part of their range, especially Tasmania.

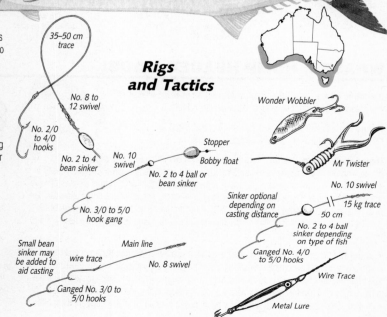

Rigs and Tactics

35–50 cm trace

No. 8 to 12 swivel

No. 2/0 to 4/0 hooks

No. 2 to 4 bean sinker

No. 10 swivel

Stopper

Bobby float

No. 2 to 4 ball or bean sinker

No. 3/0 to 5/0 hook gang

Small bean sinker may be added to aid casting

wire trace

Main line

No. 8 swivel

Ganged No. 3/0 to 5/0 hooks

Wonder Wobbler

Mr Twister

No. 10 swivel

Sinker optional depending on casting distance

15 kg trace

50 cm

No. 2 to 4 ball sinker depending on type of fish

Ganged No. 4/0 to 5/0 hooks

Wire Trace

Metal Lure

BARRACUDA ☠

Scientific name *Sphyraena barracuda*. Also known as Great barracuda, giant barracuda, giant sea pike.

Range The barracuda is found from Albany in Western Australia around the top of Australia to southern Queensland, although it is much more common in tropical waters north of Shark Bay.

Description The most remarkable feature of the barracuda is its fearsome teeth. There are two pairs of enlarged canines on the upper jaw and one pair of enlarged canines on the lower jaw. There are other large, backward pointing teeth in both jaws. The body is long and cylindrical with approximately 18 grayish cross bands on the back above the lateral line. These bands on the back and the more heavy body differentiate the barracuda from the similar snook, which is generally found outside of the range of the barracuda. The barracuda reaches 1.8 m and nearly 25 kilograms.

Fishing The barracuda is rarely specifically targeted as the flesh is of poor quality and removing the hooks is difficult. The barracuda is also prone to ciguatera and should not be consumed except from Western Australian waters. Barracuda love trolled fish baits and will also readily hit minnow, feather and spoon lures. Wire is important, especially with bait. Larger barracuda are generally found near either offshore or inshore reefs. Small barracuda form schools and are more prevalent inshore or in estuaries.

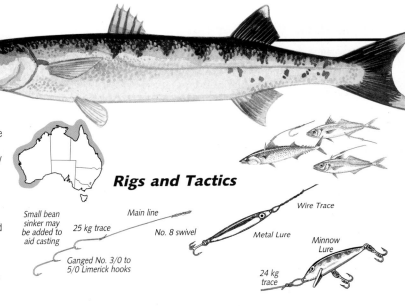

Rigs and Tactics

Small bean sinker may be added to aid casting • 25 kg trace • Main line • No. 8 swivel • Ganged No. 3/0 to 5/0 Limerick hooks • Wire Trace • Metal Lure • Minnow Lure • 24 kg trace

BONITO, AUSTRALIAN

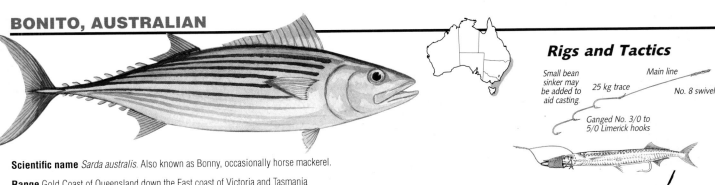

Rigs and Tactics

Small bean sinker may be added to aid casting • 25 kg trace • Main line • No. 8 swivel • Ganged No. 3/0 to 5/0 Limerick hooks • Fly fishing is successful

Scientific name *Sarda australis*. Also known as Bonny, occasionally horse mackerel.

Range Gold Coast of Queensland down the East coast of Victoria and Tasmania

Description Commonly found in large schools on the coast of NSW. Easily distinguished from other tunas and bonito species by the presence of narrow horizontal stripes on the lower part of the body. Bonito also have a single row of small but distinct conical teeth. The Australian bonito can grow to 1 m and nearly 8 kg but is usually less than 3 – 4 kilograms.

Fishing An aggressive fish which takes lures well and is less discriminating than some of the smaller tuna species. Bonito can be taken on saltwater fly rapidly stripped through the school. Minnow lures, chrome slices and feather lures either trolled or quickly retrieved work very well. Bonito will take pilchard and other fish baits such as garfish and can be taken by cubing in a berley trail. While bonito make terrific live or cut bait, they are better eating than their reputation suggest, but are prone to bruising during their after capture struggles.

COBIA

Scientific name *Rachycentron canadus*. Also known as Cobe, black kingfish, black king, crab-eater, sergeant fish, lemon fish.

Range Cape Naturaliste in Western Australia northwards, including sub-tropical and tropical waters around the top end to Sydney NSW.

Description A large pelagic species reaching over 2 m and 60 kilograms. Frequently mistaken initially for a shark in the water due to its high dorsal fin and large, dark pectoral fins. They have a relatively pointy head with the mouth at the middle of the front of the head. They have a white or creamy belly which tends to be darker around the anal fin region and a white stripe on their sides which may fade after death. They also have very short dorsal spines before the high soft dorsal fin. Other fins, except pelvic are dark and the overall colour is chocolate brown to black.

Fishing Cobia are generally encountered opportunistically. They congregate around structures such as wharves, bommies or reef tops and are renowned for traveling with manta rays and whale sharks. Many anglers chase manta rays to get a cast at these hard fighting, great tasting fish. Cobia will take a variety of baits including squid, crabs and cut or whole fish. While frequently fished to with unweighted or lightly weighted rigs, they will take baits off the bottom, especially on sand patches near reefs or jetties. They can be cast to with lures or flies but can be difficult to catch in some sight fishing situations.

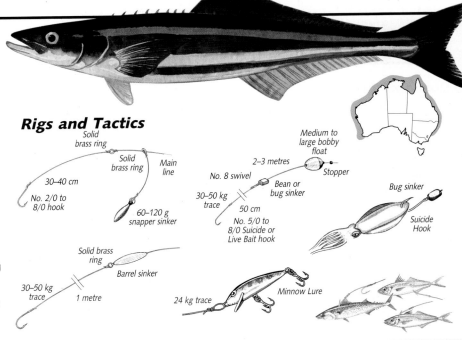

Rigs and Tactics

Solid brass ring • Solid brass ring • Main line • 30–40 cm • No. 2/0 to 8/0 hook • 60–120 g snapper sinker • Medium to large bobby float • 2–3 metres • Stopper • No. 8 swivel • Bean or bug sinker • 30–50 kg trace • 50 cm • No. 5/0 to 8/0 Suicide or Live Bait hook • Bug sinker • Suicide Hook • Solid brass ring • Barrel sinker • 30–50 kg trace • 1 metre • 24 kg trace • Minnow Lure

KINGFISH, YELLOWTAIL

Scientific name *Seriola lalandi*. Also known as Kingie, yellowtail, hoodlum and bandit.

Range Shark Bay in Western Australia and southern waters through to central Queensland with good populations at Lord Howe and Norfolk Islands and New Zealand.

Description The yellowtail kingfish is a beautiful, powerful fish which has a large, deeply forked tail. The back and upper sides are dark, purply blue while the lower part of the body is white. These two distinctive colours are separated by a yellow band which varies in width and intensity from fish to fish. The tail is a bright yellow. This can be a large fish reaching 2 m and more than 50 kg although increasing commercial and recreational fishing is affecting the presence of large fish. Any yellowtail kingfish over 20 kg will be a memorable capture.

Fishing The yellowtail kingfish is a brutal, dirty fighter which will fully test the skill of the angler and the quality of their gear. The first run of a kingfish is straight towards the nearest bottom obstruction to cut off an unwary angler. Kingfish will take a wide variety of lures such as minnow lures, soft plastics and flies. Vertical jigging with metal lures can be deadly at times. They will take a range of whole and cut fish baits, prawns, squid, octopus and cuttlefish but there are occasions when they can be finicky. At other times yellowtail kingfish will strike at bare hooks. Live bait is almost certain to attract a mad rush from any kingfish in the area. Kingfish were previously considered average eating, but they have been increasingly recognised as a quality fish, including as sashimi. Large fish are worse eating and can have worms in the flesh, especially from northern waters.

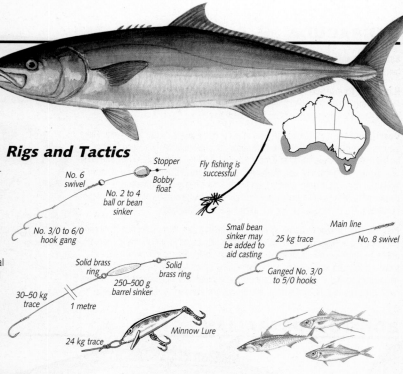

Rigs and Tactics

MACKEREL, BROAD-BARRED SPANISH

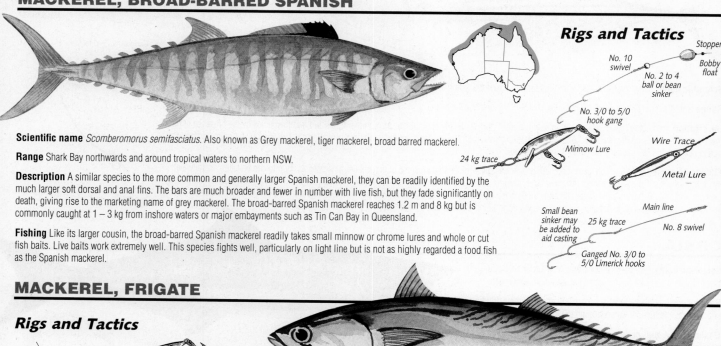

Rigs and Tactics

Scientific name *Scomberomorus semifasciatus*. Also known as Grey mackerel, tiger mackerel, broad barred mackerel.

Range Shark Bay northwards and around tropical waters to northern NSW.

Description A similar species to the more common and generally larger Spanish mackerel, they can be readily identified by the much larger soft dorsal and anal fins. The bars are much broader and fewer in number with live fish, but they fade significantly on death, giving rise to the marketing name of grey mackerel. The broad-barred Spanish mackerel reaches 1.2 m and 8 kg but is commonly caught at 1 – 3 kg from inshore waters or major embayments such as Tin Can Bay in Queensland.

Fishing Like its larger cousin, the broad-barred Spanish mackerel readily takes small minnow or chrome lures and whole or cut fish baits. Live baits work extremely well. This species fights well, particularly on light line but is not as highly regarded a food fish as the Spanish mackerel.

MACKEREL, FRIGATE

Rigs and Tactics

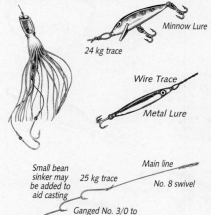

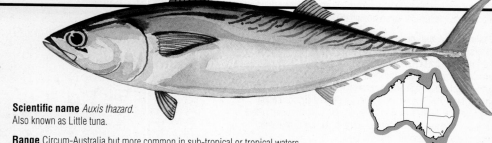

Scientific name *Auxis thazard*. Also known as Little tuna.

Range Circum-Australia but more common in sub-tropical or tropical waters.

Description A handsome fish which can reach 60 cm and around 5 kilograms. The frigate mackerel possesses the distinctive broken oblique lines above the lateral line and no markings below the lateral line. It can be easily separated from the similar mackerel tuna as the frigate mackerel has a wide gap between the two dorsal fins, no black spots near the ventral fins and a more slender body. The frigate mackerel can form large shoals in coastal or inshore waters.

Fishing The frigate mackerel will readily take quickly trolled silver or chrome lures. Christmas tree type lures work well trolled in a pattern. High speed spinning can work well. This species can be finicky at times, with large schools refusing all offerings, but on other occasions will strike savagely at any lure and will take trolled or cast dead baits. The frigate mackerel fights well for its size. It makes terrific bait, either trolled for billfish, or as cut bait for reef species. The frigate mackerel is not highly regarded as a food fish, but is suitable for sashimi or for poaching.

MACKEREL, QUEENSLAND SCHOOL

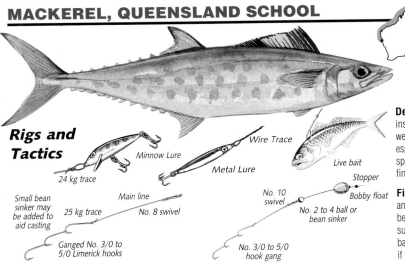

Scientific name *Scomberomorus queenslandicus*. Also known as School mackerel, doggie mackerel, blotched mackerel, shiny mackerel.

Range Shark Bay in Western Australia northwards around the top end and to around South West Rocks in NSW.

Description The Queensland school mackerel is a schooling species which frequents inshore areas. The Queensland school mackerel can reach a metre in length and a weight of 12 kilograms. However they are commonly encountered from 1.5 to 4 kg, especially on the eastern seaboard. This species is easily identified by the large dark spots on the sides and the black then white areas on the first dorsal fin. The pectoral fin is also smaller and more pointed than in the broad-barred Spanish mackerel.

Fishing Schools of Queensland school mackerel can be berleyed close to the boat and taken with live or whole dead or fresh cut bait. These fish will take lures but can be finicky. Queensland school mackerel can patrol close to the shore and can be a surprise catch from tropical beaches or creek mouths, but they can bite off lures or baits intended for other species. The Queensland school mackerel is a top table fish if filleted.

Rigs and Tactics

Minnow Lure
24 kg trace
Wire Trace
Metal Lure
Live bait
Small bean sinker may be added to aid casting
Main line
25 kg trace
No. 8 swivel
Stopper
No. 10 swivel
Bobby float
No. 2 to 4 ball or bean sinker
Ganged No. 3/0 to 5/0 Limerick hooks
No. 3/0 to 5/0 hook gang

MACKEREL, SHARK

Scientific name *Grammatorcynus bicarinatus*. Also known as Scaly mackerel, large-scaled tunny, salmon mackerel.

Range Geographe Bay in Western Australia around tropical waters and into central NSW around Newcastle.

Description A sought after fish found on shallow reef areas throughout its range. This species has a distinguishing double lateral line which divides at the pectoral fin and joins again at the tail base. The belly displays dark spots and the eye is relatively small, especially compared to the similar double lined (or scad) mackerel. The scales of the shark mackerel come away in large sheets. The name shark mackerel comes from a distinctive ammonia smell (shark-like) when the fish is cleaned but which disappears with cooking. The shark mackerel can reach 1.3 m and 11 kilograms.

Fishing Shark mackerel are good lure prospects, rising to take minnow or spoon type lure where they put up a determined surface based fight. Shark mackerel are also taken on drifted whole or cut fish baits and live baits, although shark mackerel are not the general target species with live baits in tropical waters. The shark mackerel makes reasonable eating but the quality is improved by skinning the fillets.

Rigs and Tactics

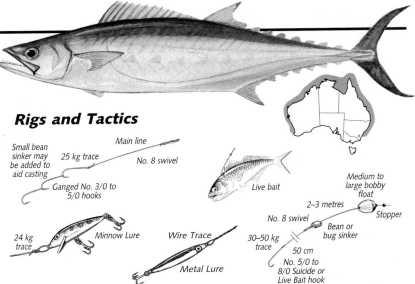

Small bean sinker may be added to aid casting
Main line
25 kg trace
No. 8 swivel
Ganged No. 3/0 to 5/0 hooks
Live bait
Medium to large bobby float
2–3 metres
No. 8 swivel
Stopper
Bean or bug sinker
24 kg trace
Minnow Lure
Wire Trace
30–50 kg trace
50 cm
No. 5/0 to 8/0 Suicide or Live Bait hook
Metal Lure

MACKEREL, SPANISH

Scientific name *Scomberomorus commerson*. Also known as Narrow-barred Spanish mackerel, blue mackerel, tanguigue, Spaniard, seer, seerfish.

Range Mandurah in Western Australia northwards and around the top end and as far south as Bermagui in southern NSW.

Description The Spanish mackerel is a highly sought after and valued species capable of reaching 2.35 m and 42 kilograms. It is commonly taken from 5 – 15 kilograms. Smaller fish travel in pods of similar sized fish. The Spanish mackerel is similar to the wahoo but has fewer dorsal spines (15 – 18 versus 23 – 27) in a shorter dorsal fin. The upper jaw of the Spanish mackerel has an obvious external bone which extends to at least the middle of the eye, while in the wahoo there is no obvious bone and the upper jaw extends to the front edge of the eye. The Spanish mackerel is found in coastal waters, frequently in the vicinity of reefs.

Fishing Spanish mackerel will aggressively take trolled lures and baits. Minnow lures, spoons and feathered lures run at 5 – 7 knots work best, while trolled garfish, slimy mackerel or other fish at 3 – 5 knots will take good catches. Spanish mackerel will also take drifted live, whole or cut baits. Land based fishermen drift large baits under balloons to take large fish. A wire trace can be an effective counter to the sharp teeth of the Spanish mackerel. The Spanish mackerel is an excellent sport fish, particularly on light line, as it runs strongly and occasionally jumps in its attempts to escape. Spanish mackerel can actively feed at different depths, so lures and baits which target a wide range will more quickly locate fish. The Spanish mackerel is a highly regarded food fish, but does not freeze particularly well, especially if cut into steaks. The quality is much better when the fish is filleted.

Rigs and Tactics

Stopper
No. 10 swivel
Bobby float
No. 2 to 4 ball or bean sinker
No. 3/0 to 5/0 hook gang
24 kg trace
Minnow Lure
Live bait
Wire Trace
Metal Lure
Small bean sinker may be added to aid casting
Main line
25 kg trace
No. 8 swivel
Ganged No. 3/0 to 5/0 hooks

MACKEREL, SPOTTED

Scientific name *Scomberomorus munroi*. Also known as Australian spotted mackerel, spotted Spanish mackerel, Japanese spotted mackerel, schoolie.

Range Abrolhos Islands in Western Australia northward and around the top end
and into NSW, sometimes reaching as far south as Sydney.

Description The spotted mackerel is smaller than the Spanish mackerel but the fight and eating qualities are at least equal to their more illustrious cousins. The spotted mackerel can reach over one metre and more than 10 kg which makes it a worthwhile light tackle target. The spotted mackerel is more commonly encountered from 2 to 6 kilograms. It can be identified by the broad band of dark spots along the middle of each side. The inside of the pectoral fin is dark blue or black. The first dorsal fin is blue with a dusky blotch on the front section.

Fishing This species is most common in summer when it follows warmer currents which extend down the east and west coasts. It takes pilchard and garfish baits well either drifted or slow trolled. Spotted mackerel take smaller live baits readily. They are frequently taken on larger lures intended for Spanish mackerel, but are good propositions with slightly smaller Rapala or Laser type minnows or spoons. The spotted mackerel is excellent eating, but should be bled and kept on ice for optimum quality.

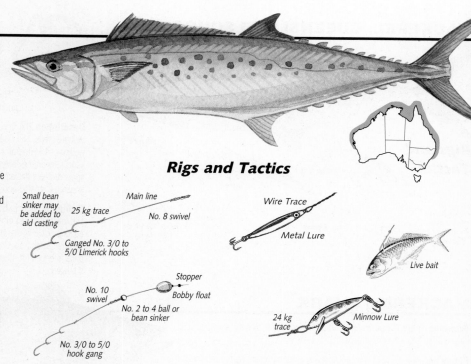

Rigs and Tactics

Small bean sinker may be added to aid casting

25 kg trace

Main line

No. 8 swivel

Ganged No. 3/0 to 5/0 Limerick hooks

No. 10 swivel

Stopper

Bobby float

No. 2 to 4 ball or bean sinker

No. 3/0 to 5/0 hook gang

Wire Trace

Metal Lure

Live bait

24 kg trace

Minnow Lure

MAHI MAHI

Rigs and Tactics

No. 10 swivel

Stopper

Bobby float

No. 2 to 4 ball or bean sinker

No. 3/0 to 5/0 hook gang

Brass ring

Main line

100–200 g barrel sinker

No. 6/0 to 9/0 hook Suicide or Live Bait hook

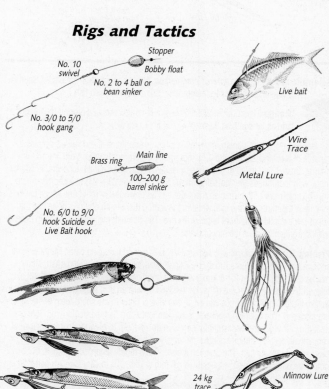

Live bait

Wire Trace

Metal Lure

24 kg trace

Minnow Lure

Scientific name *Coryphaena hippurus*. Also known as Dolphin, dolphin fish, common dolphinfish, dorado.

Range Geographe Bay in Western Australia and northwards through warmer temperate and tropical waters to Bermagui in NSW.

Description The mahi mahi is one of the most beautiful fish in the ocean when lit up, with bright yellow to blue colouration and brilliant blue flecks over most of the body and fins. The fantastic colours fade to a washed out grey after death. Mature male or 'bull' mahi mahi have a prominent high forehead and tend to be more brightly coloured. Females have a more streamlined head profile. The species is easily recognised in photographs due to its shape and brilliant colours. Other diagnostic features include the very long dorsal and anal fins and the deeply veed tail. Mahi mahi are arguably the fastest growing species in the ocean, growing as much as a centimetre a day when food is plentiful. Mahi mahi can reach 2 m and more than 20 kg but are frequently taken in Australia from 2 to 10 kilograms. In Western Australia, mahi mahi are first found in oceanic waters at less than a kilogram and within five months, those that have not been caught are more than 10 kilograms.

Fishing A brilliant blue water angling species which presents a spectacular sight as a lit up mahi mahi rises to take a trolled lure or bait. Mahi mahi are renowned residents around floating debris and Fish Aggregating Devices (FAD's) are now set in many areas to attract this and other pelagic species. Hundreds of mahi mahi can be concentrated around a floating log. These fish can be picked up by trolling or casting close to the debris with minnow, feather jigs or pusher type lures such as from Pakula. As fishing pressure increases, cut bait or whole fish and ultimately live bait are needed to take fish. An unweighted large peeled prawn drifted back to the school can take fish when all else fails. The mahi mahi provides a strong and spectacular fight, mixing dogged runs with leaps. They are a reliable light tackle standby in many parts of the world when blue water gamefishing is slow. Mahi mahi make excellent eating but should be bled and chilled immediately after the special photographs are taken. The flesh does not freeze well so only enough for immediate needs should be taken. The extremely fast growth rate and thumping which accompanies landing means that the mahi mahi bruises easily and can suffer post harvest trauma so should be released very carefully.

MARLIN, BLACK

Scientific name *Makaira indica*. Also known as Giant black marlin, silver marlin.

Range Circum-Australia, but only spasmodically recorded from the south coast. Prefers tropical waters and moves further south in summer and early autumn with warmer currents.

Description A magnificent blue water billfish capable of reaching a length of nearly 5 m and 850 kilograms. The black marlin is readily distinguished by its rigid pectoral fins which cannot be laid next to body in any black marlin and are completely rigid in all fish over 50 kg. In this fairly heavy bodied fish, the start of the second dorsal is forward to the start of the second anal fin. Black marlin are most commonly found in blue water, with many fish moving southwards with the warmer currents. Black marlin are found near current lines and where baitfish aggregations are prevalent.

Fishing The black marlin is widely recognised as the most highly prized gamefishing species. The most famous fishing ground is off Cairns, where the future of grander marlin (over 1000 pounds) has been enhanced by the almost exclusive use of tag and release fishing and the recent establishment of this species as recreational only in Australia's 200 mile Exclusive Economic Zone. Black marlin are targeted by gamefishermen along most of the east and west coasts. Black marlin are caught on trolled live and dead bait or less frequently on bait fished from a stationery boat. Marlin are also taken on trolled lures which consist of a hard moulded plastic or resin head and soft plastic skirt which travels just at or below the surface and leaves a bubble trail. Black marlin are a fast swimming pelagic species which are trolled at speeds between six and ten knots. A few marlin are caught by land based game fishermen, but only where deep, clean water comes close to shore. Marlin have a bony mouth and bill which can make setting and holding the hook difficult. When hooked, a marlin will often jump spectacularly in an effort to throw the hook and many fish are lost near the boat through the hook pulling out. Catching marlin requires patience, skill and a bit of luck. The capture of a large marlin requires perfectly maintained tackle and teamwork from all involved. They are not regarded as a food fish and almost all recreationally landed fish are released.

MARLIN, BLUE

Scientific name *Makaira mazara*. Also known as Indo-pacific blue marlin, Pacific blue marlin, beakie.

Range Albany in Western Australia and northern waters around the east coast to Mallacoota in Victoria but blue marlin are rarely found in water cooler than 20 degrees Celsius.

Description The blue marlin is one of the largest marlin, recorded as reaching a maximum weight of over 1100 kg, although specimens in Australia are less than 300 kilograms. While alive the fins and tail of the blue marlin are electric blue. The blue marlin can be separated from the black marlin by the lighter stripes on the side and the fact that the pectoral is flexible and can be laid flat in the blue marlin. The blue marlin can be separated from the striped marlin by the lower dorsal fin and the start of the second dorsal fin is behind the start of the second anal fin. The lateral line does not generally show in adults but is a distinctive chain which is apparent when scales or skin is removed.

Fishing The blue marlin is an open ocean species most commonly found along the Continental shelf, above deeper canyons and along current lines in deeper water. They can also be found by trolling around oceanic debris. Blue marlin will take trolled hard and soft plastic lures or trolled live or dead baits. Blue marlin can be taken by drifting or at anchor with live or dead baits, although this method is not generally used in Australia as fish are not common enough for a concentrated approach to be successful. The blue marlin is a tough, strong fighter whose first run may spool an unwary angler or inexperienced skipper. The blue marlin can be a spectacular jumper, but often fights deeply. When jumping the blue marlin will spin or suddenly reverse direction which can break the line. The blue marlin is not eaten, not just because of the poor quality of the flesh which is not highly regarded but because of the enormous value which gamefishermen place on these magnificent animals. Consequently, all but very few blue marlin are tagged and released. The recent national decision to prohibit the retention of all black and blue marlin by commercial fishers in Australian waters should lead to benefits to recreational fishermen.

MARLIN, STRIPED

Scientific name *Tetrapturus audax*. Also known as Striper, stripey.

Range Cape Naturaliste in Western Australia northwards and around the east coast as far south as northern Tasmania. The striped marlin prefers water temperatures of 20 – 26 degrees so is most common on the main east and west coasts.

Description The striped marlin is more compressed than the other more cylindrical marlin species. The striped marlin reaches a smaller maximum size than the black and blue marlin at 250 kg, with Australian specimens encountered to over 150 kilograms. The striped marlin has striking cobalt blue or lavender stripes which fade to a fair degree after death. The first three rays in the high first dorsal are of similar height. The striped marlin also has a single lateral line which may not be readily visible but which is raised and can be felt. The pectoral fin is longer than the body depth and can fold against the body. The tail appears squared of at the end of the top and bottom lobe.

Fishing The striped marlin can be taken at slower trolling speeds than blue and black marlin and can be an exciting catch on minnow and other lures trolled for Spanish mackerel. Striped marlin will also take traditional hard and soft plastic lures for other high speed pelagics. They can be found closer inshore, shadowing baitfish schools, and are often taken in conjunction with tuna species, especially by commercial longliners. Striped marlin are fished for with trolled live or dead baits and strip baits, particularly with plastic squids. As striped marlin are often found around baitfish schools, they are fished for with cast or drifted live baits either near worked bait fish or to cruising fish. When hooked, the striped marlin is a tenacious fighter which is a real challenge on lighter lines. They display long runs and can dive deep and tail walk across the surface. The striped marlin is excellent eating, particularly for sashimi and is therefore often retained by commercial fishing boats as it attracts a good price.

Rigs and Tactics for Black Marlin, Blue Marlin and Striped Marlin

SAILFISH, INDO-PACIFIC

Scientific name *Istiophorus platypterus*. Also known as Pacific sailfish, bayonet fish, sailfish.

Range Cape Leeuwin in southern Western Australia and tropical waters around the east coast as far south as Port Stephens in NSW.

Description The Indo-Pacific sailfish is most easily recognised by the prominent sail-like dorsal fin which forms the basis of the common name. The dorsal fin when lowered, fits into a groove. The shorter median dorsal rays are still longer than the body is deep. The characteristic upper jaw spear is slender and more than twice the length of the lower jaw. The ventral rays are very long and extend almost to the anus. The body and sail are spotted with dark and light blue. Stripes on the side may darken after death. Indo-Pacific sailfish can reach 120 kg, but any fish over 45 kg is a proud capture.

Fishing The Indo-Pacific sailfish is a spectacular fish renowned for its spectacular leaps and strong surface runs. The sailfish is one of the smaller billfish but is highly prized, especially as a light line target. Sailfish can be taken by trolling live or dead baits of mullet, mackerel, garfish, rainbow runner or other common medium sized bait fish. Baits enhanced with plastic or feather skirts seem to take more fish. Many fish are taken on lures, including pusher or doorknob type lures or even minnow lures. Sailfish are becoming increasingly targeted with fly gear, as the use of teaser baits or lures can bring lit up sailfish within casting range and their spectacular fight makes them one of the ultimate targets for fly fishing aficionados. Indo-Pacific sailfish are occasionally taken from rocky headlands adjacent to deeper water on drifted live baits or spincasting with baits or lures. Sailfish can travel in small pods and multiple hookups are possible, challenging the skills of all involved. The best sailfishing grounds are undoubtedly off Exmouth, Karratha and Broome in Western Australia, where even fairly small boats can encounter sailfish during peak periods. Sailfish flesh is palatable but not highly regarded and these days all but the record fish are returned to the water, although there are relatively low tag return rates to date.

Rigs and Tactics

SAMSON FISH

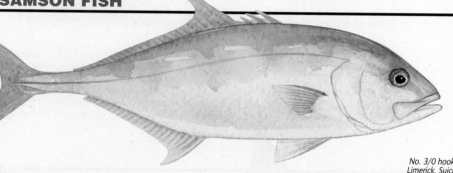

Scientific name *Seriola hippos*. Also known as Sambo, samson, sea kingfish.

Range Shark Bay in Western Australia to Yorke Peninsula in South Australia then disjointed distribution from around Bribie Island in southern Queensland to Montague Island in NSW.

Description A large and powerful fish capable of reaching 1.8 m and more than 50 kg in weight. Similar in appearance to the closely related yellowtail kingfish, but the samson fish is a much cleaner fighter which does not usually bury the angler on any available reef. The samson fish is best separated by counting the second dorsal rays which has 23 – 25 as opposed to 31 or over for yellowtail kingfish. The 16 – 17 anal rays on the samson fish distinguish this species from the amberjack which has 19 or more anal rays and 29 to 35 second dorsal rays. The samson fish also has a more rounded forehead which is more pronounced in younger fish. The flesh surrounding the teeth in both jaws in the samson fish is often but not always engorged with blood, giving the tooth patches a red appearance. The colour varies but the samson fish can often have distinct vertical blotches which, while fading with age, are not found in the other similar species.

Fishing A real challenge on light gear as skillful handling can present some extremely large fish due to their relatively clean, strong fight. Samson fish can be taken at all depths from nearshore waters to around 60 fathoms. They can be found near sand patches, around reefs or seagrass and can take whiting, garfish or other small fish from surprised anglers. Best baits are live fish, whole fresh dead fish, fillets, pilchard, octopus, squid or crabs. Samson fish can be taken on deep vertical fished jigs and rarely on trolled lures. Small samson fish make good eating, but large fish over 15 kg are best returned to fight another day. Large fish in particular can be infected with a parasite which causes the flesh to virtually disintegrate on cooking. The aggregations near Rottnest island in WA provides unbelievable sport fishing on jigs over summer. Tagged fish have been recaptured is Esperance less than a month later- which is truly remarkable.

Rigs and Tactics

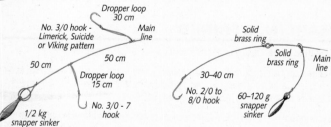

Dropper loop 30 cm
No. 3/0 hook - Limerick, Suicide or Viking pattern
Main line
50 cm
50 cm
Dropper loop 15 cm
1/2 kg snapper sinker
No. 3/0 - 7 hook

Solid brass ring
Solid brass ring
Main line
30–40 cm
No. 2/0 to 8/0 hook
60–120 g snapper sinker

Solid brass ring
250–500 g barrel sinker
Solid brass ring
1 metre
30–50 kg trace

Wire Trace
Metal Lure
Linked No. 2/0 to 4/0 Limerick or Kendall Kirby hooks
Bug sinker crimped to line

TUNA, LONGTAIL

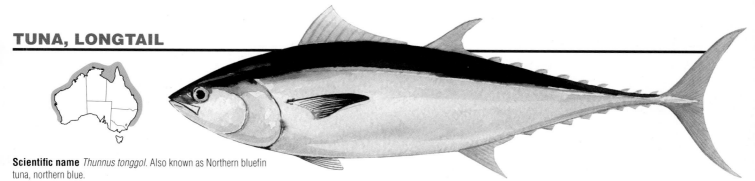

Scientific name *Thunnus tonggol*. Also known as Northern bluefin tuna, northern blue.

Range Geographe Bay in Western Australia and northwards including tropical waters and as far south on the east coast as Eden in southern NSW.

Description The name longtail comes from the light build to the rear half of this species, giving a narrow tail wrist and a slender outline. The pectoral fin is very short and finishes well in front of the start of the second dorsal fin which readily separates the species from yellowfin and bigeye tuna. This species is much more common in tropical waters but can migrate southwards in summer.

Fishing In tropical waters, small longtails can form vast schools like mackerel tuna or bonito. These schools move rapidly and fish can be caught by casting lures or trolling lures or baits near the edge of the feeding school. Minnow lures, lead slugs or Christmas tree lures, feather jigs, spoons and flies all work well with larger fish preferring larger lures and a faster retrieve. Longtail prefer inshore waters and although most are taken by anglers in boats, longtail are a highly prized land based game species. Specialised gear with live baits below large floats or balloons or high speed spinning can bring these speedsters to the rocks. As with all rock based fishing, special care should be taken of wave conditions, especially when landing large fish. Longtail love live baits fished from boats and cubing (berleying with tuna flesh and feeding unweighted cubes into the trail, one with a hook) can work well once a school is located. Longtail tuna are red fleshed and of lower quality than many species, but it is greatly improved with immediate bleeding.

Rigs and Tactics

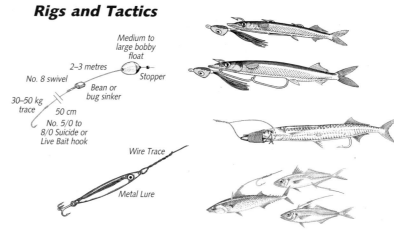

Medium to large bobby float

2–3 metres

No. 8 swivel

Stopper

Bean or bug sinker

30–50 kg trace

50 cm

No. 5/0 to 8/0 Suicide or Live Bait hook

Wire Trace

Metal Lure

TUNA, MACKEREL

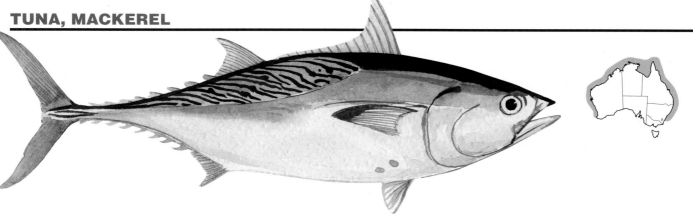

Scientific name *Euthynnus affinis*. Also known as Jack mackerel, little tuna, kawa-kawa.

Range Cape Leeuwin in Western Australia northwards and throughout northern waters as far south as Merimbula in NSW.

Description The mackerel tuna is a highly prized lightweight game species which is caught in inshore waters or larger bays, harbours and large estuarine systems as well as offshore islands or larger reefs. The mackerel tuna can reach 1 m in length and 12 kg but is much more common at 2 – 8 kilograms. The mackerel tuna has prominent wavy green lines in the rear portion of the body above the midline. The mackerel tuna is similar to the frigate mackerel but the first dorsal of the mackerel tuna reaches almost to the second dorsal while the frigate mackerel's first dorsal is short and widely separated from the second dorsal fin. The mackerel tuna has two to five dark spots above the ventral fin and more prominent teeth than the frigate mackerel which also only reaches 58 cm in length.

Fishing The mackerel tuna is a schooling fish which feeds heavily on pilchards, herrings, whitebait, anchovies, squid and occasionally krill. However, even when a feeding school is located, they can be very selective and difficult to entice to strike. Mackerel tuna are mainly taken on fast trolled or high speed retrieved lures such as plastic skirted lures, Christmas tree lures, minnow lures, plastic squids, lead jigs and feather lures and spoons. The mackerel tuna will take live baits, fresh dead baits either cast and retrieved, trolled or fished under a float. They will more rarely take cut baits. Mackerel tuna are a frequent catch of high speed land based game fishermen. Mackerel tuna have dark and sinewy meat which is best steamed and served with sauces or used as berley or cut bait.

Rigs and Tactics

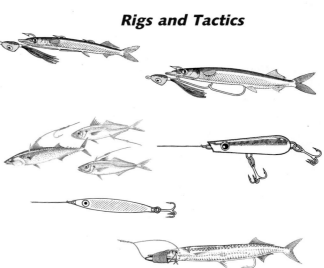

TUNA, SOUTHERN BLUEFIN

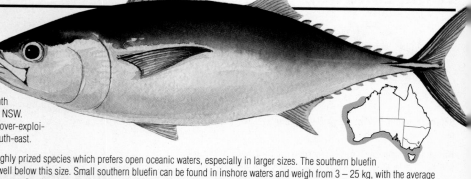

Scientific name *Thunnus maccoyii*. Also known as SBT, southern blue, bluefin, bluey, tunny.

Range A cool water species more common in southern waters but the only identified breeding area is off the north-west coast of Western Australia in International waters where they have been heavily exploited. The range is from the North-west coast of Western Australia and southwards along the south coast including Tasmania and as far as Montague Island in southern NSW. Larger fish are found near the Victoria/NSW border, but commercial over-exploitation has severely reduced the number of large fish found off the south-east.

Description The southern bluefin tuna is a heavily built and very highly prized species which prefers open oceanic waters, especially in larger sizes. The southern bluefin tuna can grow to greater than 150 kg but is most commonly caught well below this size. Small southern bluefin can be found in inshore waters and weigh from 3 – 25 kg, with the average size generally increasing as you move eastwards along the southern coast. Southern bluefin tuna have been overexploited by commercial fishing operations, especially on the high seas. The commercial overexploitation has lead to the development of extensive aquaculture, based around Port Lincoln to on-grow these fish; a process which previously occurred naturally before overfishing of juveniles removed larger adults from the south-east. Southern bluefin tuna can be identified by their heavy bodies, and the short pectoral fins which do not extend to the second dorsal. The dorsal and anal lobes are also short as opposed to the yellowfin with its scythe-like lobes in larger fish. The finlets at the rear of the body are edged with black and the caudal keels on the wrist of the tail are conspicuously yellow, especially in the sizes normally encountered by recreational fishers.

Fishing The southern bluefin tuna schools at all sizes although the larger fish form much smaller schools. Small fish can move close to shore if deeper water is nearby and can be taken by land based gamefishers. Most southern bluefin tuna are taken on trolled lures, with rubber squids, pushers and other gamefishing lures working well. They will also take minnow lures, feathers, slices and large lead slugs. They can be taken on fly. Southern bluefin tuna like offshore debris and can be taken with mahi-mahi around floating logs, shipping containers or other large flotsam in bluewater areas. The southern bluefin tuna can be taken on cast lures, but they can often hang at depth and downriggers can be productive, especially when a sounder indicates fish holding at a specific depth. Southern bluefin tuna are less frequently taken on baits, although they can be taken on trolled baits, live baits or dead baits including cubes, especially if used with berley. Deep fished live baits or whole squid can take larger fish, but local knowledge is necessary as there is lots of water between the larger fish. The Southern bluefin tuna is a highly prized gamefish species which fights hard and is a considerable challenge on lighter tackle. The southern bluefin tuna has rich dark meat which is highly prized for sashimi. These fish are much improved by being bled and chilled soon after capture.

Rigs and Tactics

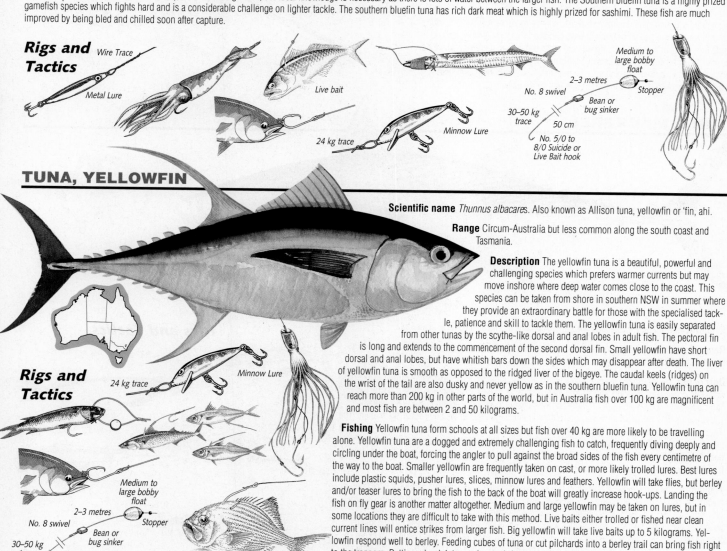

Wire Trace

Metal Lure

Live bait

24 kg trace

Minnow Lure

No. 8 swivel

30–50 kg trace

50 cm

No. 5/0 to 8/0 Suicide or Live Bait hook

Bean or bug sinker

2–3 metres

Stopper

Medium to large bobby float

TUNA, YELLOWFIN

Scientific name *Thunnus albacares*. Also known as Allison tuna, yellowfin or 'fin, ahi.

Range Circum-Australia but less common along the south coast and Tasmania.

Description The yellowfin tuna is a beautiful, powerful and challenging species which prefers warmer currents but may move inshore where deep water comes close to the coast. This species can be taken from shore in southern NSW in summer where they provide an extraordinary battle for those with the specialised tackle, patience and skill to tackle them. The yellowfin tuna is easily separated from other tunas by the scythe-like dorsal and anal lobes in adult fish. The pectoral fin is long and extends to the commencement of the second dorsal fin. Small yellowfin have short dorsal and anal lobes, but have whitish bars down the sides which may disappear after death. The liver of yellowfin tuna is smooth as opposed to the ridged liver of the bigeye. The caudal keels (ridges) on the wrist of the tail are also dusky and never yellow as in the southern bluefin tuna. Yellowfin tuna can reach more than 200 kg in other parts of the world, but in Australia fish over 100 kg are magnificent and most fish are between 2 and 50 kilograms.

Fishing Yellowfin tuna form schools at all sizes but fish over 40 kg are more likely to be travelling alone. Yellowfin tuna are a dogged and extremely challenging fish to catch, frequently diving deeply and circling under the boat, forcing the angler to pull against the broad sides of the fish every centimetre of the way to the boat. Smaller yellowfin are frequently taken on cast, or more likely trolled lures. Best lures include plastic squids, pusher lures, slices, minnow lures and feathers. Yellowfin will take flies, but berley and/or teaser lures to bring the fish to the back of the boat will greatly increase hook-ups. Landing the fish on fly gear is another matter altogether. Medium and large yellowfin may be taken on lures, but in some locations they are difficult to take with this method. Live baits either trolled or fished near clean current lines will entice strikes from larger fish. Big yellowfin will take live baits up to 5 kilograms. Yellowfin respond well to berley. Feeding cubes of tuna or cut pilchards into a berley trail can bring fish right to the transom. Putting a hook into a cube can bring a real test of gear as a large yellowfin tuna on short line tests the drag, rod and angler to the limit. The yellowfin is rated with albacore as the best tuna for cooking. For sashimi, the yellowfin is generally regarded behind bigeye and southern bluefin tuna, but a fat specimen is world class eating. Bleeding and chilling the fish greatly improves the quality.

Rigs and Tactics

24 kg trace

Minnow Lure

Medium to large bobby float

2–3 metres

No. 8 swivel

Stopper

30–50 kg trace

Bean or bug sinker

50 cm

No. 5/0 to 8/0 Suicide or Live Bait hook

TUNA, STRIPED

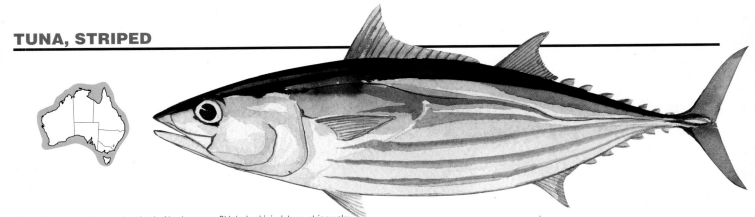

Scientific name *Katsuwonis pelamis*. Also known as Skipjack, skipjack tuna, stripey, aku.

Range Circum-Australia but more common in temperate waters between 17 – 25 degrees Celsius.

Description The striped tuna is a small, thickset schooling species which rapidly tapers at the rear of the body to a smallish tail. Sometimes misidentified as a bonito, but striped tuna lack the obvious teeth of the bonito and have no stripes on the upper flanks or back. Instead, the 4 – 6 horizontal stripes on the striped tuna are found on the lower flanks and belly. The area under and around the pectoral fin lacks stripes. The striped tuna can reach more than 15 kg, but in Australia any fish over 10 kg is exceptional and the average size is between 1 and 6 kilograms. Schools of striped tuna can be massive and may contain hundreds of tonnes of fish. This species forms the basis of significant commercial fisheries in many countries.

Fishing Striped tuna are mainly taken on lures trolled or cast from boats, deep shores or jetties which extend to deeper water. Many striped tuna are taken on heavy cord lines and Smiths jigs to be used as bait or berley. Striped tuna provide excellent sport on lighter lines as they are very hard fighting speedsters. Most bright lures which work well at around 5 knots will take striped tuna, with Christmas tree style lures working well. Slices, slug lures, feather jigs, small poppers and medium sized flies also take good numbers of fish, although striped tuna can be finicky about size and action type of lures at times. Striped tuna can be taken on pilchards, cut baits or squid, especially if a berley trail excites the fish. Larger fish can take small live baits. Striped tuna have very dark red meat which is quite strongly flavoured but is suitable for smoking, salting and canning. If bled and chilled immediately they are fair eating. However, striped tuna are excellent live baits for large pelagics and their cut flesh makes a first rate bait or berley where their oil rich red flesh attracts most species.

Rigs and Tactics

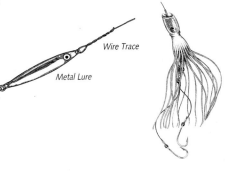

Wire Trace

Metal Lure

WAHOO

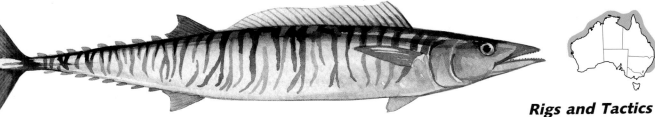

Scientific name *Acanthocybium solandri*. Also known as Ono, 'hoo.

Range Kalbarri in Western Australia and all northern waters and as far south as Montague Island in southern NSW.

Description The wahoo is a long and sleek pelagic species which is capable of very fast movement in the water. Most wahoo in Australian waters are between 8 and 30 kg but they can reach 65 kilograms. The wahoo is a solitary open water species which can be identified by the long and higher dorsal fin of approximately even height. The dorsal fin starts behind the commencement of the pectoral fin while with the Spanish mackerel it commences at the leading edge of the pectoral. The head is longer and more pointed with the wahoo and the trailing edge of the tail fin is vertical compared to the forked tail of the other mackerels. The wahoo has a number of prominent zebra-like vertical stripes along the body but these are less noticeable in some especially larger specimens and fade considerably after death.

Fishing The wahoo favours offshore blue water and temperatures between 21 and 30 degrees Celsius. Wahoo are frequently found near the surface and can be found above deep reef drop-offs and offshore reef pinnacles. Many wahoo are taken on trolled lures such as squids, pusher or Konahead type lures, bibless minnows, feather jigs or large slices. Wahoo can take lures trolled faster than for most tuna species. The teeth of wahoo can severely damage rubber skirts and wooden lures. Wahoo are criticised by many marlin trollers for their habit of coming behind a perfectly swimming bait and chopping off the tail immediately behind the hook. Wahoo can be taken on a variety of skip or swimming baits. A wire trace is an advantage, but many wahoo are hooked lightly due to their tailing tendency on baits or lures. Wahoo are seldom specifically targeted in Australia but are a welcome catch when hooked due to their blistering runs and frequent direction changes during the fight. Wahoo are excellent eating. Parasites which are commonly found in the wahoo's gut do not affect the taste or quality of the flesh.

Rigs and Tactics

24 kg trace

Minnow Lure

Wire Trace

Metal Lure

CHAPTER EIGHT

SALTWATER
BOAT FISHING

BOATING

BOATING MOBILITY AND FISHING OPTIONS

The biggest single advantage of using a boat when fishing is that it provides mobility, enabling you to fish a greater area of water and also to extend your land-based fishing options. There are also specific fishing techniques designed for use by boat anglers, such as drifting, trolling, side planing and downrigging, which give you access to fish that you would be unable to access from shore.

COMFORT FACTORS

Items that make boat fishing more comfortable include seats, flat floors, some form of shelter from sun, rain and flying spray, and adequate storage for rods and other items.

In large boats that are capable of rough water work, game chairs and boat sides sufficiently high to provide good thigh support, are additional features needed to prevent fatigue. While canopies and windshields provide shelter, they may also obscure your vision and get in the way of active fishing styles.

ORGANISATION AND CARRYING CAPACITY

Anglers can take more gear and tackle with them when fishing from a boat than when walking. Specific facilities have been designed on boats

You don't have to own a cruiser to fish effectively. A simple tinny like this will suffice for sheltered water and general fishing.

to hold or store these items, such as rod holders, livebait tanks, dry lockers and under-gunwhale sections for rod storage.

Additional benefits for boating anglers include the use of digital technology in the form of depth sounders and Global Positioning Systems (GPS) that can be used to locate fish and relocate prime

fishing spots. With the advent of electric motors, even quiet approaches to holding fish are possible.

FISHING ESTUARIES

BAIT GATHERING

Baits that occur naturally within estuaries can sometimes be gathered the same day you fish the area. At low tide, when sand and mud flats are exposed or only covered with very shallow water, you can collect squirt worms, green nippers, pink nippers ('bass yabbies') mussels, and oysters. These can then be used to fish for bream, mullet, whiting or blackfish as the next tide starts to rise. Conversely, at high tide you can catch poddy mullet or small winter whiting over the shallows, then rig them as live baits for big flathead or mulloway. Good places for these fish are the deeper holes and channels, drop-offs, breakwalls and rock bars.

BLACKFISH AND WEED

In estuaries, the most common food of luderick (or blackfish) is algae, known to anglers simply as 'weed'. The algae grow in long, thin strands that attach themselves to stationary structures such as rocks, rock walls, piers and groynes that are in the path of tidal current flows, or in shallow

Canopies make life at sea comfortable but are a hinderance in casting situations.

Sand flathead are usually encountered offshore in depths from 10 to 25 metres and are best fished for from a boat by drifting with baits on the bottom.

can minimise this nuisance by pre-soaking the bread before tossing it over the side. It will then sink quicker and offer less attraction to hovering seagulls.

BREAM AND OYSTERS

Oysters are a preferred food of bream so wherever there are oyster beds there are sure to be bream nearby. Whether the oysters grow naturally on rocks, are cultivated in racks, or are 'drift oysters', borne around on the shells of benthic creatures like whelks, bream like to eat them.

Bream inhabit a range of estuarine habitat and will move significant distances up and downstream according to tides, food availability, rainfall and seasonal spawning prompts.

HARD AND SOFT FEEDING AREAS

Without question, some spots in estuaries yield fish more consistently than others do. Often, the factor that determines where fish will feed is the extent and strength of water flow. Strong currents aggregate fish near hard structure, such as rocks, snags, wharves and jetties, while in gentler flows, fish roam over softer bottoms such as mud, sand and weed beds.

If you want to catch fish on a hook and line, you have to find fish that are either already feeding, can be persuaded to begin feeding, or fish that will react aggressively to anything that invades their private territory.

ICE CREAM TUB MULLET TRAP

Small juvenile mullet, called 'poddies', are easily caught for bait in a trap baited with bread or dough. You can buy several commercial versions

Big tidal estuaries are the places many of our species live and breed.

of these traps, or make your own from a white plastic four-litre ice cream tub. Just cut a hole in the lid (about 10 cm square) and Araldite a 12 cm square section of plastic flyscreen over the hole. When this is secure, use a sharp knife to cut a smaller hole (about 4 cm square) in the middle of the flyscreen panel, then put a slice of fresh white bread inside the ice cream tub, and wire another slice to the lid so it covers the hole. Use a sinker to weight the tub so it doesn't float or drift away, secure the baited lid and place the trap in about 30 cm of water. Sandflats bordered with weed beds are good places. Mullet will be attracted to the slice of bread on top, eat their way through the middle of the bread and enter the trap, from which they will find it difficult to escape.

bays near inflow points like creek mouths and stormwater drains. Wound onto short, small-gape hooks, this weed is terrific bait for luderick and when chopped and mixed with sand, also makes great berley. Luderick also occasionally eat crustaceans, marine worms, and even small fish.

BREAD AND BEATING SEAGULLS

When you use berley in estuaries, particularly a floating berley like bread, seagulls soon cotton on to the free meal and make a nuisance of themselves, stealing the floating bread and with their fluttering and noisy cries, scaring the target fish, which will usually be mullet or bream. You

Fish use either hard or soft terrain as feeding areas. In this photograph, there are examples of both — in bridge and rock wall areas, and sand and weed beds.

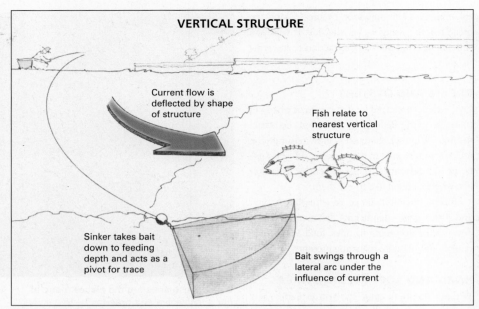

VERTICAL STRUCTURE

Current flow is deflected by shape of structure

Fish relate to nearest vertical structure

Sinker takes bait down to feeding depth and acts as a pivot for trace

Bait swings through a lateral arc under the influence of current

Fish and vertical structure

Sensible anglers make a point of releasing any fish excess to bag limits or immediate requirements. It's a way of contributing to the quality of your own future fishing.

Often the fish will end up near the mouth of large estuaries during periods of high rainfall.

LOCAL KNOWLEDGE

Estuary fishing tends to be done in a relatively short casting area. This means your choice of fishing spots needs to be fairly precise, both in terms of its location as well as the time you fish it. Local knowledge of an area is a bonus here. This knowledge comes from visiting the same places often enough to build up a reliable and accurate picture of fish movements, bait preferences and bite cycles. So rather than travel long distances and fish estuaries you have no experience of, concentrate on getting to know your local estuaries better. The results will always favour those with local knowledge.

MUFFLING SOUNDS AT NIGHT

Bream bite well at night, but are very sensitive to noise. When fishing for these or any fish at night, try to minimise the amount of noise you create inside a boat. If you are fishing from a small aluminium 'tinny', a carpeted floor will deaden the sound of your feet as you move around, or the sound of anything you inadvertantly drop. In the absence of carpet, spread some wet sacks out on the floor of the boat and these will do much the same job.

RAINFALL EFFECT

Aside from increasing water levels and downstream flow rates in estuaries, rainfall also affects salinity levels. Some estuary species can tolerate lowered salinity better than others can. Mullet for example, can survive in perfectly fresh water for long periods, while bream, flounder, flathead, leatherjacket and tailor tend to shift away from 'freshes'. When a virtual 'wall' of lowered-salinity water advances downriver, these fish are often pushed toward the river mouth. During floods, whole populations of estuarine fish are swept to sea. Here, large predators such

as mulloway and sharks, feast on them until the flood abates. As it does, saltier water starts pushes back up into the estuary and allows the smaller fish to enter the river and find sanctuary again.

SQUIRT WORMS AND FISHING TOWELS

In winter, squirt worms are a top estuary bait for blackfish, bream, whiting and mullet, but these small marine animals exude a substance that can dry and crack the skin of your hands, especially when cold, dry, winter winds are blowing. Carry a small piece of towel in the boat to wipe your hands each time after you finish baiting up and you will avoid this painful and annoying aspect of cold weather fishing.

THE FOOD ATTRACTION

When deciding which parts of an estuary to fish, try to focus your attention somewhere near places that naturally carry an abundance of local fish foods. Weed beds for example, harbour prawns and shrimp, and shallow hummocks between channels are often places where mussel beds accumulate. Oyster clumps growing on rocks and other structures will attract fish too, as will any eddies or quiet pockets of water where baitfish will seek refuge from predators and strong currents. Vegetarian fish, like blackfish, will rarely be found far from substantial growths of their favourite kinds of green weed and whiting will always be found over sandy shallows where there are beds of pink nippers.

TIDAL VARIATION

The variation in tidal heights is due to the elliptical orbits of the Earth around the Sun, and the Moon around the Earth. These variations in distance mean greater or lesser gravitational pull is exerted on coastal waters, so the water is

'lifted' to varying extents. It is possible to roughly predict the cycles of tide height on a more or less monthly basis, but several months can elapse before similar height tides will occur in the same place during the same period of the month. For identical tide heights to occur on the same calendar date can take several years.

TIDE AND TIME

Normally, estuary fishing centres round the time of day and the state of the tide. First and last

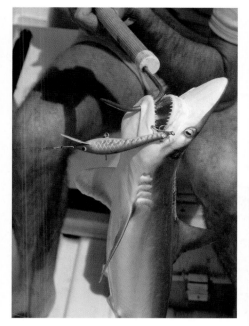

Trolling lures offshore can turn up anything. The last thing this angler expected was for a small shark to attack the lure and hook up.

These rock bars are covered at high tide and well out of the water at low tide. The fishing around such areas is always good regardless of the state of the tide.

light are both productive times, especially in the shallows where fish are easier to get at. High tides that coincide with dawn and dusk are prime fishing periods, so check out the tide charts for your favourite area and time your trips to be there when the fish are at their best.

TIDE FACTS

Tides are the alternate rising and falling of sea levels, a more or less continuous cycle of advancing and retreating water. The gravitational pull exerted on the oceans by the Moon and to a lesser extent by the Sun, causes tides. This tidal effect is greatest close to the equator and less at polar latitudes. In most places, this cycle of ebb

and flow occurs roughly twice in each 24-hour period. Exceptions are places where special tide patterns called 'dodge' tides may occur only once a day or even less.

TROPICAL ESTUARY TRICKS

In tropical waters, predatory fish like barramundi, mangrove jacks, trevally and others will lie in ambush around structure such as submerged rock bars, creek mouths, near and among clusters of bankside trees that have fallen into the river, to ambush baitfish that move up- and down-river with the tide. Casting baits, lures or flies around this structure and areas where there in a sudden change in water depth is a good tactic.

TIDAL VARIATION

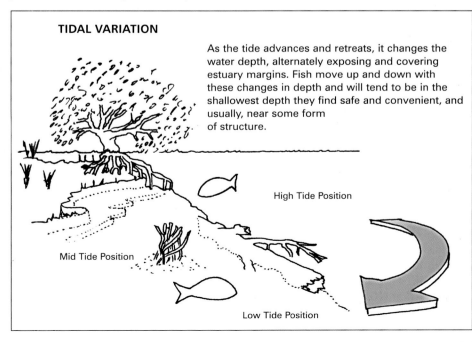

As the tide advances and retreats, it changes the water depth, alternately exposing and covering estuary margins. Fish move up and down with these changes in depth and will tend to be in the shallowest depth they find safe and convenient, and usually, near some form of structure.

High Tide Position

Mid Tide Position

Low Tide Position

Tidal movements can mean an area is bone dry at low tide, yet may be several metres underwater at high. This means you have to time your fishing trips to suit.

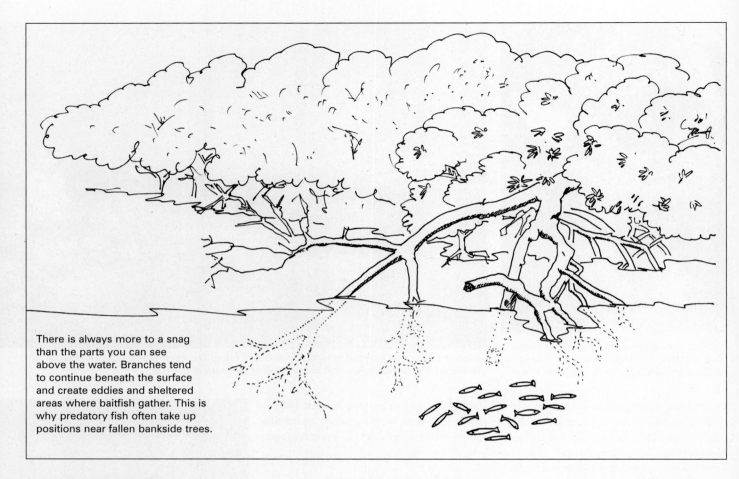

There is always more to a snag than the parts you can see above the water. Branches tend to continue beneath the surface and create eddies and sheltered areas where baitfish gather. This is why predatory fish often take up positions near fallen bankside trees.

WORKING ESTUARY 'EDGES'

Some forms of estuary fishing, such as drifting, can be successfully carried out by positioning the boat in the middle of an open stretch of water, but to a remarkable degree, you will find better fishing somewhere close to an estuary edge of some kind. Typical examples are: where current meets rocky outcrops, or rushes past sunken logs or timbers, or the edges of weed beds, the edges of channels where shallow water drops into deep and in any stretch of bankside water deep enough to afford fish some security.

FISHING THE BAYS

AMBUSHERS AND PROWLERS

Fish like bream, trevally, leatherjackets, flathead, flounder and whiting tend to take up positions

Big tropical estuaries always hold fish close to cover. Work the edges always.

where tidal currents and wave action will bring them food. Other species, like kingfish, tailor, tuna, salmon and bonito are constantly on the move, hoping to come across concentrations of prey, which they then attack, feeding on them until they disperse. Then the predators round them up again and start feeding once more or swim off to find more prey.

ANCHORING BASICS

If you anchor up with just one anchor rope, the boat will still be able to swing away from where the fish are as wind and tide move it about. You can improve your holding position by (1) using a single anchor bridle or better still, (2a and 2b) using a double anchor bridle. This requires two anchors of equal size and holding ability and will hold your boat over the desired grounds in almost wind conditions. They will not however prevent the boat swinging off the spot when the tide changes. If you need to hold over a bay fishing ground through a tide change, you'll need to employ (3) a 'fore and aft' system. This anchoring system will hold through all conditions, but many anglers do not like to use it as the anchor ropes get in the way of the fishing. In some bay fishing situations though, it may be the only way of getting a fish on in the first place.

CRAB-CATCHING IN BAYS

In large estuaries and bays, the arms of the system are prime locations to find crabs. The key features

you should be looking for when setting traps for crabs (mostly blue swimmers) are:

- sloping weed beds that run down into deeper water with an open sand or mud bottom,
- deeper holes that have shallow margins spilling water into them as the tide falls, and
- any place where flows of varying salinity collide, bringing with them the sort of detritus food concentrations on which crabs feed.

Depending on rainfall, you can position traps near creek inflows or even up inside tributaries with sufficient tidal exchange.

FLATHEAD AND FLOUNDER DRIFTS

Many coastal bays have sand and scattered reef patches near their mouths and often, schools of flathead and flounder lie along the edge of any pronounced deepening, such as a shipping channel. The best way to target these fish is to use a Paternoster rig with a heavy snapper lead or bomb sinker to keep the baits down near the bottom. This will let you cover a lot of ground as you drift with the wind or tide. Slender strips of fish flesh or small whole fish like whitebait are good choices, as are chunks of pilchard, tuna or slimy mackerel. Run one large bait and one small bait to see whether flathead or flounder are about, and then switch both rigs over to whatever is working on the day.

Right: The simpliest way to improve your holding position at anchor is to employ a bridle (1). A double bow anchor is a bit more complicated but more effective (2a and 2b), while a fore and aft anchor set will hold you on a mark through a tide change (3).

Left: Crabs can be caught from most estuaries and bays throughout the warmer months. This is a blue swimmer crab, shown belly-up to indicate the distinctive 'V' shape of the male crab's belly flap. Females have a broader, more rounded flap and if carrying eggs, should be returned to the water.

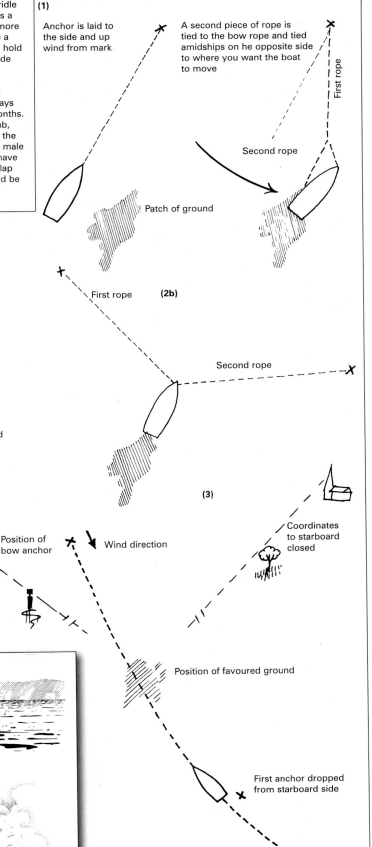

ANCHORING TACTICS

(1)

Anchor is laid to the side and up wind from mark

A second piece of rope is tied to the bow rope and tied amidships on he opposite side to where you want the boat to move

First rope

Second rope

Patch of ground

(2a)

Direction of wind

First anchor laid

Boat motors across wind

Second anchor laid

Patch of ground

First rope

(2b)

Second rope

(3)

Coordinates to starboard closed

Position of bow anchor

Wind direction

Coordinates to port closed

Position of favoured ground

First anchor dropped from starboard side

Below: When fishing for flathead over shallow or weedy sand flats, rather than rigging a bait on the bottom, try setting the bait under a float. You can use a stem float as shown here or a small bobby cork; the idea is just to keep the bait up off the bottom and out of the weed. The float should be adjustable so you can cope with different water depths and have the bait drifting just above the bottom. Flathead will readily move off their lies to take this enticing presentation.

KINGFISH AND BEACONS

Yellowtail kingfish are attracted to vertical structures like mooring buoys and channel markers. You can fish for these powerful predators with metal lures, poppers, flies or soft plastic stick-baits, but almost nothing beats a strip of fresh squid (if the squid are large) or a small whole, live squid. Position the boat upwind or up current of the structure so you will drift by it within casting distance. As you approach the beacon, cast as close to it as you can, then tweak the bait or lure back toward the boat and be ready to lift the rod and set the hook the moment a fish attacks.

HAIRTAIL

In winter, great schools of hairtail migrate down the Australian coast from equatorial waters and enter large bays and estuary systems. Here they take up residence in deep holes, feeding mostly at night, for which their slender bodies' huge light-gathering eyes and fearsome teeth equip them well. Their bodies are like polished chrome, which on dark nights actually makes them harder for their prey to see, especially as they tend to approach stealthily, in a curious swimming attitude, with their slender ribbon-like bodies hanging almost vertically in the water.

Sounders are a useful tool in finding fish in saltwater.

Yellowtail kingfish frequent vertical structures like beacons and navigation towers because these features attract baitfish and allow the kingfish to hunt efficiently.

SNAPPER AND MULLOWAY IN BAYS

Depending on available reef and other structure, snapper can take up residence in a part of a bay, but may still move around within a fairly well defined area. Mulloway tend to sit in deep caves, under wharves or in reef crevices for a good deal of the time, but when night falls or the tide begins to move, they often embark on a systematic tour of likely feeding places. Typically, they will follow bottom contours or visit known baitfish aggregation areas and so can be targeted wherever baitfish congregate or where there are sudden changes in depth or bottom shape.

TARGETING BAY TUNA

When tuna move into bays to feed, much of the action can be seen from some distance away. Often, they will bottle the bait up against the surface and rip through it, churning the water to foam and attracting a canopy of screeching seabirds, which further aids the observant angler in spotting such boil-overs. The best way of catching these fish is to approach to within casting distance of the feeding school then to cast flies, metal lures or surface poppers along its edges.

Kingfish and Beacons

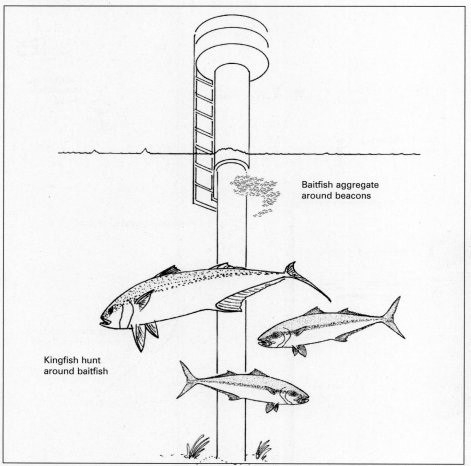

Baitfish aggregate around beacons

Kingfish hunt around baitfish

Oceanic fish like tunas will enter estuaries and bays and can sometimes be seen feeding actively at the surface, sending up splashes like these.

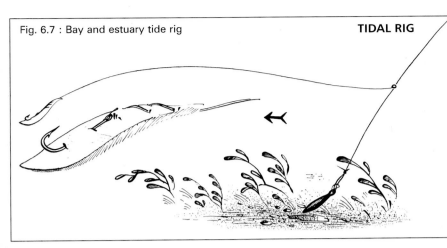

Fig. 6.7 : Bay and estuary tide rig

TIDAL RIG

When fishing in big bays and estuaries, there may be considerable tidal current and it can pay to use a heavy snapper lead to keep the bait down near the bottom. To offset any presentation disadvantage created by using this heavy sinker, rig the bait on a long dropper (two to four metres). This will pick up all normal bay inhabitants, even shy biters, like whiting and leatherjackets.

TUNA BAY INVASIONS

Each winter and spring, various species of tunas follow bait schools down the East Coast, usually capitalising on food chains that have begun as nutrient upwellings from the deep ocean, then grown into massive mobile larders of the sea, populated by plankton, crustacea, jellyfish and myriad clouds of baitfish. As this huge food chain drifts steadily southward on the East Australian current, bits of it, the food-laden water and the attendant tuna, are swept in and out of large coastal bays by tidal action and variable winds. This creates temporary but exceptionally good fishing in enclosed waters for fish that are more usually only encountered out at sea.

In suitably calm weather, taking the family out in the boat to catch fish and crabs, or just peer over the side and see all that is going on, is very enjoyable.

Casting from a small boat is a very effective way to catch small sportfish.

WEATHER

Australian coastal bays that are quite wide and exposed as the open sea to wind, should only be fished from small boats in calm to moderate weather. If these bays are also shallow, wind waves and chop can build up to dangerous levels when a squall or weather change comes through. Strong tidal flows that make the waves steeper and more likely to break, can also contribute to an already dangerous situation and in such conditions anglers should head for sheltered waters.

REEF FISHING

CHOOSING SIDES

Which side of the reef should you fish from? Generally speaking, when bait fishing, fish from the upwind and/or up current side of the reef or bombie. This makes it easier to cast your baits and to drift them toward the fish with the moving water. When casting lures, try to position the boat with the wind behind you, but with the current or water flow coming over the reef toward you. When trolling, work the edges that the current and wind are coming from.

REEFS AND FISH

Reefs are usually made of coral or rock, and often carry many forms of marine animal and plant life. This makes them ideal feeding and shelter stations for marine fish. Often too, such reefs stand in the path of oceanic and tidal currents and wave action; all of which create areas of disturbed water in the form of eddies and swirls around the reef edges. Small fish shelter in these areas of low water movement and bigger fish patrol the fringes, looking for an easy meal.

Casting poppers over reefs will often produce giant trevally.

OFFSHORE REEF TACTICS

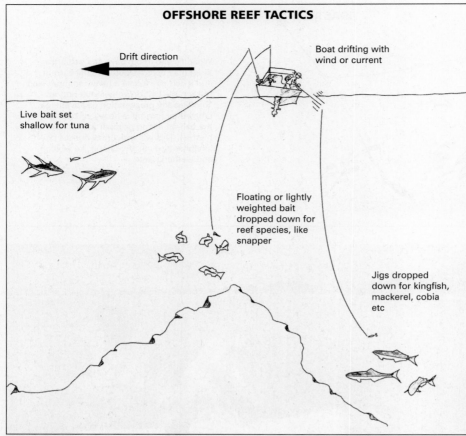

Drift direction

Boat drifting with wind or current

Live bait set shallow for tuna

Floating or lightly weighted bait dropped down for reef species, like snapper

Jigs dropped down for kingfish, mackerel, cobia etc

Reef fishing techniques

SNAPPER RIGS

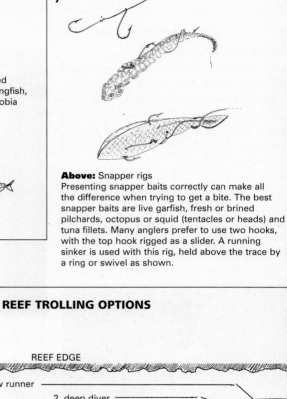

Above: Snapper rigs
Presenting snapper baits correctly can make all the difference when trying to get a bite. The best snapper baits are live garfish, fresh or brined pilchards, octopus or squid (tentacles or heads) and tuna fillets. Many anglers prefer to use two hooks, with the top hook rigged as a slider. A running sinker is used with this rig, held above the trace by a ring or swivel as shown.

REEF FISHING TECHNIQUES

You can fish reefs by anchoring nearby and casting or drifting baits or lures toward them, or you can set up trolling paths that will take baits or lures past the productive reef edges. When fishing reefs, with berley, position your boat up current from the reef and fish at anchor. When drift fishing, start your drift at some point upwind of the reef, allowing enough time for baits or lures to sink to the depth fish are holding. Trolling near reefs is often more productive along the side any wind or sea action is coming from, while bait fishing tends to be best on the edges where currents wash by.

REEF TROLLING TIPS

As most reefs slope roughly through a series of steps and edges into deeper water, the lures running closest to the reef will be in somewhat shallower water than those set on the other side of the boat. To maximise your coverage of the water, run a deeper diving lure on the outside of the boat (furthest from the reef edge) and a shallower diver on the side closest to the reef.

RIGS FOR REEFS

Depending on the depth of water over the reef and how much current is running, you may need to use enough sinker weight in the rig to get the bait down to the fish.

REEF TROLLING OPTIONS

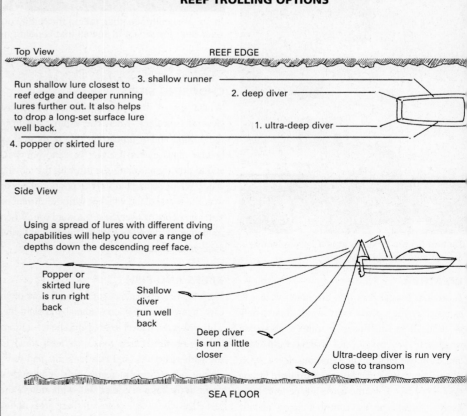

Top View

REEF EDGE

Run shallow lure closest to reef edge and deeper running lures further out. It also helps to drop a long-set surface lure well back.

3. shallow runner

2. deep diver

1. ultra-deep diver

4. popper or skirted lure

Side View

Using a spread of lures with different diving capabilities will help you cover a range of depths down the descending reef face.

Popper or skirted lure is run right back

Shallow diver run well back

Deep diver is run a little closer

Ultra-deep diver is run very close to transom

SEA FLOOR

Reef trolling techniques

Where the reef is shallow with little current but considerable wave action, unweighted baits and shallow running lures will reach the fish but be less likely to get caught up and snagged on the reef. Deep reef rigs are often based on the Paternoster style, which has the sinker hanging below either single or several dropper lines, armed with bait-laden hooks. Shallow reef covered with turbulent water can often be fished effectively with a running sinker rig that allows the sinker to slide all the way down onto the hook.

WASH FISHING

BOMBORAS

Bomboras are essentially small rocky islands that don't quite make it to the surface. They can be seen as isolated areas of white water well away from the shoreline and as such are extremely productive places to look for fish. They attract both resident species and pelagics and have the added virtue of being worth fishing in almost any conditions, provided you can do so with safety.

Calm areas off headlands are deceptive. Be wary before venturing too close, it always pays to stand off for a long while before moving in close.

Bomboras are small reefs that come close enough to the surface for waves to break across them. They are incredibly productive places to fish, but also require anglers to have good boating skills and to use commonsense.

CAMOUFLAGE AND LURE COLOUR

Baitfish use the camouflage of the bubbles and white water of breaking waves to hide from predators like tailor, salmon, kingfish, bream and snapper. This is why brightly coloured lures or those with dramatic counter-shading (light belly, dark back) can be more effective than plain chrome or white. An alternative is to use noisy surface lures, like poppers or propeller-baits that churn the water when moved. These tend to create small, open pockets of relatively clear water, which allow fish to zero in on them.

ISLANDS AND HEADLANDS

Wash areas around islands and headlands are comprised of a solid rock edge emerging from the water, a surge area of breaking water, and then a broad fringe of gradually thinning surface foam. Baitfish schools often move along the rock face under cover of this surface foam, running the gauntlet between resident predators and the pelagic species near the wash's outer edges. Depending on the direction of the weather, the seaward side of islands will generally produce more big fish than the inshore side, but with the judicious use of berley and live baits, even the relatively calmer inshore island edges can provide good fishing.

LIFT AND SAFETY

The wash areas that attract fish are caused by wave action that can pose significant

Have a variety of equipment ready rigged for fishing around washes and bomboras. You never know what you'll need next, often quickly!

risks to angler safety. As waves roll in toward bomboras, the shelving bottom makes the moving water ramp up into steep walls that can pick up a boat and dash it onto the rocks with disastrous results. If you look at such areas though, you can usually see where the waves start to lift and become steep. To stay safe, you should never bring your boat inside that line. Most times, you can reach the productive water with a good cast from beyond the 'lift' area. If you can't, then concentrate on fishing the outer fringes of the bombora or perhaps, be prudent and accept that conditions are too rough on the day to fish that place in safety.

TACKLE AND TECHNIQUE

Use relatively light line and rods with fine tips for casting when wash fishing. If you hook large, stubborn species like kingfish or cobia in shallow water, pace the fight. After ensuring a solid hookup, take things easy and maintain just enough pressure on the fish to keep a tight line while you slowly drive the boat away. In a remarkable number of cases, the fish will follow you out into deeper water, where you can afford to fight it more vigorously.

WASH FISHING AND CASTING SKILLS

The ability to cast accurately and far enough to reach fish is fundamental to a great number of fishing styles, but seldom is it more important than when wash fishing. Often, strong wave action close in to wash areas means that you will need to cast that little bit further to reach the fish while still keeping the boat outside the danger zone. Fishing with heavy-duty threadlines is a

Above: For safety, always fish down current and down wind of a wash. That way you'll never end up drifting into the hazard.

Below: Australia has many billfish species, but none as prolific or well known as the black marlin, Makaira indica. This fish weighed 149 kilograms and was an outstanding angling achievement in a small boat.

fast track to better casting performance, but you can, with practice, cast the required distances with overhead reels too. To maximise your ability to cast the distance, you will need to match line strength, casting weight and rod style and always fish your reels fully loaded with line.

OFFSHORE AND GAME FISHING

AUSTRALIAN BILLFISH SPECIES

The billfish available to anglers in Australian waters are marlin, of which there are three: black marlin, blue marlin, and striped marlin. There are also sailfish (the Pacific variety), shortbilled spearfish and broadbill swordfish. Black marlin are known to attain weights in excess of 700 kilograms, but are commonly caught between 50 and 150 kilograms. Blue marlin can exceed 500 kilograms but are common between 70 and 100 kilograms, while striped marlin are most often caught between 50 and 150 kilograms but can attain weights in excess of 200 kilograms. Pacific sailfish are mostly caught around 35 to 80 kilograms and the much rarer shortbill spearfish is usually captured in weights around 10 to 20 kilograms, only infrequently being encountered at much over 40 kilograms. Broadbill are still something of an enigma in Australian gamefishing circles, being rarely taken on regulation gamefishing tackle by recreational fishermen but appearing occasionally in catches by commercial long-liners on the NSW south coast.

BILLFISH DIET AND BAITS

Billfish are sufficiently large and fast to feed on almost anything that swims, except the largest sharks and cetaceans. They also eat diminutive forage like anchovies and garfish, as well as a range of popular baitfish, like yellowtail, cowanyoung, slimy mackerel and pilchards.

Anglers seeking seriously big billfish, such as the 500 kilogram black marlin off Cairns in far-north Queensland, or the giant blue marlin

that roam the NSW coast, can confidently troll baits as large as whole bonito, shark mackerel, striped tuna, mackerel tuna, or even school-sized yellowfin. Popular marlin baits in NSW also include whole frigate mackerel, large sea mullet, and tailor, while in the tropics, fish like long-toms and wolf herring (known as 'cricket bats') are used. All these species regularly appear in billfish stomach contents, as do stranger food choices, like boarfish, Rays bream, nannygai, snook, trevally and toadfish. Sometimes in southern Queensland, Pacific sailfish and marlin will develop a fixation for feeding on swarms of surface-schooling toadfish and more than once, stomach contents of black marlin have revealed fish as disparate as juvenile striped saltwater catfish and sand flathead.

WHERE BILLFISH LIVE

Billfish generally are distributed widely throughout Australian waters but certain species are more prevalent than others are in particular regions. For example, while there is overlap between the ranges of black, blue and striped marlin, they each do have areas in which they are most numerous and more commonly encountered.

GAMEFISHING FOR BILLFISH

Billfish, such as marlin, sailfish and broadbill swordfish are all large, fast-swimming predators that have little to fear except from the very largest oceanic sharks. They are sought by anglers mainly trolling lures and baits, but will also fall to chunk-baits or live baits fished in a berley trail at anchor or on the drift. In Australia, broadbill swordfish are usually pursued over abyssal canyons at

This mackerel tuna would make an excellent bait for marlin if rigged and trolled whole, or could be filleted or cubed into smaller baits for yellowfin tuna, kingfish or snapper.

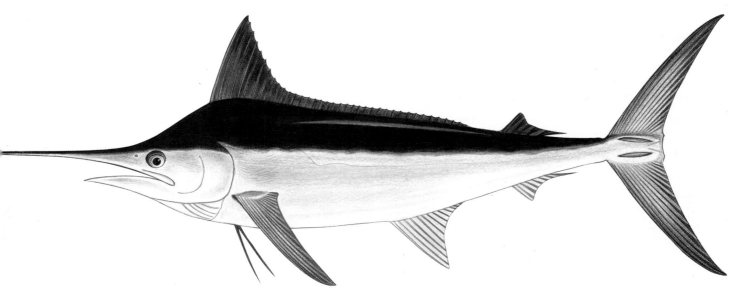

Black Marlin

night, using large live or dead squid for bait, rigged with a chemical light-stick to help attract the fish to the bait.

Sailfish will take trolled lures, but trolled baits work better, while marlin will variously take live baits, trolled lures or baits and occasionally, also chunk baits in a berley trail, aimed at other fish, such as yellowfin tuna.

BLACK MARLIN PROFILE

Black marlin are characterised by having body depths greater than the height of the frontal lobe of their first dorsal fins and for having their second dorsal fin begin just ahead of the second anal fin. Colouration is generally dark blue to black back with silver sides, exhibiting some iridescent vertical barring. The bills of black marlin also tend to be shorter and thicker than those of other marlins of equivalent size. The bulge of the forehead is pronounced and in adults, the pectoral fins are rigid and do not fold down easily alongside the body.

On the east coast, black marlin are found from the tropical tip of Cape Yorke Peninsula, right down to Tasmania, as well as the waters surrounding Lord Howe Island and Norfolk Island. They are rarely encountered in the shallow, often turbid waters of the eastern Gulf of Carpentaria, nor in Bass Strait or along the southern coastline of the Australian landmass. Their range resumes in the north from Gove, runs across the Northern Territory coastline and down through the coastal waters of the Kimberley and Western Australia as far as Albany.

There are annual migrations of black marlin down the East Australian coast, lasting from about spring to autumn, when they are thought to move offshore until the following spring and summer. Many of these fish stay within the confines of the Continental Shelf, and some come in close enough to the coast to be targeted by small boat operators or even by landbased fishermen.

Black marlin from the north-west coast of Australia are known to travel to parts of the Indian ocean south of Indonesia from March to late April and this movement is thought to be for spawning purposes, the fish returning to the north-west coast again in late spring.

'Runs' of marlin can be separated into roughly two age groups. One group comprises one to two years old (weighing from 15 to 30 kg) and two to four years old (weighing from 30 to 70 kg) and these fish are common in late spring through summer in north Queensland grounds such as Cape Bowling Green, Mooloolaba and Moreton Bay. Another group of adult fish (weighing from 70 to 150 kg) are encountered during summer and early autumn, usually around significant inshore reefs and shoals or close to the drop off where Continental Shelf waters fall away into oceanic depths. Significant grounds for these fish range from Moreton Bay wide, down through Coffs Harbour, Port Stephens and Sydney to The Sir John Young Banks off Nowra, and the far south coast grounds of Narooma, Bermagui and Merimbula. In late autumn and early winter, the usual pattern is for most black marlin to disperse eastward into the open ocean, where they are thought to remain until spring and early summer. At this time, they seem to follow the bait schools back inshore again as water temperatures rise and onshore winds concentrate feeding activity closer to the coast.

Black marlin are known to exceed 700 kg in weight, but from about 200 to 500 kg, they can be regarded as the prime breeding stock from which all spawning recruitment originates. September through October and November are the peak aggregation months for big spawning black marlin off the Queensland coast from Cairns northward. It is widely held that male black marlin mature sexually much earlier than females. The sex ratio of marlin stocks appears to change too as the fish get older; there being roughly equal numbers of males and females when fish are sampled in sizes from 10 to 60 kg, but this changes significantly as fish get older and larger. Fish less than 100 kg are usually males, while fish over 200 kg are usually females.

Black marlin are usually targeted with high speed trolling lures, skip baits, and swimming baits of mackerel and small tuna, but they will also take live baits, either slow-trolled or drift-fished. They have also been known to take large dead baits, set deep for sharks, as well as chunks of fish flesh, fed over the back of the boat in a cube trail, aimed at yellowfin tuna.

Juvenile fish (to 50 kg) can be successfully targeted on light tackle (six to 15 kg) but for fish in excess of 100 kg, 24 kg tackle is advisable and full chair-rods with 36 or 60 kg line class tackle will be necessary to tangle with the really big fish.

BLUE MARLIN PROFILE

Blue marlin share the black marlin characteristic of having a body depth greater than the dorsal height, but their second dorsal begins slightly behind the front of the second anal fin. The forehead may be slightly more concave than that of black marlin, but the most telling characteristic is that the pectorals will fold flat easily against the body. Colouration can be misleading, for while the overall hue of the back and flanks is blue to blue silver, almost any marlin can when excited flash iridescent blue. An additional identification clue with blue marlin is that its bars are often formed of light blue dots.

Blue marlin share much of the distribution range of black marlin, in terms of coastal coverage, (with the exception of the entire northern and southern landmass coastlines) but their preference for greater water depths usually see them caught further out from the coast than black marlin. Statistically, you are unlikely to encounter large blue marlin in waters less than 100 metres deep, which alone probably

All gamefish feed on squid, in fact they probably eat more squid than any other food. Yet most game fishermen, partly through convenience and partly through ignorance of this fact, are content to use lures. Even these lures however closely resemble squid — the skirt mimicking the tentacles trailing behind the body and the use of large eyes seen on many lures also emulating the large eyes of squid.

While skirted gamefishing lures are usually well made and attractive to both fish and the anglers who fish for them, nothing is as effective as the real thing, not even close. Freshly caught squid, or squid that have been quickly frozen after capture, will out-fish lures by a wide margin, if rigged correctly. This is how it is done.

To rig a squid for either drifting or trolling you will need a length of leader material — either heavy monofilament or multi-strand wire, a suitable hook such as the Mustad 7731 or Sea Demon (size 8/0 to 10/0). You'll also need about a metre of .8mm galvanised tie-wire, which you can buy from any hardware store. A sharp knife and a pair of scissors finish off the list.

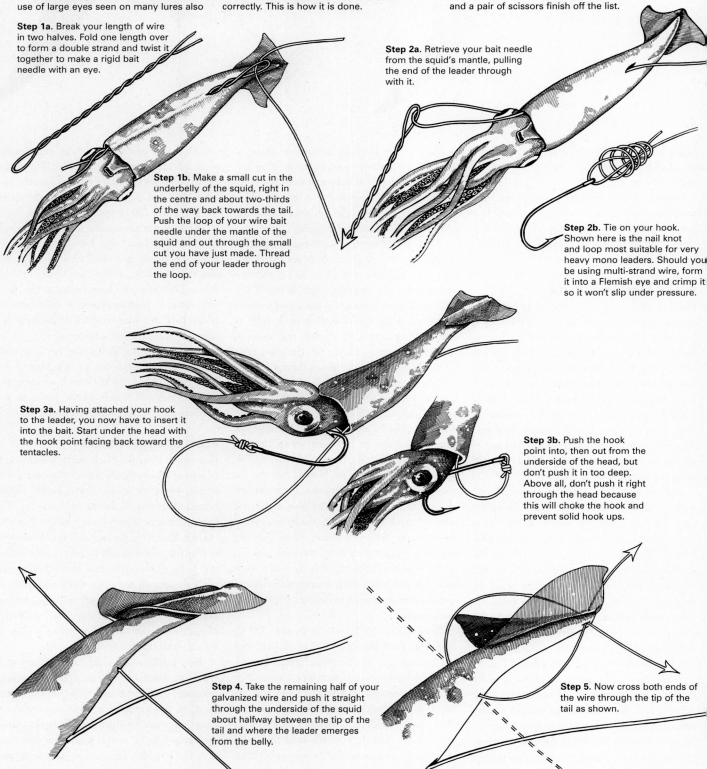

Step 1a. Break your length of wire in two halves. Fold one length over to form a double strand and twist it together to make a rigid bait needle with an eye.

Step 1b. Make a small cut in the underbelly of the squid, right in the centre and about two-thirds of the way back towards the tail. Push the loop of your wire bait needle under the mantle of the squid and out through the small cut you have just made. Thread the end of your leader through the loop.

Step 2a. Retrieve your bait needle from the squid's mantle, pulling the end of the leader through with it.

Step 2b. Tie on your hook. Shown here is the nail knot and loop most suitable for very heavy mono leaders. Should you be using multi-strand wire, form it into a Flemish eye and crimp it so it won't slip under pressure.

Step 3a. Having attached your hook to the leader, you now have to insert it into the bait. Start under the head with the hook point facing back toward the tentacles.

Step 3b. Push the hook point into, then out from the underside of the head, but don't push it in too deep. Above all, don't push it right through the head because this will choke the hook and prevent solid hook ups.

Step 4. Take the remaining half of your galvanized wire and push it straight through the underside of the squid about halfway between the tip of the tail and where the leader emerges from the belly.

Step 5. Now cross both ends of the wire through the tip of the tail as shown.

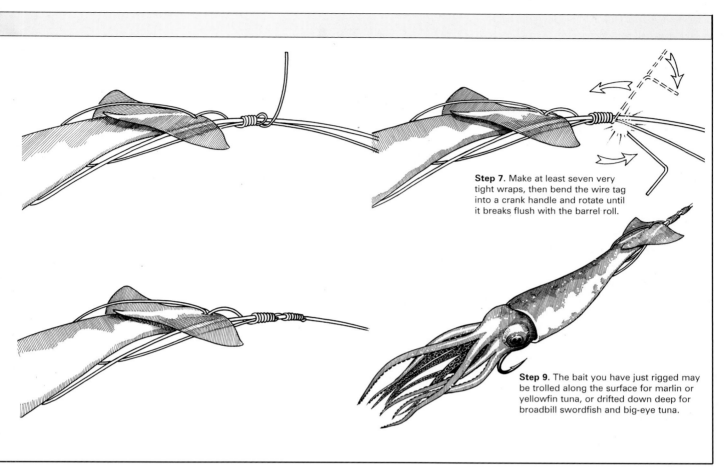

Step 7. Make at least seven very tight wraps, then bend the wire tag into a crank handle and rotate until it breaks flush with the barrel roll.

Step 9. The bait you have just rigged may be trolled along the surface for marlin or yellowfin tuna, or drifted down deep for broadbill swordfish and big-eye tuna.

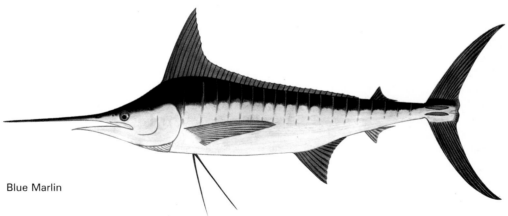

Blue Marlin

accounts for their relatively infrequent capture by recreational anglers. Large game boats, and skilled anglers equipped with heavy tackle are however, making inroads into these areas.

Little is known about blue marlin spawning locations, regimes, and periods, but there is a general belief that Australian stocks spawn anywhere north of 10 degrees below the equator and probably year round as blue marlin larvae have been found in various northern waters from October to March.

There are large southward seasonal movements of blue marlin down the coast each summer and these appear to be made up of more than just one group of fish: several groups might come, in pulses or waves, according to suitable water temperatures, weather conditions and bait availability.

Weight for age is difficult to assess with blue marlin, as research has been sketchy and significant variations in growth rate seem to occur for similarly aged fish, probably a result of highly variable food supplies. For example, research in Hawaiian waters indicates that a female of 175 kg could be anywhere between five and 17 years of age, while a 75 kg male might be either three years old or 17 years old! What is known, is that female blue marlin grow in excess of 900 kg and males rarely exceed 170 kg.

Recreational fishing hot spots for blue marlin (beyond the 200 metre depth line) are from Mooloolaba and Tweed Heads in the north, through various grounds from Byron Bay to Port Macquarie, Port Stephens, Sydney and Jervis Bay to Bermagui and Tathra. For really big

blue marlin, the far south coast of New South Wales is presently the recognised hub of activity. Angling tactics for blue marlin centre on towing large lures and large baits and anglers seriously targeting these fish should not be using less than 24 kg tackle.

STRIPED MARLIN PROFILE

Striped marlin are much more slender fish than either blue or black marlin, their body depth usually being equal to or less than the height of their primary dorsal fin. Also, the anus is quite close to the origin of the first anal fin, the lower jaw is quite long and the body is not as wide across the back as either blue or black marlin. There is often a pronounced scoop in the forehead of the striped marlin but the head shape differs from that of blue marlin in that the bill is much longer and more slender.

Striped marlin occur through much the same range as blue marlin with the addition of a population found south and east of Albany, well round into the Great Australian Bight. They spawn in the general Southwest Pacific, as far south as 30 degrees below the equator (roughly opposite Coffs Harbour). Their spawning season is somewhat shorter and later than that of black marlin, being from November through December off the East Coast and October to December off Australia's northwest coast.

The recreational fishery for striped marlin on the east coast is centred around Mooloolaba and Cape Moreton in Queensland, Coffs Harbour, Port Macquarie, Cape Hawke and Port Stephens, Sydney, Wollongong, Nowra, Bermagui and Merimbula in New South Wales, and Point Hicks in Victoria. There is also an emerging striped marlin fishery in Tasmania, from Cape Barren Island to St Helens. On the West Coast, most recreationally caught striped marlin come from around Exmouth.

Growing to 200 kg, there is not the same pronounced difference in sizes between the sexes that occurs in blue and black marlin. Hawaiian long-line research indicates growth rates for striped marlin in the order of 23 kg at two years old, 43 kg at three years old, and something like 50 kg at 4 years old. Growth rates for New Zealand (and possibly Australian) striped marlin seem somewhat better, with three year old fish reaching over 90 kg and five year old fish reaching more than 100 kilograms.

Fish off the West Coast tend to be slightly smaller than those off the East Coast and in both fisheries, striped marlin are most often targeted where deep drop-offs occur on the edge of the Continental Shelf. Localised differences arising from regional food supplies and water conditions, can mean that striped marlin may be encountered in quite shallow waters from time to time.

Since striped marlin are generally longer and more slender fish for a given weight, they are commonly targeted on lighter fishing tackle, with many anglers rating them as a worthy opponent on 10 or 15 kg tackle but somewhat over-gunned on 24 kilogram. Striped marlin are very active fish, fast and athletic, and by far the most spectacular leapers of all the billfish, often taking off on repeated, low 'greyhounding' sequences of jumps. It would be foolish to consider these elegant fish an easy target however, and expert skippers go to great lengths to prepare smaller baits and lures so they run just right and stand up to the rigours of extended trolling use. Striped marlin can sometimes be approached stealthily by a boat as they fin lazily on the surface or work surface schools of baitfish. Many anglers are taking a leaf

Striped marlin

from the book of overseas gamefishers in such situations and using heavy threadline tackle to cast live baits to these finning fish, often with spectacularly good results.

Striped marlin are also aggressive fish that can be teased up within casting range of a boat, giving rise to a small but growing number of anglers taking them on as a saltwater fly target, which may well be the pinnacle fishing experience for Australian saltwater flyfishers.

BROADBILL SWORDFISH PROFILE

Broadbill swordfish are generally brown to black in colouration with a single high frontal dorsal fin, and a long bill flattened into a sword, hence the name. Reportedly reaching weights over 500 kg, most Australian broadbill caught on the East Coast are between 75 and 100 kilograms.

The distribution of broadbill is astonishingly large being virtually right around Australia except for the top end between Cape York and the Kimberley. It is the only billfish known to be caught throughout the Great Australian Bight and circum-Tasmania, its preference for generally cooler waters obviously being a factor in this. Capable of tolerating water temperatures from five to 27 degrees Celsius, broadbill can cheerfully cope with surface temperatures that get down to 13 degrees. An astonishing fact about these fish is their ability to adjust rapidly to temperature variations of as much as 19 degrees. Acoustic tagging studies have revealed that

broadbill engage in massive vertical migrations from the surface waters at night to depths of up to 600 metres during the day. In these studies, many broadbill were found to be spending the daylight hours right down on the bottom on the drop off of the Continental Shelf, only rising into the upper water column as night fell.

This contrasts markedly with the behaviour of Eastern Pacific broadbill, which will commonly be seen swimming or lolling at the surface during the day. This enables fishermen to troll for them with whole fish baits or fillets. In Australia, the principle bait used is large squid, fished with the enhancement of a chemical light stick, to assist the fish to find the bait in the inky blackness of the night hours. Broadbill swordfish are occasional catches for commercial longliners working the deep shelf canyons off Bermagui and Eden in southern New South Wales, but are still something of a rare recreational catch. In fact, up until 1989, no one had managed to catch a broadbill in Australian waters on regulation gamefishing tackle and have it weigh more than the line class in use. Since then, several fish over 50 kg have been caught, with a 106 kg fish brought in off Eden in 1991.

Broadbill are such an uncommon recreational catch because they spend the bulk of their time well offshore in depths between 200 and 600 metres, and in places where the seas are likely to be rough. Fishing such places at night is not for the faint-hearted or those lacking in financial clout as the boats needed for this work need to be large, specially equipped for night fishing and consequently expensive.

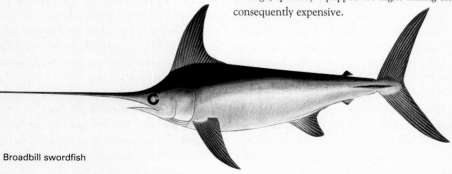

Broadbill swordfish

Indo-Pacific sailfish

INDO-PACIFIC SAILFISH PROFILE

Sailfish are the ballerinas of the billfish community—generally long and slender, with a magnificently extravagant dorsal or 'sail' and spectacular colouration. Pacific sailfish are wonderful jumpers; they can accelerate to a top speed of over 70 kilometres per hour and come to a dead stop again in mere seconds, making them always an impressive sight. Sailfish bills are thin and rapier-like and their pelvic fins are elongated into long, thin ribbons that might reach halfway back toward the anal fin.

There are two sailfishes, the Atlantic and Indo-Pacific, of which the latter is found in Australian waters. The distribution of Indo-Pacific sailfish is essentially throughout tropical and warmer temperate waters. That translates to an area from Geraldton in Western Australia to the Kimberley, with the most famed western grounds being off Exmouth. Sailfish also occur throughout Northern Territory waters, are relatively scarce in the shallow turbid reaches of the Gulf of Carpentaria but become common again to the east and south of Cape York in Queensland. From here, they occupy similar environmental niches as juvenile black marlin and striped marlin, being plentiful around all the Queensland islands in season and a possibility as far south as Sydney or some years even down at The Banks off Nowra.

Sailfish are not strong fighters, often being targeted on light line classes, with eight and 10 kg tackle being commonly used, but line classes as light as six, four, and even two kilograms have been successfully employed. The real difficulty with sailfish on light tackle is not landing them, but getting the hook to bite in that hard mouth in the first place. This leads to the popular use of such hook-friendly baits as garfish, which being slender are easily taken into the sailfish's mouth and even when folded over on the strike, do not tend to 'choke' or fill the bend of the hook. With little to prevent the hook taking a firm hold, all that remains is for the hook to be sharp enough and small enough for light tackle to pull it in past the barb.

Finding sailfish is relatively simple in season (September through May in most of their range). Experienced anglers search them out by working recognised aggregation areas, where coastal currents collide and form eddies that hold vast baitfish schools—sometimes at the surface, but more often down at some depth. These bait schools can be spotted at the surface by the appearance of 'nervous' or ruffled water or circling seabirds, or located down deep by watching the echo sounder screen as the boat is trolled through the likely areas.

When a bait school is located, the boat is stopped and multi-hook bait-jigs are dropped down to them. The live wells are stocked up with baits and a trolling pattern is set up to take either lures, dead baits or live baits close to where the bait schools are located. When several bait schools are found, the ideal trolling pattern is to run from one bait-ball to the next, trolling back and forth until fish are sighted or a strike is taken.

PACIFIC SHORT-BILLED SPEARFISH PROFILE

Looking not unlike either a juvenile marlin or a sailfish or something of a cross between the two, Pacific shortbilled spearfish have as the name suggests a proportionately shorter bill than that of either marlin or sailfish. The dorsal fin, like the sailfish's, is a continuous ribbon along the fish's back but is nowhere near as high or spectacularly coloured as the sailfish's impressive fin.

A much smaller fish than either of its near relatives too, the shortbilled spearfish rarely exceeds 45 kg and is quite often taken at weights of 15 to 20 kg. Some inevitably are taken by commercial longliners, but are rarely prized as table fish. Recreational anglers will most often take spearfish on trolled fish baits or smaller lures and oddly enough, from mostly temperate waters, making their likely range in eastern Australia from Moreton Bay to Port Stephens and occasionally Sydney or Narooma.

In plain fish fighting terms, shortbilled spearfish do not require very sophisticated or heavy tackle to catch them, the reality is however, that their capture is so rare that it is virtually impossible to realistically target them to the exclusion of larger billfish. Since every other billfish does demand the very best tackle and suitable line classes to have much hope of landing what you hook, it is inevitable that most spearfish captures will be something of an anti-climax, other than the excitement and satisfaction catching something unusual.

GAMEFISHING FOR TUNA

Tuna are among the fastest fish in the sea and, in one form or another, are distributed worldwide. Australia has six large tunas: yellowfin, bigeye, Southern bluefin, Northern bluefin, (also known as 'longtails') dogtooth tuna, and albacore. There are

Pacific short-billed spearfish

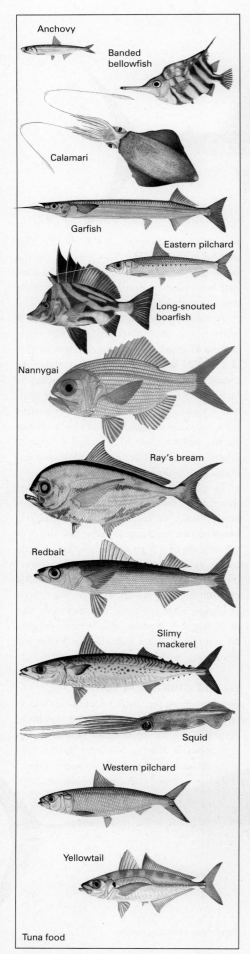

Anchovy
Banded bellowfish
Calamari
Garfish
Eastern pilchard
Long-snouted boarfish
Nannygai
Ray's bream
Redbait
Slimy mackerel
Squid
Western pilchard
Yellowtail

Tuna food

also several smaller tunas - mackerel tuna, striped tuna, frigate mackerel and bonito. Most tuna are caught by trolling or casting lures, or by setting out live baits of smaller fish or with a method known as 'cubing' - a form of chunk-fishing that involves drifting a hook-bearing chunk down a berley trail of other, hook-less fish pieces.

TUNA FOOD

Proportionally, fish dominate the diet of tunas in coastal waters, but are supplemented by seasonal runs of prawns, as far out as the Continental Shelf. Out in the open ocean, vast schools of arrow squid take centre stage, and for the very largest tunas, even roaming schools of striped tuna and frigate mackerel are simply something else to run down and eat. Mitre squid and Northwest pink squid also feature in the inshore diet of tunas, as do both Northern and Southern calamari, most often in late summer when there are vast numbers of their juveniles about after summer spawning events. In summer off the NSW coast too, schools of striped tuna may also feed extensively on planktonic lobster larvae.

The fish that tunas eat range in size from tiny slivers of life, like glass minnows and some of the smaller tuna themselves. Predictable bait species include yellowtail and cowanyoung, slimy mackerel, garfish, pilchards and marays, anchovies, hardyheads and sandy sprats (also called 'whitebait'). Tuna also eat weird offshore ooglies like Rays bream, nannygai, bellowsfish, boarfish and redbait. Anglers watching prawn trawlers haul their nets and discard their by-catch at sea will also realise that yellowfin tuna gather round such events and snap up almost any variety of other unfortunate fishes. In late spring and early summer, small tailor fall prey to tuna as post-spawn booms of two to three centimetre juvenile choppers gather around inshore reefs and estuary mouths. In an ironic twist, large adult tailor can also be caught with juvenile tuna and bonito inside them at this time of year.

STRIPED TUNA PROFILE

Striped tuna, also known as Skipjack, stripie, or 'Aku' (Hawaii) have the typical cylindrical body shape of all tunas, but carry their weight well back toward the tail. The body narrows rapidly from a fat jellybean shape to a slender, hard-scuted caudal fin. The back is black to purple, with silver sides and a series of pronounced grey/black stripes running along the flanks and belly. Most often encountered by anglers at three to four kilograms in weight, stripies can grow to a metre long and 20 kg, although it is uncommon to catch them over five kilograms.

Striped tuna are distributed extensively through most of the world's oceans, but in Australian waters are essentially a fish of the east and west coasts, with a narrower band of distribution running eastward from Cape Leeuwin in Western Australia. This presence extends into the Great Australian Bight as far as Kangaroo Island off the South Australian coast.

Spawning is thought to take place in the Coral Sea off the East Coast and in the Indian Ocean northwest of Australia's Kimberley region.

In terms of inshore distribution, striped tuna along the East Coast are most often encountered along the 50 metre depth contour and seawards, but will occasionally enter large southern estuaries and bays when there is sufficiently clean water and concentrations of baitfish to attract them. On the west and east coasts, they are known to frequent areas of coral reef shoal, seamounts and the interface areas between conflicting oceanic currents.

Striped tuna can be taken by trolling small metal slugs or skirted lures and occasionally, a very large stripie might take a live bait set out for some other fish, but by and large, they are a lure fishing prospect. Anglers in small nimble boats can enjoy astounding sport fishing by approaching to within casting distance of surface feeding schools of striped tuna and casting metal slugs and chrome lures in front of the churning school of fish. High speed spinning tackle is required — either threadline or overhead — and good knots, well set and smooth-running drags and a particular mix of angler aggression and patience.

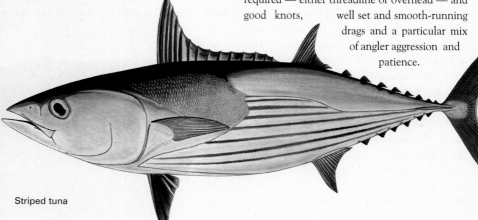

Striped tuna

Striped tuna are not only exciting sportfish in their own right; they make excellent bait and berley for a range of other species from bream and snapper to other tuna. Fished whole, live, and slow trolled around a school of their fellows, they are first-class baits for big sharks, marlin and heavyweight yellowfin tuna.

ALBACORE PROFILE

Albacore are a prized food fish, with the reputation of being 'the chicken of the sea'. Known also as longfin tuna and 'Albies', these fat, sleek fish gather in dense midwater schools, rarely feeding at the surface but often being a voracious deep and mid-water predator of planktonic crustaceans, squid and small fish.

Distributed right around Australia except for the shallow northern waters between Cape York and Darwin, albacore prefer water temperatures between 16 and 22 degrees Celsius, which they find most readily off Coffs Harbour and Eden in New South Wales. Another concentration of albacore can be found out wide of the Great Barrier Reef, roughly east of Cairns.

Growing to 40 kg or more, albacore are most often encountered at weights between eight and 15 kilograms. Their growth rates are astonishingly fast, attaining fork lengths of 38 cm to nearly 60 cm in their first year, at which size they probably weigh something in the order of three to four kilograms. They then grow at a rate of approximately 12 cm per year until aged six or seven years, at which time the growth rate slows. This means that fish of 10 kg are likely to be something like four to five years old.

Albacore frequent water depths of 100 metres or more and are often found in the upper layers of these depths, wherever forage is most plentiful and conditions of temperature and oxygen concentration are to their liking. In New South Wales, anglers mainly fish for albacore from September to December, then again from April to May. The prime area for albacore is the mid-south to far south coast of New South Wales, meaning that anglers embarking from ports such as the Shoalhaven, Narooma and Bermagui are more likely to target and find them than anglers fishing further northward. Even so, trips of considerable distance will have to be undertaken to put your boat in the best albacore country, so if you want to target these fish, you will need to own or have access to a boat in excess of five or six metres.

Albacore fishing methods vary from high speed trolling of skirted lures, to slow trolling dead or live baits, berleying and chumming with fish pieces and fishing with 'cube' baits of fish flesh. Some anglers locating a school of albacore use heavy hookless metal jigs to excite the school and bring them closer to the surface where baits can be floated down to them.

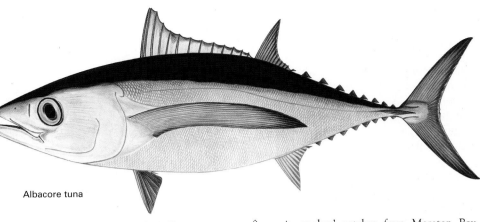

Albacore tuna

YELLOWFIN TUNA PROFILE

Yellowfin tuna are the primary target species of anglers chasing tuna. This is because they are available in generally greater numbers and sizes than either Southern bluefin or Northern bluefin tuna (longtail). The growth potential of Southern bluefin is undoubtedly greater than that of yellowfin, but stocks of this over-exploited fish were so severely damaged by commercial overfishing during the 1970s and 1980s that there are very few truly large bluefin available, even now, several decades after the damage was done. Certainly the very largest fish frequent wide offshore areas scarcely within the fishing range of recreational fishers, so the yellowfin, being much more inclined to inhabit coastal waters are more often targeted.

School yellowfin commonly run from six to 10 kg, while what most specialist tuna anglers classify as serious yellowfin start to tip the scales at around 40 to 60 kg and go all the way to 200 kilograms.

Distributed mostly along the eastern and western coasts yellowfin range from the tip of Cape York down to Eaglehawk Neck in Tasmania and from the Western Australian border in the Bight west and northward as far as the outer Arafura Sea. Principal recreational fishing areas for yellowfin tuna coincide roughly with the main commercial fishing areas, which range from north of Brisbane, throughout New South Wales, offshore from wide of Fraser Island to the outer southern edge of the Great Barrier Reef and also closer in toward Cairns. Mostly, big yellowfin (over 50 kg)

figure in anglers' catches from Moreton Bay south to Green Cape, with really big fish (over 100 kg) being more of a southern phenomenon than a northern one.

To find yellowfin, you need to look for a combination of forage (such as dense schools of baitfish or squid) and suitable depth, bottom shape and current. Add in the seasonal factors of water temperature and greater food availability and it is easy to see why some places produce big yellowfin more consistently than others do. Such places include Moreton Bay Wide, the Coffs Harbour canyons, various inshore reefs scattered from Port Macquarie to Port Stephens and the legendary grounds off Sydney of Broken Bay Wide, The Peak, Brown's Mountain, The Marley Wreck and others. There is also good yellowfin fishing throughout the south coast, all the way from the reefs off Wollongong, to the Sir John Young Banks off Nowra, Montague Island near Narooma, The Six Mile and Twelve Mile reefs near Bermagui and various reef complexes from Merimbula to Tathra and Eden.

Yellowfin take trolled skirted lures, big magnum-sized minnows, live striped tuna, slimy mackerel or yellowtail slow trolled, or skipped at high speed as dead baits. They also take slimy mackerel and yellowtail and frigate mackerel as drifted live baits and are particularly susceptible to drifted cubes or chunk baits of any of those in a berley trail. On the far south coast from Narooma downwards, the use of live reef fish, such as nannygai is also popular.

Yellowfin tuna

You can sometimes find yellowfin by looking for surface working schools of striped tuna or frigate mackerel, which the bigger tuna will shadow and prey upon. You can also utilise companion predators, such as bottlenose dolphins, which will often feed on the same baitfish schools as yellowfin. The dolphins serve as an indicator that there may be more predation going on from yellowfin, only down deeper and not showing directly on the surface.

BIGEYE TUNA PROFILE

Bigeye tuna are very much like yellowfin tuna. They are of similar colouration and it is only when both species get to adult stage that the differences become more apparent. For example, yellowfin tuna when mature, have long, graceful, sickle-shaped second dorsal and anal fins that are bright yellow and there is a blaze of yellow down the lateral line. Bigeye tuna have short, stumpy dorsal and anal fins, lack the golden blaze down the flanks and gill plates and have a markedly larger eye.

Distribution is similar to that of yellowfin tuna though not as extensive, nor are they as plentiful. Most big-eye tuna are caught by anglers fishing for yellowfin with deep-set live baits or by cubing. They generally favour offshore areas more than inshore, and deeper water rather than shallow. Baits and tackle and techniques are similar to those used for yellowfin, just fish deeper, and use slightly larger baits.

SOUTHERN BLUEFIN TUNA PROFILE

Southern bluefin tuna are a stout-bodied fish, of generally black to grey/blue on the back, silver on the flanks and belly, with a series of dots and marks that may be more apparent in some individuals than others. The median caudal keels (the flat ridges either side of the tail) are bright yellow and the anal fin and finlets are also yellow, tinged with black. A distinguishing feature of the species is the relatively short pectoral fins, something like a quarter or a fifth of the overall body length from nose to tail fork.

The distribution of this species of tuna gives the clue to its name, as on the east coast at least it is generally only found from Coffs Harbour southward, then right around the Tasmanian and Victorian, South Australian and Western Australian coasts. Curiously, the fish's range then extends right up the west coast as far as Exmouth, then further out to sea and continues northward as far as about 12 degrees south, which means it is well north of the Kimberley, hardly southern, but there you are.

Recreationally, anglers are most likely to encounter Southern bluefin tuna in schools of juvenile to young adult fish. There is an intermittent fishery for them in eastern Tasmanian waters from Maria Island down past Eaglehawk

Neck, a similarly fluky supply of fish around Port Fairy to Portland in western Victoria and around Port MacDonnell in South Australia.

The vast schools of Southern bluefin that used to be staple fare for the South Australian commercial fishing fleet were mostly an offshore proposition, beyond the reach of most recreational fishing craft. There are however some indications that inshore schools of smaller fish are starting to make a comeback, both here and in southern parts of Western Australia, as there are along the far south coast of New South Wales as far north as Sydney.

Growing to a massive 200 kg (potentially), but more often encountered by anglers in sizes from 10 to 30 kg, Southern bluefin tuna are hard fighters and excellent food fish. This last virtue is probably their undoing as a species, because the appetite people world-wide have for their flesh both as canned tuna, tuna steaks and as sashimi brought them to the edge of extinction some two decades ago. Since then, despite stringent controls and quota systems, they have still not yet fully recovered from this position.

You can target Southern bluefin tuna in these smaller sizes, by trolling small plastic squids and other high speed skirted lures, while larger fish will fall to seriously big-skirted lures and magnum minnows. Live bait in the form of slimy mackerel and jack mackerel will work for Southern bluefin tuna, as will the cubing techniques that are so effective on yellowfin.

NORTHERN BLUEFIN TUNA PROFILE

Northern bluefin, also known as Northern blues and longtail tuna, are just as highly prized as Southern bluefin for sashimi, but because of an unacceptably high level of dolphin bycatch, commercial fishing for Northern bluefin was officially suspended in 1986. This may account for the continued accessibility of Northern bluefin to recreational fishermen, that and the fact that they tend to be a lot more active inshore than Southern bluefin and so come within reach of more anglers.

A handsome and streamlined fish, Northern bluefin exhibit the body conformation that gives rise to their other more recently popular name of 'longtail' tuna. The head and body of these fish are robust and heavy-set, but the tail tapers much more gradually than that of Southern bluefin, striped tuna or even yellowfin.

Southern bluefin tuna

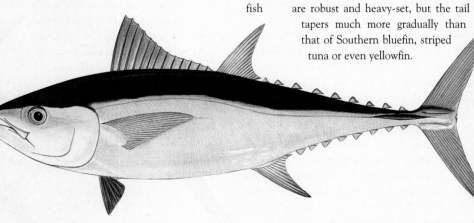

Northern bluefin tuna

Colouration is similar to Southern bluefin, tending more toward blackish blue with brilliant silver sides and belly, and the finlets are yellow tinged.

Distribution of Northern bluefin tuna overlaps that of Southern bluefin. Extending as far south as Green Cape in New South Wales, it continues northward right up the Queensland coast, across the Top End (where fish are characteristically much smaller than southern east coast specimens) and down the northern coast of Western Australia about as far south as Geographe Bay (near Busselton).

Curiously, more Northern bluefin are taken from the rocks in New South Wales than from boats, except for around Bermagui's Six Mile and Twelve Mile reefs. A thriving Northern bluefin boat fishery exists in and around Moreton Bay and to a lesser and more chancy extent in the Port Stephens estuary. In the far north of Australia vast schools of smallish (3 to 8 kg) Northern bluefin tuna are encountered just about anywhere you troll far enough offshore to find clean blue water. Average size of Moreton Bay longtails is around 8 to 10 kg, Port Stephens fish can be anywhere between 12 and 25 kg when they decide to show up, and fish to 35 kg have been taken by game fishermen in the Bermagui area.

Techniques that work for inshore schooling fish include live baiting, trolling minnows and skirted lures, and casting to pods of surface-working fish on baitfish schools. Realistic tackle for Northern blues depends greatly on the size of the fish and the circumstances in which you find them. In most cases, spinning tackle and rods two to two and half metres long and line classes from four to eight kilograms is all that is necessary. Live baiting gear can be overheads on jig stroker rods, with line from 6 to 10 kg being suitable.

MACKEREL TUNA PROFILE

Mackerel tuna are widespread, occurring from Merimbula northward to The Great Barrier Reef on the East Coast, and from Cape Leeuwin to the Northern Territory up the West Coast. Generally an inshore fish, the larger fish (from 12 to 20 kg) are nearly always encountered well offshore, but periodically, a run of bigger mackerel tuna will come well inshore even entering estuaries and bays. Typical fish in Moreton Bay run to eight kilograms with some six kilogram specimens, Port Stephens fish are usually six to eight kilograms, with sporadic occurrences of much smaller fish from two to three kilograms.

Mackerel tuna are a handsome greenish to silver fish, with the back half of their upper backs covered in thin wavy 'mackerel-style' markings. These tuna often run with schools of Spanish and spotted mackerel and thus came to be known as 'mackerel' tuna because they were always around

Above: Whilst the tuna mackerel regarded highly as a sportfish, it does not have great value as either bait or table fare.

Frigate mackerel

in mackerel season and tended to be taken by the same trolling methods used to catch mackerel.

Look for mackerel tuna around any offshore island washed by the East Australian Current and adjacent to large estuary systems that flush large quantities of baitfish in and out on the tides. Most inshore reefs carry visiting schools of mackerel tuna on a seasonal basis and peaks of activity for most inshore mackerel tuna are around late summer, and winter to spring. In places like Port Stephens, Broken Bay, the mouth of Sydney Harbour and also Botany Bay and Port Hacking, mackerel tuna can turn up any time there are large schools of baitfish around and westerly winds to create concentrations of fish for the mackerel tuna to attack.

Typical spin tackle for mackerel tuna in the smaller sizes can come right down to three and four kg line; unless you are experienced with light line and fast fish, four to six kg line is a more realistic minimum for the larger fish. Lures for casting generally need to be small chrome slugs and baitfish profiles, especially in central and southern New South Wales, but in Moreton Bay and tropical climes, minnows and slugs share top billing with surface poppers and saltwater flies.

Mackerel tuna are at best only marginal table fare, but do make acceptable sashimi or cold meat fish for salads. They are a passable bait species for bream, kingfish, snapper and other tunas, and make acceptable berley, but their chief value is as sportfish.

FRIGATE MACKEREL PROFILE

Frigate mackerel (also generally known as 'Leadenall' or simply as 'leadies') look very much like mackerel tuna to the untrained eye, right down to the carriage of wavy mackerel-type markings on the upper rear back. They are however a generally smaller fish and lack the distinguishing feature of four to five irregularly-shaped black smudges on the forward flanks, just near the pectoral fins. Mackerel tuna have these marks, frigate mackerel do not. The confusion between the two occurs most often when there is a run of exceptionally small mackerel tuna around at the same time that adult frigate mackerel are seasonally available.

Frigates make excellent live trolling baits for marlin and big yellowfin, especially when trolled around the school from which they came. They will take small trolled plastic squids, chrome slugs and baitfish profiles and tiny saltwater flies. They make first class strip baits and can be rigged as teasers for gamefishing sailfish and striped marlin as they are firm fleshed, the skin is tough and shiny and the size is perfect for rigging either as a hookless teaser or skip bait.

Distribution of frigate mackerel is mostly northward of the Victorian border.

BONITO PROFILE

There are two bonito species within Australian waters, the Australian bonito, which has grey/black line markings on both the upper and lower

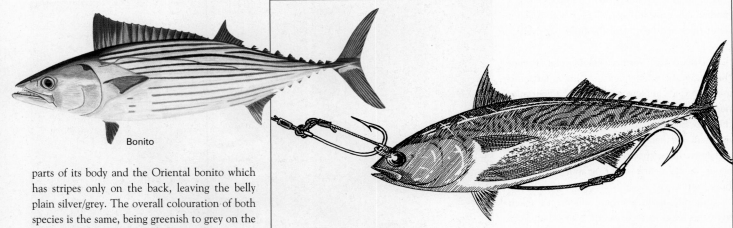

Bonito

This bait can be trolled or drifted for big sharks. The key to the rig is the use of wire and the placement of the second hook well back, just snicked under the skin, to cope with the habit many sharks have of taking the tail off a victim first.

parts of its body and the Oriental bonito which has stripes only on the back, leaving the belly plain silver/grey. The overall colouration of both species is the same, being greenish to grey on the back and silver on the flanks and belly.

All tuna have teeth, but the bonitos carry this trait a little further, having quite a mouthful of nasty little needles that can easily perforate careless fingers. They do not have the shearing teeth of the true mackerels however, so wire leaders are not necessary; heavy mono-filament is quite enough in most cases.

Bonito are excellent table fish provided you fillet them, cut the dark meat away from the area of the lateral line and skin the fillets, leaving a good centimetre of flesh under the skin. This will remove the blood-gorged outer flesh from the flesh you want to eat and leave it attached to the shiny skin, making first rate snapper baits.

Bonito will take trolled minnows and flies, and will occasionally attack surface poppers, but just love chrome jigs and baitfish profiles. You can spin for bonito around washes, drop jigs down to them over reefs and troll minnows or flies around island corners and headlands all with good effect.

Bonito will also take strip baits or live baits of slimy mackerel, garfish or yellowtail with gusto.

Most bonito encountered outside the Heads will be two to three kilograms, with some fish getting up toward six kilograms, while fish that enter large bays and estuaries can run from half a kilogram up to a kilogram and a half.

DEEP REEF FISHING

Many popular fish species can be found over deep reefs. For example snapper, while sometimes venturing into water about a metre deep, will inhabit reefs in depths greater than 200 metres. Morwong too, will inhabit both middle-depth to very deep reefs, Jackass morwong usually being found in water from 40 to 400 metres depth and Grey morwong preferring depths from 10 to 100 metres. Western Australian dhufish normally inhabit reefs in depths of 100 metres or more, except in autumn and winter, when large adults will move inshore to spawn over reefs as shallow as 20 metres. Mulloway, on the other hand, are mostly found in water of moderate depth, although some move as far offshore as the

Continental Shelf and depths up to 150 metres. To detect bites from fish in very deep water, many offshore anglers use gelspun lines, which have much greater bite sensitivity and, because of their low stretch, enable better hook setting as well.

GAMEFISHING FOR SHARKS

Gamefishers target sharks mostly by using whole dead fish baits or large fillets of fish accompanied by vast quantities of berley. Occasionally, very active and aggressive sharks, such as makos and hammerheads, will pursue trolled baits or even lures. Shark fishing offshore is usually done in very deep water, on or over the edge of the Continental Shelf. To maximise the chances of finding sharks within the relatively short time-spans allocated during fishing tournaments, several baits are set at various depths: at the surface, in midwater, and down deep as well.

NAVIGATIONAL AIDS

Initially the only navigation tools available for recreational offshore fishing were a compass and marine charts. Finding reefs was usually a combination of guesses and rough compass work, combined with line-of-sight positioning by landmarks. These days, with radar and GPS (the Global Positioning Satellite system) it is possible for anglers to plot courses to reefs, canyons and other fish-holding offshore features, even at night or in poor visibility conditions and even to places so far from shore that landmarks are irrelevant.

Below: When you are out wide at sea and there are no landmarks, you need some form of navigational aid to find your fishing spots and get back home again. A compass is a basic tool for this job, but a GPS is much better.

OFFSHORE BERLEY

Berley, offshore as elsewhere, is usually some form of natural fish food or cereal- based product that is dispensed from a boat either at anchor or as the boat drifts with prevailing wind and current. The main differences between estuary berley and offshore berley for example, are that the latter will tend to use more fish flesh and fish oil and a great deal more volume. Depending on the sort of fish you are after, you can set up a surface berley trail comprising mostly buoyant fish oils, and fish chunks. This works well for marlin, yellowfin tuna, kingfish or mackerel. Or, you can use a berley pot and some system of ladling out minced-up fish offal and lay down a sinking curtain of berley, a technique that works well for sharks. Because any surface-released berley is unlikely to reach deep bottom in any useful concentration, deep reef berleying is usually done with berley bombs–canisters loaded with berley that are lowered to a predetermined depth, where they are opened by remote trip devices.

OFFSHORE SAFETY EQUIPMENT

All State waterways authorities have mandatory safety equipment requirements for all boats heading offshore. These include such things as both smoke and rocket flares, a bright orange V-Sheet, approved life jackets for everyone on board, adequate anchoring gear, a bucket and lanyard, a fire extinguisher and a compass and some alternative method of propulsion, whether oars and paddles, an electric trolling motor or an auxiliary engine. You should also carry appropriate charts of the areas being fished, a waterproof torch, navigation lights, some form of sound signal device such as an air horn, or a bell or whistle, a marine radio, and an E.P.I.R.B. (Emergency Position Indicating Radio Beacon). It is also commonsense to anticipate being caught at sea without provisions and to carry sufficient fresh drinking water and emergency rations on board, for several days. A GPS (Global Positioning System) and a depth sounder will also facilitate your being found by a search and rescue team if you can give the depth of water under your keel and your exact position, updating both as required by marine radio.

OTHER GAMEFISHING SPECIES

There are many other species of Australian fish recognised and accepted as gamefish by National and International gamefishing associations. These include several species of tuna, various kingfish, mackerels, and other fish such as wahoo, dolphin fish (actually a true fish and nothing like a dolphin) and scores of trevallies and related species. There are scores of other fish that meet the gamefish criteria too, but these are mostly found only in some countries, some in several, but essentially all in places other than Australia.

Large and sharp-toothed fish like this Spanish mackerel should be gaffed to bring them aboard.

TUNA FOOD

Proportionally, fish dominate the diet of tunas in coastal waters, and these are supplemented by seasonal runs of prawns, as far out as the Continental Shelf. Beyond the Shelf, in the open ocean, this food is substituted by vast schools of arrow squid, and for the very largest tunas, roaming schools of striped tuna and frigate mackerel as well. Mitre squid and Northwest pink squid also feature in the inshore diet of tunas, as do both Northern and Southern calamari, most often in late summer when there are vast numbers of their juveniles about after summer spawning. In summer off the NSW coast too, schools of striped tuna may also feed extensively on planktonic lobster larvae.

The fish that tunas eat range in size from tiny slivers of life, like glass minnows to some of the smaller tuna. Predictable bait species include yellowtail and cowanyoung, slimy mackerel, garfish, pilchards and marays, anchovies, hardyheads and sandy sprats (also called 'whitebait'). Tuna also eat weird offshore ooglies like Rays bream, nannygai, bellowsfish, boarfish and redbait. Anglers watching prawn trawlers haul their nets and discard their by-catch at sea will also realise that yellowfin tuna gather round such events and snap up almost any variety of other unfortunate fishes. In late spring and early summer, small tailor fall prey to tuna as post-spawn booms of two to three centimetre juvenile choppers gather around inshore reefs and estuary mouths. In an ironic twist, at this time of year large adult tailor can also be caught with juvenile tuna and bonito inside them.

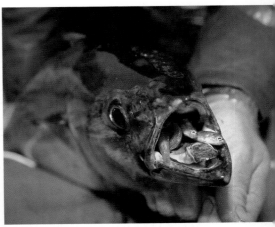

What any fish eats is of interest to anglers because it tells you what form your bait or lure should take to be successful. This mackerel tuna fed so vigorously on sandy sprats that they were spilling from its mouth when the fish was caught.

USING WIND AND CURRENT LINES

Wind can be a nuisance out at sea if you have to fight against it, but it can also be a fishing ally, enabling you to set up good drifts for fishing with baits out. Current lines are often quite visible on the sea surface, usually as slicks of relatively smooth water when the wind and current are both moving in the same direction, or as unusually ruffled strips of water when they are opposed. It can be very productive to set up trolling courses for gamefish along the edge of current lines or to even deliberately criss-cross them to maximise the likelihood of exposing the baits or lures to hungry hunting fish.

DRIFT FISHING

CUBING ON THE DRIFT

This form of drift berleying works best when the wind is gentle and blowing in a slightly contrary direction to the prevailing current. Chunks of fish flesh, cut neatly into cubes or into small, flat pieces are fed over the back or side of the boat, one chunk at a time, just as the last one is disappearing from view. Among these innocent hookless pieces of bait, you then feed back another identical-looking chunk with a razor sharp hook carefully buried inside it. When you feel the take, the fish is given a little line before the reel is shifted into gear and the hook is set with a firm upward sweep of the rod tip.

Cubing on the drift is sometimes used for yellowfin tuna when water depths are too great for anchoring.

DRIFT-FISHING WITH BERLEY

The key to berleying (dispensing some form of natural fish food or cereal-based product into the water in order to attract feeding fish) on the drift is to have the boat drifting a little slower than

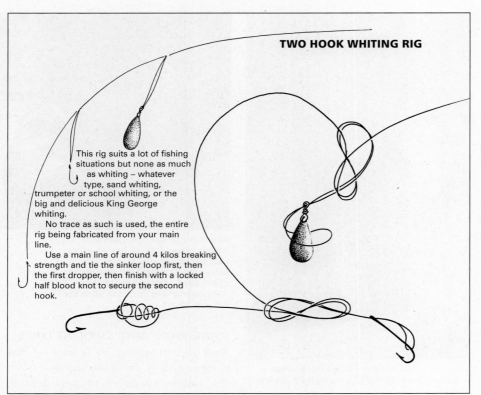

TWO HOOK WHITING RIG

This rig suits a lot of fishing situations but none as much as whiting – whatever type, sand whiting, trumpeter or school whiting, or the big and delicious King George whiting.

No trace as such is used, the entire rig being fabricated from your main line.

Use a main line of around 4 kilos breaking strength and tie the sinker loop first, then the first dropper, then finish with a locked half blood knot to secure the second hook.

You can use any form of fish flesh for 'cubing' or 'chunking', as it is also known. In this instance, the fish is a sweep, but prime bait choices for this work are tuna, pilchards and slimy mackerel.

the berley stream, so that fish are excited to feed before your bait gets there. Simply drifting with a cloud of berley falling under the boat will mean you are relying on the fish to follow your boat to take a bait, something that small and nuisance fish might do, but worthwhile angling targets seldom will. Worse, if the boat is drifting much faster than the berley, you can be leaving a layer of food behind the boat, attracting fish to it and actually keeping them away from the baits you have out.

DEEP WATER DRIFT FISHING

In deep sections of estuaries, such as tidal channels, float rigs are used to present weed-baits to luderick. In some waters, the boat is allowed to drift on the tide with the distance between the float and boat more or less constant. By far though, the most common method of fishing for luderick from a boat is to anchor the boat, but drift the bait rig, paying out line behind the float as it is carried away by the current. Out at sea, you can drift fish for flathead in depths around

40 metres with a snapper lead rigged Paternoster-style and two droppers carrying chunks or strips of fish flesh. Deeper water still, well offshore, is drift-fished too, with very large baits for oceanic sharks.

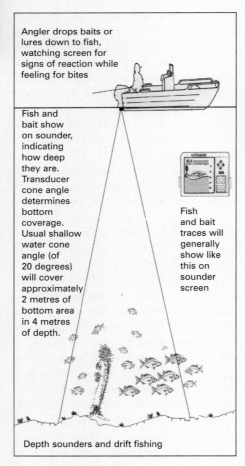

Angler drops baits or lures down to fish, watching screen for signs of reaction while feeling for bites

Fish and bait show on sounder, indicating how deep they are. Transducer cone angle determines bottom coverage. Usual shallow water cone angle (of 20 degrees) will cover approximately 2 metres of bottom area in 4 metres of depth.

Fish and bait traces will generally show like this on sounder screen

Depth sounders and drift fishing

DEPTH SOUNDERS AND DRIFT FISHING

Depth sounders can be used to good effect when drift fishing. You can use them to run over an area prior to fishing it and determine the mean water depth so rigs can be set to travel close to or just occasionally hitting the bottom. Another use of sounders when drift fishing though is to locate schools of fish suspended between the surface and the bottom and to fish baits or lures down to them as the boat drifts over their position.

SETTING RODS FOR DRIFT FISHING

Drift fishing can involve covering a lot of ground, which can take time. Holding a rod constantly while drifting can be tiring and prevent you from carrying out other activities such as rigging another outfit, preparing fresh replacement baits, steering the boat and so on. Good rod holders that keep the rod securely on board will free your hands up to do all these jobs. If a fish takes an interest in the bait as it passes by, the rod tip will nod, giving you plenty of notice to pick it up and set the hook. Sometimes you will need to feed line to a hesitant fish before striking, but in other cases, the fish and the rod holder will do the job for you quite effectively.

Drift fishing for species such as flathead and flounder can be a restful way to fish or as much hard work as you want to make it. The more rods you have out, the harder you will be working to bring all the fish in.

SHALLOW WATER DRIFT TECHNIQUES

Drift fishing in shallow water requires the rigs to be either buoyant or snag-resistant so you don't constantly have to stop and go back to extricate the rig from the bottom. Drifting over weed, or rough bottom, requires rigs that use very little weight, if any, and reasonably buoyant baits, or the use of appropriate floats. You can afford to have a sinker bouncing or skidding along the sea-floor when drifting over clean bottom but the bait in such cases is usually rigged above the sinker, Paternoster-style. This keeps it at a depth the fish can easily see it and take it without being impeded by the bottom.

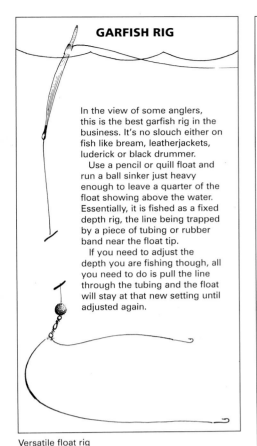

GARFISH RIG

In the view of some anglers, this is the best garfish rig in the business. It's no slouch either on fish like bream, leatherjackets, luderick or black drummer.

Use a pencil or quill float and run a ball sinker just heavy enough to leave a quarter of the float showing above the water. Essentially, it is fished as a fixed depth rig, the line being trapped by a piece of tubing or rubber band near the float tip.

If you need to adjust the depth you are fishing though, all you need to do is pull the line through the tubing and the float will stay at that new setting until adjusted again.

Versatile float rig

TROLLING TECHNIQUES

FINDING YOUR WAY TO FISH

Usually, the starting point for any trip to new fishing grounds is to refer to a marine chart, figure out your position relative to where you want to go, then use dead reckoning to get you there. To do this you'll need marine charts, a set of compass bearings, a reliable timepiece and a sum-log to measure how far you have travelled and to tell you when you should be 'there'. These days with GPS, the process is much simpler, as all you need do is punch in the destination co-ordinates, hit the 'go to' button and allow the screen plotter to show you which course to steer to get to that place. Once you've found a spot, you can enter it into the GPS unit's memory and simply hit 'go to' the next time you want to go there. Even with all this electronic wizardry, it is unlikely you will drop right in on the exact spot without landmarks, so you may need to instigate a localised search pattern to find the precise spot you need to be over.

FOLLOWING SEARCH PATTERNS WITH GPS

Often there is a need for precise location of some specific fishing target, such as a reef or wreck near which to anchor or to fish on the drift, or a depth contour line along which to set up a trolling course. Assuming your destination is say 70 metres deep, a normal sounder transducer of 20 degrees cone angle will give you about 35

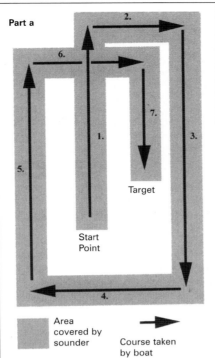

Part a

Area covered by sounder

Course taken by boat

Sounder with 20 degree transducer covers 35 metres of bottom in 70 metres of water, so continue doing rectangular circuits – a set distance less each time until target is found. To allow for course deviation or other error, reduce the distance travelled on each leg by only 25 metres.

Part b

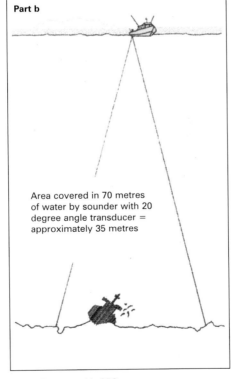

Area covered in 70 metres of water by sounder with 20 degree angle transducer = approximately 35 metres

Search Patterns with GPS

metres of bottom coverage. Allow some margin for error, and set up a rectangular search course, reducing each pass by 25 metres at a time. As you approach the search area, turn on your sounder, create an 'event mark' on the GPS as a starting point and continue through that point

on the same course for about 100 metres. Now turn right and travel for 50 metres, turn right again, and travel for 200 metres, turn right and travel for 100 metres, then turn right again and travel for 175 metres. This is the outer extent of your search pattern. If the target hasn't shown on the sounder by this stage, turn inside that rectangle again, but this time travel just 75 metres, turn right, travel for 150 metres and so on, gradually reducing the search area by 25 metres each time. The nearby illustration shows this quite clearly.

HIGH SPEED TROLLING

Generally, 'high speed' offshore trolling is regarded as being anything over 10 knots, with true high speed trolling starting about 13 knots and peaking around 17 or 18 knots. Very slender, symmetrical and well-weighted skirted lures with long tails can even be effectively trolled at speeds in excess of 20 knots, but strike impacts at these speeds can be so brutal that most popular line classes simply can't withstand the strain and part on the hit. Conversely, close inshore, trolling speeds of 8 to 10 knots with bibbed or bibless minnows (for tuna, kingfish and mackerel) can be considered 'high'. In estuaries, 'high-speed' trolling for tailor, salmon or flathead can be as little 7 or 8 knots.

High speed trolling was evolved to attract the big, fast-swimming oceanic predators like marlin and tuna. It works on the general principle that predators instinctively respond aggressively to 'escape behaviour' by prey. High speed trolling also enables the coverage of much larger tracts of ocean, which puts mathematical probability in your favour of coming across large predators. The thinking is, the more water you cover, the more likely you are to show the lures to active (feeding) fish.

TROLLING DEAD BAITS

The boat speed when trolling dead baits is usually slower than that used for lures. An exception is when trolling skip baits, which can be successfully towed in combination with lures. Unlike a hard-bodied lure, which can be slid through the fish's mouth to drive the hooks in, a bait most often requires that the angler is alert enough to knock the reel out of gear and feed the bait to the fish. This allows the fish to get the bait well down before the skipper guns the boat forward again and the angler strikes to set the hook.

The difference between baits and lures in this situation is more one of texture, feel and smell rather than one of function. Another difference between trolling lures and baits is that when the fish takes the bait into its mouth, it feels and tastes right, and can be firmly gripped, if not crushed by the fish's jaw pressure.

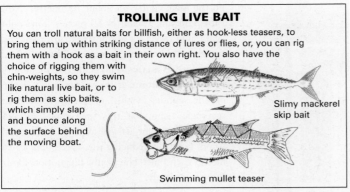
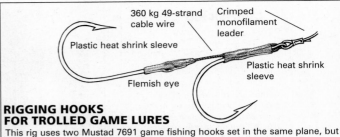
TROLLING LIVE BAITS

Most bluewater, livebait trolling is done by rigging a live fish with a bridle that positions the hook well clear but just forward of the fish's forehead. When trolling live baits, troll speeds generally have to be slower again than that for trolling dead baits to avoid overstressing and killing the bait. It is difficult to troll skirted lures effectively at these low speeds, so live baits tend to be a 'single tactic' kind of fishing. You can use various kinds of teasers (effectively hookless lures) to add to the impression of a school of bait and draw more fish to your offering.

Live yellowtail trolling rig

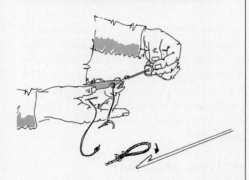

TROLLING LURES

The size and type of lures trolled for saltwater fish varies in relation to the target species, For example, flathead will readily take bib-minnows slow-trolled within particular areas of estuaries and bays. The key is to choose models that resemble local forage and with depth capabilities that mean they will run close to the bottom or just touch it occasionally. Marlin, tuna and other gamefish on the other hand, need to be searched for over a much wider area, and at much higher troll speeds. The lure types that respond best to this faster trolling style are more or less cylindrical in head shape and carry multi-coloured skirts that are slit into tails that resemble the many tentacles of a squid.

TROLLING PATTERNS – THE 'V'

In this sense, the expression 'patterns' refers to the way the group of lures is arranged behind the boat when viewed from above. Classic examples include 'V' trolling patterns, where the centre lure is set close to the boat transom while other lures, run from the transom corners, are set further back, and the 'shot-gun', which is an inverted 'V' pattern i.e. the middle lure is set furthest back and the two corner lures are set closer to the boat. The 'V' pattern suits small boats and inexperienced trolling crews, as it is relatively simple to stagger the two outside lures and avoid tangles when turning the boat.

TROLLING PATTERNS – THE 'W'

The 'W' pattern adds another two lures to the spread, usually by employing outriggers to run the two outer lures well back, with a lure set off each transom corner – one about half the maximum distance out and another one slightly more or less than that. The centre and fifth lure in the pattern is then set slightly further back than either of the two transom corner lures but not as far back as those run off the outriggers. The result is a 'W' shaped pattern when viewed from above, say from the boat's flybridge. This arrangement increases the amount of water being covered by the lures, adds to the general noise and attraction and often results in more hookups than trolling

fewer lures. It also makes higher demands on the boat driving and tackle management skills of the captain and crew, as setting lures too close to one another can result in tangles and lost fishing time. Special care must also be taken when turning the boat, and when one angler gets a hookup, those lines without fish on them must quickly be cleared away to give the best chance of landing that fish.

TROLLING TEASERS

Teasers are basically lures (or baits) that are trolled without hooks in them, to create more noise and increase the fish-calling appeal of the lures or baits with hooks. They include winged styles called 'birds', flashing darter style teasers, such as Marlin Magnets and Witchdoctors, lures with revolving bodies and mirrored panels on them to create flash and groups of squid or skirted lures called 'daisy chains'. You can further increase the density (and effect) of teasers by running them off spreader bars or dredges, which are essentially metal rods that provide multiple towing points for several daisy chains. Whatever you are using for a teaser though, you must be able to get it in and out of the angler's way quickly when a fish does come up into the pattern and take a hook-fitted lure or bait.

Trolling teasers

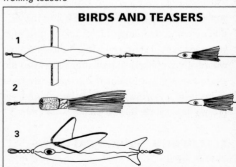

CASTING TO FISH

When casting to structure-holding fish like bream, mangrove jack and barramundi, make the lure splash down as close to the structure as possible. With open water feeders like tuna, tailor, salmon and kingfish, the fish will mostly be on the move when feeding and it is important to throw the lure so it lands ahead of the school's direction of travel.

When casting to fish that you can see in the water or see feeding by the surface disturbance they leave behind, make sure to throw in front of the fish so it comes across the lure naturally and doesn't have to double back to pick it up. Depending on the species, you may have to 'lead' the fish with your cast by a few inches, or as in the case of this fast-swimming tuna, by a couple of metres.

CASTING TO STRUCTURE

Casting lures towards structure, such as reefs, bombora, coral edges and wash areas, can be very productive as many species of fish gather around such features just waiting for something edible to pass within reach. When casting to steeply dropping rock formations like island corners and mainland rock platforms, allow the lure to sink a little before retrieving as it will be easier for fish to see if it sinks beneath the white water. Poppers cast toward submerged coral edges should be thrown beyond the drop off and up onto the shallows, then ripped back quickly over the edge into deep water again.

DROP AND LIFT JIGGING

Many species of lure-eating fish will hold at a particular depth when feeding and the best presentation for such fish is to work the lure within close range of this preferred depth. You can do this by free-spooling a jig down to where the fish are. This can be indicated by your depth sounder readout, or by counting the lure down to where the lure is hit. After the lure reaches this critical depth, it is bounced by starting a sharp lift and drop motion with the rod tip, this will make the lure dance invitingly right in the fish's face, where it cannot be ignored.

You can improve your results even when fishing without being able to see fish, if you cast toward some form of structure known to hold or attract your target species. Casting up into the weedy shallow of the bay in this picture and bouncing the lure back along the bottom caught this flathead.

FULL SPOOLS AND LINE MANAGEMENT

You can cast further when the spool of the reel is full. With 'over-the-lip' style reels such as sidecasts and threadlines the line will not have to climb as far to slide over the spool lip and with less line drag comes greater distance. Even overhead reels cast better when full, as a full reel spool does not have to accelerate to the same high revolution speeds involved when the diameter of the line load is down. However, you need to be careful not to overfill a reel spool or loose coils of line can spring or be blown off the reel by wind.

HIGH SPEED JIGGING

This energetic form of jigging begins like lift and drop jigging, but the lure is then speedily cranked all the way back up to the surface, while sudden and vigorous upward sweeps of the rod tip are made. The technique suits aggressive and competitive feeders like tailor, kingfish and mackerel and can result in bone-jarring hits as fish chase the lure upward, roll over the top of it as they strike and head for the bottom at top speed.

HIGH SPEED SPINNING

All lure fishing depends on imparting movement to the lure to simulate life and stimulate attack by predatory fish, but high speed spinning targets the faster-swimming species like tuna, mackerel, cobia and kingfish. Reels with high ratio gearing (6:1 or even faster) are ideal for this kind of work as they greatly reduce the handle speed required to get the lures moving fast enough to draw a strike. You can get by with lower gear ratios of 5:1 or even 4.6:1 or 4.2:1, provided the spool diameter of the reel is large enough to generate the required line recovery rate.

OVERHEADS VERSUS THREADLINES

Overhead reels such as baitcasters, jig reels and surf reels are best for throwing heavy metal lures and will give less trouble if you can manage to throw down-wind. If the lures to be thrown are light, threadline reels will often prove a better choice, especially when casting up into the wind.

BOATING SAFETY AND SKILLS

BAR CROSSINGS

Many Australian coastal ports open to the sea through areas of breaking surf, known as 'bars'. When crossing a bar toward the sea, wait inside the line of breakers to gauge the rhythm and size of the sets and then when you have chosen to go, don't waste time that might leave you in a vulnerable position with a large wave bearing down on you. As for all head seas, use enough power to climb the wave at a slight angle and back off the throttle as the boat reaches the wave crest, applying power again smoothly once over the wave, so you are ready to line up the next one.

When returning from the sea to the bar, try to position the boat on the back of an advancing wave, and use enough power to overcome wave suction from behind. If you don't, the wave behind your boat will overtake it and you will be shooting down the face, probably out of control and in danger.

BOAT MAINTENANCE

When fishing in salt water, boats are subjected to all manner of wear and tear, some of it quite subtle. Rust and corrosion and salt encrustation all work pervasively to cripple engines, electrical equipment and various moving parts, like hinges, anchor shackles, throttle and gear change controls and so on. Always wash your boat down after use in salt water and flush the engine out with fresh water before stowing the boat away. Regularly spray exposed metal parts with WD-40, or RP7 or Inox or similar (even painted ones) and apply waterproof grease to steering cables, anchor shackles, trailer winches and rollers and make a point of washing the undercarriage of the trailer, including the springs and axles and wheel hubs. Lift the engine lid and spray well with aerosol lubrication and de-watering compounds, then wipe excess oil and grease up and your fishing boat will be much less likely to let you down when you can least afford it.

If you go to sea, sooner or later you are going to have to cross the line where the bay or river becomes the open ocean. Such places often shallow up and are known as 'bars'. It takes strong nerves, a good boat and considerable skill to handle bar crossings without disaster. Make sure you are equipped with all three before tackling water this rough.

GOING OUT AND COMING BACK

You need to drive a boat differently into advancing seas than you do when running before seas that are following the same direction you are travelling. Head seas, usually encountered when heading out to sea, are best taken at an angle slightly off 90 degrees. This reduces the steepness of the wave face a little and allows the boat a more comfortable and controllable turning moment as the hull tips over the peak of the wave and slides down the back. Apply enough power to climb the wave and make headway against it but be ready to drop that power off quickly as you reach the peak or you risk leaping off the wave top like a launching pad.

When in big following seas, try to avoid having the boat picked up by a wave and speared forward like a surfboard. Out at sea in following waves, it is better to drop some speed off and let fast moving swells pass beneath the boat rather than try to ride them down the face.

HANDLING TIDE AND CURRENTS

Tides in some parts of the Australian coast are quite large and the currents they generate can be unbelievably strong. In some tropical locations and parts of Western Australia for example, tides can run with all the force of a big river in flood, creating overfalls, whirlpools and considerable boating danger. Use enough power to maintain steerage and try to skirt around the worst eddies and pressure waves. Wherever possible, try to steer around areas of water that appear to bulge ominously. They may simply be pressure waves, but in unfamiliar areas, it's not easy to tell which bulges are water pressure and which ones have solid rock beneath them.

KEEPING YOUR BALANCE

This refers not only to the need to maintain your own balance within a boat and avoid falling over or worse, overboard, but also to how you distribute weight throughout the boat to keep the hull flat and level. When travelling slowly into advancing waves, it can pay to have passengers move back a little so the bows are able to rise up over the wall of water rather than bury into it. When running before a sea, the bulk of the weight being carried, whether people, fish, or tackle and fuel, should be neither right at the stern nor at the bow but at a point slightly astern of dead centre.

OVERLOADING

It is sheer folly to load more people or other freight into a boat than it can safely handle; yet many boating tragedies bear testimony to this frequent and needless error of judgement. By law, all boats now come with safe passenger load limits advised on stickers or compliance plates and you should adhere to these guidelines.

TELL SOMEONE

Whenever you go out fishing in a boat, always tell someone where you are going, what time you expect to be back and make sure if you change that arrangement you are able to ring or radio and tell someone why you will be late. Whenever you go to sea, you are required to carry a marine radio and it is simply good sense to call in to the local coastguard advising them how many people are on board, the size and type of your vessel, your likely destination and your projected return time. It is very important too that you make sure you sign off at the end of the day so the coastguard can take you off its books and not risk life and limb needlessly mounting a 'rescue' for someone already safely on shore!

WHAT YOU NEED

Besides regulation safety gear, you should carry basic tools needed to effect simple and common repairs, such as spark plugs and spanners, de-moisturising sprays, spare boat bungs, emergency food and water rations, and plenty of warm dry clothing. It also makes very good sense to think ahead and make contingency plans; such as where you might be able to make landfall if you break down or for some reason cannot make it back to your original port. The old military adage of planning for the worst is a good rule of thumb and far better than being caught short by unexpected problems.

In any sized boat, you need to work on keeping your balance when the water becomes joggly. In small boats like this one, balance is critical if you are to avoid injury or a dunking.

CHAPTER NINE

SALTWATER
SHORE FISHING

BEACH FEATURES AND FISHING

You will rarely find fish distributed right along the full length of a surf beach. Far more often, fish will be concentrated around beach formations, where wave action and longshore currents shape the bottom. These features create feeding opportunities Any sort of sudden deepening, such as a gutter, channel or hole in the sea floor along a beach is a good place to start fishing. You can detect these places by looking for the darker water, which is deeper, or isolated white water patches, which indicate shallow areas surrounded by depth.

BEACH FISHING BY FOUR-WHEEL DRIVE

Some beaches are so long that the only feasible way of fishing their remote sections is by using a four-wheel drive vehicle for access. Beach ecosystem are sensitive areas, so enquire first about allowable access and secure the relevant permits before taking a vehicle onto any beach. Drive above the water line to prevent rust damage from salt water but keep to the lower flat hard pan area rather than the soft sand of the upper beach or dunes. To prevent bogging, lower the air pressure of your tyres to between 14 and 20 psi so the wheels 'float' over the sand. You should also time your trips to avoid being caught by advancing tides.

Low tide provides the opportunity to gather bait from sand flats like these and to do some reconnaissance of an estuary's bottom features.

These anglers have been able to get at the best surf gutter on the beach by using a four-wheel drive vehicle. It is important when beach driving to observe entry and permit regulations and to practise dune conservation.

BREAD FOR BAIT AND BERLEY

You can use bread for bait and catch a huge number of fish species from the shore. Using bread also for berley helps bring travelling fish within reach of your fishing position. That's real bread and butter fishing in more ways than one.

BREAM TACTICS

The key to bream fishing is to keep your bait or lure moving in a stop-start retrieve. Usually bream will take your lure or bait on the pause. You can fish for bream with baits of fish strip, shellfish, prawns, shrimp and squid pieces or cast small lures and flies for them. Regardless whether you use natural or artificial baits or them, try to cast close to structure and either drift or retrieve your offering through known bream habitat, such as sandy shallows, deep channels, near rocky reefs and shorelines and around weed beds, oyster leases and creek mouths.

Bream are widespread throughout Australian coastal waters and are well within the reach of shore-based anglers, whether fishing in estuaries, from the rocks or in the surf. There are three main kinds: the pikey bream of the tropics, so named for its stout anal spine and gill spikes, the yellowfin or silver bream, which inhabits the coast from sub- tropical to warm temperate regions and the black and southern bream, the predominant bream species south of about Sydney.

BUS-STOP BREAKWALLS

Along the coast of Australia, there are many rocky training walls, built to break the force of the sea and protect harbours or river entrances. Migratory fish call in at these places as regularly as clockwork on a seasonal basis. These movements are so predictable that breakwalls are almost like bus stops for fish. Casting and retrieving metal lures is the best way to catch one of these pelagics. Tailor, Australian salmon, small tunas, barracouta, trevallies and barracuda are just a few that will take metal lures.

Estuarine species also gather around them, but their movements are more frequent, being based around rising and falling tides. Bream usually bite on the lead up to the top of the tide and continue on the very first part of the run out. After that luderick will often take over and feed all through the run out to the bottom of the tide.

Mulloway are a prize catch off breakwalls and using live baits such as mullet, salmon, slimy mackerel or pike either suspended under a float or just free swimming are preferred methods.

CATCHING BEACH WORMS FOR BAIT

Some surf beaches offer the angler a ready supply of first class bait in the form of beach worms. Beach worms can grow up to 2 metres in length and the thickness of a man's finger, but are more

Bream

usually encountered at a metre or less and about 3 to 6 mm thick. They are caught by using a stink-bait of fish scraps in a loose-weave bag and a finger bait of either fish or pipi flesh.

The stink-bait is dragged along he water line, dispersing aromas from the bag and bringing the worms to the surface of the sand. Any worms present will stick their heads out looking for the food they can smell, betraying their location by a 'V'-wake as the wave recedes past them. If you are alert enough, you can present a small piece of hand held bait to the worm, allow it to grab hold, then quickly seize it behind the head with thumb and forefinger, and draw the worm right out of the sand. Some anglers use pin-studded pliers for this job, but others prefer to develop the hand-catching method, believing that pliers break as many worms as they catch.

CHECK THE SEA CONDITIONS

When going down to the ocean rocks to fish, always be aware of the power and danger of sea swells that can sweep up and over rocks, taking the unwary angler into the water. Serious injury or even death can result from such wash-ins, so the risk should not be taken lightly.

Before going down to the water level, always spend enough time watching to see whether the waves cover the place you are intending to fish. Any rock spot that is already wet when you get there is definitely a bigger risk than one that is dry.

FISHING FROM JETTIES

Jetties and wharves are great places to fish from, usually giving landbased anglers direct access to deep water and providing an inbuilt attraction

Beach worming

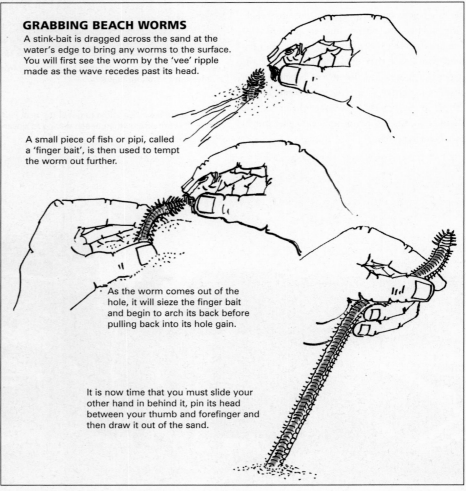

GRABBING BEACH WORMS

A stink-bait is dragged across the sand at the water's edge to bring any worms to the surface. You will first see the worm by the 'vee' ripple made as the wave recedes past its head.

A small piece of fish or pipi, called a 'finger bait', is then used to tempt the worm out further.

As the worm comes out of the hole, it will sieze the finger bait and begin to arch its back before pulling back into its hole gain.

It is now time that you must slide your other hand in behind it, pin its head between your thumb and forefinger and then draw it out of the sand.

Huge mulloway like this are a real possibility from river breakwalls, beaches or ocean fronting rock platforms. You need to get your tackle, baits and tactics right though.

These anglers are fishing temporarily from a small sandbar exposed at low tide. The channel separating it from the mainland is fairly shallow and easily waded, but they will have to keep an eye on the time to avoid being trapped by the rising tide.

for fish because of their shelter and current deflection properties. Knowing that you'll always find the best fishing next to and under the jetty where the fish live.

For best results, employ direct drop fishing styles, which means rigging so that you can drop a bait straight down. This makes the Paternoster rig a good choice as you can use enough weight to hold the line out of everyone else's way. Add a berley sinker or feeder to attract more fish to your baited hooks.

It also pays to fish a lighter outfit rigged with a pencil or waggler float. This rig is perfect for garfish, tommy ruff, salmon, leatherjacket and many other smaller species that move and feed vertically around jetty pylons.

FISHING FROM SANDBARS

In temperate regions, landbased anglers can sometimes find good fishing some distance from shore, by fording minor channels at low tide and fishing into much deeper water on the other side of the sandbars. These areas of high ground may be fully exposed at low tide or perhaps covered by only shallow water, enabling you to get amongst the fish just as well as a boat angler. In particular, look for sandbars that have some sort of current running over or past them, as fish will often congregate near such features and feed avidly on anything the water washes down to them.

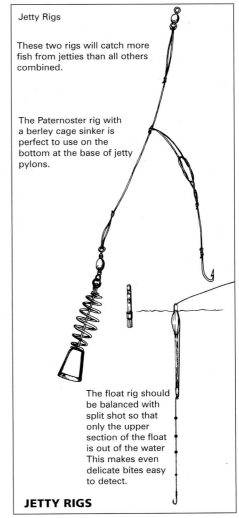

Jetty Rigs

These two rigs will catch more fish from jetties than all others combined.

The Paternoster rig with a berley cage sinker is perfect to use on the bottom at the base of jetty pylons.

The float rig should be balanced with split shot so that only the upper section of the float is out of the water This makes even delicate bites easy to detect.

JETTY RIGS

It is prudent to spend time watching wave patterns before venturing down onto low ocean rocks. This angler is taking no chances and will probably fish for years without risk or dangerous incidents. Less careful anglers are often injured or even killed.

FISH THE BEACH FOR VARIETY

Surf beaches offer good fishing, both in terms of fish size and numbers, but also in variety. The best hint to any surf fisherman is to always carry some surf popper flies and a range of metal lures. With such a simple range of terminal tackle you can take advantage of anything that happens to come along.

FISH THE EDGE WATER VISUALLY

When fishing from shore, it pays to be observant and watch for signs of fish working close in to the water's edge. In the tropics for instance, barramundi and threadfin salmon will often use the riverbank or a sloping sandbar to help them herd baitfish and prawns into concentrations that are dense enough to make easy pickings. The ideal situation when this happens is to try to quickly get ahead of the feeding fish's line of travel, so you can throw a bait or lure into the feeding area and pull it away in the same direction the natural prey is trying to escape. If you can't do this because of the terrain or some other reason, try to cast well past the feeding activity and then jink and flip the lure or bait into the fish's path, as if it were injured or confused prey.

This photo shows a typical northern NSW bechfront interspersed with broken rock platforms and points. Fish typically cruise such places on a rising tide ans feed where the two different kinds of terrain adjoin.

Surf beaches fish best where wind and wave action have created holes and gutters in which fish can hide or hunt.

FISH THE TERRAIN CHANGES

Very often, fish will gather where the local terrain changes in character, say from rocks to sand as shown in this photograph. This is why the corners of beaches where they abut a section of rocky shore are favourite fishing spots, yielding species such as bream, tailor, drummer, blackfish and sometimes, mulloway. Fish these places with unweighted baits of fish flesh, cunjevoi, green weed and cabbage or small baits such as mullet or chopper tailor.

FLATHEAD IN CLOSE SHALLOW WATER

Big dusky flathead will hunt in astonishingly shallow water at times, especially when light levels are low enough to afford them cover. Many anglers make the mistake of throwing their baits and lure too far out. In fact, they often throw right past where the fish are lying, and unwittingly frighten them away by blundering into the water just so they can cast further, when what they need to do is cast smarter.

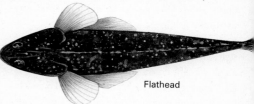

Flathead

FLATHEAD SHOREFISHING TACTICS

A good lure choice for this sort of fishing is one like a Rio Prawn, or lead-headed jig with a soft plastic tail. Retrieve prawn style lures with a slow twitch and glide presentation, and hop lead-head jigs along the bottom with gentle, short lifts of the rod tip. The best time for this style of fishing is the last half of the falling tide, low tide and the first half hour of the incoming tide. It can be productive to walk the banks of small coastal creeks, casting baits or lures out into midstream and working them with the current, so they appear to be part of the natural food supply. That means walking and casting upstream on a falling tide, and fishing the opposite direction as the tide is rising.

If you can see shallows and channels clearly (polarised sunglasses help here), it is a good tactic to cast up onto the shallow area and work the bait or lure back into the deeper water. Flathead will sit in deeper water right at the base of these ledges. In broad shallow flat areas, a common feature of many coastal lakes, try wade fishing, but as flathead conceal themselves by burying partway in the bottom, make sure yo explore an area thoroughly with several casts before advancing, otherwise, you will simply scare more fish than you catch.

Before you assume there are flathead away out 'there' somewhere, stay well back from the water's edge and try a few exploratory casts in he margin water You might catch something as big as this.

This flathead took a soft plastic imitation prawn in a shallow sandy bay. A lead-head jig provided the casting weight and enabled the lure to be hopped along the bottom where the fish was waiting in ambush.

GATHERING BAIT FROM THE SHORE

Landbased anglers can gather many kinds of bait from the same shoreline they are fishing, some at low tide, others when the tide is full. There are restrictions however on taking some kinds of bait roam certain rock platforms and estuary sanctuary zones, and a total prohibition on bait gathering in some other places. Most such areas are clearly signposted but it can pay to check your local Fisheries regulations to find out where these protected places are. Where bait gathering is permitted, small baitfish can be caught at high tide in funnel-traps baited with bread.

At low tide, pink nippers and squirt worms can be pumped from sand and mud flats, black crabs can be gathered from beneath flat rocks and soldier crabs can simply be scooped up before they can bury themselves in the sand. If you are sufficiently fleet of foot, you can catch ghost crabs from sandy beaches as they scurry toward their holes, while green weed can be collected around many storm water outlets that drain into estuaries. Crabs and octopus can be caught in rock pools, squid can be jigged from rocky shorelines and cabbage weed can be picked like so much lettuce from ocean-fronting platforms. Cunjevoi can be collected by slicing open their leathery casings with a sharp knife and removing

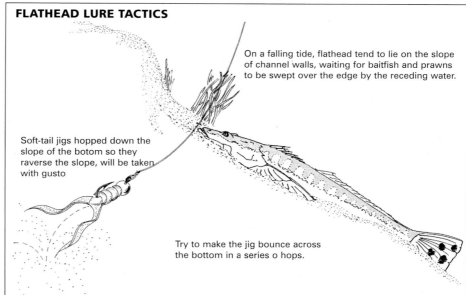

FLATHEAD LURE TACTICS

On a falling tide, flathead tend to lie on the slope of channel walls, waiting for baitfish and prawns to be swept over the edge by the receding water.

Soft-tail jigs hopped down the slope of the botom so they raverse the slope, will be taken with gusto

Try to make the jig bounce across the bottom in a series o hops.

the soft purple meat inside. From beaches, you can gather pipis, and beach worms, but there are now bag limits on these in most States and you should consult local regulations to ensure you do not exceed the limit and incur a fine.

HIGH AND LOW TIDE GUTTERS

Some beach gutters have water deep enough to hold fish only when the tide is high. The fishing in such places tends to be good for only short periods at high tide.

Gutters that retain fishable depth at low tide can be productive at either end of the tide cycle.

MULLOWAY METHODS

Mulloway can be caught from breakwalls on slabs of fish or live baits. The tactic is to drift the bait with the tide by casting it out then walking along the wall after it as the flow carries it past likely fish-holding territory. It is very important to keep the bait up of the bottom to avoid snagging and to have it travel close to the rockwall face, so some anglers like to use a large bobby-cork rig to achieve better drift control.

Above: On the north coast of New South Wales, big mulloway like this one regularly patrol along the rock faces and breakwalls and take live baits such as slimy mackerel, mullet or pike.

High tide gutters like this one are likely to hold bream and whiting, with flathead under the first blanket of foam. It would be a long throw however to reach surface fish like tailor or salmon, which would more probably be patrolling the clean water beyond the more extensive second break.
This angler is fishing a high tide gutter, indicated by the fact that there is softer sand immediately behind his feet, and that it is well-churned with the tracks of four wheel drives that have driven well up from the water level at low tide. Low tide gutters tend to have a considerable apron of hard pan between the water and the soft sand, unless recent storms have eroded a beach and shaped it into a steeply sloping ramp.

MULLOWAY AND BREAKWALLS

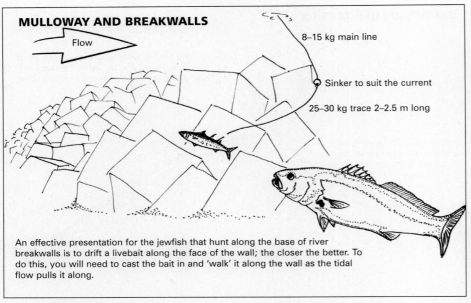

Flow

8–15 kg main line

Sinker to suit the current

25–30 kg trace 2–2.5 m long

An effective presentation for the jewfish that hunt along the base of river breakwalls is to drift a livebait along the face of the wall; the closer the better. To do this, you will need to cast the bait in and 'walk' it along the wall as the tidal flow pulls it along.

Jewfish and breakwalls

SAFETY

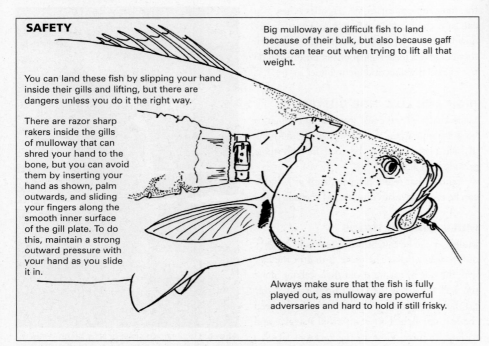

Big mulloway are difficult fish to land because of their bulk, but also because gaff shots can tear out when trying to lift all that weight.

You can land these fish by slipping your hand inside their gills and lifting, but there are dangers unless you do it the right way.

There are razor sharp rakers inside the gills of mulloway that can shred your hand to the bone, but you can avoid them by inserting your hand as shown, palm outwards, and sliding your fingers along the smooth inner surface of the gill plate. To do this, maintain a strong outward pressure with your hand as you slide it in.

Always make sure that the fish is fully played out, as mulloway are powerful adversaries and hard to hold if still frisky.

Gilling jewfish

Fish such as bream often cruise along close to riverbanks or hold near structure like snags. Wearing polarising sunglasses like this angler, you will see more fish and if you are alert, you will catch more too.

POLARISED SUNGLASSES HELP YOU CATCH FISH

Polarised glasses cut the surface glare and let you see into the water much more effectively, sometimes revealing fish, but always giving you a much better understanding of the bottom shape and structure.

The best lens colour for salt water viewing is the copper or penetrator tint. This colour has proved to contrast fish best against a variety of backgrounds in typical saltwater environments. This is especially so when wading flats or spinning off the rocks.

Often, what you will see is not an actual full visual profile of a fish, but hints and suggestions of a fish, such as moving shadows, flashes from scales or sometimes, the flip and skitter of baitfish or shrimp.

SHOREFISHING PROBLEMS AND SOLUTIONS

The biggest single problem presented by fishing from the shore is limited reach. You can only cast so far, and, being bound to the shore, yo will also have limited options about the direction in which you can fish. Unlike boat fishing, which allows you to shift your position so you are fishing a spot from virtually any direction, you are obliged when shorefishing to fish from a single plane range of positions. In other words, you can move up or down a shoreline, but you can't move further out than the water's edge.

When you are making a cast over line-cutting objects like rock outcrops, or trying to bring in a fish, you can sometimes keep the line out of trouble by climbing higher if the terrain allows it. Rock fishermen use this ploy often when trying to steer troublesome fish around dangerous water. There are other tactics available to the fixed-position shore angler too. You can for instance, confuse a fish or influence it to change the direction it is swimming by suddenly putting the reel in free spool and taking all pressure off it. This tactic works very well when fishing for tuna off the ocean rocks. Under heavy rod pressure, many tuna will swim an arcing run back and forth across the face of the rocks. On these and other open water swimmers, such as snapper and jewfish, you can avoid having the line wrapped around sharp rocks by suddenly releasing all pressure, causing them to react by veering out and away from trouble. The tactic doesn't work with all fish though. For instance, when you take the pressure off groper, kingfish and drummer they may simply bury the line in the rocks completely.

TAILOR AT DAWN AND DUSK

Tailor on surf beaches usually keep to the first deep longshore gutter, where there is water clean enough to accommodate baitfish schools. Dense spawning concentrations occur from May to October and tailor can be caught from beaches during daylight hours.

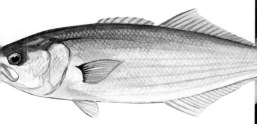

Tailor

In the warmer months, their main feeding activity takes place at night. To help efficiency at night many beach fishermen use head-set torches that leave their hands free to bait hooks, work fishing rods and land fish.

TARWHINE

Tarwhine, a close relative and look alike of the yellowfin bream, can be caught from estuary breakwalls, in shallow coastal lakes near sandy channels and weed beds and around areas of isolated estuary reef or bridge pylons. Use small baits and hooks, and weight the rig lightly so the current can wash it along the bottom where these fish feed.

Tarwhine

THE CHANNEL AND TIDE GAME

Many estuary channels have a deep, rocky side with steep walls and a more gently sloping sand or mud bottom, rising to extensive shallow flats. Fishing channels from either shore is most difficult in mid-tide, when the flow is strongest. At either end of the tide cycle, tidal flows reduce enough for fish to feed with less effort. This lets you present baits and lures more easily. Let's assume for now that we are fishing such a channel from the deeper or rocky side. In fast water, standard cast and drift techniques will require too much weight to hold near bottom for the to behave naturally and be attractive to a wide range of fish. Whiting may be caught this way by allowing the bait to sweep the channel floor, but through the strongest part of the run, fish like luderick and bream will probably have taken up station along the steep rocky side of the channel. To get at these, you may need to use a float rig that enables you to run baits down through a narrow corridor of seam water where irregularities in the channel wall create holding eddies.

Above: Tailor will bite during the day, but are a much surer bet during periods of low light such as dawn and dusk, particularly if those periods of low light such as dawn and dusk, particularly if this periods coincide with a rising tide. Note that this angler came prepared with a head-lantern, enabling him to work in good torch light but with both hands free.

High speed spinning and live baiting from the rocks is very popular along the New South Wales coast.

TIDE TACTICS

Tailor and other fast swimmers at this time will be in or near the channel system of an estuary but will hang around points of land or reefs that create pools of slower water where they can circle and wait for disoriented prey to be carried to them From half-tide up towards full, as the run slows, the main body of the channel will again have several species of fish roaming around more freely, and standard bottom rigs can be used again.

If a rising tide is big enough, it will spill over the channel lip and onto adjacent shallow flats. From half-tide down to low, casting into the channel itself from the deep-side bank starts to work again. Adult whiting will have resumed their side to side drift across the channel floor, bream and luderick will be in transition mode between roaming and tucking in to cover. Because mullet, juvenile whiting and other small baitfish will be spilling back over the drop off into the channel, this is also a good time to cast baits and lures up onto the shallow flats and pull them back into the channel. Mid water retrieves will likely take tailor, while rigs bounced down the sloping channel wall will attract flathead. A live bait drifted down the channel may take flathead during the day, while at night, around points of land where the channel drops into a deep hole, school mulloway are a real prospect.

Wading and casting soft plastics for flathead at high tide in the upper reaches of estuaries will result in some big dusky flathead.

Lure casting into deep channels at high tide will soon find whether pelagics are present or not

USING LAND NETS

The best way to get a fish into a net is to submerge the net mouth in front of the fish and swim it in. Chasing the fish around with the net is pointless. Instead, tire the fish out enough to lead it slowly along the surface toward the waiting net and you will land a lot more fish than you lose.

WADE FISHING

You can catch a lot of fish in estuaries by casting from the bank or shoreline. If you can't reach out to where the fish are though, you can sometimes wade out within casting distance, provided the bottom strata is firm and the water is shallow enough. The trick with wading is not to wade so far that you find the fish are now moving about between you and the bank. If this happens, they will nearly always be keenly aware that you are there and will be much harder to catch.

Wear a peaked cap or broad-brim hat and polarising sunglasses to cut surface glare and you will spot fish much more readily, as well as being able to pick up important bottom detail, such as channel edges, weed beds, and rock clumps.

Here's a tip when wade-fishing. Wear an army surplus ammunition belt or buy a nylon bum-bag to carry a handful of lures and small tackle items like spare hooks, sinkers and swivels. A belted pouch too can let you take a pair of pliers and a knife for releasing unwanted fish.

WADING IN SAFETY

Wading is safe enough, as long as you know what you are putting your feet on. It is quite pleasant to wade in bare feet, but given that oyster-covered rocks, razor fish, and stingrays can be lurking down there, it is more prudent to wear sandshoes, robust sneakers, or in bad country, even purpose-built wading shoes. The tropics present special

hazards, such as the venomous stonefish and the lethal box jellyfish. Anywhere north of Rockhampton in Queensland or Exmouth in Western Australia, you need to be aware of the danger of saltwater crocodiles too. Wading in our far northern estuaries, bays and mangrove shorelines is extremely inadvisable. When the water is discoloured, as is often the case, it can be quite foolhardy.

WET WADING VERSUS DRY

You can wade fish an area with protective clothing or without, and there are good reasons for doing either. In winter, when water temperatures are low, waders can provide comfort and some insulation and definitely prevent body heat from being stripped directly from your legs. Rubber waders provide less insulation than neoprene but are usually much cheaper. In summer though, both rubber and neoprene can be stiflingly hot and waders of lightweight nylon polyester would be better, or alternatively, no waders at all.

Wading without waterproofing is known as 'wet wading' and allows you to detect subtle changes in water temperature. This can be important, as if you can detect cold patches of water within estuaries, you can avoid areas where fish are less active and therefore harder to catch. Even when wet wading though, it can pay to have some protection in the form of lightweight track pants, especially in warmer regions where stinging jellyfish can be a problem.

WHITING SHORE FISHING TACTICS

Whiting can be consistently caught from the shore wherever there is deep moving water close by. The ideal bottom is either sand or a mixture or sand and mud, with some weed beds nearby. Fish for whiting from the shore with baits of bloodworms, mussels, cockles, live nippers, thin fish strips or small peeled prawns. The best rig here is a running feeder with a loop to loop trace attached to a size 8 long shank whiting hook. The feeder can be packed with mussel or cockle for

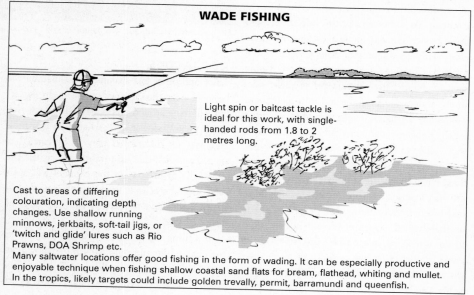

WADE FISHING

Light spin or baitcast tackle is ideal for this work, with single-handed rods from 1.8 to 2 metres long.

Cast to areas of differing colouration, indicating depth changes. Use shallow running minnows, jerkbaits, soft-tail jigs, or 'twitch and glide' lures such as Rio Prawns, DOA Shrimp etc.

Many saltwater locations offer good fishing in the form of wading. It can be especially productive and enjoyable technique when fishing shallow coastal sand flats for bream, flathead, whiting and mullet. In the tropics, likely targets could include golden trevally, permit, barramundi and queenfish.

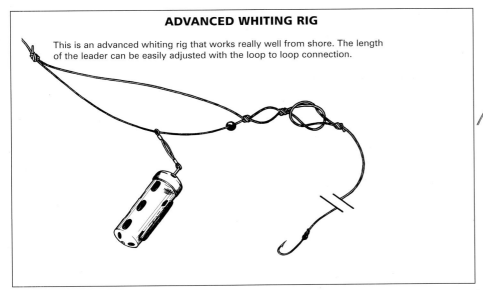

ADVANCED WHITING RIG

This is an advanced whiting rig that works really well from shore. The length of the leader can be easily adjusted with the loop to loop connection.

WHITE WATER RIG

Whether you are using a free floating bait or one under a float the best way to hook your bait is with a ganged series of hooks.

WD-40, CRC, or Inox, but do not lubricate the internals with anything except water or a few drops of household detergent. Even this however must then be flushed out to avoid contaminating and killing the baits on subsequent trips. Buy spare washer sets and replace them as soon as the old ones start showing signs of perishing.

added berley. This rig is cast slightly up current and allowed to wash back towards you through the deep water, in such a way that the bait bowls along naturally, down near the bottom.

As the current sweeps the rig down towards you, stay in touch with the bait by winding in the slack line. This is so you can set the hook on any tentative bites. Don't wind line in so much that you pick the bait up and swing it clear of the bottom, just enough so you can feel any bites, and set the hook by smartly lifting the rod tip. In still or slowly moving water, you will need to cast and slowly retrieve the bait to impart the necessary movement that whiting prefer.

YABBIES—PRIME SPOTS

Yabby beds occur in estuaries where the bottom is of a suitable sand and silt constituency. Steep beach fronts will not hold good yabby beds, but gently sloping or flat beaches usually will. Often, the best yabby beds are over extensive tidal sand flats that are inundated with each high tide.

You can spot which yabby holes are likely to produce baits by the pattern and density of hole clusters. The more random and densely grouped, the better. Look particularly for those that are positioned along drainage gutters and slightly up the rising sand wall of any high spots in the sand flat and select those holes with a domed appearance or those with haloes of differently coloured sand piled up around them. These indicate a busy digger is in residence. When pumping over shallow submerged flats, you can pick active holes by looking for slender 'smoke trails' of sand particles rising from the clusters of holes. When pumping nippers over submerged flats, it's a good idea to tow a floating sieve around and discharge the pump contents into that. Nippers are good swimmers and in water more than 20 cm deep can easily escape to the bottom and bury again before the suspended cloud of silt clears enough for you to spot them.

YABBY PUMPS— USE AND MAINTENANCE

Yabby pumps are a section of tubing with side handle, a tee-handled vacuum plunger attached to an internal rod, applying suction through a compressed stack of soft-rubberised washers. Security and adjustment of the compression on these soft washers is by means of two metal pressure plates and a wing-nut. Don't buy a plastic-bodied yabby-pump, get a stainless steel one, look after it, and it will last you a lifetime. The yabby pump is placed over a yabby hole and pushed downward into the sand while the plunger is simultaneously pulled upward. This sucks sand (and hopefully, yabbies) up into the pump body. The pump is then lifted away from the hole, and the plunger is pushed back down to eject a slug of sand, along with any yabbies that have been sucked up with it. It is best to pump where there is subsurface water permeating the sand, as without this, the sand will be too solid to lift into the tube. Wash the pump in salt water immediately after each bait gathering session and later at home, hose it out with fresh water, strip the washer assembly and wipe away any residual sand. It is helpful to wipe down the outside of the pump with a rag sprayed with

Pilchards are a top bait for many species.

WHITE WATER AND WASH AREAS

The wash areas around rocks can be very productive fishing spots because they create eddies and surface cover where fish can feed in safety. The correct way to fish these areas is with an unweighted pilchard or garfish. You don't always have to throw very far either to reach fish. Sometimes, unweighted baits cast right at your feet and allowed to wash around with the surge, will be taken by quite large fish.

If the sea floor is too craggy to allow this or you have to cast a little further, rig with a bobby cork to keep the bait and hook up off the bottom. The best tackle for this job is a medium to slow action surf rod with a sidecast or threadline reel.

After a long absence through commercial over-fishing, big kingfish are now making a comeback and willingly hit lures or livebaits fished from the rocks.

BOAT FISHING

BARRAMUNDI AND BILLABONGS

During the Wet season, many barramundi within freshwater rivers move into backwater areas in search of cover and food. As monsoon rains ease and water levels drop, these backwaters, called billabongs, become separated from the main river system, trapping fish within them. During the Dry season, fishing in billabongs at first and last light may not be as productive. Barramundi are disinclined to feed when water temperatures drop below 23 degrees Celsius. You can experience excellent fishing though in the middle of the day, or again, from nightfall for a few hours when surface lures can produce explosive strikes.

BARRAMUNDI AND CASCADES

During the transition from the Wet season to the Dry, waters that have covered the low flood plains will begin to drain back into the major river systems. River levels tend to drop faster than the flood plain water, creating countless cascades off the riverbanks and into the main stream. These are renowned aggregation places for barramundi (and other predatory fish), which strike unhesitatingly at lures cast into the fringe water.

BARRAMUNDI AND CURRENT

Like many fish that feed from cover, barramundi will seldom be found right in a current, but frequently will hold position just off the edge of the strongest flow. You can target them wherever current flows past rocks or snags, or where points of land jut out and create eddies and turbulence.

In the run-off period at the end of the Wet season, swirls and boils occur where conflicting currents meet in streams. Here, you can sometimes find very large barramundi that are attracted by the plentiful food carried to them by the water flow. Position your boat just off to one side of these areas to best fish them.

BARRAMUNDI TROLLING TRICKS

When trolling for barramundi, use an echo sounder to locate submerged snags, trees and rock bars. Barramundi use these places to hide in ambush and wait for baitfish, crustaceans or other prey to come past. If the current is swift, such features will be distinguished by roiled surface water. Where the current is slow, or in the still waters of billabongs and lakes, the 'underwater eyes' of an echo sounder can prove invaluable.

The immediate advantage of an echo sounder is that it will indicate water depth and enable the correct choice of lures for particular running depths. Choose lures that will swim along as close to the bottom structure as possible without snagging. Work your lures too—hold the rod in your hand and push it forward then let it fall back, then repeat the procedure—the trolled lures will alternately dart forward then wobble back briefly and this erratic jigging action will produce more strikes.

BARRAMUNDI, BOATS AND BLOOPERS

Quite often, fishing from a boat is the only way you can reach productive sections of water, particularly pockets of water margins where extensive weed beds or lily pads prohibit shore casting. A very good lure for this style of fishing is a cup-faced popper. It can be cast into tight little corners of open water between rafts of floating vegetation, and be worked out from the bank with repetitive, short stabs of the rod tip. This will make the popper dive under, trapping air and creating a 'blooping' sound that can bring barramundi in from some distance away to strike the lure.

BASS AND ALGAL BLOOMS

In many large water storage impoundments, there is a daily cycle of algal blooms generated by fluctuations in water temperature and light levels. When these high points in temperature and light coincide with suitable pH levels, algal growth is stimulated. Algae is a food source for invertebrates and baitfish, and through photosynthesis, it also generates localised surges in dissolved oxygen. Bass are attracted to these areas of dams by the smaller prey that have gathered to feed on this algae and also react to high-oxygen levels with greater activity.

Anglers can see the algae by watching a sounder screen and looking for 'clouds' forming in midwater. Sometimes, you will also see denser signals, indicating baitfish or shrimp, or even arches, blips and dashes that show there are also big fish feeding there. By trolling lures past such showings, or dropping jigs down to these levels you can fish directly to these concentrations of bass that are already primed and in a serious feeding mood.

Barramundi in billabongs can be taken by casting to bankside cover or trolling channels.

BASS AND BAITFISH

The vast majority of bass lures sold in Australia are 'bug-shaped'; some are actually intended to represent insects, such as cicadas and beetles. But in rivers a very large proportion of bass food consists of small fish, such as snub-nosed garfish, hardyheads, rainbow fish, glass-fishes, gudgeons, jollytails, mullet and herring, which are staple foods of bass, as are introduced fish like goldfish, gambusia and others. In large freshwater impoundments, smelt and bony bream figure largely in the bass diet. Swimming plugs and minnows imitate the general shape and sonic pulses of baitfish, while bladed lures such as Celtas and spinnerbaits offer that same throbbing sound with the added flash of the blade. The halting, erratic movement of jerkbaits and soft plastic lures is much like the escape behaviour of many types of baitfish too. So wherever you see baitfish milling around river margins, or showing as clouds on a sounder, hungry bass won't be too far away.

BASS AND HEAVY TREE COVER

In some rivers, bass hang around willows and other trees. Willows aren't especially the very best kind of bass cover, but they tend to dominate natural bankside vegetation once they are established. The trick with willow fishing is to look for gaps in the drooping foliage and fire flat, accurate casts right in underneath the canopy. This is not easy but if you use heavy lures, such as spinnerbaits, or jigs with soft plastic tails, you can sometimes punch a cast past the hanging fronds and land it in the critical zone next to the tree trunk. As willows also have a mass of roots under the

Heavy bankside foliage provides lots of habitat for bass, but casts must be accurate and land as close as possible to the cover.

surface you need to control the depth of your lure. Retrieve it close to the roots, but just clear of them.

BASS AND STEEP BANKS

To catch bass, find them, then make them bite. In early morning and late afternoon, bass will move in close to steep banks next to deep water, and feed along the water's edge. Lures that work well in such places include short, deep-diving plugs and spinnerbaits. Stand the boat a comfortable casting distance off the bank and toss these lures as close to the shore as possible.

Bring them back down the steeply sloping bottom with a slow retrieve. In the middle of the day, you can still catch fish from these places, but the boat will need to stand a little further out to avoid being right on top of the fish. Work the lures down through the deeper water further down the slope. Select areas of bank with tree cover or shade.

BASS BETWEEN THE WEED BEDS

Weed beds tend to be avoided by beginner bass anglers, usually because the lures get tangled in the vegetation and it takes time to get them out. However bass frequently use weed beds for cover and as feeding grounds, chasing the small fish, shrimp, water snails and other benthic creatures. Where weed beds are continuous along a bank, cast along the outside edge, or use sinking lures that you can pitch to the weed edge and drop down the outer face of the weed. Most weed beds will have intermittent breaks and gaps between them, and you can often pick up fish by casting to the water behind the weed beds and bring the lure through these openings.

BASS IN POCKET WATER

Recent advances in bass fishing techniques include open water fishing and fishing at depth, but the classic bass technique is still to fish for them in small, secluded pockets of water—where a riverbank follows a wobbly line with distinct indentations or cuttings. Bass like these places because they provide cover on three out of four sides, leaving only the outer, water side open for a feeding charge. The best of these will have overhead cover or significant water depth, or a combination of both. Overhead cover can be bankside trees and bushes that hang over the water like a canopy, or even floating weeds and grass fronds.

Small boats open up the enormous fishing potential of our many freshwater impoundments. Here two boats have rafted up for company to baitfish some drowned timber in Lake Glenbawn NSW.

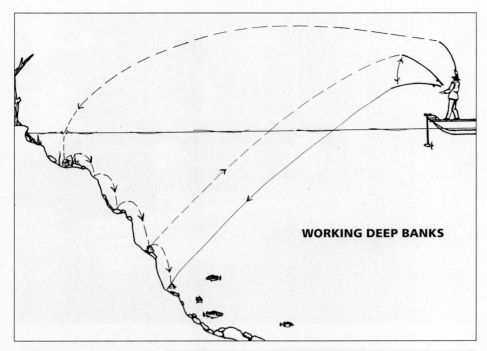

WORKING DEEP BANKS

Above: Cast a sinking lure, such as a spinnerbait, as close as possible to the bank. Let it sink to the bottom, then hop it down the slope with lifts of the rod tip, winding line in slowly after each lift and drop.

Right: Spinnerbaits allow you to fish vertical bank faces as they can be cast in close and will sink within the fish's strike zone.

Below: This angler in Copeton Dam NSW has just trolled up a nice trout by working his lure along the edge of a drop off.

CARP AND MUD BOILS

On sunny days, carp can often be spotted cruising in clear water; when they are feeding down deeper, on the bottom the clouds of suspended mud and silt indicate their presence. A well placed nymph, small lure or bunch of wriggling worms cast to the clear water at the leading edge of the mud boil should expect to be hit.

CARP ON CORN

To bring fish to your area, berley or 'ground-bait' it before you start fishing. Sweet corn is one of the very best baits for carp. Use the kernel type of sweet corn as bait (the mushy style is okay for berley but too hard to keep on a hook). Rig with a short shank, round-bend hook such as a Suicide pattern in sizes #10 to #4 and try a variety of presentations. Bottom rigs can be weighted with split shot to get them down; waggler float rigs suit fish that are feeding just off the bottom. For very active fish that are feeding close to the surface, a simple unweighted rig comprising just a hook, line and bait can be cast close to the action and will often be picked up without hesitation.

COWBELLS AND FORD FENDERS

The idea behind attractors such as Cowbells and Ford Fenders is to represent a school of fish swimming fast with a straggler in pursuit. The 'straggler' is a lure or fly set back from the rest of the attractor, which makes it a prime target for a predator. Remember to only troll Cowbells and Ford Fenders at a very slow speed (around 2 – 3 kilometres per hour) -electric trolling motors are an ideal propulsion choice for this kind of fishing.

DEEP AND SHALLOW TROUT TROLLING

You can troll for trout with several lures at a time and set the boat up for either shallow and fast trolling, or deeper and slower trolling. Here's how: For shallow and fast trolling, try running a small Rebel Crawdad some 10 metres back from the boat, a Rapala CD5 at 15 metres and a Tassie Devil at 20 metres. Ideal trolling speed for this set up is 3 – 5 mph (a good brisk walking pace).

To troll a bit slower and deeper, run a slightly larger Crawdad: again at 10 metres, a high-action floating minnow behind a Downunder sinker at 15 metres and at 20 metres, a Cowbell with a bladed spinner on the tag end.

DODGERS INCREASE LURE ACTION

Try using a dodger when trolling spoons and Tassie Devils. Apart from creating extra flash and attraction in the water, they will also give extra action to your lure and it is often this additional darting movement that induces a strike. The shorter the drop between the lure and the dodger, the more erratic the path of the lure.

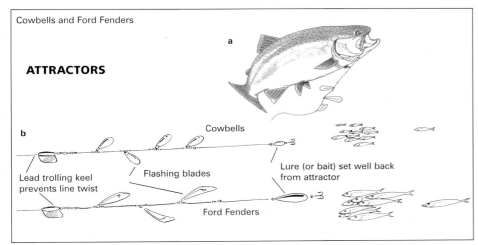

Cowbells and Ford Fenders

ATTRACTORS

a

Cowbells

b

Lead trolling keel
prevents line twist

Flashing blades

Lure (or bait) set well back
from attractor

Ford Fenders

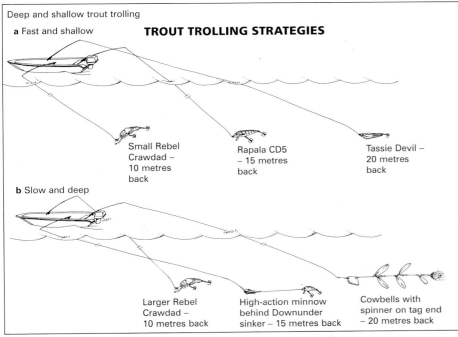

Deep and shallow trout trolling

a Fast and shallow

TROUT TROLLING STRATEGIES

Small Rebel
Crawdad –
10 metres
back

Rapala CD5
– 15 metres
back

Tassie Devil –
20 metres
back

b Slow and deep

Larger Rebel
Crawdad –
10 metres back

High-action minnow
behind Downunder
sinker – 15 metres back

Cowbells with
spinner on tag end
– 20 metres back

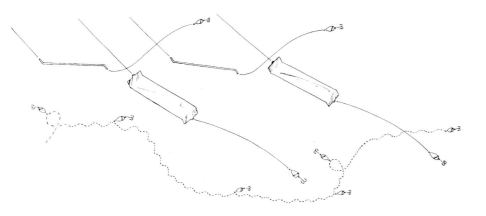

Dodgers increase lure action

As the dodger is trolled along, it
kicks the lure from side to side
On a short leader, the lure's path
can be quite erratic.

Above: A range of boat types will serve for
fishing freshwater dams. Only calm days like
this however would be suitable for fishing from
a canoe.

DOWNRIGGER RELEASE CLIPS

There are a number of different types of release
clips for downriggers. The two main styles are the
button type and the clothes peg type. Of these,
the clothes peg type is by far the most popular.

FIGURE-8 TROLLING

Native fish often hold over rocky points and one
tactic that really works well is to steer the boat
in a sort of Figure-8, crossing and re-crossing
the point from slightly different angles. Don't
assume there are no fish there if you aren't hit
on the first or second pass. You can afford to
make up to 20 such passes before moving on to
another spot. Murray cod for example, will often
let a lure run right past their noses several times
before striking. It can take time to annoy the
fish sufficiently to produce a strike and get the
angle and speed of approach just right. If you are
marking fish on the sounder however, keep trying
and you should eventually get a result.

FRESHWATER PATERNOSTER

The Paternoster rig is great for fishing in fresh
water for redfin perch. It is a particularly good rig
for boat fishing around trees and using shrimp
for bait.

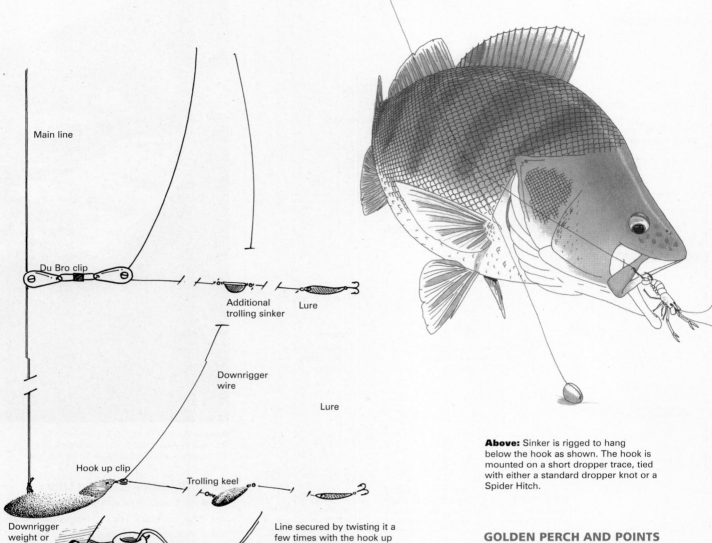

Main line

Du Bro clip

Additional trolling sinker

Lure

Downrigger wire

Lure

Hook up clip

Trolling keel

Downrigger weight or 'bomb'

Line secured by twisting it a few times with the hook up clip before inserting it into the holding clip.

Above: Downrigger release clips

Below: Figure-8 trolling

Above: Sinker is rigged to hang below the hook as shown. The hook is mounted on a short dropper trace, tied with either a standard dropper knot or a Spider Hitch.

GOLDEN PERCH AND POINTS

Anglers targeting golden perch from a boat in dams can often find these fish feeding actively along the submerged slopes of points of land. The depth at which the fish will feed varies according to time of day, weather and light conditions. The most common mistake is to assume these fish are always in deeper water. Quite often, golden perch will forage up along the sides of points in water as little as a metre or so deep, particularly if there are heavy weed beds close by or drowned trees that they can use for cover. Troll across these points at an angle so the lure covers each side of the slope, or stand off and cast lures up onto the shallows and bring them down the slope.

GOLDEN PERCH AND SUMMER SHALLOWS

In summer, at first and last light, golden perch will often enter shallow bays and forage in water barely deep enough to cover their backs. In calm, foggy conditions, you can even sight-fish these perch as their tails break the surface while they pursue shrimp and small baitfish amongst the weed.

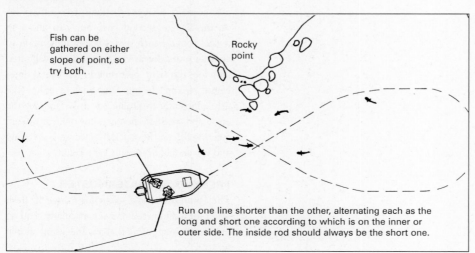

Fish can be gathered on either slope of point, so try both.

Rocky point

Run one line shorter than the other, alternating each as the long and short one according to which is on the inner or outer side. The inside rod should always be the short one.

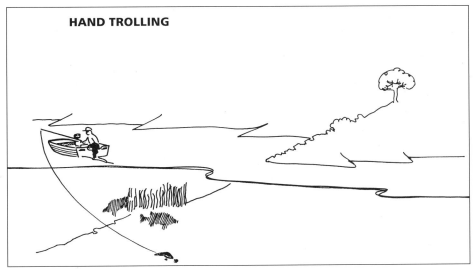

HAND TROLLING

Above: Watch the sounder to establish actual depth, but also keep an eye on the surrounding banks so you can anticipate when the bottom will shallow. Always troll with the rod in your hand in such situations, so you can drop the tip back to float the lure over any obstacles.

Left: Big golden perch like this tend to sit around points of land or close to the bank and tree lines.

CASTING LURES IN SHALLOW WATER

Inset

Best done either early morning or late afternoon when sun is low. Stand well off the shallow water and use long rods and light line to cast well up into the shallows, with jerkbaits or other shallow- running lures. If you see a fish tailing, aim your cast beyond the fish and far enough ahead of it so it is not spooked.

GOLDEN PERCH AND THE 5-METRE CONTOUR

You can catch golden perch in a variety of depths, from less than 30 cm to well over 20 metres. However, when trolling dams in an exploratory manner, use your sounder to locate the five metre contour and to troll along that. Golden perch often favour this depth because it offers enough diffusion of strong sunlight to be comfortable, easy access to deeper water for a quick escape if danger threatens, and frequently, the edges of weed beds. Since golden perch habitually patrol the outer edges of weed beds, this is as good a place as any to start looking for them.

GOLDEN PERCH AND WEED BEDS

Weed beds provide both cover and food for golden perch and many other fish too. Sometimes the fish will be located on the outer edge of the weed beds and occasionally in a deep trench that sometimes forms between the weed bed and the bank. Gaps in the weed are prime spots to cast to as fish often sit in these waiting to ambush any prey that decide to shift from one weed bank to another.

JIGGING FRESH WATER

Fish in large impoundments tend to behave differently to those in rivers— they school more readily and move around in search of aggregations of prey. Often, these clusters of baitfish and crustaceans assemble in mid water, well away from any recognizable structure and can be discovered by using an echo sounder. You can catch these fish by dropping sinking lures down to the school and jigging them back up again. Depending on the fish type, you might need to use spinnerbaits, leadhead jigs with soft plastic tails or chromed metal bar lures. Even European ice jigs will take fish in this situation and you should experiment with lure choices, sizes and presentations until you find what the fish want on the day.

WORKING WEED BEDS

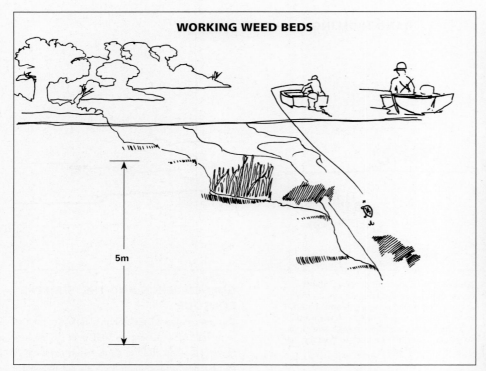

5m

Golden perch will often sit just outside a weed bed, on the five metre contour line. To find this productive strip of trolling water, you can use your sounder or make an estimate of depth, based on your observations of the immediate bankside terrain. If you can't see the bottom because of turbidity, start your trolling run a distance off the bank you judge will give you that ideal depth. Usually, the bottom profile on dams will resemble that of the hillside immediately above the water, so whatever distance up the hill will result in a five metre climb, the same sort of water depth will usually be found a similar distance off the bank.

CASTING STRATEGIES

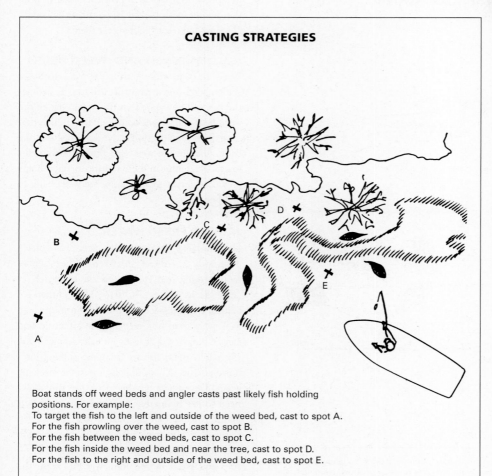

Boat stands off weed beds and angler casts past likely fish holding positions. For example:
To target the fish to the left and outside of the weed bed, cast to spot A.
For the fish prowling over the weed, cast to spot B.
For the fish between the weed beds, cast to spot C.
For the fish inside the weed bed and near the tree, cast to spot D.
For the fish to the right and outside of the weed bed, cast to spot E.

Bass in dams will school up and take metal jigs like this one. The trick is to first find the fish on the sounder, then drop the lures down to them.

MULLET AND BERLEY

Mullet in rivers can be caught from the bank, but are particularly susceptible to anglers fishing from boats, since they can travel to where they are already gathered and feeding. You will do much better though and keep the fish within reach of your chosen fishing position if you use berley. The two very best berleys for mullet are pollard (or poultry laying mash) and plain white bread, especially if using bread for bait. If you are using garden worms for bait, mix a few cut-up worms in with the berley so the fish get a taste for the worms as well and they will then more readily take baits of the same type.

MULLET FLOAT FISHING AND WEED EDGES

A boat allows you to fish the very productive channel water that can be out of reach for bank fishermen sometimes because of distance, or because it is situated on the outer edge of dense bankside weed beds. If surface activity reveals there are mullet schools in the pool you want to fish, tie the boat or anchor it just outside the weed beds and a little way (say, 10 to 15 metres)

JIGGING FRESHWATER

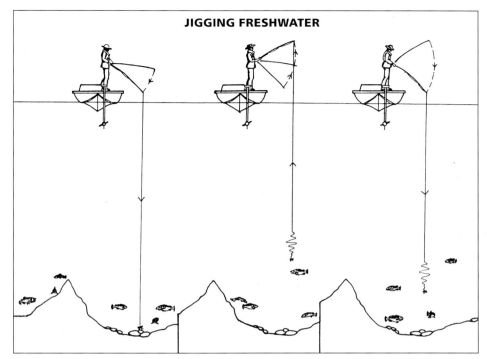

Drop jig down to either the bottom, or the depth at which fish are schooling.
Lift the rod tip briskly to raise the jig, then drop it again to allow the jig to fall.
Work the jig at various depths, by counting down for say twenty seconds, then on the next drop let it fall
for only fifteen, then ten and so on. This way you will present the jig to specific depth ranges.

up-current of where the fish have been spotted. If there is no current, position the boat upwind. This allows you to cast or drift float-rigs right down the edge of the weed bed and down to where the fish are. Use suitable baits, such as dough or garden worms, and set the float depth so that the bait travels about 10–15 cm off the bottom in the deepest water and just clear of the bottom where it shallows.

Murray cod are not always taken from muddy water. This fish took a lure cast towards cover in water that was crystal clear.

This golden perch took a lure cast towards the bank from a boat in a small, secluded bay.

Golden perch can be fished for with baits, such as worms or crayfish tails

MURRAY COD AND FALLEN LOGS

Murray cod like to hide beneath, inside or next to some substantial form of cover, mostly horizontal cover if any is available as it provides them with protection from above. This is why fallen logs often hold good cod. Fish the structure by drifting baits down past the log or bringing lures past it, preferably diving deep enough to pass lower than the log and close alongside. It can even be helpful to have the lure bump the log a few tines as it passes as Murray cod can take some stimulating before they rouse themselves to strike. In the absence of horizontal cover they will use vertical structure.

MURRAY COD AND MOONLIT NIGHTS

It's something of a secret among experienced cod fishermen that you can catch Murray cod at night. You can do this most nights with bait, but there is a truly exciting form of fishing awaiting you if you choose to fish for them with lures on bright, moonlit nights. Big surface lures that create a lot of commotion are ideal for this sort of fishing and these should be fished slowly, with frequent pauses and lots of subtle twitches and bloops.

MURRAY COD AND ROCKY SHORES

Areas of dams and rivers that have rocky edges dropping into deep water can be Murray cod hot spots. The rocky edges provide cover for the cod as well as food, in the form of small of

In Lake Mulwala on the NSW and Victorian border, there is an enormous amount of habitat for cod in the vertical timber.

trolling speed needed to get the lure working properly will end up being too fast for the cod to chase the lure. It can also be difficult to troll the sort of lures that cod like up into a strong flow because there may be too much water pressure for the lures, making them lose their balance, and skid up and out of the water. Try tying up to a tree and casting snag-resistant lures such as heavy spinnerbaits into the pocket water between the timber. You will find it easier to control these lures in the current if you switch the blades from the round Colorado type to the more slender Willow-leaf style.

NATIVE FISH TROLLING TACTICS

When you troll more than one lure at a time for native fish, run the deepest-diving lure the furthest back on the outside or deeper side of the boat. When you turn around and troll back along the bank in the opposite direction, remember to change the position of the deep and shallow

baitfish and yabbies. The cod often prowl along such areas, on the lookout for anything that might be edible to dart out from cover and make and easy meal. Anglers can capitalize on this by using sinking lures, such as spinnerbaits, Mann's George-n-shads, weighted soft plastic lures like lizards, shads, worms and grubs. Cast these right in hard against the rock walls and let them sink to the bottom before beginning a slow, halting hop and crawl retrieve along the bottom. Discipline yourself, to wind slowly and deliberately, working the lure down deep all the way back underneath the boat. Cod will sometimes follow a lure for some distance before taking it—often just as it starts to leave the bottom and rise toward the surface.

MURRAY COD AND STANDING TIMBER

Many dams have areas of steep bank with rows of drowned but still standing trees just off the bank. These submerged tree trunks are a favourite place for Murray cod to sit in ambush and wait for passing food. To catch these fish, you cast repeatedly so the lure lands right alongside the tree trunk and sinks well down before retrieval, or, you can troll right along the row of trees, keeping the lure in close to the bottom of the tree.

MURRAY COD IN STRONG CURRENT

The rivers in which Murray cod are found are often prone to flooding or significant changes in current speed. The best river fishing is often when the rivers are in spate and running fairly quickly, so you will need to rig up and adapt your techniques to suit this situation.

It is difficult to troll for Murray cod in the same direction as a strong river flow because the

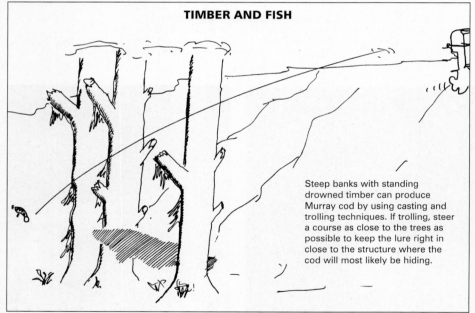

TIMBER AND FISH

Steep banks with standing drowned timber can produce Murray cod by using casting and trolling techniques. If trolling, steer a course as close to the trees as possible to keep the lure right in close to the structure where the cod will most likely be hiding.

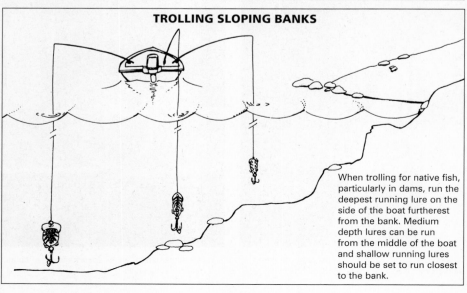

TROLLING SLOPING BANKS

When trolling for native fish, particularly in dams, run the deepest running lure on the side of the boat furtherest from the bank. Medium depth lures can be run from the middle of the boat and shallow running lures should be set to run closest to the bank.

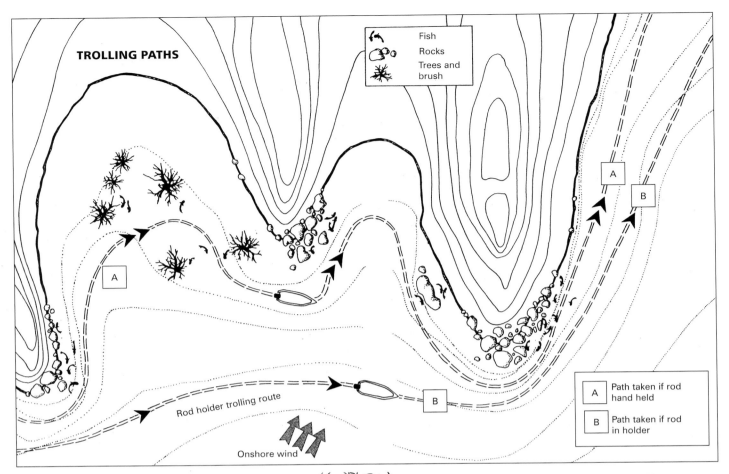

TROLLING PATHS

Fish
Rocks
Trees and brush

A — Path taken if rod hand held
B — Path taken if rod in holder

Rod holder trolling route

Onshore wind

Rod holders or hand held?

running rods. This way, all three lures will be running near the bottom where native fish are often found.

ROD HOLDERS OR HAND HELD?

While it is easier to troll with the rod in a rod holder, it is not as effective as holding the rod in your hand. This is because a hand-held rod can be manipulated as the boat follows the fish-holding contours. With the rod in a rod holder this sort of intensive searching pattern is almost impossible. This technique is particularly useful if trolling along a windblown shore.

SARATOGA AND SECRET WATER

Saratoga often position themselves in deep undercut bankside channels. Often, these are tucked in tight beneath thick overhanging foliage, such as pandanus clumps, making it impossible to fish them from the bank and difficult even to see from the water. Observant anglers however will notice that there are usually small areas of open surface between the outer fringes of the pandanus and the inner edge of any stands of lily pads. By casting lures into these small pockets of secret water, you can often find that a big, bad-tempered saratoga that is ready to pounce on anything that falls into its domain.

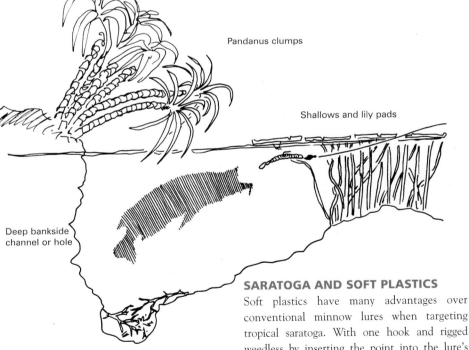

Pandanus clumps

Shallows and lily pads

Deep bankside channel or hole

Saratoga and secret water

SARATOGA AND SOFT PLASTICS

Soft plastics have many advantages over conventional minnow lures when targeting tropical saratoga. With one hook and rigged weedless by inserting the point into the lure's body, soft plastics can be cast into classic saratoga habitat more safely, since they won't hang up on weed or lily pads as much. Most soft plastic lures also respond well to short-range twitches and jiggles, a retrieve that saratoga find irresistible. Lastly, the soft body of these lures encourages hard-mouthed saratoga to take the lure in deep where the hook can find a secure hold.

SARATOGA IN THE LILY PADS

Many tropical rivers in far north Queensland and the Northern Territory have shallow mud-bottom sections covered with vast stands of lily pads. Saratoga often swim around freely under them but to fish such places with conventional minnow lures, you need lure types that can penetrate this living barrier and get to the fish-holding water underneath, such as spinnerbaits and weighted soft plastic lures, rigged weedless, with the hook point inserted into the soft lure body.

SARATOGA SURFACE TRICK

If you look at a photograph of a saratoga, you can't help but be struck by the way the eyes are mounted right on top of the head. The fish spends most of its life looking upwards. The almost dead flat line of its back allows the saratoga to cruise undetected just beneath the surface, while the large top-mounted eyes and upward slanting mouth are for spotting and taking food from below. This means they are a walk-up start for surface lures such as poppers, fizzers, paddlers, sliders and frog imitations. A very effective and low-cost lure option for saratoga is to use an unweighted double tail with a z-bend hook. This is cast to likely cover and brought back with the rod tip held high and steadily retrieved, just fast enough to make the twin tail tips ripple enticingly across the surface.

Big silver perch may need the stimulus of a big lure to get them to strike. It doesn't matter if the fish is feeding or defending its territory, the hit is savage and the fight strong either way.

This saratoga took the surface popper seen in the background and jumped repeatedly during the fight.

SILVER PERCH AND LURE SIZE

There are two schools of though about choosing lures for silver perch. One is to take their relatively small mouths and usual diet of small creatures into account and use lures that are small enough for them to inhale in a single fast strike, which is their usual feeding style. The other tactic is to use lures that are large enough to represent a territorial threat and produce a strike that is not a feeding charge so much as a defensive reaction against what is perceived to be an invader.

The first tactic targets schooling silver perch in sizes from 250 grams to one kilogram, while the latter technique works very well on solitary big fish that have set up a territory and will aggressively repel any intruders.

SILVER PERCH AND SHRIMP BAITS

Silver perch will take a variety of freshwater baits, but none as readily as a nice bunch of live kicking freshwater shrimp. Use a minimum of two shrimp per bait, and rig them belly to belly, so they kick against one another. This draws silver perch in from considerable distances away. If you do rig with a single large shrimp or several small dead ones, add some appeal to the presentation by dropping the bait down and jigging or bobbing it up and down several times at a particular depth. If you don't get a bite at that depth, raise the bait a metre or so and bob it there for a while. Continue to vary the depth at which you are bouncing the bait until you get a hit or until you have covered all the water depth from top to bottom. Then, cast to a slightly different spot and repeat the process. Since silvers often gather in bays that have a lot of dead standing timber in them, you can go from tree to tree, tying up at each and fishing it thoroughly before moving on to the next.

SILVER PERCH AND STRUCTURE

Silver perch relate strongly to structure as much of what they eat is found near sunken trees, weed beds and rocky shorelines, as well as any hard structure that deflects current and creates feeding eddies. This is why in rivers, silvers are often found near weirs and barrages, especially those with relief pipes and culverts that allow a percentage of the river's flow to be maintained. In dams, small to young adult silvers move in schools throughout heavily timbered bays, while larger adults favour weed beds and rocky points or jumbles of fallen logs and drowned tree stumps.

SILVER PERCH SCHOOLING BEHAVIOUR

Younger fish are more mobile and gregarious than older, larger specimens and may shift from bay to bay within a dam or cruise up and down a river looking for forage. Larger fish seem to alter their diet to include significant amounts of vegetation and may simply browse over and around dense weed beds, or take up residence around suitable rocks and stumps from where they charge out and grab passing food. As juveniles, silvers need the protection of numbers to avoid predation by larger golden perch, Murray cod and shags. The schools

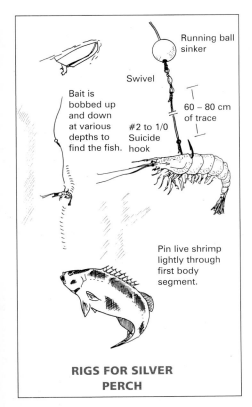

Running ball sinker

Swivel

Bait is bobbed up and down at various depths to find the fish.

60 – 80 cm of trace

#2 to 1/0 Suicide hook

Pin live shrimp lightly through first body segment.

RIGS FOR SILVER PERCH

Silver perch and shrimp baits

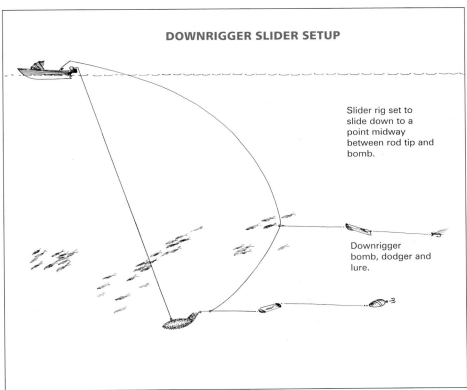

DOWNRIGGER SLIDER SETUP

Slider rig set to slide down to a point midway between rod tip and bomb.

Downrigger bomb, dodger and lure.

Slider rig

they form tend to function as a single unit, and the food needed to sustain such a voracious corporate 'body', can only be found by the school being almost constantly on the prowl. Paradoxically, the food requirements of a single larger fish are much less, allowing big adults to settle in some productive place or another. Such food resources must be vigorously protected however, which explains the extremely territorial behaviour of the large adult fish.

SLIDER RIGS

A slider rig (in this sense) is a lure or fly (and a dodger if needed) attached to one end of a monofilament trace about 1.5 metres long that is set on a downrigger to run between the surface and the downrigger bomb. To deploy the slider, set the downrigger bomb and lure at the chosen depth, then while underway, simply clip the slider rig onto the downrigger wire. Toss it over the back of the moving boat and allow it to slide down to a point mid-way between the rod tip and the bomb. This allows you to effectively double the amount of water being covered by any trolling run.

SMELTING FISH

In many deep freshwater reservoirs, a native freshwater forage fish called the smelt (Retropinna semoni) is abundant in the surface layers, but mostly well away from the bank. This makes it of most interest to boat anglers, who on a glassy calm can come across literally thousands of tiny dimples being made in the surface by these important prey.

Most smelt are less than 60 mm long and when there is a surge in the juvenile population in late spring through summer, there may be absolute clouds of tiny silver-grey slivers hovering at or just below the surface. Not so common in highland dams as those at lower altitudes, smelt are mostly of angling significance to impoundment bass and yellowbelly anglers.

When bass target smelt right on the surface, it is usually very early in the morning or late in the afternoon, and small streamer pattern flies can be successful, but between October and February, they may attack schools of smelt at depth at any time of the day. When this deeper feeding occurs, ice jigs, slender soft plastics and deep-fished flies on high-density lines are better choices.

SOOTY GRUNTER'S COMPETITIVE STREAK

There are few fish as pugnacious and willing to strike at lures as sooty grunter. These fish have enormous appetites and when in schools will compete ferociously for food, even attacking an inanimate floating object, like a stick or fallen berry, if one fish in the school so much as shows a passing interest in it. Understandably lure selection does seem not to be critical to catching these fish, but you will improve your catch rate by using smallish lures and casting as close to structure as possible. Prime spots are the bases of small waterfalls and cascades, wherever the stream narrows, accelerating flow and funneling food, and near fallen logs or weedy corners.

This tiny sooty grunter gives some idea of how aggressive these fish are. The lure is quite large for something as small as this fish to hit, but it was taken without hesitation.

SOOTY GRUNTER, COVER AND TACTICS

Boat fishermen can target sooty grunter in any of the coastal freshwater drainages of north Queensland. In the upper reaches of such streams, access for large craft is limited, but canoes can provide excellent angling for those prepared to paddle and portage and to cast toward rocky shorelines, rapids and large mid-stream boulders. Downstream, bankside trees, logs and weed beds near sandbars are worth casting to or trolling near.

Most river sooty grunter weigh something less than a kilogram but may approach two kilograms. In dams where sooty grunter have been stocked, they grow to enormous size and can exceed four kilograms. They are mostly targeted by boat fishermen and can be caught on baits of peeled crayfish tail, whole small crayfish and large Macrobrachium shrimp, or simply garden or scrub worms. They will also vigorously take lures and flies, notably, spinnerbaits, diving minnows and small soft plastics. Successful flies include streamers, Crazy Charlies and Dahlberg Divers.

SOOTY GRUNTERS LOVE SHADE

If there is one sure way to find sooty grunters during the middle of the day, it is find shaded water of the right depth. In really dense shade, sooties can be found in water as little as 30 centimetres deep, but in more open spots with scattered shade water over 60 centimetres will produce much better. Target banks that are lined with large trees, steep rocky banks or large mid-stream boulders, or logs that have fallen down from the bank to the water, creating shaded areas beneath them. Often, the hits will come just before the lure wriggles out of the shade and into the sunlight, so apply retrieves that feature a lot of short, and intermittent rod movements.

SOUNDERS AND JIG FISHING

Developed to a marked degree in recent years for impoundment bass, jig and sounder techniques are also applicable to golden perch and trout. In most cases, jigging for bass involves finding mid-water schools of fish, often well away from any obvious structure. There will be some form of irregular bottom shape relevant however, whether a submerged hilltop or drowned forest, or as subtle as a slight bump in the bottom. Even slight humps in the dam floor can set up feeding eddies as they deflect convection currents created by the heat of the sun or prevailing winds at the surface. Golden perch are frequently jigged around tree lines, whether bankside or mid water, and quite often in association with the original riverbed, that still serves to direct sub-surface water movements in dams.

Trout tend to gather in mid water around suspended schools of daphnia (water fleas) or in some lowland lakes, schools of smelt. They will also

Modern freshwater fishing boats are marvels of sophistication and equipment. This one shows how you can pack sounders, electric motors and casting platforms neatly into a stylish and effective fishing boat.

Sooty grunter love shade

SHADE AND SOOTIES

A – shade under trees

B – shade alongside rock faces

C – shade beneath bridged logs

forage around drowned standing timber, where they target other small baitfish, crustaceans and emerging insects such as dragonfly nymphs.

Part of the trick with all jig fishing is to use the sounder to locate the fish school. The rest is learning to interpret what is showing on the screen so you can make appropriate lures choices and presentations. When bass are on large active prey like bony bream, chromed metal jigs such as Raiders (up to 40 grams) are often the best choice. When the prey is smaller, or the fish are not feeding so aggressively, ice jigs like the Rouhala and NilsMaster models can work well. Golden perch respond well to soft plastic jigs like Mann's George'n'shads, or to spinnerbaits or sinking Rattling Spots. Trout will take micro-jigs with either Marabou feather tails or soft plastic grubs attached, ice jigs, tiny tail spinners, or even at times simple chrome spoons like Wonder Wobblers and mini Tobys.

THE GPS TRICK

It has only become apparent in the last decade just how effective a fishing tool GPS can be in freshwater impoundments. This is because fish in large dams tend not to be biting equally well (or even distributed evenly) in all parts of the lake at once. This means that without some speedy system of reconnaissance, you can spend a lot of time fishing where there are few or no fish instead of fishing to the greatest concentrations of active fish possible. GPS, when used in conjunction with a depth sounder, can help you by allowing you to do a quick tour of a dam with both units switched on. As you drive the boat over an interesting structure that might hold fish or an actual showing of fish, you simply punch a key and the GPS registers that location as an 'event' mark. This way, you can cover a great deal if not all of a lake in a very short time, then go back and fish the best and most promising of those marks by simply calling up the appropriate entry and hitting the 'go to' navigation button. The GPS will have fixed that spot as a set of latitude and longitude coordinates and will provide an unerring course right back to the spot from wherever you are on the lake.

THE SHAG-DRIVE SYSTEM

Many inland freshwater dams attract and support large populations of fish-eating birds, including several species of shags and cormorants. Little Black Cormorants (Phalacrocorax sulcirostris) flock in sometimes huge numbers and will work cooperatively as a team to 'drive' scattered baitfish into dense shoals that can then be chased and caught more easily. Some anglers become agitated when they see this happening, believing that the shags are unfairly making things tough for them. More informed anglers accept these events as a natural consequence of creating food

In rivers that have lots of shallows and tight spots, canoes are a very suitable form of fishing boat. You may need to get out from time to time though and portage it through rapids like this one.

resources for native fish—birds and further, are intelligent enough also to realize that wherever baitfish are compressed into such dense rafts by the birds, that predatory fish like bass, silver perch and yellowbelly will be drawn to the melee and can be trolled and jigged from underneath such activity.

TROLLING DEEP

There are many devices available to anglers to enable lures and baits to be trolled down deep. Downriggers are one such method, but there are also three other systems that allow you to do much the same thing. These are; the Downunder sinker, the Paravane and the Trolling Board.

TROLLING MUDEYES

Trolling mudeyes (the aquatic larvae of the dragonfly) is an effective way of catching trout in lakes, but you need some additional gear to get the bait down below the surface, provide some action and also make the bait more visible. All of these things can be done by rigging the mudeye behind either Cowbells or Ford Fenders. This deadly method of trout trolling was developed by well-known Victorian angler Fred Jobson. How you hook the mudeye is critical. A long shank hook, such as the Partridge, Reddich, or Tyrall style is required. The knot used to attach the hook is also very important, as the tag should close away from the hook shank. This helps to hold the mudeye on the hook.

Little Black Cormorant

DEEP TROLLING ACCESSORIES

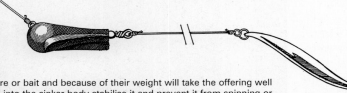

1 Downunder sinkers
These are rigged ahead of the lure or bait and because of their weight will take the offering well below the surface. Fins moulded into the sinker body stabilise it and prevent it from spinning or weaving off-line. A towing eye allows it to be tied or clipped to your main line while a swivel moulded into the tail of the unit can accept a trace leading to the bait or lure.

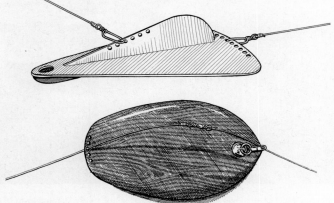

2 Paravanes
A paravane is a delta-shaped 'wing' weighted at the front to keep the unit nose down and on track when trolled, with a broad horizontal flat wing topped by a vertical fin. Various attachment holes along the upper edge of the fin allow the towing angle to be precisely adjusted, while a row of attachment holes across the trailing edge of the flat wing provide the choice of several towing points. Choosing the central one will mean the unit tracks straight and in line with the boat, while attaching the trace clip progressively further to one side of centre or the other, will tilt the unit and make it swim off to that side a little. Paravanes can be used to send a lure or bait down as far as 10 metres. Factors that affect this depth capability include the size of the paravane, the diameter of the main line and the size and resistance of the lure or bait being towed.

3 Trolling boards
Trolling boards may be rigged ahead of a bait or lure and can take them down about four metres. Unlike downrigging and other forms of depth-presentation, trolling boards tend to have a weaving action of their own and can impart substantial action to the lure or bait as well as simply presenting it down deep. For this reason, they are popular with many trout anglers.

TROLLED MUDEYES ON FORD FENDERS OR COWBELLS

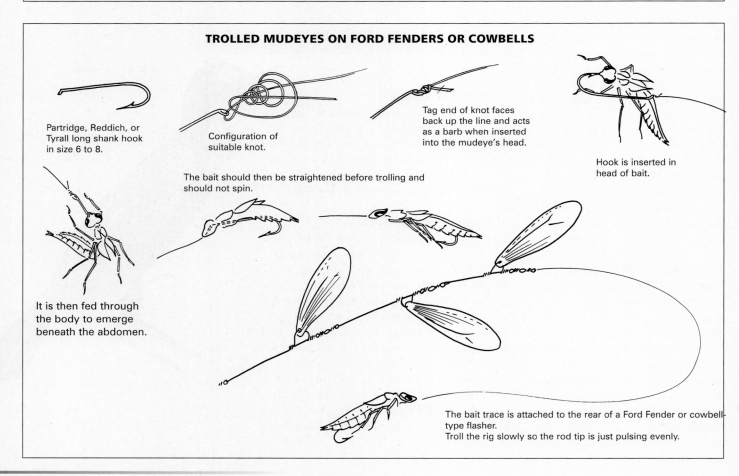

Partridge, Reddich, or Tyrall long shank hook in size 6 to 8.

Configuration of suitable knot.

Tag end of knot faces back up the line and acts as a barb when inserted into the mudeye's head.

Hook is inserted in head of bait.

The bait should then be straightened before trolling and should not spin.

It is then fed through the body to emerge beneath the abdomen.

The bait trace is attached to the rear of a Ford Fender or cowbell-type flasher.
Troll the rig slowly so the rod tip is just pulsing evenly.

Right: Example 'A' shows two metal spoons, set deep on downriggers, two 'Cobra' style lures (one set short on the Port side and the other set long on the Starboard). A third lure type, a deep running plug, is set down the middle in what is sometimes called, the 'shotgun' position. The rear-most three lures are running without any depth enhancing aids, and are therefore classified as 'flat-lining'. By staggering the lures like this you are not only covering various depths, but also an extensive area of water behind the boat.

Example 'B' shows a flat-lined diving plug in the shotgun position, a metal spoon behind a paravane on the inboard Port side and a Cobra behind a trolling sinker on the inboard Starboard. Set back from those another Cobra is flat-lined on the on the outer Port side and a metal spoon is flat-lined well back from the outer Starboard corner.

Example 'C' shows a much simpler arrangement, with two lures flat-lined, a metal spoon on the Port side and a Cobra on the Starboard.

TROLLING STRATEGIES

Freshwater trolling options can include various kinds of equipment, each designed to set the lure to troll at a particular depth. These devices include downriggers, flatlines and paravanes, and each requires a suitable trolling strategy to get the most from the technique and gear.

TROLLING WHITEBAIT

Trolling a minnow or fish bait such as a glassie or whitebait is a deadly freshwater tactic. This rig produces well on both rainbow trout and Chinook salmon in Victorian lakes and was developed for use in Lake Bullen Merri in Western Victoria.

Below: This rainbow trout was taken by trolling a small brown 'Spicky' lure that approximated the appearance and size of the goldfish on which the trout was feeding.

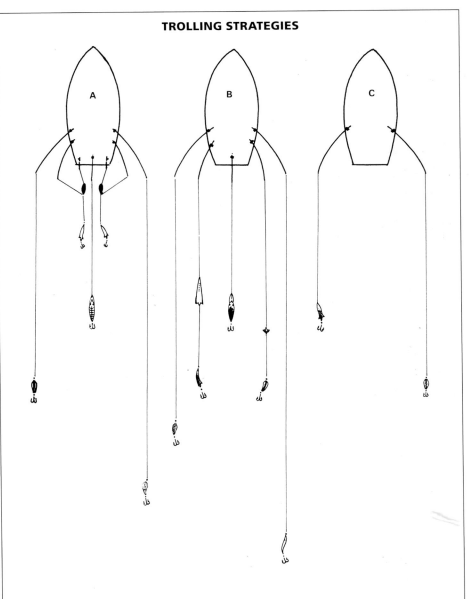

TROLLING STRATEGIES

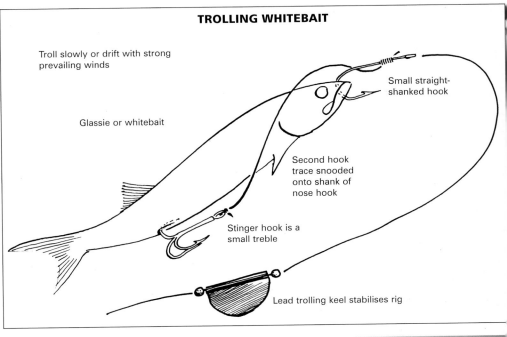

TROLLING WHITEBAIT

Troll slowly or drift with strong prevailing winds

Small straight-shanked hook

Glassie or whitebait

Second hook trace snooded onto shank of nose hook

Stinger hook is a small treble

Lead trolling keel stabilises rig

CHAPTER ELEVEN

FRESHWATER
LANDBASED FISHING

Lure manipulation — This golden perch was goaded into striking by lifting the rod tip briskly to make the floating lure dive, then pausing the retrieve and allowing the lure to rise toward the surface. This routine was repeated all the way back in to the bank until the fish hit. Often, such strikes will come while the lure is still slowly rising.

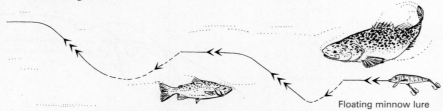

a Pausing with a sinking lure lets it drop and flutter down, then winding again makes it surge upward.

Sinking metal lure

b Pausing with a floating lure lets it rise momentarily then winding again makes it dive and swim again.

Floating minnow lure

c Zig-zag retrieves   Interrupting a steady retrieve with aggressive sideways movements of the rod will make a lure zig-zag in toward the shore. This duplicates the evasive behaviour of many bait fish.

ADD LIFE TO YOUR LURES

While all lures have some action built into them, you can enhance their fish-catching potential by adding extra movement or 'life' to them during the retrieve. As you wind them in, try pausing the retrieve and dropping the rod tip, or, move the rod tip aggressively from side to side. Sometimes, just twitching the rod tip as you retrieve the lure will be enough to prompt a strike from a fish that is following without hitting.

BAIT FISHING FOR MURRAY COD

When baitfishing big rivers for Murray cod, always position yourself well upstream of a snag. Cast out and allow your rig to swing around in the current so it comes to rest close to the snag but some little way upcurrent. This will avoid having your bait hang up in the snag and the subsequent frustration of losing the rig and having to rig up again.

Fig. 9.1 left: You can prompt strikes when spinning by varying the retrieve pattern.

Below: Murray cod baitfishing spots — Often, good baitfishing spots for Murray cod are in discoloured water, which is why aromatic baits such as bardi grubs and crayfish work so well. Another component of these spots is heavy timber snags such as trees that have fallen into the river after bank collapses during heavy rain. Use heavy line and fish close to the timber to catch these fish, as they seldom stray far from cover.

BARDI GRUBS

A selection of rubber bands is essential for freshwater bait fishing. For example if you're using bardi grubs for native fish, a couple of rubber bands can be really handy to make an attractive and presentable offering.

FISHING TACTICS IN RIVERS FOR NATIVE FISH

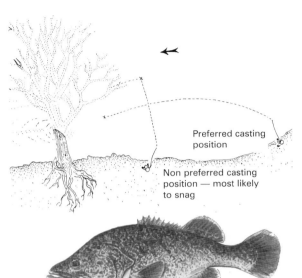

Preferred casting position

Non preferred casting position — most likely to snag

Bait fishing for lake trout at dawn and dusk — In the gloom, the trout move inshore with more confidence, which brings them within reach of anglers' baits.

BAIT FISHING FOR TROUT IN LAKES

When bait fishing for trout in lakes, always set the reel so line can peel freely from the spool. Baitcasters will need to be set out of gear with a light ratchet on, but spinning reels are simply set with the bail arm open. This free spool technique works as well with delicately hooked mudeyes (dragonfly larvae) set under floats as it does with a lightly weighted worm, rigged to sit on the bottom.

Trout prefer to take a bait that offers little or no resistance. To avoid having a trout drop the bait in fright, you may need to feed out as much as 10 metres of free line when the bait is picked up, before setting the hook by raising the rod tip smoothly and slowly. You can use various kinds of strike indicators to alert you that a fish has your bait. An empty aluminium drink can be set up to fall noisily when the line pulls tight around it, or if you want to keep things quiet, hook the line

over a blade of grass, then watch the grass like a hawk. You can also buy commercially made line clips that snap onto the rod grip.

BANKSIDE JIGGING

When fishing small creeks or rivers with deep water right alongside the bank, you can sometimes drop sinking lures straight down and take fish that are hiding deep inside bank undercuts. Typical places are those with logs running out

TROUT TACTICS

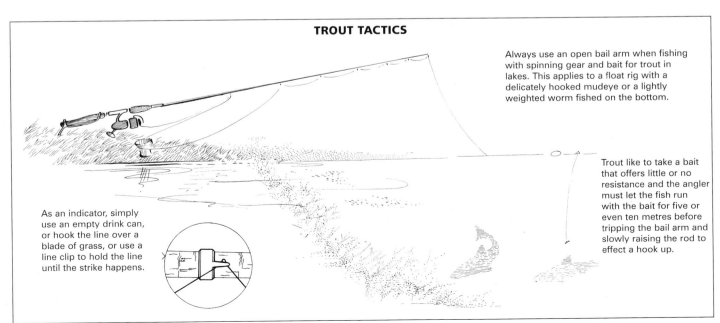

Always use an open bail arm when fishing with spinning gear and bait for trout in lakes. This applies to a float rig with a delicately hooked mudeye or a lightly weighted worm fished on the bottom.

As an indicator, simply use an empty drink can, or hook the line over a blade of grass, or use a line clip to hold the line until the strike happens.

Trout like to take a bait that offers little or no resistance and the angler must let the fish run with the bait for five or even ten metres before tripping the bail arm and slowly raising the rod to effect a hook up.

Lift and drop spinnerbait tactic — Spinnerbaits can be worked in deep rocky clefts like this one in the New England district to catch Murray cod. This fish hit after the lure had been cast and allowed to sink to the bottom, then brought in slowly by lifting it with the rod tip, letting it sink again, then winding in the slack before repeating the lift, drop and wind routine.

COLLECTING BARDI GRUBS

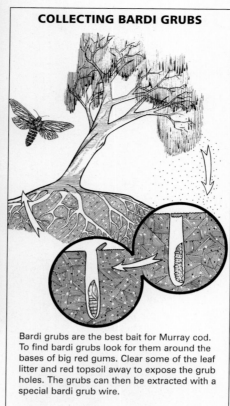

Bardi grubs are the best bait for Murray cod. To find bardi grubs look for them around the bases of big red gums. Clear some of the leaf litter and red topsoil away to expose the grub holes. The grubs can then be extracted with a special bardi grub wire.

MAXIMISING GRUB BAITS

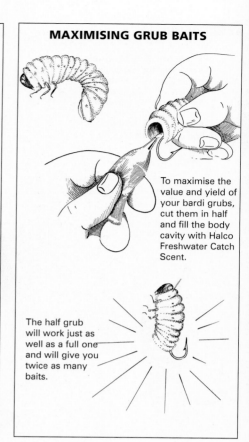

To maximise the value and yield of your bardi grubs, cut them in half and fill the body cavity with Halco Freshwater Catch Scent.

The half grub will work just as well as a full one and will give you twice as many baits.

from the bank at an angle, creating a small pocket of deep water between the log and the bank. Try dropping down bladed lures like Celtas or spinnerbaits and jigging them up and down for a few seconds at various levels.

When rivers are in flood and the water is discoloured lures are not appropriate. The best technique is to use a lightly weighted scrub worm. Again, present the bait right against the deep banks. In flooded rivers the trout move in right against the bank.

BARDI GRUBS ARE GREAT BAIT

Bardi grubs are the larval stage of a large native moth and are quite large and meaty baits, ideal for many freshwater fish. They are particularly effective baits for Murray cod, but don't discount their attractiveness to big trout.

Some anglers gather and use their bardi grubs fresh; they can be kept alive for long periods if stored individually in something like a cigarette packet or better still in the hollow of a Rangoon cane. If given a 'home' and left in a cool environment under the house they will live for months.

Others prefer to pickle them in brine or other preservative solutions so they can be stored for longer periods and used when required. Pickling bardi grubs toughens the skin and enables the bait to last much longer on a hook than the fresh grub too.

Another method is to simply freeze them. Before freezing it is imperative to blanch them in boiling water for 40 seconds. If this isn't done the bait becomes unmanageable and unusable when thawed.

BEING INCONSPICUOUS

A large part of getting close enough to fish to catch them relies on not alerting them to your presence. This means wearing clothing that blends in with your surroundings.

CASTING ACCURACY AND CREEKS

Often when fishing small freshwater rivers and creeks, you will need to thread a cast between overhanging bushes or tree branches to land a lure or bait in just the right spot. For better casting accuracy, always take your time, don't rush the cast and think about where the bait or lure is going before you let fly.

To cast accurately use thinner line and fill the reel spool to within three or four millimetres of the lip. You will find it easier to cast light weights with reasonable control. It helps to practise your casting in more open water until you can hit whatever target you are aiming at, then to try for those difficult to reach places that seem to hold all the big fish.

COUNTDOWN CASTING

Fishing big open freshwater lakes from the shore can sometimes mean fishing into quite deep water. Many of the lake fish, such as trout, may be suspending at a particular depth and will feed more readily there than they might down deeper

or closer to the surface. It is a good idea to cast and count your rig down until you know the depth at which the fish are feeding. First cast to one depth — say a count of three — then if that doesn't produce, count the next cast down to four and so forth. When you catch a fish, make your next few casts to the same area and count the rig down to that same depth and often, you will pick up another.

Camouflage — Wear clothing that blends in with the backdrop of the country around you. This angler's dull brown and tan clothing allowed him to get close enough to this large wary trout to catch it.

BIG TROUT

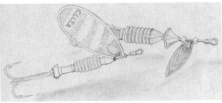

Big trout in rivers show a definite preference for spinners in winter and early spring. There are a variety of spinners that work, including Mepps, Celta and Jensens. If you are spinning on rivers during the cooler months, always be prepared for an occasional big trout to grab these tiny lures.

Big trout and small spinners

COMFORT LIFT

If you practise catch and release fishing then the comfort lift is a technique you should learn. You can lift a lot of Australian native fish quite simply and without injury to either the fish or yourself by positioning your hand under the side of the fish so it is balanced on your palm, before carefully lifting it from the water.

Most times, the fish will lie quite still while you work a hook out of its jaw and then it can be released simply by lowering it into the water.

COARSE ANGLING RIGS

Coarse angling rigs have proved to be very effective on many species in Australia. Redfin, trout, estuary perch and carp are just a few species that are targeted. The techniques and tackle associated with coarse angling are probably more effective than any others. Part of the reason for this is that even the slightest bite is registered. They are balanced with shot to sit the float with just the tip out of the water, so that any bite is registered, even a lift bite.

DEEP WATER RIG

The problem associated with presenting a big bait in deep water is that often the excess line will sink and snag in the shallow water. This can be overcome by greasing your monofilament with floatant and using the deep water rig.

The bubble float helps hold the line off the bottom in the shallow water.

DIVE AND RISE RETRIEVES

When fishing shorelines, there may be deep water right to the bank, but more often there will be various submerged obstructions, such as weed beds, rock piles and sunken shrubbery a little way out from the bank before the deep open water starts. You shouldn't avoid fishing such places though as such bankside features provide habitat and feeding opportunities for many freshwater fish. With high buoyancy floating diver lures, you can explore the deep water and also effectively fish this difficult but productive zone. Cast the lure out, and wind it down as far as you can without getting it fouled. If you wind carefully, you can bring the lure in close to all that fish-holding structure without getting snagged by feeling for any touch of the lure on the submerged objects. When you do feel something, stop the retrieve and allow the lure to float up and over the trouble spot. This technique will often take golden perch and silver perch from large rivers and dams.

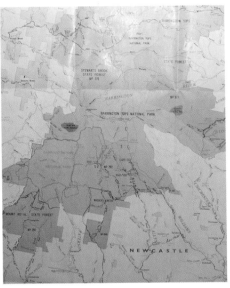

When planning trips to freshwater destinations, aids like forestry maps are invaluable.

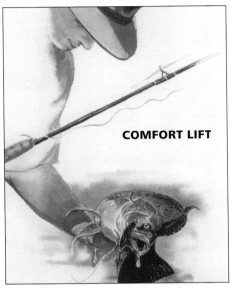

The Comfort Lift

COARSE ANGLING RIGS

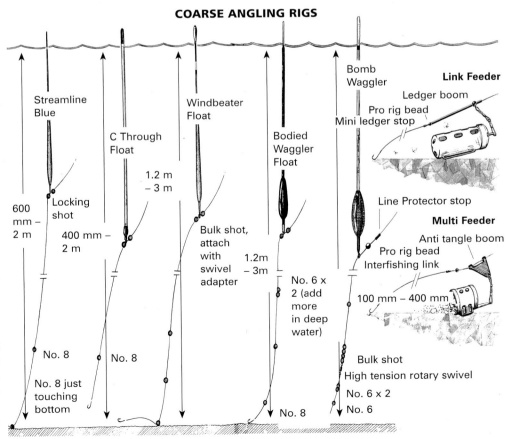

AUSTRALIAN FISHING ENCYCLOPEDIA **341**

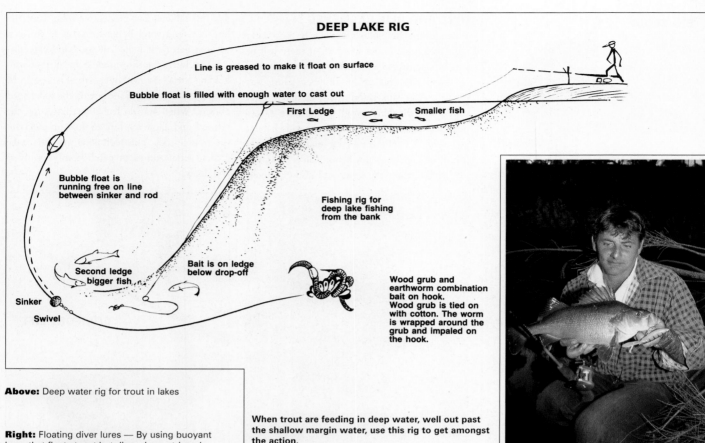

DEEP LAKE RIG

Line is greased to make it float on surface

Bubble float is filled with enough water to cast out

First Ledge   Smaller fish

Bubble float is
running free on line
between sinker and rod

Fishing rig for
deep lake fishing
from the bank

Second ledge
bigger fish

Bait is on ledge
below drop-off

Sinker

Swivel

Wood grub and
earthworm combination
bait on hook.
Wood grub is tied on
with cotton. The worm
is wrapped around the
grub and impaled on
the hook.

Above: Deep water rig for trout in lakes

When trout are feeding in deep water, well out past
the shallow margin water, use this rig to get amongst
the action.

Right: Floating diver lures — By using buoyant
lures that float at rest but dive when retrieved,
you can fish effectively in even small deep rocky
pools like this one. Despite there being lots of
submerged rocks and sunken tree branches to
negotiate, this angler is able to bounce and thread
the lure through the trouble spots and pick up this
fine redfin perch.

DRIFT FISHING

Drift fishing for trout in our rivers is a rewarding
and productive method. The idea is to present
a bait or fly in a natural manner using standard
spinning tackle. The split shot weight in all cases
should be kept to a minimum so that it takes the
bait or fly to the bottom but not all the way. The
rig can then drift naturally across the bottom to
entice trout to strike.

FISHING FOR CATFISH

Catfish can be caught with baits of worms, peeled
crayfish tail or shrimp, all of which they usually
find by smell. The eel-tailed catfish are found in
clear-flowing coastal and inland streams, mostly
around sandy channels and weed beds in one
to two metres of water. They are more common
however in many of the large water storage dams
of the eastern inland of Australia, where they
inhabit the margins in depths from several metres
to shin deep, depending on the time of day. You
can set baits day or night for catfish in dams and
fishing for them in shallow muddy or sandy bays
is always worth a try. A good rig for this work is
simply a running ball sinker above a swivel with
about 0.5 m – 1.0 m of trace below that to a
number #4 to 1/0 hook.

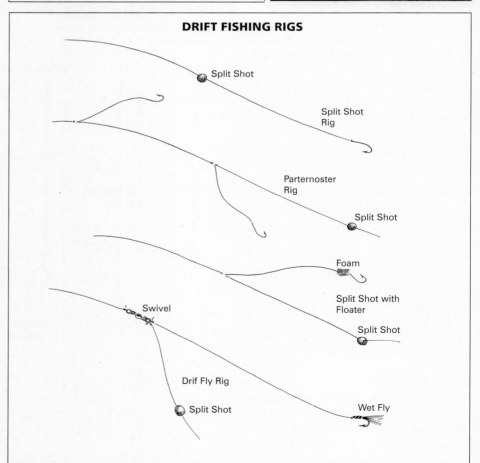

DRIFT FISHING RIGS

Split Shot

Split Shot
Rig

Parternoster
Rig

Split Shot

Foam

Split Shot with
Floater

Split Shot

Swivel

Drif Fly Rig

Split Shot

Wet Fly

There are some great rigs for drift fishing for trout in rivers. They are searching rigs that can be used
with baits such as worms, mudeyes, crickets and other lightweight baits, as well as with flies.

FISH'S SENSE OF SMELL

Fish use their sense of smell to locate food and this is why many odorous baits work so well.

The nostrils of fish like trout and Murray cod are located forward of the eyes and toward the top of the head near the nose.

FISH NEAR THE WEEDS

Some anglers try not to fish near or in weed as they always get snagged. This is a mistake as many fish species live and feed close to underwater vegetation. It can be a problem to fish near weed if you simply use a bottom bait rig that sinks into the weed and becomes lost, or if you are fishing with diving lures and winding them thoughtlessly into the thicket of underwater growth.

However, if you approach fishing near weed intelligently, you will catch a lot more fish. The trick is to use bait rigs that float the bait above the weed or choose lures that can be worked close to but clear of the entangling foliage.

FISHING WITH ARTIFICIAL FLIES

Fly fishing uses small fur and feather dressed hooks called 'flies' to simulate various fish foods. These flies weigh almost nothing and specialised tackle has evolved to cast them. A flyfishing rod is generally long and whippy so it can transmit the casting forces smoothly and allow the delicate presentations that are sometimes needed in this sort of fishing.

What provides the casting weight necessary is not the weight of the fly but the weight of a thick, heavy flyline. When in motion, the mass of the flyline increases dramatically and as the rod propels the line forward, it carries the tiny fly with it. In order to facilitate the connection of the flyline to the fly, a length of nylon leader is used. Often, like the flyline, this leader is tapered, being thicker at the butt end and finer where it is attached to the fly. This tapered line shape is what allows the power of the casting force to be translated into the smooth presentation of a fly to its precise target.

FLY FISHING WITH SPIN TACKLE

One way for a newcomer to quickly get amongst trout on flies is to use a fly and bubble rig so it can be cast on standard spinning gear. It's a great way to get amongst the trout when a new chum has no experience with fly tackle. It's also a serious technique used by many top anglers in many situations.

An occasion for using this technique is on a lake when a fly needs to be cast well out from shore, which can't be achieved on conventional fly casting tackle.

Right: Fish's sense of smell

Catfish locations — Catfish in eastern flowing streams prefer clean water with noticeable flow. The channels and runs shown between rocky outcrops and grass stands in this photo, as well as the hole near the large mid-stream boulder, are all likely eel-tailed catfish haunts.

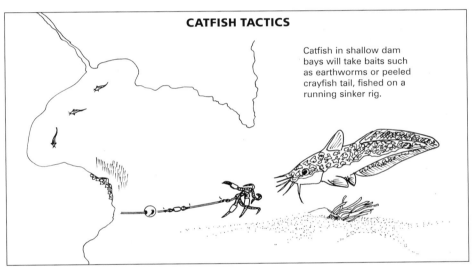

CATFISH TACTICS

Catfish in shallow dam bays will take baits such as earthworms or peeled crayfish tail, fished on a running sinker rig.

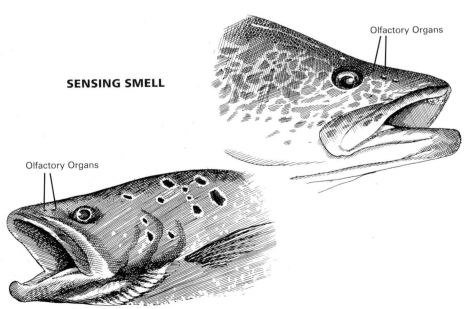

SENSING SMELL

Olfactory Organs

Olfactory Organs

Fish and foliage — It is always worth tossing a lure or bait in near bankside foliage such as reed stands or submerged plants like water weeds. These plants harbour fish foods like shrimp and small fish and also provide shade and shelter that the fish need. This silver perch was caught in a farm dam by targeting just such country.

HOOK PROPORTIONS

It's really important to get the hook proportions just right on your lures. Today, most manufacturers do get them right but a lot don't. If the hook is too big, it will tangle and if it is too small, it will miss too many strikes.

IDENTIFYING RIVER HOT SPOTS

In short, fish are attracted to places where water changes flow, depth, speed or direction. This means they are rarely distributed evenly along a length of river. Instead, they are drawn to specific places such as rapids, holes, channels, rock-piles, snags, and weed beds. Other productive areas are: corners or bends in rivers, junctions with feeder creeks, areas of high bank with deep water adjacent, or places where fallen trees lie across the main river flow.

Many of these river hot spots are obvious at a glance, but others offer more subtle signs of their presence. These can include swirls on the surface, where flow is deflected from a rising bottom or submerged objects, or flotsam lines that indicate an eddy where the current slows, allowing easy fish feeding. It is not only deep water that holds fish either. Shallow glides above rapids can often hold fish that lie in shallow bottom depressions, picking off food sluiced down to them by the accelerating water.

IN-STREAM CASTING

Wade fishing is often much more productive than fishing from the bank. Invest in a pair of waders

WEEDY LAKE RIGS

When fishing in a lake with a low aquatic weed cover or with a rough rocky floor, you can make your scrub worm bait suspend above the weed or rubble by injecting it with air.
Use a standard hypodermic needle and rig a running sinker with a drop of around one to two metres on the trace.

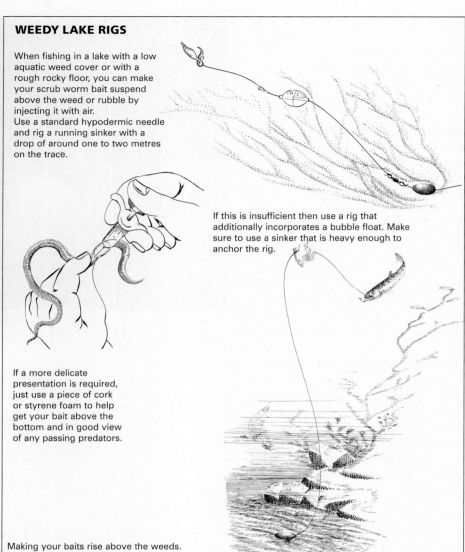

If this is insufficient then use a rig that additionally incorporates a bubble float. Make sure to use a sinker that is heavy enough to anchor the rig.

If a more delicate presentation is required, just use a piece of cork or styrene foam to help get your bait above the bottom and in good view of any passing predators.

Making your baits rise above the weeds.

Fishing with flies — Flies are simply hooks dressed with various natural and synthetic fibres and materials to resemble small creatures that fish eat. This fine brown trout was taken on a small brown nymph pattern, one that approximates the immature sub-aquatic stage of the mayfly.

Below: Flyfishing with spin tackle

Lure casting with flies
Use only two to three kilogram lines and a small bubble float. Half fill the bubble float with water to give the right casting weight.

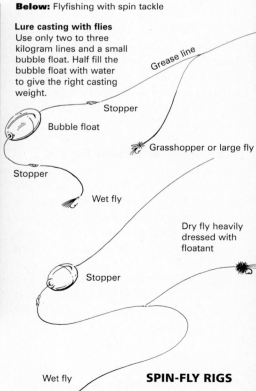

Grease line

Stopper

Bubble float

Grasshopper or large fly

Stopper

Wet fly

Dry fly heavily dressed with floatant

Stopper

Wet fly

SPIN-FLY RIGS

Even though they may only yield small fish, small streams can be a delight to fish on foot.

and add this string to your bow. You'll catch more fish.

You need to proceed carefully though, as river stones and sunken logs can have slippery algal growth on them, making your footing insecure. You also need to move slowly to avoid alerting fish to your presence. The rewards of getting it right though are worth the trouble as wading can open up casting opportunities, allowing you to reach all kinds of productive water.

REACHING THE FISH

It is a widely held belief that the best fish are always further away from the bank, and while this is seldom true, there is sometimes a real and practical need for anglers to make long casts. For instance, you might need to reach a spot right up in an otherwise inaccessible nook or a river, to reach the far bank of a river or lake bay or some feature such as a snag or weed bed well away from the shore.

The basic rules for making long casts are the same as those for making accurate ones. The reel spool must be full, the line needs to be neatly laid down, not bunched up in coils or loops and it must also be fine and light enough for the casting weight in use to pull the line off the reel without difficulty. It is also important to match the casting weight and line size to the bending characteristics of the rod. A rod must not be so stiff that it will not bend enough to load and catapult a light lure, or so thin or flexible that it will not handle casting heavy weights either.

There is a skill involved in loading a rod during the cast. To obtain optimum distance when casting, think not in terms of 'swinging' the rod but instead in terms of 'slinging' the lure or bait. To do this, the rod must be bent during the casting stroke, not just waved around.

RIVER TEMPERATURE

Trout prefer cool to cold water (from 11 to 15 degrees Celsius) which accounts for them being more active in highland regions. This is particularly so in summer, when lowland streams can heat up considerably.

One of the main reasons water temperatures are lower in the highlands is that the amount

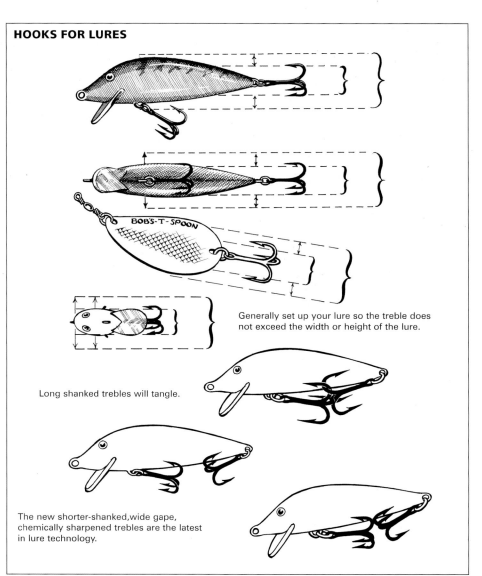

HOOKS FOR LURES

BOB'S-T-SPOON

Generally set up your lure so the treble does not exceed the width or height of the lure.

Long shanked trebles will tangle.

The new shorter-shanked, wide gape, chemically sharpened trebles are the latest in lure technology.

Lure Hook Proportions

In-stream fishing — This angler has managed to circumvent the casting problems of steep banks and heavy foliage by getting into the water and wade fishing. While some casting targets in this patch of river were accessible from the shingle bank in the background, the best hole that held this fish was only open to a cast made from mid-stream.

Reaching the fish — Fish were found in this rocky pool, by casting underneath the waterfall in the background and along a less obvious rock shelf that drops vertically on the extreme right of the picture. Being able to make casts as long as needed will get you more fish.

of sunshine they receive each day is reduced because of the terrain. In more open regions at lower altitude, waters are exposed to much longer periods of direct sunlight and hence the waters are generally warmer.

Take a thermometer with you when you fish for trout in summer and use it to seek out the cooler waters.

SHADOWS AND FLASH

Freshwater fish are vulnerable to attack from above the water and often, the only warning they get of danger is the moving shadow of a fish-eating bird, or the unnatural wink of reflected light from something foreign to the normal backdrop of bankside foliage. You will catch more fish if you prevent your shadow falling across the water you intend to fish and by keeping your wristwatch or any shiny fishing tools obscured. Some anglers even go to the extent of sanding the gloss finish from their fishing rods in case the flash of a moving rod will scare the fish.

SHORELINE FOLIAGE FISHING

Bankside foliage creates shelter and feeding opportunities for fish. Sometimes it just provides some much-needed shade and a cool spot out of the direct heat of the sun. Other times it can interrupt water flow and form eddies in which fish can sit and rest away from the main force of the current. Most times, such growth patches will also harbour food like small fish and crustaceans. In any of these cases, fishing around such features is always worthwhile.

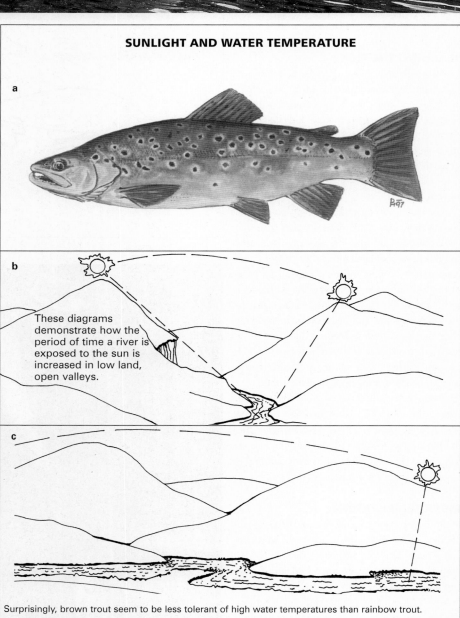

SUNLIGHT AND WATER TEMPERATURE

a

b

These diagrams demonstrate how the period of time a river is exposed to the sun is increased in low land, open valleys.

c

Surprisingly, brown trout seem to be less tolerant of high water temperatures than rainbow trout.

SHORELINE RETRIEVE TACTICS

It might seem that fishing from the shore restricts your options, and from a mobility point of view it can. There are many other options you can exercise from a fixed casting position however, notably in the way you aim the cast, or even more importantly bring the lure or bait back toward you. Try varying your retrieve between casts. First slow, then fast, then one where you stop and twitch the lure and so on. Changing something simple may also produce fish, like the direction you cast and whether you bring the lure in with the flow or up against it. The idea is to experiment and the aim is to find what the fish want in that spot at that particular time.

SHORELINES AND SNAKES

From late spring through to early autumn, there is always the chance of encountering snakes near the water's edge. Shore fishermen should be aware of this and take precautions. Keep an eye out for any movement at ground level and listen for any pronounced rustling in dry grasses or leaf litter. It might only be a lizard, but it could be something more dangerous.

The best defense against snakes is to assume that every tussock has a snake in it and to act accordingly. When you approach a riverbank through tall grass, walk slowly, and make sure you can see where you are putting your feet. If you are concerned there are snakes about, tread heavily enough for them to hear you coming and get out of your way. Most snakes will simply slip away from you when they hear you coming,

The deeper water just above the rifle should hold fish and the prime place to cast would be along the bubble trail that skirts the bank and willow fronds.

but for those that don't, the answer is waders or at least heavy, loose fitting jeans or long legged cargo pants.

SHORELINE STEALTH FISHING

Fish have excellent hearing and can pick up vibrations through the ground, so stamping about a lot will ensure that you catch very few. With the possibility of snakes (see previous tip 'Shorelines and snakes') you need to strike a balance between being too noisy and being so stealthy even snakes don't hear you coming. Believe me, you don't want to surprise a snake. Even if it doesn't bite you, its sudden departure will probably give you a fright you could do without. There is more to stealth than sound however. A good deal of fishing stealth is visual, wearing suitable clothing, keeping yourself down below the brow of a hill so you aren't silhouetted against the sky and keeping far enough back from the fish's location to avoid being seen. Interestingly, fish are easier to get

close to in shallow water than they are when they are sitting down deep. This is because their cone of vision gets broader, the deeper they go.

SIGHT-FISHING LAKE MARGINS

There can be few methods of fishing more absorbing or exciting than seeing a fish first, then getting into position to cast to it without scaring it away. With good polarising sunglasses and sunlight falling at the right angle, you can walk the shoreline of many freshwater lakes and see well into clear water, locating fish well ahead of your position. This gives you time to study where and how they are feeding and to devise which fly or lure, and which approach to use to make them strike.

Stealth fishing — This angler has approached to within casting distance of a feeding trout and is completely unseen because of his inconspicuous clothing and careful movements. The reward was this hookup.

Fish the bushes — This clump of bankside pandanus in Australia's tropical north created a narrow alley of deep water with cover on both sides. Enough reason for this outsized saratoga to be lurking there when a speculative lure swam through the gap.

Shoreline snakes — This black snake was curled up asleep on a riverbank and spotted as the wading angler drew abreast of it. As a matter of interest, the shot was taken from several metres away, with a telephoto lens. Getting this close with a wide angle lens would put you well within strike range!

Sight fishing lakes — Despite the clear water, the glass-like calm of the surface and the natural wariness of trout, this angler has managed to spot a feeding fish in this shallow bay, present his fly and have it accepted by the fish as confidently as if it were the real thing.

There are many variants on the main kinds of soft plastic hooking arrangements, but really, there are only a few basic types.

Soft plastics will catch everything from Murray cod to trout. Generally trout prefer micro plastics suspended under a bobber float while Murray cod are more interested in a macro on a Texas rig enticingly moving through their territory.

STREAM FLOW STRATEGIES

When fishing rivers or any body of water with a constant stream flow, you can use the current to help you present baits and lures attractively to fish.

Casting upstream and bringing the lure down with the current makes it behave like natural food items being bowled along by the flow.

Casting downstream and bringing it up against the flow rarely works as well but when it does, it is usually because you have imparted some irregular jerks and darts to the lure's movement instead of simply winding in steadily.

Casting across stream, you can allow the current to carry the lure downstream and stop this travel any time by commencing the retrieve. As the lure or bait is pulled back in across the

STRATEGIES FOR SHOREFISHING POINTS AND BAYS

Fish in large bodies of water tend to move around a fair bit. Depending on weather conditions and other factors like seasonal runs of prey items, fish may gather around points of land, or enter bays and prowl about looking for food. Generally, shallow bays are favoured by native fish species in the warmer months and when light levels are low early in the morning and late in the afternoon.

Trout however can cruise right into shallow water in bright sunshine and you need to assume they are there rather than not or you will scare them before you even get to cast. Fish generally favour points when there is some wind blowing or where currents force water past a promontory. Golden perch love feeding over shallow points in summer, while bass in dams seem to prefer slightly deeper points or submerged hilltops. Fish in bays by twitching shallow running lures past weed beds and reed stands. Points can be fished with deeper-running lures and it is a good strategy to cast out along one side of the point and bring the lure back in a series of rod lifts and pauses, then work the other side of the point in case the fish are over there.

SOFT PLASTIC RIGS AND TACTICS

There are several ways to rig soft plastic lures and all of them work at one time or another. The trick is to select the lure size and shape that suits the species being sought and then to rig those lures with the appropriate hardware so they can be fished to their best effect.

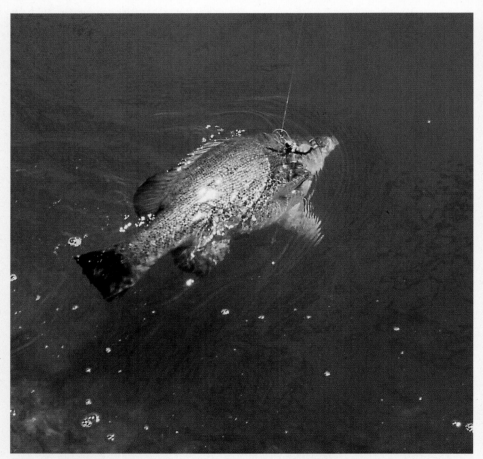

Skimming the bottom — On rocky shores that drop into deep water, golden perch will often be stationed some distance out from the bank and down near the bottom. You can tempt these fish by casting a deep-running lure out some distance, then cranking it down until it is close to the bottom, even bumping it a little if necessary. Pause the retrieve, allow the lure to rise slightly, then lift the rod tip hard to drive it down and bump the bottom again. Wind in the slack line you create with each lift and pause and continue until you have brought the lure all the way back in. Then re-cast and start the procedure all over again. Making the lure bump and skim the bottom all the way into the shore, can turn up big golden perch like this one.

WORM HOOKS

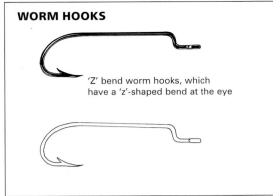

'Z' bend worm hooks, which have a 'z'-shaped bend at the eye

RENOSKY 'EASY WORM' HOOK

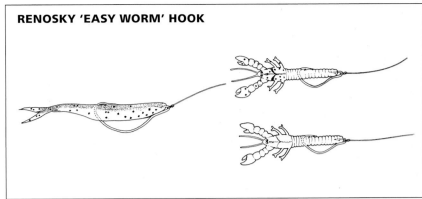

Choosing a hooking style

Depending on the depth and movement of the water you are fishing, you may need to fish soft plastics with plenty of weight, or just a little, or sometimes none at all. When you need to get a lure down to the bottom fast and to operate it within a fairly small area, or in relatively short movements, a lead-head jig may be the best hooking method.

If you still need weight in the rig but are able to present the lure with more of a lateral sort of movement so it covers a bit more ground area, then either a Texas rig or a Carolina rig might be the answer. The Texas rig mounts the soft plastic on a worm hook with a bullet sinker running down onto the nose of the lure. This rig is fished in a series of hops and glides, each covering a somewhat longer distance than is possible with a standard lead-head jig set up. At the hook and lure end, the Carolina rig is identical to the Texas rig, but where it differs is that the bullet weight is rigged to slide down to a swivel, some little distance ahead of the lure. This enables the lure to glide further with each movement, and because of the short leader arrangement, it will also react more slowly than the Texas rig, making it suitable for more subtle and less vigorous presentations.

You can also rig a standard straight fishhook as a 'stinger' by attaching it to the leading hook with a short nylon trace.

Should the fish you are after prefer to strike at a slender lure that maintains a horizontal attitude when moved, then weighting a 'z' bend worm hook with strip lead wound around the shank will deliver this sort of action. The amount of lead strip wound on will determine both the casting weight and sink rate of the lure. This is a surprising amount of casting weight just in the body of a soft plastic lure and the bare hook, so for surface to near surface presentations you may not require the use of lead at all.

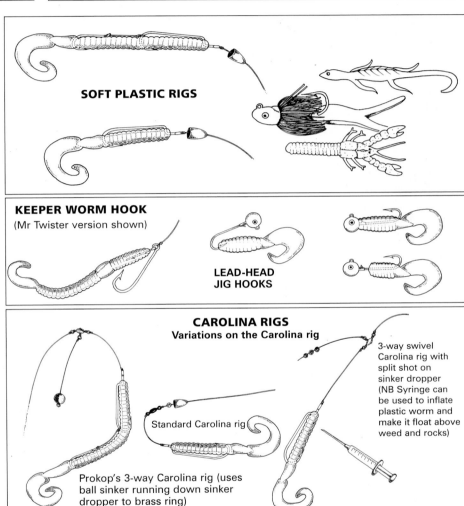

SOFT PLASTIC RIGS

KEEPER WORM HOOK
(Mr Twister version shown)

LEAD-HEAD JIG HOOKS

CAROLINA RIGS
Variations on the Carolina rig

3-way swivel Carolina rig with split shot on sinker dropper (NB Syringe can be used to inflate plastic worm and make it float above weed and rocks)

Standard Carolina rig

Prokop's 3-way Carolina rig (uses ball sinker running down sinker dropper to brass ring)

Making soft plastic lures weedless

You can rig a soft plastic lure so it doesn't hang up in snags or weed. This can be done by attaching the tail to a jig that is fitted with weed guards (usually an array of stiff plastic bristles embedded in the lead-head of the jig) or, it can be done by burying the point of the hook completely inside the lure body. This latter kind of rig requires the use of specially designed worm hooks that have the eye directly in line with the hook point.

WEEDLESS SOFT PLASTICS

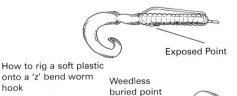

Exposed Point

How to rig a soft plastic onto a 'z' bend worm hook

Weedless buried point

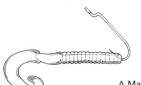

A Mann's Shadow, rigged through the side with a 'z' bend worm hook

Above: Fishing running water — You can utilise rapids and flow-funnels like the one in this photograph to present lures in a natural and enticing manner. Casting above the mini waterfall and allowing the lure to be washed down over the lip into the hole beneath will generally result in an unhesitating strike from any fish sitting there under the turbulent flow.

current it will swing from the far side to the near side of the stream and will also tend to rise in the water.

All methods will prompt strikes from fish at one time or another, so vary your approach until you hit receptive fish.

WIND CAN DETERMINE WHERE FISH ARE

In lakes and rivers, wind can position fish on one shore or the other because of several factors. One is that the most oxygenated water will always be on the lee shore — that is the one with the wind blowing onto it. Also, thermal layering of the water within lakes can be pushed about by wind, resulting in fish's preferred temperatures being concentrated on one side of the lake or another. Lastly, wind creates turbulence that dislodges food items from cover and disorients them, making them easy prey for prowling fish.

Fishing windward shores — This trout water is Brumbys Creek, in central Tasmania, When the wind blows in from the mountains like this, trout tend to feed aggressively along the wave-pounded shore, snuffling up all manner of prey that the rough conditions have made easier to catch and eat.

WINDWARD SHORE TROUT RIG

This rig, with the sinker above the bubble, allows the bait to be positioned out in deep water despite the onshore wind, the live mudeye being suspended enticingly below the now-tethered bubble float. Try this, it is a great technique.

Big trout are often found on windward shores. This can create problems with the standard bubble float rig as the float will tend to wash up onto the shore all the time.

WORKING WATER SYSTEMATICALLY

When confronted by a considerable amount of water, it is best to fish it systematically. First identify where you think fish are most likely to be, given the prevailing conditions. Then start to eliminate areas that are least likely to hold fish — for reasons of depth, access, water quality and so on, until you have pin-pointed a finite and manageable number of likely casting targets. Then start to work your way through them, being meticulous, even with those you have little faith in, because you never know for sure which ones the fish will prefer on the day.

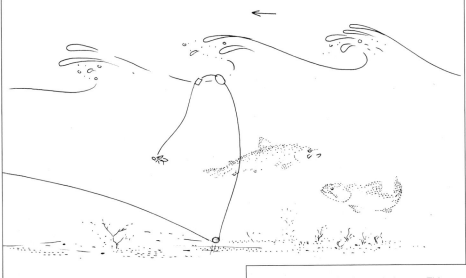

Right: The elimination technique — This backwater off the Swampy Plains River, near Corryong in Victoria, held many good fish the day this photograph was taken. Hardly any of them were seen before being hooked. Most had to be winkled out by systematically working through the most obvious and likely spots. To do this, the least likely spots had to be eliminated first. What was left was then worth fishing.

CHAPTER TWELVE

FLY FISHING

ACCURATE FLY CASTING

While being able to cast a good distance is helpful, it is not all there is to practical and successful fly fishing. A cast of moderate length can also reach your targeted fish if your approach has been sufficiently skillful and if your casting is accurate. Fortunately, the same casting principles that deliver distance are at the heart of accurate casting as well.

The two aspects of casting that ensure accuracy are: correctly judging the length of line required to reach the intended fishing spot and, controlling the plane of the cast, i.e. the path that the rod follows during the casting stroke.

Getting the right amount of line in the air is achieved by 'false casting' (see heading: 'false casting'). Basically this involves trapping the fly line lightly against the grip with the forefinger of your rod hand and pulling extra line from the reel. This line is progressively paid out as you keep the fly line in the air by casting back and forth. False casting is normally used to get your fly line into

the air initially, and then to increase and decrease the amount of line being cast while the rod is in motion.

Your accuracy will be determined by the direction and movement of your rod tip as that is what the fly line follows. At the end of your final casting stroke, the rod tip should be pointing directly at your target. Judging distance and direction when casting is made far easier if you practise casting, perhaps in a some open space, such as your own back yard or maybe a nearby park. However be mindful of other people possibly walking behind you as a whistling fly line flying around them would be unexpected.

'BELGIAN' CASTING

This casting style was developed to overcome the problems of fly casting when wind is blowing the fly and line off their intended trajectory, often into the casting angler's face.

The Belgian cast involves moving the plane of the cast several degrees off the vertical to one

side or the other to counteract the effects of the wind. This is achieved by moving the rod tip away from the vertical and downwind. Casting in this plane will cause the fly line to punch back into and against the wind and counteract the situation of the wind blowing the line and leader off course and causing the fly to land down wind of the projected target.

The more you lower the rod tip the greater the line will punch back into the wind and the greater the counter to the wind will be. The stronger the wind the lower you will need to lower the tip. It is particularly useful on big rivers when the wind is blowing strongly along the bank, and can also be used when swirling winds blow on the open banks of large dams and impoundments.

BRAIDED DACRON LOOPS

Join fly lines to leaders or backing line quite easily and quickly with braided Dacron loops. To make a Dacron loop, take about 250 mm of 60 pound braided Dacron and double it, to form a

Sometimes you have to really thread the needle with a cast to get it in past obstructions such as trees, bankside bushes and so on. This fish came from a pool guarded by a heavily overgrown bank and a fallen tree. There was less than a 40 cm hole through which to fire the fly and land it a metre or so inside the gap, but the cast was on line and this fine fish was the result.

MAKING A DACRON LOOP

You can make easy and quick leader changes if you use this system of loops. You can join flyline to leader and even leader to tippet sections with loop to loop connections as shown. Be sure to connect the loops correctly though as shown in the detail sketch.

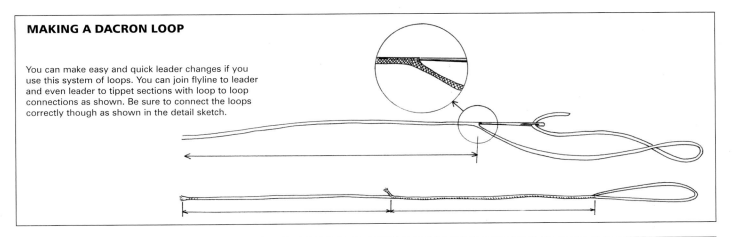

ATTACHING A DACRON LOOP TO A FLY LINE

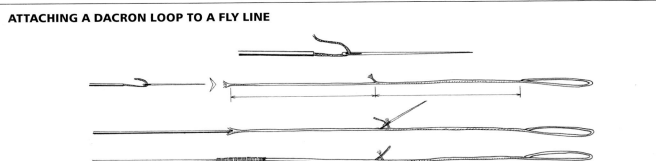

To join the Dacron loop to the end of the fly line, use a sharp knife or razor blade to strip about 25 mm of the plastic sheathing from the fly line, exposing the woven core inside. Thread this through the eye of the needle, and use the needle to push it up into the other end of the Dacron for about 120 mm, before pushing the needle out through the side of the Dacron tube. This should position it somewhere near the tag end of the loop you formed before. These two tag ends should then be trimmed so they overlap by about 5 mm and then whip-finished with fly tying thread and secured with a small drop of fly tying cement.

LOOP TO LOOP CONNECTION LEADER TO DACRON LOOP

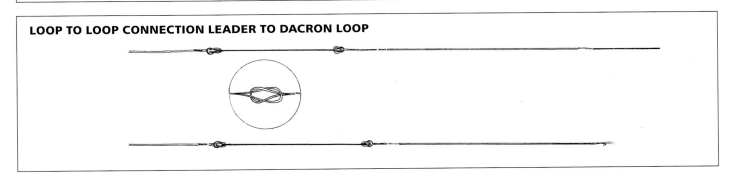

loop. Thread one end of the Dacron through the eye of a large blunt needle and insert the needle into the centre of the hollow Dacron cord. Feed this up the centre at least 80 to 100 mm before exiting through the side of the Dacron tube. Adjust this loop until it is about 35 to 50 mm long. (Tip: Make up a few of these loops for later use.)

CASTING PROBLEMS

Tailing loops: If you allow the rod tip to droop on the back cast, the tail end of the fly line loop will drop below the rest of the line and create what is known as a 'tailing loop'. Tailing loops can tie knots in your leader and you can lose fish from the resulting weak spots in the leader as well as fishing time when your tackle has to be re-rigged.

If the rod tip drops further on the backcast, the fly can hit the ground or shrubbery behind you, becoming snagged. To prevent this, keep the rod hand rising at the end of the back cast. This drives the fly line up into the air behind you. If the problem continues, check that your wrist is not pivoting, or cocking backwards at the end of the stroke as this will pull the rod tip down and the fly line into the ground. Shock waves: Shock waves in the fly line are caused by the incorrect application of power during the cast, and will rob you of distance and accuracy. Trying too hard is often the seat of the problem. Power, applied smoothly and moderately, will let the loaded rod throw the line. Brute force is not needed. Think instead in terms of a smooth start, an acceleration, then an abrupt stop. Failing to stop the rod and let it unload,

or continuing to apply power after the rod has passed the optimum point in the cast, is simply wasting energy and contributes to a host of casting problems.

Lastly, whether casting overhead or out to the side, make sure that the rod always travels backwards and forwards in the same plane. If you move out of that plane you risk an inefficient cast.

DISTANCE CASTING

Distance casting is entirely reliant upon line speed, and to achieve the greatest line speed, a relatively open stance is called for, and a much wider sweep for the rod hand. What really delivers phenomenal line speed and distance however is the practice of 'hauling': pulling the fly line with your free (line) hand as the casting stoke begins. Using just one haul (for either the back cast or forward cast) is called 'single-hauling'; using a haul for both the back cast and forward cast is 'double hauling'.

To keep more than 20–25 metres of fly line in the air can be difficult but necessary. To accomplish it, strip the amount of line you need (and can cast) from the reel. Coil it neatly at your feet, or lay it carefully into a stripping basket. This loose line is 'shot' or flows through the rod guides when you deliver the final forward cast. If enough line speed has been generated, the moving fly line will have the necessary mass and force to drag the loose line out behind it. Twenty metres of fly line moving fast enough, will easily drag as much fly line out behind it again.

This practice of 'shooting' line is much easier with short, heavy fly lines, weight-forwards and shooting heads because most of their bulk and weight is concentrated at the front end of the line. Moving quite rapidly they can generate enormous casting force with the right casting technique.

EFFECTIVE FLY CASTING

To make an effective casting stroke, apply enough force to actually bend the rod as it progresses through the casting arc. When you stop the rod (once it passes your shoulder), it will straighten or 'unload', flinging the fly line straight out behind you. The same thing happens on the forward cast.

The timing of this forward cast is important. To effectively load the rod for the forward cast, begin to do so while the fly line is in the air behind you and still moving. If you start this forward movement too early, the line will accelerate at the end of its backward flow and crack like a whip with the sudden change in direction. This whip-cracking will damage the leader and probably snap the fly off.

On the other hand, don't wait too long before starting the rod's forward movement or the energy you have put into the back cast will be lost, causing the fly line to droop and fall to the ground behind you.

Ideally, the forward cast should begin just as the back cast fully straightens. One way to determine when this occurs is to turn your head and watch for the line to straighten so you get this timing right.

The application of power in a fly casting stroke is different to that in most other forms of casting. It begins slowly, accelerates smoothly to its top speed, and then stops abruptly, so the line and fly are catapulted towards the target. To transfer casting energy efficiently, both the rod tip and fly line must be made to travel in a straight line. This can only happen if the rod is made to bend during the first part of the casting stroke, then made to straighten suddenly at its conclusion.

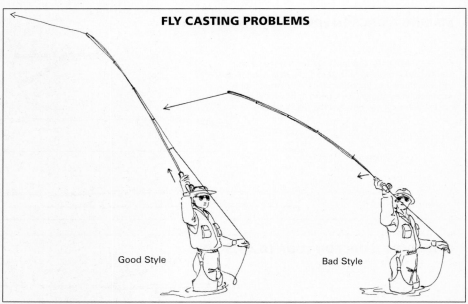

FLY CASTING PROBLEMS

Good Style

Bad Style

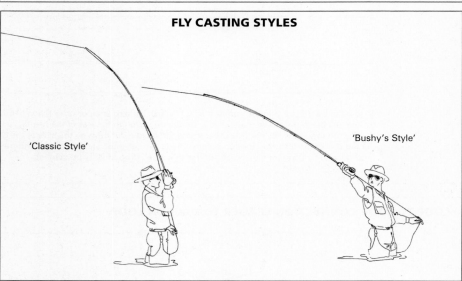

FLY CASTING STYLES

'Classic Style'

'Bushy's Style'

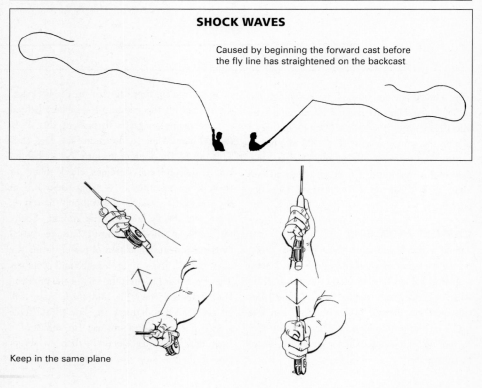

SHOCK WAVES

Caused by beginning the forward cast before the fly line has straightened on the backcast

Keep in the same plane

The main problem most people have with fly casting is a tendency to swing the rod like a bat. To fly cast effectively, you need to make the rod bend by pulling it back toward you on a back cast and pushing it forward on a forward cast—the rod hand acts like a piston moving through a flat plane. High-speed filming reveals that the rod-bend changes shape, dragging the tip back and forth in virtually a dead straight line. The fly line always follows the path of the rod tip.

If you find the fly line is not straightening properly when you cast, then stop the rod suddenly just past the mid-point of the casting stroke, allowing it to unload and catapult the line. Beyond this mid-point you cannot impart any more energy to the cast. This translates casting effort into distance and a clean cast.

FALSE CASTING

Most times, you should be able to deliver a fly to a chosen target with just one back cast and one forward cast. Occasionally though, when you do not have enough line out to reach a target or when you need to change the direction of a cast, you might need to cast back and forth more than once or twice to achieve it. This repeated casting back and forth without actually delivering the fly or allowing it to settle on the water is called 'false casting'. False casting is also used initially to get line through the guides when beginning to fly fish.

As a general rule of thumb, try to keep false casting to a minimum. Every time the line sails back and forth is an opportunity to get it wrong and scare a fish or make some other casting mistake. It might look impressive to be able to keep a lot of fly line in the air, but it doesn't catch fish! The idea of casting is to reach fish with the fly.

FLIES FOR FRESH WATER

There are many kinds of flies used in fresh water. These include a range of 'dry flies' (those tied with foam, stiff hackles and deer hair so they float and are fished on or in the surface film). Dry flies include representations of mayflies, caddis, stoneflies, beetles, cicadas, frogs, mudeyes (the larval stage of dragonflies) and water snails. Then there are 'wet' flies, which include a range of winged (or un-winged) flies that imitate spent mayflies, various ants, beetles and such like, or various crustaceans like crayfish, shrimp and scuds. Nymphs are another broad group of wet flies, representing the sub-adult and larval stages of various aquatic insects, such as mayflies, caddis, stoneflies, damselflies, midges and the like.

Small baitfish are imitated by another groups of wet flies, classified loosely as streamers. Sometimes frogs, mice, big bulky terrestrial insects and injured baitfish are represented by popping bugs or sliders, deer-hair or cork or foam bodied confections that are intended to create as much surface disturbance and wake as possible.

FLIES FOR SALT WATER

The main group of saltwater flies is the streamers. These include the legendary Deceivers, Brook's Blondes, Flashy Profile Flies and others. Shrimp and crab patterns are becoming more widely used now that saltwater fly rodders are beginning to target species like bream, permit and golden trevally that are particularly susceptible to such flies.

Various fast-sinking flies are used for saltwater bottom fishing. Most use either beadchain or lead dumbbell eyes for weight and are tied so the hook points ride uppermost. Notable among these are Crazy Charlies, Keel flies, and an up-hook version of the Baited Breath pattern. Smaller, slim-tied

Flycasting tackle is amazingly versatile and quite capable of subduing even strong saltwater fish like this longtail tuna, caught in Moreton Bay, Queensland.

flies using sparse dressings of Flashabou, Polar Fibre and Mylar can be grouped together under the heading of baitfish profiles, and these include Surf Candies, various Whitebait patterns and so on.

Floating saltwater flies include poppers, from slender models aimed at bream, to larger, 50-cent piece sized bloopers that get the attention of big trevally, queenfish, kingfish and cobia. A small floating fly tied with densely-packed white deer hair can be used to good effect on schooling mullet or even bream that have been excited into a feeding spree by bread berley.

FLY CASTING BASICS

The basic principle of fly casting is to use the weight of a heavy fly line to bend and load a flexible rod so that it catapults the fly line, its leader and the attached fly towards a target. The fly line itself is the casting weight that delivers the almost weightless fly where it has to go.

To start, thread the fly line from the reel through the runners of the rod, and shake or pull several metres of fly line out through the tip to provide some casting weight. Lift the rod (and line) crisply up then backward in what is called a 'back cast'. The momentum of the fly line thrown out behind is what loads the rod for the following forward cast. When the line cast back is just about to straighten, the rod is then pushed forward and stopped, which catapults the fly line and fly past the rod tip and out over the water in front of you. As the energy of the cast dissipates, the fly line and fly should settle gently down onto the water and the fishing can now begin.

Fly casting differs from other forms of casting such as lure or bait fishing that use a heavy weight to load the rod and tow out a length of thin line behind them.

You can gradually adjust the amount of line you have out by false casting until you have just enough line in the air to reach your target.

Form in fly casting is vital to efficiency. This angler is aiming his back cast straight and high to avoid tailing loops and is focussing on where the fly will fall.

HARD LEADER
Hard Leader Presentation

Good for wet flies

Straight Leader

SOFT LEADER
Soft Leader Presentation

Good for dry flies on lakes

HARD/SOFT LEADER
Hard/Soft Leader Construction

'S' Curves   Hard butt

Good for dry flies on rivers

Soft Tippet

Hard leaders or soft leaders

FLYFISHING LEADERS

The same bulk and thickness that gives a fly line the necessary casting weight, also makes it too thick to be tied to the tiny hook-eyes of flies. Instead a tapered nylon leader is used, which is thick at the butt (fly line) end and thinner at the tippet (or fly) end. This leader configuration also enables the force of the cast to be transmitted smoothly down from the fly line to the fly. In some flyfishing situations (saltwater fly especially) heavy 'shock leaders' are used to terminate the main leader at the fly.

The use of a 'hard' monofilament leader will aid in forming a straight leader, while using a 'soft' leader will cause lots of curves, which is useful when presenting cross-current and drag is a problem. Combining both types will give the direct striking capabilities of a straight leader with the curves needed when presenting flies in fast currents.

It is important when fishing for skittish fish that the fly is delivered without alarming the fish and putting it on its guard.

FLYFISHING STREAMS 'ACROSS AND UP'

Some flies are most effectively fished by casting them upstream and allowing them to drift down on the current toward you. In doing this, you may be casting over fish that are lying in the stream, and scaring them. So, determine where they are most likely to be first and then cast a little to one side, allowing the flow to carry the fly and less conspicuous leader over them in a natural manner.

Most upstream casts also tend to be made a little across the stream as well, again, to ensure the fish are not spooked. The precise angle at which you cast across the stream, will be dictated by where you think fish are, and by how fast the current is flowing. Gather in the slack fly line as the current brings it downstream, so you can stay in direct touch with the fly and set the hook should a fish grab it.

Dry (floating) flies work well when flyfishing streams 'across and up' as you can see when a fish takes them.

FLYFISHING 'ACROSS AND DOWN'

Wet flies and nymphs can be fished by casting them upstream but the conventional method is to cast these fly types across and downstream of your position. The water flow and the effect of line drag, may put curves in your line and stop the natural drift of your fly. Eliminate this by 'mending' the line (see note on 'mending'

line). The idea is to try to keep a straight line between the rod tip and the fly so that when the fly is taken, the angler's strike sets the hook.

As the current sweeps the fly downstream, it will tend to sink near the bottom but be pulled along by the effect of the flow on the fly line. When the line reaches its limit and stops, the flow starts to lift the fly toward the surface. This is often the precise moment a trout will take the fly, as this rising motion mimics the hatching of many aquatic insect nymphs.

FLYFISHING BARE BANKS

Because water levels rise and fall significantly in many large freshwater storage dams, their banks are often bare and open, offering anglers little cover to disguise their presence. Despite this, it is possible to get close enough to the water's edge to spot fish and cast to them. The trick is to keep low, on your hands and knees if necessary, and to move slowly and only when you can see that the fish is moving away from you. This will place you in its 'blind spot', i.e. directly behind it.

FLYFISHING OPEN SALT WATER

Flyfishing tackle can be taken to sea and used to catch large open-water species such as tailor, salmon, kingfish, tuna and many tropical species.

Fly lines need to be heavier to cast the larger flies involved and overcome the breezes that often accompany such fishing. Rods should be correspondingly more powerful too, both to cast the heavier lines and flies and to handle the bigger and stronger fish. Weight-forward floating lines or shooting heads will handle surface feeders, while sinking lines will prove more useful for fish that feed deeper. Flycasting outfits that suit 8- to 10-weight lines are better for larger fish while smaller fish may only require 6- or 7-weight outfits, providing you take your time with them once they're hooked.

Casting from an open boat in rough water takes some doing. You must keep your fly line under control. Working on your line management skills or using a stripping basket to hold the fly line up off the deck as it is pulled in will help.

FLYFISHING SALTWATER ESTUARIES

Anglers who like to fish in temperate saltwater estuaries can use flycasting tackle with good

Polarising barren lake shores for trout is exciting and very rewarding for skilled fly fishers.

Flyfishing in salt water in the Australian tropics can yield almost any of the local species, but few are more willing to hit a fly than the giant trevally.

This flathead took a barred-tail green streamer fly, fished on a sinking fly line down into a deep gutter that traversed a sand flat in a north coast tidal lake.

This brown trout took a fly fished down the tail-end glide of a river pool just as evening fell and the river came alive with feeding fish.

This angler, wearing dull green and tan clothing, has used camouflage to get close to the stream edge and make his cast. The fish was hooked near the deep bank on the other side, which required a cast to be made upriver and slightly across, so the moving water carried the fly right past the fish's lair.

effect on species such as flathead, bream, tailor, mullet and whiting and even luderick.

Fly tackle is most effectively used in water that is less than 10 metres deep, so concentrate on the shallow areas such as sand flats, weed beds and bankside drop offs. Flathead require a fly that sinks well, so weighted flies like Clouser minnows, Crazy Charlies and so forth are popular. Bream will take suspending flies such as Baited Breaths, small Dahlbergs and various semi buoyant shrimp patterns. Whiting will take bloodworm and shrimp imitations, while if you berley with bread, mullet will aggressively hit small white flies tied to imitate bread scraps. Luderick will take worm imitations, small shrimp flies and also green flies tied to look like their favourite food, green weed.

FLYFISHING TO RISES

The diet of many freshwater fish is predominantly insects and when 'hatches' of insects occur, it can signal intense fish-feeding periods. Hatches can happen almost any time of the day should conditions become suitable. The wind dropping or changing direction, or changes in the degree of sunshine and cloud cover can bring on hatches. When clouds gather and obscure the sun, light levels and air temperatures drop slightly; when clouds clear, air temperatures and light levels will rise again. Such fluctuations in the waterside environment can prompt hatches at any time, but the two most significant periods of environmental change on any freshwater streams or lakes, are dawn and dusk. You need not confine your fishing activity to these peak periods, but your fishing opportunities will certainly improve if they are included in your fishing time.

FLYFISHING VEGETATED BANKS

Where waters have heavily overgrown banks you will need to employ a very high back cast (when fishing across the stream), or alternatively, get into the water so your back cast area is clear and the line can move unhindered above the water. Approaching fish from downstream in rivers is always a better option, since the fish will spend most of their time facing up into the current, creating the opportunity for you to sneak within casting range.

FLY LEADER BASICS

While some fly fishing leaders are the same thickness from tip to butt, most are tapered, being thicker at the butt than the tippet. This mimics the taper of the fly line itself and allows a smoother transfer of power from fly line to fly, which aids in presentation.

Leaders come in many forms, some factory-made leaders are solid nylon, extruded in a single tapered length. Others are made of tapered braids. Angler also make up their own leaders, according to their ideas and preferences, using short lengths of gradually thinner lines. These sections of different thickness line are knotted together in various proportions or 'formulas' to produce particular desired results.

There are dozens of different leader formulas but a popular and workable version known as the 'Gibson Leader' suits both wet and dry fly fishing. This style of leader is constructed in thirds. The first or butt section is close in thickness to the end of the fly line, the next, intermediate section (also a third of the total length) is made up of three equal sections of line, each slightly thinner than the preceding one. The final third of the

leader's overall length is the 'tippet' or thinnest part of the leader.

If you look at the other leader illustrations nearby, you will see that the dry fly leader shown differs from the wet fly leader example. The dry fly leader incorporates an extra fourth section of taper before the tippet, which tends to be lighter than that used for wet fly fishing.

This dry fly leader formula best suits delicate presentations and calm water, whereas the wet fly leader example can be used with larger flies and in rougher water. Braided leaders are generally more supple than mono leaders and are growing in popularity. They are however also more expensive and on occasions can reflect light, causing flash that may frighten fish.

FLY LINES

Flyfishing lines are much thicker than conventional fishing lines and more complex in construction. Most fly lines consist of a woven core and an extruded outer sheath or skin of plastic.

At one time, fly lines were made of woven silk and before that, of woven horsehair. With the advent of plastics in the 1940s, mass-produced synthetic fly lines became available and their widespread availability, relatively low cost, durability and consistent strength saw a huge expansion in the popularity of fly fishing through the latter half of the Twentieth Century. Fly lines with various degrees of buoyancy were now available on demand and this is when dry fly fishing ceased to be the province of the upper-classes and spread like wildfire throughout the ranks of everyday anglers.

Most modern fly lines are made of a woven

Leader Formulas

LEVEL LEADER

Basic 3m (10ft) Level Leader

KNOTLESS TAPERED LEADER

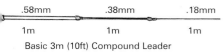

Basic 3m (100ft) Knotless Tapered Leader

LEADER COMPONENTS

Butt   Taper   Tippet

COMPOUND LEADER

.58mm   .38mm   .18mm

1m   1m   1m

Basic 3m (10ft) Compound Leader

GIBSON LEADER

1/3   1/3   1.3

1/3   1/3   1/3

Basic 3m (10ft) Gibson Leader

GIBSON LEADER

.58mm   .48 mm   .38mm   .28mm   .18mm

100cm   33 cm   33cm   33cm   100cm

DRY FLY LEADER

.58mm   .48 mm   .38mm   .28mm   .18mm   .15mm

100cm   33 cm   33cm   33cm   30cm   100cm

3.3m Dry Fly Leader

WET FLY LEADER

.58mm   .48 mm   .38mm   .28mm   .18mm

100cm   33 cm   33cm   33cm   50cm   100cm

2.5m Wet Fly Leader (rough)

BRAIDED LEADER

Fly Line   Tippet

LOOP TO LOOP

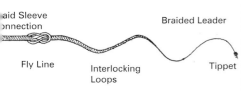

aid Sleeve
onnection   Braided Leader

Fly Line   Interlocking   Tippet
            Loops

---

nylon core, sheathed in an extruded plastic coating. Industrial advances have meant the availability of alternative core materials, including Dacron, Kevlar, and even some gelspun polyesters. Exterior sheathings have also become sophisticated; some enough so to be blended seamlessly with inbuilt monofilament and copolymer extensions. These are good for when a perfectly clear fly line is required to fish for sight-sensitive species. Australian examples include bonefish, giant herring, permit and golden trevally. Similar lines are also sometimes employed when fly fishing for yellowfin, longtail and mackerel tuna. Some early work has also been done with these low-visibility fly lines on bream.

The ability of manufacturers to control line density and formulation means that lines can be produced for a wide range of flyfishing situations. Fly lines types can be fully floating, or those that float for most of their length and just sink at the tip end. They can also be made to sink at various rates, from slow sinkers to lines that plummet to the bottom like stones. Note: floating fly lines are relatively less dense than sinking lines of similar weight, so a sinking 8-weight fly line is likely to be much thinner than an 8-weight floater.

Fly lines come in a range of shapes and weight distributions. One type of flyline shape is the 'double taper', which has identically-tapered end sections and a fatter, heavier middle section. These are excellent choices for short-range delicate presentations of tiny flies to spooky fish such as trout. Fly lines can also be made with their fatter and heavier section well forward of the middle and these are known (naturally enough) as 'weight-forward' lines. Weight-forward fly lines are easier to cast in short-range fishing situations since most of the line's mass is concentrated in a relatively short length of line.

Fly lines used for bream and flathead in salt water and species other than trout in fresh water are usually of this type. Still others are made with a short, very heavy section of the line up front and a trailing thin section of line. These are known as 'shooting heads' and the thin section of line behind them is called a 'running line'.

Shooting heads are popular with saltwater fly fishers who need to make quick, long casts with a minimum of false casting, even in adverse wind conditions. At one time, shooting heads were only available as short head sections to which a separate running line had to be attached. Nowadays, there is a trend toward lines that combine the shooting head and running line in the one integral unit. 'Bug' or 'Bass' tapers are simply weight-forward lines with a shorter and more pronounced thickening of the forward casting head. These fly lines are designed for the effective presentation of bulky wind-resistant flies

---

ANATOMY OF A FLYLINE

When discussing fly line configurations, there are certain terms used. The diagrams below show the relationship of these terms to a basic fly line configuration. All of our fly lines have a core of braided monofilament, braided monofilament or extruded monofilament. The core is coated with a PVC in which we impart the taper design. Within the PVC we add hollow glass microspheres (floating) or various density compensating additives (sinking).
Variations in the amount of additives used account for some of the differences in the characteristics of our lines, i.e. higher float or faster sink.

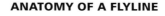

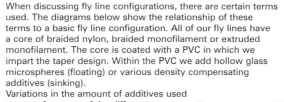

Hollow glass microspheres

CORE

HEAD
The head is the combination of the front taper, body and the rear taper. The weight of the front thirty feet dictates the line-weight designation.

TIP
Connect the leader to the tip, which is thin and short (usually 6–12 inches).

BODY
Most of the weight is concentrated in this section. It's the longest section of the head and has the largest diameter. Its weight is what carries your cast.

FRONT TAPER
The front taper decreases in diameter from the body to the tip. This gradual change in the line's mass (weight) effects how your casting energy is transferred to the fly and how delicately or powerfully the fly is delivered.

REAR TAPER
This section decreases in diameter from the thicker body to the thin running line. This gradual change provides casting smoothness on casts beyond 30 feet.

RUNNING LINE
When you make a long cast, the weight and energy in the head pulls the running line out through the guides. Being lightweight and small in diameter, it passes through the guides easily on long casts.

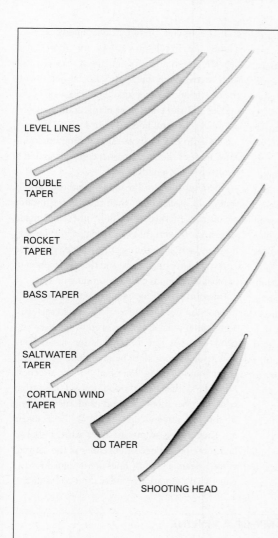

LEVEL LINES

DOUBLE
TAPER

ROCKET
TAPER

BASS TAPER

SALTWATER
TAPER

CORTLAND WIND
TAPER

QD TAPER

SHOOTING HEAD

LEVEL LINES
No Tapers or Belly. When Delicate fly presentation or long cast are not essential.

DOUBLE TAPER
A reversible fly line with an identical taper at both ends. Easy to mend

Rocket Taper
Specially designed wieght forward line with long front taper foe delicate presentation. Weight distribution of body section allows extra distance.

BASS TAPER
Weight forward line with short front taper to 'turn over' heavier, wind resistant cork and hair body bugs. The mosy practical choice for bass bugs.

SALTWATER TAPER
Weight forward line forcasting larger flies during windy conditions. Small diameter running line feeds through rod guides with less frictional resistance.

QD TAPER
Weight forward design that combines a 24 foot sinking head with a 6 ft. rear floating section. Allows mending of line.

CORTLAND WIND TAPER
Weight forward design that has a compound taper allowing easier casts into the wind.

SHOOTING HEAD
Specialized for long distance casting. It is a 30' or 40' head with a factory spliced loop for attaching modifilament or running line.

Above: Types of Fly Lines

Below: Which Fly Line do I use?

such as large–faced poppers, 'bug' patterns and big freshwater streamers.

FLY REELS

Flyfishing reels are usually centrepins with holes drilled in the side plates to minimise weight and allow the fly line to dry quickly when not in use. Some are quite simple in design, with nothing more complicated than a ratchet check to control the spool's movement and to prevent overruns. Other fly reels, designed for large gamefish or species that are likely to be hooked in fast flowing water, can have sophisticated drag mechanisms built into them. This facility takes over from the angler's hand on the reel rim to prevent the light leader being snapped when a fish makes a concerted run, and some fly reel drags can be set to slip line smoothly under precise and controlled pressure to wear down a strong fish. Most fly reels are machined from various alloys and anodised or painted in finishes to suit a particular style of fishing.

Saltwater fly reels are usually of more robust design, with larger spools and better drag systems than are required for freshwater types. Their external finishes are also usually more impervious to saltwater damage and, where metal parts are used, they are normally of stainless steel or similarly corrosion-resistant metals, such as titanium or phosphor bronze.

A freshwater reel can be used for light saltwater fly fishing but greater care has to be taken to wash down and lubricate it after each trip to avoid it corroding and becoming unserviceable.

CHOOSING A FLY LINE

SURFACE FEEDING (#12 – #22) FLIES
2 to 6 weight-forwrd (WF) or double-taper (DT) floating. Make extra-delicate presentations of small flies on light tippets.
• 444 Laserline floating • 444 floating • 444 clear creek
• 444 sl

FEEDING JUST BELOW THE SURFACE
4 to 10 weight weight-forward intermediate lines or sinking-tips Type 1.
•444sl ghosttip •444sl clear •444clear camo •444sl20' intermediate sink tip

FEEDING DEEP IN STILLWATER
5 to 10 weight weight-forward uniform-sinling or shooting-taper lines or QDs
•444SL quick descents •444sl steady sinks •444sl xrl sinking
•444 sinking shooting taper

FEEDING NEAR BOTTOM IN MOVING WATER
5 to 10 weight sink tip Type I-VI
• 444 Nymph tip • 444sl sink tip 5', 10' or 20' • lazerline sink tip
• deep nymphing line • 444 sink tip 10' & 20'

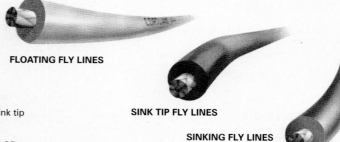

FLOATING FLY LINES

SINK TIP FLY LINES

SINKING FLY LINES

ABOUT SINKING FLY LINES
Fish take a majority of their food below the surface. Full sinking and sink tip lines ae often the only way to get the fly to where the fish are feeding. Eventually, all sinking lines reach the same depth. However, the speed in which the line reaches the various depths is often the deciding fctor in whether or not the fish are being caught.

LINE SIZES AND THEIR USES

1–2	Trout, panfish, fly sizes #26–#18
3–6	Trout, bass, panfish, fly sizes #24–#2
7–8	Trout, Steelhead, bonefish, redfish, Atlantic salmon, bass, fly sizes #12–#1/0
9–11	Steelhead, Atlantic salmon, Pacific salmon, bluefish, small tarpon, dorado, stripers, permit, fly sizes #6–4/0
12–15	Tarpon, billfish, tuna, fly sizes #2/0–#8/0

TYPE CHARACTER	SINK RATE
1-Slow (Intermediate)	1-1/4 – 1 3/4 inches/second
2-Fast 2-1/2 – 3 inches/second	
3-Extra fast	3-1/2 – 4 inches/second
4-Super Sinker	4-1/4 – 5 inches/second
5-Super Fast	5-1/4 – 6 inches/second
6-Extra Super Sinker	6-1/4 – 7 inches/second

Fly reels are all centrepins, some quite simple and others very sophisticated. Most have holes in the side plates that lighten the reel and allow the fly line to dry more easily.

FLY RODS

Rods for fly casting are generally long and slender and designed to 'load' (bend) and 'unload' (straighten) very smoothly. The reel seat is located at the butt end of the rod so the reel's weight acts as a sort of counterbalance to the forces generated by casting. Locating the reel right on the butt also allows the maximum length of rod to bend freely during the casting process.

In theory, flycasting rods can be any length, and some specialised versions are as short as 1.8 metres or as long as 4 metres, but the vast majority of flycasting rods are between 2.5 and 2.7 metres long. At such lengths, transportation of these slender rods would present difficulties and present a high risk of breakage, if they were once-piece, so most are made in multiple pieces. It is possible to buy rods manufactured in several multi-piece configurations, sometimes as many as six or seven, but two pieces of equal length are more common. In recent years, the growing popularity of air-travel to far-flung fishing destinations, has popularized three- or even four-piece flycasting rods, which can be taken on board aircraft as carry-on luggage.

INDICATORS

An 'indicator' is a short piece of wool or other buoyant, fluff that can be knotted around the leader before you cast out a nymph. The indicator will float on the water above the nymph until a fish takes or hits it. The indicator then drops out of sight, indicating to the angler that it is time to strike.

The indicator knot must be secure while in use and easily undone when it needs to be adjusted up or down the leader to another position as water depths and conditions change.

You can use any colour wool or fluff you like, but on clear water rivers, you might like to take a leaf from the book of New Zealand fly fishers, who use raw sheep wool because it is more buoyant than processed wool or artificial fluff.

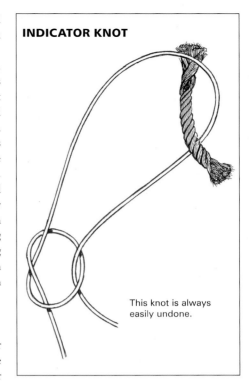

INDICATOR KNOT

This knot is always easily undone.

There are two advantages to this choice, the raw colour is less conspicuous to the fish and its better natural floatation means you can use less of it for the same effect. These facts ensure that the indicator is amply visible to the angler but much less likely to alarm spooky trout.

LANDING FISH ON FLY TACKLE

Landing fish on fly tackle can be difficult because of the length of the rod, so bring the fish within a rod's length and use a net. If the fish is small enough, grab the line down near the fly and swing

Fly rods should suit the weight of line being thrown and the species of fish being targeted. This 9 foot 8-weight graphite rod is ideal for the golden trevally and permit.

it ashore. You can slide fish that are docile in toward your feet and pick them up by hand. Do not make the mistake of trying to use the thin fly rod as a lever and pole the fish out of the water.

LOCH STYLE FLY FISHING

Loch style fly fishing involves fly fishing from a boat while it drifts down wind. The technique involves using a drogue or sea anchor to slow and control that drift. Many anglers also use an electric motor to manoeuver the boat. There are two main styles employed: the first is simply dapping with a single dry fly to entice a strike. The second method is classic loch style which involves fishing up to three flies, the point, the bob fly and the dropper fly. The point fly is attached to the end of the tippet, the dropper fly is located between the point fly and the bobber, which is on the surface of the water. The idea is that the fish can be attracted to any of these flies – the anglers simply provide alternatives.

The effectiveness of this method has opened up new trout fisheries in still waters in Tasmania, Victoria and New South Wales.

LINE MANAGEMENT

As you strip fly line from the water back to land, you create coils of fly line that accumulate around your feet. Stepping on these or get them tangled around rocks and twigs on the ground will waste your valuable fishing time and frustrate you. When standing in the water, you can sometimes dump some line at your feet and let it float, but this too create tangles as the line gets wrapped around and between your legs.

Saltwater anglers, especially those making long casts while wading, or when fishing from the deck of a boat, use a stripping basket, a free-draining pouch, held across the angler's stomach with a belt to solve this problem. With shorter casts, say less than 20 metres, this much paraphernalia is more trouble than it is worth, so many freshwater fly anglers use a method of retrieval that gathers the fly line in the free (non-rod) hand. The line is woven into the palm of the free hand in a series of figure-eights, a method of line gathering that allow the coils to be easily and cleanly slipped free on the next cast. The hand in effect becomes a temporary

storage place for the loose fly line as it is stripped in. The rolling hand movement required to gather the line in this way usually provides sufficient retrieve speed for most freshwater fly fishing situations and the intermittent gathering of line with pauses in between also provides a fish-attracting cadence and tempo to the retrieve.

Note that the fly line is not pulled directly from the first rod guide into the free hand, but run between the rod grip and the forefinger of the rod hand under light pressure. By trapping the fly line against the rod grip in this manner, the angler is able to control the fly line at all times. If a fish happens to hit during one of the brief pauses between strips, the line can be instantly clamped to the rod to set the hook. An alternate method of gathering in the line is simply to use the free hand and the forefinger of the rod hand in concert to form large loops that are hung from the free hand until the next cast is made.

'MENDING' A CAST

'Mending' is the process of creating slack line in a presentation, to overcome the problems of line drag in a strong current.

As the current carries a fly line downstream, some parts of the water will move faster than others. The slower-moving section of the water tends to hold the fly line back, while the faster section carries the rest ahead of it, creating a loop or bow of line in the water. This creates a surface disturbance and a wake that alarms fish and can prevent them taking the fly.

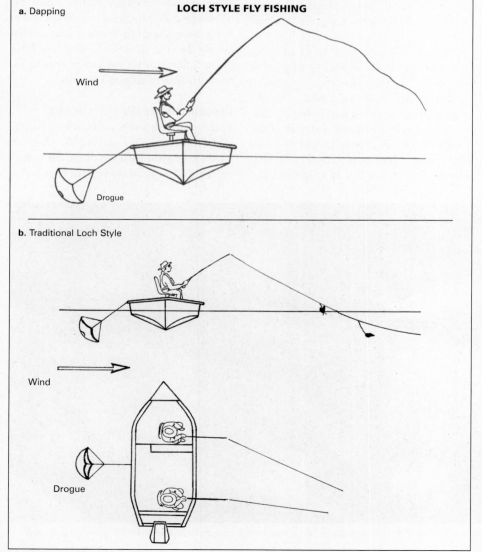

LOCH STYLE FLY FISHING

a. Dapping

Wind

Drogue

b. Traditional Loch Style

Wind

Drogue

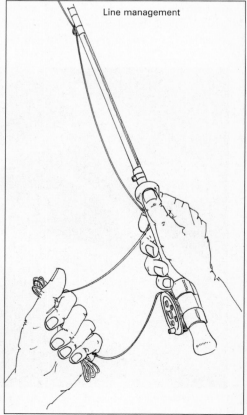

Line management

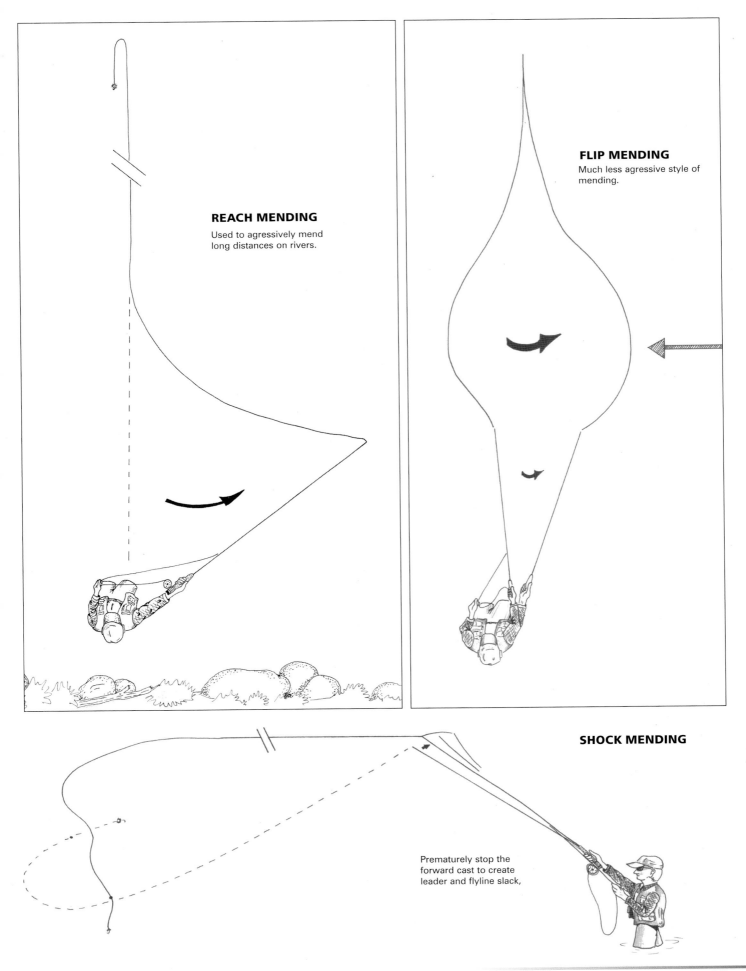

REACH MENDING

Used to agressively mend long distances on rivers.

FLIP MENDING

Much less agressive style of mending.

SHOCK MENDING

Prematurely stop the forward cast to create leader and flyline slack,

The solution is to throw an extra bit of line into the presentation in the form of a loop to begin with. This gives the fly an extended amount of drag-free drift before the line is gripped by the current and begins to drag across the surface. This little extra 'clean' drift is often enough for the fish to be fooled into taking the fly without a qualm.

You can sometimes throw this 'extra' line into the cast as it is being made, by giving the rod tip a sharp upward flip just as the line straightens which causes the line that falls on the water into an S-shaped wriggle. Small amounts of drag can be counteracted this way. For more serious drag, created by stronger flows and longer casts, you can use a 'reach mend' or a 'flip mend'. A reach mend involves lifting the rod to the side, upstream, after the line lands on the water. A flip mend is essentially the same process, except instead of a gentle, slow reach with the rod to lift a long length of line off the water, a small loop, (like a mini-roll cast) is sent upstream by flipping the rod tip up and across.

The reach mend is best used when fishing a section of stream with a broad current stream and a short line to a fish, while the flip mend suits presentations where a narrow stream of fast current runs down through a generally slow and meandering flow. This situation is common where rivers carry a wide, general weed growth, with isolated clear channels that flow much more quickly.

POLARISING TACTICS

Polarising or sight fishing trout in lakes is a very popular and exciting form of fly fishing. Polarising sunglass lenses are used to cut through much of the surface glare to reveal what is going on beneath it, though the angler's ability to see into the water is limited by the angle of incidence (the angle at which the line of vision strikes the water). The optimum angle of incidence is 37 degrees and, as that angle reduces, so does the angler's ability to penetrate the surface glare. This means that in flat calm conditions, your vision will be able to achieve optimum surface penetration fairly close in to the bank. As you train your vision on spots further and further out from the shore, the angle of incidence reduces, until once below 30 degrees, you ability to see into the water is also reduced considerably.

In reality, you will see and catch more fish if you are able to see into the water some little distance off the bank as well. For this to happen, you need to take advantage of rougher water, which stands the surface up into waves. As the wave rises, it presents the angler with a lens, through which that optimum angle of 37 degrees can be achieved, allowing fish to be spotted even in considerably deep water and from some distance away. This is the 'secret technique' of some of the very best fly fishers.

The accompanying diagrams show how this works and should help you come to grips with this theory. So don't become despondent about

polaroiding when wind creates surface chop on a lake, learn to look through those wave faces and you'll see more fish. The bigger the waves in fact, the better you will be able to see through them.

ROLL CASTING

Often when fly casting from the shore, you will have trees, dense foliage or a hillside behind you, which can prevent you from making a conventional back cast. You can get around this problem by using the drag of the fly line on the water to load the rod. Lift the rod towards you and slowly upward to a point just beyond the vertical — just past your head and shoulder — drawing the fly line across the water and creating a large loop from the rod tip to the line still on the water's surface. Then push the rod forward and down in a short, sharp movement. Essentially, you will be rolling the loop of fly line across the water until the loop unrolls and the fly and leader fall back out where they were. The resistance provided by surface tension allows you to load the rod and propel the fly line forward. Unlike conventional back and forth casting, this cast applies the power all the way through the forward rod stroke, gradually feathering the force from the cast as the rod tip drops below the horizontal. It is still more of a push than a snap or a swing though; it just takes place over a smaller range of movement and a shorter space of time.

If you use this cast when wading along a

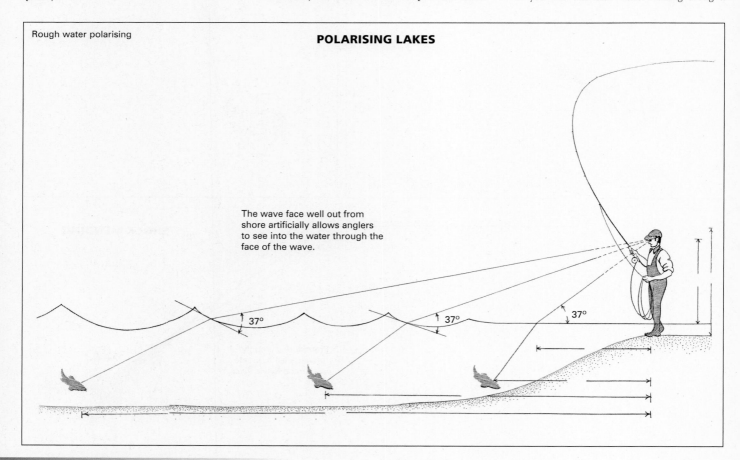

Rough water polarising

POLARISING LAKES

The wave face well out from shore artificially allows anglers to see into the water through the face of the wave.

37°   37°   37°

To get past the reed stand along the river's edge and the steep bank behind him, this angler has moved into the water and fished from a wading position. Be sure when doing this though to wade slowly and carefully to minimise wake and to explore water ahead of you with the fly.

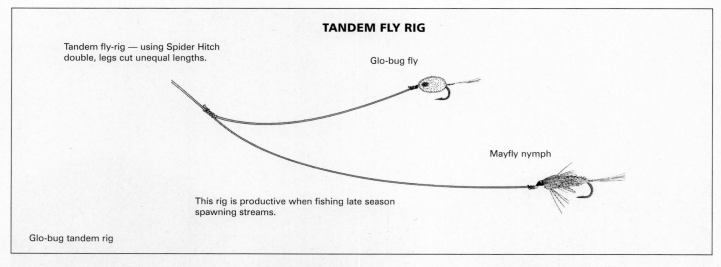

TANDEM FLY RIG

Tandem fly-rig — using Spider Hitch double, legs cut unequal lengths.

Glo-bug fly

Mayfly nymph

This rig is productive when fishing late season spawning streams.

Glo-bug tandem rig

river, you can advance the coverage of each successive cast by taking one or two steps between each cast.

STEEPLE CASTING

This cast is an alternative to the roll cast and used in similar situations, say, where high banks or trees behind the angler make a conventional back cast impossible. It is not an easy cast to master, but with practice, it can become a useful tool. As the name suggests, the back cast is not thrown horizontally out the back of the angler but more or less vertically. The casting stroke is an upward sweep of the rod, which begins with the casting hand well in front of your body before being brought toward you in a sharp upward curving path. It ends with the rod hand stabbing the rod tip toward the sky. When properly executed, this cast will extend the fly line straight up from your position. As the line is straightening, the rod tip drifts up toward the extended fly line then punches back down at an angle of about 45 degrees. It is critical not to make this forward cast a slow or a long movement. It is the shortest and sharpest of all the fly casting strokes, the rod hand usually travelling 30 to 40 centimetres or so up and back down again.

TANDEM GLO-BUG RIGS

Often, when fishing for spawn run trout, it can pay to use a combination of an egg-pattern fly such as a Glo-bug with a trailing nymph in the rig. Most often, the nymphs will be a compact pattern, such as a brown nymph, seal's fur nymph or a pheasant tail nymph, but virtually any nymph that represents a locally prevalent forage item will suffice. The tandem rig is simply constructed by first tying a double in the end of the leader with a Spider hitch, then cutting one leg of the double shorter than the other so you have two leader strands of unequal length. The Glo-bug is attached to the shorter of the two and the nymph is tied on the longer one so it trails a short distance behind.

WADE FISHING

Sometimes the very best way to get a good fly cast away to a fish-holding spot is to be standing in the water. Provided that depth and water movement make this possible, you will lower your profile and also let you feel and register nuances such as current and water temperature that can help you work out where fish will be. But there are some things you should keep in mind. The first of these is safety. When wading, move one foot first, then make sure it is secure before you move the other one. Do not wade in deep water where currents are strong, or you could lose your footing and get into difficulties. Be mindful also when wading lake shores, especially at night, that the bottom may drop away sharply leaving you floundering at best and drowning at worst.

The other consideration has more to do with not spoiling fishing chances for yourself by creating unnecessary disturbance. Always wade slowly, to maintain your footing, and to minimise the waves created by pushing the water away with your legs and body. Also, instead of blundering across or through a stretch of water because you assume there are no fish in it, make a cast and check it out first. You might be pleasantly surprised.

WEED GUARDS ON FLIES

When fishing flies around weedy water or amongst sticks and drowned brush, it can pay to incorporate some form of weed guard on the fly to help shed any weed that might otherwise foul the hook tip and render the fly unattractive. Small flies can be tied with a loop of nylon attached at the eye and looped around the hook bend, securing it under the tail of the fly. There are special flat-sectioned monofilaments made for this purpose.

Larger flies, intended for use in heavy brush or around dense rafts of flotsam can have a light springy wire weed guard tied in at the eye and extending toward the hook point. Thin and stiff stainless steel wire is good for this job, and should be bent into a narrow 'U' shape, so there are two springy legs of wire to deflect any rubbish away from the hook point. The wire can be arranged as shown so the open legs rest near the hook point or for fishing in very heavy brush country, it can be reversed, so the open legs are tied in at the hook eye and the stronger looped end rests against the hook.

Weed Guards on flies

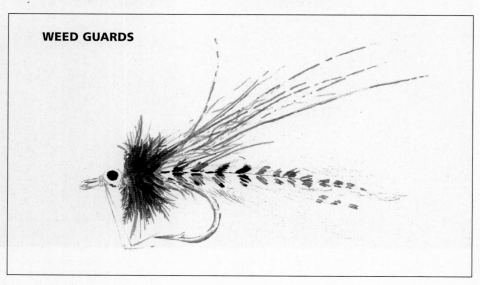

WEED GUARDS

STATE BY STATE TOP FISHING
LOCATIONS

NEW SOUTH WALES

CAMDEN HAVEN

The local estuary system comprises the Camden Haven river, Queens Lake to the north, Watson Taylors lake to the west and Gogerlies Lake to the south. Bass fishing exists upstream in the Camden Haven, Johns, and Stewarts rivers.

Fishing is consistently good from the breakwalls either side of the river entrance. Beyond those to the north and south, there is excellent surf beach fishing north to Grant's Beach, and south from Camden Head, a glorious stretch of beach to Diamond Head.

Good rock fishing can be had at Diamond Head, Camden Head and Pilot Head south of the river, and at Grant's Head to the north. Care is needed however as these places can be risky to fish in rough weather.

Offshore, a maze of small scattered reefs spreads some five kilometres seaward, to the 40 metre line, where an erratic line of drop-offs and gradually descending bottom falls eastward for another 20 kilometres or so in a broad sea slope to the 200 metre line.

Target species include bream, flathead, whiting, mullet, jewfish, snapper, kingfish, cobia, pearl perch, cod, billfish, sharks, tuna and both spotted and Spanish mackerel. Bass in freshwater.

Principal towns are Laurieton, North Haven and Dunbogan.

View of the Camden Haven Estuary

PORT STEPHENS

A large, deepwater coastal bay with scattered islands offshore, several good surf fishing beaches and rock-fishing headlands, Port Stephens offers most saltwater table species, excellent game fishing offshore and access to hinterland bass fishing in rivers an hour and a half or so west of Nelson Bay.

There is northern shore access from Tahlee, Tea Gardens and Hawks Nest, but facilities are much better on the southern shoreline. Small suburbs strung along this shore from west to east are; Soldiers Point, Salamander Bay, Nelson Bay, and Shoal Bay. Fingal Bay to the south faces the sea itself. Anna Bay, Birubi Point, Fisherman's Bay and Boat Harbour, are separated from Port Stephens by the Tomaree National Park, and are accessed from Nelson Bay Road or Gan Gan Road.

Offshore, Cabbage Tree Island, Big Island, Little Island and Broughton Island offer excellent sport, game and bottom fishing, there is good fishing for a variety of species within the massive confines of the bay itself while from Yacaaba Head, Bennetts Beach extends 12 kilometres northward to Dark Point, and south of Birubi, Stockton Beach runs for nearly 30 km. Zenith, Wreck Box and Fingal beaches sit between Tomaree and Fingal Head.

SOUTH WEST ROCKS

South West Rocks sits on the southern side of the Macleay river mouth and is a popular jumping off point for boat trips southward towards Smoky Cape and Hat Head and northwards toward Grassy Head and Scotts Head.

Easter usually sees big migratory schools of Spanish and spotted mackerel arrive, while kingfish and cobia can turn up any time. Juvenile

Above: Green Island SWR

Green Island SWR

black marlin gather here to feed on vast schools of baitfish around Christmas and through into February. Snapper and cod fishing is available year round but is best from spring through summer.

The Macleay is a prolific fishery for most common estuary species and the breakwalls consistently produce numbers of mulloway, which are known to peak whenever the river is in flood.

Beach fishing is excellent from Nambucca to Crescent Head and bass fishing is accessible and rewarding anywhere upstream from Smithtown early in the season, but better from Kempsey to Bellbrook upwards as the season progresses.

A feature of the region is that from Scotts Head to Hat Head, the rock platforms and headlands, though sloping and difficult to fish, offer excellent spinning, live baiting and conventional bait fishing for surface species, bottom feeders and seasonally, even game fish.

FORSTER/TUNCURRY

These twin towns straddle the entrance to the enclosed waters of Wallis Lake, a huge tidal expanse fed by the downstream flows of the Coolongolook, Wallingat and Wallamba rivers.

Essentially, the area is known for its estuary fishing, with bream, blackfish and flathead high on the list of most commonly caught species, but whiting, leatherjackets, jewfish, flounder and small tailor are also frequently found.

Offshore, there are few classic-form reefs, but additionally, seasonal sand movement can occasionally expose low rubble and reef areas and these can fire if uncovered long enough for food

chains to develop. Snapper, teraglin and tailor are commonly caught, over reefs, as are kingfish, longtail tuna and marlin in season.

Beach fishing is very productive from Nine mile beach north of the entrance and also from Forster Beach, Pebbly Beach, One Mile Beach and Burgess Beach on the southern side. Elizabeth, Boomerang and Bluey's beaches are also worth a look.

The breakwalls fish well for mulloway on live and dead baits and also of late, on soft plastic lures. Bream spinning is very popular and several catch and release tournaments are held at Forster each year.

Bass are available in the Wallamba, Coolongolook and Wallingat rivers.

COFFS HARBOUR

The creek and estuary fishing in the immediate Coffs vicinity can be interesting, with mangrove jacks, bream, mullet, flathead, trevally and small tailor on offer. It is probable though that offshore fishing is the big drawcard for the area.

There are many island and reef groups surrounding the Coffs area and while the fishing can be excellent, you will need to ensure that emerging Marine Park exclusion regulations do not prohibit you entering certain areas. Up to date information can be obtained by contacting Fishing Tackle Australia 02665 24611 before your visit.

South of Coffs Harbour, are Sawtell, Urunga and Nambucca Heads. Seasonally, very big Spanish mackerel roam these waters, while in winter, runs of super sized tailor are often encountered here too. A superlative inshore snapper fishery exists from spring through summer, with other quality reef fish like pearl perch available to seaworthy boats and experienced skippers.

Beach fishing is good along Boambee, North and Valla beaches to the south of Coffs, while to the north, Woolgoolga, Corindi and and Wooli beaches can be very productive.

Bass are available in the upper Bellinger, Kalang and Nambucca rivers and ardent local trout fishers drive up into the New England highlands.

BOTANY BAY

Right in the heart of industrialised Sydney, Botany Bay surprisingly yields fishing that ranges from very good to exceptional. Tailor, salmon, kingfish, bream, leatherjacket, flounder, trevally and tuna have all managed to adapt to man-made changes in bottom shape and depth as the bay's shipping and transport use has been evolving.

Exclusion zones include between the runways of Mascot airport, and within the container wharf area of Brotherson Dock on the northern shore and there is a 100 metre no-go zone skirting the

Above: Leatherjackets are just one of Botany Bay's fishing options

Below: Luderick inhabit the weedy creeks and cabbage-covered ocean rock shelves

The moorings in Great Turriel Bay are productive fishing places

oil refinery wharves on the bay's southern edge. This still leaves vast areas for fishing, including the channel markers off Molineaux point for kings, and general fishing over Watts Reef, the flats of the Monterey foreshore, Dolls Point and Towra Point and the Kurnell groynes.

Rock fishing requires a weather eye but places from Cape Banks through to Bare Island on the northern headland and from Sutherland Point round to Tabbegai produce luderick, snapper and drummer.

The Georges River flows into the bay underneath both Tom Ugly's and Captain Cook bridges and is very productive for bream, flathead and whiting. Upriver, around Como and Alfords Point, there are bream, tailor, mulloway, flathead, leatherjacket, whiting and luderick.

JERVIS BAY

Jervis Bay is some 20 minutes south and east of Nowra on the NSW mid south coast and represents one of the largest, cleanest and most pristine marine environments on the east coast.

Fishing restrictions have applied in the bay since the implementation of the Jervis Bay Marine Park in 2003, resulting in several shoreline areas being either placed totally off limits or proscribing certain fishing and boating activities. Despite this, 'JB' as it is known, still offers exemplary fishing for flathead, bream, whiting, leatherjacket, snapper, tailor, bonito, kingfish, Australian salmon, seasonal marlin and occasional visiting schools of tuna.

Maps with specific access and activity restrictions are available at www.mpa.nsw.gov. au/jbmp/jbmp.htm but, put simply, angling is only specifically forbidden in the areas gazetted as 'Sanctuary Zones'. These comprise about 40% of the bay's internal shoreline and something less than a third of its total area.

Obviously, shoreline fishing has been most affected by these closures, but significant fishing areas, like the central bulk of the bay and the land-based gamefishing at the Torpedo Tubes on the northern shore have remained open to anglers. The general Commonwealth Waters area at the bay's southern end allows for public access, subject to Defence requirements.

NAROOMA

Narooma, on the southern shoreline of Wagonga Inlet, is famed for offshore fishing around Montague Island and further south, the 12 Mile reef system. Bermagui, some 40 minutes south by road provides an alternate access point. The Continental Shelf is only 10 nautical miles off this part of the NSW south coast, providing access to yellowfin, big-eye and southern bluefin tuna, blue, black and striped marlin and many shark species. Big yellowtail kingfish, albacore, dolphin fish and longtail tuna also inhabit these waters and bottom fishing for snapper, mulloway and big trumpeter can be exceptional.

Wagonga Inlet offers flathead, bream, whiting, small tailor, school mulloway, luderick and estuary perch. The inlet is forked and deep upstream of the highway bridge but shallow and broad near the ocean bar, which can be challenging and even dangerous to cross when seas build with onshore winds and a run out tide. Local advice should

Above: Launching into Wagonga Inlet

Left: Tailing a brown trout in Hatchery Bay

always be sought before attempting it.

In the hinterland that separates the far south coast from the elevated plains of the Snowy region, several coastal rivers carry bass. These include the Tuross, Brogo, Deua and Clyde. The Brogo also has a small dam in which bass have been stocked.

PORT HACKING

A generally overlooked jewel in Sydney's galaxy of waterways, Port Hacking has no significant industry on its shores and serious urbanisation only on its north shore, making it a very clean estuary for a major city.

Flathead bream whiting, luderick, tarwhine, tailor and mullet make up the enclosed water fishing options, while occasional Australian salmon and small tuna zip inside the Port on a making tide. In one notable period, some seriously large yellowfin tuna were caught well upstream in the deep waters of South West Arm. At other times, oddball captures of usually tropical species like giant herring, queenfish, golden trevally and even bonefish have been made from the deceptively fishy area around the Deer Park church camp at Gogerlys Point.

Nippers can be pumped by hand from sand

flats that dry at low tide from Costens Bay to the Ballast Heap, but there is an Intertidal Protected Area (IPA) on the southern side of the port from Simpsons Bay Beach to the Bundeena Ferry Wharf.

Outside Port Hacking, south from Jibbon Bommie, there is good snapper fishing and kingfish, bonito, salmon, tuna and marlin. Shark Island off Cronulla is a good bait ground for slimy mackerel and yellowtail.

SYDNEY HARBOUR

Once erroneously thought to be past its best, Sydney Harbour can turn on blisteringly good fishing. Areas of interest include the two 'Wedding Cake' channel markers, the nearby Sow and Pigs reef, the drop off in front of Nielsen Park, the general trolling and spinning area between the Western Channel, Middle Head Dobroyd Head and Quarantine head and the rocky shoreline along the foot of the cliffs at the Old Man's Hat on North Head.

Tailor, bream, luderick, flathead and occasional goat fish can be caught around the Sow and Pigs, while adventurous anglers pit their gear and wits against the sometimes huge kingfish that prowl around the Wedding Cakes and Nielsen Park.

Out in The Sound (the broad open area between the heads and leading westward toward Middle Head and Grotto Point) you can often find surface-feeding schools of tailor, frigate mackerel, and Australian salmon.

LAKE JINDABYNE

The second most famous trout lake in New South Wales, Jindabyne offers good fishing for fly fishers and for bank-fishers using either bait or lures. It serves trollers well too—both the seriously set up kind and the casual 'drag and hope' variety.

For trollers, depth control of your presentation is a critical part of success. Techniques such as trolling with lead-core line and even down riggers, using echo sounders to indicate the presence of fish beneath the boat, show how deep they are and even to an extent suggesting how actively they might be feeding.

In the absence of such sophisticated gear, many anglers still manage to troll up good fish by 'flatlining' i.e, simply trailing a lure out the back off the rod tip and relying on the diving and running characteristics of the lure to reach whatever trout happen to be at that depth.

In late winter and early spring, flyfishers, equipped with polarising sunglasses to cut surface glare, stalk edge-swimming trout (usually) along the western shoreline points, casting ahead of the cruising fish.

Bait fishers also do well off the shore, early mornings and late afternoons, with mudeyes, worms or paste baits fished under floats.

OBERON/LITHGOW

About three hours west of Sydney, over the Blue Mountains and on the elevated western slopes, the Oberon/Lithgow district offers excellent trout fishing in a series of dams and rivers.

Trout dams include Lake Oberon—within a kilometre of the town itself, Thompson's Creek Dam and Lake Lyell, which are much closer to Lithgow.

There is an extensive network of rivers in the area. Around Oberon you'll find the Fish River, the Duckmaloi, the Campbells and a host of smaller waters, like Solitary Creek at Tarana, Sewell's Creek and Wiseman's Creek running into the Campbells river and beyond those, out past Ginkin, on the Jenolan Caves Road, idyllic little streams that flow into wild back canyon country—streams such as the Hollanders, the Tuglow, Kowmung and Boyd.

The Cox's River flows down out of the tailrace of Lake Lyell, through the Megalong Valley and down into the Burragorang catchment where it picks up the Jenolan and Kowmung and empties into Warragamba dam.

Fluky and occasionally torrential rainfall can mean that these streams typically run slightly discoloured compared to other trout areas. Exceptions are the freestone rivers, like the Hollanders and Coxs, provided they get adequate, gentle rainfall over time.

Landmarks like the Harbour Bridge are also productive fishing spots

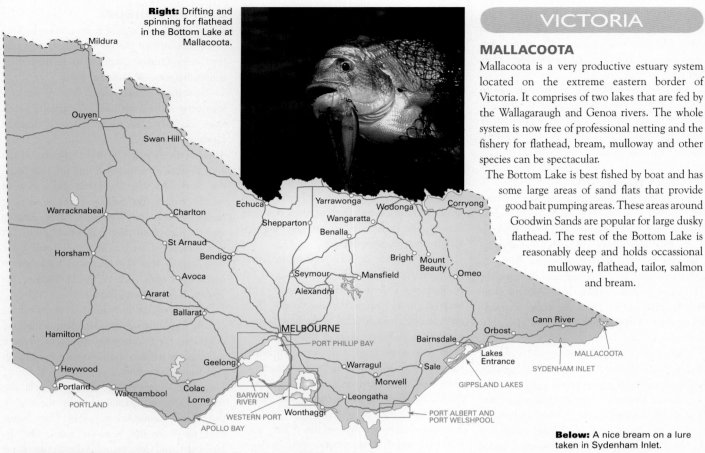

Right: Drifting and spinning for flathead in the Bottom Lake at Mallacoota.

MALLACOOTA

Mallacoota is a very productive estuary system located on the extreme eastern border of Victoria. It comprises of two lakes that are fed by the Wallagaraugh and Genoa rivers. The whole system is now free of professional netting and the fishery for flathead, bream, mulloway and other species can be spectacular.

The Bottom Lake is best fished by boat and has some large areas of sand flats that provide good bait pumping areas. These areas around Goodwin Sands are popular for large dusky flathead. The rest of the Bottom Lake is reasonably deep and holds occassional mulloway, flathead, tailor, salmon and bream.

Below: A nice bream on a lure taken in Sydenham Inlet.

The Narrows is a 1.5 kilometre long channel connecting the Bottom and Top lakes and during the summer mulloway are a real prospect here. The shallower Top Lake is a haven for lure and bait anglers chasing bream, flathead, estuary perch and luderick. A boat is necessary to access most of the prime target areas including Double Creek Arm, Cape Horn and the Genoa and Wallagaraugh rivers.

There is excellent land based fishing along the western shore at Robertsons Bight, at Captains Point, the Mallacoota boat ramp and wharf and Bastion Point. There are also several surf beaches close to Mallacoota providing good fishing for salmon, gummy shark and tailor. These include the Entrance surf beach, Betka Beach and Tip Beach.

When the entrance is open and safe to navigate the offshore fishing can be very good. There is bottom fishing for gummy sharks and flathead and at times it is worthwhile trolling for tuna, kingfish and marlin.

The township of Mallacoota is right on the shores of the Bottom Lake and there is a huge caravan park that fronts onto the water.

SYDENHAM INLET

Sydenham Inlet is the lagoon estuary of the Bemm River. The bream fishery at Sydenham is one of the best in Victoria with bream, mullet, luderick, whiting and estuary perch all present in large numbers. It is a shallow estuary and boats to five metres are all that are required. The majority of anglers also position their boat on the fishing grounds will long poles driven into the mud rather that using anchors. The Bemm River is much deeper than the estuary and there are always good catches of bream to be had from the entrance to the river and upstream to the falls. Surf fishing in the area is also productive and the Pearl Point surf beach is particularly noted for good catches of gummy sharks and salmon. Access is via a 4WD track from the settlement at Bemm River.

GIPPSLAND LAKES

Gippsland Lakes are Victoria's most extensive estuary system and encompass Lake Wellington, Lake Victoria, Lake King, Lakes Entrance and the rivers Tambo, Mitchell and Nicholson. The major towns in the area include Lakes Entrance, Metung and Paynesville, all of which have plenty of facilities, accommodation and boat launching. Both southern and black bream are present throughout the system and despite immense pressure from commercial operators they are still the mainstay for recreational anglers. Snapper enter the system over the summer months and can be caught as far into the system as Lake King.

There are abundant land based opportunities around Lakes Entrance. Bullock Island is a great place to catch a bream and the footbridge crossing the Cunningham Arm gives easy access to the surf beach and the east entrance wall. The Kalimna Jetty is another great spot to catch bream and flathead.

For boat angling the channels around the South Channel, Metung, Raymond Island, Carstairs Bank and Lake King will provide plenty of scope to score a bag of fish. Tailor and salmon

Anchoring up and baitfishing in Gippsland Lakes.

The jetties at Paynesville.

are often taken on the troll and flathead, whiting, silver trevally, snapper and even mulloway are always present for anglers fishing bait. Bancroft Bay, near Metung is a deep bay that produces the odd mulloway in autumn.

The town of Paynesville located on McMillan Strait is an ideal base to fish the Strait and the surrounding sheltered areas of Raymond Island. These waters hold lots of opportunities for soft plastic fishing for bream.

The three major rivers feeding the system— the Tambo, Nicholson and Mitchell are all well known for some of the best bream fishing in the state. Anglers base their accommodation at Johnsonville, Swan Reach, Nicholson and Bairnsdale. All three rivers can be fished land based and from a boat depending on your preference. There are lots of options and the best time is during the colder months when the bream are in the rivers in increased numbers.

PORT ALBERT AND PORT WELSHPOOL

The vast Port Albert and Port Welshpool channels and banks support a fantastic and varied fishery. Snapper, whiting and flathead are the mainstay species but salmon, gummy shark, pike, snook, trevally and kingfish are also present.

There are excellent fisheries in the main channels around Sunday and Dog Islands as well as the smaller islands Pelican, Sheep, Scrubby and Cyril. The No 3 starboard marker on the Port Albert Channel now marks the site of the old Basket Beacon on Sunday Island. This is a land mark off which many good snapper are caught over the November to January period.

The Snake Channel, which extends some eight kilometres to the west of the entrance is the deepest part of Port Albert and is one of the best places to try for snapper. The area really requires a boat to get to the best fishing spots. However the Port Albert jetties are well worth fishing from, especially at high tide.

The Middle Ground is a shallow stretch of water between One Tree Island and Port Welshpool and is barely navigable at high tide. It is however one of the best areas to lure and fly fish for big flathead.

Port Welshpool has an excellent boat ramp which accesses directly into the Lewis Channel which in turn leads to the massive Corner Inlet and onwards to offshore and the Seal Island Group.

Fishing in the Lewis Channel will see snapper and gummy shark as well as some lovely King George whiting and flathead on the edges of the channels. The channel between Little Snake and Snake islands provides great shallow water fishing for big flathead and whiting.

Land based anglers are lucky at Port Welshpool as there is a very long jetty extending right out into the Lewis Channel. Whiting are found in the shallower water and silver trevally are to be found in the deeper water around the pylons. Anglers fishing the end of the jetty at night at high tide can catch snapper and gummy sharks.

WESTERN PORT

Western Port is the second largest bay in the state and consists of a series of sand bars and channels, making it often difficult to navigate. Being so close to Melbourne there are plenty of facilities and boat ramps all around its extensive shoreline. King George whiting are the most popular fish in Western Port, closely followed by snapper. Elephant fish are very popular in season and recently a very solid mulloway fishery has been discovered.

Phillip Island is situated at the entrance to Western Port and effectively creates the two entrances to the bay. While the main waters of Western Port require a boat there are ample of opportunities for the land based angler on Phillip Island. At San Remo you can fish from the beach directly into the deep channel downstream from the bridge. The jetties at Newhaven, Cowes and Rhyll can all produce flathead and very occasional snapper.

The main areas around Western Port that produce snapper and whiting are Corinella on the eastern side and Hastings and Stony Point on the western side. Both have good ramps that are suitable for craft of all sizes. Other launching ramps are at Tooradin, Warneet, Blind Bight,

The Port Welshpool Jetty extends right out to the Lewis Channel.

A blue shark taken offshore from Apollo Bay.

Fishing for silver trevally off Wild Dog Creek.

Lang Lang and Grantville and access the upper areas of the system so local knowledge when using these ramps is very handy. On Phillip Island there are three excellent ramps at Newhaven, Rhyll and Cowes.

There are literally hundreds of fishing marks in Western Port, the upper area of the system is very productive for King George whiting, while snapper tend to become more prevelant further down.

The Flinders Jetty is one of the best places in Victoria to catch squid and anglers fishing from this jetty will also take whiting and garfish.

Finally there is a very good surf beach on Phillip Island, Gunnamatta surf beach is approximately three kilometres west of Cape Schanck. This beach has gained a solid reputation amongst anglers for good catches of salmon.

PORT PHILLIP BAY

Located right on Melbourne's doorstep, the bay covers some 2000 square kilometres and is Victoria's main saltwater fishery. Every year around early November there is a huge influx of snapper into the bay that are highly sought after by thousands of anglers. Apart from snapper there are solid populations of King George whiting, sand flathead, gummy shark, salmon, bream and many other species.

As the season progresses the snapper spread out across the bay providing quality angling in all areas.

The shallow sandy areas around Sorrento, Queenscliffe, Swan Bay, Indented Head, Kirk Point, Werribee, Point Cook, Brighton and Black Rock all have good fishing for whiting over the summer months.

Early in the season the snapper will run into the bay and then spread out into Corio Bay off Point Wilson and Point Richards and on the eastern side off mount Martha and Mornington.

Later in November the snapper grounds extend all around the bay with the very popular areas off Frankston, Sandringham, StKilda and Altona.

Generally the fishing in the bay for snapper after Christmas slows a little with species like flathead and whiting being targeted . As the weather cools the fishing becomes concentrated in certain areas. Two very good general areas in autumn are Hobsons Bay and Beaumaris Bay where there are excellent fishing prospects over the cooler months.

The bream fishery in the Yarra River and Patterson and Werribee rivers is also very good and anglers using soft plastic techniques do very well.

The bay also offers an outstanding amount of land based fishing from dozens of piers and jetties. These extend all around the bay and are very popular.

BARWON RIVER

The Barwon River estuary is famous for its large mulloway. These can be taken from a small boat using live baits. There are however opportunities for land based anglers fishing the mouth, the bridge, the Ozone Jetty and at the Sheepwash.

The nearby township of Barwon Heads has accommodation as does Ocean Grove on the other side of the estuary. There is a good ramp into the estuary at Ocean Grove and the main fishing for mulloway is downstream from there to the road bridge.

APOLLO BAY

Apollo Bay is a small man made harbour protected from the prevailing south westerlies by Cape Otway. Anglers basing themselves at the township of Apollo Bay can fish some great close inshore marks for whiting, silver trevally, snapper, flathead, salmon and much more.

There is excellent surf fishing on the Apollo Bay surf beach at the mouth of the Barham River.

The beach between Wild Dog creek and Apollo Bay can also be quite good with salmon during the day and silver trevally after dark. The Barham River itself supports a good estuary perch and bream fishery.

The Apollo Bay harbour can be a phenomonal fishery as well with barracouta, salmon, warehou, garfish and flathead all being taken from the harbour walls. Offshore there are numerous marks that produce quality bags of snapper and bottom fish including Cape Patton, Big Henty Reef, Hayley reef, Bald Hill and Blanket Bay.

PORTLAND

Situated far to the west, Portland harbour is a major shipping harbour behind Western Port and Port Phillip Bay. Portland Bay is relatively sheltered from the prevailing south westerlies and over summer has a great fishery of flathead, mulloway, yellowtail kingfish, snapper, salmon, trevally and pike. All sized trailerboats can be launched safely in the Portland boat harbour and the harbour gives easy and safe access to the close inshore fishing grounds of Portland Bay.

There is a good run of kingfish usually every year between Danger Point and Minerva reef. There is also a good run of snapper over Christmas and into the summer. Drifting for flathead can be very productive and there are some great spots to anchor in between Whaler Point and Snapper Point that will produce snapper, salmon, whiting and flathead.

For land based anglers the breakwaters around the Portland harbour offer some great fishing from October until April. Snapper and whiting are prime targets with silver trevally and warehou also there in large numbers at times.

During February and March the breakwalls can see some numbers of large yellowtail kingfish present, these can be taken on heavy gear using squid under a bobby float.

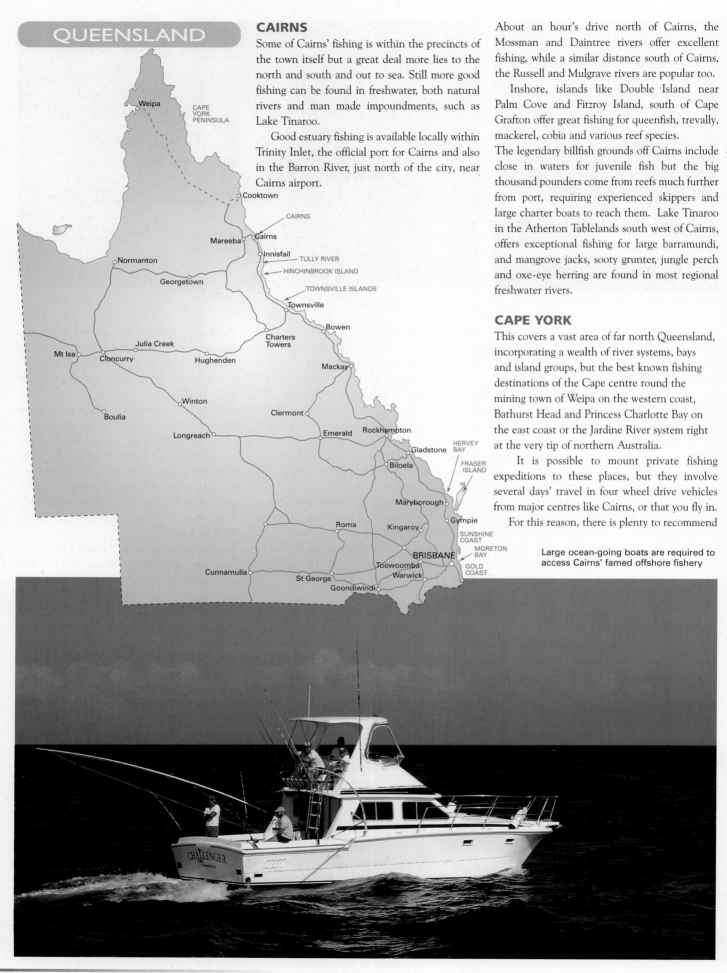

Weipa
CAPE YORK PENINSULA
Cooktown
CAIRNS
Cairns
Mareeba
Normanton
Innisfail
TULLY RIVER
HINCHINBROOK ISLAND
Georgetown
TOWNSVILLE ISLANDS
Townsville
Bowen
Charters Towers
Mt Isa
Julia Creek
Cloncurry
Hughenden
Mackay
Winton
Clermont
Boulia
Emerald
Rockhampton
Longreach
Gladstone
HERVEY BAY
Biloela
FRASER ISLAND
Maryborough
Roma
Kingaroy
Gympie
SUNSHINE COAST
Cunnamulla
Toowoomba
MORETON BAY
BRISBANE
St George
Warwick
GOLD COAST
Goondiwindi

CAIRNS

Some of Cairns' fishing is within the precincts of the town itself but a great deal more lies to the north and south and out to sea. Still more good fishing can be found in freshwater, both natural rivers and man made impoundments, such as Lake Tinaroo.

Good estuary fishing is available locally within Trinity Inlet, the official port for Cairns and also in the Barron River, just north of the city, near Cairns airport.

About an hour's drive north of Cairns, the Mossman and Daintree rivers offer excellent fishing, while a similar distance south of Cairns, the Russell and Mulgrave rivers are popular too.

Inshore, islands like Double Island near Palm Cove and Fitzroy Island, south of Cape Grafton offer great fishing for queenfish, trevally, mackerel, cobia and various reef species. The legendary billfish grounds off Cairns include close in waters for juvenile fish but the big thousand pounders come from reefs much further from port, requiring experienced skippers and large charter boats to reach them. Lake Tinaroo in the Atherton Tablelands south west of Cairns, offers exceptional fishing for large barramundi, and mangrove jacks, sooty grunter, jungle perch and oxe-eye herring are found in most regional freshwater rivers.

CAPE YORK

This covers a vast area of far north Queensland, incorporating a wealth of river systems, bays and island groups, but the best known fishing destinations of the Cape centre round the mining town of Weipa on the western coast, Bathurst Head and Princess Charlotte Bay on the east coast or the Jardine River system right at the very tip of northern Australia.

It is possible to mount private fishing expeditions to these places, but they involve several days' travel in four wheel drive vehicles from major centres like Cairns, or that you fly in.

For this reason, there is plenty to recommend

Large ocean-going boats are required to access Cairns' famed offshore fishery

the use of professional fishing charter operations. These can get you to where the fishing is best, provide assisted fishing camps or mothershipping, or alternatively, operate in tandem with remote resorts.

All the tropical salt and freshwater species are on the cards in this largely untouched area. In the freshwater rivers, barramundi, mangrove jack, sooty grunter, and catfish are plentiful, with barramundi, jacks, several species of trevally, grunter, queenfish, threadfin salmon and mudcrabs and even permit in most estuaries. Offshore, you can find mackerel tuna, longtail tuna, Spanish and school mackerel, cobia, giant herring and lots of sharks.

FRASER ISLAND

This huge sand island (the largest in the world) sits offshore from the Queensland towns of Maryborough and Bundaberg. It is best known for its marvelous beach fishing, but also offers rock fishing from Indian Head and Waddy Point, offshore fishing on the east coast, excellent bay fishing in Hervey Bay, between the island and the Queensland coast and even some limited estuary creek fishing at Wathumba Creek and Moon and Moon Point.

From the island's western shore, you can catch sand whiting, bream, flathead and other estuarine species.

Principal fishing targets from the island's vast eastern sand beaches are; Tailor, mackerel, mulloway, permit, flathead, whiting and bream. Indian Head can provide sizzling action at times with huge tailor, plentiful mulloway and big Spanish mackerel. Queenfish also visit this headland, as do golden trevally, cobia, occasional kingfish and seasonally, some very big bream.

Although having several perched freshwater lakes and a substantial freshwater spring fed outflow on the east coast at Eli Creek, Fraser Island is not regarded as a legitimate or worthwhile freshwater fishery.

Pipis and beach worms however, are plentiful right along Fraser's east coast beaches, so providing you have the knack, gathering super fresh bait is not a problem.

THE GOLD COAST

The Gold Coast attractions for general tourism don't detract from its fishing appeal.Good surf fishing can be had from most of the metropolitan beaches, while offshore, there is an alluring mix of tropical and temperate species of bottom dwellers, like pearl perch, snapper, emperors, sweetlips, golden snapper, mulloway. There are also plentiful surface fish, like tailor, dolphin fish, various tunas, many species of mackerel as well as billfish and sharks.

Offshore access is via the Southport Seaway, which, together with ongoing sand dredging, has made the crossing of the notorious Southport bar much less hazardous than it was previously. Care is still needed however when an onshore wind meets an outgoing tide.

The estuaries comprise some natural river mouth systems such as Tallebudgera Creek and the Nerang and Tweed rivers but an astonishing amount of coastal tidal water intrusions are in the form of man-made canal estates, which, to the surprise of many, have turned out to be extremely productive recreational fisheries.

To the west of the Gold Coast, there is also good freshwater fishing in dams like Moogerah, Hinze and Maroon. All these have been stocked with Australian bass, golden perch, and silver perch and offer excellent fishing.

HERVEY BAY

Hervey Bay stretches from the inside northern tip of Fraser Island (Rooney Point) to the Queensland coast at Burnett Heads, southward as far as Urangan and east again to Sandy Point on Fraser Island.

It's a huge body of water, playing host to several pods of migrating whales each year and offers a great variety and extent of fishing, suitable for boats ranging from small car-toppers to large sea going craft – very much needed, out in the vast open stretches of water in the bay's northern half.

Above: Mother-shipping is a very workable way to fish these remote locations

Below: Vehicles parked at Indian Head for an early morning session

Above: Mulloway can be caught from the beach or rocks of Fraser Island's eastern shore

The waters off Southport can be challenging and dangerous but offer great fishing

Golden trevally are plentiful in Hervey Bay

water called collectively, The Great Sandy Strait. These offer excellent fishing for flathead, bream, whiting, grunter and in the creeks either side of the Strait, mangrove jacks and trevally.

HINCHINBROOK ISLAND

Located just off the coast near Cardwell, two hours north of Townsville, Hinchinbrook Island offers small boat anglers a variety of fishing locations, a wide range of tropical saltwater species and some of the most spectacular scenery in all of coastal Queensland.

Waters immediately off Cardwell tend to be shallow and the foreshore is quite soft bottomed. Scattered rubble and hard bottom starts to appear some distance off shore from Cardwell towards Hinchinbrook and firms into rising rock and coral where Garden, Goold and Brook islands emerge from the sea to Hinchinbrook's north and north-west.

Trolling the drop-offs of these small islets will produce coral trout, trevally and various other species at times, but the waters around Cape Richards are more consistently productive for

Within Hervey Bay, there are several islands, and productive channel markers too, which offer excellent small boat fishing for species such as kingfish, giant trevally, golden trevally, mackerel, queenfish, and some reef fish, like sweetlip, emperor and snapper. Woody Island in particular has small satellite islets and outlying bommies. These attract huge trevally that will smash surface poppers retrieved through the tidal races and over shallow tide washed ledges.

To the south of Woody Island, there are many islands, channels, sand flats and open

Above: Saltwater crocodiles are a part of life around Hinchinbrook. Treat them with respect

Threadfin salmon are sometimes encountered in the Hinchinbrook Channel

Mangrove jacks can be caught in many of the tidal inlets

queenfish and mackerel. The waters surrounding Hinchinbrook Island are subject to management of the Great Barrier Reef Marine Park but angling access is permitted in Macushla Bay, the Hinchinbrook channel, and across the shallow flats at the southern end of the channel near Lucinda. Fishing is limited in Zoe Bay – consult current GBRMPA zoning regulations for up to date regulations.

Species available around Hinchinbrook include barramundi, mangrove jack, fingermark, GT's, queenfish, estuary cod and golden trevally.

SUNSHINE COAST

This stretch of Queensland coast runs from Tewantin to Caboolture and takes in Bribie Island. Much of it is excellent beach fishing country with several estuaries and rock spots as well and first rate inshore and offshore fishing.

The Noosa River offers bream, flathead, whiting and bass in its upper reaches – note there is a closed season for bass here from 1st June to 31st August. Mangrove jacks, permit and various trevallies also inhabit this system. Offshore from Noosa, schools of mackerel tuna and longtail appear seasonally , while mulloway and cobia are frequently caught from reefs like Chardons and North Reef.

Working down the coast, Peregian beach, Coolum beach and Yaroomba beach (near Point Arkwright) set the tone for the major surfing and fishing beaches as far down as Caloundra. All offer dart, flathead bream and occasional whiting, with tailor periodically available as well.

Coolum creek has good bream fishing on lures and flies in summer, while the river at Mooloolaba will provide trevally and flathead .

There are excellent billfish grounds offshore from Mooloolaba and the best way to find them is to look for working birds, surface splashes or use your sounder to locate deep bait schools.

MORETON BAY

Queensland's biggest urban bay, Moreton Bay is a staggeringly good fishery. It offers most warm water reef and estuary species, as well as plentiful surface fish, ranging from mackerel and tuna through kingfish, cobia and tailor.

Whiting are a walk up start from almost any sandy part of the foreshore and bream and flathead are plentiful too. Mackerel tuna and longtail tuna frequently bust up throughout the bay but particularly in the centre and southern half around Peel Island, Mud Island, St Helena Island and Green island. Longtail also inhabit the Rous Channel and South Passage area.

The recent phenomenon of snapper on soft plastics had its start around the mouth of the Brisbane River but has now spread right round the bay, taking in most of the islands as far

Longtail tuna are challenging targets for serious spin and fly-fishermen

Queensland dam barra vary in size but can be huge

south as Coochiemudlo. Bigger fish come from the shipping channels together with kings and cobia round the four beacons. The spoil grounds are also worth a look as are Harry Atkinson and Curtin reefs. The coffee rock ledges north of Tangalaooma have also produced snapper in excess of eight kilos at times.

The bay can cut up in a strong breeze, so keep a careful eye on the weather.

TOWNSVILLE ISLANDS

North of Townsville and stretching as far up as Lucinda, a group of islands takes their collective name of the Palm Islands from Palm Island, the largest in the group and an Aboriginal Reserve. Orpheus island boasts an exclusive resort as well as a marine science research facility associated with James Cook University and Pelorus and Fantom are also worth fishing.

Boats of five or six metres are well able to reach the Palm group from launching points such as Rollingstone Creek, or even Townsville on exceptionally good days. Northern islands in the group can be accessed from Lucinda.

Mostly the fishing is for reef species, with a lot of surface fish thrown in. Species such as mackerel, queenfish, giant trevally and others can be spun from coral ledges, from tidal passages between the islands or caught by trolling poppers, minnows or chrome lures over the shallow fringing reefs.

Best fishing with lures is when a tide change occurs, funneling water past points and through narrow gaps. This bunches up baitfish and encourages feeding sprees by the predatory species. A particularly effective technique is to cast poppers over a shallow coral flat and rip them back quickly into deeper water.

QUEENSLAND BARRA DAMS
AWOONGA

Thirty kilometres south of Gladstone—covers 3500 ha–7.7 metres deep—barramundi, forktailed catfish, golden perch, saratoga, silver perch and sooty grunter. Fishing is excluded 200 metres upstream of the dam wall and 400 metres downstream.

CALLIDE
Situated 12 kilometres east of Biloela—covers 1200 ha–depth 6.8 metres—stocked with barramundi, golden perch, silver perch and Saratoga.

KINCHANT
Thirty kilometres west of Mackay, covers 900 ha –depth 10 metres—stocked with barramundi and sooty grunter.

MOONDARRA
Approximately 16 kilometres east of Mount Isa —stocked with barramundi, saratoga and sooty grunter and covers 2300 ha–6 metres deep.

PETER FAUST
Twenty-six kilometres north west of Proserpine township, covers 4300 ha–11 metres deep and features heavy stands of timber. Stocked with barramundi and sooty grunter.

TEEMBURA
Situated 60 kilometres west of Mackay, covers about 1000 ha and is usually about 14 metres deep. It is stocked with sooty grunter and barramundi,

TINAROO
Fifteen kilometres northeast of Atherton, 13 metres deep–covers 3300 ha–stocked with barramundi, archer fish, pikey bream, redclaw, snub nose gar and sooty grunter

OTHER BARRA DAMS
Burdekin Falls, Eungella, Koombooloomba, Monduran, Boondooma, Wuruma and Fairbairn dams.

QUEENSLAND BASS DAMS
BAROON POCKET 5 kilometres southwest Montville–400 ha–15 metres deep.
BORUMBA 12 kilometres Southwest Imbil –500 ha–6 metres deep.
CRESSBROOK – 20 kilometres east Crows Nest –500 ha–15 metres deep.
EWEN MADDOCK — 5 kilometres Southeast Mooloolah—370 ha–4.5 metres deep.
HINZE — 8 kilometres southwest Nerang–970 ha–7 metres deep.
LAKE MACDONALD – 6 kilometres northeast Cooroy–260 ha–6 metres deep.
MAROON — 24 kilometres south Boona —325 ha–9.6 metres deep.
MOOGERAH — 15 kilometers southeast Kalbar —880 ha–10.5 metres deep.
SAMSONVALE — 4 kilometres west Petrie —2180 ha–9.8 metres deep.

Above: Shark mackerel are plentiful off the islands and reefs north of Townsville

Adult bass from Somerset Dam can easily attain 50 cm and four pounds in weight

SOMERSET — 25 kilometres northeast Esk — 4210 ha–9 metres deep.

WIVENHOE — 9 kilometres northwest Fernvale — 10750 ha–10.8 metres deep.

BJELKE-PETERSEN — 12 kilometres southeast Murgon—2150 ha–5.8 metres deep.

BOONDOOMA — 20 kilometres northwest Proston—1920 ha–11 metres deep.

CANIA — 37 kilometres northwest Monto — 720 ha–12.4 metres deep.

GORDONBROOK — 20 kilometres northwest Kingaroy —235 ha–2.8 metres deep.

LAKE GREGORY — 26 kilometres southwest Bundaberg — 200 ha – 3.1 metres deep.

LENTHALLS – 20 kilometres south Howard – 400 ha – 3.9 metres deep.

MONDURAN — 21 kilometres northwest Gin Gin — 5340 ha – 11 metres deep.

WURUMA — 36 kilometres northwest Eidsvold — 1780 ha – 9.3 metres deep.

TULLY RIVER

The Tully River is a classic tropical coast stream. It starts life high in the rainforest of the Cardwell Range, grows in volume and pace as it enters boulder-strewn rapids and rock bars and as it slows into its more fishable midwaters, it is sleek, clear and green. Deep holes and snaggy corners are interspersed with sand and gravel shallows until, running under the Bruce Highway just south of Tully, it spills into the sea at Rockingham Bay.

Carrying barramundi, sooty grunter, mangrove jacks and tarpon, the Tully is a bewitching fluid statement of what a wild river ought to be. Despite some residual pollution from past cane farming practices, the Tully remains an awesome place to fish or even to simply experience the wonder of a fully functioning tropical river.

Accessible at various points, the upwaters are best negotiated in plastic canoes, kayaks or inflatable rafts, but once down into cane country, it is very suitable for shallow-draft aluminium punts. It should be noted that this river is natural habitat for estuarine crocodiles, which can become a serious danger for canoes and small craft. It is definitely not recommended for anglers to disembark and fish this river from the bank!

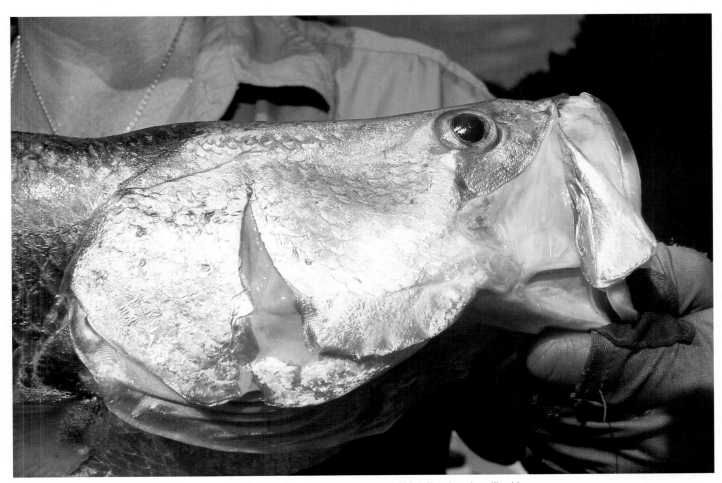
Below: Barramundi are a feature of Tully River fishing. Fish taken closer to the entrance will be silver in colour, like this.

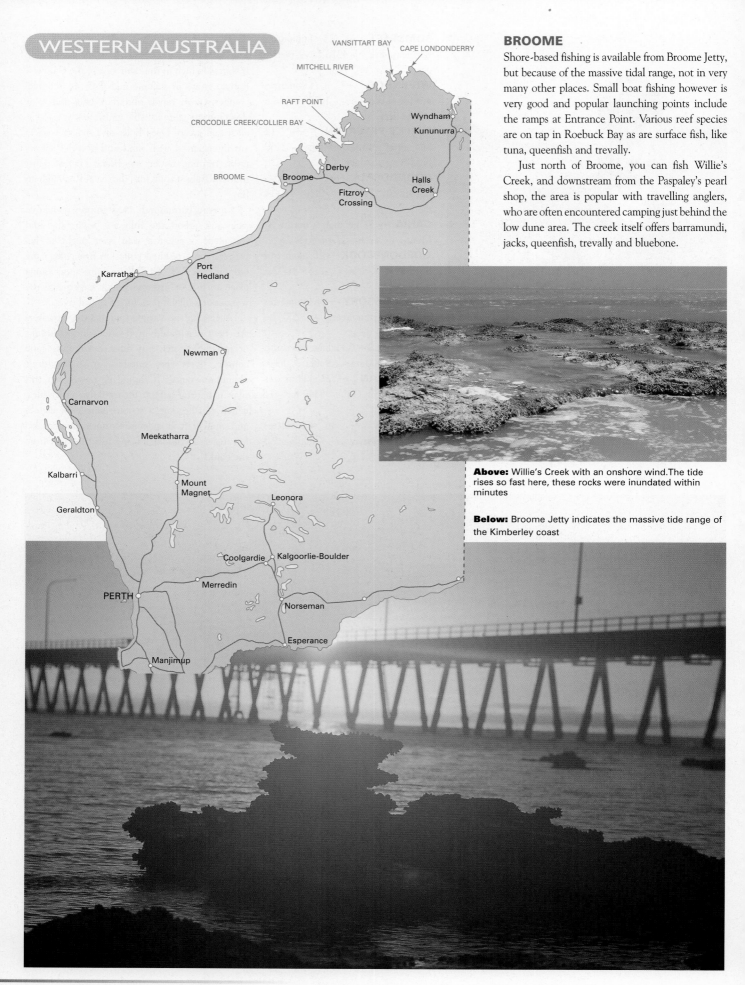

VANSITTART BAY

CAPE LONDONDERRY

MITCHELL RIVER

RAFT POINT

CROCODILE CREEK/COLLIER BAY

Wyndham

Kununurra

BROOME

Broome

Derby

Halls
Creek

Fitzroy
Crossing

Karratha

Port
Hedland

Newman

Carnarvon

Meekatharra

Kalbarri

Mount
Magnet

Geraldton

Leonora

Coolgardie

Kalgoorlie-Boulder

Merredin

PERTH

Norseman

Esperance

Manjimup

BROOME

Shore-based fishing is available from Broome Jetty, but because of the massive tidal range, not in very many other places. Small boat fishing however is very good and popular launching points include the ramps at Entrance Point. Various reef species are on tap in Roebuck Bay as are surface fish, like tuna, queenfish and trevally.

Just north of Broome, you can fish Willie's Creek, and downstream from the Paspaley's pearl shop, the area is popular with travelling anglers, who are often encountered camping just behind the low dune area. The creek itself offers barramundi, jacks, queenfish, trevally and bluebone.

Above: Willie's Creek with an onshore wind. The tide rises so fast here, these rocks were inundated within minutes

Below: Broome Jetty indicates the massive tide range of the Kimberley coast

Bluebone will readily take baits of crab but can also be targeted with soft plastic lures. Getting them out on light casting tackle though can be difficult since much of the creek's margins are overgrown with mangroves or fringed with rough rocky shelves.

Watch the tides here as they can rise quickly and catch you out if you've picked a fishing spot that can be cut off as the water rushes in.

Further north again is Barred Creek, notable for the remains of a petrified forest on the northern approaches, but also for good fishing. Watch for big crocs and sandflies!

CROCODILE CREEK/COLLIER BAY

Fishing in the remote wild places north of Broome is blindingly good but is no place for the ill prepared or inexperienced. That considered,

Above: Water is still cascading from Montgomery Reef even as the next tide is rising

Left: Freshwater pool on Crocodile Creek with saltwater in the background

the expense of hiring guides or even taking one of the various mother-ship packages is an option well worthwhile. Mother-shipping can deliver you to a range of locations in safety and comfort, with guides, food accommodation and transport all rolled in.

One place opened up by such long range craft is Collier Bay, where possibly the world's biggest queenfish live. Captures of queenfish in excess of 15 kilos are not uncommon here and the sheer numbers of golden trevally, mackerel, GT's and queenies will leave you gobsmacked.

Crocodile Creek is tucked away at the back of an inlet, above a low waterfall that only rarely allows saltwater intrusion. A steel ladder here gives you access to a large rocky pool full of pure fresh water, This pool has warm water vents like a spa and interestingly, small mangrove jacks — which have the endearing habit of sneaking up behind bathers and giving them a nip.

In the inlet below, reef species live close to the sheer rock-walled shoreline and the wider bay has loads of surface fish.

MONTGOMERY REEF

Montgomery Reef lies offshore from Raft Point, the closest mainland point to the reef and the place from which Aboriginal fishermen would raft across to Montgomery Island to fish, hunt and collect turtles.

The turtles are still in evidence and as the Reef dries at low tide, you can see hundreds browsing on the weed along the channels that lace the reef's higher ground.

In those deep channels, huge cod and bluebone swim along crevasse-like walls. Across shallow

Bluebone and parrot fish smack squid baits and often break fishing lines

flats, golden trevally do head-stands, waving their tails in the air as they forage amongst the weed and coral and alarmingly large sharks swirl and hunt amongst them.

Fishing the tidal run off from this reef complex is like spinning into the torrent of a salmon river. Often, large barracuda, sharks and other reef species lie in wait, ready to pounce on anything swept down to them by the water pouring off the reef top.

Trolling the outer edges of the reef produces mackerel, queenies and tuna and, in the brief time it takes for the reef to drown again, you can see whole armies of fish swarming up to feed on the reef top until the next run out tide.

MONTALIVET ISLANDS

Offshore from Bigge Island, a group of islands called the Montalivets studs an area of deep channels where coastal currents rip through, carrying bait schools and attracting sailfish and other large marine predators.

While fishing for the sails can be patchy, the reef fishing is both reliable and spectacular. Huge fingermark (called 'golden snapper' in the west) vie with coral trout, bluebone, emperors, sweetlip and others to grab any bait you drop to them. Don't even think about light tackle here. Wipeouts are common on 15 kg braid and inevitable on 10 kg.

The routine is to use fresh baits (whole small squid are best) rigged on a sliding bean sinker rig, with 60 pound trace or better. Drop the baits down until they hit bottom – or are eaten first, as can happen, then lift them a foot or so, bounce once or twice and get ready to be creamed. If

you land half of what you hook, you'll have done well.

Small sharks often get into the act here and you generally know you've got one if you either (a) get bitten off quickly or (b) find that the 'fish' is coming in a bit too easily. Great fun!

MITCHELL RIVER

The Mitchell is a major river at the southern end of Admiralty Gulf. It's a generally muddy and rock strewn stream, which can be difficult to navigate at anything other than high tide but seems to fish best as the water drops and the fishes' location options are reduced.

Expect barramundi, mangrove jacks, threadfin salmon, and around high water, GT's and queenfish. Large boulders sit in the main river bed and create awesome tidal eddies in which both bait and fish become bottled up. Casting into nooks and crannies and rock crevices of such structures will produce most fish.

Crocodiles are both plentiful and fearless in this river, so if you do run aground, do not

under any circumstances get out of the boat to push it off. Providing you have a spare props (yes, plural, 'props' in this part of the world) it makes more sense to grind your way off any stranding. You can minimize the seriousness of any such event by travelling slowly in the first place. Well upstream of the mouth, the Mitchell is barred by a significant rise in landform that creates a challenging passage at high tide and an mpenetrable one at low tide.

RAFT POINT

Broad rock shelves and sand platforms are a feature of the bays near Raft Point and these have enormously violent tidal races that sweep across them at high speed.

With care and good boatmanship, you can negotiate these turbulent waters and either spin into surface working schools of fish or simply troll them in a criss-cross fashion. Poppers are best as the water depth varies and diving lures can hang up, and in any case, the mackerel, queenfish and trevally that haunt and hunt this place will take

Fishing the Mitchell River on a low tide. It is tricky to navigate the narrow channels, but worth the effort

After an hour or so of this slam dunk fish brawling, you may well find your tackle box is depleted, you've gathered a few bumps and bruises and that you are pretty well exhausted and ready for a quiet spell in the shade somewhere. Thank God for mother-ships, hot showers and ice cold beers!

VANSITTART BAY

Getting close to the northern limits of the Kimberley coast, Vansittart Bay lies just inside Cape Talbot and is probably the premier shallow water fishery of the whole Kimberley region's coastline.

Seasonally, vast clouds of golden trevally, permit and mackerel enter the bay and swarm across the sandflats, harassing local bait populations and creating champagne sport fishing for anyone with a penchant for casting lures and flies at fast moving and challenging fish.

The shallow rock flats near the mouth produce queenfish and mackewrel with tuna schools just outside them on the first major drop off. Spanish

Above: Saltwater flyfishing at Raft Point. It's easy to have your flies eaten—not so easy to stop what eats them.

Below: The islands off Raft Point are feeding grounds for literally thousands of surface fish like queenfish, mackerel and trevally

Below: A tropical storm builds at the mouth of Vansittart Bay

poppers as readily as any other lure type.

It's really something to surf the boat along past boils and upwellings and have the lures slammed by great mobs of fish. At times, the melee becomes so intoxicating that you can find yourself getting the boat into quite questionable conditions, so some control is necessary to avoid endangering yourself.

Below: Within Vansittart Bay and virtually any Kimberley inlet with sand and rock bottom, golden trevally are a good bet

remain submerged if they stood vertically on end, simply erupt from water that you might otherwise write off as too shallow for anything of any size.

Along the bay's northern shoreline, there are colonies of black-lipped oysters – not to the taste of some, but like seafood heaven to others These can be gathered at low tide and are so huge that a half dozen of them is a meal for some people.

erupt from water that you might otherwise write off as too shallow for anything of any size.

Along the bay's northern shoreline, there are colonies of black-lipped oysters – not to the taste of some, but like seafood heaven to others These can be gathered at low tide and are so huge that a half dozen of them is a meal for some people.

CAPE LONDONDERRY

The point at which you start to leave the Kimberley coast and enter Northern Territory waters, Cape Londonderry is subject to strong currents and at times, quite strong winds too. When these are opposing, passage can be rough and even dangerous in all but very large craft, but, as is often the case with such places, the fishing can be phenomenal.

Inshore, the water is moderately shallow but

further out to sea it both clears and deepens dramatically. Sailfish and marlin hunt the drop off walls at these deepenings and schools of tuna and mackerel often gather to hunt in the massive eddies that form here, trapping bait in vast arenas of colour-change water.

A little-known fishery also exists right in close along the rocky shoreline here for barramundi. When sea conditions allow it, getting small boats within casting range of the rocks can turn up very good fishing and occasionally quite large fish.

Wherever scattered reef breaks up the generally shallow sand and mud bottom of the larger bays, cobia and other reef fish are suckers for either live or dead baits and sometimes, manta rays can gather over the shallows, where cobia and golden trevally will shadow them.

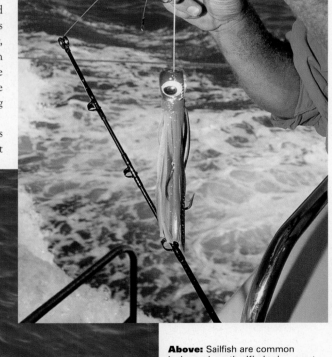

Above: Sailfish are common inshore along the Kimberley coast wherever deep, clean water is channeled by coastal gutters

mackerel will at times hunt schools of mullet across the shallows, blasting from the water like missiles as they charge through the bait and it's unforgettable to see fish that couldn't

Left: Free-swimming sailfish can often be seen on or just below the surface in this area

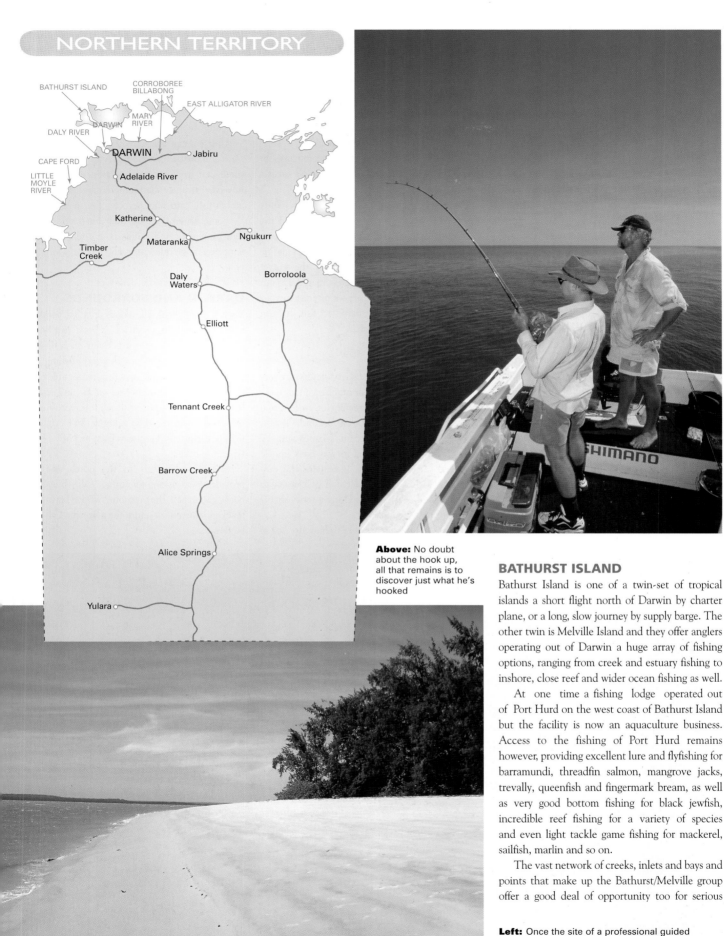

Above: No doubt about the hook up, all that remains is to discover just what he's hooked

BATHURST ISLAND

Bathurst Island is one of a twin-set of tropical islands a short flight north of Darwin by charter plane, or a long, slow journey by supply barge. The other twin is Melville Island and they offer anglers operating out of Darwin a huge array of fishing options, ranging from creek and estuary fishing to inshore, close reef and wider ocean fishing as well.

At one time a fishing lodge operated out of Port Hurd on the west coast of Bathurst Island but the facility is now an aquaculture business. Access to the fishing of Port Hurd remains however, providing excellent lure and flyfishing for barramundi, threadfin salmon, mangrove jacks, trevally, queenfish and fingermark bream, as well as very good bottom fishing for black jewfish, incredible reef fishing for a variety of species and even light tackle game fishing for mackerel, sailfish, marlin and so on.

The vast network of creeks, inlets and bays and points that make up the Bathurst/Melville group offer a good deal of opportunity too for serious

Left: Once the site of a professional guided fishing lodge and now an aquaculture centre, Bathurst Island and Port Hurd remain great fishing destinations

saltwater fly anglers and many existing and pending World fly tackle records have been captured here. In the freshwater lagoons and creeks of Melville Island, saratoga are also available.

CAPE FORD

This productive spot lies to the south and west of the Daly River entrance and Anson Bay. It offers small boats and mother-ships a good protected anchorage in the often prevailing south-west winds and excellent fishing right on tap when you wake up in the morning.

Golden trevally often boil along the beachfront here, while a string of rocks and reeflets extend roughly north-east, where they entrap eddies and bait balls. These bait schools come under attack from mackerel, trevally and other predators and north and northwest beyond that line of foul ground, a vast shallow basin of sand and reef bottomed water often carries massive schools of big queenfish. Large Spanish mackerel can also be trolled or live-baited some distance further offshore where a drop off line steers sea currents past the Peron Islands and Cape Blaze.

CORROBOREE BILLABONG

This is actually a series of waterholes, connected or not at various times by prevailing water levels that spill from the Kakadu floodplains. These flood waters are channeled via numerous creeks and rivers, many of which rise below the higher ground of Mount Goyder to the south.

Barramundi enter these water holes when water levels are high and can become trapped when the waters drop again. Such fish take on very dark colouration due to the local water pigments and lack of salinity and they may not be as good for table fare as fish from more saline environments.

Successful techniques include trolling lures along the outer edge of lilypad fields, or casting to drowned timber, pandanus-fringed banks or the points of land where the river course takes a sudden bend.

Besides barramundi, expect to find plenty of fork-tail catfish, some sooty grunter and the occasional mangrove jack. In common with many floodplain waterholes, Corroboree is home to a great many saltwater crocodiles, the danger of which should never be underestimated. Do not hang about if a large croc shows interest in your boat and never walk the banks to fish. It's not worth the risk for a few fish.

DALY RIVER

This famous barramundi fishery deserves every bit of its reputation, both for numbers and quality of fish. With better management of professional and recreational fishing, barramundi stocks have recovered through recent decades and the fishery has gradually worked its way back up the glory days of years gone by. It remains the very best place within easy road reach of Darwin to present a good chance of catching a seriously big barramundi.

Huge tidal movements over the hundred or so kilometres of river between the river mouth and the Daly River Crossing causeway mean that fish can at different times of the year, be scattered, bunched up, or inclined to shift en masse up or downstream according to local conditions of rainfall and food supply, as well as water temperature and clarity.

Upstream of the Crossing, the water is pure fresh and the behaviour and location of fish varies somewhat from the tidal section. Both sections however produce barramundi, mangrove jacks, archer fish, catfish and crocs – lots of crocs.

Some fishermen park their boats and fish on foot from rock and sandbars in the Daly but it is not recommended as a way to live a long and pain-free life.

DARWIN AND SURROUNDS

With a small boat and some creative thinking, you can catch an awful lot of good fish within the immediate vicinity of Darwin itself. Darwin Harbour for example provides good fishing over sunken wrecks for black jewfish, reasonable creek fishing for barramundi and jacks and almost limitless access to queenfish schools, occasionally remarkable runs of mackerel and virtually nowhere you can get away from trevally of one type or another.

Shoal bay, slightly to the north and east provides good fishing for surface fish while larger boats can reach the Vernons, where barracuda, mackerel, queenfish and some awesome GT's can be found.

Above: Small boats like this can handle the fishing conditions of Corroboree but don't offer much protection from crocodiles

Barramundi from the Daly are often still silver from their time in salt water

In the creeks and backwaters of Darwin harbour estuary cod are common

To the south west of Darwin, in Turnbill Bay, Bynoe harbour and the waters between Indian Island, Grose island and Dum in Mirrie Island, the fishing is probably limited most by what you decide you want to catch.

It's probably a measure of how spoiled Territorians are for fishing choices that so little is made of this local fishery. Although at any time, you are likely to find a good number of boats clustered in any of these places, which means that the locals can't all think that the fishing is poor. They're right of course, it's not.

LITTLE MOYLE RIVER

South of Cape Scott, the Little Moyle is a great place to set up a fishing camp, using a large vessel as home base and making day trips in smaller boats. Several mother-ship operations service this area and the better ones like M.V.Cannon have earned a well-deserved reputation for producing excellent and safe fishing for their clients, both local and those that fly or drive in for holidays.

Barramundi are a given in this river system as are good jacks, exceptional threadfin salmon schools and a variety of trevally, queenfish small mackerel and

estuary cod, with occasional bigger mackerel in the open water offshore from the Little Moyle.

Mudcrabs are plentiful, and can be trapped easily but don't set traps for too long - crocodiles are partial to mudcrabs (and even just the bait sometimes) and aren't too tidy about how they get at either of them.

Boats that anchor overnight are almost certain to be visited by resident cod. These fish are huge and great fun to play with on (hookless) rope. Tie off a fish frame, splash it a few times on the water and wait for the big boys to turn up. Just don't fall in!

MARY RIVER

The Mary River runs through the wetland areas of Corroboree and Shady Camp, becoming Sampan Creek below this junction. It carries barramundi, saratoga and some jacks and is best known for the fabulous fishing it offers as the post-wet season flood load drains off into the main river channels as the dry season gets underway.

If you cruise the Mary River at this time, look for anywhere that water is cascading from the floodplain, and you'll find innumerable places where fish are literally stacked up underneath the inflow points, ready to pounce on any lure, fly or bait you toss in there.

Be judicious about how you approach shallow

The Mary River provides excellent fishing along its edges during the run-off period after the Wet

weedy sections of bank. Quite large crocodiles can lie hidden in just a few feet of water and can erupt from these shallows in an alarming manner if they sense a boat coming over the top of them.

Fish the direct inflow points, but also any obvious downstream channels or gutters of deeper water that might be in between the bank and the first line of weed. Fish will often sit in here and ambush food that has made it past the first line of hungry mouths below the waterfalls.

EAST ALLIGATOR RIVER

Named in error by early settlers who couldn't tell the difference between crocodiles and caymans, the Alligator series of rivers do nonetheless help drain the Kakadu National Park and the associated Magela Plain. They are all excellent fisheries and the East Alligator can often be the equal of the Alligator and South Alligator, although because it is further afield than either of them from places like Cooinda and Kakadu Holiday Village, it sometimes receives less attention.

This relative neglect is not justified, as the fishing can be extremely good at times, especially in the build up to the wet when barramundi can gather in numbers at the river mouth. Because of its isolation though, the East Alligator requires a higher level of self-sufficiency by visiting anglers, whose last point of provisioning and outside help is at the Border Store and Cahill's Crossing, reached from Jabiru from the Mudginberri/Cahill's Crossing road.

Crabbing is excellent in the East Alligator and well set up anglers could keep themselves supplied with fresh fish quite easily. It's prudent though to carry plentiful supplies of alternative food – and sufficient fresh water, since fishing here can be off, just like anywhere else. Being prepared means surviving.

Left: Threadfin salmon are often caught here and can be seen herding schools of jelly prawns around creek mouths

PORT MACDONNELL

Situated around 500km by road from Adelaide and just south of Mount Gambier, Port MacDonnell is primarily a base for commercial lobster fishermen, but it's also becoming popular with recreational anglers. You'll need a big, capable trailer boat to fish safely and comfortably in this area and a degree of experience and local knowledge is also desirable. The harbor is quite shallow and just outside there are several reefs and bommies that demand care and common sense.

Port MacDonnell (or 'Port Mac' as it's more commonly known down this way) provides ready access to the Continental Shelf. In fact, it's the closest point to the Shelf anywhere in SA. Season migrations of southern bluefin tuna often bring these great sportfish within trailer boat range and members of the local gamefishing club hold an annual tournament in May to take advantage of the tuna run. World class albacore turn up with the bluefin some years as well, making it a very attractive fishery for those with the right boats and equipment.

Just recently, a few more adventurous Port Mac' locals have begun plumbing the depths of the Continental Shelf for hapuka and blue eye trevalla. These are caught in depths to 500

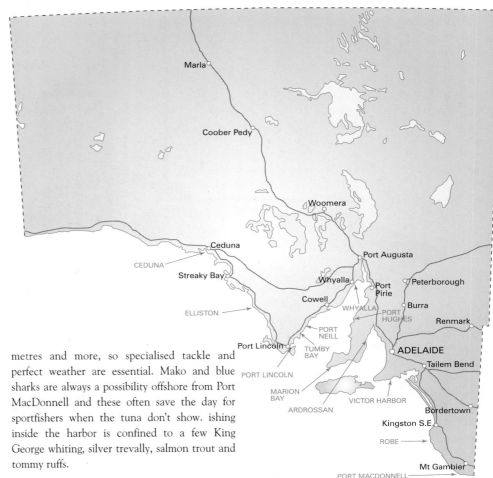

metres and more, so specialised tackle and perfect weather are essential. Mako and blue sharks are always a possibility offshore from Port MacDonnell and these often save the day for sportfishers when the tuna don't show. ishing inside the harbor is confined to a few King George whiting, silver trevally, salmon trout and tommy ruffs.

Bluefin tuna are the mainstay of Port MacDonnell's sportfishery

Above: School sharks are always a welcome deep water catch
Below: Medium snapper and big King George whiting are often hooked together in SA

ROBE

The natural harbor at Robe, about 350km from Adelaide, is one of the most picturesque in South Australia. It's home base to many commercial lobster boats and also produces some entertaining light tackle fishing. Yellow eye mullet, salmon trout and small silver trevally are the main catch from the wharf, but it's outside that the real action occurs. Like most of SA's South-East, Robe can be severely affected by wind and swell and only those with proven blue water boats should contemplate heading well offshore.

Small to medium snapper and big King George whiting are the main target species, but many anglers also set amateur lobster pots to add delicious variety to the catch. It's not unusual to hook whiting of better than a kilogram off Robe and although the snapper are rarely giants like those caught in SA's gulf waters, they are still good fish of up to seven kilos or so. Locating a productive reef system is the key to hooking reds in good numbers.

Robe's deep water fishing is very much a lucky dip proposition. Knife jaw, gurnard, kingfish, silver trevally, morwong, nannygai and even latchets are a possibility and when the bluefin tuna run through these waters in autumn, they can also be

Charter boats are now available right around SA. This one is from Marion Bay.

accessed in reasonable conditions.

Mako sharks are relatively common and at times both albacore and skipjack tuna will venture close enough to the coast for trailer boat anglers to catch. As is the case throughout SA's South-East, perfect weather conditions are a prerequisite for any offshore expedition from Robe.

VICTOR HARBOR

These days, Victor Harbor is almost considered a southern suburb of Adelaide. It's a pleasant hour and a half drive from the city to this delightful little resort on lower Fleurieu Peninsula and although it cops plenty of pressure from the angling masses, it seems to keep producing quality fish. You can catch a feed from rock, river, beach or jetty around Victor, but a decent trailer boat will obviously open up a different range of possibilities.

Bream specialists are well catered for in both the Hindmarsh and Inman Rivers. The fish may not be as plentiful today as they once were, but those who persist with light tackle and the right baits can expect to do well on bream up to a kilogram. Salmon trout, mullet, garfish and barracouta are taken from Granite Island's Screwpile jetty year round, along with the odd nice snapper and mulloway by those with the right gear.

The short wharf at Rosetta Head (commonly known as 'The Bluff') produces some huge

calamari at times, along with salmon, flathead and snapper. Surf fishers still manage to find salmon at nearby Waitpinga and Parsons Beaches, but they are neither as large or as plentiful as they were a decade ago.

Victor Harbor's offshore fishing isn't perhaps as reliable as it once was, but there are good numbers of snapper, trevally, snook and slimy mackerel caught on the Seven Mile Reef in the warmer months. For those with smaller boats, salmon trout, garfish and King George whiting are available inside Encounter Bay.

ARDROSSAN

Ardrossan is one of Yorke Peninsula's major bulk grain loading centres, but it's also significant for both commercial and recreational anglers. Situated about two hours' drive from Adelaide, it is within easy reach of the weekend fisherman. There are two piers at Ardrossan, but only the smaller town jetty is open to the public and it produces tommy ruffs, squid, garfish, snook, mullet and the occasional school mulloway.

King George whiting is the most popular offshore variety and indeed there are plenty to be caught if you know where and when. Winter and spring are probably the best whiting seasons, but they can be expected year round in varying numbers and sizes. Owners of small boats can often pick up a good feed of whiting by fishing the

shallow water north and south of the town and concentrating on fishing the sand patches. Berley is the key in this situation.

Ardrossan's offshore snapper fishing is excellent, particularly from December through until March. A sunken barge about eight miles offshore (put down in 1984 to replace fishing access around the historic 'Zanoni' shipwreck site) produces some thumper reds in the summer months. It's not unusual to pull a boat limit of snapper to 13 or 14 kilos from the barge when the tides and weather are right.

Blue swimmer crabs and calamari are easy pickings from a small boat and it's also possible to 'rake' crabs in the shallows on foot. Optimum crabbing time is November through until after Christmas.

MARION BAY

Although launching and general boating facilities at Marion Bay are poor, it remains one of the best offshore angling locations within reach of Adelaide. It's roughly a three hour drive without a boat in tow and now has plenty of quality holiday rental accommodation, a great tavern and general store. You won't necessarily need a boat to catch a feed of fish around Marion Bay, as the jetty, rocks and nearby beaches all yield a good variety of table species. Snook, squid, salmon, mullet, tommy ruffs and garfish are all

Whyalla is nationally famous for its brilliant snapper fishing.

their luck. Garfish, snook and squid are also on the list of likely jetty targets, along with small yellowtail kings that escape regularly from Spencer Gulf fish farms.

With a top notch launching facility now on line, boat fishing at Port Hughes has never been easier. King George whiting and snapper are the traditional offshore target species and both come in good numbers and sizes at certain times. Summer is the most likely season for big reds, but it's invariably windy at this time of year and boaties often have their activities curtailed by incessant south-easterlies.

Whiting are at their best in the winter months and there are usually plenty of nice salmon down near Cape Elizabeth for those who enjoy some light tackle sport. The salmon generally vary between 2-3 kilograms and are eager lure chasers. Big snook can be trolled in the same area, while the Tiparra light is a regular venue for those chasing garfish and squid.

WHYALLA

The 'Steel City', about 380 kilometres by road from Adelaide, is known around Australia as the home of big snapper. Snapper have made Whyalla famous in national angling circles and not without good reason. Each year at Easter time, hundreds of competitors from around the country line up for substantial cash prizes in the Australian Amateur Snapper Championship and, more often than not, the heaviest red for the weekend tops the magic 15 kilogram mark.

But Whyalla offers anglers a lot more than simply snapper. There are some massive yellowtail kingfish out at Point Lowly, plenty of medium-size King George whiting, squid, salmon, garfish, snook and blue swimmer crabs. It's very much a 'mixed bag' fishery and those prepared to diversify generally do well.

Shore-based anglers can expect nice yellowfin whiting during the warmer months, plenty of squid, snook, garfish and tommy ruffs from the rocks and jetty, salmon out near the Point Lowly lighthouse and razor fish and crabs along the city foreshore. Wading for crabs with purpose-built 'rakes' is very popular on Whyalla's beaches and sand flats. It's something anyone can do and has become a traditional family activity.

Whyalla's boat launching facilities are good, with a multi-lane ramp set within a well sheltered marina. There's another ramp out at Point Lowly, which puts boaties within easy reach of the 'Rip' and other famous snapper fishing locations. There are several kingfish farms adjacent to Point Lowly and these often yield huge snapper for those who know when to be there.

PORT NEILL

Although it's not exactly a household name, Port Neill is one of SA's most consistent fishing

available according to season. The legendary Browns Beach is a short drive to the west around the foot of Yorke Peninsula and still produces plenty of big salmon.

If you intend to venture to the wider grounds out in Investigator Strait and beyond, you'll need a good, seaworthy boat and a measure of offshore experience. Thumper King George whiting, snapper of mixed sizes, nannygai, morwong, sharks and samson fish are caught regularly to the east and south-east of Marion Bay, but only when both swell and wind are down.

The launching ramp is very poor and you'll need a four wheel drive to launch or retrieve at low tide. Seaweed builds up regularly around the launching area, making things extremely difficult and if there's significant swell running outside, chances are there will be an annoying surge up

and down the ramp. Most Marion Bay locals use old tractors to launch and retrieve their craft and this can be arranged at the local tavern for a small fee.

PORT HUGHES

Port Hughes is about two hours by car from Adelaide and now offers a host of facilities for visiting anglers. It has its own general store, tavern and marina facility with dual lane boat ramp, as well as a long jetty for those land-based. The town is enormously popular with holiday-makers and its population swells markedly over the Christmas, Easter and other significant vacation periods.

Tommy ruffs are the staple catch from the jetty, especially on warm summer evenings when there may be a hundred anglers or more trying

venues, particularly for boaties. Located on Eyre Peninsula, about 560km from Adelaide and 90km north of Port Lincoln, it's a quiet, friendly country port with heaps to offer the offshore enthusiast. Snapper and whiting are the big drawcards offshore and both varieties can be caught all year round.

Port Neill now has a neat little dual lane, all tide boat ramp with ample parking and wash down facilities. From the ramp it's possible to be catching big reds in under ten minutes. There's a wreck just north-east of the town that fishes well between October and Christmas time and several wider grounds which fire up as the weather gets warmer. Snapper of mixed sizes are the norm out wide, with fish to eight or nine kilos pretty

Left: Brett Mensforth with a typical Port Neill red.

Below: At anchor off Reevesby Island (Sir Joseph Banks Group) after a great day on the whiting

common. For those with smaller boats, there are a couple of inshore reef systems to the south of the town which produce plenty of nice snapper in early summer time.

King George whiting are generally at their best in the winter and spring and these are much bigger fish than you'll find off Adelaide of further up Spencer Gulf. Yellowfin whiting turn up on the inshore sand flats and beaches around Christmas time and, provided you can pump live yabbies for bait, catching a bag limit of 20 per angler is easy. Although the Port Neill jetty isn't long and doesn't reach deep water, it still produces good numbers of squid, along with tommy ruffs, garfish and snook in the evenings.

TUMBY BAY

There are few other locations in SA that offer so many angling possibilities in such a confined area as Tumby Bay. Just a half hour drive north of Port Lincoln, it's the closest stepping off point to the famous Sir Joseph Banks group of islands — an archipelago consisting of more than 20

islands, islets and semi-submerged reefs. It's a 12 mile run from the new Tumby Bay marina out to the nearest islands in the group and, provided you have the necessary equipment, camping out overnight can be both pleasant and rewarding.

King George whiting are the preferred target of most who visit Tumby Bay and there are plenty of thumpers caught all year round. Kilogram-plus specimens aren't uncommon and achieving the personal daily bag limit of twelve fish is rarely difficult. King George can be caught from the shore both north and south of Tumby, as can the closely related yellowfin whiting during the warmer months. Number one bait for yellowfin is salt water yabbies, but they will also take pieces of green prawn.

Tumby Bay's long pier is a very popular and productive venue for those who enjoy a feed of calamari, tommy ruffs, garfish or snook. Salmon and flathead are taken from the rocks to the south of the town, while the new marina sometimes yields school mulloway and the odd silver trevally. Escapees from yellowtail kingfish farms also turn up in the marina and around the jetty from time to time, but these are generally undersize and have to be thrown back.

PORT LINCOLN

Famous Australia-wide as the home of the biggest bluefin tuna fleet in the country, Port Lincoln is also renowned for its gamefishing and inshore sportfishing. Boston Bay, its magnificent natural harbor, is a great place to catch snapper, King George whiting, squid, salmon, trevally, garfish and snook. The bay is deep, its water is pristine and although there are plenty of anglers on or around it, the catch remains consistent.

Land-based anglers can find yellowfin whiting for much of the year, particularly in the shallow areas from the town jetty westward, but live yabbies are essential bait. Schools of salmon visit the bay regularly and fish of varying sizes are caught from the main jetty by anglers of all ages and levels of experience. The salmon action is invariably at its peak when commercial pilchard boats are tied up at the jetty to unload their catch. With pilchard blood and oil in the water, the salmon often go crazy, grabbing any bait offered.

Port Lincoln's offshore gamefishing action is unparalleled. Southern bluefin tuna, samson fish, yellowtail kings and sharks are targeted by both recreational and charter boats, with some of the best action coming from remote locations such as Rocky and Greenly Islands. Kings to over a hundred pounds have been caught near Greenly Island and there are giant blue groper available for those with the tackle to hold them. Several large charter boats now work out of Lincoln Cove Marina, so accessing the offshore action is easier than ever.

Above: South Australia is famous for its snapper. This one, caught by John O'Keefe, came from wide of Port Lincoln.

ELLISTON

Thousands of anglers who enjoy tangling with big salmon in the surf regularly travel westward from Adelaide to spend several days in or around the small port of Elliston. It's a quaint little place that's well geared to accommodate visitors, with abundant accommodation and a host of first class facilities. The Elliston jetty is a consistent producer of big tommy ruffs, trevally, snook and garfish, but it is the surf beaches to the north and south that seem to lure the bulk of angling visitors.

Locks Well, Sheringa, Talia and Mount Camel Beaches are all legendary surf fishing locations. The fish are generally at their best through the cooler months and they regularly top four kilograms — great sport in heavy surf. The Elliston community holds an annual salmon fishing competition, with rich prizes on offer for the heaviest fish, and this attracts a lot of hopeful anglers to the area.

Above: Big nannygai (red snapper) are common on Elliston's offshore reefs.

Left: Port Lincoln's Billy Lights Point boat ramp is a first class facility.

Although the offshore scene isn't as accessible as in some other Eyre Peninsula locations, boaties launching at Elliston regularly catch big nannygai, whiting, snapper, groper and samson fish.

Pearson and Flinders Islands are within reach of larger tailer boats and these produce some fabulous fishing at times. Whiting to over 60 centimetres and two kilograms have been caught around Pearson Island and there are also huge blue groper, yellowtail kingfish, sharks and giant flathead. Naturally, accessing both islands is very weather dependent and local knowledge is desirable, but there are charter boats available with experienced skippers and guides.

CEDUNA

Ceduna is the last substantial settlement as you head westward toward the WA border. It marks the beginning of the Eyre Highway and is often referred to as the gateway to the Nullabor Plain. It's a long drive from Adelaide, but the fishing is about as unspoiled as anywhere in the state. It has plenty to offer, including fabulous surf fishing, two productive jetties, countless rock fishing options and a host of offshore fishing for those with large or small trailer boats. Launching facilities are barely acceptable, but a new marina facility is currently in the planning stages and this will improve things dramatically for all boat owners.

Some of Australia's biggest mulloway are caught each summer on the surf beaches west of Ceduna. Fish to 35 kilograms are reasonably common in some areas and most anglers who are well informed and adequately prepared catch at least one of these giants on an annual visit.

The surf salmon fishing is fantastic, too, especially on beaches like Scotts, Tuckamore and Cactus. If it's salmon you're after, the biggest fish (often topping ten pounds) are at their peak in July and August, but they are essentially a year-round proposition.

Those with big trailer boats can catch bluefin tuna outside Ceduna in the summer months and plenty of medium snapper. Big snapper come into Murat Bay in late spring and these are best tackled from the edges of the Thevenard shipping channel. White sharks are regular visitors to this part of the world and all small boat anglers should take care while snapper fishing. King George whiting are prolific in the bay for much of the year, although they aren't generally as big as those caught in offshore areas.

TASMANIA

NORTH TASMANIA

This large area extends from Stanley in the west to Bridport in the east. Launching at Stanley one can fish offshore around Hunter Island and Three Hummock Island. Expect to catch salmon, flathead, barracouta, trevally, tailor and there have been reports of snapper and kingfish. There is also a reasonable shark fishery out in deeper water. It is over twenty kilometres out to these islands, so caution and common sense needs to be taken when undertaking this journey.

Closer to Stanley in Sawyer Bay the fishing can be just as good and it's much closer to the ramp. Other good fisheries are at Perkins Bay and Robbins Passage that have the added attraction of flounder and whiting.

There is excellent land based fishing from the jetty at Stanley.

Burnie is the main deepwater port on the north coast and there is no fishing allowed from the port jetty. The boat ramp is to the east of the town and the breakwater there has good land based fishing. Apart from that one really needs a boat and offshore here you can fish for anything from sharks to salmon to flathead.

Devonport is on the large Tamar River and its large estuary – Port Dalrymple – offers flathead, whiting and, surprisingly, some snapper. The fishing outside is quite good too with flathead and whiting being the main targets, but also salmon, barracouta, flathead and trevally can be added to the list. The Tamar River is huge and is navigable all the way to Launceston. There are plenty of boat ramps along its length.

Bridport supports a reasonable professional fleet and there are plenty of jetties there to fish from. There are some good bream there as well as flathead, mullet and at times small salmon. There is a boat launching ramp and just offshore in Anderson Bay there is a reasonable fishery for flathead, salmon, whiting and flounder.

ANSONS BAY

This is the most northerly fishery on the east coast of Tasmania. It is a picturesque, shallow estuary that hosts some huge bream in the Ansons River that flows into the estuary. In the estuary itself, there are some flathead and flounder.

ST HELENS

St Helens is at the end of a reasonably large bay – Georges Bay – and is the launching point for the offshore fishing on the north coast. Offshore there are tuna, marlin and sharks as well as deep water reef species, while close inshore fish such as flathead, salmon, silver trevally and many others abound. Good inshore spots are just offshore from Grants and St Helens points.

In the bay there is a great salmon fishery for long periods of the year, as well as flathead, whiting, mullet, trevally and garfish. The George River is a noted bream fishery and is one of the best in Tasmania.

There are plenty of land based opportunities from the jetties around the town.

SWANSEA

The township of Swansea offers access to Great Oyster Bay and offshore. The bay is ideal for small boat fishing for flathead, Australian salmon, barracouta, slimy mackerel, warehou and occasionally silver trevally and small kings.

Swansea has a quality, concrete boat launching

A huge Tassie bream well over 2 kilos caught at St Helens.

Mike Stevens nailed this Derwent bream at one of the AFC Bream Series Tournaments.

ramp and from there it is about a ten kilometre run to Schouten Passage and offshore. The Passage can experience rougher water on run tides but just back inside there is an excellent fishery for the species just mentioned. On the western side, Thouin Bay offers similar fishing and species range.

Land based anglers should look at Wineglass Bay for flathead, mackerel and occasionally salmon and barracouta.

For the bream anglers there are the estuaries of Great Swanport Bay and the Swan River just north of Swansea. There are two ramps that enable soft plastics anglers to launch directly into the river and estuary. To the south there is the Little Swanport River, which has its own ramp as well.

Even further south at Triabunna one can launch and fish for flathead, salmon and mackerel and further out, either inshore or offshore of Maria Island, there is more good fishing. The offshore areas of Maria Island are particularly good for southern bluefin tuna.

TASMAN PENINSULA

This is a large and very picturesque area just north east of Hobart. There are over fifteen launching ramps around this peninsula and the area offers plenty of safe inshore bays fishing for flathead, salmon, barracouta, trevally and at times ling, garfish and cod.

On the seaward side of the peninsula there is excellent deep water bottom fishing for reef species. For those sport and game fishers launching at Eaglehawk Neck and travelling offshore there are the game fishing grounds where tuna and occasionally marlin can be found in season.

HOBART

The Derwent River estuary is a jewel on Hobart's doorstep and in the extensive middle reaches is one of Australia's best bream fisheries. Added to that there is always the possibility of some excellent sea run brown trout.

However, there is also the added attraction of salmon, flathead, cod, pike, mackerel and trumpeter. The Sandy Bay area right at Hobart's doorstep also has a significant population of whiting, silver trevally and flounder.

There is some good fishing from the jetties around Secheron and Selfs points. Many anglers fish from shore in this extensive estuary for bream, trout and indeed all the other species. The areas around the Tasman and Bowen bridges have good land based locations and the East Derwent highway runs along the river in places again offering good access.

The whole estuary is also very popular with boat fishers and there are plenty of boat ramps all along the Derwent.

D'ENTRECASTEAUX CHANNEL

This area is below the Derwent and extends from the mouth of the Derwent, past the mighty Huon River and all the way down to the road's end at Cockle Creek.

The fishing here in the protected bays is best done out of a boat with flathead, trevally, salmon and barracouta being the principle targets.

There is great trout fishing to be had in the Huon, Esperance, Lune, D'Entrecasteaux and Catamaran rivers. All are best fished out of a small tinnie.

NORTH EAST RIVERS

Often called the lowland rivers of Tasmania, this extensive network offers predictable fishing and much more predictable weather than that on the high plains. There are over one hundred rivers in this area ranging from the large drainages like the Macquarie, the South Esk and North Esk systems to some delightful little creeks.

The larger rivers are sometimes best fished from a drifting raft or rowboat. Brumbys Creek, the Macquarie River and the South Esk River are three examples that recently have been targeted from drifting boats. Doing so opens up a lot of water previously unfished by shore based anglers. However, having said that there is still kilometre after kilometre of bank fishing along these major rivers.

For those after accessible fishing for brown trout averaging a bit under half a kilogram look to some of the tributaries – the Meander, Liffey, Lake and Break o' Day rivers all have great reputations for trout whether you use fly, soft plastic, light lure or spinner techniques.

Of the lakes in the area, there are the well known Tooms, Leake and Trevallyn systems that all hold very good stocks of brown trout. However, don't forget Brushy Lagoon, Four Spring Lake and Curries River Dam near George Town.

Laurie Matcham with a great Swan River bream.

SOUTHERN TASMANIA

This area is dominated by the Derwent and Huon rivers and lakes Gordon and Pedder. The Derwent has been dammed along its way for hydro purposes with the better trout lakes being Meadowbank Lake and Wayatinah Lagoon where the best approach is trolling lures from a boat. Access to the Derwent's plentiful trout can be made from the Lyell Highway from New Norfolk to Rosegarland.

The Huon River is more remote and difficult to fish. In its lower reaches at Huonville there is quality sea run fishing for larger trout, but a boat is a boon while not being absolutely necessary – trout can be taken right at the bridge area at Huonville. The middle reaches can be accessed via Geeveston and a tributary, the Weld, offers Tasmania's best rainbow trout river fishing.

The massive Impoundments Lake Gordon and Lake Pedder are within this area. Lake Pedder is dammed on the Huon River and Lake Gordon is dammed on the Gordon River. Both are best fished from a boat as land based access is limited, except at the southern end of lake Pedder.

CENTRAL HIGHLANDS

This huge lakes area of Tasmania is world-famous and there are so many lakes here (over two thousand) that not all have been fished or even named. The largest lake is Great Lake, which offers excellent boat fishing, whether trolling, fly fishing or downrigging. There is also plenty of shore based access all around the lake.

Not far from Great Lake is Arthurs Lake. Smaller than Great Lake, for many years Arthurs

Trolling minnows is the best bet if you want to catch trout in the West Coast rivers.

has had the reputation of being Tasmania's most productive trout lake. Arthurs is a great boat fishery and equally as good a land based fishery.

Recently Woods Lake has developed a daunting reputation of being a better producer of trout that Arthurs, but it has much less shore based access and a boat is almost mandatory to get amongst the Woods' trout.

To the south, Penstock Lagoon has blossomed in recent years with solid catches of quality browns and rainbow trout. Penstock is one of the few lakes on the Central Highlands where

one can catch a quality rainbow trout. The other is Dee Lagoon in the Bronte area south west of Great Lake.

In this area are the quality trout lakes such as Little Pine, Pine Tier, Bronte, Brady, Binney, Echo, Laughing Jack, King William, St Clair and Tungatinah all offer good land based fishing for trout as well as boat fishing.

There is an area in the Western Lakes called the Nineteen Lagoons – an area that is remote but accessible by vehicle. The remote waters of lakes Augusta, Ada, Botsford, Double, Kay and many smaller lakes and tarns are accessible by day trip in a vehicle from Miena. Here there is quality 'back country' fly fishing for sight fishing to trout.

Further west from Ada are a thousand remote lakes and tarns that can only be accessed by hiking.

Such places as Pillans, Olive, Naomi, Tin Hut and hundreds of others offer opportunities to fool a remote Tasmanian trout.

WEST COAST

There are some famous west coast rivers in Tasmania that hold some very large sea run brown trout. The Arthur River on the northwest coast is accessible via Stanley and has land based fishing at its mouth, but to fish its extensive waters further inland from there a boat is required.

At Corinna there is the Pieman, and again a boat is required to either venture further upstream or downstream towards the mouth. Above Queenstown there are opportunities in the Henty and Little Henty rivers.

Above: When Little Pine Lagoon fires the results are great trout like this.

Left: These anglers are fishing a wind lane on Little Pine Lagoon, one of Tasmania's great trout lakes.